CW00375834

BIBLE PROBLEMS AND ANSWERS

Bible Problems and Answers

WILLIAM HOSTE, B.A.,
and
WILLIAM RODGERS

JOHN RITCHIE LTD
CHRISTIAN PUBLICATIONS

40 Beansburn, Kilmarnock, Scotland

ISBN-13: 978 1 909803 25 1

Copyright © 2013 by John Ritchie Ltd.
40 Beansburn, Kilmarnock, Scotland

www.ritchiechristianmedia.co.uk

All rights reserved. No part of this publication may be reproduced, stored
in a retrievable system, or transmitted in any form or by any other means
– electronic, mechanical, photocopy, recording or otherwise – without prior
permission of the copyright owner.

Typeset by John Ritchie Ltd., Kilmarnock
Printed by Bell & Bain Ltd., Glasgow

PREFACE

Amongst the gifts which the Risen Lord was pleased to raise up for the edification of His people in the earlier part of this century, two of the most sane and balanced teachers, to whose oral and written ministry, saints in many parts of the world owe a debt of lasting gratitude, were the late Mr. Wm. Hoste, B.A., London, and Mr. Wm. Rodgers, Omagh, Northern Ireland.

For a number of years these brethren contributed Answers to "The Question Box" of *The Believers' Magazine,* of which periodical Mr. Hoste was for some seven years prior to his Home-call the esteemed Editor. This feature of the *The B.M.* is one which has ever been much appreciated by readers, and it is generally agreed that for scholarly ability, critical acumen, breadth of thought, painstaking accuracy, and above all, spiritual insight, the Answers by Mr. Hoste and Mr. Rodgers rank amongst its best. One has not been surprised, therefore, that many students of the Word have from time to time expressed the desire that these should be bound in a more permanent form. The compiling of the present selection has been undertaken in order that this laudable desire might in measure be satisfied. It is regrettable, however, that the work of revision and preparation for publication has not the advantage of being executed by the authors themselves.

For convenience, the Questions are divided into two parts. In the first, Subjects are dealt with, under their appropriate titles. The second part is devoted to queries about the meaning of texts and portions of Scripture, the Answers to which are arranged in regular Biblical order. Some Questions are of such a nature, or are so worded, that it was difficult to decide with which group they should be classified. Any Question, however, can be found easily by referring to the Indexes at the end of the book. Each Answer bears the initials of its author.

In certain cases it will be seen that the same, or a very similar Question, is answered twice by the same pen. The dates of such Answers were usually years apart, and as the earlier is always placed first, the reader has in the later one the writer's more mature thoughts upon the subject. Moreover, while in such cases a certain amount of repetition is unavoidable, the second Answer often treats of aspects of the subject not touched upon in the earlier one. Where both writers answer the same question, the reader, of course, has the advantage of being able to compare the different viewpoints expressed, whether or not the writers agree. The value of many of the Answers is not only the help they give concerning the particular Scriptures with which they deal, but the light they cast upon other passages of the Word. Some Questions were not too clearly stated. These have been revised, although it was deemed best to leave them as near as possible to the original, consistent with clarity of thought. In no case has the view or interpretation of either author been modified, and the compiler does not necessarily endorse, or hold himself responsible for every opinion and exposition here set forth.

It remains for one to express sincere thanks to Messrs. J. Ritchie Ltd., Kilmarnock, for permission to reproduce these Answers from their valuable periodical, to Mr. A. Borland, M.A., its present Editor, for his kindness in writing the Foreword, and to my friend Mr. T. W. Ball, B.A., for his willing help in correcting the proofs of the entire work.

The volume is sent forth with the consciousness of many imperfections in its compilation, but with the prayer that it may prove to be a useful work of reference, and a rich treasury of Scripture knowledge to all who may read it, to the end that the Name of our Lord Jesus Christ may be glorified.

WM. BUNTING.

January, 1957.

CONTENTS

FOREWORD

by Andrew Borland, M.A.,
Editor, *The Believers' Magazine*.

The compiler of this book of Questions and Answers is to be heartily congratulated. He has completed a work which will meet the needs of many an inquiring mind, a work which contains material that will not readily be found elsewhere in such convenient form. Here is a compendium of truth arranged in sections and with most helpful Indexes, that almost any subject may be studied both directly and with reference to allied themes.

The subjects cover a wide range, and the fact that some questions are duplicated adds to the value of the volume. Sometimes various aspects of the same truth are tackled, and light is thus shed on a theme from different angles. That is all to the good, for the exercise involved in referring to the different sections of the book cannot but produce a studious attitude towards the Scriptures.

There is great need to-day to give careful attention to certain aspects of truth which are apt to be neglected in an age of easy-going compromise, and special attention should be drawn to the very wise counsel contained in the answers dealing with Church and kindred subjects. Both the writers responsible for the answers were men of deep scholarship, wide experience and sane judgement. For many years they were accredited leaders among the Lord's people, and acceptable writers in *The Believers' Magazine*, of which William Hoste was most capable Editor for a number of years. The present generation cannot properly assess the value of their ministry, but can now through their collected writings learn from them how to contend earnestly for the faith. They were men who avoided extremes, yet remained inwardly faithful to principles which they believed were derived from the Scriptures. They never wavered in their adherence to what they had learned; and both were men who had bought the truth at no inconsiderable personal sacrifice.

It cannot be expected that there will be agreement with all the answers, but the present writer has found himself mentally stimulated and spiritually enlightened by a perusal of the book. I have no hesitation in heartily commending the volume, and pray for it a wide circulation, especially among younger Christians who will find many of their problems dealt with by men of understanding wisdom and knowledge.

PUBLISHER'S NOTE

Grateful acknowledgement is made of the vast amount of work involved in the compilation of this volume. Special thanks are due to Mr. Bunting, and those who in any way assisted, for the valuable service rendered in making this work of reference available for the Lord's people.

THE HOLY TRINITY

GOD

Is God invisible? Please explain the seeming contradiction of the following passages: 1 John iv. 12; Exod. xxxiii. 11, 20, 23; Gen. xxxii. 30.

There can be no contradiction in Scripture, therefore when we have a positive statement in 1 John iv. 12, we must seek to understand apparent discrepancies in the light of it. Now Exod. xxxiii. 11 does not say that Moses SAW the face of God, which would contradict vv. 20 and 23. Would it not be possible to speak face to face with a blind man, or with a friend in the dark, and yet in neither case for your face to be seen? If a man cannot gaze on the sun, how could he gaze on its Creator! But to His creatures "He made darkness His secret place" (Psa. xviii. 11). Moses drew near the thick darkness (Exod. xx. 21; see also Deut. v. 22; 2 Chron. vi. 1). Is there not a seeming contradiction between such verses and 1 Tim. vi. 16? But what light is and what darkness is are mysteries not solved to-day. In any case we may be sure that wherever God has made Himself visible, as at Peniel, it was in the Person of "the only Begotten Son."   W.H.

The Old Testament Theophanies are the only possible explanation of these seeming contradictions. All of these were Christophanies, *i.e.*, an invisible God appearing to His creatures in human form. The One who ever thus appeared was the only Begotten Son, the Second Person in the Godhead (John i. 18). In Exod. xxiv. 10, "They saw the God of Israel," and in v. 11, "They saw God, and did eat and drink." In Ezek. i. 26, the seer saw the form of a man upon the throne, and in Ezek. x. 20, says that man was "The God of Israel," the one who is our Lord Jesus Christ.—Mr. J. Ritchie, first Editor of "The Believers' Magazine."

Is it scriptural to speak of God as "the breasted God"?

No doubt those who use such a term wish by so doing to impress a sense of God's bountiful providence to His creatures and especially to His people, but the expression is, I am sure, most objectionable, like that other phrase one has heard, "the motherhood of God." Both are quite unscriptural. The one before us is in fact based on a mistaken derivation of **Shaddai,** used as an epithet of the Divine Name in "El-Shaddai", and always translated in the Authorised, "Almighty God."

Indeed, the fact that the Septuagint, Vulgate and our own translators give respectively, **"panto-krator"**, **"omnipotens"** and **"Almighty"**, all meaning the same thing, might suffice to rule out a term so derogatory to the Divine Majesty as "breasted". None of us know very much; it is good when the little we do know leads us to distrust ourselves, and especially amateur translation and derivations, unknown to the grammarians and lexicographers, but which seem to have a great attraction for some minds. The epithet "breasted" is based, as I say, on a derivation, which has just enough appearance of reality as to make it a pitfall to the unwary. No doubt **Shaddai** is derived from a word **šad**, but there are two such words in the Hebrew quite distinct in meaning and derivation, the one meaning "breast", derived, as some believe, from a disused root, **shah-dah** (with one d), meaning to irrigate; and the other meaning "powerful", from **shah-dad** (with two d's)—to oppress, spoil—a verb rarely used of God, though see Jer. 25. 36; 47. 4; 51. 5. **Shaddai** however, is used **exclusively** of Him, whereas **šad**, a breast, is never so applied. Now the dual number of **šad**, a breast, is **shadayim** (with one d), but **shaddai** (plural of excellence) has two d's, proving its derivation from **šad**—powerful. Really **Shaddai** has no more connection with **šad**, a breast, than the word "manna" has with our word "man".

W.H.

THE TITLE EL

Does the title El apply only to any singular Person of the Trinity, or does it apply to the Trinity as being One in nature and essence? (See Mr. Newberry's note on the Divine titles).

It seems that Mr. Newberry's note is correct and instructive as far as it goes. Though El is a singular form (but not of Elohim, which is Eloah), I do not think it necessarily expresses a single Person of the Holy Trinity, though this is true in some cases (e.g. Immanu—El, with us—God). It means a "mighty one," or simply "might," and even any deity; but is used often too of the true God. The special emphasis of the word is the Divine Unity, whereas that of Elohim is plurality in Unity. It is hardly ever used in prose writings without some adjunct or attribute, as Mr. Newberry's references show.—Almighty God—El-Shaddai; the Everlasting God,—El-'Olam; a jealous God, El-qanna', and so on. El-Elohe-Israel, is a special name of God—"God the God of Israel." The word is however much more frequent in poetical books such as the Psalms and Job—and sometimes with the definite article—"The God"; see Psa. 18. 32—"The God girdeth me with strength"; 68. 21—"The God shall wound the head of His enemies"; Job 8. 3—"Doth the God pervert judgment?"—where the thought represented seems to be the True God. There are gods and gods, gods many and lords many, but our God is THE GOD—the only God. Perhaps the true key to the use of the word is that it may mean simply "a god". The adjunct or attribute shows that the One True God is meant. W.H.

GOD'S GOVERNMENT OF THE UNIVERSE

Is it scriptural to teach that God has ceased to hold the reins of government relative to the universe (presently)? If so, give a little enlightenment on such verses as Jeremiah 27. 5-8; Dan. 4. 25 and 26; Matthew 22. 21; Romans 13. 1-7; 1 Timothy 2. 1 and 2; 1 Peter 2. 17.

I should say it is very unscriptural. There is no such thought, that I know of, in the Scriptures. If Satan and man are in rebellion against God and try to usurp His authority, and apparently succeed to a certain extent, it is only by His permission and within strictly prescribed limits. I think Jer. 27. 5-8; Dan. 4. 25; Matt. 22. 21; Rom. 13. 1-7, verses quoted by the questioner, are quite sufficient to prove that God has never relinquished the reins of government of the Universe or of this world even. Satan is certainly called the "Prince of this World," but it was only by God's permission, Who "makes the wrath of man to praise Him," and he is never called this since the Cross and resurrection of our Lord. But nowhere is Satan entitled as Prince of the Universe. How could it be said "The Lord reigneth" (Psa. 93., 97., 99.), had He ceased to hold the reins of government? W.H.

THE PERSONS OF THE GODHEAD

Are there three distinct Persons in the Godhead, to be distinguished from one another?

It behoves us to tread with unshod feet as we approach the high and holy subject of the Being of God. Anything savouring of a mere discussion of Him, before whom the angels veil their faces, the Three in One and the One in Three, cannot be too strongly deprecated. We must not try to define or explain or measure where the Word of God is silent; in fact our wisdom is to limit ourselves as far as possible to the words of Scripture. We cannot by searching find out God, except in so far as He is pleased to reveal Himself. God has never condescended to prove His existence, nor yet explain His mode of Being; but He reveals Himself in His Works and Word; and even then we need God the Spirit to teach us. The great truth of the Old Testament is the Unity of the Godhead. "The Lord our God is one Lord" (Deut. 6. 4), and we believe this as strongly as any Jew or so-called Unitarian. But from the very first verse of Genesis we are made aware of a Plurality in that Unity. The word for "created" is in the singular, but "God" is a plural word—Elohim, though when this stands for strong ones or false gods, it takes a plural verb (e.g., see Exod. 32. 4). In verse 2 a Personal Being in the Godhead is differentiated: "the Spirit of God." Then in verse 26 we read, "Let us make man in our image." Later, in Exodus we become aware of another Person—the Angel of the Lord, to whom Divine honours are paid (chap. 23. 20-22)—and yet He is distinct from Jehovah. In Mal. 3. 1 the word "messenger" ("messenger of the covenant") is in the Hebrew the same as "angel". We are brought face to face with a Personal Wisdom possessed by Jehovah "before His works of old" (Prov. 8. 22-31); and in Prov. 30. 4 we are asked, Who is the Creator and "what is His Son's name?" Who then is this Angel of His presence—and Who this Spirit against whom Israel rebelled and Who was grieved with their ways? (see also Zech. 12. 10 and 13. 7). Clearly even in the Old Testament there are in the Unity of the Godhead, three Personal Subsistencies.

In the New Testament this becomes clearer. In Matt. Jesus is identified with Immanuel—"God with us." But "God so loved the world that He gave His only-begotten Son" is equally true, so that the Giver and the Given One are both God. Again in John 1. 1 we read "The word was with (or in relation to—pros) God, and the Word was God" and in v. 14, "the Word became flesh." To Him at His baptism the heavens were opened and He saw the Spirit of God descending like a dove . . . and heard a voice from heaven saying, "This is my beloved Son in whom I am well pleased" (Matt. 3. 16, 17). Later, He "by the Eternal Spirit offered Himself without spot to God" (Heb. 9. 14) and then after the Lord ascended, the Father sent the Spirit, in His and His own name, to testify of Christ. All who believe are to be baptized into the Name of the Father and of the Son and of the Holy Ghost (Matt. 28.), and to such comes the message, "The grace of the Lord Jesus Christ and the love of God and the communion of the Holy Ghost be with you all" (2 Cor. 13. 14). "For through Him we both have access by one Spirit to the Father" (Ephes. 2. 18). We do not confound the Persons nor do we divide the Substance. There is a distinction in the Divine Functions. The Father preordains—determines "the times and seasons," and gives the Son; The Son creates, redeems, intercedes; The Spirit calls, gives life, indwells. But those three Divine Persons are coequal, co-eternal, co-substantial in the Unity of the Godhead.　　　　　W.H.

THE PERSON OF CHRIST

THE DIVINITY AND HUMANITY OF CHRIST

How are we to reconcile the truth that Christ is God and Christ is Man, in one Person, or rightly to estimate what belongs to each? Again, how could our Lord be tempted in all points, like as we are, sin apart, if, as we believe, sin had no appeal to Him, as it has to us?

It is noticeable that when our Lord affirms that "no one knoweth the Father save the Son," He at once adds, "and he to whomsoever the Son will reveal Him." Why did He not, when affirming as he had just done, that "no one knoweth the Son but the Father" add "and he to whomsoever the Father will reveal Him"? Is it not that there are mysteries in the Union of the two Perfect Natures, Divine and human, in the **One Person** of our Lord Jesus Christ, which the Father nowhere promises ever fully to reveal? Not only are they too deep for us (we do not even understand our own tripartite being), but it is unnecessary for us thus to analyse His Being. One thing we aught never to forget, our Lord was not a **dual personality,** that is two Persons, Divine and human, but ONE DIVINE Personality, in equal relation to His two perfect natures. "The Word was God . . . the Word was made flesh and dwelt among us." (John 1. 1, 14). The Modernists, and alas, they have their representatives everywhere to-day, will not brook to be told that there are things their highest powers cannot grasp, and they so attempt to reconcile what has never been out of harmony, and explain what they ought rather to believe. To some persons a glib bad answer, seems preferable to saying "I do not know." As we read the Gospels under the influence of the Holy Spirit, it is not like chemists, with our test-tubes and reactives analysing all the mysteries of Christ, or like physiologists with our instruments dissecting His Personality, but as disciples and as worshippers. The human sympathy of Christ is not a mere theory, which we must make real to ourselves by a certain manipulation of His Person to satisfy the logical deductions of some shallow minds, but a blessed reality, which He makes true in our experience when we embrace Him by faith. The effect of this wrought by the Spirit in our souls, will not be some philosophical demonstration that after all "He is **altogether such an one as ourselves**—sin apart," but the adoring cry of Thomas, "My Lord and my God." The question of the temptation of our Lord is not after all so far beyond our grasp, if we remember that temptation is used in two distinct senses in the New Testament: **of allurement**—"Every·man is tempted when he is drawn aside of His own lust and enticed" (James 1. 14), and **of testing** —"He was tempted (or tested) in all points," according to the similitude, "apart from sin." (Heb. 4. 15). When we read that "God did tempt Abraham" (Gen. 22. 1) it was in this latter sense. He put him to the test. So Christ was tested by Satan in the wilderness, and proved to be the Son of God; but He was never tempted in the sense of being "drawn away of lust and enticed," for He had none—He was "holy, harmless and undefiled." (Heb. 7. 26). "He did no sin" (1 Peter 2. 22); "He knew no sin" (2 Cor. 5. 21); "In Him is no sin" (1 John 3. 5). I am sadly convinced that the attempts of modernist teachers to emphasise the humanity of our Lord, on the plea of establishing His power of sympathy with us, is for the most part quite unreal; for, taken as a class, they are a self-sufficient, self-satisfied type of man; but rather, unconsciously to themselves it may be, and we trust it is, they "cast Him down from His excellency," through undermining His Divinity.   W.H.

Had the Lord Jesus Christ, a spirit, a soul, and a body, as a perfect Man, together with, yet different from, His being God?

This is no unnecessary matter for consideration, for not only is the Deity of Christ attacked to-day, but also His true Humanity, and that in circles where one might hope for better things. This arises partly from ignoring the labours of God's servants in the past, especially in the first centuries of the Christian era, which we cannot afford to do. God overruled the early attacks on the Person of His beloved Son to consolidate and define the truths of His Deity and Humanity, and we owe a debt of gratitude to those whom He raised up to "contend earnestly for the faith." One truth which emerged as Scriptural from these conflicts was what is known as the "Hypostatical Union," that is the union in the Lord Jesus Christ of two whole and perfect natures, the Divine and the Human, in equal relation with One Divine Person, the Eternal Son of God, of one substance with the Father. We cannot penetrate this mystery for "No man knoweth the Son but the Father;" we believe what is written. However, even the Arian heresy of the 4th century turned to the furtherance of the truth. The Arians taught the quasi-Godhead and quasi-Manhood of Christ. For them He was neither perfect God, nor true man, but something less than the former and more than the latter; and the spiritual element in His manhood (i.e., the spirit and soul) was replaced by His imperfect Godhead. The Arian controversy was a matter of life and death. Arius was a popular soft-spoken man and exercised a notable influence, as such men do to-day. However, the truth prevailed, and the Godhead of Christ, of the same substance as the Father, was established on a firm Scriptural basis, but His Manhood remained undefined. It was the heresy of Apollinarius of Laodicœa (in Syria), an earnest opponent of Arius, that led to this. He taught that in the manhood of Christ the rational soul was lacking, and was replaced by the Godhead. This is virtually the error taught in some circles to-day. It was proved to be entirely unsatisfactory and unscriptural. If Christ were truly man, He must have been in possession of all that constitutes complete humanity—spirit, soul, body, will, etc. Indeed, His own words testify to this: "This is **My body**"; "**My soul** is exceeding sorrowful, even unto death"; "Father . . . not as **I will**, but as Thou wilt"; "Father, into Thy hands I commend **My Spirit**." (Matt. 26. 26, 38, 39; Luke 23. 46). Thus the words, "The Word became flesh", imply something much more than that a Divine Person took a body, which might have meant little more than a Theophany of the Old Testament, but rather that He entered into manhood, that He became incarnate as truly "born of a woman," a virgin, with all that perfect **unfallen** humanity implies. He was not less man, because sinless; not less experienced in human joys, sorrows, affections, weariness, hunger, pain, because truly God; not less capable of death, because not liable to death. He was, moreover, not a dual Personality, as Nestorius of Constantinople taught (430 A.D.), but one Divine Person, in equal relation with His dual natures. As man, He is able in all points to sympathise with His people's infirmities; as God, He is able to succour them.   W.H.

Was it only at His incarnation that our Lord became (1) "The Image of the invisible God"; (2) "The Firstborn of every creature"; and (3) "The express Image of His Person"?

This I believe to have been the view taken by Mr. Hoste. Personally, I believe that all three expressions were true of Him before then; and this is the opinion of most commentators on the passages, both ancient and modern.

With regard to Col. 1. 15-20, it seems to me that the simplest and most useful division of the attributes of Christ contained in these verses, and of the verses themselves, is into two groups.

(1) Those which were true of Him from the beginning (vv. 15-17).

(2) Those which were true of Him from the Cross (vv. 18-20).

In the first of these groups He is "The Image of the invisible God"; in the second He is "The Head of the Body, the Church." In the former He has the title, "Firstborn of every creature"; in the latter He has that of "Firstborn from the dead." In each case a reason is appended for the application to Him of these titles. He is "Firstborn of every creature, for by (or 'in') Him were all things created that are in heaven and that are in earth." He is "Firstborn from the dead . . . for it pleased the Father . . . by Him to reconcile all things unto Himself . . . things in earth or things in heaven."

Now since the reason assigned for the title, "Firstborn of every creature," is that all things were created by Him, I cannot see how that title, or the one coupled with it, "Image of the invisible God," can be referred to His incarnation only. Both declare His dignity as Originator and Sustainer of the first creation, just as those in verse 18 declare His pre-eminence in connection with the new creation.

As to Heb. 1. 3, it is agreed by Mr. Hoste that Christ was always "The Brightness of His glory," and when once this is granted I cannot conceive how the next clause, "The express Image of His Person," is to be divorced from its fellow, and referred to something which only became true of Him at His incarnation. Both clauses hang closely united upon the same participle, "Being," which precedes them; and if the view

B

mentioned were correct, this participle would be bearing its literal meaning in the one clause, and then would have to be thought of as though it meant "becoming" in the next clause. On the other hand, when we take them together, as is usually done, we get in them an interesting contrast with the two opening expressions of v. 1. In time past God spake in the prophets "by divers portions" (a portion now and a portion again), and "in divers manners" (some less clear and some more clear than others). But now God has spoken in His Son, in whom is, not merely a few rays shining out from time to time, but the whole effulgence of His glory; and not merely dim outlines and shadows, but the exact "image" of His substance. And of course it is implied that the revelation thus made is, like Himself, both full and perfect. On this the subject matter of the entire epistle is based. The passage should be read in the R.V., and its connection noted with the word "enlightened" in chap. 6. 4, and "illuminated" (same Greek) in chap. 10. 32.   W.R.

Is there anything wrong, when seeking to defend the real Deity and true humanity of our Lord, in making use of the statement, "He is very God of very God, and very Man of very man?"

The words, "very God of very God" were inserted in the creed of the Nicæan elders and teachers at the council of Nicæa in A.D. 325, for whose faithful contending for the faith we may well thank God. They were intended to safeguard the true Deity of Christ, in opposition to the soul-destroying heresies of Arius, which denied it. They affirmed that the Son, though truly said to be the only begotten of the Father, is no less truly God—co-equal, co-substantial, and co-eternal with the Father and the Spirit. The creed, like every human writing must be tested by the Word of God. In this case, I judge, the expression in question to be quite legitimate and laudable. But the expression, "very Man of very man," stands on other footing. It does not, for one thing, occur in the Nicene creed, nor, as far as I know, in any other, and in my judgment ought to be avoided. It is an attempt to express "the secret things" of the Incarnation, but seems to ignore the part the Holy Spirit had in the conception—"That which is conceived in her is of the Holy Ghost." We must and do insist on the true humanity of our Lord, but without attempting to *define* how it was produced.   W.H.

THE ETERNAL SONSHIP

Does the doctrine of the Eternal Sonship of the Second Person of the Divine Trinity involve inferiority or subsequence to the Son?

It is on such strange affirmations that the deniers of the Eternal

Sonship of our Lord rest their theories, and is exactly what the arch-heretic, Arius, rested on to deny the deity of the Son. But what is eternal cannot be subsequent to anything, and what is divine cannot be inferior to anything, and the Son partakes of the whole Divine Essence equally with the Father and Spirit. Really Arius was more subject to the Scriptures than the present-day deniers we refer to, for he saw that the Lord's Sonship, as prior to His incarnation, was so clearly revealed in the Word of God that it could not be denied. His only escape from the dilemma he had manufactured for himself was then to deny the Lord's deity. He was exceedingly exalted, but because He was clearly said to be the only-begotten Son, and that long before He came into the world, there must have been a time when He was not begotten, and therefore did not exist. By the mercy of God the followers of Mr. J. Taylor do not, up to now, deny the deity of the Lord; therefore they must invent another loop-hole of escape: the Lord was only Son as the result of incarnation. It is really fortunate that Arius is not still in the flesh, for one would tremble for this whole company in face of his sophistries, to which they seem to have some strange affinity. It is hard to conceive of men, with any pretence to weighing the words of Scripture, being satisfied with the reasonings they allege, involving as they do the modelling of the Divine and Eternal relations in the Godhead on the human and temporary expedients of earthly relationship. The human relations of any father and son, involve, so they assert, inferiority in the son, therefore the Divine relations of Father and Son must also involve inferiority in the Son, as though anyone thought of the eternal generation of the Son in terms of the human. It is a complete reversal of the true order of things. Sonship in its highest possible human development, that is where all thought of even a conventional inferiority of the son has passed from view, is only a faint shadow of the Eternal and Divine Sonship, where neither subsequence nor inferiority could have ever existed. When the Lord claimed in John 5. 17, to have worked also, as the Father ("My Father worketh hitherto and I work"), the Jews sought the more to kill Him, because such words could only mean that, by speaking of Himself in the same breath with God as His Father, He did clearly assert His **equality** with the Father, and our Lord accepted the inference, while asserting that such equality did not preclude subordination for mutual purposes. If the Lord was only speaking of a relation established on the earthly plane at Bethlehem, then, according to these teachers, He would not have been equal to His Father and proves by their own showing that He was speaking of Divine relationships existing before His birth. It is surprising that any Christian teacher should fail to differentiate between eternity and the divine on the one hand and time and the human on the other, and try to import into the former, ideas attaching to the latter.   W.H.

It is being taught in some quarters that our Lord was "God the Son in eternity," and became the "Son of God in incarnation." Is this distinction scriptural?

I do not know where the phrase, "God the Son," occurs in Scripture, though no serious objection need be raised to it. As a Trinitarian Person He was God the Son, but THEN, too, He was in the relation of Son to the Father, and was therefore Son of God. There are those who deny the Eternal Sonship of Christ, which is a very serious error, but clearly the teacher referred to here admits this important truth. But I believe it is unscriptural to limit the expression "Son of God" to incarnation. To the Son He saith, "Thy throne, O God, is for ever and ever," and to the Son also, "Thou, Lord, in the beginning hast laid the foundation of the earth" (Heb. i. 8, 10)—uttered to the Lord centuries before His incarnation. I doubt if the Sonship of Christ is ever made to depend on His incarnation. He was CALLED the Son of God in incarnation, because He was the Son of God before incarnation (Luke i. 35), just as the "Son given" is called "Wonderful, Counsellor, the Mighty God," because He was all this before being "the child born" of the virgin (Isa. ix. 6). The above teacher has been referred to as to the phrase this question is based on, and he replies that what he intended to be printed was, "Christ was God the Son in eternity, and became the Son of God as Man," which seems only to mean that personally He was unchanged, but now as Son of God He entered into Manhood and became changed in condition.   W.H.

Some say that the word translated, "only begotten", in such phrases as, "The only begotten Son which is in the bosom of the Father" (John i. 14), merely means, "beloved," and should be so translated especially in all passages relating to the Eternal Son—the Second Person of the Divine Trinity. Do you think this is so?

My own conviction is other, though I know esteemed brethren who maintain it. I doubt indeed if such an opinion would ever have been broached, had it not been for the mistaken notion that to apply such a term as "only begotten" or even "begotten" to our Lord in a past eternity, necessitates the thought of a time before the begetting, and therefore must infringe on the eternity, and therefore on the true Deity, of the Son. This, however, is only so, if we insist on defining and explaining Divine relations by the human, whereas, the latter are the vaguest shadows of the Eternal and Divine: as soon measure the fixed stars with a foot-rule. The same objection applies to the terms "Father" and "Son". Such terms do imply priority and subsequency in earthly relations, but there cannot be priority or the reverse in the case of Eternal Persons. The same objection would apply to the epithet, "the

Word," for does not such a term necessitate to our minds a time before the word was uttered, and when consequently the word had no existence? I was reading only the other day two writings, one by a denier of the Deity of the Son, the other by a denier of His Eternal Sonship, who both refused to believe, because their minds forsooth could not comprehend the possibility of such things. There must be no unsolved mysteries to this type of person, though one wonders how such can believe at all in the God of Revelation, for surely His existence is beyond their comprehension. Such might also lay to heart the limitation imposed by the Lord Himself, "No man knoweth the Son save the Father." However, to return to those who, while holding firmly the Eternal Sonship of Christ, yet refuse the term "only begotten,"* and substitute for it "well-beloved." This is indeed a secondary meaning springing, as we see, directly from the primary, for who is more beloved than an only child? Now although "only-begotten" is the literal translation of the Greek word, it would be permissible, under certain conditions to abandon this—the etymological meaning—if usage justified it. But if the predominant usage agrees with the original philological meaning, then we must keep to that. That this is the case here, can, I think, be clearly shown by a reference to our three chief sources of information (not to mention Latin ecclesiastical writers who translate—uni-genitus "only begotten")—the Hebrew Scriptures, the Septuagint Greek version, and the New Testament. (a) The Hebrew word, **"yahidh,"** occurs twelve times in the Old Testament, and is translated in A. V.: twice, "my darling"; margin "only one" (Psa. 22. 20; 35. 17); twice "desolate" or "solitary" (Psa. 25. 16; 68. 6); once "only beloved" (Prov. 4. 3); and six times "only son" (Gen. 22. 2, 12, 16, of Isaac; Jer. 6. 26. Amos. 8. 10, and Zech. 12. 10); and "only child" (Judg. 11. 34, of Jepthah's daughter); and with all these the R.V. agrees. (b) The Septuagint translates the two Genesis, the Proverbs, and the three prophetic occurrences by **"beloved,"** and the remaining five by "only child" or "son" (**monogenēs**). It may be added that the LXX in their translation of Gen. 22. 2 have, "thy loved son, whom thou lovest," the tautology of which translation might alone have raised a doubt as to its correctness. (c) In the New Testament the word **"monogenēs"** occurs nine times: once of Isaac (Heb. 11. 17)† and thrice of only children (Luke 7. 12; 8. 42; 9. 38), and five times of the Son of God (John 1. 14, 18; 3. 16, 18 and 1 John 4. 9), translated in each case both in A.V. and R.V. as "Only Begotten." Lest anyone should

---

* From two Greek words, "monos," only, and "genos," offspring (see Acts 17. 28).

† A rather shallow objection has been raised against the translation here, on the ground that Isaac was not the "only-begotten" of Abraham, seeing that Ishmael was also his son; but I think the principle of Rom. 9. 7 clearly counts here, "Neither, because they are the seed of Abraham, are they all children, but in Isaac shall thy seed be called." Ishmael was a son of the flesh, and simply did not count in the purposes of God.

imagine that this is the ordinary word for "beloved", when applied to the Lord, I would mention the significant fact that on the two occasions on which the Father bore audible witness from heaven to the Lord as His beloved Son (Matt. 3. 17; 17. 5), He does not use the word we are considering (**monogenēs**), but the ordinary word for "beloved" (**agapētos**). Surely these two occasions would have been specially suitable for the use of the word "only-begotten," if the Lord's Sonship depended, as is falsely taught in some quarters to-day, on His incarnation!   W.H.

CHRIST AS AN ANGEL

Is the Lord Jesus sometimes spoken of as an angel? How can this be, seeing He is the Son of God, higher than the angels, and the Object of their worship?

We cannot be too jealous for the glory of our Lord Jesus Christ. The first chapter of Hebrews establishes His superiority over the angels in various ways, which we need not recapitulate. He has a place, a relation, prerogatives, and glory far transcending those of the highest angelic beings. But the Hebrew word, "malak," from a root "to depute," and the Greek word, "angelos," from a root meaning, "to announce," both usually translated "angel," are also frequently translated "messenger," *e.g.*, Gen. xxxii. 3; Num. xx. 14; 1 Kings, xix. 2; 2 Kings v. 10; Hag. i. 13; Isa. xlii. 19 (presumably of Christ Himself); and in N.T., Matt. xi. 10, referring to John Baptist; Luke vii. 24, messengers of the Baptist; ix. 52; 2 Cor. xii. 7; James ii. 25. So that when we affirm that there are places where the words "malak" and "angelos" represent the Lord Himself, we are not bringing him down to the level of His own creatures, the angels, but emphasising the fact that He was the MESSENGER OF JEHOVAH. There is indeed a number of O.T. passages where we are obliged to understand the angel mentioned as a Divine Being. In Gen. xlviii. 16, for instance, could it be a mere angel of whom Jacob speaks as His Redeemer, whose blessing he invokes on his grandsons? Is not this to place an angel on the level of God? Then in Exodus 3, "the angel of the Lord" of v. 2 becomes "God" in v. 4. Later on Jehovah speaks of sending an angel before Israel, and adds, "Beware of him and obey his voice; provoke him not, for he will not pardon your transgressions, for My Name is in him" (Exod. xxiii. 21). Could all this apply to a mere angelic being? In the case of Manoah, how could anyone but a Divine Person dare to identify Himself with the burnt offering? Certainly Manoah and his wife believed they had seen God (Jud. xiii. 20-22). To assert that God made Himself known by merely angelic beings is a flagrant denial of the truth of the words, "The only begotten Son who is in the bosom of the Father, HE hath declared Him" (John i. 18). He did not cease to dwell there. When thus revealing God, the Son of Man was in heaven, though on earth (John iii. 13). Blessed paradoxes! Human reasonings stumble at them; faith bows to God's word and adores. To close I would refer to Mal. iii, where the word "malak" is translated twice "messenger"—(1) as applying to John the Baptist, (2) to the Son of God manifest in flesh as the Messenger of the covenant," exactly the same Hebrew expression as is used in the rest of the O.T. for the "angel of the covenant." Is it not conclusive then that this Being is Divine, and represents Him whom we know to-day as the Lord Jesus Christ? W.H.

THE CROSS

Could our Lord have returned to heaven without going to the Cross?

This idea used to be put forward as a possible suggestion for illustrative purposes. What a wonderful ending to our Lord's life it would have been had He gone straight up to heaven without dying! but without asserting that this was a possibility. Of later years this supposition has become an affirmation, put forward as though there was a clear "thus saith the Lord" for it. Especially have speculative teachers, who love the sensational, asserted this in connection with the Transfiguration on the Holy Mount. In reality this was the most unlikely moment for such a thing to occur, had it been otherwise within the range of God's purposes, for such an event is never hinted at in any of the three Gospel accounts of the Transfiguration. In Matt. 17 this comes just after the Lord's first clear announcement of His passion: "Jesus began to show unto His disciples, how that He must go unto Jerusalem, and suffer many things", etc. (chap. 16. 21). In Mark 9 likewise the account is preceded by the words of chap. 8. 31, "The Son of Man must suffer," etc., and so in Luke 9—the reference to the sufferings in verse 22 as a necessity, is followed by a glimpse of the coming Kingdom glory. Far then from a choice being offered to our Lord on the Holy Mount of returning to heaven without dying, I believe this prophetic view of the coming Kingdom glory was to cheer the disciples in view of the certainly coming Cross. There is an additional fact given us in Luke, namely, the subject on which Moses and Elias conversed with our Lord in the glory —"They spake of His decease which He should accomplish at Jerusalem." Certainly Peter tried to turn Him from this purpose in Matt. 16, but was met with a stern rebuke. The momentous scene in Gethsemane clearly shows, however, that the Lord was a free Agent in redemption. He was under no fatalistic necessity to redeem men, but He was "the Lamb slain before the foundation of the world," and He had said to Nicodemus, "The Son of Man must be lifted up." Later we hear Him saying, "For this cause came I unto this hour," and "The Son of Man came . . . to give His life a ransom for many." These two sides of truth are seen at Gethsemane. His holy human will rightly shrank from contact with sin, and the Divine abandonment involved; but as a Divine Person His will was able to say, "Nevertheless not My will but thine be done." When Peter sought by the use of the sword to defend His Master, the latter says, in Matt. 26. 52, "Thinkest thou that I cannot now pray to My Father, and He shall presently give me more than twelve legions of angels?" but immediately adds, "But how then shall the Scriptures be fulfilled, that thus it must be?" In John 18. 11 we have an additional word, "The cup which My Father hath given Me, shall I not drink it?" which, coming either before or after the other words, gives us the balance of Scripture. It was with "wicked hands"—the voluntary act of murderers—that men crucified and slew Him; but it was also with holy hands that He by a voluntary act, and by the Eternal Spirit, offered Himself without spot to God (Heb. 9). He could say with equal truth, "No man taketh My life from Me, but I lay it down of Myself," and "this commandment have I received of My Father" (John 10). There was no fatalistic necessity for our Lord to lay down His life, but there was a moral necessity, and it is very unprofitable and unsound speculation to assert the contrary.   W.H.

Was the Cross on which our Lord was crucified the cross as shaped to-day? Is the word used that for a stake and not a cross, a word only implying that which stands up?

It is true that the first meaning of *"stauros,"* the word translated, "cross," in the New Testament, is a "stake" (from *"histēmi,"* to stand), and this was occasionally used in executions, the victim being sometimes impaled on it. But this stake, called "the simple cross," was not the Latin cross, which was in the shape of a T, and had an upright above the crossbar, on which the title of accusation was displayed. This was the form of cross the Romans used, and, on which there seems no room to doubt, our Lord was crucified. Because the cross is found in Babylonian cults is no good reason for denying that the Romans crucified Him on the ordinary Latin cross. We are certainly not to wear a cross or display it on "religious buildings," but to learn the meaning of Christ's Cross, and bear our own.   W.H.

CHRIST'S BURIAL

As regards our Lord's burial, is it right to say that, "Burial is a necessary part of our Lord's vicarious work"? "The Gospel includes it as we see in 1 Cor. 15. 3, 4. Adam being guilty, the judgment of God required that he should return to the earth whence he came. The burning outside the camp of the sin-offering when its blood was taken inside the veil, points to this" (so a Mr. J. T. asserts).

It is important to distinguish between the penal and governmental consequences of sin. The former are defined in the words of the Lord God, "In the day that thou eatest therefore **thou shalt surely die.**" There is no mention till later of dust returning to dust, if we must take that as the equivalent of burial, though it is more a putting out of sight, than physical dissolution. Nor indeed was physical death the death primarily referred to in the above warning: additional precautions had to be taken to ensure that, namely the prevention of access to the Tree of Life—"Now lest he put forth his hand and take also of the tree of life and eat and live forever (i.e., exist in a sin-haunted body), therefore the Lord God sent him forth from the garden of Eden." Nothing of an outward physical change seems to have taken place at the Fall, but a mysterious moral gulf had appeared between the creature and his Creator; he was afraid of God and hid himself. This was spiritual death.

In verses 16 to 19, the governmental consequences of the Fall are detailed quite distinct from death. The Christian is saved from the penal consequences of sin whereas he often has to know its governmental consequences. I believe the former were exhausted at the cross as the words, "It is finished," declare, and as the rending of the veil proves. The Lord before breathing out His spirit was now no longer forsaken of His God for He commends it to His Father. But as the writer Mr. J. T. well says, "The forsaking would not have been a public matter, had not our Lord uttered the cry." So the death of the body was the outward and visible sign of that other death which had the much deeper significance of separation from God. I am surprised that Mr. J. T. should understand the meaning of the burning of the sin-offering outside the camp in Lev. 4 as burial. The word for "burning" is "śaraph," representing Divine judgment; it is Christ's suffering under God's righteous judgment, outside the camp.

It is difficult to conceive our Lord Jesus as under Divine judgment when with reverent and loving hands He was laid in Joseph's tomb. We may remark that His grave with the rich man was not a penalty for sin, but, "because he had done no violence neither was there any deceit in His mouth." It is perfectly true that Christ's burial is an eloquent testimony to the complete setting aside of the old man; but could it be said that our Lord was buried vicariously? I trow not. It is part of "the **truth** of the Gospel," but as far as I remember, is only once referred to by an apostle in any public address in the Acts, which seems to show that it is not a significant part of the Gospel for the unsaved. But the Gospel is very great and extended, and has a close application to the believer. Perhaps we would be right in saying that the cross is the refuge for sinners, the sepulchre, the receptacle for the old man— signified by baptism; and "in Christ" risen, the residence of the new man.   W.H.

DID GOD DIE?

Is it wrong to assert that God died on the cross? If so, we must revise some of our hymns, e.g., "Save in the cross of Christ, my God," and "When Christ, the Mighty Maker, dies."

It is quite possible that some of our hymns (though not perhaps above) need revising; at best they are human compositions, but let it be done by those capable for such work. Not every amateur possesses the poetic gift. Better leave out a hymn, than maul it. Certainly it is quite unscriptural to say that "God died on the cross," for "God only hath **immortality**," and as such of course cannot die, but this does not imply that the One who hung upon the cross was not God, for He was, and Thomas was perfectly right when he exclaimed later, "My Lord and my God."

Perhaps an illustration will make the matter plainer. We read twice in Psa. 121 that "Jehovah slumbers not nor sleeps." Are we then to assert when we read in Mark 4. 38 of our Lord that "He was asleep on a pillow," that God was asleep, or that He who was asleep was not God? Neither the one nor the other, for both assertions would be false. Hebrews 2. 14 teaches that He who in chapter 1 is spoken of as the Son, the Heir of all things, the Creator and Sustainer of all things, and Who as such possessed Immortality, and was therefore immune from death, did Himself in order to purge our sins "take part of flesh and blood, that **through death,** etc." He did not cease to be what He was before; but He became flesh, and so far capable of death, though never subject to death, as we are.   W.H.

CHRIST'S PRIESTHOOD

When did the High Priesthood of Christ begin, at the offering of Himself on the cross, or upon His sitting down at God's right hand?

If I were to ask, at what point in the record given us in the 8th and 9th chapters of Leviticus did the high priesthood of Aaron begin, I should probably receive various replies. Some possibly would tell me that he was high priest from the very beginning of the first day of the eight mentioned in these chapters, when he was put forward, before the congregation (chap. 8. 2-5), as the one God had "called" (Heb. 5. 4) for the position. Others might say that his priesthood should be reckoned from after the bathing, and clothing, and anointing, and offering (including that of the ram of consecration) on that first day had been completed. Others still might think that only at the end of the seven "days of consecration" (chap. 8. 33) could he be called high priest; while some perhaps would suggest that his priesthood did not effectively begin until he commenced to act on the people's behalf during the transactions of the eighth day (chap. 9. 15). If I got these replies, could I say that any of them was entirely wrong? I do not think so.

Let us then see what the Hebrews epistle has to tell us about the beginning of the High Priesthood of Christ. In chapter 9. 11, after a description of the ministry of the Old Testament high priests, we read, "But Christ having (R.V.) come a High Priest . . . entered in . . . having obtained eternal redemption." Here the expression "having come a High Priest" seems to suggest that, right from the commencement of His Activities in connection with obtaining redemption, He was acting in priestly character; and definitely so, before He "entered in." Then in chapter 2. 17 we get, "It behoved Him to be made like unto His brethren, that He might become (see Greek, or Newberry) a . . . High Priest . . . to make propitiation (R.V.) for the sins of the people." In this passage His becoming High Priest is made consequent on His having been made "like unto His brethren," and yet it was as High Priest that He made propitiation for sins. Again, in chapter 6. 20 (R.V.) we read, "Whither as a forerunner Jesus entered for us, having become a High Priest"; which appears to imply that His "entering" followed immediately upon His becoming Priest. Next, in chapter 5. 10, after having "learned obedience by the things which He suffered" (this, in light of Phil. 2. 8 surely including His death), and after having thus been "made perfect"; He is then "named (R.V.) of God a High Priest after the order of Melchizedek," probably in the sense that there was a proclamation of His Priesthood at His ascension. Lastly, in chapter 8. 4 we are told that His Priesthood is not "on earth," and in chapter 7. 26 that it is in a sphere where He is "separated (R.V.) from sinners, and made higher than the heavens."

In view of all this, would I be safe in setting down as wrong: (1) the person who says that when Christ offered up Himself He was Priest as well as Sacrifice; or (2) the person who tells me that His Priesthood is part of the outcome of His death; or (3) the person who states that for the exercise of His Priesthood, He required to be where He now is, in the heavenly Sanctuary? In each case, I do not think so.   W.R.

CHRIST'S GLORIFIED BODY

Does the Lord still bear in His glorified body the marks of the Cross?

Most certainly. In Revelation 5. 6 John was granted a vision of the Lord in ascension on the throne of God, and He was seen as a living Lamb, **standing,** and yet as having been slain, that is, as plainly bearing in His body the sacrificial marks, or in other words, the scars, of Calvary. Besides, how could we admit for a moment that the marks in His resurrection body to which He made appeal again and again to prove

His identity, have been removed since? How, moreover, could such appeal be real, unless the marks were something more than temporary and indeed an essential part of His spiritual body? It would be like some one appealing to imitation scars, to prove identity with someone who had received real wounds. We should lose, too, antitypically in a very serious way were we to admit the possibility hinted at in the question. For then how explain the blood on the live bird let loose into the open field in the day of the leper's cleansing? (Lev. 14. 7). Or what would there be in the Heavenly temple to correspond to the blood on the earthly mercy seat, if the One on the throne no longer bore the marks of Calvary? When the Lord arose He had the same body that was crucified and slain, but under new conditions, that is, it was now a spiritual body. Again in ascension He had the same body as before, but once more under new conditions, for it was a glorified body, but still bearing as its highest glory the scars of Calvary.

It is indeed the presence of the Lord on the throne, which gives it its character as a throne of grace, and how appropriate then that He should retain His scars of atonement!   W.H.

THE HOLY SPIRIT

THE DISCIPLES AND THE HOLY SPIRIT

Were all the followers of Christ indwelt by the Holy Spirit before the day of Pentecost?

The true answer is, not one of them was. No doubt, as we shall see, the Spirit was with them in a sense, but the Lord distinguishes between this and His indwelling, in John 14. 17: "He dwelleth with you and **shall** be in you." But earlier we read, "The Holy Ghost was not yet given, because Jesus was not yet glorified" (chap. 7. 39).

Later the Lord said, "It is expedient for you that I go away, for if I go not away, the Comforter will not come to you, but if I depart I will send Him unto you" (chap. 16. 7). Does this mean that the Spirit had never been working on the earth before? No, far from it—He had, as we have seen, been always with His people, for we read of His workings throughout the Old Testament. He it is "Who moved (or brooded) on the face of the waters," preparatory to the renovation of the earth (Gen. 1. 2); "who strove with men" (chap. 6. 3); who filled His servants and came mightily upon them for special service, e.g., Bezaleel, Joshua, Samson, etc.; who moved holy men of God in the Old Testament to speak, and to write, e.g., David: 2 Sam. 23. 2 (see 2 Peter 1. 21); and who was vexed with the rebellion of Israel (Isa. 63. 10). These various actions He performed as an Omnipotent and Omnipresent Divine Person. But it was later at Pentecost that He came down, Personally to indwell His people and baptise them into "the One Body," and thus unite them to the Risen Christ in glory, in answer to the request of the Lord Himself. W.H.

THE SIN AGAINST THE HOLY SPIRIT

What is blasphemy against the Holy Spirit?

Our Lord's words about the blasphemy against the Holy Spirit arose from the ascription by the Jewish leaders of His works to "Beelzebub," implying that "He had an unclean spirit." Whether they KNEW intelligently He was actually working by the Holy Spirit is not said, but they were no doubt speaking deliberately against the Lord, and that was a very heinous sin, leading on to His cruel death at Calvary. Could a more dreadful sin be imagined? Yes, there was one greater. That could be forgiven, and many of His murderers were indeed forgiven on repentance (Acts ii. 38), through the testimony of the Holy Ghost sent down from heaven. What, then, is this more grievous sin, for which there is no forgiveness? It is the deliberate rejection of the testimony of the Holy Spirit; it is the sin of apostasy. When this sin has been reached, "It is impossible to renew again to repentance" (Heb. vi. 6). It is not that those guilty want to repent and are refused, but it is impossible to get them to want to repent. They become adversaries (see Heb. x. 27). One thing seems certain, that no one who desires forgiveness has committed the unpardonable sin. Where there is the desire, confession is still available, with immediate forgiveness and cleansing for the Lord's sake (see 1 John i. 9; ii. 1, 2). W.H.

Can the Sin against the Holy Spirit be committed to-day?

The possibility would seem greater in the present day, as the Holy Spirit is now in Person on the earth. This sin seems to be a deliberate ascription, not necessarily aloud, but perhaps in the heart, to Satan of the Spirit's work. For those who refused the Lord Jesus, as Messiah there was forgiveness, as witness the early chapters of the Acts. But when once the apostolic testimony to a risen Christ by the Holy Ghost was definitely and nationally refused, we hear no longer of such mass conversions, and the blessing moved more and more from Jerusalem to the Gentiles, though the grace of God lingered over the beloved city, as the glory had done in the time of Ezekiel. There may be a point in the experience of many, when they finally resolve to refuse Christ and probably never experience the Spirit's drawing again. They will henceforward believe any lie, but the truth, never. Such individual apostasy will become the mass movement of the very last days. They will believe the lie, and take the mark of the Beast and their eternal doom will be finally sealed. This is apostasy, from which there is no recovery, a giving up of Christianity, sometimes, as one hears to-day, for Mohammedanism, Buddism, Hinduism, Spiritism or what not. One thing, however, is, I believe, certain, that such apostacy is never marked by a fear of having apostatised. That is not the sign of apostacy, but rather the belief that the truth has at last been found. Where a poor soul dreads having committed the unpardonable sin, and still desires to be saved, there is no apostacy, and no doubt there is still mercy in the heart of God to such an one, and a full offer of salvation by faith in our Lord Jesus Christ. Let such an one come to Christ and he or she will not be cast out.   W.H.

Does God ever refuse to forgive in this life? If one is conscious of having resisted the call of God, may not that make it impossible for Him to forgive?

It is quite certain that God will never refuse forgiveness in this life to anyone who comes to Him as a sinner in the Name of the Lord Jesus, pleading in faith His atoning work. No other plea can suffice, but that will always reach the ear of God. "To Christ give all the prophets witness, that through His Name, whosoever believeth in Him shall receive remission of sins" (Acts x. 43). "We have redemption through His blood, even the forgiveness of sins" (Eph. i. 7). This is the forgiveness of God as Judge. Then to believers, the Father's forgiveness, for the restoration of communion, is granted on confession. "If we confess our sins, He is faithful and just to forgive us our sins and to cleanse us from all unrighteousness" (1 John. i. 9). As to Divine forgiveness, there may seem to be an exception in Matt. xii. 31, where the assurance of "forgiveness of all manner of sin and blasphemy" is qualified by the Lord with the words, "but the blasphemy against the Holy Ghost shall not be forgiven unto men," the reason of His saying this being, "because they said He hath an unclean spirit." I know this is usually taken as proving that the Pharisees had actually committed the "unpardonable sin;" for myself I feel more and more persuaded, taking other Scriptures into consideration, that the Lord was rather warning them of the terrible danger of refusing the future testimony of the Spirit, at and after Pentecost. The rejection of Christ did not shut the door of forgiveness, for the Spirit was poured forth; but if His testimony were rejected there could only remain judgment. No one who finally rejects that testimony will ever, I believe, feel the need of forgiveness, much less ask for it. How many there are who did at first resist the offers of God's mercy, and the pleadings of His Spirit, but who afterwards were led to repentance. Was not Paul's "kicking against the pricks" a case in point? But it is not poor, timid, anxious souls who have finally resisted the appeal of the Spirit, but hardened and impenitent sinners like the murderers of Stephen.   W.H.

THE SEALING

Is the sealing of the Holy Spirit in this dispensation, a sealing on the forehead, seen outwardly, or is it experienced inwardly? Does not Bunyan refer to an outward sealing?

The sign of the old covenant was circumcision, an outward mark in the flesh. It is said in the case of Abraham to have been the "seal of the righteousness of the faith, which he had yet being uncircumcised" (Rom. 4. 11), which was of course exceptional, as infants of eight days old have no righteousness. The Lord seals His people as His own by giving them His Holy Spirit. "In whom having believed ye were sealed with that Holy Spirit of promise" (Eph. i. 13, R.V.; see also chap. iv. 30; and 2 Cor. i. 22). This is not an experience subsequent to conversion, but at conversion; nor is it an outward mark on the flesh, but a spiritual reality, which no doubt will come out in life. John Bunyan's "Pilgrim's Progress" is an allegory: that is, a spiritual truth conveyed under the form of a literal story. We should get into no end of difficulties, if we interpreted the figures literally. Are all sinners, for example, to wade through a literal "Slough of Despond" on their way to the wicket gate? Besides, even Bunyan must be checked by the Word of God, and no less, "experiences" that pious persons claim to have passed through. There is no such thing taught in the Bible, as a Christian "being sealed on the forehead," and for anyone to claim such a thing is a mistaken pretension, which he should seek grace from God to abandon. W.H.

THE HOLY SPIRIT AND THE CHURCH

Does the Holy Spirit go back to Heaven with the Church at the close of the present Dispensation, or, does He still remain here, to convict of sin, righteousness, and judgment? In other words, is He here in Person only from Pentecost until the "Rapture"?

We learn from 2 Thess. 2. 5 that the common view that the apostle in this passage was correcting the teaching of the first epistle is quite mistaken. Exactly the reverse is the case; he was confirming it; "Remember ye not, that when I was yet with you, I told you these things?" Add to this the fact that in verse 1 he actually appeals to "the coming of the Lord and our gathering together unto Him," as revealed in 1 Thess. 4, to counter the false teaching abroad "that the day of the Lord" was then present (see R.V.), for the other must take place first. Verse 6 teaches, I believe, the same truth. Some suggest that "that which letteth" is law, and "he who letteth" the executive of law, government But this seems forced and unnatural. Is it not more in harmony with the context to interpret "that which letteth" to be the Church indwelt by the Spirit, and He who letteth, the Spirit indwelling the Church? When the Church goes at the coming of the Lord, the Holy Spirit will, as an indwelling Person, go too. He will therefore be no longer in this scene as the One in Whom the Church is baptised and united to a Risen Christ. That wonderful and unique work of God belongs only to the present dispensation. But the departure of the Spirit in this sense does not mean that He will cease to work in the world. He will resume His activities of pre-Pentecostal times toward God's people and the world. What we read in Rev. 7 and 14, shows clearly that He will carry on a mighty work of conversion, through the sealed of Israel, far beyond, it would seem, anything known in the present dispensation. This began with 120 sealed ones, that will begin with 144,000, and the zenith will be, "a multitide that no man can number." We must, however, avoid the thought that the wicked one will be revealed at the **moment** of the rapture of the Church. This chapter warns us against such an idea, for the apostacy will first fully develop and then the way will be open for the manifestation of the Man of Sin.   W.H.

ANGELIC BEINGS

SATAN

SATAN'S FALL

Is it right to teach that Satan fell first of all in Eden's garden?
Perhaps there is scarcely any subject which lends itself more readily
to speculation, and concerning which speculation ought to be more
carefully avoided, than the mysterious fall of Satan. No fact is more
clear; hardly one mentioned with more reserve. If the above question
means whether his fall took place in the actual Garden of Eden of
Genesis ii, the answer can only be, "No." Satan comes on the scene
in it as a fallen being, already the enemy of God and man. His fall had
taken place long before, and, as I believe, in another scene. This
fall is referred to by our Lord in Luke 10. 18: "I beheld Satan as lightning fall from heaven." This would indicate that heaven was his original
abode. The reason of his fall is given in 1 Tim. iii. 6, to be pride, but
nothing is said specially of his pride in the Eden episode. His fall is
referred to also in Isaiah xiv, in words which must go far beyond the
Assyrian: "How art thou fallen from heaven, O Lucifer, son of the
morning!" Again in Ezekiel xxviii, his fall is described, no doubt in
symbolic language: "By the multitude of thy merchandise, they have
filled the midst of thee with violence, and thou hast sinned" (v. 16).
"Thine heart was lifted up because of thy beauty; thou hast corrupted
thy wisdom by reason of thy brightness" (v. 17). Pride, corruption,
and violence characterised his fall, as they have also our fallen race.
What has probably given colour to the idea referred to above are the
words in Ezekiel xxviii. 13 addressed to Satan concerning his fall:
"Thou hast been in Eden the garden of God." If God prepared for
Adam, the head of the earthly creation, a delightful abode suitable for
his highest enjoyment, is it not likely that He would do the same for the
head of the angelic creation? Just as there is now, besides the earthly
paradise that was, a heavenly paradise, so there may have been two
Edens. It has been suggested that Lucifer's Eden may have occupied
the same site in the original earth of Genesis i. 1, as the Eden of the
Adamic earth. Some think there would be a fitness in this. Certainly
heaven and earth were not so wide apart once as now, but the idea
seems to lack direct scriptural support.   W.H.

**Had Satan any history previous to his appearing in the Garden
of Eden—or does the expression in Ezekiel 28—"Eden the**

garden of God," mean the Garden of Eden where Adam and Eve were?

Such a thought as that Satan fell in the earthly Eden is entirely foreign to the Genesis account, where Satan is presented to us at once as the seducer of man. His fall is always considered in the Scriptures as from heaven not on earth. To rest such a theory as that Satan fell in the Eden of Genesis 2, on the words, "Thou wast in Eden," (Ezekiel 28. 13), is like balancing a pyramid on its apex. The word Eden is 'edhen (from 'adhan, to be delighted), and simply means a place of delight. It would be like saying that when Paul was caught up into Paradise, it must have been into the garden of Eden, for the same Greek word paradeisos is used there. As there is a heavenly and an earthly paradise, we may believe there is a heavenly as well as an earthly Eden. It is noticeable that "the garden of Eden" does not necessarily mean that the garden and Eden are the same, for in ver. 8 we read, "God planted a garden in Eden", and in ver. 10, "A river went out of Eden to water the garden"; thus the two are distinguished. This garden is never called "the Garden of God", as in Ezekiel 28. 13 ("In Eden, the garden of God . . . thou wast.") The Genesis "garden" is rather the garden of man. The description of Lucifer in Ezekiel 28. 12-15 (for it is surely he) must be taken as a whole, revealing his created glories (v. 12), and the place of delight, perfectly suitable to his nature prepared for him by God. Next his covering is described. The beauty of the place seems to have been rather mineral than vegetable. He was the anointed cherub that covered (i.e., the throne of God?). "He was in the holy Mountain of God and he walked up and down (same word and mood employed of Enoch) in the midst of the stones of fire." All this is perfectly foreign to the earthly paradise of Genesis 2. The account goes on—"Thou wast perfect in all thy ways, from the day that thou wast created till iniquity was found in thee." The earthly "garden of Eden" was prepared by God for man at his creation, and we have no reason to believe he was long in Eden before he fell. Is it not a fantastic theory that all that we have read in Ezekiel, beginning with "Thou was in Eden . . . till iniquity was found in thee", must be squeezed into man's unfallen sojourn in the garden! We do not make ourselves responsible for speculations attributed to those who believe Satan fell long previously to man. We do not profess to be "wise above that which is written," but we regard the theory of Satan's fall in the Adamic garden of Eden as quite untenable and as subversive of all sane scriptural interpretation.

W.H.

PRINCIPALITIES AND POWERS

Is there a difference between the "Principalities" and "Powers" mentioned in Eph. 1. 21; 3. 10; 6. 12, Col. 1. 16; 2. 10;

2. 15? Some of the statements made concerning them suggest that they are good, others that they are evil.

The words "principalities" and "powers," when used together, define the status of certain who hold high place of rule, whether among men, or among angelic beings. In the former connection they are found in Titus 3. 1, where we are exhorted to be subject to them; while of the latter the clearest example is perhaps Eph. 6. 12, in which they are definitely set in contrast with "flesh and blood." In some passages, as Rom. 8. 38, Eph. 1. 21, Col. 1. 16, they occur in a statement of such a character that it might perhaps be thought of as inclusive of both.

With regard to those principalities and powers which are angelic, there certainly does seem to be a difference on the lines indicated in the question above. Against those mentioned in Eph. 6. 12 we have to fight, and verse 11 shows that their leader is the Devil. But on the other hand, the principalities and powers of Eph. 3. 10, who are even now learning lessons through the Church of the manifold wisdom of God, can scarcely be thought of as other than good, especially when comparison is made with the similar statement of 1 Pet. 1. 12, "Which things angels desire to look into." It must not be thought however that their being described as "in heavenly places" is sufficient proof of their goodness, since this is the very same term which is rendered "high places" in connection with those of chapter 6. 12 (see R.V.).

According to Col. 1. 16, all principalities and powers were created by Christ, and this of course implies that they were all good originally. But we read in Jude 6 (R.V.) of "Angels which kept not their own principality," an expression which will at once suggest a reason why there should now be found both good and evil amongst them. Then in Rev. 12. 7-9 we read of a conflict between good angels under the leadership of Michael and evil angels led by the Devil, in which the latter and his host will be defeated, and cast down to the earth from the heavenly position until then occupied by him. W.R.

What is the difference between fallen angels, demons, unclean spirits, and familiar spirits?

This is a matter concerning which many seek to be wise beyond what is written, with results that are not profitable, either to themselves or to others. That Satan is a fallen angel, and a leader of other angels who fell with him, just as Michael is of unfallen angels, seems to be definitely proved by Rev. 12. 7. That the sinning angels of 2 Pet. 2. 4 and Jude 6 are a different company, whose fall took place at a different time, is a view held by some, but without sufficient proof. That Satan is identical with Beelzebub the prince of demons is implied in Matt. 12. 24-28 and Mark 3. 22-26, where Christ uses the terms interchangeably; and if that be so, the demons are most probably of the number of those who fell with him. These demons are otherwise called "unclean spirits," because of their character, as may be seen by comparing verses 12 and 13 of Mark 5. As for "familiar spirit," it is a term used in the Old Testament of demons who, by entering into diviners, enabled them to carry on their evil work. See 1 Sam. 28. 7, etc.. The "spirit of divination" in the damsel of Acts 16. 16 is similar. W.R.

THE DEMON POSSESSED

Were those of whom we read in the New Testament that they were demon-possessed responsible for being in that condition?

Certainly not in every case. In that of the boy in Mark 9. 20-22, his father in reply to the Lord's question said that he had been thus from childhood. What was true with regard to the other miracles of healing wrought by Christ was probably true of the demon-possessed also, that in some instances the trouble was due to sin on the part of the person concerned, and in others not so. Contrast the warning to the impotent man in John 5. 14, "Sin no more, lest a worse thing come unto thee," with the words spoken of the blind man in John 9.3, "Neither hath this man sinned." W.R.

GOOD ANGELS

Are we to believe that God the Father has angels (Rev. 3. 5), Christ some (2 Thess. 1. 7), and Michael some (Rev. 12. 7)? Or are they all the same?

Though we recognise in the Scriptures that the Divine Persons are co-equal, co-eternal, and co-substantial, that is that each possesses the whole Divine essence in the Unity of the Godhead, we equally see distinctions between the Persons, and differences of relation and function; also conditions of subordination between them for mutual purposes, and this not only since the Incarnation, but eternally and necessarily so by the Divine law of their Being. Thus the Father is revealed as Source—the Fountain of all things. He originates, He purposes, He is the Creator of all things. He is the Father of Spirits, and therefore of the angels, who belong to the spiritual creation, so that they may with the utmost propriety be termed "The Father's angels." Then on the other hand, the Son was the Agent in Creation—"All things were made by Him," including "all things that are in heaven, and in earth, visible and invisible, whether they be thrones or dominions, or principalities or powers: all things were created by Him and for Him" (John 1. 3; Col. 1. 16). He, too, is said to be "Head of all principality and power" (Col. 2. 10). In such phrases are inclusively described "the innumerable company of angels—the general assembly" (Heb. 12. 22, 23). These may then be equally called Christ's angels. To say that they are the Father's and not the Son's, or the Son's not the

Father's, is to ignore our Lord's words, "All that the Father hath are Mine" (John 16. 15), or "All Mine are Thine and Thine are Mine" (chap. 17. 10). That is, even when the Father is said to give anything to the Son, it does not cease to be the Father's. In the cases cited above— Rev. 3. 5, the Lord is speaking of His Father and naturally He speaks of the angels in relation to Him (His angels), but in 2 Thess. 1. 7, the Spirit is describing the return in glory of the Son, and here the angels are spoken of, as we should expect, as His angels, because related to Him. But we do not for that conceive of the angels as divided into two companies, the Father's and Christ's. The case of Michael's angels is very simple and quite distinct. They are not his in the same sense as above, but they are the angels put under his command for a certain purpose. Michael is five times mentioned in the Bible—thrice in Daniel—10. 13: "One of the chief ("the first" of marg.) princes"; v. 21, "your prince"; and chap. 12. 1, "the great prince which standeth for the children of thy people." Then in Jude 9 as "the archangel"; and lastly, in Rev. 12. 7 as the leader in the war in heaven, when Satan and his angels (those who followed him in his fatal choice), will be cast down. Satan is always the bitter enemy of Israel, God's earthly people, and Michael, the archangel (he is the only one so named) is specially seen as opposing him, and is, as leader of the angelic hosts, called to fight against him. In this sense they are Michael's angels, that is, under his leadership. W.H.

BIBLE DOCTRINES

How does Scripture present Predestination? Is it true, as I have heard it said, that "we are not out to save souls, God will do that; we teach believers"?

As for the latter part of the question, we believe it to be a most dangerous perversion of the truth. If it were so, why did the Lord tell His disciples, "Go and make disciples of all nations" (Matt. 28), and "Go into all the world and preach the Gospel to every creature" (Mark 16), and again, "Ye shall be witnesses unto Me" (Acts 1), where clearly the thought is evangelising? True, we cannot save souls, but what is an evangelist for, if not to evangelise? All believers are called to this publicly or privately in their measure. Directly we allow election to tinge our gospel, the latter is spoiled, and is no longer "glad tidings of great joy, which shall be to all people," and our election becomes fatalism. We preach Christ as a Saviour available for all sinners. "Whosoever" is the word for the unsaved; all might be saved did they repent and believe the Gospel. This being so, we equally believe in the electing grace of God. We do not need to understand in order to believe; we believe and so we understand. But not only is "election" a truth by itself, but it is to be distinguished from "Predestination." Thus in Ephesians 1. 4 we read that the saints are "chosen (eklegō) in Him before the foundation of the world, that we should be holy and without blemish before Him." But they are also said in the next verse to be "Predestinated." Now this has to do with their adoption, or receiving a place as sons. Thus the distinction would seem to be that Election determines eternal blessing to the objects of it, whereas Predestination determines the special character of the blessing. All the elect are chosen to be holy, but the special character of their blessing varies according to the class of elect persons to which they belong. We do not gather from Scripture that the angels, though they are certainly called, "sons of God," are that, except in the sense of creation. Israel belongs to the earthly family, the Church to the heavenly. So we see later in the chapter that the saints of the present dispensation are predestinated to the inheritance (i.e., the heavenly), and in Rom. 8, are predestinated to be "conformed to the image of His Son," which is not the portion of the redeemed of every age. The same word is found in Acts 4. 28 with reference to the "sufferings of Christ," of which it could not be said that they were "elected," but "determined to be done," i.e., mapped out or planned beforehand. Again the word is used in the same sense in 1 Cor. 2. 7, of the wisdom of God revealed in Christ, which is said to be "ordained before" the world unto our glory. We who have by mercy believed, are exhorted to "make our calling and election sure," by adding to our faith the practical graces of Christian life (2 Pet. 1. 10). W.H.

ELECTION

Some have become concerned as regards their unsaved relatives and the doctrine of election; they cannot understand how the difficulty of God's sovereignty and man's responsibility is to be met.

That, however, is a poor reason for not believing them both. We do not need to range ourselves in men's categories and take sides with Arminians, those who hold the responsible freedom of man's will, or with Calvinists who believe equally firmly in God's sovereignty; we believe in both, not as a mixture, but as entireties. Directly our gospel is limited or hampered by views of God's sovereignty, we may be sure that we hold it wrongly. As has been said, we pray as though all depended on God's grace; we preach as though all hinged on man's faith. Really the difficulty need not trouble us. It meets us, if we think of it, in every action of our life. Certainly God is Sovereign; "Known unto God are all His works from the beginning of the world" (Acts 15. 18). God knows what will happen; He forsees; He chooses; He disposes. What can we do therefore? What is to be, will be. "We must wait for Him" to do all. On the contrary, we know we have a responsibility to fulfil and no accusations of Arminianism need turn us aside. Let us take a simple illustration:—Supposing we have friends returning to the homeland from U.S.A.; but within sight of land the ship catches fire and everyone on board is in great peril. Now nothing is more certain than that God knows all, who will be saved and who will not be, but will that deter the most convinced Calvinist from seeking to bring help to those in danger and straining every nerve to reach them in time? We ask God's help, and we thank Him when our friends are brought safely to land, but if everyone sheltered behind the purposes of God, and sat down and did nothing, then most probably those in danger would be lost. Now, if we would not act like this in temporal affairs, why do so in spiritual things? We are not called to examine the book of God's decrees, but by prayer and effort to bring our relatives under the sound of the Gospel. The Lord did not send His disciples to preach election to every creature, nor the Gospel to all the elect (for we do not know who they are), but the Gospel to every creature. When Paul thanked God for the election of the Thessalonians in chap. 1. 4 of the first Epistle, he did not cite some wonderful vision or spiritual experience through which they had passed, to justify this conviction, but he based it on: (1) the way they received the Gospel, and (2) the effects of the Gospel on their lives, summed up in verse 9 as "turning to God from idols to serve the living and true God, and to wait for His Son from heaven." Generally when man's responsibility and God's electing grace are mentioned on the same page of Scripture, it is the former that comes first. Thus in John 5. 40 the Lord said to the Jews, "Ye will not come unto Me that ye might have life" (not ye cannot), and in the following chapter (v. 44) we hear His words, "No man can come to Me, except the Father, which hath sent Me, draw him." See also Acts 13. 46, "Seeing ye put it (the Word of God) from you, and judge yourselves unworthy of eternal life, lo, we turn to the Gentiles"; and then two verses on, "As many as were ordained to eternal life believed." In chapter 18. 8, "Many of the Corinthians, hearing, believed, and were baptized," and in v. 10, "I have much people in this city." We must not limit the Gospel message as a **bona fide** proclamation of Christ's death, burial, and resurrection as the means of salvation, available for all, for "God wills all men to be saved and to come to the knowledge of the truth," and "Christ gave Himself a ransom for all," that "whosoever believeth in Him should not perish, but have everlasting life"; and the last message in the Scriptures to the unsaved is, "Let him that is athirst come. And whosoever will let him take the water of life freely." Those who have believed the Gospel and who have the humble confidence that they are amongst God's chosen ones, give glory to Him alone, and seek to make their calling and election sure. Perhaps there was never a more direct and specific promise from God of safety to any company than to Paul's ship-companions: "There shall be no loss of any man's life among you." "God hath given thee all them that sail with thee"; and Paul added, "I believe God." This was God's sovereign act (Acts 27. 22-25), but in verse 31—when the sailors were about to flee out of the ship—Paul uttered the warning words, "Except these abide in the ship, ye cannot be saved." This gives the human responsibility side, to which both saint and sinner should give good heed. It should be understood that this reply is limited to the subject of the question before us, and hardly touches on the great subject of the eternal counsels from the believer's standpoint.   W.H.

THE ATONEMENT

It has been stated that Atonement is an Old Testament truth, which has no place in the New Testament, Is this so?

I am surprised that any Christian "apt to teach," should make such a statement. Perhaps it is owing to the fact that in the one place in our Version, where the word "atonement" occurs, it ought to be "reconciliation": "By Whom we have now received the reconciliation" (Romans 5. 11). This however, does not prove that the truth of atonement is not expressed in other passages of the New Testament, under a different form of words, for which "atone" or "atonement" might be correctly substituted. The fact is that the atonement of the Old Testament is only a shadow of the truth, and that if we had not the substantial, divine thing in the New Testament, we could not have the shadow in the Old. The Hebrew word for atonement constantly occurring in the Old Testament, especially in Leviticus is the root, "Kaphar," which primarily means "to cover," then by a simple transition, it gets to mean that by which alone God can righteously cover sin—namely by full satisfaction being offered to His holy claims, or in other words, by atonement. The word, "atone," has long since lost its philological, or derived, meaning of "at-one," for that by which God and the sinner can be "at-one"—the atoning work of Calvary.

This root, "Kaphar," also occurs in the substantival form, "Kapporeth" (mercy-seat)—the place where the blood of atonement was sprinkled, therefore, one would suggest, better translated the "atonement-seat." The verb is sometimes translated in our version—"make reconciliation" (e.g. Ezekiel 45. 15, 17; Dan. 9. 24), "purge" (Psa. 79, 9), "pacify" (Prov. 16. 14), "appease"—"I will appease him (Esau) with the present" (Gen. 32. 20), but in the vast majority of occurrences "atone" or "make atonement." What then, we may enquire, is the Hellenistic Greek equivalent used in the Septuagint? In nearly every case, **"exilaskomai,"** or in a few cases simply, **"hilaskomai"**—which is, we see, the same verb without the preposition "ek"—denoting here "entirely," "perfectly"—though we need not press this, as "hilaskomai" means practically the same thing, for atonement, if of any value, must be complete. Turning to the New Testament, we find this same root (hilaskomai) employed (and N.T. Greek is much the same as found in the Septuagint) in six passages: In the publican's prayer we read, "God **be merciful** to me a sinner" (Luke 18. 13, lit. be propitiated). As the publican was standing in the temple area—"afar off," i.e., probably outside and in full view of the altar of burnt offering, we can see no reason to assert, as Alford does, that the publican could not have had any idea of the ground of his acceptance—though he would naturally not know what the lamb prefigured. Then in Rom. 3. 25 and Heb. 9. 5 there occurs the substantival form—**"mercy-seat."** In Heb. 2. 17 we have, "A merciful and faithful high priest ... to **make reconciliation** for the sins of the people"; and finally in 1 John 2. 2 and 4. 10 the translation is, **"propitiation** for our sins." I think it is clear and reasonable that we have in these passages the sense of atonement, applied, except in the case of Heb. 9. 5 and Luke 18. 13, directly to the work of Christ, as the ground on which God can come out to man in grace and the gospel be preached to every creature. W.H.

RECONCILIATION AND ATONEMENT

Is "Reconciliation" the same as "Atonement"?

No, they are as distinct as cause and effect. Atonement is the ground on which reconciliation becomes possible. Unfortunately the Greek equivalents are not always correctly translated in our version. In fact in the only place (Rom. 5. 11) where the word "atonement" occurs in the Authorised Version it is a mistranslation for "reconciliation." On the other hand, "make reconciliation," in Heb. 2. 17 would be quite correctly translated, "make atonement" (hilaskomai), as it is the same root and nearly always translated so in the LXX, Greek Version of the Old Testament. This, too, is the word the publican uses in his prayer (Luke 18. 13), and goes much deeper than merely asking for compassion. It might be translated, "Be propitiated by sacrifice." Some shallow teachers having sufficient acquaintance with Hebrew, to know that Kaphar (making atonement) means primarily "cover," have thought this was its only meaning and have whittled "atonement" down to "covering," and asserted that it is a purely Jewish thing. They ignore the fact that the word has a secondary meaning, denoting that by which alone God can cover sin, namely, by making full satisfaction for His broken law. This has alone been effected by the blood-shedding of the Lord Jesus Christ: "He poured out His soul unto death." The Old Testament has the word again and again but only typically and prophetic-ally; the New Testament alone has the reality (see 1 John 2. 2; 4. 10:—hilasmos, the same root again). Reconciliation becomes possible by atonement, but practical when the sinner turns to God with repentance and faith. The word for "reconciliation" (Katallagē) "points habitually," as Dr. Moule reminds us, "to the winning rather the pardon of an offended King, than the consent of the rebel to yield to His kindness." 'Be ye reconciled to God' would then mean, secure while you can His acceptance."*   W.H.

It has often been stated, and generally accepted, "That God did not need to be reconciled." Now Trench, in his "Synonyms," points out that *katallagē* has two sides:—(1st) God laying aside His holy anger against our sins and receiving us with His favour; (2nd) The daily depositions under the Holy Spirit of the enmity of the old man toward God. Did God need to be reconciled?

No question is raised as to God's love to sinners, nor as to His willingness that all should be saved (the death of Christ does not make God love sinners. He "so loved that He gave"). But whether EFFECTIVE "reconciliation" is made in Scripture simply to depend on the sinner's willingness to "make it up" with God, it is certain that our Lord by His

---

* "Outlines of Christian Doctrine," pp. 79 and 80, and also ''The Atonement" (by present writer) pp. 7 and 8.

atoning death has fully met POTENTIALLY all the claims of God on account of sin. This, however, only becomes ACTUALLY true for those sinners who individually acknowledge their guilt, and believe in the Lord Jesus Christ, and until they do, God's attitude toward them is not one of complacency, but of righteous displeasure. As the late Dr. Moule puts it—"Reconciliation (*katallagē*) habitually points to the winning rather the pardon of an offended king, than the CONSENT of the rebel to yield to his kindness." "Be ye reconciled to God," would then mean, "As the offending party, secure while you can His acceptance through the atoning work of Christ." This is borne out by Matt. v. 23-24, where it is the offender who is told to go and be reconciled to his brother, ostensibly by confession and amends. We, too, are the offenders: in order to be reconciled we must come to God, confess our sinfulness, and believe the Gospel, and then we have peace with God. As Trench (Syn. p. 292) writes of reconciliation: "To make the secondary meaning (that is the breaking down of the enmity of the carnal mind to God), the primary, is based . . . on a foregone determination to get rid of the reality of God's anger against the sinner" (*i.e.*, Psa. vii. 11, "God is angry with the wicked every day"). W.H.

SINS OF IGNORANCE

Is it right to teach that the Lord will not hold man responsible for sins of ignorance?

The answer depends on the cause of the ignorance. Leviticus 4 is taken up with sins of ignorance and the sacrifices to be offered in order to obtain forgiveness. Such are specified as "sins of ignorance"— **"against any of the commandments of the Lord,"** which every Israelite was responsible to know. See v. 17 of chap. 5: "If a soul sin and commit any of these things, which are **forbidden to be done by the commandments of the Lord,** though he wist it not, yet is he guilty and shall bear his iniquity." Ignorance in such cases does not spell innocence. See chap. 4. 28 (R.V.): "If his sin . . . be made known to him." His attention would be called to the commandment he had broken, but he does not then become guilty, but responsible to bring a sin-offering. Ignorance of the law of the land is no excuse for disobedience. The first question then is how far is a man responsible for being ignorant? Evidently an Amalekite or Moabite would not be responsible for offending against the ceremonial law of Israel. They might eat pork, for instance, without defilement. They would not be responsible to keep the Sabbath; but in matters of moral right and wrong, "The Gentiles which have not the law . . . are a law unto themselves, which shew the work of the law written in their hearts, their conscience also bearing witness." (Rom. 2. 14, 15). Mr. F. Arnot once said that he found a good way of showing an African that a certain course was wrong, say stealing his neighbour's goods, was to ask him whether it would be right for his neighbour to treat him so? It will be a sorry excuse for those who live in a land where the New Testament can be had for a penny, to allege that they did not know what God's will was for them, when it is all contained in the Book. Ignorance, if not voluntary, may lessen responsibility, but not annihilate it, if it could by any means have been avoided; so "he that knew not his Lord's will, and did commit things worthy of stripes, shall be beaten with few stripes."   W.H.

FORGIVENESS

Is there to be forgiveness without acknowledgment of wrong?

There are various categories of forgiveness in the Scriptures, which must be distinguished—God's forgiveness of sinners; the Father's forgiveness of His children; ecclesiastical forgiveness; and personal forgiveness. As to the first named, though it is a mistake to apply to the conversion of the sinner, the words of 1 John 1. 9: "If we confess our sins, etc.," which have to do directly with God's children, yet it may be confidently affirmed that no sinner ever received divine forgiveness without acknowledgment of sin in one form or another, tacit or explicit, leading on to faith in our Lord Jesus Christ, when revealed. But here it is not so much a confession of particular sins, as of sinnership—"God be merciful to me a sinner." This corresponds with "repentance unto life," the result of the Holy Spirit's work in conviction, without which there can be no true conversion to God. In the case of the Father's forgiveness to His erring children, it is conditional on confession of sins; then "He is faithful and just to forgive us our sins and to cleanse us from all unrighteousness." It is perfectly true that God's forgiveness has already covered the sins in question, but His forgiveness as Father is needed, if communion with Him is to be restored. The confession should be real and full, and at once forgiveness and cleansing follow, though not often realised to the full at once. David was forgiven the instant he confessed his sin in the presence of Nathan, but later he wrote the 51st Psalm. This may correspond to the application of "the water of separation" on the third and seventh days (Numbers 19. 12, 19). As for ecclesiastical forgiveness, this is that which is referred to in Matt. 18. 18 and John 20. 23—the "binding or loosing," the remitting or retaining, of sins, not by ecclesiastical officials, the pretended priests of Christendom, but by the local church. Nothing is said in these passages of the condition attaching to the forgiveness, but the case that arose in the Corinthian Church (see chap. 5. 1), throws light on this, for in the second epistle, the restoration of the offender is recommended by the apostle on the ground of his repentance—"lest perhaps such an one should be swallowed up with over-much sorrow"—and if they forgive him, he (Paul) will forgive also (2 Cor. 2. 7-10). Paul does not appeal to some leaders in the Corinthian Church, but to the Church as a whole. This ecclesiastical forgiveness has been perverted into what is known as auricular confession, and priestly absolution, things, as we believe, totally foreign to the New Testament and Christianity. As for individual forgiveness, there should be from the first a forgiving spirit on the part of the offended person; he must not bear a grudge or count the offender as an enemy, but be ready to forgive (Matt. 18. 15, 21, 22), but he must not **express** his forgiveness until the offence is acknowledged. To do so would be a subtle way of putting your opponent in the wrong, and be an insult rather than a favour. "If thy brother tresspass against thee rebuke him, and **if he repent forgive him**" (Luke 17. 3, 4). W.H.

If a Christian falls into sin for a longer or shorter period, and is restored to communion through confession, will this entail loss in eternity, or will all be forgiven and forgotten at the Judgment Seat of Christ?

It seems very important to distinguish between God's government and God's grace. When a sinner is led to repentance and faith in Christ, he is forgiven all iniquities: he possesses eternal life; he "shall not come into judgment, but is passed from death unto life." (John 5. 24). He is a child of God. He is "in Christ Jesus" and there is "no condemnation" to him; this is grace. But if he sins as a child of God, whether for a longer or shorter period, it will lead to chastening in one form or other. This is government. He needs the forgiveness of the Father and it is for such a circumstance that the advocacy of Christ exists: "If any man (i.e. Christian) sin, we have an Advocate with the Father, Jesus Christ the righteous." (1 John 2. 1). This advocacy produces conviction by the Spirit, confession and restoration, and "If we confess our sins, He is faithful and just to forgive us our sins and to cleanse us from all unrighteousness." (1 John 1. 9). This again is grace. But though forgiven and cleansed, it does not follow that the **effect** of the sin is at once removed governmentally. David confessed his sin and was straightway forgiven, but the Lord dealt with him governmentally in three ways: "the sword would never depart from his house," the child would die, and he would receive the same treatment he had meted out to others (2 Sam. 12.). So that though sins are forgiven and forgotten in one sense, they are not in another. The time that the soul is away from God, is lost time, for it is fruitless. What has been occupied in sin and self-will, might have been filled with service and fruit for God. The believer stands in different relations to God and Christ. He is not only a member of Christ, a child of God and a temple of the Spirit, but he is a steward, a servant, a builder, etc., to the Lord. If his "work be burnt up he shall suffer loss, but he himself shall be saved, yet so as by fire" (1 Cor. 3. 15); that "every one may receive the things done in his body according to that he hath done, whether it be good or bad." (2 Cor. 5. 10). It seems very hard to believe that this will not entail an eternal difference. Some are preparing themselves for a high position in the millennial and everlasting kingdoms, which others could not possibly fill, owing to their unbelief, self-will or disobedience to the Lord's commands.   W.H.

WRONG TEACHING

What are we to think of "British Israelism," and what should be our attitude towards adherents of it?

The hypothesis is that "Anglo-Saxons are the lineal descendants of the Ten Tribes of Israel and inherit the wonderful promises made to them. These promises the Anglo-Saxons possess nationally." This can hardly be "dignified" with the name of "heresy"; it is rather one of those "imaginations" which we are to seek to cast down in the Name of Christ. As far as truth is concerned, it is of "the stuff that dreams are made of;" a simile not so far-fetched, when we consider that the B.I. theory's prime foundation stone is, as we shall see, confessedly, **an invented dream.** Alas! how sad it is to see even pious Christians thus snared by the great fowler, as also numbers of wordlings, taking up as a sort of fashionable pastime the slogan, not "We are **lost sinners,**" but "We are the **lost tribes.**" It thus provides for the world another gospel, which captivates and hypnotises them with the thought of capturing great earthly blessings for themselves and the British Empire, apart from repentance and faith in Christ, as though He had never died and risen to procure us blessings, and we must needs make out a fancied identity with the lost tribes (bereft of blessings themselves) in order to get a few for ourselves and the British Empire. Certainly Christ did not die for the glory of the British Empire. If God has blessed our country so signally in the past, the reasons are not far to seek: (1) His Sovereignty; (2) the comparative good treatment England has bestowed on the Jews; (3) the fact that she has been a harbour of refuge for persecuted Continental Christians; (4) because, by His mercy, the Word of God was accepted at the Reformation, and became our national Book for centuries; (5) and because of His many people in our country and their prayers; though now she is on the way to forfeit all this by her national sins and apostasy. But not one blessing did Britain ever inherit for the "British-Israel" reason, because even if she were the lost tribes, she has not kept God's laws and statutes, the very condition of blessing (see Deut. 28. 15) and would have put herself outside the covenant, if ever under it, by neglecting circumcision. British Israelism is no mere harmless delusion; its logical effect is virtually to exclude Christ (not He, but the British Empire looms at the centre of things), and to supersede the gospel to sinners with some fancied national position, with its naked abandonment of the heavenly calling of the church and a complete confusion between her and Israel. Even, if we were Israel, she is set on one side nationally for the present so far as earthly blessing goes, and so should we be. If space allowed, I would gladly take up the general arguments for or against the much vaunted "identifications," but before examining the ornaments of a building, it is well to enquire as to the foundation. I believe no castle-in-the-air ever had a flimsier base than this theory. Is there any historic proof that the ten tribes migrated from the latitudes where the Assyrians placed them, to England or anywhere else? There is not a scintilla. No mention is made of their doings either in Scripture or secular history from about 720 B.C., when their Assyrian captors settled them in Assyria, etc., though we have promises in the Scripture of their future restoration, e.g. Isa. 11. 12, where Jehovah promises to gather back again to their only land of blessing the **"outcasts of Israel,"** along with **"the dispersed of Judah,"** from whom they are thus carefully distinguished. We may be sure the Assyrians, as long as they had the power, would not allow their captives to wander away at their own sweet will to some other land. Until we have some serious proof that the ten tribes ever **started** on their journey for the British Isles, it is futile to spend time in proving they never **arrived** there. On what then does the B.I. theory rest? On a passage in an Apocryphal book, the 2nd of Esdras,* purporting to have been written by Ezra the scribe, but really **forged** 700 years after the captivity by some unscrupulous impersonator living in Egypt. The passage (see chap. 13. 1-12; 39-46) purports to be the interpretation of a **fictitious** dream ascribed to Ezra, to the effect that the ten tribes took counsel to leave the heathen country where they were in captivity and go off into a land where no one dwelt; where they might keep God's statutes. They crossed the Euphrates miraculously and after a year and a half arrived at some unknown region called Arsareth. "Then dwelt they there until the latter time." The whole chapter reads like an unholy parody of Scripture, as indeed it is, naturally bereft of all spiritual power, and bristling with the wildest improbabilities. And yet this fake dream and its fictitious interpretation is admitted by the writers of **"British Israel Truth"** (chap. 7.) to be the "one only **tradition** of their fate (i.e., of the lost tribes) which past ages have handed on to us."† That a whole system should rest ultimately on a **"tradition"** would be bad enough, but when that "tradition" is a dream, that nobody really ever had, the edifice must be in a parlous state. As to how to deal with a Christian "in fellowship," who becomes inoculated with this unscriptural, unhistoric theory; it may be said that as far as is apparent, it does not effect **directly** fundamental truth as to the Person of Christ, though what it may lead to is difficult to say. Any attempt to propagate it in an assembly, could not be tolerated and anyone persisting in such a course

* Esdras, Greek form of Ezra.
† See "British-Israel—Under New Searchlight," by Avary Forbes, M.A.

would bring himself or herself under the open rebuke of the elders. Certainly the theory "causes divisions and offences contrary to the doctrine, which we have learned" and we should "mark" and "avoid" those who are in active sympathy with this sad delusion.   W.H.

THE PROTOCOLS

What are the Protocols?

The word is derived from the Greek: **prōtos**, first, and **kolla**, glue, and originally meant the first leaf glued to a papyrus roll. This bore the year of the king ruling at the time, and thus dated the roll. Reading the other day of the discovery of some papyri, the words occurred: "They found a stray leaf close by which was supposed to be a protocol of one of the papyri." Later the name was applied to the original copy of any writing, e.g., a treaty, and then it came to mean the rough draft of any transaction.

As showing the importance of these dated "protocols," the following facts are of interest. The Higher Critics have sought in their general attack on the Old Testament Scriptures to unsettle the Biblical dates of the books of Ezra, Nehemiah and Daniel. "Their scholarship makes it impossible (!) to believe it otherwise." "All (!) scholars are agreed" that these books could not have been written in their place, as we have them. Such persons as are described in the two former books did not exist, and two Greek words for musical instruments* in the book of Daniel most probably bring its date down to the second century instead of the sixth, in which it claims to be written (!). However, in 1904-1907, some papyrus rolls written in Aramaic by Jews of Jeb were discovered in the island of Elephantine or Jeb, in the Nile, opposite Assouan, all dated with the names of Persian Kings of the fifth century, B.C.. In these occur the names of Biblical persons such as Sanballat and the high priest, Jehoiada, and his son, Jehohanan, and also three Greek words† more unlikely in their character to be found, than the two Greek words occurring in Daniel. These flimsy papyrus-leaves, preserved in the dry sand of Egypt, are found to negative the premature conclusions of the critics. Daniel belongs to the same epoch.

The word "Protocol" has come rather prominently before the public in late years in connections with "The Protocols of the Elders of Zion," a book purporting to be records of a world-wide conspiracy engineered by Jews. This work has proved to the satisfaction of very many to be a forgery by enemies of the Jews. It is, however, still used by Anti-semites on the Continent‡ (e.g., in German schools to-day) to stir up race-hatred against God's earthly people.   W.H.

---

* "Psaltery" and "Symphony."

† For a coin, colour and article of dress.

‡ This was written before the Second World War. [Ed.].

D

EVOLUTION

Can a Christian believe in Evolution?

It is sad to think that anyone "naming the name of Christ" should forsake the clear testimony of God's Word for the fable of "Evolution"—"Science falsely so-called." The former declares that "In the beginning God created the heavens and the earth" (Gen. 1. 1; see also Heb. 11. 3). Later we read, "And God said, Let there be light, and there was light" (v. 3); "Let the waters bring forth abundantly" (v. 20); "Let the earth bring forth the living creature" (v. 24); "God created man in his own image" (v. 27); and in chap. 2. 7, we have the detailed account of this; "And the Lord God formed man of the dust of the ground, and breathed into his nostrils the breath of life and man became a living soul." Of course the most cursory reader of Gen. 1, can see that God's method in Creation was one of progression, from—the inorganic to the organic,—vegetation, fish, fowl, beasts, and lastly, man. We know, moreover, by experience of the things around us, that there is room **within the species** for the most wonderful variations (e.g., men, dogs, pigeons, etc.). Ill-informed persons confuse this with "Evolution," and they profess to be "evolutionists" because of such facts, which are undisputed. But "Evolution" properly so-called is supposed to account for the development of **new species** of plants or animals, either by mutation or by minute modification. Its teaching is that everything organic began with a cell (possibly more than one, but perhaps only one), and evolved by minute variations, into the myriads of "species" in the world, brought about by "natural selection," securing "the survival of the fittest" during the course of "a struggle for existence." Can anything be conceived more wildly improbable? It is only one more proof of "the Fall," that otherwise sensible men can be found gullible enough to believe it. For such a process has **never been proved to have taken place in nature.** Now, Science is something **known,** so that **it is very unscientific to be an Evolutionist,** seeing that evolution is not something known; it has not even attained to the dignity of a theory, but is a mere hypothesis. The late Lord Kelvin, perhaps the greatest scientist since Newton, said in one of his last addresses, "I marvel at the undue haste with which teachers in our universities and preachers in our pulpits are restating truths in terms of Evolution, while Evolution itself remains an **unproved hypothesis** in the laboratories of Science" (my emphasis). Not only is Evolution a direct attack on the Creatorship of God, negativing the Scriptural account of the origin of things, but it denies the fall of man, and so inevitably the need of atonement and also, logically, the work of Christ. Shallow thinkers may profess to be able to believe the Scriptures and Evolution, but intelligent believers subject to the Word, and clear-headed agnostics, like Huxley, see clearly that the two are mutually incompatible. Evolutionists in the meanwhile continue to utter discordant cries hardly agreeing upon a single point, except that their pet hypothesis is true. Our choice simply lies between God as Creator and His Word for it, or everything its own creator and man's word for it. W.H.

OXFORD GROUP

What do you think of the Oxford Group movement?

Much has been written for and against this religious cult. It ought not to be difficult for anyone who has experienced true conversion to God and found peace with Him by faith, on the ground of the precious blood of Christ, to form a correct view of a movement in which, no doubt, as in Freemasonry, Roman Catholicism, Seventh Day Adventism, etc., some true children of God are entangled. But the crucial question is, what place has Christ and His atoning work in it? It is the Sermon on the Mount, vaguely grasped, not the Atonement of Calvary, which is the favourite watch-word. It is "the Spirit" as a sort of "familiar spirit," whispering in the ear, rather than the Holy Spirit of God testifying to Christ through the Scriptures. As far as we learn, no questions are raised to aspirants as to their doctrinal belief. A Unitarian is just as welcome as a Trinitarian; a Roman Catholic, as a Protestant; an Anglo-Catholic, as an Evangelical. It is as though the prodigal son had staged a home-coming scene, with confession, reconciliation, best garment, shoes, fatted calf, etc., all complete, but remaining the while in the far country. It is Cain offering the fruits of the earth and making himself believe it is he, not Abel, who is accepted. It is a building without foundation, but 'best hotel accommodation' provided for all. It is assuming the name and privileges of the family without being born into it. It would indeed be surprising were such a system anything but attractive to decent worldings. W.H.

KESWICK TEACHING

What is meant by the following exhortation:—"There is the surrender that claims the filling of the Spirit"? Is this "Keswick" teaching?

Though never having been present at what is called the Keswick Convention, one naturally has a certain acquaintance with the so-called "Keswick" teaching. The motto, "All one in Christ Jesus," is a commendable recognition of that blessed unity created by the baptism in the Holy Spirit, which exists between all true believers in this dispensation (1 Cor. 12. 13) in spite of the sad divisions which rend them externally. It is good to recognise this at least during one week of the year, and better still during the remaining fifty-one. In fact, we are responsible to do so on the basis of the seven-fold unity of Ephesians 4. 4-6, and to put away everything which man has set up in addition to, or in diminution from, these seven basal facts, which may mar that unity of the Spirit, which we are enjoined to keep in the bond of peace. We are never told to keep the Unity of the Body, but to recognise it, and carry it out practically, not by forbidding the introduction of any subject, or Bible truth on which people differ, but by separation from everything which will not bear the test of God's Word.

No doubt God has blessed the meetings at Keswick, and that, not because of any particular **panacea** of sanctification, peculiar to the place, but because the Word of God is generally preached on evangelical lines, and Christ presented as the object of faith and as God's sufficient resource for every need. It is impossible for this to be done without blessing resulting. When we come to details. I fear it must be said that "Keswick" teaching concerning the reception of the Spirit by an act of faith subsequent to conversion and based on "absolute surrender" is seriously at fault. The case of the twelve disciples at Ephesus in Acts 19 is adduced as a typical example of this. On the contrary, it is quite unique. I never heard of such a case happening in any country in the world since. The question which seems to lend itself to the erroneous notion here combated, "Have ye received the Holy Ghost **since ye believed?**" is a mistranslation, as the R.V. (based on the literal Greek) shows, for, "Did ye receive the Holy Ghost when ye believed?" The normal order is given in Ephesians 1. 13: "in whom having believed, ye were sealed with that Holy Spirit of promise."

The case of these twelve disciples may be taken up later. It may suffice here to remark that the filling of the Spirit is not an attainment reached once for all, and which may puff up the recipient, or put him on a pedestal above his fellow Christians, as some spurious fillings of the Spirit seem apt to do, but a humbling and self-emptying experience, true to faith and which makes Christ more real to the soul. Such an experience is repeated and progressive. Directly that teaching on the Spirit puts Him forward as the object of faith, and eclipses the Lord Jesus Christ ever so little, the teaching is so far off the lines. Certainly "full surrender" is good and reasonable, but how much it implies is perhaps realised by few who claim to have made it. It is generally associated in men's minds with going out as a missionary to the ends of the earth; it is needed as much and perhaps more, for the humdrum tasks of everyday life in the home, or for separation from "religious" practices and associations, which have no divine authority.

There is always danger of connecting blessing with some spiritual "Mecca," some sacred geographical spot on earth, instead of with the Person of Christ of whom the poet sings:

> "Where'er they seek Thee, Thou art found,
> And every place is hallowed ground."   W.H.

THE "FALLING AWAY" DOCTRINE

Is it possible for one who has been truly converted and has eternal life to be eternally lost?

Surely the terms "eternal life" and "eternal perdition" are incompatible and mutually exclusive. A life that can be lost cannot be eternal. The Lord says of His sheep: "I give unto them eternal life, and **they shall never perish**" (John 10. 28), and again, "He that heareth my word and believeth on Him that sent me hath everlasting life, and shall not come into condemnation (lit. judgment) but is passed from death unto life" (John 5. 24). Christ is the life of His people ("Christ, who is our life"—Col. 3. 4) and each true believer is "baptized in one Spirit into one body," and is a temple of the Holy Spirit and a child in the family of God. Not one such then could be lost, for if so, the Church would be blemished; the temple marred; and the family broken for all eternity. The Word says, "He that hath begun a good work in you, will perform it until the day of Jesus Christ" (Phil. 1. 6). It behoves us then to be sure that this good work has truly begun in us, for as there were false brethren crept in unawares in the primitive churches, so there may be spurious Christians to-day even in the most scriptural assemblies, men who can pass muster with their fellow-men, but who are only counterfeit professors, and who will one day be exposed as such—"Every tree that my Heavenly Father hath not planted, shall be rooted out." We should not then take ourselves too easily for granted. Perhaps a few doubts about ourselves now and again are not a bad sign, though we should never, never doubt Christ. I question whether false professors often doubt themselves. How then does God begin His work in a soul? By convicting of sin by His Spirit and then revealing Christ crucified as the all-sufficient Saviour. He continues, however, to shew us increasingly the evil within, till we find that we must look away to Christ for **everything,** and be content to have **Him** for our All in All. But if we want to convince others that we are indeed true believers, something more is needed than a profession of faith. We read of some who became antichrists, who had no doubt professed faith, been baptised and broken bread: "They went out from us, but they were not of us, for if they had been of us they would no doubt have continued with us, but they went out that they might be made manifest, that they were not all of us" (1 John 2. 19). Not even great gifts, successful preaching and mighty works prove reality. Judas Iscariot had all these, and so also have the wonder-workers of Matt. 7. 22, 23, of whom the Lord utters one of His most solemn warnings: "Many will say unto me in that day, have we not prophesied in Thy name, and in Thy name cast out demons, etc.?" Yet He will say to them "I never knew you." They were never possessors of eternal life through faith in Him. Gift is of great profit, where there is grace, but gift without grace is nought. There is a number of tests in the Epistles of John, which we may apply to ourselves, if we would be assured that we have truly been born of God, of which I will here quote two or three: "Every one that **doeth righteousness** is born of Him" (1 John 2. 29). If a man is crooked in his ways, unrighteous in his acts and untruthful in his words, he may well tremble for himself. Then here is another test: "Whosoever is born of God **doth not commit sin**" (1 John 3. 9). This does not mean that a true child of God never sins, for in chapter 1. 9 we have God's gracious provision for the failures of His people, but it means he does not continue in it, like a swine in his wallowing. Alas! with what warning voice to us all do the sad exposures of years of immorality and dishonest dealing of which we sometimes hear, even among professed believers, speak. It is not for us to say glibly of such that we know them to be children of God, because they have long passed as such. The hidden life which has come to light, seems to give the lie to any such theories. One more such test will we quote: "Whatsoever is born of God **overcometh the world**" (1 John 5. 4). The overcomer is not one who is never overcome, but who, like Joshua, overcomes at last (Exod. 17. 11). The final overcomers are not some extraordinary kind of Christians; they are true Christians who prove themselves to be such by continuing to the end. For other tests we may see chap. 3. 1 and 14; 5. 1; 2 John 9. Enough has been said to remind us of the solemn words: "Let him that thinketh he standeth take heed lest he fall"; "Watch and pray lest ye enter into temptation!" Thank God for the words of our Lord Jesus, "Him that cometh to Me, I will in no wise cast out"; which not only mean that He will not **reject,** but that He will not **eject** the one who comes to Him.　　　　　　W.H.

UNIVERSALISM

Do not scriptures such as Col. i. 20, Eph. i. 10, 1 Tim. ii. 4-6, iv. 10, Rom. v. 19, 1 Cor. xv. 22-28, Phil. ii. 9, 10, 11, teach the universal salvation of the race? Will not all men be saved?

This writer is clearly a "Universalist," believing that all fallen creatures will one day be restored to Divine favour, and brought to heaven. He quotes seven passages, which, he says, teach his doctrine, and accuses us of finding difficulty in believing them. This is not so. We believe them all, but not in his sense. Thus, to go through them: there is nothing in Phil. ii. 9-11 about willing submission. All will bow the knee and confess Christ as Lord, if not willingly, then unwillingly. When the Lord utters the terrible words to certain ones, "Depart ye cursed into everlasting fire, prepared for the devil and his angels," is there a hint that this will mean their conversion and restoration? Certainly 1 Cor. xv. 22-28 is a strange passage to prove the salvation of all. It refers to the terrible scenes in Rev. xx, when Satan and the impenitent will be judged and cast into the lake of fire. It is said that Christ at the end will "put down all rule and all authority and power" (v. 24). If this meant their reconciliation, then death would be reconciled too, for "destroyed," in verse 26, is the same in the Greek (*Katargeō*) as "put down" in verse 24. The real meaning is explained in v. 25: "all His enemies will be put under His feet," or "made His footstool," as in Psa. cx. This would be a peculiar way of expressing reconciliation. It was not thus that the father in Luke xv. welcomed the prodigal. Joshua did treat the Amorite kings just in this way, and it sealed their doom, and they were executed before nightfall. Rom. v. 19 does not say a word about all being saved, but merely that "as many were made sinners by the disobedience of Adam, so many will be made righteous by the obedience of Christ". The condition of repentance and faith is enforced throughout the epistle. How divorce it from this verse? Rom. ii. 5 tells us of those who refuse to repent. 1 Tim. iv. 10 simply says that God is the Saviour of all men, "specially of them that believe." Why "specially," if all are equally saved? Many believe, and I think they are right, that Saviour here means "Preserver."* The Lord cares for all, and in a special way for His people. 1 Tim. ii. 4-6 does not say that all will be saved, but that God is willing that all should be saved. We glory in this truth, and we are sure that wherever He can righteously apply the saving efficacy of the blood of Christ, He will do so. The ransom is paid for all. It is suffic- ient for all, efficient for them that believe. But those who refuse to be- lieve will perish in spite of the work of Christ. To some the Lord had to say, "Ye will not come to Me that ye might have life". Neither Eph. i. 10 nor Col. i. 20 says a word about "things under the earth," or infernal things, as Phil. ii. 10 does, when the *subjection* of all is in view. It is, moreover, "all *things*" that are to be reconciled. How could heavenly persons need it? But sin has entered the heavenly sphere; discord has marred the harmony there as here, and things, so far, need adjustment or harmonising. Certainly, all things in heaven and earth will be "headed up" in Christ (Eph. i. 10), but the impenitent are not included. They will be vessels of wrath to display God's power and wrath. The questioner allows there are some verses which seem to teach otherwise, and quotes one—John iii. 36—which he really explains away by leaving out the first part, and dwelling on the fact that "the wrath of God abideth in the unbeliever" is in the present. But it is clear that the future is referred to from the first words, "He that believeth not, shall not see life." This cannot refer to the present, for as long as breath is in the body, a man may turn, believe, and see life; but once the unbeliever passes from this scene he will never see life, but will exist under the wrath of God for ever. Space will only allow me to point out, that our Lord gave no hint of a future probation and restoration of all. Do His words (to quote only one Gospel) in Matt. x. 28, xiii. 42, xviii 9, xxv. 46, teach universal

* The French version has usually "Conservateur," i.e., Preserver.

salvation? The Lord spoke of many passing down the broad road to perdition; of a "closed door," and of many asking in vain for admission; of "a great gulf fixed," which none might pass! The hope of Universalists is a false hope, as all who trust in it will one day find. "He that believeth and is baptized shall be saved, He that believeth not shall be damned."   W.H.

HOUSEHOLD BAPTISM

Are those who teach what is known as "household baptism" justified in using the crossing of the Red Sea, referred to in 1 Cor. 10, as a type of Christian baptism, and in asserting that, as undoubtedly infants were carried across the Red Sea by their mothers, they therefore were baptised unto Moses, and so infants now should be baptised?

Certainly these friends must be hard put to it to find authority for their practice of baptising households to-day, if they have to go back to this far off Old Testament event to justify it. We are asked, moreover, to believe that had Moses and the elders held Believer's Baptism, they would have been obliged cruelly to leave all the infants on the west bank of the Red Sea to the mercy of the pursuing Egyptians, on the plea that such were not fit subjects for baptism. I remember one well-known clergyman in Brighton (the "Reverend" H. B.), who wrote a tract to justify the sprinkling of infants, and he built his argument on the probability of the wind sprinkling the Israelitish infants, as they were carried through the Red Sea. It seems hard to believe that fancy could go further. We may be sure that no-one from Moses to the youngest Israelitish mother had the slightest idea that a figure of Christian baptism was being carried out during the crossing of the Red Sea. But if for the sake of argument, all who shared in the crossing were baptised, then this was true of "the mixed multitude" and of the flocks and the herds. Perhaps those who christen bells and ships rely on this passage. We see, however, from Numbers 14 that the children did not count, but only those of Israel who were numbered "from twenty years old and upward," for in verses 29 and 33 a difference is made between those who were numbered (v. 29) and their children (v. 33). Whereas the former (except Caleb and Joshua) would be excluded for good, all the children would be brought in when their fathers' carcases were wasted in the wilderness. We may be sure that the infants no more shared in the baptism of the Red Sea, than in the daily eating of the manna and drinking from the rock that followed them. No doubt it is legitimate to see in the crossing of the Red Sea a figure of the death and resurrection of Christ and of believers' association with Him, but it is not, properly speaking, a figure of Christian baptism, for that would be a case of a figure representing a figure. Rather what is set forth is what has already taken place for all believers, namely, their baptism in the Spirit. Christi n baptism is in no way in view in 1 Cor. 10, and it is a great mistake to think that wherever the slightly different word, "baptismos" occurs in our Authorised (e.g., Mark 7. 4, 8; Heb. 6. 2; 9. 10), that the Christian ordinance is referred to. The reference clearly is to the ceremonial purifications of the Levitical service. W.H.

MAN AND HIS FUTURE STATE

Explain the difference between the terms "flesh" and "body"? What is meant by the "redemption of the body"?

If the inquirer can examine, in any good Lexicon of New Testament Greek, or better still, in Mr. Vine's Expository Dictionary, the great variety of meanings which each of the two words "sarx" (flesh) and "sōma" (body) may bear, according to the context in which they occur; he will realise that it would be difficult to reply to his question adequately, within the bounds of this page. And if he can avail himself of a Young's or Wigram's Concordance to go through all the occurrences of each word, he will probably glean more help in that way than he would from any formal answer.

The fact is that, as used in some passages, there is little or no difference between the two words; and yet in certain other passages a clear distinction is made between them. For instance, in 2 Cor. 4. 10 we have the phrase, "that the life also of Jesus might be made manifest in our BODY"; while in the parallel statement of the next verse it is, "that the life also of Jesus might be made manifest in our mortal FLESH." Here the two words are practically synonymous. The opposite extreme may be seen in Col. 2. 23 (R.V.), where one can show "severity" to the BODY, and at the same time be showing "indulgence" to the FLESH.

Taken in its most literal sense, the "body" is the physical or material part of man, viewed as an organised whole (see 1 Thess. 5. 23). The "flesh" is the substance of which this body is to a large extent composed (see Luke 24. 39). But either word may be used to represent the entire man, as "body" in Luke 11. 36, and "flesh" in Luke 3. 6.

It is when the thought of evil, either in state or in tendency, is suggested, that a deeper distinction is at times made between the two words. For example, the expression "in the flesh" may be employed as in Rom. 7. 5 and 8. 8, 9, of the moral standing of the unsaved, but "in the body" is never so used. The latter phrase may refer to one's bodily presence in some particular place, as in 1 Cor. 5. 3, or to the present earthly life of man, as in 2 Cor. 5. 10; but this is not distinctive of it, for "in the flesh" may also have either of these meanings, as in Col. 2. 1 and in Phil. 1. 24.

Again, "tendency to evil" may sometimes be signified by the term "the flesh," especially in such phrases as "after the flesh," etc.; but "the body" is not so used, except in a few remarkable expressions, "the body of sin" (Rom. 6. 6), "the body of this death" (Rom. 7. 24), "the deeds of the body" (Rom. 8. 13), and "the body of the sins of the flesh" (Col. 2. 11).

The body is frequently spoken of as capable of being used for God (Rom. 12. 1; etc.), and so are its members (Rom. 6. 12, 13); but this is never predicated of the flesh (see Rom. 7. 25), the members of which seem rather to be those named in Col. 3. 5. Moreover, the body of the saint is called a temple of the Holy Ghost and a member of Christ (1 Cor. 6. 15, 19), but it is his "flesh" that lusteth against the Spirit (Gal. 5. 17). Finally, the saint's body, having been "bought with a price" (1 Cor. 6. 20), awaits its full "redemption" when our Lord Jesus comes again (Rom. 8. 23). Then He "shall fashion anew the body of our humiliation, that it may be conformed to the body of His glory" (Phil. 3. 21, R.V.); and when He has done so, "WE (not merely our bodies) shall be like Him" (1 John 3. 2).   W.R.

THE BODY OF MOSES

What do you understand is intended to be conveyed to us by the dispute of the archangel Michael with Satan over the body of Moses?

We have the full account of the death of Moses in Deut. 34, but no account of his public funeral, for he had none, but, as is expressly stated, "He (i.e., the Lord) buried him in a valley in the land of Moab, over against Beth-peor, but no man knoweth of his sepulchre unto this day." There must be a reason for this. I think it is that were it possible to examine the grave of Moses to-day it would be found empty. But someone will say, "How could Moses have been raised from the dead seeing that our Lord Jesus Christ is in 1 Cor. 15 called 'the first-fruits' of the resurrection, and in Colossians 1, 'the first-born from the dead'?" This is an important question. It was impossible for anyone to be raised on to true resurrection ground till our Lord rose. Then if Moses was raised, it could only have been back on to the death plane, as the various cases of resurrection of the Old and New Testaments prior to our Lord's resurrection, such as the son of the widow of Sarepta, that of the Shunammite, Lazarus, and the widow of Nain's son, etc. All came back on to the death plane and died subsequently. I think the incident narrated in Jude refers to the raising of Moses back on the earth plane. If he is one of the witnesses he will die again. No man can die physically after true resurrection. This gives an added completeness to the scene on the Holy Mount: The Lord the centre, Elijah representing them who will never pass in death, Moses the raised one. Satan might legally contest a premature resurrection of Moses in the true sense, while he could not possibly urge any legal objection to Moses being temporarily delivered from the state of death. "It is appointed unto men once

to die." If Moses is to be one of the witnesses, his death will be true
death.   W.H.

IS MAN A TRIPARTITE BEING?

**Is man dual or tripartite in nature? If the latter, how are
spirit and soul distinguished?**

Certainly tripartite, as 1 Thess. 5. 23 proves—"I pray God your
whole Spirit and Soul and Body be preserved blameless unto the
coming of our Lord Jesus Christ." An attempt was made by the late
Dr. Bullinger to shew that man is dual:—the combination of Spirit
and Body forming the Soul—but it was clearly untenable, for if that
were the case, the order of the words would be Spirit and Body, even
the Soul; and at death the personality would be dissolved, a doctrine
even worse than the so-called "sleep of the soul." The Spirit and the
Soul represent the spiritual side of man, which is sometimes called by
one name, sometimes by the other. They are distinct, but only divisible
in a metaphorical sense by the Word of God "piercing even to the
dividing asunder of soul and spirit" (Heb. 4. 12), that is, they are
never viewed as separated one from the other. The Spirit is the higher
part; with it, man understands (1 Cor. 2. 11), and is in touch with the
unseen:—"God is Spirit: and they that worship Him must worship
Him in spirit and in truth" (John 4. 24). The Soul is the other side of
man's spiritual being, and links it with the body—it desires, loves,
sorrows, etc. "My soul is cast down within me" (Psa. 42. 6; see also
1 Sam. 18. 1; Num. 21. 4; 2 Sam. 5. 8).

The personality is sometimes connected with the soul (e.g., "few,
that is, eight souls* were saved by water"), or with the body. When
Stephen fell asleep, we read that "devout men carried him (i.e., his body)
to the burial" (Acts 8. 2), but Stephen in a higher sense was not in the
graveyard, but with Him to Whom he had just committed his spirit."
                                                               W.H.

THE INTERMEDIATE STATE

**If we enter at the very moment of death into our Lord's
presence, do we enter bodily? If so, in what kind of body do we
enter? If this immediate entry were true, would not resurrection
be superfluous; and how reconcile it with 1 Thess. 4. 15-17?**

Certainly the Scriptures do not teach that at the moment of death the
believer enters "bodily" into the presence of Christ, and yet the
Apostle Paul says very plainly, "To depart and to be with Christ, which
is far better" (Phil. 1. 23). He adds however, "nevertheless **to abide
in the flesh** is more needful for you;" so that the presence with Christ
is **not "in the flesh,"** it is **not bodily:** the body is laid in the grave, it

---

* This was without prejudice to the fact that hundreds of anima souls—but of a lower order—
were saved also in the Ark (see 1 Pet. 3. 20).

sleeps awaiting the resurrection. Then again in 2 Cor. 5. 1-8 the apostle describes his earnest desire to depart and to be with Christ, which was so great, that he was willing even to enter the disembodied state, so as to be with Christ, even in that imperfect condition. "We are confident and willing rather to be absent from the body, and to be present with the Lord." The passage in 1 Thess. 4. 15-17 describes quite another thing, namely, the coming of the Lord; the raising of the sleeping saints (sleeping, that is as to their bodies and whose spirits God will bring with Christ); and the changing of the living saints—two companies which will be caught up together to meet the Lord in the air. This will be the perfected condition. 2 Cor. 12. 2-4 is clear proof that the human spirit can exist consciously and intelligently apart from the body, for Paul, when he was caught up, knew perfectly that he was at the third heaven, and in Paradise, and heard unspeakable words, which it is not lawful for man to utter, and yet he twice assures us that he could not tell whether he was in the body or out of the body. This shows that he believed in the possibility of spiritual existence apart from the body.

W.H.

Do all spirits at death go to God? Num. 16. 22; 27. 16; Job 34. 14, 15. Eccl. 3. 21; 8. 8; 12. 7. When are the spirits of the unsaved dealt with?

It is a good thing to "purge our references." I am not sure for instance whether Num. 16. 22 or 27. 16 proves that "all spirits go to God." The expression in Job 34. 14, however, "gather unto Himself man's spirit," describing dissolution, certainly favours the belief that at death all spirits go to God. So in Eccl. 3. 21 the word "upward" points the same way. Eccl. 12. 7 is very distinct that "the spirit returns to God Who gave it." Heb. 12. 23 refers only to the spirits of just men. I do not think there can be any question that the spirits of all men are "dealt with" at death, as regards their final destiny, but the measure of reward or punishment awaits a later day. Lazarus of Luke 16 was at once comforted; the rich man was at once tormented, but at the great white throne he will be judged according to his works. Paul knew for himself, and so did the saints in general, that "to depart" was "to be with Christ, which is far better" (Phil. 1. 23). But I know no Scripture which describes this as having "gone to God," and I think the propriety of anyone publicly pronouncing on the spiritual destiny of any man, who has died without giving satisfactory **proof** of repentance, may well be questioned. Certainly it is gravely wrong to speak of one who has led an ungodly life, and died without visible repentance, as "this our brother," and assert he is now "at peace." We may not affirm that such a one is saved, but is it within our province to affirm that such a one is lost? God alone searches the heart and knows what has passed between a soul and

Himself at the last. To anyone who had not heard what passed between our Lord and the repentant thief, he was clearly a lost soul, but we know that grace intervened and snatched him as a brand from the burning. Even of Judas, whose sin was manifested and his awful death a matter of common knowledge, Peter refrained from saying anything more than that "he went to his own place." This, though it left no doubt of his fate, was said among the Lord's disciples. As far as we know the apostles never referred to the traitor in public.   W.H.

Man is composed of spirit, soul, and body. When he dies where does the spirit go?

The spirit and the soul must not be confused, nor yet divided. They together form the spiritual part of man. When a believer falls asleep he only does so as regards his body. The spiritual part of him, with which the personality is really connected, goes at once to be with Christ (see 2 Cor. v. 8). "Absent from the body, and to be present with the Lord." This, of course, cannot refer to the resurrection state, as then no believer will be absent from the body. Paul describes dying as departing to be with Christ which is far better (Phil. i. 23). It is a most serious denial of God's truth to describe the condition of the believer who dies, as that of sleep, except as regards his body.   W.H.

Is there any scriptural authority for saying that at death only the spirit of the believer returns to God, while the spirit of the unbeliever remains with the soul in hell (Hades)?

I do not know of any Scripture which would justify this distinction; for one thing I would ask—Is the spirit ever spoken of in Scripture as separated from the soul? They are regarded on the contrary, though distinct, as inseparable. They together constitute the spiritual side of man's tri-partite being, according to the words of the Apostle Paul, "I pray God your whole spirit and soul and body be preserved blameless unto the coming of our Lord Jesus Christ" (1 Thess. 5. 23). The only passage I know where spirit and soul are presented to us as divisible is Heb. 4. 12—"The word of God is quick and powerful, and sharper than any two-edged sword, piercing even to the dividing asunder of soul and spirit." This is a supreme proof of the separating power of the Word of God, but even this does not imply an actual separation, so much as the ability of God's Word to differentiate between the movements and actions of the soul and spirit. As for the actual question proposed above, which is taken, I presume, from Ecclesiastes, chapter 12. 7 ("The dust shall return to the earth as it was, and the spirit shall return unto God who gave it"), I do not think it can be shown that this refers only to a believer. It is a general statement and is true of all. Naturally the return of the spirit to God is different in character in the two cases, but in both they return to God. Here I gather that "spirit" simply means the spiritual part of man, including the soul. The questioner does not mention the soul of the believer; he agrees, it may be hoped, with the above thought. As for the difference between spirit and soul; the former is that which understands: "No man knoweth the things of a man, but the spirit of man that is in him" (1 Cor. 2. 11). It is by his spirit that man has intercourse with the Father of Spirits, whom "he must worship in spirit and in truth" (John 4. 24). The soul is the lower side of the spiritual part of man, by which he loves (1 Sam. 18. 1), hates (2 Sam. 5. 8), and is sorrowful (Matt. 26. 38), etc. It is the soul which is in immediate contact with the bodily senses. But again I would repeat, though the two are distinct, they are inseparable. Sometimes the spiritual part of man is termed spirit, sometimes soul. Occasionally, it is true, you read of souls as the equivalent of persons—"Eight souls were saved by water" (1 Pet. 3.), but that in no way invalidates the sense of the word as discussed above. W.H.

HADES

Does there seem sufficient scriptural warrant for the teaching that "Hades is in the heart of the earth"? (Matt. 12. 40 being cited). In the Old Testament the passage of souls to it is frequently spoken of as a descent.

The word **Hades** (from two words, "a," not and, "idein," to see) means the Unseen world. It never represents "the grave" in the sense of a tomb, but "grave-land," the place of departed spirits. This was the Greek classical use and there is no proof, but that exactly the same sense was carried on into New Testament Greek. Certainly a burial place is not unseen. It is the equivalent of the Hebrew, Sheol. There are rare places, e.g., Psa. 49. 14, 15 where this may seem to be equal to a mere tomb, but with the large majority of cases before us, we may say that even in such, the tomb is viewed as the gate for the particular soul into the underworld. David's words in Psa. 16 bear out the ordinary meaning: "Thou wilt not leave my soul in Sheol, neither wilt thou suffer thy Holy One to see corruption." Sheol then was the place where the spiritual part went; the grave, where alone corruption is seen, where the body was interred. The Annihilationists try to confuse the two; and deny any existence between death and resurrection; but this is plainly contrary to many Scriptures. "The wicked shall be turned into Sheol" (Psa. 9. 17), surely means more than mere burial. "Shall burn unto the lowest sheol" (Deut. 32. 22)—graves don't burn. "Speak to him out of the midst of Sheol" (Ezek. 32. 21)— so it is not then a place of silence, as a grave certainly is. Jacob in Gen. 37. 35, knew his son Joseph was devoured by some beast and so had not been buried at all, and yet speaks of going down (**yaradh**) to his son to sheol. This word, yaradh (always to go down or descend), certainly favours the thought that we are intended to conceive of Hades as in the heart of the earth. It is the word used of Korah, Dathan and Abiram "going down alive into the pit (sheol)," (Num. 16. 33). The Spirit of Samuel was also seen to ascend, when the witch of Endor, for the first time in her miserable career, was permitted, to her own horror, actually to call up one of the departed, instead of the lying familiar spirit, who usually impersonated them—"An old man cometh up" (1 Sam. 28. 14). Also in Psa. 55. 15, we read, "Let them go down quick into Sheol." But the passage which may well settle the matter for us is Ephes. 4. 9: "Now that Christ ascended, what is it but that he also descended first into the lower parts of the earth?" There does not seem to be any real difficulty to those who believe in God's Word. Naturally those who deny there is such a place as Hades, are unwilling to allow anyone to assign it a location. What they want is that someone should prove it does not exist at all.   W.H.

If Hades be "in the heart of the earth," as some have thought, how can we reconcile this with Jonah's experience, who went down into the whale's belly (symbol of Sheol), spirit, soul and body, while the Lord's soul went to Hades (Sheol) and His body to the grave?

There is really no contrast, still less contradiction in the two thoughts. Though Jonah speaks of being "in the belly of hell" (Sheol), I think those are mistaken who deduce that he actually died in the belly of the whale, as I think the rest of his prayer shows. The Lord does not say that the prophet died, though so terrifying was his experience, that he might have imagined he was in the unseen world. But the death of the prophet was quite unnecessary to justify the Lord's comparison between Himself and Jonah. Jonah's disappearance in the belly of the whale was a figure of the disappearance of the Lord, when His body was laid in the grave and He in spirit descended into the place of departed spirits—Paradise—as it was for Him and for all of His own, who had already died. But the exact location of this it does not seem necessary for us to define, even if it were possible. Our Lord's words were, "As Jonah was three days and three nights in the whale's belly, so shall the Son of Man be three days and three nights in the heart of the earth" (Matt. 12. 40), and this came to pass.   W.H.

IMMORTALITY

Is it so that "Immortality in God's Word has no reference to the soul"? If this be so will you kindly explain Matthew 10. 28: "Fear not them which kill the body, but are not able to kill the soul."

Immortality is immunity from death. Clearly man did not then possess immortality in that sense, when created, for he was warned he would die, if he ate the forbidden fruit. But what is death then? It certainly is not "annihilation" or a cessation of existence, for Adam and Eve continued to exist after the fall. In fact no external change apparently took place in them. But a marked spiritual change occurred, for "They heard the voice of the Lord God walking in the garden . . . and Adam and his wife hid themselves from the presence of the Lord God" (Gen. 3. 8). Death therefore is not cessation of existence, but separation of existence, that is existence out of harmony with God. This spiritual death has been the condition of the whole human race ever since. When a man believes the gospel "he passes from death unto life" (John 5. 24). He now possesses eternal life and has the assurance from God that "he will never perish" (John 10. 28). This is immortality in the spiritual sense. "Verily, verily I say unto you, If a man keep my saying he shall never see death" (John 8. 51). But the fall did not kill the body. To assure this, man was shut off from the tree of life and now "it is appointed unto men once to die" (Heb. 9. 27). Even the body of the Christian "is dead, because of sin" (Rom. 8. 10). If he dies, his corruptible body will put on incorruptibility at the Lord's return, if he survives till then his mortal body will put on immortality. He has the immortality of the spiritual side of his being already included in the gift of eternal life, for that immortality is not only a bodily attribute is clear from the words, "God Who only hath immortality" (1 Tim. 6. 16) —that is in Himself, though, of course, He does communicate it. The special verse referred to, Matt. 10. 28, merely states that the soul survives the body. Man may kill the latter, but cannot kill the former. This would be equally true of an unconverted man, who will never cease to exist away from God, as of a converted man who will never cease to live with God. W.H.

Does Matthew 10. 28 teach the immortality of the soul? I have been challenged in the open air by Christadelphians who deny the immortality of the soul, and though I entirely disagree with their Christ-dishonouring doctrines, I cannot find on this point a more direct Scripture than Matt. 10. 28. I would esteem further light thereon.

I hardly think Matt. 10. 28 touches on the "immortality" of the soul, but rather on its survival, which probably the Christadelphians deny too. Man can kill the body, but to kill the soul is beyond his power. "Fear Him Who can **destroy** (it does not say kill) both soul and body in hell." The word for "destroy" (apollumi) never means "to annihilate," but to render useless for its original object. Thus the same root is applied to "the **lost** sheep of the house of Israel" (Matt. 10. 6), "the **marred**

E

bottles (Mark 2. 22), and to the one who may "**lose** his life" (Luke 9. 24). I believe the true doctrine of immortality has been misrepresented as well as denied. The words, "God only hath immortality" merely mean that He alone has it intrinsically, in Himself, underived, but do not deny that He communicates it to men and angels; but immortality is sometimes used as though it merely meant the faculty of never-ending existence. I believe Adam certainly had the latter at creation, but he clearly did not possess "immortality" for that means "immunity from death." Now, had he possessed this by creation, the words, "In the day that thou eatest thereof, thou shalt surely die," would have had no meaning, for he could not have died. It is clear he was capable of death. The whole crux of the question is, "WHAT IS DEATH?" Is it a ceasing to exist or is it existence out of harmony with, or in separation from, God. Consider what happened when Adam sinned. He did not cease to exist. He did not die physically (that had to be provided for later by cutting him off from the tree of life). Externally and physically he was apparently unchanged. But a marked and mysterious change took place in his moral being. He knew he was naked, and he was afraid of God, and sought to hide from Him. That is, a moral gulf had yawned between him and his Creator. Death is not cessation of existence but separation of existence. This condition of death has passed on the whole human race. Man is alive to the world, but dead to God—Paul reminds the Ephesians of this their state before conversion. Then God raised them up into a new life, having quickened them together with Christ (Eph. 2.). This accords with what our Lord says happens to him who hears and believes. "He has eternal life . . . He has passed from death unto life" (John 5. 24). This eternal life includes immortality. The believer becomes immune from Spiritual death, but he has not yet immortality, physically speaking. That he will receive when Christ comes (see 1 Cor. 15.). The unbeliever will never regain immortality, but will exist in alienation and separation, physical and spiritual, from God for all eternity. "This is the second death." That this is not a cessation of existence or annihilation of being is clear from many scriptures, e.g., "Where **their** worm dieth not and the fire is not quenched"; "These shall go away into everlasting punishment"; "The devil that deceived them was cast into the lake of fire and brimstone, where the beast and the false prophet are, and **they** shall be tormented day and night for ever and ever" (Mark 9. 44; Matt. 25. 46; Rev. 20. 10 and compare v. 15).   W.H.

PARADISE

Is there any truth in the idea that the Lord, when He arose, changed the place of the Old Testament saints from some Paradise below, to be with Himself in a Paradise above?

We may eliminate from this consideration, Enoch and Elijah, who are clearly exceptional. Exactly into what part of the heavenly sphere they were introduced is not revealed. Even did we know, it would tell us nothing about the dead. It is clear, however, that the Old Testament saints did not go at death to be "with Christ," not for the reason alleged by some, that they were not forgiven, etc., for they clearly were (see Psa. 32. 1, 2), and that on the ground of the work of Christ, yet to be accomplished. The reason was that as yet there was no Christ, in the Theanthropic sense, for them to be with. He had not yet died and risen nor "brought life and immortality to light, through the gospel," though ever in the bosom of the Father as the only-begotten Son of God. As for those who died in Old Testament times, such expressions are met with as, "He slept with his father," "He fell on sleep," "Descended to the grave," the idea being that the dead went down into Sheol, the unseen world (Hades of New Testament). See Jacob's words (Gen. 37. 35), where he could not have meant a literal grave, as he believed Joseph devoured, and so, not buried. In Num. 16. 33 we read that Korah, Dathan and Abiram went down alive into the pit (Sheol). The case of Samuel (1 Sam. 28) may occur to some. The Scriptures do not say that the **witch** brought up Samuel. On the contrary, when she saw the strange apparition, she cried out, presumably in fear. I have no doubt that God in his sovereignty did bring Samuel's spirit **up** from Paradise (not his body, for that was buried at Ramah, fifty miles away), for the express object of conveying to Saul the news of his approaching end. On the morrow, Saul and his sons would be with Samuel in the unseen world.

Sheol never* represents the literal grave, but some other word is always used of it, like **"Qeber"** or **"Šakath."** Psalm 16. 10 makes it plain that the Lord in spirit went to Sheol, and His body to the grave. That saint and sinner went to one general place, before the resurrection, is clear from Luke 16, where our Lord lifts the veil of the unseen world in the intermediate state. The word there is "Hades." True the saved were far-off from the lost, there being "a great gulf" fixed between the Paradise of the blessed and the place of torment, but still they were within seeing and speaking distance. Why should this be incredible, even if we had not our Lord's words for it? The Tower of London was for a long period in two sections—a royal palace and a state prison. It meant everything, which part a man went to. It was into Paradise that the Lord descended in Spirit, and where He welcomed the repentant thief. Can we suppose that only three days after, He left this trophy of grace behind? Did no benefits accrue to the saints confined there? The

* Psalm 141. 7 (though the Authorised Version gives "grave" for "sheol") is no exception. Bones are not scattered at the grave's mouth, but buried in it. The idea is rather of bones left unburied, on the brink of Hades—the unseen world, where the owners of the bones had entered. Dr. Tregelles translates sheol here as elsewhere—Hades.

resurrection of Christ had mighty effects on the universe—He filled it: on the Church—He bestowed on her His spiritual gifts: on the Old Testament saints—"He led captivity captive," that is, I believe, He set them free from their cabined and confined condition, and took them to be with Himself, henceforth in the Paradise above. This may throw light on the words in Heb. 2. 14, "to **deliver** them who through fear of death," etc. The word here translated, "deliver," denotes usually a change of place, a release, a removal. The change did not mean, of course, that they were raised, but translated to be "with Christ" in a new sphere. Thither Paul was caught up, temporarily (2 Cor. 12. 4), and permanently at His decease—"Absent from the body . . . present with the Lord," awaiting the perfect condition of glory at the resurrection day.   W.H.

CHRIST BETWEEN DEATH AND RESURRECTION

Where was our Lord Jesus Christ between His death and resurrection?

His body, as all four Gospels agree, was in Joseph's new tomb; His soul, according to Acts 2. 27, 31 (with Psalm 16. 10), was in Hell (Gr. Hades; Heb. Sheol), a place or rather state, the significance of which in the Scriptures is much wider than in our present-day usage of that word. The Revisers, in their preface to the Old Testament, say that it means "the place of departed spirits," and they warn the reader that although, in such passages as Gen. 37. 35, they have left in the text the A.V. "grave," yet it does not signify "the place of burial."

Jacob (Gen. 37. 35; 42. 38) expected to go there at death; Job (Job 14. 13-15) requested that God would hide him there until the time of resurrection would come; whilst in other passages (such as Psa. 9. 17; Job 24. 19, etc.) it is looked on as the portion of the wicked dead. We must therefore conceive of Hell as comprising two distinct regions or conditions, separated according to Luke 16. 26 by an impassable gulf, the one containing the souls of the righteous, and the other the souls of the unrighteous. Probably it is the latter which is spoken of as "the lowest hell" in Deut. 32. 22 and Psa. 86. 13; and doubtless it is the former which is called "Paradise" by our Lord in Luke 23. 43, when He said to the repentant and believing thief, "To-day, thou shalt be with Me in Paradise."

This last statement, taken with Acts 2. 27, 31, shows that the Scriptural reply to our question, so far as the soul of the Lord Jesus is concerned, is that between death and resurrection He was in the region of Hell called Paradise, in which were also the souls of all saints who had died previously.   W.R.

DEPARTED SAINTS AND EARTH

Do saints with the Lord "look this way"? Are they cognisant of what is taking place on earth, as the hymn puts it, "Some one in glory LOOKING this way"?

I do not know any Scripture, which shows that those with Christ are cognisant of what is going on on the earth, or are "looking this way." Samuel, when called up from beneath, as I believe he undoubtedly was, did not know why, but had to be told the circumstances by Saul (1 Sam. xxviii. 15). He was not "looking this way," he called it being "disquieted." The rich man in Hades did "look this way," as far as remembering he had five brethren still alive, who, though he could not see them, he instinctively felt were on the wrong road. Lazarus was in Abraham's bosom, and gave no indication of "looking this way" (Luke xvi). From Ecclesiastes we learn that "the dead know not anything" (chap. ix. 5), that is, of world happenings; not that they are unconscious, but as v. 6 tells us, they have no more "a portion for ever in any thing that is done under the sun." If we take our ideas from hymns, we may get some strange ones; but if we disapprove of a hymn, it is better not to sing it, or else to omit the offending verse, than to tamper with it. It is a serious matter to tinker a hymn, without the author's leave.

W.H.

THE RESURRECTION BODY

Will the resurrection bodies of the saints be the same as those in which they lived and died?

In our Lord's resurrection we have the pattern of our own. Was the Lord's resurrection body the same as that in which He lived and died? Yes, it **was the same body**; there was nothing left in the tomb but the grave-clothes, and our Lord took pains to show that His body was truly the very one that had died, by calling attention to His hands and feet which bore the marks of His cruel death on Calvary.

But though the same, **it was not under the same conditions.*** It was a spiritual body, not subject to the same laws as before. It could disappear at will; it could pass through closed doors; it could be seen and not be recognised, and then suddenly become recognisable; but also it could be touched and felt; it could eat, it had flesh and bones, it was a real body. When the Lord ascended "God gave Him glory," and His body was also glorified, as Paul saw Him on the way to Damascus. It was the same body, but under new conditions (see Luke 24. 36 to 43; John 20. 5, 7, 13, 19, 25, 27; Phil. 3, 20, 21). Really the buried body is the sown grain, and the glorified body the flower, the

---

* Certain elementary substances such as sulphur, phosphorus, oxygen, carbon have the quality of existing in distinct forms, known as allotropic modifications. Thus carbon exists as diamond, graphite, or soot. There may be a distant analogy between this and the existence of the body under different conditions.

same, yet not the same. God gives to the grain a body as He pleases. But what goes to form the flower, was once in the grain. A gardener can recognise the flower from the seed, and vice-versa. And so every saint will have a glorified body that will be recognisable, as coming from its particular seed sown in the graveyard. There will be no confusion: "to every seed his own body," and all "like Him" (1 Cor. 15.37, 38, 44, 49). W.H.

RECOGNITION IN HEAVEN

Will the friends and relations of this world recognise one another in heaven?

This is an old question, often cropping up, which seems to show that the replies need reinforcing to carry conviction, or that the knowledge demanded would satisfy curiosity, rather than minister edification. However we give our judgment. Three Scriptures come to mind (1), Luke 13. 28: "Ye shall see Abraham and Isaac and Jacob and all the prophets in the Kingdom of God and ye yourselves thrust out"; (2), Ch. 16. 24: "Father Abraham . . . send Lazarus"; (3), Matt. 17. 4: Peter said, "Let us make here three tabernacles; one for thee, and one for Moses, and one for Elias." The Jews would know the patriarchs and all the prophets; the rich man recognised Lazarus and knew Abraham; the apostles knew Moses and Elias. It is a fair deduction that, if in a future state, or even here under spiritual conditions, there is recognition of those not known before, there will be not less of those already known. But the conditions being entirely altered, and new relations established, the old would disappear. Even now this is temporarily the case in an assembly of saints, gathering to the name of the Lord. When they are thus "in church" the earthly relations are in abeyance, but the personality persists, and so will it be I believe in the future state. Earthly relations and affections will be for ever superseded by heavenly, but the personality will never lose its identity. "Now we see through a glass, darkly; but then face to face; now I know in part; but then shall I know even as also I am known (1 Cor. 13. 12). W.H.

In light of Matt. 22. 30 and 1 Cor. 15. 50-54, shall we know one another in heaven?

This is an oft-raised question and one that shews how diverse are men's minds. To many the very possibility of non-recognition seems unthinkable. If we are to know as we are known, does not that bespeak a deeper and wider knowledge than before, not a feebler and narrower, "when the mists have rolled away"?

Abraham knew Lazarus and the "rich man," and all about their past; and the "rich man" knew Abraham and Lazarus, and can we suppose that Lazarus, did not know on whose bosom he was pillowing his head?

(See Luke 16. 23, 25). This speaks, no doubt, of the intermediate state, but the principle is the same. The apostles knew Moses and Elias on the Holy Mount. What point would there be in making to ourselves friends with our money, that they may receive us into everlasting habitations? (See Luke 16. 9), for how could these "friends" do so, if they could not recognise their benefactors? I think the true conclusion is that we shall know those whom we have known and all others of the redeemed besides. This does not mean that earthly relations which are of a temporary character, will continue, and this is I think all that Matt. 22. 30 teaches, but nothing is hinted as to a change of personality or a loss of identity. As for 1 Cor. 15. 50-54, surely no changes wrought in the saint by the putting on of immortality or incorruptibility, will exceed the wonderful change wrought in Christ by His glorification, and yet "He is the same" and is recognisable through it all, as John experienced (see Rev. 1).

W.H.

ETERNAL PUNISHMENT

It is believed by some that Eternal Punishment is only for a certain period, and that the doctrine of Eternal Punishment is Brethrenism and not fundamental. How should this be answered, and how should those in our assemblies who hold these views be treated?

The test of a doctrine is not what the world thinks of it, or even the professing church, but what the Word of God declares. Judged by that test, I have not the slightest doubt that a condition of never-ending punishment awaits those who reject the grace of God in whatever form presented, and die in their sins and self-righteousness; and this has been the general belief of the church down the ages. That a committee of determined criminals or weak sentimentalists should decree the impossibility or injustice of life-sentences might be comprehensible, but would not affect the course of the law in any degree. Nor will the divine administration be affected in the slightest way by man's opinions of His decrees. When the opponents of never-ending punishment are asked, "What then will become of the wicked?" they cannot agree among themselves: one party say all will eventually be saved—they are the Universalists; another that all who refuse the grace of God will eventually cease to be—they are the teachers of what is known as "Conditional Immortality." I believe both these theories are in conflict with the Scriptural teaching throughout, e.g., "He that believeth on the Son hath everlasting life (i.e. life in harmony with God, more than mere existence); and he that believeth not the Son shall not see life (which refutes universalism); but the wrath of God abideth on him" (John 3. 36). The wrath of God cannot abide on a nonentity, which

refutes annihilationism. Space will not allow here any lengthy consideration of this tremendous theme. One or two points may, however, be
raised. If we believe in the never-ending bliss of the redeemed, we must
believe in the never-ending punishment of the wicked. The Lord's
own words make this plain, for He uses the same word in the same
context of each: "These shall go away into everlasting punishment,
but the righteous into life everlasting" (Matt. 25. 46). Some again say
that the devil and his angels will suffer eternally, but not human beings;
but in this same chapter our Lord classes them together: "Depart ye
cursed (He will say to wicked men) into everlasting fire prepared for
the devil and his angels" (v. 41). That fearful punishment, here so plainly
revealed by Him who was the embodiment of holy love, was not prepared for men, but for the devil and his angels, but those who deliberately choose to follow him will find themselves with him for ever. A
great effort has been made to show that the word translated here "everlasting" or "eternal" only means "age-lasting." That may be perfectly
true by derivation, as is true indeed of our word "everlasting," but
what matters is the usage of the word. It is used of "God" (Rom. 16.
26); His "honour and power" (1 Tim. 6. 16); "covenant" (Heb. 13.
20); "kingdom" (2 Pet. 1. 11); "gospel" (Rev. 14. 6); the "weight of
glory" of the redeemed (2 Cor. 4. 17); the unseen world (2 Cor. 4. 18);
the glorified body (2 Cor. 5. 1); "glory" (2 Tim. 2. 10); "salvation"
(Heb. 5. 9); "Spirit" (Heb. 9. 14), etc., etc., on the one hand, and
on the other, of future punishment, as above (Matt. 25. 46); "fire"
(Matt. 18. 8); "damnation" (Mark 3. 29); "destruction from the
presence of the Lord" (2 Thess. 1. 9). What honest believer, subject to
the Word, but must admit that the never-endingness of God, His
Spirit, salvation, redemption, and the consolation and the inheritance
of the redeemed, stands or falls, with the never-endingness of the
future punishment of the finally impenitent! Is it not strange that men,
instead of repenting of their sins and believing on the Lord Jesus Christ
as their Saviour, should rather spend their time in trying to disprove
what the Saviour so clearly taught (none more clearly than He)—the
fearful future of those who refuse Him, whom God has provided in
His infinite love as a Saviour from "the wrath to come!" As for the
second part of the question, we must "make a difference" between those
who may be for the moment perplexed over a doctrine and those who
doubt it as part of their fixed belief. It is noticeable that among "the
principles of the doctrine of Christ," in Heb. 6. 1 and 2, which are clearly
considered as fundamental ("not laying again the foundation," etc.),
the doctrine of "eternal judgment" closes the list. This, therefore, is
a fundamental question, and those who deny it have so far departed
from the faith, and deny the clear and unmistakable words of Christ.
How can such then claim a place among the people of God? Their denial

of God's truth raises the solemn question whether they have ever truly known His grace. May God in His infinite mercy preserve the feet, both of writer and readers, from straying from His Word, on this or any other truth! W.H.

Do Scriptures such as Luke 12. 47, 48 and Rev. 20. 12 teach that there are degrees in punishment for the wicked dead?

They certainly do. The former passage especially lays down what is doubtless a general principle of God's dealings in judgment, namely, that the punishment varies, not so much according to the amount of evil inherent in the act itself, as according to the amount of knowledge of right and wrong possessed by the sinner. It is worthy of note that "the servant which knew" is beaten with many stripes, merely for not doing things he should have done, i.e. for sins of omission; while "he that knew not" gets his few stripes for wrong things done by him, i.e. for sins of commission. Another passage in which the same principle is strongly emphasised is Matt. 11. 20-24, where Christ pronounces woes on the cities in which He had preached most, and in doing so says that it shall be more tolerable for Tyre, Sidon, and even Sodom in the day of judgment than for them. W.R.

RESURRECTION AND RAPTURE

A circular to hand asserts that Christ will come FOR His saints "immediately after the tribulation of those days," and challenges anyone to point out in Matt. xxiv., Mark xiii, or Luke xxi, any verse where Christ said He would come SECRETLY or "at any moment." Please throw light upon this subject.

The circular is composed of a number of verses, referring to the coming of Christ *with* His saints, and the events preceding it, and it is naturally vain to look in such passages for what is quite distinct from and subsequent to it, namely, the descent of the Lord from heaven to take away His sleeping and living saints from the earth, to be for ever with the Lord, as is revealed in 1 Thess. iv. 13-18. It will hardly be believed, that the writer of the circular does not once refer to this or similar passages (*e.g.*, John xiv. 1-3; Phil. iii. 20-21; 1 Thess. i. 10), nor yet to 1 Cor. xv. 51-54, where the "mystery" of this first stage of the Lord's return is revealed: "Behold, I shew you a *mystery*, we shall not all sleep, but we shall all be changed, in a moment, in the twinkling of an eye." This is not referred to in Matt. xxiv., etc., for the good reason, that the time had not come to reveal it. The coming there described is that of the "Son of Man" to the earth, to deliver Israel, which was not a mystery at all, but had been plainly revealed in the Old Testament, *e.g.*, Zech. xiv. 4, 5. where we read that "His feet shall stand upon the Mount of Olives, and that "all His saints will be with Him," that is clearly all the saints already caught up to be with Him. It is true that the words "secret rapture" do not occur, but if, as is stated, the whole event will be over in "the twinkling of an eye," clearly only those taken away will know of it at the time, though their absence will doubtless be noticed later. They will be delivered thus from the Great Tribulation.   W.H.

If we are right in taking the expression, "in Christ," as a New Testament term, and therefore "the dead in Christ" (1 Thess. 4.) as referring only to New Testament saints, when will the Old Testament saints be raised?

In 1 Cor. 15. 23 we have the general truth that Christ is "the first-fruits" of the Resurrection, "afterward, they that are Christ's at His coming." This expression seems to include here the whole completed Second Coming, when the first Resurrection will be finished. This will have taken place in different stages and categories. Thus, supposing the Resurrection in 1 Thess. 4. is of the saints of this dispensation alone since Pentecost (to such only applying the expression—"dead in Christ), that will be the beginning of the first Resurrection, which will not reach its final stage until Revelation 20. 4, where the Resurrection of more than one category of saints is indicated, of which we read in verse 5, "this is (i.e., completes), the first Resurrection." This will no doubt include the Old Testament saints. To conceive of Old Testament saints however, being included in the first Resurrection, at the same time as the Church, is very difficult and indeed impossible. How could such be caught away to meet the Lord in the air along with the Church? In that case there would be two distinct companies, each in a distinct relationship with the Lord. W.H.

When will the Old Testament saints rise?

This question was replied to by Mr. Hoste in "The Believers' Magazine," October, 1933. He pointed out that what is spoken of in Scripture as "The First Resurrection" takes place in different stages and categories, of which the raising of saints at the Lord's coming to the air is but one, and of which the final one is seen in Rev. 20. 4, 5, to take place when He comes as Son of Man to earth. He took the view that Old Testament saints will not be raised until this final stage is reached; and he added, "To conceive of Old Testament saints being included in the first resurrection at the same time as the Church is very difficult and indeed impossible, as there would be two distinct companies in a distinct relationship to the Lord."

Personally, I cannot see that this last point presents any difficulty; but on the other hand I do feel it difficult to think of the twenty-four elders of Rev. 4, clothed in white raiment, and wearing victor's crowns (see Newberry), as representing saints of the Church period only; and indeed to even conceive of the Lord leaving any of His saints still in their graves, when the glorious event described in 1 Cor. 15. 51-53 and 1 Thess. 4. 15-17 takes place. I therefore, with the late Mr. J. Ritchie, and many others, believe that when our Lord comes to the air, all the saints who up till then have died will be raised again. W.R.

CHILDREN AND THE RAPTURE

Is it scriptural to say that the children of believers shall be caught up when the Lord comes? Some evangelists say they will, while others say they will not. I mean children not old enough to understand.

Does not the difference of view among the Lord's servants arise from the fact that there is no clear revelation in the Word of God? It would seem unthinkable that the small children of unconverted parents throughout the world should be all caught away when the Lord returns, for if any go all must go. It is equally unthinkable that the irresponsible children of Christians, the subjects of believing prayer, should be all left behind when their parents are taken, for if any are left all must be left. Can we not leave the matter to God in the assurance that the Judge of all the earth will do right? In the meantime diligently point the little ones to the Saviour.   W.H.

The resurrection of 1 Thess. iv. 16 is qualified by the expression "the dead in Christ," so "we who are alive and remain," and are caught up together with them, must also be "in Christ." This is a Pauline expression peculiar to His Gospel, and necessitates the having heard the Gospel and having put faith into the Son of God.

J. Ritchie, first Editor of "The Believers' Magazine."

THE JEWS

When and how did the name "Jew" originate, and to whom does it apply to-day?

The word is an abbreviation of "Judæan" and occurs first in 2 Kings 16. 6, where we read that "Rezin recovered Elath and drave the Jews" thence. A reference back to chap. 14. 21 tells how Azariah, made King by **"the people of Judah,"** had smitten Elath and restored it to Judah, which shows that Jews and people of Judah are synonymous terms and represented the Southern Kingdom, after the separation of the ten tribes under Jeroboam. After the Captivity, those who returned though no doubt including Levites, Benjamites and representatives of other tribes, were all known as Jews, the Judæans being predominant (see Ezra 4. 12; Neh. 1. 2; 4. 2).

Only twice in the Synoptic Gospels do we find the word (Matt. 28. 15; Mark 7. 3), if we except a few occurrences of the phrase, "King of the Jews," but the name is common in John and the Acts. I believe it is a great mistake to meet the British Israel "hypothesis" (which I believe for many reasons, historical and scriptural, to be a complete delusion), by denying any difference between "the lost tribes of Israel" as they are usually and properly termed, and the scattered Jews. Certainly many Israelites had lapsed to the Southern Kingdom, before their captivity by Assyria, under Sargon, but in spite of this the Northern Kingdom of Israel was able to withstand a three years' siege from the greatest of the then world-powers. We are distinctly told that they were taken captive, except a feeble remnant, and placed "in Halah and Habor, by the river of Gozan, and in the cities of the Medes." Considering that these places were far-removed geographically from Babylon, at a distance of 300 or 400 miles to the north, and that the captivity of Israel took place in 721 B.C., that is a century-and-a-quarter before that of Jehoiachin, it is very unlikely that the two captivities mingled or even came in contact. When a thing is lost it is not a bad idea to seek for it as near where it was lost as possible, and probably the representatives of the lost tribes may still exist in or near those parts. The difference between Judah and the ten tribes of Israel is preserved in the accounts of the final return to the land, e.g., in Isa. 11. 12, we read of "the outcasts of Israel" and "the dispersed of Judah." See also Isa. 27. 13; Zeph. 3. 19, and especially Ezek. 37. 16-22, where God commands prophetically the two sticks to be taken, one "for Judah and the children of Israel his companions" (representing those individual members of the ten tribes who had lapsed to Judah and are confused sometimes with those tribes themselves), and the other "For Joseph, the stick of Ephraim and for all the house of Israel his companions" (i.e., the lost tribes). To meet this British-Israel delusion with a defective argument is to strengthen it, for its advocates will surely take notice of it, though they usually leave the sound arguments, which abound against their theory, severely alone.   W.H.

THE TEN TRIBES

Were the ten tribes restored after their dispersion? In the "Believer's Magazine" of July, 1927, the statement is made that they were never restored. Is this correct? (see Acts iv. 27; v. 21; ii. 36).

It is clearly impossible in this column to track out the deplorable delusion of "British Israelism," which is occupying so many minds to-day with earthly hopes and national ambitions, to the exclusion of Christ and the HEAVENLY calling of the church. This church is being called out from all nations, including the British Empire, which, however, as a whole, is fast apostatising from God. At the same time, I think it is quite indefensible to contest this error by denying that the tribes of Israel were ever lost. All admit numbers of them seceded to Judah, but it is equally certain they existed as a separate kingdom till 721 B.C., when they were carried away by Shalmaneser into Assyria. They were no skeleton tribes then, but able to resist a siege of three years to their capital by the greatest world power of the time (2 Kings xvii. 6). The fact that the generic name of Israel is sometimes applied to the remnant of Judah, etc., who returned from Babylon, proves nothing; they were as truly descended from Israel as the other tribes, and they were the representatives of the whole nation in the land. This explains the expression the questioner refers to "as to the lost sheep of the house of Israel." At that time large numbers of Jews were scattered throughout the civilised world. The Lord was not sent to these, for He never stepped outside the promised land, but He of course fulfilled His mission perfectly to such as were within its limits. In the prophets, Israel and Judah are constantly distinguished (e.g., Jer. iii. 8-14; Zech. x. 6; etc.). To faith the twelve tribes existed still even to New Testament times, and do still, though mostly lost to sight.

The breaking of the covenant between the two nations of Judah and Israel was only finally consummated at the crucifixion, i.e., when "Beauty" was cut off, "Bands" cut asunder, and (see carefully Zech. 11. 10-14) "the brotherhood between Judah and Israel" broken. That state of alienation will continue till the restoration of both in the last days. In Isa. 27. 13 we read, "They shall come which were ready to perish (Heb. 'abhadh. see R.V. Marg., 'lost.' This is the first meaning Gesenius gives to the word—like 'a wandering sheep which gets lost and disappears,' and quotes this verse in support) in the land of Assyria."

If you lose a thing, it is not a bad idea to look for it where you lost it. There is no record, biblical or historical, of the tribes of Israel ever having returned to the land, or having migrated to other lands, or being scattered, as the Jews have been; in fact, they are called "OUTCASTS of Israel," in distinction from the "DISPERSED of Judah" (Isa. xi. 12-16). It is only in Ezek. xxxvii. 16-22, after the vision of the dry bones, that is, in quite the last days, that the two peoples are once more reunited— "For Judah, and the children of Israel, his companions (*i.e.*, the seceders to Judah from the other tribes), and for Joseph, the stock of Ephraim and all the house of Israel, his companions" (*i.e.*, the great majority of the ten tribes). I think a careful consideration of this passage alone is sufficient to show that up to that point, the two leading companies will have been separate peoples, leading a distinct existence, and with no attempt to coalesce. It is noticeable that in Zech. xii, when the Lord comes in glory to deliver Jerusalem, only "Judah and his companions" will have returned the land, and they are addressed as "Israel" in verse 1.   W.H.

How could there be ten tribes in revolt in Israel, when the tribe which provided the priests and Levites remained for the worship of the Lord in the Temple, in addition to Judah and Benjamin?

When thinking of this matter of the revolt from Rehoboam, and the division afterwards into two kingdoms, have you not for the moment forgotten that there were actually thirteen tribes in Israel?

Jacob had of course only twelve sons, but the giving of tribeship to Joseph's two sons, Ephraim and Manasseh, brought the number of the Tribes to thirteen. See Gen. 48. 5, 22. This is described in 1 Chron. 5. 1, 2 as giving the birthright. (i.e. the double portion, as in Deut. 21. 17) to the sons of Joseph. And Ezek. 47. 13 shows that the arrangement will persist even in Millennial times.

The expression "The Twelve Tribes," as used in Exod. 24. 4; Matt. 19. 28; James 1. 1; Rev. 21. 12; etc., became a kind of ideal description for them, and that the more readily because of Levi having no possession in the sense that the other tribes had. But when a list of twelve is given, either one tribe is omitted, as Dan in Rev. 7. 4-8, or Manasseh and Ephraim are joined in one, as in Deut. 27. 12, 13.

This thought of twelve as an ideal number is also the most probable explanation of the statement, "He was seen ... of the Twelve", in 1 Cor. 15. 5, since Judas was not present on the occasion referred to.   W.R.

THE RESTORATION OF ALL THINGS

When does the restoration of all things by Elias take place?
The answer is given in Malachi 4. 5: "Behold I will send you Elijah
the prophet before the coming of the great and dreadful day of the
Lord." The Lord seems clearly to refer to this promise, see Matt. 17. 11:
"Elias truly shall first come and restore all things." As to what
this coming represents we must refer to other Scriptures. The first
time historically that Elias is mentioned in the N.T. is in Luke 1, in the
angel's message to Zacharias that his promised son "shall go before
Him in the spirit and power of Elias to turn the hearts of the fathers to
the children, etc." John's mission was to resemble in spirit and power
and result, the mission of Elias as described in Mal. 4. 6. Now, we
remember that when later the apostles James and John proposed to call
down fire from heaven, even as Elias did, and consume the Samaritans,
the Lord rebuked them on the ground that they knew not what spirit
they were of. It was the spirit of Elias, which was perfectly right in his
dispensation, but not that of the Son of man (see Luke 9. 54). Does
not this supply one more Scriptural reason against the new theory that
John, had he only been faithful, would have become one of the twelve
apostles? Had he been so, there would have been two incompatible
"spirits" in the twelve, one, that of Elias in the person of John the
Baptist, and another foreign to it, the spirit of Christ. In Matt. 11. 14,
the Lord said, "If ye will receive it, this (i.e., John the Baptist) is Elias
which was for to come." The words, "if ye will receive it," are important,
as they also throw light on our Lord's words in chap. 17. 12: "I say
unto you that Elias is come already, and they knew him not." This
cannot, I submit, mean that John was a reincarnation of Elias. They are
separate entities to-day. Elias will surely come again, but he will not be
born, as John was, of a mother. He will come again as he went and probably as secretly, as far as the general world will be concerned. John
did up to a certain point fulfil the role of Elias. To use a modern phrase,
he was his "double," but none the less it remains true that "Elias will
come before the great and dreadful day of the Lord," and most
evangelical interpreters of the Revelation are agreed that he will be one
of the two witnesses of Rev. 11. Their ministry will last 1260 days or
3½ years, that is, during the first half of Daniel's last week of years,
beginning with the Covenant between the Head of the Roman people
and the Jews. The ministry of the two witnesses will be a ministry
enforced by judgment and plague, and bearing down all opposition and
crushing their enemies by miraculous power. It will also be wonderful
in its success. There will be a revival in Israel, such as has never yet
been known, and a world-wide testimony through, I might suggest,
the 144,000 equipped for this service by that Pentecost (see Joel 2), of
which that of Jerusalem was the foretaste, and vast numbers will be

brought to repentance. It will only be when their ministry is finished that the "Beast," then manifested as such, will slay them. This will inaugurate the day of Jacob's trouble and the great tribulation, running concurrently, only to end in the appearing in power and great glory of the Son of man—"the great and terrible day of the Lord." W.H.

MILLENNIAL SACRIFICES

What will be the nature of the Jewish sacrifices offered at Jerusalem during the Millennium? They cannot, of course, in any way be connected with sin since Christ has died and "their remaineth no more sacrifice for sin." Will they be sacrifices of praise and adoration or of remembrance?

Here again we see the importance of dispensational truth—according to the oft-quoted words of Augustine: "Distinguish the dispensations and the Scriptures will agree." Here, what is quite out of place in the present Church era, will evidently from Ezekiel 43. 26 once more be in vogue. After the measures of the altar are given (chap. 43. 13), the ordinances of the altar are laid down, and the sin offering is mentioned again and again (e.g., vv. 21, 22, 25, and chap. 44. 27, 29), but certainly not in the sense of taking sin away. The Old Testament dispensation was characterised by an altar on which typical sacrifices (a shadow of good things to come) were offered, the present is characterised by a table, on which the memorial symbols of bread and wine are presented, and partaken of, in remembrance of the One Sacrifice of Christ, the only and sufficient ground for the atonement and taking away of sin. But the future millennial age, when the earthly people are once more restored to the place of testimony and blessing, will be characterised once again by an altar of remembrance—on which literal sacrifices will be offered, no longer pointing forward, but backward—and that by earthly priests—the sons of Zadok alone (chap. 44. 15). So that we see that what is a Satanic delusion to-day:—the pretended offering up again and again of the sacrifice of Christ, will in a future dispensation be renewed in a figurative and memorial sense. W.H.

F

THE KINDGOM AND THE HOUSE OF GOD

THE KINGDOM

THE KINGDOM OF GOD AND THE KINGDOM OF HEAVEN

Some hold that there is a difference between the Kingdom of God and the Kingdom of Heaven, and that only those who are born again are in the former, while all who profess are in the latter. If such be the case, how can they explain Matt. 5. 20 and 18. 3? I was under the impression that both were the same, and that conversion and regeneration also were the same. Am I correct?

Some, I believe, maintain that the Kingdom of God is the real thing and the Kingdom of heaven inclusive of all profession. But does not the first Beatitude seem to refute this? "Blessed are the poor in Spirit for theirs is the Kingdom of heaven" (Matt. 5. 2). A comparison of Matt. 13 and Luke 13 shows that in the two chapters the same parables—of the mustard seed and of the leaven—are referred, in the former to the Kingdom of heaven, in the latter to the Kingdom of God. This would seem to indicate that the difference cannot be vital. In the one phrase, the seat of the authority exercised is emphasised. It comes from "the heavens": In the other, the one who exercises the authority is the predominant thought—it is God Himself. I believe both are real. How could it be otherwise when both belong to God? It is dangerous, however, to shuffle Bible terms. But in the Kingdom of Israel remnants of the Canaanites, e.g., the Gibeonites remained, but were not subjects of the Kingdom. In the Kingdom of this land, foreigners, enemy spies, alien communists, ever hostile to our king, may live and lurk; they must recognise the law of the land, but they are not recognised as British subjects and they can be repatriated at the will of the Sovereign. So there are doubtless some who profess the name of Christ who are not really subjects of the Kingdom. They will be purged out, but it does not follow they were ever included in the Kingdom. As regards the terms, "conversion," and "regeneration," they may coincide and I believe do, but they are far from being synonymous.

Conversion is the turning of the sinner to God and represents the man-ward side of things; regeneration is the new-birth wrought in the soul by the Holy Spirit, when conversion takes place. This represents the God-ward side.   W.H.

What is the significance of the terms "Kingdom of Heaven" (Matt. 3. 2) and "Kingdom of God" (1 Cor. 15. 24)?

The expression "Kingdom of God" does not actually occur in 1 Cor. 15. 24, but I believe the Kingdom there referred to is the same to all intents and purposes as that proclaimed by John the Baptist. Any godly Jew, versed in the Old Testament Scriptures and especially Daniel's prophecy, knew that God had transferred the Kingdom from Israel, for their sins, to the four great Gentile Powers—Babylon, Medo-Persia, Greece and Rome, the last of which was exercising its sway at the time of the Baptist's mission. It would also be known from Daniel that the next event on the divine programme was to be the smiting and total destruction of the great-powers, regarded in their integrity as an image, by the stone cut out without hands, to be followed by the "setting up of a Kingdom which shall never be destroyed," and "which shall not be left to other people,"—"it shall stand for ever." What else could a godly Jew understand then by John's proclamation, "The kingdom of heaven is at hand," but that God was about to introduce His, the fifth Kingdom, upon earth? For that, God had His King ready, but the King was also the Lamb of God—for atonement must be made, the only ground on which the Kingdom could ever be set up on this sin-stained earth. Had the Jewish nation received the post-pentecostal testimony to the resurrection of the Lord, God would have sent back the Lord Jesus to destroy His enemies and set up His millennial Kingdom. It is that Kingdom to which reference is made in 1 Cor. 15. 24, at the close of which the Lord will put down all His enemies—human and angelic—and then deliver up the Kingdom to God, purged of every "evil concurrent." This will not be as is so often mistakenly asserted, in the sense of ceasing to reign, for the millennial reign will only be the first stage of the everlasting Kingdom of our Lord and Saviour Jesus Christ, but in the sense of restoring it to Him. Then no less than before, God will be (not become) All in All, and the Lord will reign as universal King. God's throne will for ever be the throne of God and the Lamb.   W.H.

Please give a clear understanding as to the terms Kingdom of God and Kingdom of Heaven?

These two expressions refer in the Gospels to the same thing, from a slightly different standpoint, as is seen by comparing Matt. xiii. 31-33 and Luke xiii. 18-21, where the same pair of parables describe in the former, "the Kingdom of Heaven," and in the latter, "the Kingdom of God." When we read, "Kingdom of Heaven," the place from which the kingly rule is exercised is in view, when "Kingdom of God," the Divine Person who exercises that rule. Both expressions in the Gospels represent generally the condition of things produced in the world by the preaching of the Gospel in the absence of the King. This is always true, I believe, of the expression Kingdom of Heaven, which only occurs in Matthew. In the Kingdom of Heaven there is a mixture of good and bad—tares are sown by the evil one; worthless fish are caught with good; but when the King comes, He will cast out of His kingdom "all that offends and all that work iniquity." The kingdom aspect of truth represents the responsibility side of things and includes profession, which must be tested. To enter the real thing the new birth is needed. The Kingdom of God in this aspect is "not meat and drink, but righteousness and peace and joy in the Holy Ghost." The kingdom includes the Church, but is greater than it, in that it began before it. Abraham, Isaac, and Jacob will sit down in the Kingdom of God, but they will not be in the Church. The kingdom will continue when the Church is taken, but will only be visibly established when the King returns.   W.H.

THE KINGDOM LIKENED UNTO LEAVEN

In what sense is the Kingdom of God "like unto leaven which a woman hid in three measures of meal till the whole was leavened", if leaven is the symbol of evil, and the kingdom of God embraces only that which is "born again" (John iii. 3)?

When John the Baptist began his ministry, the Jewish people were, and had been for some time, under the domination of Rome, the fourth of the great world powers who were foretold by Daniel, of which the first three were Babylon, Medo-Persia, and Greece. Rome, the last, was to be superseded on the Divine programme by another of a totally distinct character. "In the days of these things shall the God of heaven set up a kingdom which shall never be destroyed" (Dan. ii. 44). What other meaning could the Baptists' words, "Repent, for the kingdom of heaven is at hand," have to an intelligent Jew, who knew the Old Testament prophecies but that this kingdom was about to be set up? The Lord took up the same testimony, and in due course presented Himself to Israel as their Messiah and King. That He was present in power as King was evidenced by His miracles, but by twice deliberately attributing these works to Satan, (see Matt. ix. and xii.) the leaders of the nation rejected His claims. Consequently, at chap. xiii. there is a break, the MYSTERIES OF THE KINGDOM being introduced, and parable to a great extent replaces miracle. The King is rejected, but a kingdom is set up, notwithstanding, in the hearts of men. The kingdom, as we have it in the seven parables of Matt. xiii, is the condition of things produced in the earth as the result of the preaching of the Gospel, including very much of a mere profession of Christianity, which is not all the genuine work of the Spirit, for when the Lord comes "He will gather out of the kingdom all things that offend and them which do iniquity." Clearly these were in the kingdom, BUT NEVER OF IT. The seven parables present to us the progress of the spurious, as well as of the real. In the first two parables we see the effects of the good seed being hindered by the mixed qualities of the soil, or by an imitation seed. In the second pair, the mustard seed and the leaven, we see the monstrous growth and insidious spread of the bad, as exemplified all around us in Christendom to-day. Far other is the real Divine kingdom, entered only by the new birth. That is a different phase altogether, misunderstood and despised of men, if not hidden altogether from their view. This is exemplified in the parables of the treasure and the pearl, first in its relation to Israel, and then as the whole aggregate of the children of the kingdom. The seventh parable, the drag-net, represents the last great testimony for God in the world. Multitudes will be gathered in, but here too, as with the tares, there will be a sorting out needed. Of course, it is impossible in the space available to take up all the aspects of this great kingdom subject, distinct from those touched upon here—"the kingdom of the Son of His love;" "the everlasting kingdom of our Lord and Saviour Jesus Christ;" "the kingdom of the Father," etc. There is much to learn and unlearn.   W.H.

"THY KINGDOM COME"

Why did our Lord teach His disciples to pray "Thy Kingdom come" (Matt. 6. 10), yet later say to Pilate in John 18. 36, "My Kingdom is not of this world"? How reconcile these statements?

It may be said on the face of it that, if we take the expression, "Thy Kingdom come," by itself, there is nothing to affirm that the Kingdom referred to is of this world. The expression is often used to-day of what would be termed "God's cause"—"not meat or drink, but righteousness and peace and joy in the Holy Ghost." When we speak of the Kingdom of God coming, why, it may be asked, should we not be referring to the spiritual Kingdom? However, I am not advocating this use of the term, as we ought to take the words in their context. Such a question as this shews how important it is "rightly to divide the word of truth," and to recognise the dispensational change, which occurred even in the brief space of our Lord's ministry. The kingdom that John, and subsequently our Lord and His apostles, proclaimed, was the Kingdom for which the disciples were taught to pray. This Kingdom, as we have shewn more than once lately, was the fifth Kingdom foretold by the prophet Daniel (chap. 2. 44). Babylon, Medo-Persia and Greece had lost their power, and for nearly a century Jerusalem had been subject to Rome. The Lord Jesus was born King of the Jews. Born of the seed of David according to the flesh, He was the rightful heir to the Throne. He offered Himself as such. His miraculous works were His credentials, but these were in Matt. 9 and 12 imputed by His foes to Satan, and His rejection on the day of His entry into Jerusalem became a foregone conclusion. This in no way set on one side the necessity of atonement, but that is kept in the back-ground till chapter 16. 21: "**From that time forth** began Jesus to shew unto His disciples how that He must suffer . . . be killed and be raised again the third day." The Lord could not reign over an unrepentant people, and only, if repentant, on the ground of atonement. The setting up of the Messianic earthly kingdom was then postponed, so that the Lord's words to Pilate fit into their place: His Kingdom had then for the time being lost its earthly character. When once more He claims the Kingdom, it will be as the Son of Man, coming in glory, and then it will be established by force. It will be said in that day, "The kingdoms of this world are become the Kingdom of our Lord and of His Christ; and He shall reign for ever and ever." The Millennial Kingdom will be the vestibule of the "Everlasting Kingdom of our Lord and Saviour Jesus Christ."   W.H.

ASPECTS OF THE KINGDOM

To what time do the references to the Kingdom belong in Matt. 26. 29 ("My Father's Kingdom"); Mark 14. 25 ("the Kingdom of God"; see also Luke 22. 16); and 2 Pet. 1. 11 ("the Everlasting Kingdom")? Are these terms interchangeable?

It is evident that the expression, "My Father's Kingdom" in Matt. 26. 29 refers to the same Kingdom as "the Kingdom of God" in Mark 14. 25, for the same occasion is referred to. It may be noticed that the Lord does not say "**our** Father's Kingdom," but "**My** Father's Kingdom." It reminds us of "My Father and your Father," where there is a distinction with a difference. We might refer also to Matt. 13. 43: "Then shall the righteous shine forth as the sun in the Kingdom of **their Father.**" The One whose Kingdom it is, will be in special relation to the redeemed—His own children—who will share in it; but as the Kingdom in its millennial aspect (which is specially in view here) will embrace in its scope many, who will not be children of God, born in the earth during its course, it is called also "the Kingdom of God." He will be God of such, but not Father. Though the Millennial Kingdom is only the first stage of the Everlasting Kingdom, of 2 Pet. 1. 11, and though our Lord Jesus Christ will reign over both in the Father's Name, the two are quite distinct. In the Millennial Kingdom, though Satan will be excluded, evil will still be present, and the reign will close with the last great rebellion under Satan, who will be liberated for a short space. Then will all the enemies of God and of His Christ be subdued for ever under His feet and judged, so that in the Everlasting Kingdom, in which Christ will continue to reign for ever, there will be no "evil concurrent," no opposing will, and righteousness will no longer "reign" as in the Millennium, but "dwell."   W.H.

THE HOUSE OF GOD

Do you think that the House of God is regarded in Scripture as "the place of profession," as is sometimes taught?
A good deal is taught on this subject, which we do well to test by the Word of God. It is laid down that the House of God is the place of Christian profession, and that God recognises this as a "third something" between the true Church and the world. What is known as Household-Baptism, for instance, thus seeks to justify the baptism of children and unconverted household servants. These are brought, they assert, into the House of God—they are "in the ambit of the Church of God," as the strange expression goes. They are there on the ground of profession; but what profession can infants make? And if unconverted persons make any, it can only be false. That man has made a mixed thing of it by carelessness in reception, or by neglect of Scriptural discipline, is sadly true; but to make out that God is responsible for, or connives at such a state of things is indeed serious. Now, the expression "House of God" refers in the Old Testament, if we except Gen. 28. 17, 22, where Jacob uses the expression in a figurative sense, to the Tabernacle or to the Temple, and though uncleanness and even idols (2 Chron. 33. 7) might invade that House, they never formed part of it, and at every revival were drastically removed and cleansed away (e.g., 2 Chron. 24. 13; 29. 16; 33. 15). Paul in writing to Timothy speaks of his knowing "how to behave himself in the house of God, which is the church of the living God, the pillar and ground of the truth." This is the local aspect—the Church of God, viewed as the place of responsibility. Undesirable elements did incorporate themselves, alas too easily, in the local "house" (see Jude), but though the condition was detected, it was not approved of. Ecclesiastics justify the sad lack of discipline in their organisations by the parable of the tares and the wheat—"Let both grow together until the harvest"—but they seem to forget that "the field is the world," **not the church.** Undesirable visitors, thieves, and such-like, may find entrance into a house, but it is contrary to the desire of the head of the house, and they form no part of the household and must be removed as soon as detected. In Hebrews we read, "But Christ as a Son over His own house: whose house are we, if we hold fast the beginning of our confidence firm unto the end" (Heb. 3. 6), that is, those who continue in the way prove themselves to be the House of God, the rest have no part in it. It is indeed a blessed privilege of the people of God no longer to be "strangers and foreigners, but fellow-citizens with the saints, and of the **household of God**" (Eph. 2. 19). And this is His purpose in gathering saints to Christ —"To whom coming as unto a Living Stone . . . chosen of God and

precious; Ye also as living stones are built up a spiritual house" (1 Pet. 2. 4, 5). "Ye are God's building . . . ye are the temple of God" (1 Cor. 3. 9, 16). When the apostle speaks of the "House of God," does he then view it as possibly or even probably including "false brethren crept in unawares," or ideally? I believe the latter, for whatever is not God's building is an extraneous element to be purged out. For instance, in Heb. 10. 21, Christ is presented as "High Priest over the house of God"—surely He is not the High Priest of false worshippers—trespassers in that house. Again, Peter reminds us that "judgment must first begin at the house of God." Has he in view the heterogeneous company, that some seem to see almost exclusively, in the place of profession—a mixture of believers and unbelievers, because they all profess and call themselves Christians? I think the context shows rather that the true House of God is in view—contrasted with those that "obey not the gospel of God," and paralleled in the following verse with the righteous—"If the righteous scarcely be saved, where shall the ungodly and the sinner appear?" (1 Pet. 4. 17, 18). Where is there room in this verse for a third something, neither righteous nor ungodly, but "professors." The original from which this quotation is taken bears this out: "Behold, the righteous shall be recompensed in the earth; much more the wicked and the sinner" (Prov. 11. 31). These latter, including false professors, will be recompensed not now, but in the future. But someone will say, "Does not Paul speak of 'the great house of Christendom' in his Second Epistle to Timothy?" Certainly not in so many words, though such a form of words has been dogmatically attributed to his writings. What he does say, I believe parenthetically, is, "But in **a great house** there are not only vessels of gold and of silver, but also of wood and of earth; and some to honour and some to dishonour" (chap. 2. 20). This passage and the 'parable of the tares seem to be the sheet anchors of ecclesiastics to justify their mixed systems. To them "the great house" is "the Church" in their broad sense of a great ecclesiastical, christened organisation, reciting the apostles' creed and practising "the sacraments." Others, as we have seen, understand Paul to mean "the great house of Christendom," though I believe such an idea springs from a misreading of the passage. I submit again that verse 20 is in the nature of a parenthesis, explaining the use the apostle is about to make of the term, "vessel unto honour" in verse 21. "In a great house" (that is in any great house in Rome, where he was in prison, or in Ephesus, where Timothy is supposed to have been), there are vessels of various materials and of varied uses. At this point the apostle resumes his exhortation, "If a man purge himself from these"—the evil things and men above referred to—he shall be something corresponding to the literal material vessels of gold and silver of any great house, namely a spiritual vessel unto honour in the House of God, "sanctified

and meet for the master's use, and prepared unto every good work."
One does not wish to dogmatise, but I would ask my readers, who
desire to be still subject to the Word of God, apart from the glamour
of great names, carefully to weigh above with the Scriptures.   W.H.

THE LORD'S SUPPER

Did the Lord Himself partake of the emblems when He instituted the Supper?

In none of the three synoptic accounts is it said that He did, though the words of Matthew 26. 29 and Mark 14. 25: "Verily I say unto you, I will drink no more of the fruit of the vine, until that day that I drink it new in the Kingdom," may be taken to convey an inference that he did at least partake of the cup. Equally well they might be taken as explanatory of His not doing so. In any case, I believe it is a false inference, for in Luke 22. 18, where we have, I judge, the true order, both these words and similar ones in v. 16 referring to what He had just eaten, **are connected with the Passover.** This order in Luke is, I believe, determinant, and permits us to give weight to two moral considerations. Why should the Lord need to partake of the **memorial** of His own sufferings? and how could He suitably partake of the emblems of His own body and blood?   W.H.

Why did our Lord, though not partaking of the bread when instituting His supper, drink of the cup? Can there be some spiritual truth hidden in this?

We think the idea that the Lord partook of the cup (as above) is based on a misunderstanding of the accounts of the Institution, and on a false inference. The misunderstanding arises from the position of the words, "I will not drink henceforth of this fruit of the vine," in the Matthew and Mark accounts, and the false inference, from the idea that the Lord had necessarily that moment drunk of the cup in question. It is clear from the Luke (chap. 22.) account that there were two cups, that in the 17th verse which was the passover cup, and the other the cup of the new supper, the memorials of His body and blood. It was to the former (see v. 18) that the Lord's words, above quoted, refer. The Lord did not Himself partake of the emblems of His death in either kind, as Luke's account shews.   W.H.

Was Judas present at the institution of the Lord's Supper?

This is a much debated point, on which godly men have differed, so one would hesitate to dogmatise. Before giving what I believe to be the correct answer, I would say that the anxiety to prove that Judas was not present seems to rest on the false assumption that his presence would sanction to-day the admission of the ungodly to the Lord's table. I believe this to be an entire mistake. Judas was a professed disciple of the Lord and one of the twelve apostles. He had passed all the tests and was apparently the most trusted of all by his fellow apostles, though the Lord knew from the beginning that he was a devil and would betray Him (John 6. 64, 70). He did not, however, use His omniscience to expose Judas before the time, in fact not till he had irretrievably committed himself. IIis presence then at the Lord's table would no more justify the reception of those known to be ungodly, than his being sent forth to preach would sanction the sending forth of the ungodly for this purpose. Matthew 26. 25 seems to shew he was present up to the institution, and verse 26 begins, "As they were eating." That is, the passover was not yet formally over; is it conceivable then that Judas would have left the room thus prematurely, as he must have done, to bar his being present at the institution of "the supper"? However, whether he did or not is not clearly stated in this Gospel, nor yet in Mark 14. 22. It is true that before that, the Lord had said plainly that the traitor would be found "among them that dipped with Him in the dish"; and He had said to Judas, "Thou has said," in answer to his query, "Master (not Lord) is it I?" which for very decency's sake he must have felt bound to make, lest he should draw attention to himself by his silence (Matt. 26. 25). But this was probably only to Judas' ear, who sat next to Him. This must not be confounded with the Lord's definite sign to John, in answer to what I believe was his subsequent question, "Lord who is it?" "He it is to whom I shall **give a sop,** when I have dipped it." This revealed definitely to John the name of the traitor, and he alone narrates the incident (John 13. 26, 27). When we come to Luke's Gospel we have a definite statement which must be allowed to have its influence, and I believe, its determinative influence with us. After the Lord has instituted the supper of remembrance, He immediately adds, "But, behold the hand of him that betrayeth me is with me on the table." The force of this definite statement is met at once by some who assert that Luke does not give us things in historic, but in moral order. Certainly there is a measure of truth in this, though it can not mean that the historic order in some detailed account by Luke is never to be followed, but only has weight when Luke gives us an order of events (as he does, e.g., in the last journey to Jerusalem) which seems to clash with the other Gospels. But what moral order is concerned in such a statement as that of our Lord? (Luke 22. 21). It would seem to be going out of the way to introduce **confusion,** rather than moral order, unless we are to take it literally. If Matthew and Mark had clearly stated that Judas had left before the supper was instituted, then such an argument might have force, and Luke's testimony be discounted. John 13 does not seem really to help us, as there is no hint that Judas went out before the first "breaking of the bread," for nothing is said of it. He did go out when the Lord had given him the sop and that was, I believe, **after** he had partaken to his own condemnation of the bread and the wine, symbols of that very body and blood, of which by his betrayal he became guilty.

W.H.

Did Judas partake of the Lord's Supper when it was instituted?

The only reference to the actual time when Judas left the upper room occurs in John 13. 30, where we learn that he did so "immediately" after the conversation as to who would be the traitor, a conversation which ended by the Lord giving the "sop" to him.

This conversation, according to Matt. 26. 21-26 and to Mark 14. 18-22, took place before the institution of the Lord's Supper; and if we possessed these three Gospels only, we should have no doubt that Judas did not partake of it.

But when we turn to Luke 22. 19-23, we find the order reversed, and the paragraph regarding the institution of the Supper (vv. 19, 20) placed before the one which mentions the conversation about the traitor (vv. 21-23); and thus an element of uncertainty is introduced. It is evident that either in Luke on the one hand, or in Matthew and Mark on the other, the order followed is not that of time; and from what we know of their Gospels elsewhere, it is much more probable that the adoption of an order other than that of time is in Luke.

In the circumstances, however, we cannot say with certainty that Judas did not partake of the Supper; but why it should be a stumbling block to any if he did so, is not apparent. His profession of being a believer in and a follower of Christ was as loud and as clear as that of any of his fellow-disciples. They had accepted him as their treasurer (John 13. 29). One or other of them had preached the Gospel in company with him (Matt. 10. 1-5). And he certainly in any case partook of at least some portion of the Passover feast (Matt. 26. 23).

If he did partake of the Lord's Supper, we have in that fact the most solemn warning possible that our being accepted by brethren as worthy to partake is not, however careful they may be, a sure proof that our hearts are right with God, and that we have been truly born again. Luke elsewhere mentions those who shall say, "Lord, Lord, . . . we have eaten and drunk in Thy presence"; and to whom Christ shall reply, "I know you not, . . . depart from Me."   W.R.

THE HOUR — THE BREAD

Ought we not to observe the Lord's Supper only at night, and only with unleavened cakes, seeing this was the case at the institution?

Of course all admit that the Lord's supper was instituted "the same night that He was betrayed," "while they were eating," that is, as the passover meal was drawing to its close. This was in the evening by a definite direction of Jehovah, but no direction was given that the Lord's supper should be observed at any special hour of the day. Acts 2. 42 and 46, where the "supper" is, I think, certainly in view, makes no mention of the evening, but simply states that "they broke bread at home" (R.V.), in contrast with the daily public meeting in the temple. In Acts 20. 7 the first day of the week is specifically mentioned, but we are left to gather incidentally that the observance was in the evening. There is, moreover, a very simple reason, quite apart from any spiritual significance, which I have never heard attached to the hour, why the evening was probably the time usually chosen in those early days, because it was the most convenient or the only time free in the day. The observance of a "Sunday" on which shops were shut, and work closed down as to-day among men of all creeds or no creeds, was then quite unknown. For those who stickle for an exact imitation of the institution, one wonders why they do not celebrate the feast on the Thursday, the original day of its institution. We certainly only have custom rather than **direct command** for the first day of the week, though I do not question that this is the right day. Christianity is not like Judaism, a religious system of "days and months and years," worked on a time-table, but a life to be lived on spiritual principles in the power of the Spirit, and governed by the Word, but not by inferences or deductions merely. Of course believers are perfectly free to break bread in the evening, if convenient, but it is not the only time, for the Word is "as oft as ye do it," which cannot be limited to any particular hour of the day.

As for the necessity of using only unleavened bread, there is not a hint in Scripture for making this a **sine qua non.** Christians, no doubt, may use it if they see fit, but they have no right to impose it on their brethren. It is mere ceremonialism. The word, "artos," used for the bread or loaf, simply stands for any mixture of flour and water, baked. There is nothing wrong about leaven itself, though, in the Scriptures typical of evil, but its anti-type is not leaven (to interpret a type by itself is not very helpful exegesis), but "malice and wickedness" or some such defiling sins (1 Cor. 5. 8). What we are called to do, is, not, like a company of Jews before the Passover, to search for literal leaven, but to examine ourselves for unjudged sin. To be occupied with the hour of the day, or the exact components of the bread and wine is to substitute the accidents* for essentials, and human inferences for Divine commands. I would close with the following weighty words of the well-known

---

* A property or quality of a thing which is not essential to it, as whiteness to paper, the texture of cloth, the exact composition of bread.

servant of Christ, John Wesley: "What the Bible commands is good, what the Bible forbids is evil: what the Bible neither commands nor forbids, either in plain words or in undeniable inference, is a thing in itself indifferent, and neither good nor evil. The Bible is our sole guide and our adequate guide in faith and conduct."

Matters on which the Bible does not legislate are left to the judgment of believers. The course good for one, may not be so for another. We are "by reason of use to have our senses exercised to discern between good and evil." If the above principle were understood, it would help us to distinguish between things commanded, things commended, and things left entirely open, like the hour of the breaking of bread, or the exact kind of bread to be used, and it would prevent the harmful habit of judging one another on matters where even an apostle would confess he had no commandment from the Lord.   W.H.

Why is the Lord's Supper kept on Lord's Day morning when according to the Book it was always celebrated in the evening?

The hour for the observance of the Passover was definitely laid down by Jehovah. It was to be "in the evening" (Ex. 12. 6), but no such order is given for the celebration of the Supper. No doubt, our Lord instituted His supper at the close of the paschal feast, but He neither enforces the time on the Apostle, nor does Paul in 1 Cor. 11. When he reminds the Corinthian saints that it was "the same night that He was betrayed" that our Lord took the bread, etc., the emphasis seems clearly on the proximity to His betrayal, rather than to the fact that it was eventide. In other words, it was not the time of day, but the time in relation to what was to follow. Christianity is not a system worked on a time-table, like Judaism—"Ye observe days and months and times and years" (Gal. 4. 10). Certain ceremonialists are intensely occupied with the time of the observance, the colour, etc., of the bread (it must not be white, and it must be unleavened!), the kind of wine (it must be "unfermented"). But this verges at best on a mechanical imitation. One wonders why these good folk do not insist on reclining on couches, as no doubt our Lord and His disciples did, or at any rate observing the Lord's supper on the very day He instituted it. Nothing we can make in the way of bread or wine could adequately represent the holiness or purity of Christ. To interpret the leaven of the Old Testament by literal leaven is not an intelligent understanding of the types. An Old Testament type refers to a New Testament reality. No, we are not to examine the table to see if there be any leaven or "ferment" thereon, but ourselves, lest there be any old leaven of wickedness in us, or malice or untruth. The early disciples may always have broken bread in the evening, but if so, it was for convenience sake (as they were working all Lord's Day, as all other days), and that is quite legitimate, but I have never heard that any teaching is supposed to depend on evening communion. But how the legal mind of man loves to enforce its enactments on all! "Stand fast in the liberty wherewith Christ hath made us free and be not entangled again in the yoke of bondage," and if men insist on legislating where the Word of God does not, let us not follow them or be moved by them. W.H.

THE BREAD

At the Lord's Supper is the loaf a symbol of the human Body of the Lord, and also a symbol of His mystical Body—the Church? When thus gathered, are we an expression of that Body on earth? It has been stated by a well-known teacher that "the Church which is Christ's Body" (Eph. 1. 22-23) is spiritual, and spiritually discerned, lying altogether beyond the range of the natural senses and is without organisation or expression on earth."

It has often been remarked that the order of things in the 10th chapter of 1 Cor. differs from that of the following chapter, in that in the 10th the cup precedes the bread, whereas it is the bread which comes first in the 11th chapter, where we have the actual order of the celebration. In the former chapter, it is a question of communion which rests on the blood; in the latter, of remembrance, which views primarily the Person. Certainly in chapter 11, the loaf represents the literal human Body of the Lord, according to His words: "This is My body, which is given for you." How else could such words be understood, than as referring to His literal Body, which was crucified for us, and in which He bore our sins, and which the bread represents?

But in chapter 10. 17, we read: "For we being many are one bread, and one body: for we are all partakers of that one bread," or as the R.V. margin has it, more clearly and I judge, more correctly: "Seeing that there is one bread, we, who are many are one body." I do not think it is necessary for us to assert that "we are an expression of the body on earth," for this may, as it has too often done in the past, savour of pretension, but rather that the one loaf is the expression of the one mystical Body of Christ. I do not think that this is out of harmony with the statement quoted above by the "well-known teacher." The one loaf does not define the unity of the Body, it affirms it and we say, "Amen"! W.H.

"BROKEN" OR "GIVEN"?

Is it right or wrong to say, as we find in some hymns, "Thy body broken"? With us, some substitute the word "given," on the ground that "broken" contravenes the prohibition, "A bone of Him shall not be broken."

The expression in the said hymns is based on the A.V. of 1 Cor. 11.

24: "This is My body, which is broken for you." Whether or not this is correct, it is difficult dogmatically to decide, but I think we are safe in refusing "given" as a substitute for "broken" in the Corinthian passage, for there is no serious manuscript authority for it, and it is only supported by three versions—the Latin Vulgate, the Egyptian and the Ethiopic, and the editor of the 4th or 5th century—Euthalius. This reading, however, has the bulk of authority in Luke 22. 19. The choice then lies between "broken" and simply, "This is My body for you" (lit. the one on behalf of you), though one cannot help feeling that this sentence seems to need completing with some verb. However, although some good authorities like Drs. Tregelles and Christopher Wordsworth, refuse to give up "broken," which has a considerable body of weighty authority behind it, there seems still more authority for omitting. Then again there is the prohibition: "A bone of Him shall not be broken," which some quote as conclusive against our reading, "broken," as the verb in 1 Cor. 11. 24. It is perfectly true that the bread is broken, but surely this is not as a symbol of anything that occurred at the cross, but simply for purposes of distribution. It is the breaking of bread which stands for the communion or sharing of it by those participating. Whether again the breaking of the body, i.e. of the skin and flesh, as was undoubtedly the case at Calvary, might take place, without the unity of the body being compromised, is a question. It is the bones which matter, for they are the foundation of the bodily frame, and alone preserve its unity. I have sometimes wondered whether the prohibition as to breaking a bone of the Paschal lamb (Exod. 12. 46 and Num. 9. 12) did not mean that the carcase should preserve its entirety, the bones being not only unbroken, but unsevered. The flesh would be carved off, the bony frame remain intact. It seems as though nothing short of this would represent the unity of the Body of Christ symbolised by the Lamb. Our Lord's prophetic words in Psa. 22. 17, "I may tell all my bones," no doubt refer primarily to His physical bones, but they go further to those whom He in His omniscience even then knew as His members, and as being crucified with Him. In Psa. 34. 20, we have the assurance, "He keepeth all His bones, not one of them is broken"— where "broken" might well bear the sense of "severed." In the next Psalm we have the testimony of each and all of these "bones"—"All My bones shall say, Lord, who is like unto Thee, which deliverest the poor from Him that is too strong for him" (v. 10).

Our conclusion must be on the whole that while "given" is doctrinally correct (vide Luke 22. 19), it cannot be upheld by the textual authorities of the Corinthian passage as what Paul wrote by the Spirit. As for "broken," though well supported, it certainly has the general understanding of the prohibition of John 19. 36 against it, as well as the larger bulk of manuscript authority. I think we are safer then in accepting with the R.V. the version of the words in question as, "This is My body, which is for you," though we may not be able to do so with absolute conviction. W.H.

BREAKING THE BREAD

Is it right to take the loaf, that which answers to the Body of our Lord and break it in two, and then hand it round the Assembly?

In Matt. 26. 26; Mark 14. 22; Luke 22. 19, we read that the Lord took bread and gave thanks (or blessed) and brake and gave unto His disciples saying, "This is my body," and Luke adds, "which is given (not broken) for you." In 1 Cor. 11. 23, 24, the Lord Jesus is said to have followed the same order, with the words, "which is broken for you," but this, R.V. changes simply (and with sufficient MS. authority) to, "which is for you." Now, compare this with Luke 24. 30, where a simple meal was about to begin (for it can hardly be maintained that the two disciples had spread the table of remembrance that evening at Emmaus, in the condition in which they were of unbelief and ignorance of the true meaning of all that had taken place), and where we read that the Lord took bread and gave thanks, as he sat down to the meal, and then brake it. I do not, therefore, think we must put undue emphasis on the breaking of the bread even by the Lord, though far be it from us to affirm that any act of His was not significant. However, the brother who gives thanks in the Assembly for the bread or the cup, would shrink from any pretention to be taking the place that the Lord rightly took. His giving thanks is no official act, but only as representing the Assembly, and his breaking the bread is only for the convenience of distribution. The true breaking of bread is done by all, each one for him or herself, as we read in 1 Cor. 10. 16: "The bread which **we** break, is it not the communion of the body of Christ"? What is important is that the giving of thanks should take place before the loaf is broken for distribution, for the loaf is one, and this must be maintained, for it not only represents the one holy Body of the Lord given for us, but His mystical Body, the oneness of which is thus witnessed to. "The bread which we break is it not the communion of the Body of Christ? seeing that there is one bread, we who are many are one body" (1 Cor. 10. 16, 17, R.V., margin).

To pass a whole loaf around would be very inconvenient, and would necessitate its being divided in some way by the one who received it first, which would come to the same thing as that to which the questioner objects. The breaking of the bread by the saints is not a dividing of the Body of Christ, but a communion in it ("Him we all in common share"), a remembrance of Him in the act, and a proclamation of His death. W.H.

G

Ought the brother who gives thanks for the loaf, to break it before it is passed round?

In all the accounts of our Lord's institution of His supper in the synoptic Gospels and in 1 Cor. 11, the order is: "He took the bread," "He gave thanks" (or blessed, i.e., for it), "He (then) brake" and "gave to His disciples." Now it is quite true that he who gives thanks for the bread at the Lord's supper does not put himself in the place of the Lord. But was the "breaking" a ceremonial act with some symbolical meaning? I cannot find any hint that such was the case; in fact it is the point rather that the loaf remains unbroken up to the last moment before the partaking, which is insisted upon as symbolising the unity of the mystical Body of Christ: "Not a bone of Him shall be broken." See also the margin of 1 Cor. 10. 17, R.V.: "Seeing that there is one bread, we who are many, are one body, for we are all partakers of the one bread," which seems clearer than the R.V. text which is one of those little gems of ambiguity, which the Revisers so delight in, and which they mistake for "faithfulness," but which are really failures of translation. The bread is then not broken till the thanks have been given, in other words, till it must be broken. For what is the alternative suggestion? I suppose it is to hand an unbroken loaf to the first brother or sister seated where the loaf usually begins to go round the circle. But to break a small portion off an unbroken normal loaf is to most people a physical impossibility, so that the first recipient is forced to do the very thing objected to—break the loaf. Now the same order was observed when the Lord in the Gospels multiplied the loaves. He took, He thanked, He brake, He gave. That he did so for convenience of distribution seems evident, and I believe he did so at the first "Supper" for the same reason. If this be so, then the brother, who for the occasion gives thanks and follows the act with breaking the bread, is not infringing on some prerogative of the Lord, but following His example in a matter of useful order. Were there some important teaching in the dividing of the loaf, we should expect something analogous in the case of the cup, but as the division of this presents no difficulty, nothing is said about dividing it; or the same thought applies as was expressed of the Paschal cup: "Take this and divide it among yourselves." If there be brethren who attach a great importance to the loaf being handed round whole, they ought to find a command to this effect, and to explain the symbolical meaning of so doing? If the dividing the loaf for distribution prevented each one breaking the bread for himself or herself, then I could see an objection, but not otherwise.   W.H.

Should the loaf be broken before being passed around?

This question, put in a somewhat different form, has been replied to by Mr. E. W. Rogers in the words, "The initial breaking of the loaf is but an act of convenience for the saints. Someone of course must be the first to break the loaf, but it is no official act." With that reply I fully agree.

The preliminary dividing into two or more sections has become necessary in most of our larger Assemblies, but has no spiritual significance beyond that which the breaking off of the individual portions has. And it does seem from 1 Cor. 10. 16, 17 as though the saints at Corinth were accustomed to breaking their portion from an undivided loaf. Because the expression, "Breaking of Bread," is used by us to-day exclusively for the ordinance, we are in danger of forgetting that in the time of the apostles it was used of ordinary partaking of food (See Luke 9. 16; 24. 30; Acts 27. 35), and of attributing to the "breaking" more significance than it necessarily bears.   W.R.

It has been laid down in certain circles that in order that the Lord's Supper be scripturally observed, the bread must be a loaf, that this must be lifted and held in the hands of the brother who gives thanks, and that after thanks are offered, he must then break it before passing it to those who partake. How far do you judge such order as above to be scriptural?

The word, **"artos,"** translated **"bread"** in Matt. 26. 26, is usually so in our Authorised Version, though sometimes **"loaf."** But in the three synoptic accounts of the Institution, as also in 1 Cor. 10. and 11., we always have **"bread."** The Revised Version adds "loaf" in margin, in above cases, except in 1 Cor. 11, where "bread" stands alone. Grimm's Standard New Testament Greek Dictionary gives as the meaning of artos—(1) Food composed of flour, mixed with water and baked, so that a biscuit would seem adequately to meet the case. Certainly a pass-over cake would, being presumably the bread at the first occasion, though not strictly a loaf according to our ideas. (2) Food of any kind. The important point for us is that the bread should be a whole (not cut up, or broken into pieces), as representing the Lord's perfect human Body, of which "a bone should not be broken," as also His mystical Body, in its spiritual unity (1 Cor. 10. 17). As for the loaf being necessarily **"lifted,"** the verb for "take," one of the commonest in the New Testament, is not once so translated therein, and certainly not in any of the five references to the Lord's Supper above mentioned. It is the same word as, **"Take,** eat!"—where there is no thought of **lifting,** but rather of receiving.

As I have already pointed out in a previous answer, I do not see from Scripture that the breaking of the bread **by the one who leads the assembly in thanks** is a ceremonial act, but only for convenience. It is "the bread which **we** break." All break the bread; the thanksgiver for the house divides the bread, so as to make it available for his fellow-saints. Such questions as these show the importance of holding revealed truth in equal balance, the omitting of nothing, but not making additions either.   W.H.

SHOULD WE USE A COMPLETE LOAF

Should we have a complete article in the Lord's Supper to represent His Body? Is there any indication in the Scriptures to show that it was a whole loaf which Christ used Himself when instituting the feast? Would the bread cut round not be equally the same as a small loaf?

It is important, where possible, to have a whole article, some kind of small loaf or roll, not a piece or bit of it, for the observance of the Lord's Supper, because the bread not only represents the Lord's physical Body, but also His mystical Body—the Church. This seems plain from Revised Version margin, which follows the original closely, "seeing that there is **one** bread, we who are many are **one** body." The one bread or loaf represents therefore the oneness of the Body. To cut the bread seems clearly contrary to the thing symbolised; for that would represent a sect, rather than the whole Church. Probably the Lord used a flat passover cake. All we read is, "As they were eating Jesus took bread" (or, "a loaf," Greek) (Matt. 26. 26). While observing these details, how important it is not to become mere sticklers for minor points—ritualists in fact—while perhaps failing to discern the Body of Christ, as we should or the unity of the mystical Body. "These ought ye to have done, and not to leave the others undone."   W.H.

HANDING OUT THE EMBLEMS

Is it necessary that the brother who gives thanks for the bread or the wine should himself hand out the emblems, no matter where he is sitting?

The only Scripture I know of, which deals with this matter, is 1. Cor. 14. 40: "Let all things be done decently and in order." It is an exhortation one would like to see framed and hung on the walls of assembly meeting-rooms everywhere, with that other one of verse 26 hung over against it, "Let all things be done unto edifying." Together, they should help in the settling of many such points as that in the question—points about which no separate rule has been laid down in the Word of God.

It would scarcely be in keeping with them that a brother who is sitting in a distant part of the company, or in the midst of others past whom he has to make his way, should of necessity hand out the emblems; that is, unless a definite Scripture can be produced which says it must be so. One's feeling of what is "in order" would suggest that it be done by someone in a convenient position, and at the same time one who has the confidence and respect of his fellow-saints.   W.R.

THE BREAD AND THE WINE THAT ARE LEFT

Has Exodus 12 any reference to the Lord's Supper? If so, has verse 10 anything to do with the bread that is left after the morning meeting? Can it be used for other purposes and should the wine be put back into the bottle?

Certainly Christ is the centre both of the Passover and of the Lord's Supper, and that in His death. The slain Lamb is the figure, and the bread and the wine the symbols of His death, but it does not follow that the ordinances of the former have any direct reference to the latter, though, no doubt, spiritual lessons drawn from Exod. 12 may helpfully apply to 1 Cor. 11. The disciples in the Gospels, as members of the House of Israel, with their Lord "made under law," were observing the Passover, in memory of the national deliverance from Egypt, and from the judgment of God by the blood of the Lamb, but when at the conclusion of that Feast the Lord instituted His memorial Supper it was a new thing never heard of before. In 1 Cor. 5 the Apostle shows that Christ is the fulfilment of the passover: "Christ our passover is sacrificed for us"; and the passover, being followed by the feast of unleavened bread, the Apostle goes on—therefore let us keep the feast, not with the old leaven (perhaps gross sins common in the world), neither with the leaven of malice and wickedness, but with the unleavened bread of sincerity and truth." It is only later in the Epistle that the Apostle introduces the Lord's Supper (see chaps. 10. and 11.). It is common to hear the word "feast" applied to the Lord's Supper both in ministry, prayer and hymn, nor do I feel that there is any grave objection to so doing, but neither in the institution of the Supper, by our Lord, nor in the order transmitted to us by the Apostle Paul, is the expression found. The expression in 1 Cor. 5, as to the putting away of leaven (i.e., moral evil) is a general exhortation to a holy life, etc., among saints. We should be going far from the authority of Scripture were we to apply literally to the Lord's Supper the ordinances of Exodus 12. 10 except, as I have said, in the sense of spiritual principles. As for Exod. 12. 10, the Paschal lamb was unique and belonged to the passover feast and must not be dissociated from it, but I do not think this applies to our loaf. Superstition makes the "consecrated" bread something to be adored, or vests it with certain magical qualities as bread, but this is going entirely beyond Scripture. There is no "consecration" properly so-called; the Lord gave thanks for, or blessed it, and we do the same; but what is left should not be wasted, but used for purposes of nourishment. As for putting the wine back into the bottle from the glasses which have been handed round the assembly, this, I should say, should be carefully avoided, not on any conscientious principle, but on a sound principle of hygiene.   W.H.

Is it right to take the wine that is left in the cup, after all in the assembly have taken their share, and put it back into the bottle for further use?

I hardly think that rightness or wrongness enters into such a question, but healthiness or unhealthiness. One would judge it the reverse of hygienic to put back a few drops of wine from a glass from which various persons have drunk. It is lawful, but not expedient. The Pharisees made of their washings before meals, which of course is a cleanly and commendable practice, a religious observance, saying it was **wrong** to eat with unwashen hands, and **right** to wash; and it was just then that the Lord controverted them and unveiled their hypocrisy, for they were leaving their inner lives uncleansed, while stickling for their outward washings. Perhaps someone may justify the custom referred to in the question by the Lord's words, "gather up the fragments that remain that nothing be lost." I hardly think this principle would apply, for I judge that those fragments were not half-chewed scraps from the leavings of the multitude, but what was over and above of His abundant provision for the hungry ones, fresh and clean. Can we imagine the Lord telling His disciples to gather up ought else? (see Mark 8. 8). However, if brethren like to preserve wine for future use that has already played its part, none can say they are morally wrong.   W.H.

REFERENCES IN THE BOOK OF THE ACTS

Among the various passages where "breaking bread" is mentioned, in Acts and elsewhere, please distinguish, which do, and which do not, refer to the Lord's Supper.

Whatever difficulty there may be of settling this point in any particular instance, is due to one or both of two considerations. On the one hand, it is clear that the usual Jewish method of eating bread was by first breaking it up into convenient portions; and therefore the statement that a person had "broken bread" might with them signify merely that he had had a meal, with bread as its prominent feature. On the other hand, it also seems to be beyond doubt that in the apostles' days the Lord's Supper was often associated with a meal, of which the saints partook in fellowship together; and therefore, when the phrase "break bread" is linked with some other one about taking food, it is open to question whether this, or an ordinary meal only, is meant.

In Acts 27. 35, and of course in the references in the Gospels to the Lord breaking bread to feed the hungry multitudes, there can be no suggestion of the Ordinance; and to these occurrences I would add Luke 24. 30, 35; for although the Lord there took bread, blessed, brake, and gave to the two disciples; and although their eyes were opened to recognise Him as He did so; they could not, even in thought, connect this with the Supper which had been instituted a few days previously; since none but the apostles had been present on that occasion.

Over against these instances we may place Acts 2. 42; Acts 20. 7; and 1 Cor. 10. 16; as passages in which the reference to the Lord's Supper cannot reasonably be denied; and we then are left with Acts 2. 46 and Acts 20. 11, as the only occurrences about which there may be difference of opinion, In each of these there is an additional word or phrase about the partaking of food; and although in the view of some, this rules out any reference to the Ordinance; it seems to me that its effect is just the opposite. For why, if an ordinary meal, and nothing more, is intended, should the two separate expressions have to be used at all? Either of them, in that case, would have said all that was to be said, without the other.

In Acts 2. 46 the significance of the statement appears to be that, while some of the activities of the early disciples could be carried on in the precincts of the Temple, the Breaking of Bread could not; and so it took place in their homes (see R.V.). As for Acts 20. 11, the insertion of "the" (R.V., "had broken the bread"), which is according to the reading of all the most ancient authorities, links the statement with verse 7, and implies that here too the Ordinance is meant; though some may find a difficulty in the fact that Paul's long address would thus have been given before the Supper, transgressing certain views they hold as to it being out of place for a brother to speak, or even to read the Scriptures, in the part of the meeting which precedes it.   W.R.

UNFERMENTED WINE

Are not Christians who believe that unfermented or non-alcoholic wine is nearer that used by Christians in the early days justified in using such at the Lord's table?

It is well not only to have beliefs, but also to be able to justify them from the Word of God or from real facts, admitted as such. Otherwise our "beliefs" may degenerate into personal opinions or even fads. I have never heard any proof that the wine used in the Scriptures was not ordinary fermented wine, as is produced in all wine-producing countries to-day. Fermentation is an ordinary process of nature and cannot but occur when wine is made. The wine used in the Bible made persons intoxicated, if taken in excess, and that used by the Corinthians, when they came together ostensibly to keep the Lord's supper, was of the same character, as 1 Cor. 11. 21 ("another is drunken") shows. It was indeed a sad state of things, but the apostle did not solve the difficulty by changing the liquid used, but by changing their ideas of the Lord's supper from a meal to an act of remembrance. Really "unfermented wine" is a contradiction in terms. If it is not fermented, it may be a red liquid, it may be even a concoction of raisins, but it cannot be true wine. The late W. Hunter of Manchester, used, I believe, to say that "unfermented wine," was on a par with "unfrozen ice." This being said, the wine need only be of such a strength as will preserve it sufficiently, so as not to necessitate the opening of a new bottle every week.

W.H.

Am I right in refusing to take the cup at the Lord's Table because it is not "non-alcoholic"?

That the wine used by the Lord at the institution of the Lord's Supper was the ordinary wine of the country, nothing but special pleading can deny. The vintage was then long past, so that any idea of fresh grape juice and water is ruled out. At Corinth (see 1 Cor. xi), the erroneous idea had crept in that the Lord's Supper was to be a meal, and each brought his or her provisions, and "one was hungry and another drunken"! How does the apostle meet this scandal? Not by advocating the use of some substitute for the ordinary wine used, but by showing that it was not a meal, but a memorial act, for which a morsel of bread or a sup of wine sufficed. I am not advocating the habitual use of wine as a beverage; on the contrary, but for anyone to refuse to partake of the cup, which the Lord Himself instituted, because it contains wine, which some have abused, seems like setting up himself to be wiser than God, and to incur a serious responsibility.

W.H.

HOW MANY CUPS?

Is it not as much a departure from the scriptural practice to use two or so cups at the Lord's table, as it would be to use fifty-two?

Though the unity of the cup is not insisted upon in the Scriptures in the same way as that of the loaf, which in 1 Cor. 10 represents the one indivisible Body of Christ, nevertheless it is always "the cup" that is spoken of—the unique receptacle of that which represents the blood of Christ. But even in the case of the loaf, as each member present partakes, the outward unity of the loaf is not preserved. Indeed, even before that, as the brother who gives thanks, breaks the loaf, and for convenience places the portions on different plates, the figure of the unity of the body is in no way affected, as it would be were the loaf originally cut up in in bits. No more would the unity of the cup be, even though it stood on the same ground as the loaf, by being poured into different glasses or cups, for convenience of distribution. It is still "the cup," each being filled from the one original receptacle. But by the introduction of what is called "the individual cup" for each "communicant," the receptacles are multiplied and the identity of the wine in them is completely lost and the thought of fellowship hindered. As we practise it, though there be two or more cups, for purposes of distribution, all are filled from the original receptacle and still constitute "the cup"—the communion of the blood of Christ. W.H.

Is it scriptural in the light of 1 Cor. x. 16-17, to have more than one cup on the table? If so, how can we give thanks for "THE cup"?

The expression, "cup," in the various accounts of the institutions of the Lord's Supper refers, not to the containing vessel, but, by the figure of metonomy, to the wine contained (*e.g.*, Matt. xxvi. 27, and 1 Cor. xi. 25, "This cup is the New Testament in My blood"). We speak of "a good table," meaning the food on it. The Romanisers who insist on our taking literally the words, "This bread is My Body," should also force the words, "This cup," to mean the literal *vessel* holding the wine, rather than the wine, which is not once mentioned. Now, there is certainly an important truth which demands that there should be only one loaf, "For we being many, are one bread and one body, for we are all partakers of that one bread" (1 Cor. x. 17). The R.V. margin seems still clearer, "Seeing that there is one bread, we, who are many, are one body." But there is no corresponding truth which obliges us to have only one original receptacle, no idea of unity being bound up in the "oneness of the wine." Indeed, the blood of Christ was not shed on the Cross as a unity, but gradually, though finally all was poured out from His pierced side. However, any division, beyond what is absolutely necessary for the convenience of distribution, should be avoided. What is called "the individual cup" seems abhorrent to the idea of communion one with another. W.H.

IS THE SUPPER FOR THIS DISPENSATION?

Some teach that the Lord's Supper is not for Christians now— of "this dispensation of the Mystery," whatever that exactly means. Do you think there is any scriptural authority for this?

It is indeed a grievous thing that the Lord's people should be disturbed with these unscriptural vagaries—part of the Dead-Sea fruit of Bullingerism,* which asserts that baptism and the Lord's Supper are Jewish ordinances. In U.S.A., however, we understand that most of this cult, though still rejecting baptism, now teach that the Lord's Supper is for Christians to-day. They are mostly "Universalists" out there, while the British section hold what is known as "Conditional Immortality" or "Annihilationism," so the system is divided against itself on more points than one. One reason these teachers give against the Lord's Supper is that the Lord instituted it directly after partaking of the Passover—a Jewish feast of age-long standing; but there is no reason

---

* The late Dr. Bullinger no doubt adopted these notions from others, but he it was who popularised them, hence the term "Bullingerism."

at all why a new ordinance ostensibly appointed to suit the new dispensation about to dawn should be Jewish too. The Lord's death and resurrection are not limited in their application to Jews, because they occurred in close connection with His earthly ministry to Israel. The fact that the Apostle Paul was commissioned to lay down afresh the order of the Supper, in writing to a church of the Gentiles, was probably to guard against the very error combated here. The words, "For as often as ye eat this bread and drink this cup, ye do shew the Lord's death till He come," surely prove conclusively that the Supper was to be observed by Christians till then. The theory seems to be "begun, continued and ended" in a series of fallacies. First there is the fallacy that a new dispensation began in Acts 28, during Paul's imprisonment at Rome; that it was inaugurated, not by a new Pentecost or something analogous, nor by signs and miracles, as we might expect, but by the Epistles—which Paul wrote while in prison, which they call "the Prison Epistles"—the Ephesians, the Philippians, the Colossians, and Philemon. All others they tell us are not for us. There is also the unsound argument that only in prison-letters is revealed the mystery of Christ, that the Gentiles were to form one Body, etc., with believers from Israel (Eph. 3. 5). No one denies that the teaching of the Epistles is progressive, but it is also cumulative. Already in Rom. 12. 5 and 1 Cor. 12. 13 the "one body" is spoken of, and there is not a second, nor could there ever be. This is the "one body" of Eph. 4. 4. Is it not remarkable, if so much depended on those letters, that nothing is said of them in Acts 28, and that millions have read them, without knowing or enquiring when they were written? Another fallacy on which this system rests is that Paul here told the Jews that henceforth he would turn to the Gentiles, as though that was the first time this had been announced. On the contrary, he uses almost the same words as in verse 28 to the Jews at Antioch (chap. 13. 46), and at Jerusalem (chap. 22. 21). The same truth was patent at Caesarea through Peter (chap. 10), and indeed by the commission of the Lord Himself to His apostles (chap. 1. 8), not to speak of Romans 11, where the setting aside of Israel nationally had been clearly taught. Yet another fallacy is that Paul was the sole repository of the Mystery of Christ, and that in the prison-house at Rome. But Paul does not say so—but rather just the opposite, e.g., Eph. 3. 3-5, where he distinctly says it was "made known to **His holy apostles and prophets by the Spirit.**" There was then no great gulf between Paul and "the apostles that were before him," though, as we all know, Paul was set apart specially as the apostle of the Gentiles, which would affect the manner of his ministry, while the essential truth which he and they preached was the same. Still one more fallacy is the teaching that only in the Prison Epistles is "the Mystery" made known, but it is not once mentioned in the Philippians, or Philemon,

or 2 Timothy, whereas years before, Paul had written in Romans
16. 25, of "my gospel . . . according to the revelation of the Mystery,
which was kept secret since the world began, but is now made manifest."

We are firm believers in dispensational truth, but what we are com-
bating here is not that, but rather dispensational fancies, that is, dispensational distinctions which are in sober fact non-existent. The church
period began at Pentecost; believers were then baptised in the Spirit
(Acts 1. 5; 1 Cor. 12. 13) to form the church, the one and only Body of
Christ, of which all believers in the present dispensation form part,
and in which baptism and the Lord's Supper are the two ordinances
ordained by Christ—"till He come."   W.H.

MINISTRY AT SUPPER

**Could we support the thought of ministry before the breaking
of bread from verse 9 of Acts 20, or was Paul's visit a special one?**

Do not many of our difficulties arise from legislating, or allowing
others to legislate for us, where the Scripture is silent or by being wise
above that which is written? Making laws in the things of God, in the
place of the Lord, is as much lawlessness as breaking the laws He has
made. I cannot think for a moment that Paul would have neglected
any principle the Lord had laid down on a special, any more than on
an ordinary, occasion.

The disciples had come together to break bread, as was their custom,
and that would be their first object before the Lord, apostle or no
apostle being present. How thankful we may be that no precise account
of the meeting is given, for that would with little doubt have become
the rule for succeeding ages of formalists.

In 1 Cor. 11 nothing is said of praise or hymns or worship or reading
of the Scriptures, nothing but of the manual acts of breaking the bread
and drinking the cup. Strictly speaking then, according to the letter
of the Word, to be "perfectly scriptural," no one should utter a sound,
no hymn should be sung, no Scripture read, no ministry given at the
breaking of bread. But clearly the Spirit of God has left the order of
things indeterminate, so that with spiritual minds we may carry out
the **principles** of God's Word in dependence on the Spirit. Thus
on the one hand, we shall not have brethren with little intelligence of
what is fitting, introducing things foreign to the occasion, nor on the
other, men laying down fleshly regulations by which all must be
bound.

Personally, I am convinced that the passage in Acts 20 does not
profess to give the details of all that passed. The disciples no doubt
fulfilled the intentions of their gathering together with worship, hymns
of praise, words of Scripture, ministered or merely read, and breaking
of bread. Then I suggest followed Paul's long address, interrupted by

Eutychus' fall, and the miracle that brought him back to life. This serves to remind Paul, not of the object of the meeting (which must by this time already have taken place), but of his and their bodily needs. He was therefore led to wind up his discourse and break the bread in a new way, as the expression, "and eaten," seems to show—the word signifying, as Alford translates, "having made a meal." If we all came together "well-examined," to meet the Lord and show forth His death, there would be neither licence nor legislation, but "the liberty of the Spirit." The ministry and the question of the number of speakers would be controlled by the fear of God, the Word, conditions of edification, time, and the judgment of spiritual men who correspond to the "prophets" of the early days.   W.H.

CARRYING THE SYMBOLS TO THE SICK

Is there anything in Scripture that might give light on the practice of two or three of an assembly taking the symbols of the Lord's death to the sick-bed of a fellow-member? Is such a practice to be encouraged or not?

I cannot think of any instance of such a thing in the Scriptures, nor of anything analogous to it. No doubt the Lord is present "where two or three are gathered together in His Name," but both in the institution of the Lord's Supper in the Gospels and in the directions given by Paul, in 1 Cor. 11, the breaking of bread seems a collective act when the people of God are "come together"* "in church" rather than the act of two or three detached from the assembly. The case before us in the question is, moreover, of a special order. It is not merely a few saints perhaps abroad for the time, finding themselves in a place where no assembly exists, and breaking bread together thus, but of carrying the Supper to a sick-bed. Now, to be confined to the house or even to bed is the normal course of things for the Lord's people, as they get on in years, and is often for such the highest class in the divine school. Some of the Lord's brightest saints are bedridden. But in 1 Cor. 11. 30 we read of certain believers who were under the judgement of God on account of a careless observance of the Lord's Supper: "For this cause many are weak and sickly among you and many sleep." The apostle explains this as the chastening of the Lord, that the afflicted ones should not be condemned with the world, the effect of this temporal judgment being that the believers were removed from their place of privilege and could not break bread with their fellow-believers. Now, of course, it would be very reprehensible to assert that such and such a case of physical weakness or illness fell under the above three categories, for there are other explanations of illness, besides that of definite chastening for the

---

* See 1 Cor. 11. 17—14. 26, in which section, the phrase "come together" occurs a number of times, and in different forms, and seems to characterise it.

reason named. But on the other hand, it would be difficult positively to assert that one laid aside by weakness or infirmity, was not thus being dealt with by the chastening hand of God. If so, are not those who advocate carrying the bread and wine to the sick believer, running a risk of nullifying the purpose of God in segregating one of His children from the privileges of the House of God, by carrying to them those privileges? Perhaps in visiting sick believers there is sometimes too great precipitancy in pouring in the oil of comfort, rather than in seeking first to exercise the patient as to the cause of the affliction. The sick believer is not deprived of remembering the Lord and His dying love, even though bereft of the breaking of bread; there is always the testimony of the Word upon which to meditate, in communion with the Lord.

Perhaps it should in fairness be added that the 1 Cor. 11 passage refers to persons in health laid aside, more or less suddenly by illness, rather than to aged believers, infirm by the lapse of years, etc., and that the above argument from 1 Cor. 11 applies more directly to the former class. On that ground we must so far avoid any dogmatic conclusion, though our opening remarks as to the collective character of the ordinance hold good. W.H.

ISOLATED COMPANIES

Is it scriptural for small companies of believers, isolated from assemblies, to meet together on the first day of the week to remember the Lord?

As far as I have received light on the question, I believe that the Lord's Supper was **primarily** intended as a collective church act; but the words "as often as ye do it" seem to give a certain extention to the observance. Thus in some assemblies there is a breaking of bread in the evening for those unable to be present in the morning, and I cannot see that this (though we have no instance actually in the Scripture) is out of harmony with the intention of the Lord. Can we divorce from the Lord's Supper such words as "Where **two** or **three** are gathered together in My name, **there** am I in the midst of them"? We may **infer** that this can only refer to a church gathering, but it does not say so. Personally I feel at liberty under circumstances such as you indicate to gather with a few of the Lord's people meeting at a place for a holiday, and break bread together, when there is no assembly, of course. I remember on July 16th, 1916, breaking bread with Dan Crawford on a native path in the wilds of Central Africa, and there remembering our Lord. We were on trek far away from civilisation of any sort. I know that the fact that one does a thing does not make it right, but it seems to me there is a great danger of trying to be wise above that which is written. "Let every man be fully persuaded in his own mind." W.H.

Is there anything in Scripture that would condemn or justify two or three believers from an assembly, who are on holiday, and not within reach of an assembly, meeting together according to Matthew 18. 20, at their hired house, to break bread and drink wine in memory of their Lord?

This is a question on which godly brethren differ, so that we must not be too dogmatic. The incident of the two disciples at Emmaus is often quoted as an instance of two persons remembering the Lord together in the breaking of bread apart from an assembly, and the phrase, "He was made known to them in the breaking of bread," is quoted as an encouragement to saints to expect the same. But I think this is a mistaken view. Were these two likely to be "remembering the Lord" and "shewing forth His death in the breaking of bread," in the condition of despondency and unbelief in which they were, and before they knew that the Lord was indeed risen? On the other hand, dogmatically to forbid such a thing as a few persons breaking bread together under certain conditions seems to be legislating, where the Lord has not, and seeking to "be wise above that which is written." To ignore an assembly already existing in the place would be wrong, but there are many places abroad say, where there is not and could not be an assembly in default of believers. If we accept as a binding principle that the breaking of bread is purely and only an assembly matter, how many servants of the Lord, engaged in pioneer work, or in journeying in the Lord's service, would be deprived of it for weeks together?   W.H.

Is it scriptural for a number of brethren on holiday to meet together to remember the Lord, or should they go to the nearest assembly?

When the Lord Jesus instituted the Supper, He laid down no code of laws as to when, and how often, and in what circumstances, it was to be observed. This, however, does not mean that we are left without guidance; it means that in this, as in certain other matters of church order, instead of direct commands we have the practice of New Testament believers, as recorded for us in the Acts and the Epistles. That practice, if our hearts are loyal to the Lord, we shall seek to follow in all things, so far as is possible.

With regard to the Supper, we see that almost at once it came to be looked on as an ordinance which should be carried out by each local assembly (Acts 20. 7; 1 Cor. 11. 20-34); and we find no reference to its taking place in any other circumstances. Paul in Acts 20 was in haste to reach Jerusalem (v. 16), yet he waited seven days at Troas, evidently with a view to being present at the Breaking of Bread (v. 7); although he might have passed on, and arranged to observe the ordinance with his companions as they went, had he inclined to do so.

Indeed, the Supper appears to have been, more than any other part of their service or testimony, the badge of an assembly, and the focus around which all the other activities of its members revolved. And this is very much the case with ourselves at the present day, because the formation of a new assembly is invariably linked with the first occasion on which the believers who are to compose it meet together to break bread.

The question above, in the form in which it is stated, contains a hint that a local assembly is somewhere within reach of the holiday-makers; and if so, it is surely becoming that as visitors they should strengthen the hands of those already there; rather than that, by organising a separate meeting, they should proclaim that they do not desire to have fellowship with these, or alternatively that they are too lazy to make an effort to do so.

On the other hand, if saints when arranging their holidays have not sufficient interest in the things of God to make sure that an assembly will be within reach, it is unlikely that such will feel it a hardship to be without a Breaking-of-Bread meeting until their return.   W.R.

A SHADOW OF THINGS TO COME?

Is the Lord's Supper a shadow of things to come? In other words, does it portray His heavenly feast in which we shall participate with Himself?

We do not think so. The Bible rather limits it to the present—"ye proclaim the Lord's death, **till He come**" (1 Cor. 11. 26). In 1 Cor. 5 we read the words, "therefore let us keep the feast," but this follows the statement, "Christ our Passover is sacrificed for us," and the reference would be to the feast of unleavened bread which followed the passover, to which should correspond the holy life which befits the child of God.   W.H.

THE LORD'S PRESENCE

Do you consider that there is a deeper significance in the presence of the Lord at His table on the first of the week than when the saints meet for prayer or a Bible reading?

Perhaps it is not quite clear what the questioner means by "a deeper significance." The Lord's words, "Where two or three are gathered together in (or unto) My Name, there am I in the midst of them" (Matt. xviii. 20), apply primarily to the Prayer Meeting (v. 19). Perhaps the Lord's presence is often more real to the saints at His table, because they are more occupied with Him there, than with their needs. Besides, there is often more real exercise of soul before going to the Lord's table, than to the Prayer Meeting or Bible Reading. "Let a man examine himself, and so let him eat." We get what we go in for. But the prayer meeting and Bible Reading ought not to be neglected, as is too often the case, by the majority of the assembly, or treated lightly even sometimes by those who attend. Surely there would be a greater spirit of prayer poured out and more edification in the Bible Reading if all went in a spirit of soul preparation and waiting upon God.   W.H.

THE SPIRIT'S GUIDANCE

Is the Breaking of Bread meeting open for ministry, etc., under the Spirit's guidance, in a way which would not equally apply to a Conference, a Gospel meeting or a Prayer meeting?

I certainly think it is; but in order to understand why, it is necessary to apprehend the special character attaching to meetings of different kinds. Each has in effect its special character, which predominates, though there is a certain latitude, and other things may have their place up to a point. Thus a Gospel meeting is for the preaching of the good news to sinners; that should characterise the meeting, though a short word to believers present may sometimes be in place and cannot be forbidden. A teaching meeting is for teaching the truth of God to believers, and need not be taken up too much with long prayers and hymn singing; an exhortation meeting is for exhortation, also to believers. In these cases it is a question of the exercise of gift manward. All are not evangelists or teachers; all are not called to exhort, etc. "He gave some, evangelists, some, pastors and teachers" (Eph. 4. 11); and in Rom. 12. 6 we are reminded that "we have gifts differing according to the grace given," either for prophesying (a foundation gift that no longer exists) or for ministry of various kinds—teaching, exhortation, etc. To apply the principle of equality of opportunity to all in such cases is clearly to set on one side the Lordship of Christ, who has given gifts according to His own will. We may invite men known to be qualified to evangelise or teach to the more general meetings for teaching (wrongly called "conferences," for rarely does anyone confer). Where there are several teachers present, unless some special brother has been invited to minister the Word, there may well be an opportunity for open ministry, not however to all present, but only to those known to possess the gifts needful for edification. Too often what is called "the open platform" has been abused, either because of too much liberty granted by elder brethren convening the meetings, or because of too much liberty taken by brethren present, who are not truly qualified to teach, but who get up on the plea of "the liberty of the Spirit," and waste valuable time by unedifying talk. Let those who are gifted to teach wait on their ministry, and consider their brethren. The liberty of the Spirit is not anybody's liberty to do as they like, but for the Spirit to do as He wills and use whom He chooses. The breaking of bread meeting is quite different; it is not primarily for ministry, though there may be secondary opportunities for this, when the true object of the meeting is over, which is to "shew the Lord's death" (thus remembering Him in the breaking of bread), and to worship the Father. The object of those present is not to receive instruction, but to obey the Lord's command, and as priests to offer spiritual sacrifices acceptable to God by Jesus Christ. As all believers, by the fact of the new birth, are constituted priests, the meeting is left open for all present to worship the Father, whether silently or vocally. In the 1 Cor. 11 passage there is not a hint of any arrangement of speakers for ministry, and much less of anyone to preside and, as clergyman, minister, or pastor, "administer the sacrament" or "dispense the elements." The bread is "the bread which **we** break," the cup is "the cup of blessing which **we** bless." These are terms which make breaking the bread and giving thanks for the cup a general privilege, rather than an ecclesiastical monopoly. The same principle applies to a prayer-meeting. All may pray, the women silently (1 Cor. 14. 34), the men "everywhere lifting up holy hands, without wrath and doubting" (1 Tim. 2. 8); that is, it is they who lead in prayer. How can a prayer-meeting be rightly anything but "open" for the Spirit's guidance? He alone knows the state of each soul; He alone knows the particular needs, and can make known that need to each and give suitable words to express it. Accordingly, there is not a hint in 1 Tim. 2 of anyone presiding over or directing the prayer-meeting.   W.H.

H

PRAYER AND WORSHIP

In this dispensation, to which Person in the Godhead should the worship of the assembly be directed?

Without question our Lord Jesus Christ is a true and proper object of His people's worship. The wise men from the east came to worship Him (Matt. ii. 2), and "when they saw the young child with Mary His mother, they fell down and worshipped (not them, as the Romanist and Ritualist would have it, but) Him"—not to mention such cases as occur in chap. viii. 2; ix. 18, which perhaps would hardly mean more than an act of deep reverence (for "worship" etymologically means "worth-ship," and is thus used in law courts—"your worship"). In chap. xiv. 33 we read that those in the boat recognised Him as "Son of God;" as did the healed man of John ix. 38 when he exclaimed, "Lord, I believe, and he worshipped Him." In each instance it is the revelation of the glory of His person, which draws out the adoring worship of His own. This was the case on earth after His resurrection (Matt. xxviii. 9), and never did the Lord disclaim such worship, as did Peter (Acts iv. 12), but accepted it as His rightful due. This is all perfectly true and most blessed, and wherever to-day God is worshipped, our Lord Jesus Christ receives His part, for He is God the Son. But this being so, we must not confuse the Persons of the Trinity. Each has His proper place and function, and in John iv the Lord clearly indicates that it is God the Father who is seeking worshippers, and it is "in spirit and in truth" that the true worshipper must worship Him. The worship of the Old Testament saints was figurative. The worship of the Lord when on earth was direct and personal, but there was another worship, even then beginning, true and spiritual. The Lord Jesus is the Way to the Father. If in our priestly worship we habitually stop short of Him, we fall below what the Lord wills for His people. He is the High Priest over the house of God, delighting to present their worship to the Father. The object, the way, and substance, the power of worship are all indicated in that most inclusive verse, Eph. ii. 18, "For through Him (the Lord Jesus) we both (Jew and Gentile) have access by one Spirit unto the Father."

W.H.

Is it scriptural to teach that when we come together to remember the Lord, our worship should be directed to the Father only, and that even hymns addressed to the Lord Jesus should not be sung?

Our Lord when censuring certain leaders in Matt. 15. 9, applied to them the words of God through Isaiah, "In vain they do worship Me, teaching for doctrines the commandments of men." And there are many rules being laid down in connection with worship to-day, regarding which the last clause of this quotation might fittingly be used; since they are nothing else than "the commandments of men." Of such the teaching referred to in the question is a typical example; for there is no command whatever in the Word of God to the effect that the Son should be excluded from worship. On the other hand, there is the statement that "All men should honour the Son, even as they honour the Father"; and also many examples of worship directed to Christ, such as Heb. 1. 6; Matt. 2. 11; 28. 9, 17; Luke 24. 52, etc. If it be objected that none of these examples has reference to a breaking of bread meeting, we ask the objector to point out where in the Scriptures is the word "worship" at all used in connection with such a meeting? It will then be possible to consider what special limitation, if any, is placed on our worship in that connection. W.R.

Can we approach the Lord Jesus to worship Him apart from the Father?

We are on holy ground when considering any aspect of divine truth, but especially do we need to approach "with unshod feet," when it is a question of the Being of God! We can only know what He is pleased to reveal, and even then it is "as in a glass darkly," and "in part." There is one God—that is, one Divine Essence; but in that unity there are three Divine Persons or Subsistencies, the Father, the Son, and the Holy Ghost; co-equal, co-eternal, and co-substantial: that is, each of the three possesses the whole Divine substance. We must neither divide the substance, nor confound the persons. These three Persons are in necessary relations to one another, and it is important not to confound these relations. Each possesses the Personal properties essential to Himself, and which cannot be predicated of or communicated to the others. Thus it belongs to the Father to "beget:" His are the eternal counsels; the Son is the Only-begotten, the Incarnate One; He alone suffered for sin. The Spirit proceedeth from the Father and the Son. The Spirit reveals the Son, by whom the Father is declared or interpreted. Now, it is not derogating from one Divine Person to refrain from attributing to Him what the Holy Scriptures assign to Another. Thus we never read of worship being offered to the Holy Spirit, though He is omnipotent, omnipresent, omniscient, eternal, divine as the Father and the Son. But we do read, even in the days of His humiliation, of worship being rendered to the Lord Jesus, and He accepted it. And in Revelation, e.g., chap. v. 8, 12, 13, Divine worship is paid to the Lamb in heaven. Nevertheless, the Lord proclaims in John iv. 23, 24, that the true worshippers will worship *the Father*, and that it is the "*Father* who is seeking worshippers"—"God is Spirit, and they that worship Him must worship Him in spirit and in truth." The apostle Paul indicates, too, in that pregnant verse (Eph. ii. 18), the true Divine order. "Through Him (Christ Jesus) we both (believers from Jew and Gentile) have access by the Spirit unto the Father." The Lord is the way to the Father and the substance of worship; the Spirit the power; the Father the recipient of the worship of the people."   W.H.

PRAYER TO THE LORD JESUS

Is it scriptural to pray to the Lord Jesus Christ continually in a Breaking of Bread meeting, and for a believer to confess privately to saints that he does not believe in praying to the Father in such a meeting, seeing that we gather there to remember the Lord?

I believe the custom referred to, though doubtless many godly persons are addicted to it, is due to a defective view of what the atoning death of Christ entailed on the other Persons of the Godhead. It is true that our Lord Jesus alone suffered directly for sins on the cross. There the Divine judgment fell on Him; there He was forsaken of His God. But who can estimate what it cost the Father "not to spare His own Son"?—nor should we forget that it was "by the Eternal Spirit that He offered Himself without spot to God." It seems clear that to limit our worship, or nearly to limit it, to the Lord Jesus is to come short of His definite purpose, communicated by Him in revealing the Father. Far from desiring that His own should concentrate on Him their worship, He indicates the contrary. "The hour cometh, and now is, when the true worshippers shall worship the Father in spirit and in truth, for the Father seeketh such to worship Him." (John 4. 23). By so doing we do not set the Son on one side. "At that day ye shall know that **I am in the Father,** and ye in me, and I in you." (John 14. 20). Again, to maintain that we ought only to worship the Lord Jesus, because we are gathered to remember Him, seems to embody a fallacy. Does not the very act of breaking the bread lead us to the Father? As the Son is revealed to our souls in His love and preciousness, we adore the Father for such a gift; "Through Him we both (i.e. believing Jews and Gentiles) have access by one Spirit unto the Father" (Eph. 2. 18). One of the greatest needs of our hymn books to-day is, I submit, that God would raise up Christian poets, to add to them more hymns of the type of our departed brother Deck's, "Abba Father, we approach Thee."   W.H.

PRAYER TO THE HOLY SPIRIT

Is it right to pray to the Holy Ghost? Which Scriptures, if any, can be cited to justify this, either directly or by implication?

It is not according to God's order as laid down in His Word. The glorious Three in One, though co-equal, co-eternal and co-substantial (that is each possessing the whole Divine substance), are not identical in function and relation, as any thoughtful reader of the Scripture will allow at once. The Father sends the Son, the Son by the Eternal Spirit offers Himself to God, the Spirit proceedeth from the Father, Who sends Him forth in the name of the Son. The Father desires worshippers. Such can only come through the Son, and in the power of the Spirit. All these purposes and functions are also the work of the Divine Being in the Unity of His essence.

It is therefore quite beside the mark to insist on predicating of each of the Blessed Divine Persons the same relations, lest we dishonour any One of Them. We pray to the Father and the Son (John 14. 13, 14), but never are we told to do this to the Holy Spirit; nor have we one instance so far as I know, of any such exercise. Whatever pious ecclesiastics, often governed as much by their feelings as by the Word, may say, we cannot presume to be wiser than God, or to go beyond His Word, or honour Him by going outside what He has revealed. The ultimate divine order is given in Ephesians 2. 18: "For through Him (the Son) we both (Jew and Gentile) have access by one Spirit unto the Father."

W.H.

"YOU" OR "THOU"?

Is it right to address the Lord, in prayer and praise as, "You," rather than as, "Thou," as some occasionally do, and as certain hymns are worded, e.g., "I'll say what You want me to say, dear Lord—I'll be what You want me to be," etc.?

Certainly the general custom has always been to address the Lord as "Thou," but then the question arises whether this custom is based on Scriptural usage? In the case of the prayer which the Lord taught His disciples, the Father is addressed all through in the second person singular—"Thou," and this may well serve as a model for us, though it is true that the prayer, not being offered in the Name of the Lord Jesus, lacks something appropriate to the present dispensation. It was certainly never intended to be used as a sort of conventional formula at the close of every public exercise of prayer, as it is to-day in some circles, sometimes twice or thrice in the same morning. Surely this is to make a repetition of what was specially given to avoid such. The disciples' request was not, "Teach us a prayer," but, "Teach us to pray." "After this manner pray," were our Lord's words. When we come to the recorded prayers of our Lord in the Gospels, e.g., His prayer at the grave of Lazarus (John 11. 41, 42), or that offered in the next chapter, verses 27 and 28, or once more, His sacerdotal prayer in chap. 17, we find that He always addresses His Father in the second person, singular

—"Thou." The same is true of the apostolic prayers of Acts 1. 24, "Thou, Lord, who knowest the hearts of all men," and chap. 4. 24, where the apostles address God as, "Thou art God who has made heaven," etc. Likewise the prayer of Stephen in chap. 7. 60, "Lord, lay not this sin to their charge", is literally, "Lord, lay not Thou this, etc.". The same is true of praise in Psalms or Songs like Simeon's (Luke 2. 29; see also the songs of the elders in Rev. 4. 31, and of them and the four living beings in chap. 5. 9). Those of Mary and Zacharias are in the third person. We conclude that the general custom is right and not to be departed from. Hymn-books are not always models of good English or true poetry or sound doctrine, and ought to be revised, if they depart from the standard of God's Word. We should instinctively shrink from anything common or familiar in addressing the Great God and Father of our Lord Jesus Christ.   W.H.

Would it be right to accede to the request of a sick brother, to send for the elders of the church to pray for his recovery?

I should think that the question ought rather to be, "Would it be right to refuse such a request?" Surely the Scripture is very plain, "Is any sick among you? let him call for the elders of the church; and let them pray over him, anointing him with oil in the Name of the Lord: and the prayer of faith shall save the sick, and the Lord shall raise him up; and if he have committed sins, they shall be forgiven him" (Jas. 5. 14, 15). We must not evade Scripture or twist it out of its simple meaning, as is sometimes done, because if taken as it stands, it may seem to favour some false notion. There is scarcely a heresy in the world which cannot quote some half-truth or twisted text n its favour. No doubt James 5. 14* has been used as a basis for the many erroneous systems of bodily healing abroad to-day, and so some have fallen into the erroneous idea that it must be evaded. "For instance," says one, "James does not give us 'church truth.' " That is no doubt in a sense the case, but he seems to speak here of a church custom, for we cannot admit that "church" in its local and technical sense, means one thing in the Acts and another in the Epistles, and we accept without hesitation for ourselves to-day other exhortations of the Epistle. Another evasion, as it seems to me, is to ask, "Where in the scattered condition of the church are the elders?" The answer is that in nearly every scripturally-ordered assembly there are some who are known and act as such, and who bear the character of elders in a greater or lesser measure. Others point out that the epistle is addressed to the

---

* In order to have a full view of this whole subject we must not limit ourselves to this passage, but must join with it such passages as 2 Cor. 12. 7-9; Phil. 2. 25-27; 2 Tim. 4. 20; 1 Tim. 5. 23, etc., in which there is neither mention of any miraculous intervention nor of sending for the elders. No scripture contradicts any other nor can it dispense with any other.

twelve tribes. Yes, but to them as actual or potential believers in Christ. See, for example, chap. 2. 1: "My brethren have not the faith of our Lord Jesus Christ . . . with (or along with) respect of persons." The R.C. Church, of course, bases on this passage the "Sacrament of Extreme Unction." But for this they have to read—"Is any among you dying?" because they only administer the rite to those **in extremis.** For any-one to recover after the reception of Extreme Unction is quite unlooked for and out of order, whereas the anointing in "James" is in view of recovery—"The prayer of faith shall save the sick, and the Lord shall raise him up, and if he have committed sins they shall be forgiven him." This last promise seems to give character to the whole passage. It is as though it were a case where the sufferer* suspected that the Lord was dealing with him on account of some sin, and sent for the doctors of the soul, rather than of the body. I do not know any faith-healing systems which teach the sick to send for the "elders of the church." It is generally rather some leader, who professes to be a "Healer," who sends for the sick; or else it is a faith-healing home, often under female control, where the sick are taken in as boarders, awaiting their turn to be healed at some public service, which savours rather of an advertise-ment for man than as a testimony for God. One is, of course, not ques-tioning the earnestness of many of these people, but is comparing their methods with our passage. Here it is the sick one who desires the fellow-ship in prayer of his brethren. These make no claim to be "faith-healers," but they pray in simple fashion for the sick one, in submission to the will of God, anointing him with oil in the Name of the Lord. They cannot command the prayer of faith. It may not be the Lord's intention to raise up the sick brother, but the prayer of faith (if they are able to offer it) shall save the sick, and the Lord shall raise him up, and if he have committed sins they shall be forgiven him. Nothing is said as to other means being unlawful, and the word for "anoint with oil" is not the sacred word—used, for instance, in Heb. 1. 9 (the "Christ" word). It is noticeable that the most outstanding example in the Bible of heal-ing, granted to the prayer of faith—that of Hezekiah—was in no way incompatible with the use of means—a fig poultice. The faith-healing systems would entirely rule out this as a lack of faith. The case that follows in James 5 is still more simple. Here there seems no doubt as to the cause of the illness, and there is no question either of physician or elders. "Confess your faults one to another, and pray one for another." Any godly person will do, for "the effectual fervent prayer of a righteous man" (though he be not an elder) "availeth much." There ought surely to be more exercise among us as to the why and the wherefore of our sicknesses. They may not all be sent in chastisement, they may be part

---

* The word is "weak"—the first condition noted in those under the chastening of the Father: "for this cause many are weak and sickly, and many sleep" 1 Cor. 11. 30).

of our salutary and daily discipline, but there can be no loss in enquiring of the Lord, "Why am I thus laid aside?" We cannot leave the subject without a note of warning. Many erroneous teachings prevail to-day in the "faith-healing" world, e.g., that disease does not exist (how then cure what does not exist?); that disease in a Christian is a sin (!); that bodily healing is included in the Atonement (then why does any believer die?): and healing pilgrimages—little "Lourdes—are being encouraged to-day within the fold of the Protestant State-Church. The fact that cases of miraculous healing are claimed for all these systems, even if genuine, is not conclusive, for miraculous powers are not limited to the Spirit of God. We must test teachings, methods and results by the Word of God. What strikes the student of the faith-healing systems around us is the distant resemblance they bear, if any, to apostolic healings.   W.H.

CHURCH TRUTH

WEAKNESS IN TESTIMONY

Is "The Church of God" in ruins, as held and taught by many?
If by the "Church of God" is meant "the Church which is His
Body," the statement is quite erroneous, for that is preserved for ever.
But "Church of God" is used by Paul in 1 Cor. xv. 9; Gal. i. 13, in
an extended sense of all Christians he could get at, though the term
generally refers to the local expression of the Church. Thus, in 1 Cor.
x. 32, the inhabitants of the city are divided into "Jews," "Greeks,"
and "the Church of God" (see Acts xx. 28; 1 Cor. i. 2; xi. 22). We have,
too, the expression the "Churches of God" (see 1 Cor. xi. 16; 1 Thess.
ii. 14). The expression, "IN RUINS," would apply rather to some WORLD-
WIDE ORGANISATION. When that breaks down, they say the Church is in
ruins, but it is THEIR ORGANISATION. None of God's assemblies, low as
their state was, was ever said to be in ruins, though Ephesus was
warned lest her lampstand be removed. The testimony, too, is of a
remnant character, and in weakness; but such as it is, it is not "IN
RUINS," nor ever need be. Such an expression is not applied in the
Scriptures to a Church of God.   W.H.

**Can a company claim to be an assembly of God, where Church
truths and fundamental truths are not taught?**
Of course, we understand that such truths are not denied, but simply
neglected for others, such as exhortation, or prophetical and dispensational teaching. Where fundamental truth is generally denied in a
company, such loses its character as an assembly, just as the individual
does his character as a Christian. But what constitutes an assembly, is
a company of true believers who seek to gather to the Name of the Lord,
know no other Centre than He, and no other Leader than the Spirit of
God (while welcoming those whom He has called to rule, or qualified
to minister the Word), and no other rule than His Word. But why
should not these truths be taught? Are there not elders among the saints,
who though not exactly "teachers," in the sense of possessing a distinct
gift, are nevertheless "apt to teach" (1 Tim. 3. 2) and able to explain
both church and fundamental truths? There is a call for prayer that the
Lord would raise up "gifts" in His churches able to instruct the saints.
But it is not "light" which constitutes an assembly, but life in Christ
of those composing it. On the other hand, we need "all the counsel of
God" as revealed in His Word, not merely certain favourite truths, for

"all Scripture is given by inspiration of God, and is profitable for doctrine, for reproof, for correction, for instruction in righteousness, that the man of God may be perfect, throughly furnished unto all good works" (2 Tim. 3. 16, 17).   W.H.

If an assembly is dwindling away, and there are now eight survivors, of whom only one is a brother, ought the breaking of bread to be continued?

In principle I would judge in the affirmative. Why should not eight persons, though only one of them be a brother, remember the Lord in the breaking of bread? "This do in remembrance of Me," would address itself to each. They might not be able to pay their way in a hall, but there is usually some private house available. In practice it would depend on whether the brother had spiritual energy and gift to go forward, in spite of the disabilities. I remember years ago in the South of England, it was felt by neighbouring assemblies that there was a call to form a small assembly in a seaside place, where a number of godly persons, already in fellowship, resided, of whom, however, only one was a brother, and he a foreign Christian Hebrew, quite unqualified to lead the assembly. Neighbouring assemblies used to help in turn each Lord's Day. It was not, however, normal to find oneself the only one to take part. I made it plain that if the sisters looked to me, I could not promise to carry through, but if they would look to the Lord, I felt sure He would, and I do not think there was any lack. The meeting gradually grew, and it has been I believe, fairly prosperous for some time. There is no fixed rule in the Scriptures that the meeting must last so long as the conventional hour or hour-and-a-half, which would be no doubt beyond the spiritual energy of the one brother. The essential is that the breaking of bread should be carried through in the power of the Spirit; "decently and in order"; a good deal depending on the godliness of the sisters present. If they know what it is to wait on the Lord, they will not be disappointed. The crucial difficulty comes in if the brother is not spiritual, and thinks that he can carry things through like a little "parson", simply because he is a brother: then I fear the sisters will go empty away, and a poor remembrance of the Lord be enjoyed. In the particular case under review, are there no meetings in the district that could come to the help of their weak neighbour?   W.H.

Can an assembly go on without brethren's meetings?

It does not seem quite clear what is meant here by "brethren's meetings." If there are those, whom God has raised up to do the work of oversight in the meeting, surely it is they who ought to exercise this ministry; but they should avoid acting in a high-handed way, or shutting out any younger men whom the Lord might be calling to this service.

It is always a happy thing to consider one another, and not even to appear to ride rough-shod over the feelings of fellow-believers, be they old or young, but rather to take others into counsels as far as possible in the arrangements for the welfare of the meeting. I do not, however, know of any meeting of "the brethren" apart from the Assembly as a whole, and clearly all the brethren are not likely to be called to oversight. When Paul and Barnabas came to Jerusalem to get help in the serious Judaising trouble at Antioch in Syria, we read that "they were received by the church and the apostles and elders," and they then and there declared all things that God had done with them (Acts 15. 4). Incidentally, the matter that had troubled them at Antioch seems to have cropped up here too, and at once Judaizers at Jerusalem took the same line and agreed with the troublers. Instead of continuing an argument before the whole church, which could not have edified, we read that "the apostles and elders came together for to consider the matter." There being no apostles now the elders can alone meet. But from verse 22 we learn that when they had reached oneness of mind, "the whole church" was called into their counsels and shared in their action.   W.H.

If a company of Christians is keeping close to New Testament order in church matters, we should suppose that amongst them many souls would be saved, and every kind of good work would abound. Yet in actual experience the reverse is sometimes the case, and the company is little more than dead-alive. Why is this?

We have here no new experience, but a trouble nearly as old as the dispensation itself. The Church of God at Corinth was not long existent, when the Apostle had to write to them these two messages in successive paragraphs of the same letter:—

(1) "Now I praise you brethren that ye . . . keep the ordinances as I delivered them to you" (1 Cor. 11. 2).

(2) "Now I praise you not, that ye come together not for the better, but for the worse" (v. 17).

Nor was the Church of Sardis very ancient, when the Lord had to say to it through His servant John, "Thou hast a name that thou livest and art dead."

Right church position and order will surely be sought after and maintained by anyone who really loves Christ and desires to please Him; but right church position does not of itself necessarily ensure continuance in a good state of soul. This also must be sought after and maintained, otherwise we cannot expect to be accounted "vessels unto honour, sanctified and meet for the Masters' use, and prepared unto every good work."

On the other hand, we have to remember that an outward show of fruitfulness in the way of many professing conversion at our meetings, is no guarantee that we are walking in a path pleasing to the Lord. When Moses in his disobedience of Num. 20 struck the rock, it is stated that "the water came out abundantly," which is more than is said in Exod. 17, on the occasion when he acted in strict obedience.

My business, both in regard to church truth, and to all other truth, is to humbly walk in the path the Lord has laid down for me in His Word, and leave the results with Himself. And if the company of saints with which I am connected has become such as the last part of our question describes, I have to remember that the character of the said company is just that of the aggregate of the units composing it; and the first step towards getting it right, is to get right myself.   W.R.

RECEPTION AND FELLOWSHIP

Should a Christian be a Freemason? and is a Freemason eligible for fellowship?

Only those unaware of what Freemasonry really stands for could ask such questions. True, there is a talk of God, the great Architect of the Universe, and the Bible is among the symbols of the craft, but it is perhaps not generally known that this "God" is not the God of the Bible, but a composite deity, or trinity, fashioned of Jehovah, Baal (the abomination of the Zidonians), and Osiris or On, a god of Egypt. I understand that the great secret of Masonry is the "divine" name, which it takes three initiates to pronounce. It is true that "Jesus" is recognised, but only as one of a list of great benefactors of the human race, along with Buddha, Vishnu, Baldu, Osiris, Adonis, etc., etc.. A niche in their pantheon has always been offered by the world to "Jesus," but unfortunately for them He claims the universal throne. "My glory will I not give to another." "There is none other name given among men whereby we must be saved." As for the Bible, it lies amongst their symbols, but one of the foundation tenets of the craft is that "no effort must be made to change the belief of any person." In the Masonic charge we read, "Masonry encourages each man to be steadfast in the faith his heart loves best." In this system, Unitarians, Hindus, nominal Christians, Jews, Moslems, Theosophists, live happily side by side. All have their place in it, except true believers in our Lord Jesus Christ. It is the boast of Masons that theirs is not a religion, but that it is "Religion," that is, the essence of all creeds. Certainly it jealously guards that which is the basis of all human religion, the denial of atonement by the blood of Christ, and the claim that every man is his own saviour and no one else. The blood-curdling oaths the neophytes have to utter on the first night of initiation ought to open the eyes of any Christian to the godless character of the whole system. That Freemasonry will provide a religion for the Antichrist, we need not doubt, but the truth of God will prevail. W.H.

Why is it some assemblies will not admit believers to the Lord's Table, until they have been baptized? Is this scriptural?

The question ought, I judge, to be reversed. Why do some assemblies admit believers who have not been baptized? It can hardly be questioned that baptism was ordained by Christ Himself as the initial rite in the Christian life. "Go, disciple the nations, **baptizing them** (i.e., the disciples when made), in (or into) the Name of the Father, and of the Son, and of the Holy Ghost" (Matt. 28. 19). "Go into all the world and preach the Gospel to every creature: He that believeth **and is baptized** shall be saved" (Mark 16. 15, 16). Accordingly, in the Acts a profession of faith in Christ in one form or another was always followed by baptism, e.g., "Many of the Corinthians hearing believed, and were baptized" (Acts 18. 8). The twelve disciples of Ephesus, having been wrongly baptized, were re-baptized in (eis) the name of the Lord Jesus. There is not a single case mentioned of an infant being baptized. Baptism ought undoubtedly to be put before all candidates for fellowship. With young converts there is rarely any difficulty, but when we come to older Christians seeking fellowship, who have perhaps formed part of some evangelical denomination for a number of years, the case is more complicated. Many such firmly believe they have been truly baptized, either as children before faith, or by sprinkling after faith. The question then arises whether it can be right altogether to refuse fellowship to such undoubted believers, who seem unable to see the need for "re-baptism." I judge that such passages as 2 Chronicles 30. 18; 1 Sam. 21. 6; Num. 28, 9, etc., with our Lord's comment on the last two passages in Matt. 12. 3-7, shew that there are cases where God's strict order may be modified by special circumstances. "I will have mercy and not sacrifice." Each case, however, must be judged by spiritual men, who will surely have wisdom from God how to act; but certainly there should be no reception into the local fellowship without this question being raised. W.H.

Ought children who say they are saved and ask for baptism, to be baptized and received into fellowship without delay, or ought they to be asked to wait for a time?

The Scriptures teach the baptism, not of adult believers, but of believers—"He that believeth and is baptized, shall be saved" (Mark 16. 16). "Many of the Corinthians hearing, believed, and were baptized"

(Acts 18. 8). "When they believed Philip preaching . . . they were baptized, both men and women" (Acts 8. 12). It is true that children are not mentioned here, only "men and women"—but this, I think, merely emphasises the fact that both sexes were baptised, or perhaps there was no child believer on the occasion. But the fact that we never read of children as such being baptised, merely arises from the fact that it is not the age of a candidate that is in question, but the faith. Can a child of thirteen believe the Gospel? Undoubtedly it can; and many such have been brought to faith, confession, baptism and fellowship, and have stood well. We do not know if there were children in the households of Lydia and the Philippian jailor, etc., but if so, they were old enough to hear the Word, believe, and be baptized. On the other hand, children are easily impressed and are apt to follow the example of their elders, and I am afraid it is a fact that few would contest, that some children have been too lightly received as believers and baptized, and their after-history has not been encouraging, but has rather cast doubt on the reality of their confession of faith. Is not then the evident lesson that no rule can possibly be made? Each case must stand on its own merits. If the parents and elder brethren, whose advice may well be asked, are satisfied, let them go forward in faith and count on God! But if there be not unamity of judgment, further waiting would be indicated. At the same time, there is a danger of discouraging true faith and putting the child back from a step, which might under God's blessing be a deciding factor in its whole future. The word, "saved," in Mark 16. 16 goes further than "forgiven" or "justified," it seems to include the thought of deliverance, which is connected so closely with the truth of death and resurrection, in baptism, and it would be sad to deprive a real believer, be it young or grown-up, of this help in the Christian life. Some parents who have perhaps too easily encouraged their children to be baptized have later on regretted it, and some who have discouraged their children have lived to regret it, too. We are cast upon God for each case, and if we definitely wait on Him, He will surely give oneness of mind to those concerned.   W.H.

I read lately in the records of a certain London assembly, of visits paid to them by a well-known Christian editor, now with the Lord, who would occasionally break bread with them and minister the Word, though unwilling to take his place among them. I cannot see how such spasmodic ministry was likely to build up the saints in "the ways that be in Christ," or establish them in separation from the religious world, with whom the said editor was obliged to be hand in glove. What do you think?

Some to-day seem impatient of any attempt to preserve a line of demarcation between the simple gatherings in the Name of the Lord, and the denominations of Christendom. Such is denounced as narrowness and pharisaism: "The Lord has His people everywhere," they say, "and they are just as much saved as anybody else!" This is no doubt true: many of us were converted in one or other of these systems; but there are other important questions in the Scriptures besides the forgiveness of sins. The simple assemblies of the Lord's people, with whom many of us are associated, originated in a movement of the Spirit calling the people of God back to the simplicity of the truth, and to the rejection of all else. Thus the great truth of the sufficiency of the Lord Jesus as our Centre of gathering; of the Holy Spirit as our Power for worship; of the Scriptures as our rule of faith and worship, and of many other important truths, including the common priesthood of all believers, became acknowledged. These truths seemed so vitally important to us, and so contrary to the surroundings in which we had been brought up, that we were led out of the denominations in which we had perhaps been converted, and that, we believe, by the Lord's own hand. If such a step were justified at the time, certainly the Word of God has not changed back to something else now. We stultify ourselves and the truth itself, if we go back to what we once left. How could this good editor, only partially instructed in the truth, be likely to "build up the saints in the ways that be in Christ," which he was himself unwilling to follow? Of course, the editor of an interdenominational paper simply cannot afford to speak the whole truth. Were he, for instance, to testify against the sectarian and clerical systems, he would lose half his subscribers. **But sectarianism is a work of the flesh** (see Gal. 5. 20), and clericalism, seeing it practically quenches the Spirit and renders null and void the common priesthood of believers, denies the true Christian position, and makes **collective** Christian worship not only difficult, but impossible. When we compare with the Scriptures, for instance, the official services, say of the Established Church, even when the clergyman is a truly converted man, who can pretend that the common priesthood of believers is respected or allowed scope? Such a thing is impossible. The presiding cleric, even if converted, and sharing the common priesthood of his fellow-Christians (Rev. 1. 6), is obliged to fill the role of a priest of another order; he takes a privileged position, even when he makes no claim to be a **sacerdos** or sacrificing priest; he wears a distinctive garb—a relic of Rome, half Jewish, half pagan; he claims a title, which no apostle claimed; he holds the exclusive right to pronounce the absolution or administer "the sacraments," and he alone may set his foot within the communion rails, a sort of holy place; whereas all true believers have equal liberty "to enter into the holiest by the blood of Jesus" (Heb. 10. 19). We are all priests; we worship in the heavenly temple not made with hands, and as Luther used to say, "If any man claim to be a priest in any other sense than all the true people of God are priests, let him be anathema!" The conditions described above constitute no mere surface differences, but fundamental divergencies between what is Christian and what is not, and never could be, Christian. It is sometimes advanced, we believe, by those who would break down all the distinctions the Word of God has set up, that our brethren in these denominations are enquiring after further light, and that it is our privilege to bring it to them by frequenting their "places of worship," and sharing their platforms. Such has not been our experience. To quote one instance: many years ago we wrote a book in a spirit, we hope, of moderation and charity, pointing out the vital differences between the Levitical and Christian economies, and that the churches of Christendom, to judge by their practices, are based on the former, rather than on the latter. A relative of ours lent a copy to a business friend of his, known also to me: a prominent C. of E. Evangelical, father of one of the best known London clergymen of to-day. He brought it back a day or two later in a high state of dudgeon, with words I can never forget, though I should be quite prepared to hope that they travelled beyond his true thought. "Never lend me such a book again!" he cried to my relative; "I hate the book, and I hate the man who could write it." The language is extreme, but I do not think the attitude exceptional. But someone may say, "Why touch on these matters? Why not be content to limit ourselves to the "simple Gospel"? If we do, **we betray the truth and disobey the Lord.** These differences lie at the root of all Christian progress, and are vital to the present enjoyment of our true Christian position. If the systems of men are right, then the work of Christ has stopped short at obtaining forgiveness for us, leaving things much as they were in the Old Testament times; but if Christ has gloriously triumphed, and He has, then we are delivered from every chain, brought to God by the blood of Christ, to offer to Him, as spiritual priests, acceptable worship by Jesus Christ.

W.H.

It has been taught that an unbaptized believer, who comes seeking fellowship, should be received if sound in doctrine; but should be taught afterwards his responsibility to be baptized. (1) Is this statement scriptural? (2) Can a person who remains unbaptized be said to be "sound in doctrine?"

The question of receiving an unbaptized believer into an assembly, like one or two other questions recently answered in this column, is for the most part of theoretic rather than of practical value. Possibly the experience of others may have been different, but the present writer, after having had to do with cases of reception into assemblies for forty years past, cannot remember a single individual who desired to come into the assembly but refused to be baptized. A few cases there were in which, for one cause or another, the baptism was deferred; but it was not objected to, and did in fact take place later.

I should not make, in that particular form, the statement which is cited in the question; but on the other hand I would certainly refuse to be bound by a "Medo-Persian" law that none may ever, in any circumstances, be received, unless they first submit to baptism. To take that stand would constitute us a sect of Baptists, and this of the "strictest" kind. Indeed one might as readily hold that baptism should be refused to any believer, unless he will undertake to come into the assembly immediately afterwards. These things are both the commands of the Lord, and meant to be obeyed; but neither is intended to be hung around the neck of the other.

As for the second question, the term "sound in doctrine," when it is used in statements about reception into an assembly, is generally meant to convey "sound in such doctrines as are fundamental," that is to say, doctrines the denial of which would involve the glory of our Lord's person, the value of the Gospel, or the dependability of the Holy Scriptures. For if one's meetness to be in an assembly depended on being correct in one's views on every possible doctrine, small or great, scarcely two saints in the world would have the right to come together, since scarcely two could be found to agree on every point, prophetic or other, that might be raised; and if not, one or other of the two is bound to be "unsound" on that particular point. Now the necessity of being baptized could not be called a fundamental doctrine in the sense above described, and therefore an unbaptized person might in that sense be said to be "sound in doctrine."

There is, however, another side to this. If I ever have to deal with a candidate for reception who refuses to be baptized, I naturally shall inquire into his reasons for such an attitude. Possibly I may find that it is mere ignorance of the Scriptures, and if so I shall endeavour to instruct him in what they teach concerning it. But just as likely I may discover, that behind his unwillingness there are views or doctrines, which are definitely erroneous in a fundamental way, as for example, baptismal regeneration or one of its newer equivalents. If so, he is unfit for present reception, not because of his refusal to be baptized as a believer, but because of his fundamentally unsound doctrine. Or again, I may discover that his desire to come into the meeting, while he has none to be baptized, is because he has some ulterior object in view, to which end he thinks the former will be an aid. In that case also, it is unlikely that good will accrue, either to himself or to anyone else, through his being brought into the assembly.   W.R.

Is it right for an assembly to receive to its fellowship one coming from a distance, without a letter of commendation, and should such a one be allowed to partake of the supper?

I

The use of letters of commendation is a most scriptural one. Paul recognises this in 2 Cor. 3, by the fact of protesting against being required to bring such a letter when visiting Corinth, where he had "laid the foundation." "Need we, **as some others,** epistles of commendation to you or from you?" They were his letter, written on the heart, when he came to them; when he left them, they were his letter too, known and read of all men. We have the cases of Apollos in Acts 18-27, and of Phoebe in Rom. 16. 1-2, which will occur to all. This last case is helpful to our consideration, because the apostle's was no mere formal commendation, but he adds her titles to special care from the saints—"Which is a servant (diakonos) of the church, which is at Cenchrea." Letters then were not the stereotyped things they usually are to-day, mere forms filled up. Not that these are not better than nothing, nay often sufficient; but sometimes more would be better. Here Paul adds to "receive her as becometh saints," "assist her, etc., for she hath been a succourer (prostatis) of many and of me also." Ought not one, who has been regular at the meetings, diligent in service and helpful to the saints, get a better commendation than one who has been irregular in attendance, no special help, and even perhaps a trouble, on occasion? If "fellowship" means sharing others' privileges and responsibilities, how far can one who is hardly ever seen at the Gospel, Prayer, or Teaching Meetings consider oneself in full fellowship? As for the question whether no one can be received without a letter of commendation, as no rule is laid down, it is not for us to make one. It is rather strange that Paul, though he took letters from the high-priest to Damascus, did not think of getting one from thence to Jerusalem. It would have been easier for him had he done so, but Barnabas knew him and could answer for him, which did instead. But there can be no doubt as to the advisability of always carrying a letter when going to a strange place. Otherwise you can only be received on a principle which Scripture does not recognise—self-commendation. Really I should judge, no truly humble, godly person would wish to impose himself or herself on the saints and force fellowship, unless there were full confidence. A good letter imparts this. Where there is a godly walk, there will be godly consideration for fellow saints, and the more they are in touch with the Lord, the more they will share His mind in receiving those whom they believe to be His own and right with Him. "Receive ye one another, as Christ also received us, to the glory of God." No one was ever so glad as He to receive, nor so careful as to whom and on what conditions he did receive.   · W.H.

Do you not think a distinction should be made between those in fellowship and those not in fellowship (children excepted)? It always was so 60 years ago. Should not those breaking bread

sit near the table and not in the last row of seats, while children and the unsaved occupy the front row?

The apostle in writing to the Church of God at Corinth recognised a "within" and "without" (see 1 Corinthians 5. 12-13). The one, hitherto called a brother, is put away from among the people of God as "a wicked person." Such a one should also be separated from by the saints in the various relations of life—"not to keep company . . . with such an one no not to eat" (1 Cor. 5. 11)—nor should he be received in the house, nor wished God-speed (2 John 10.). Is not this principle to extend to the Lord's table? Is there not to be a difference then, very clearly marked, between those recognised as "in fellowship" and others not breaking bread? Are worldlings and believers to be mingled there as in the religious denominations? Have not the words, "What fellowship hath righteousness with unrighteousness; what communion hath light with darkness . . . what part hath he that believeth with an unbeliever?" (i.e., not necessarily "infidel" in the modern sense) (2 Cor. 6. 14, 15), any application to such an occasion when the saints are gathered to the name of their Lord, and He is in a special sense in their midst? Surely they have. The saints belong to and love Him, and are met according to His command to remember Him. May they not then hope to do so, undisturbed by and unmingled with those who are still of the world and at enmity with Him? If, as our correspondent asserts, "those breaking bread sit on the back row of the hall, and children and unsaved ones sit at the front, and these hand the bread and the wine to those in fellowship," does not this bespeak a serious lack of godly order? How can it be claimed by the elders that "all things are done decently and in order"? and how can confusion be avoided or proper care be exercised, as to those who partake of the bread and wine? Let not the unsaved be given a place which may deceive them into supposing that all is mostly well with them, or countenance given to what most of them think at heart, that there is no difference worth speaking of between those who "think they are saved" and themselves. It is not a world-feast at all. It is "the disciples coming together to break bread" (Acts 20. 7), in remembrance of their Lord whom the world rejected. Doubtless the world should have entrance to the hall, but only as spectators of what is in reality a testimony against themselves. Can it be imagined to be godly order that such should be in a position even to be allowed to pass the bread and the wine to others? It is opening the door in the churches of the saints to the Babylonian confusion, which exists in Christendom.   W.H.

Is the divided state of the Church a sufficient reason for receiving to the Lord's Table Christians from the denominations, who have no intention of continuing in the assembly?

The so-called "divided state of the Church" has been made an excuse for various things, but I doubt whether it could be called a "sufficient reason" for any of them. God's standard of what is right does not rise and fall, according to the faithfulness or failure of the saints.

As to the matter with which the question is concerned, I have never been able to understand why this has to be set up for a bone of contention so frequently as is the case. I have been in association with assemblies of the Lord's people for a long time, and have been present at the remembrance feast in very many meetings, large and small; but never yet have I met with anyone who came with the deliberate purpose of breaking bread once, and then returning to the sect to which he or she belonged. What is more, I cannot understand the viewpoint or mentality of one who would have such a purpose.

The very existence of an assembly is a testimony that sectarianism and clericalism are wrong. On the other hand, if the sects and their clerics are right, the assembly must be entirely wrong. Why then should any conscientious person, who believes his own sect to be right and scriptural, wish to join himself, even for once, with a company which, according to his view, is quite in the wrong. If, on the other hand, he has discovered that it is the assembly that is in the right, then his sect must be wrong; and why should he purpose to return to it?

There are perhaps two other possibilities. He may be not really particular as to whether he is doing what is right or what is wrong, and if so, the "back seat" is the most fitting place for him, until his conscience becomes exercised; or he may be in doubt as to which thing is right and which wrong, but in that case he will surely prefer to remain a looker on, until such time as he sees clearly that what is being practised there is according to the Scriptures.   W.R.

ASSEMBLY FELLOWSHIP

Would it be correct to say that there is only one Fellowship in Scripture, into which all believers are brought upon accepting Christ as their Saviour? If this be so, how are we to understand the Fellowship of 1 John 1? Again, does not the New Testament teach Assembly Fellowship, into which a believer can be received, and from which he can be put away? and are letters of commendation necessary? Further, does the local church in any district include all the Christians in that district? and should a professed believer who belongs to a sect, but who comes to our Lord's Day Morning Meeting and expects to get breaking bread, be received, though he has no intention of severing his ecclesiastical association?

The statement that **"There is only one fellowship in Scripture, into which all believers are brought on accepting Christ as their Saviour,"** is absolute nonsense. The particular kind of fellowship implied in any passage where the word "Fellowship" occurs has to be gathered from the context there; and an examination of this will reveal that there are various "fellowships" spoken of in the New Testament. Moreover, it is to be remembered that the Greek word **"Koinonia,"** which is usually translated "fellowship," in the N.T. is also rendered, "communion," "communication," "contribution," and "distribution."

The first occurrence of the word is in Acts 2. 42, where it is said that the new converts "continued steadfastly in the . . . fellowship." Here we have a "fellowship" in which one may "continue" or not continue; and to apply it to the fellowship of life in Christ, in which all true believers cannot avoid continuing, is to make the statement in the verse meaningless.

It is next found in Rom. 15. 26 (where in our English Version it is rendered "contribution"). Could it be said that every saint of the present dispensation, or even every saint then living, had fellowship in the gift which the saints of Macedonia and Achaia sent to those of Jerusalem?

The epistle to the Philippians supplies perhaps the most interesting examples of the various uses of the word "fellowship." In ch. 1. 5 we read of their **Fellowship in the Gospel.** Are all saints in this? In ch. 2. 1 we have mention of **Fellowship of the Spirit.** If all have this, why does Paul say, "If there be any"? In ch. 3. 10 he speaks of the **Fellowship of His Sufferings,** which he himself desired to know. But could saints who never had the least experience of persecution for Christ's sake, claim to be in that fellowship? Lastly in ch. 4. 15 (see R.V.) we get the **Fellowship of Giving.**

As to the passage in 1st John 1, in which we have the last four occurrences of the word "fellowship" in the Scriptures, the expression in verse 3, "that ye also may have fellowship with us," implies a fellowship which they might or might not have, according to the extent of their knowledge of Christ and His Word; or perhaps it would be more accurate to say, of which they might have more or less, according to whether they knew more or less of Christ and His Word. The further references in verses 6, 7, are clearly to a fellowship in which we can only claim to be, so long as we walk in the light. The man who says he is in it, while yet he is not walking in the light, is described as lying.

As to the next question—whether there is such a thing as "Assembly fellowship, into which a believer can be received, and from which he can be put away"—only a person of warped mind would deny this. When Paul said, in 1 Cor. 5. 13, "Put away from among yourselves that wicked person," and the Corinthians obeyed him, was the one who was so "put away" to continue in the circle and insist on breaking bread, as being a member of the so-called "local church?" And if, while yet in the position of having been "put away," he goes to reside in another town, must the Assembly in that town also set him down at the Table, because since he now has his home there, he is a member of their "local church?" If these things are so, we may leave the first epistle to the Corinthians out of future editions of our Bibles.

With regard to the meaning of the word "church," when used locally, I have to say what already I have said about that other word "fellowship." What it includes or does not include in any particular case must be judged from the context there. In 1 Cor. 10. 32—it evidently takes in every saved person in the district, just as the other two terms in the verse, "Jews" and "Gentiles," take in all the others in the district. But in the same epistle at ch. 11. 18 and ch. 14. 19, 28, 35, it just as plainly means none but those who come to the Meeting; and this is made even clearer by ch. 14. 23, in which, after **the whole church** has come together, there may still come in one who is spoken of as "unlearned," yet who is distinguished (by the little word **"or"** that follows) from an "unbeliever." In other words, he is a saved man, but not yet in the "local church," in the sense in which the term "church" is used in this verse.

Moreover, not only can a person be put out of a local church when he deserves it, but according to 3 John 10, he may be **"cast out of the church"** even when he does not deserve it. One might well ask, Who were still "in" this local church after Diotrephes had cast these brethren "out" of it? Or were the cast out brethren "out" and "in" at the same time?

As to "letters of commendation," is it not clearly enough stated in 2 Cor. 3. 1 that some needed them, though Paul, being well-known to everyone, did not? How often would some require a thing to be stated in Scripture, in order to feel themselves bound to act accordingly?

With regard to the other matter—the case of a professed Christian who belongs to some sect, but comes to our meeting and expects to get breaking bread for one Lord's Day only, and then returns to his own company—I would need a good deal of convincing that the one who wished so to act was an honest man. If he believes that we are right, why should he not come to stay with us? If he believes us to be wrong and his own sect right, why should he want to do wrong even for one Lord's Day? And if he can do without "breaking bread" on fifty-one Sundays in the year, why should he be insistent on being allowed to do so on the remaining one?   W.R.

SEPARATION

Is sectarianism sin? I am in an assembly of so called "open brethren" who invite "Reverend" gentlemen from the sects, also a sister, to address them. Is this right?..

Sectarianism wherever found, is a work of the flesh (Galatians 5. 20). To whom but God Himself should confession be made? The beginnings of it were seen at Corinth—"I am of Paul, and I of Apollos and I of Cephas; and I of Christ" (1 Cor. 1. 12). In the first three cases men were attaching themselves to human leaders, instead of to Christ alone; in the last case, while attaching themselves to Christ, they were detaching from Him true members of His Body and pretending to belong to Him in some peculiar sense, in which others did not. This is also sectarianism against which we must watch. The whole idea of dividing up the Body of Christ is condemned by the Holy Spirit (see chap. 3. 3, 4). It is condoned to-day and we are told that the different sects are only regiments in God's army, as though regiments recruited from one another and were sometimes found fighting against one another. The only true Christian position is to know no other centre than Christ, and to recognise all believers as equally belonging to Him, though lamenting the broken-up condition of things around. No doubt there are men truly gifted of Christ, who occupy sectarian positions, but that does not make those positions right, and to invite such to teach the saints is a complete anomaly and certainly not calculated to "build these up on their most holy faith," but rather to break down the land-marks between truth and error and lead the Lord's people back on to sectarian ground. This is especially dangerous when the invited brethren are men who were once in the simple assemblies themselves, but have become popular preachers or even "Reverends," wearing all the insignia of their declension. They are often strongly opposed to the truth they once professed. It is not for us to judge their conscience, nor should we put a salve to their conscience by inviting them to teach or preach, thus approving of their position, or be present, when they officiate, as is apparently the case in some places. As for inviting a sister to teach the gathered saints, it is so clearly contrary to our Lord's express prohibition, through His apostle: "I suffer not a woman to teach, nor to usurp authority* over the man, but to be in silence" (1 Tim. 2. 12; see also 1 Cor. 14. 34-35), that comment is needless.   W.H.

How is it we say that it was a movement of the Holy Spirit which caused Christians to come out from the churches a century

---

* The word "authenteō" does not properly mean "usurp," but merely "occupy a position of," or "exercise authority" (R.V. has "have dominion.")

ago, but now we say the Holy Spirit leads us into the Church? Can both be right?

The wording of the above question is somewhat ambiguous. By the very fact of our getting saved, we then and there became part of that Church which is described by our Lord in Matt. 16. 18; and as this great transaction was the work of the Holy Spirit, it may in that connection truly enough be said that "the Holy Spirit leads us into the Church." Used thus, it would in no wise contradict the statement in the first part of our question; since there the word "Churches" evidently refers to the sects or denominations of Christendom. Neither would it be a contradiction, were we to say that the Holy Spirit leads God's people into what we may call the local expression of that great Church, i.e. a company of saints in a particular place, "gathered together unto the Name" of the Lord Jesus, as was "the Church of God in Corinth" and other similar ones in New Testament days.

But we suppose the inquirer has in mind the principles and practices of those who, professing to have once learned that sects and denominations are unscriptural, afterwards are found joining up with them in various ways. Possibly some of these may make the claim that "the Holy Spirit leads them so to do"; but this would certainly not be the view of any who desire to hold fast the truths which they have found in the Word of God. Much might be quoted from the Scriptures to condemn it, but we shall refer to one passage only, which even if there were never another, is sufficient to cut the ground from beneath the feet of all who do such things. It is the statement wherewith Paul at Antioch confronted the turning back of Peter, Barnabas, and others to Judaistic sectarianism: "If I build again the things which I destroyed, I make myself a transgressor" (Gal. 2. 18).

The real causes of this "building again" are to be found, neither in the leading of the Spirit, nor in the teaching of the Word of God, two things which will ever be found to agree together; but in various kinds of fleshly and spiritual weakness, many of which are seen illustrated, either in Israel's history, or in that of the early Church. In Peter's case, for example, it was the fear of man which led him to build again at Antioch the things he had destroyed, as is plainly stated by Paul in Gal. 2. 12. In that of Barnabas on the same occasion, it apparently was his regard for Peter which led him to follow his bad example (v. 13). With the Galatians themselves, as is shown in Gal. 4. 9, 17, it was the clever persuasion and reasoning of certain teachers who had come amongst them.

These, and many similar causes, are just as operative to-day as they were in the early church; but perhaps the most frequent of all is one of which we have an illustration in Judges 2. There in verse 7 we read that "the people served the Lord all the days of Joshua, and all the days of the elders that outlived Joshua, who had seen all the great works of the Lord." But in verse 10 we are told that there "arose another generation after them which knew not the Lord, nor yet the works which He had done for Israel." Then did declension set in rapidly, until they were "mingled among the heathen, and learned their works" (Psa. 106. 35).

So to-day in many places the older saints, who had "bought" the truth (Prov. 23. 23) at much cost to their earthly comfort and prospects, and who would have given their lives for it, have one by one passed away; and their places in the assemblies have been filled up by "another generation," many of whom are in them for no better reason than that their parents were there before them. These have not in any real sense bought the truth for themselves, and so it means little or nothing to them. Is it to be wondered at that such should "mingle" with the sects, and "see no harm" in it?

The safeguard and remedy in such circumstances would appear to be this, that all who do still set value on the truths they have learned, should seek to let their power over their own lives be seen, in an all round separation from worldliness of every kind, religious or otherwise; and to teach them graciously and in the fear of the Lord to younger ones, as they find opportunity.   W.R.

Ought speakers from the denominations, styling themselves "Reverend," or otherwise, to be invited to the halls where the Lord's people gather, to minister the Word or preach the Gospel, provided they be true Christians?

The whole question of the existence of the simple assemblies of Christians, accepting no other name, is involved in this query. Why do such meetings exist? What was their origin? Are they merely "the Brethren": one of the many sects in Christendom? If that were so, of course it would be quite legitimate to invite their "Reverends" and other speakers, for many such are brethren in Christ and gifted at that, and also to go to them to preach and teach, etc.:—in other words, to enjoy "interchange of pulpits," as it is termed. But little as it may be admitted by the religious world, or even understood in some quarters by those forming part of the said assemblies, their origin was something quite different. It was the result of a distinct work of the Holy Spirit, opening the eyes of some of His people to the sad and evil conditions of Christendom in general, and, to see in Christ God's one and only centre of gathering, for His saints, as He is God's only Saviour for sinners. This resulted in many of the Lord's people coming out of the various denominations in which they found themselves, to gather to His Name alone. Christendom in all its sections as such, is only part of Mystery Babylon, the great whore of the Apocalypse (see chap. 17), soon to be manifested in all the hideousness of its Satanic "Reunion." It is quite beside the mark to point to the fact that many of God's people are in it; they ought to be out of it. It would have been as reasonable to argue that the remnant had no reason to return to the land under Zerubbabel, because so many excellent Jews remained in Babylon, or to accuse them of being narrow and wanting to form a new tribe, because they obeyed God's call to go back to His only centre—Jerusalem. It is true that great weakness characterised those who returned, as to-day it characterises those who profess to have come out to the name of the Lord from the sects of Christendom. They had many difficulties within and without; they suffered sin among them, lost their power, and eventually degenerated into the sad condition described in Malachi, but still there was a remnant among them who feared the Lord and thought on His name. And they were not recommended to go back to Babylon, because of the general failure. Much the same has characterised the movement of the last hundred years. There was, at the beginning, great spiritual joy, power and blessing to saint and sinner, and much glory was brought to the Name of the Lord. But through lack of vigilance and mutual forbearance, Satan at an early date sowed seeds of discord, and divisions have taken place which are very dishonouring and grievous to the Lord and humbling to His people. Much of the freshness and joy has been lost; there is no longer the same attractive power to the Lord's people in the sects, but God's principle is the same, and it is significant that the Lord did not say (Matt. 18) where "two or three thousand" are met together in My name, but where "two or three," as though He had foreseen the divided condition of things. God is ever the same. His grace is sufficient, Christ is still His centre, the Word His rule, the Spirit His power, and wherever the people of God count on Him they find Him true, and His presence and blessing assured.

But to return to our question, can we imagine the returned captivity inviting some Levite, who had preferred to stay in Babylon, to take "a week-end return," to help them in their services at Jerusalem? or that Ezra would have accepted a call from Babylon to help in some synagogue services there? If such practices are current in any assemblies to-day it only shews how little the saints know why they are where they are. Is it likely that temporary helpers from some denomination could be able to help on the saints in the ways of Christ, or that Ezra, accepting a call to Babylon, would be likely to bring back any with him when his visit was over? He would be much more likely to encourage some of the remnant to pay a visit to Babylon, which might end in their staying there. We can ask the Lord to raise up gifts among us, but we cannot expect things to be the same as at the first when all were united, as in Acts 2. The Lord's word to Philadelphia was, "Thou hast a little strength and hast kept my word and hast not denied my name." Happy are all they to whom the Lord may say **such** words to-day.   W.H.

Is it according to Scripture for a brother in an assembly to preach in missions or denominations?

This question is one concerning which we might quote, " 'Tis old, yet ever new"; since it, or something similar to it, is asked so frequently. Briefly, I would reply that it is according to Scripture to preach anywhere on earth, providing that two conditions are fulfilled:

(1) That there is no barrier, expressed or implied, against my declaring "all the counsel of God" (Acts 20. 27) there.

(2) That my presence there does not link me in fellowship with something not according to the Word of God; and that it does not tend to draw other saints into the snare of a fellowship of that kind (1 Cor. 8. 9).

Let me add, however, that it has always seemed to me peculiar that so many in our assemblies appear anxious to squeeze themselves into such places as those referred to in the question. If these brethren were fishing in a stream where the trout were plentiful everywhere, but in the course of which were a few spots with the notice "Dangerous," I wonder would they find themselves drawn inevitably to those spots, in preference to all the rest of the water? I have found, and so have many thousands of other workers, that we can get all the spiritual fishing we are able to do, without being under any necessity to touch upon either dangerous or muddy spots.   W.R.

Is it expedient that we should associate ourselves, in any form of public testimony, with those who in preaching and practice ally themselves with a considerable measure of unscriptural doctrine?

The expression, "Those who in preaching and practice ally themselves with a considerable measure of unscriptural doctrine," is a wide one, and might be used of various kinds of people, many of whom differ as much from one another as they do from the truth. Here are some of those whom the Scriptures themselves mention, and do so for the very purpose of telling us what our attitude towards them should be.

In 2 John 9-11 some are so far wrong that they are unsound with regard to "the doctrine of the Christ." Receive not such into your house, nor bid them Godspeed, lest you become partaker of their evil deeds.

In Rom. 16. 17 there are some who foster divisions, contrary to the doctrine which you have learned from the Word of God. Mark these, with a view to avoiding them.

In Titus 3. 10 we have a man who seeks to build up a sect. If you have the ability of a Titus, admonish him once or twice. For the rest, keep away from him.

In 2 Thess. 3. 6, 14 some are mentioned who walk "out of rank," and will not obey the apostolic word in the Epistles. Withdraw from such, and have no company with them, that they may be ashamed. Yet count them not as enemies, but admonish them as brethren.

It is evident from the above passages, and from their context, that we must, as Jude says, "make a difference," with regard to the persons described in them and to our attitude towards them. But in no case would it be in keeping with the injunctions given, that we should make companions of them, either in public testimony or in any other way.

There are three questions which, if we put them to ourselves honestly, should immediately settle for us the right or wrong of any particular case which may present itself to us:

(1) Shall I be able to say afterwards to those with whom I would be brought into association in this matter, "I have not shunned to declare unto you all the counsel of God"? Acts 20. 27.

(2) Is there any danger that, by connecting myself with it, I would be helping to "build again the things which I destroyed"? Gal. 2. 18.

(3) Might not "this liberty of mine become an occasion of stumbling to them that are weak"? 1 Cor. 8. 9.   W.R.

Is it advisable for Christians in an assembly to associate themselves with "The Evangelical Alliance Week of Prayer"?

Being unaquainted with both the circumstances and the object of the matter named, I shall endeavour to reply in a general sense, which may in any case be the best method.

In the New Testament the local activities of the saints are all of them linked with the local assembly, and there is nothing else. To-day, however, the Lord's people are offered opportunities of associating with all sorts of "united" efforts outside of the assembly, some of them with aims which are most praiseworthy, and others not so. In such circumstances, it seems to me that there are just three courses open to us:—

(1) If we are not too particular as to either conscience or the Scriptures, we may incline to run wherever invited.

(2) If we have a conscience that will not permit us to go so far as this, we may try to sort out the good from the bad, associating with the one, and keeping clear of the other.

(3) If we go for our guidance to God's Word, we shall find none there to take us into any of these "unions" which are external to the assembly, and we shall not feel free to join ourselves with anything, which does not run within the lines laid down in the

Acts and the Epistles, as God's path for His people during the present Church period. At the same time we shall heartily rejoice at every sincere effort made to get God's people to seek His face; and shall ourselves be stirred up by knowing of such, to increase our activity in the same direction. W.R.

I read in a daily paper where a missionary (in fellowship in the local assembly) at a united service in a theatre, read the lesson, the address being given by an Anglo-Catholic bishop, while on the platform were modernist clergymen. Was his presence there taking part in that meeting a testimony for God, or service for God, in any way?

The querist does not explain what the object of this united service was; yet one would be interested to know what possible occasion could bring together on the same platform such heterogeneous elements as an Anglo-Catholic bishop, a missionary in fellowship in our assemblies, and a few modernistic clergymen as well. I can imagine that just now in some High Church magazine a reply is being sought to the question, "Is it right for an Anglo-Catholic bishop to join in a service with an unordained missionary connected with those wretched folk known as 'Brethren'?" and both in that paper and in this the answer of course will be in the negative. If the incident has really taken place just as described, neither the missionary nor the bishop has been much concerned about acting in accordance with the principles they profess to hold. We cannot understand the hankering which some appear to have after getting their names associated with Rev.'s and D.D.'s, and bishops; but in the case above it is no matter of differing with regard to these titles, or to Church order, but of fundamentally different views as to the Word of God itself and all contained in it. Anglo-Catholics, like Romanists, set the Church above the Bible; while Modernists set themselves above it; and a missionary who can feel at home in the company of such should stay there permanently, and leave the assemblies of God's people alone. He would do much less harm that way. W.R.

ASSEMBLY OVERSIGHT

DEACONS

What is the office of a Deacon? Would it not be more scriptural to name what is called "oversight" by "deaconate"? Further, is it right for an elder to appoint, or should the assembly appoint, brethren to this position?

We must carefully distinguish between elders (or OVERSEEING brethren) and deacons (or MINISTERING brethren) (see Phil. i. 1; 1 Tim. iii, where somewhat different qualifications are described for each class). No doubt an overseer can be a deacon, too, and *vice versa*. Paul was an overseer; he had "the care of all the churches," but he calls himself and Apollos "deacons by whom ye believed" (1 Cor. iii. 5). "Let the ELDERS who RULE WELL be counted worthy of double honour, ESPECIALLY THEY WHO LABOUR in the word and doctrine" (1 Tim. v. 17), *i.e.*, who minister as deacons. It is the Holy Spirit who appoints elders (Acts xx. 28), but there is also the human side: the one who desires oversight work should shew the scriptural qualifications (see 1. Tim. iii.), if he wants his brethren to acknowledge the appointment of the Spirit. The assembly does not choose its overseers, but should be able to recognise those who are truly called of God to the work. The deacon is one who has some special gift of ministry, as a preacher or teacher, and if he is to be publicly recognised in the assembly, he too should have the character and qualifications laid down by the Spirit (1 Tim. iii. 8-12). But only the risen Lord can appoint him, for they are His gifts which he is administering. A deacon, however, may also be one who acts as treasurer or almoner for the assembly (Acts vi 1-8), and in this case the assembly ought to have a voice in his appointment, as it is their money and gifts he is taking charge of. Phœbe was a deacon of the church of Cenchrea: that is, she had definite, recognised service in the assembly, suited to her sex.   W.H.

RULE

Do the Scriptures teach that an overseer is to rule the Church? Does "obey them that have the rule over you," imply that we have rulers in the Church to-day?

Three words are translated "RULE" in the New Testament in reference to oversight: (1) POIMAINŌ (from POIMĒN, a shepherd), used by our Lord to Peter—"Feed (better, 'shepherd') my sheep" (John xxi. 16). The word in vv. 15 and 17 for "feed," is BOSKŌ; but feeding, though of the first importance, is only one item of shepherding. POIMAINŌ also occurs in Acts xx. 28 and 1 Pet, v. 2, "feed the flock"; also in Matt. ii. 6, "RULE"—"that shall rule (marg. feed) my people Israel." (2) PROISTĒMI, as in 1 Tim. iii. 5: "If a man know not how to RULE his own house, how shall he take care (EPIMELEOMAI) of the church of God?" This word for "take care" occurs only here and in Luke x. 34, 35, of and by "the good Samaritan." PROISTĒMI is used too of the RULE OF THE CHURCH in 1 Tim. v. 17. (3) HĒGEOMAI (from AGO, to lead), to be a leader, to rule (in New Testament this latter only in present participle), is used of Barnabas and Silas—"CHIEF MEN among the brethren" (Acts xv. 22); of Joseph—"GOVERNOR over Egypt" (Acts vii. 10); and in Heb. 13. 7, 17, 24 in the expression, "them that HAVE THE RULE OVER" (marg., in two latter verses, "guides," which seems to do well). Overseers, then, are shepherds, feeding, guiding, tending the flock; also ruling, but not in the self-assertive, domineering way of a Gentile king, "not as lords over God's heritage," but with gentle control for the good of the sheep, whom they love, because they belong to the Chief Shepherd who has entrusted them to their care (1 Pet. v. 2-4), and it is for the sheep to be subject to this godly rule. W.H.

OVERSIGHT

Is it scriptural for overseeing brethren to hold that, and to act as if, they and they alone are responsible to God for the carrying on of the affairs of a local assembly? Does attendance at a monthly oversight meeting constitute one an overseer?

It is not attendance at an oversight meeting which makes a man an overseer, nor the appointment of anyone, even an apostle, but the call of the Holy Spirit to the work (Acts xx. 28). There will also be a desire for the work (not an "office") (1 Tim. iii. 1), though there will be doubtless a consciousness of insufficiency. In addition, there must be also certain qualities in a man to enable his brethren to recognise his fitness and call. He must be blameless, patient, not domineering; apt to teach (that is, not necessarily a teacher, but able to instruct in sound doctrine). He must be able to rule well his own house; he must not be a neophyte, that is, a newly converted person; and he must have a good report in the world (see 1 Tim. iii. and Titus i.). These chapters are an integral part of God's Word, and it is quite a gratuitous assumption to say that they are in abeyance, because we have no apostles or apostolic delegates. Why should all these directions be left, if not to guide us on this very point? What is proposed to take the place of an elders' meeting?—a mere human arrangement without, I believe, one line of Scripture to authorise it—a meeting of the male members of the assembly. Surely it is evident that some of the men in a gathering may correspond very slightly indeed, if at all, with the conditions laid down in the Scriptures. They may be new converts; they may lack the power to keep their own homes in order; they may be lacking in the qualities and grace needed for the work of oversight; they may, perchance, not have a good report in the world. If so, they are as clearly excluded from oversight as the sisters. I was once long ago in a meeting where the leading brother, having come from a circle where the arrangement in question had vogue, insisted on all the males being invited to the "business meeting." I remember still the hindrance this was to a true oversight meeting. Only two meetings are known to the Word—(1) That of the "apostles and elders" (Acts xv. 6; xx. 18), but because we have no elders of apostolic gifts, this principle is in no way affected. What excuse can there be for introducing mere "males," whom the Scriptures exclude? (2) That of the assembly (Acts xiv. 27; xv. 4; xx. 7; xxi. 22). What is known as the "oversight meeting" is a matter of convenient arrangement between brethren who have mutual confidence, but it ought not to be what is called "a closed oligarchy," nor should it prevent anyone else, who believes himself called to the work of caring for saints, and of giving proof of his ministry; but such would naturally not force fellowship on others, but would wait to be assured of their welcome. Overseeing brethren ought to be on the look-out for Spirit-called helpers.   W.H.

Could we support the thought of a paid overseer, who "labours in the Word and doctrine," from 1 Tim. 5. 17, 18; 1 Peter 5. 2-4? and why the mention of "filthy lucre," if the pastorate were not a paid office?

The word translated, "honour," (**timē**) in 1 Tim. 5. 17, is in forty occurrences, out of fifty, so translated; in eight others, "price"; "sum" in Acts 7. 16, and in 1 Pet. 2. 7, "precious." It is always, "honour," in the Epistles to Timothy (see 1 Tim. 1. 17; 6. 1, 16; 2 Tim. 2. 20, 21). There does not appear any necessity to change the word here: "honour," "respect," "consideration," are quite adequate. However, even if we adopted the sense of monetary payment, it would only be in recognition of spiritual services rendered, not as a fixed salary. The form of the exhortation seems to preclude the idea of money due, whether the services have been well done or perchance left undone. "Let the elders that rule **well** be counted worthy of double honour, **especially they who LABOUR in the word and doctrine.**" The principle that a teacher or evangelist has a right to "live by the gospel" is clearly taught in the Scriptures (see 1 Cor. 9. 7-14), provided he teaches or evangelises. There is no idea of a "living" or ecclesiastical title or office. Assemblies which utilise their brethren's gift are quite right to remember these adequately, and not to take too easily for granted that the preacher does not need anything beyond his bare expenses. As for the "Peter" passage, we can see no hint that what the questioner calls "the pastorate" was to be filled by a salaried official. The **elders,** in the plural, are addressed here, as in the other passage, nor can we find the idea of the "presiding elder" or of "**the** pastor" of a church in this or in any other Scripture. Here the exhortation, "not for filthy lucre," seems to preclude a stated salary. A servant of the Lord truly looking to Him for his support, is not serving for filthy lucre. The man who is receiving so much salary according to an arrangement, is bound, if he is a conscientous man to give a good money's worth. The only man that I can find in the Scriptures, who agreed to do so much spiritual work (in this case as "a priest") for so much pay, was Jonathan, the grandson of Moses (though not of the family of Aaron), and his salary was ten shekels of silver per annum, a suit of clothes and his meals (Judges 17. 10). He broke the contract, only when a better living was offered him (Chap. 18. 19).   W.H.

Is it scriptural to call the whole assembly together to discuss business matters in the assembly?

I do not know of any Scripture which would favour such a custom, and judged merely by ordinary standards of common sense and business principles, I should think it very unlikely to result in good to the business or to the assembly as a whole. What profit could come from listening perhaps to differences among elder brethren? An assembly of God is not a debating society nor yet a democracy, in which rule is from beneath, it is a theocracy in which rule is entrusted by the Holy Spirit to those whom He has fitted for the work. "Take heed . . . to all the flock (not **your** flock), over the which the Holy Spirit hath made you overseers" (Acts 20. 28). "Remember them which have the rule over you" (the guides), "Obey them that have the rule" (Heb. 13. 7, 17). "Know them which labour among you and are over you in the Lord and admonish you, and esteem them very highly in love for their works' sake" (1 Thess. 5. 12, 13).

Acts 15 seems to throw light on the matter before us. Paul, Barnabas and certain others had come to Jerusalem about a troublesome matter, and they were received of the church, clearly the whole assembly, not excepting the apostles and elders. It was a meeting to hear "all things that God had done with them," but apparently at this general meeting certain Judaizing brethren, of the sect of the Pharisees, which believed, rose up and introduced the very matter that had troubled the saints at Antioch. It would clearly not have been for edification to discuss the differences before the church, so the next verse tells us that "the apostles and elders came together to consider of this matter" (v. 6). The results must have been communicated to the whole assembly (ver. 22), for otherwise they could not have had fellowship in sending Judas and Silas to Antioch with Paul and Barnabas, with letters in their name. "The apostles and elders and the brethren send greeting to the brethren of the Gentiles in Antioch and Syria." These arrived in Antioch, and when they had gathered the multitude, that is, I take it, the whole company of believers, they delivered the epistle. We gather, therefore, that matters of business and discipline are not discussed before the whole church, but that the results should be communicated to them, when it is a matter which calls for general knowledge. W.H.

Does the procedure followed in Acts 15 throw light on the question, whether business and oversight matters of an assembly should be settled solely by its elders, or whether they should for final decision, come before the entire meeting? Verses 2 and 6, with chapter 16. 4, appear to favour the former view, but verses 4, 22, and 23, the latter.

K

Acts 15 should certainly prove helpful in this connection; but before we thus use it, let us clear our minds of any thought that the gathering which is described at length in verses 6-29 was an ordinary business or oversight meeting of a local Assembly. It was a conference presided over by apostles, the decisions of which were intended to be binding upon saints and gospel workers everywhere. Paul and Barnabas did NOT come all the way from Antioch to Jerusalem to obtain the views of the Jerusalem church on the questions which had been a cause of disturbance, but to consult with "THE APOSTLES AND ELDERS" (v. 2) regarding them. And they did this NOT because they had any doubt as to the correctness of what they had been teaching (see Gal. 2. 5), but to prevent a schism arising among the churches, which might become the means of rendering much of their work ' in vain" (Gal. 2. 2).

Yet widely different though this meeting was from any to which we are accustomed, there is much to be learnt from the wisdom with which the apostles and elders acted in order to bring harmony out of what in verses 2 and 5 seemed to be hopeless discord. Let us note first that there was a manifest desire on the part of all those who were the real leaders to do everything they could to promote the unity of the saints, as well as to maintain "the truth of the gospel." There was nothing to be seen of the spirit of "I-must-have-it-my-way" amongst them. And let us note further that these leaders were after all, in substantial agreement as to what "the truth of the gospel" was, though each might express it in his own particular fashion.

Moreover, it seems clear from the first clause of verse 7 that the lesser men, among whom were those who thought that circumcision should be imposed on the Gentile converts, were first permitted to say all they had got to say in furtherance of their point of view. Not until then did Peter speak, and remind them of how this work of God among Gentiles had begun; so providing an opening for Paul and Barnabas to relate the story of how it had gone on and increased, and of how the Lord had set His seal upon it. Finally James, the one of all their leaders in whom the saints with Jewish tendencies seem to have had most confidence, signified his agreement with the others, that the Gentile converts should not be brought into bondage, but at the same time suggested that they should go as far as they reasonably could to meet the prejudices of their Hebrew brethren, by abstaining from eating of blood, etc. With this all were in agreement; and from its wording, James appears to have been the one chosen to draft the letter, in which their decision was to be made known to the churches.

With regard to the specific point referred to in the above question, it will be helpful to notice who are the parties named in each of the verses mentioned, and what is there said about them. In verse 2, as already remarked, it was to "the apostles and elders" that the mission of Paul and Barnabas was directed. In verse 4 a meeting of "the church" was held to welcome them, at which, of course, "the apostles and elders" were present, and at which Paul and Barnabas gave a report of their work among the Gentiles. This account stirred up the Jewish extremists present to protest that converts who were uncircumcised must submit to the rite, so raising the very point that had caused trouble at Anticoh. When verses 5 and 6 are read together, it will be clear that the matter was not allowed to develop or be dealt with at this open meeting; but that "the apostles and elders" came together later, to discuss it more privately; and what took place at that gathering has already been described.

Having come to a decision, verse 22 suggests that they made it known to the rank and file of the saints in Jerusalem, and that these heartily acquiesced in it. For we are told that it pleased "the apostles and elders with the whole church" to send to Antioch the letter and the men that are mentioned in it. As for the superscription of the letter as given in verse 23, the A.V. has it, "The apostles and elders and brethren," but the R.V. follows the most ancient MSS. in reading, "The apostles and the elder brethren." The latter is also in keeping with the purpose of the visit of Paul and Barnabas, as stated in verse 2, and with the expression afterwards used about the matter in ch. 16. 4.

Thus the order indicated is that questions of importance, or of difficulty, should first be considered by the leaders, and a united decision come to, which should then be communicated to the assembly as a whole. Where things are in a normal or healthy condition, the judgment of the leaders will be assented to by all, and will thus become that of the entire body. And if, as was the case in Ezra 10. 15, R.V., one or two "stand up against" their brethren, they will have as little power to hinder as the men there mentioned had. Generally speaking, however, action should not be taken in any matter, until there is substantial agreement among the saints regarding it; and when this is lacking, the Lord should be sought in prayer that it may be brought about. Above all, there should be no thought of settling the affair in the world's way, by putting it to the vote, in which the young person, brought into the meeting but a few weeks before, would have the same weight as the oldest or wisest present. That would be a complete negation of all godly rule, as set forth in 1 Timothy and elsewhere.   W.R.

Should the oversight meeting be open to all elder brethren of consistent walk in life, or only to a few, who "assume" the care and rule of the meeting?

1 Timothy 3. 1-7; Titus 1. 6-9; and 1 Peter 5. 1-5 give us the qualifications of an overseeing elder: first, he must" desire" it (or "stretch forward" to it, as the original expresses). But that is not enough; he may

even be "consistent in walk and life," and yet fail to manifest the necessary qualification for eldership. Does he rule his home well for instance? or is it a matter of common knowledge, that he is ruled in the home? An overseer of this type is a great hindrance, for sometimes it is the power in the home that seeks to rule the church by his means. Has he a "good report of them that are without"? Does he "hold fast the faithful Word"? Has he a pastor's heart, to feed the flock of God? I think one qualified by God for such a work would be very slow to "assume" anything; he would be apt to do the work, show fitness for it, and have a heart for the Lord's people, but it would not be for him to push himself into a prominent position; rather his fellowship would be sought. Elders caring for the saints should be on the look out for brethren who are manifesting any spiritual activities, and seek to encourage such, remember that age comes on apace, and that soon perhaps their work will need other hands to take it up.   W.H.

Is it scriptural to appoint Elders and Deacons in our assemblies by a system of voting amongst the brethren and sisters, the number of votes being counted up and determining the result?

Surely such a question only needs to be asked, to be answered in the negative, for what possible basis could be found for such proceedings in the Scriptures? If there be an instance or direction for such a thing in the New Testament, we do not know it, and should value the citation of chapter and verse.

The nearest approach to such a thing that could possibly be alleged would be the words of the apostles to the multitude of the disciples in Acts 6. 3, and yet even here, there is not a word about **voting** by the saints or even appointment by them—the word of the apostles was to the **brethren:** "Look ye out among **you** seven **men** of honest report, full of the Holy Ghost and wisdom, whom **we may appoint** over this business." It is to be noted that it was a question here of the appointment only of a certain kind of ministers, namely, managers of the daily distribution of monetary help to the widows in the assembly. They are usually called "deacons," though the word is not actually used except in the substantival form, **"diakonia,"** in verses 1 and 4 (**"ministration," "ministry** of the Word"). In verse 2 we have the verbal form, **"diakonein"**—to **serve**—(from a verb "diōkein," to pursue a course). These seven were chosen to distribute the gifts of the saints to the needy widows, as the givers of the gifts had a right to a little part at least in looking out suitable men, to act as their almoners. But when it is a question of spiritual "deacons" (v. 4, **"ministers** of the Word"), such as evangelists, pastors and teachers, who are the gifts of the Risen Christ, only He, the Giver can "look out" and "appoint" such men.

As for **elders,** they come under a different category. They are quite distinct from **deacons,** it not being a question of exercising gift, in the technical sense, but of godly care, oversight, feeding and guiding the flock. In Acts 20 Paul exhorts the elders, "Feed the flock of God, over which the Holy Ghost hath made you overseers."

We never read of a church appointing its elders, any more than of a flock appointing its shepherds. But we do read in Acts 14. 20-23, that when the Apostles Paul and Barnabas returned on their **second** visit to Lystra, Derbe, Iconium and Antioch, then and only then, "they ordained (or pointed out) elders in every church." Why was this only on the second visit? were they not needed on the first? Surely, but it naturally took a little time for these men to come to the front, whom the Holy Ghost was fitting and calling to the work. The apostles, I take it, only recognised His work and endorsed it. In writing later to Timothy and Titus, the apostle gives the description of men called to the work of oversight or eldership. These chapters (1 Tim. 3, and Titus 1) form part of the sacred canon, and are to-day for the guidance of men, themselves leaders, who are to be on the look out for younger men, who are aspirants to eldership work, and encourage those who manifest the divine calling and qualification.

It seems clear, however, in all this that there is not the smallest precedent or direction for canvassing a church and registering the votes of the saints for certain men who are to take the place of "elders" and "deacons" of the church. Such a church will never fall "from its excellency," **it has already fallen.** It has exchanged dependence on the Lord to give the needed gifts to His Church, for the carnal methods of **a degenerate** Christendom. May the Lord so encourage us all in the path of faith as that such devices of the flesh should not be so much as once named among us, as becometh saints! W.H.

DISCIPLINE

What should be our attitude to a neighbouring assembly, where moral or doctrinal evil is allowed to go on unjudged?

I presume what is meant by "moral or doctrinal evil" is something grave and fundamental, and not merely differences of judgement as to such questions as the exact rules to be followed at the Lord's table, or regulations as to ministry. We have no authority in God's Word as far as I can see, for cutting off an assembly, but we are not obliged to **have fellowship** with every assembly. The Lord in His messages to the Seven Churches of Asia has to reprove Ephesus for "leaving her first love"; Pergamos for allowing among them those holding the doctrine of Balaam, or the doctrine of the Nicolaitanes; Thyatira for

"suffering that woman Jezebel . . . to teach and seduce God's servants";
Sardis for dead-alive profession; and Laodicea for luke-warmness and
self-satisfaction. Yet, though in each case appeal is made to him "who
hath an ear to hear what is said unto the churches," in no case is one
church, or alliance of churches, instructed to deal in discipline with some
other church. Not even in the case of Smyrna or Philadelphia, with
which no fault was found, is any such instruction given. Is there then
nothing to be done? Clearly the exhortation "to hear" what is said to
the churches, shows that no church should be indifferent to the state
of other churches. Prayer for the erring church must be ever in season,
and godly exhortation by word or letter always permissible. But what
should be done if all prove abortive? Then all direct contact with the
assembly as such must be avoided. It is she who is morally responsible
for shutting her doors against those who stand for truth and righteousness. Can we imagine Smyrna having practical fellowship with Pergamos, or Philadelphia exchanging platforms with Thyatira? But the
modern method, if we rule out "inferences" and "logical deductions",
of excommunicating churches or groups of churches, is profoundly
foreign to Scripture. W.H.

**What should be the attitude of those in oversight with regard
to new converts who continue to attend worldly amusements,
and whose manner of life shows no change?**

If what the questioner means is that these so-called converts have
already been received into the fellowship of the assembly, then the only
fitting attitude for the leaders and others, who in such circumstances
allowed them to come in, is one of humiliation before God for their
negligence and sin. If, on the other hand, they are still outside the
assembly, this is the place to keep them, until they show some satisfactory sign that they have become "a new creature," in Christ, with
the "old things passed away," and "all things become new."

There is a regrettable lack, amongst both Gospel preachers and assemblies, of giving due emphasis to the truth that there can be no real
conversion to God, without changed interests and changed conduct. W.R.

**How should an assembly of God act, according to the Scrip-
tures, in the case of a member who has married a Roman
Catholic?**

To us it may seem worse that a professed Christian should marry a
Roman Catholic, than that one should marry an unconverted Protestant;
and generally it means much more in the way of trouble in the flesh to
the one concerned. But we have to remember that, from the point of
view of the Scriptures, and of the principle involved, the one act is as

wrong as the other; and whatever may be said as to the assembly's attitude in the case mentioned in the question, would be applicable in the other case also. Not only so, but since the evil in the act is that of being "unequally yoked together" with an unbeliever, it would to a large extent be applicable to other cases of the unequal yoke as well. A clear understanding as to all this would prevent an assembly from acting with undue harshness in the one instance, while perhaps entirely ignoring the others.

Yet, that a member of an assembly of God's people should at all wish to marry a Roman Catholic is very strange, and suggests some grave considerations. One may well wonder whether such a one has divine life; for if so, it is difficult to imagine what common interest there could ever be to bring the pair together in the first instance. At least there must have been much preliminary declension from God's ways, ere such a thing could be possible. And that suggests another matter for thought, namely, what kind of guides were in an assembly where departure from God on the part of a member could reach to such a climax as this, without faithful warnings having been given at an earlier stage which might have prevented it.

But the most surprising feature of all would be if the one who had done this thing, afterwards desired, as the question seems to imply, to remain in the fellowship of the assembly. The Roman religious authorities exercise such pressure on their people in the matter of a mixed marriage, that it would almost certainly have taken place in one of their own places of worship, and only after the non-Roman party to it had climbed down very low in agreeing to all their demands. Therefore it is not easy to understand why anyone who has gone so far should wish to continue the former associations.

If, however, all this has occurred or should occur, the assembly should certainly not ignore what has taken place. I do not think that (unless other complications are present) the Scriptures would warrant putting away from the fellowship of the meeting on that account alone. But the guilty individual should be rebuked; and since it is an evil to which a large amount of publicity is necessarily attached, I suggest that the rebuke should in like manner be public, i.e. in the presence of the assembled saints (see 1 Tim. 5. 20 and Gal. 2. 14).   W.R.

What attitude should one adopt towards an overseeing brother who absents himself from the weekly feast, in order to speak at the morning service of a denominational church near by?

This is a question of the type that suggests others which one would like to ask and have answered before dealing with it. To begin with, how did a brother such as is described, one who either has never learned the first thing about separation to the Name of the Lord Jesus, or who, having learned the truth, is prepared to set it aside for the sake of displaying his preaching ability, ever come to be recognised as a leader in an assembly of God's people? If he considers the sects, or any of them, to be right and scriptural, he should never have left them; while if he knows them to be wrong and unscriptural, he is deliberately disobeying the Lord when he goes back to them. Or, putting it in Bible language, "If I build again the things which I destroyed, I make myself a transgressor" (Gal. 2. 18).

Again, what adequate reason would such an "overseeing" brother give, if he were asked why should not the entire assembly, to which he professes to be an ensample, follow him on the Lord's Day to the sect he favours, and close down their own meeting completely?

Then from another point of view, one would require to ask, What is the standing in the assembly of the inquirer himself? Since it is his personal attitude towards the other that is in question, the answer would naturally depend to some extent upon this. If he himself is a leader and experienced, he should do what he can to bring before the inconsistent one the evil of his course, and the bad example he is setting to others; and should in his own ministry give prominence to Church truth, while at the same time carefully avoiding anything like personal allusions. If on the other hand he is one who has but recently come into the fellowship of the assembly, he should be all the more careful to hold fast what the Lord has taught him from His Word, and to follow no leader, or "overseeing brother," except in so far as he himself follows Christ (1 Cor. 11. 1).   W.R.

How do the Scriptures look upon such as habitually absent themselves from the Breaking of Bread, and are seldom or never seen at the Gospel Meeting or the Prayer Meeting? Has Numbers 9. 13 any application to them?

I do not think that we could apply Numbers 9. 13 to them, unless by way of pointing out from it how seriously neglect of obedience to God's commands was dealt with under law, in any case where there was no legitimate excuse for it. It must, however, be understood that "shall be cut off from among his people", does not necessarily imply that his fellow-Israelites were to slay him. See Lev. 20, where in various verses a clear distinction seems to be drawn between "shall be cut off" and "shall be put to death," the former referring to action taken by the Lord Himself. Something similar is seen, even in the days of grace, in 1 Cor. 11. 30, where certain members of the assembly had been taken away by death, not indeed for absence from the Supper, but for irreverence when present.

Where there is habitual absence from the meetings, something else lies behind it, the absence being merely a symptom of a deeper disorder

In some instances it means that the person concerned is beginning to turn away from all that he once professed to have and enjoy. In Heb. 10. 25-31 the "FORSAKING OF THE ASSEMBLING OF OUR-SELVES TOGETHER" seems to be viewed as the first manifestation outwardly of a course which ends in apostasy; and the individual who is guilty of it may eventually prove to be an "adversary" (ver. 27). In other cases the staying away is due to some real or imagined grievance, and if there is any substance whatever in this grievance, an effort should be made to remove it if possible. Between these two extremes lie many differing degrees of backsliding by which the trouble may be caused, and which should give scope for the exercise of any pastoral gift or activity there may be in the assembly. And in the course of this it may possibly be discovered that due allowance has not been made for the circumstances of the person, and for hindrances which may make regular attendance a difficult matter.

On the other hand, where absence from the meetings has been entire, and for a prolonged period, the point might require to be considered, whether the one concerned is still to be looked upon as a member of the assembly, or whether it should be made clear that he is no longer such. Otherwise, unnecessary reproach may be brought on the saints through his actions, even years afterwards.   W.R.

Can you give any Scripture for the "silencing" of a brother? For what "crime" is he to be "silenced"? and who is to do it?

This is an important enquiry. I suppose the questioner does not mean literally a "crime," for surely no one guilty of a serious moral offence against the law could be allowed to preach or teach, even if he were allowed for the time being to remain in the assembly, which could hardly ever be the case. But I suppose what is meant is some brother, against whom, perhaps, no real accusation can be made, but who has been requested not to minister the Word. Now, of course, we cannot judge of any particular case without knowing the details. I believe in general that no one would be silenced, unless there were good reasons—some manifest lack of gift, some recognised inability to edify the saints, some habit of too lengthy and unprofitable ministry, which had wearied hearers, or some clear moral defect. Sometimes a man may insist on reading and commenting on long chapters of the Bible, or always the same chapter, as we have known in one case, or always the same disputed doctrine, which in an unruly way he persists to inflict upon the saints. Perhaps Paul refers to some such men in Titus 1. 10, as "unruly and vain-talkers and deceivers . . . ," and then adds, "WHOSE MOUTHS MUST BE STOPPED." It is not necessary to fill every line of this indictment, to deserve the form of discipline here pre-scribed. A man would seem to fall within it, who is known as an unprofitable talker, or as pushing some doubtful or controversial teaching. I do not think this silencing ought to be done by an individual acting on his own responsibility. It is a case where "two are better," and they should act only as representatives of the assembly. The phrase, "the liberty of the Spirit," is sometimes quoted to show that the Spirit gives liberty to anyone who likes to teach, but in their context the words only refer to seeing Christ without a veil. Certainly the Spirit does not give liberty to those whom He has not qualified to speak. However, it does not always follow that the one silenced will never again be able to minister, for sometimes it may be that a young man may have been too quick to come forward into this service, and may develop a true gift later. I know of one such case, where the one silenced (and he submitted himself humbly to the ruling of his elders) became afterwards universally recognised as a true minister of the Word.   W.H.

The phrase, "to put away," is ambiguous, because this can be done either by "expulsion" or "withdrawal," as we are told in 2 Thess. 3, in the case of every brother "which walketh disorderly". Do not the various denominations owe their existence to this "putting away", and to the outcast members setting up another table?

Not only are the words "put away" in 1 Cor. 5. 13, and "withdraw yourselves" in 2 Thess. 3. 6, quite distinct in the original, but the context shews clearly that they are not at all two ways of describing the same action, but rather two ways of describing distinct actions in reference to very different degrees of evil. In 1 Cor. 5 there was serious immorality, and the offender was regarded, at his face value, as a "wicked person", though afterwards he proved to have the root of the matter in him; whereas the evil at Thessalonica was not at all immorality, but "walking disorderly", that is, "out of rank" with their brethren, and not according to the order laid down for their guidance in the Word of God ("Working not at all but are busybodies"). Such are not to be treated as enemies or wicked persons, but as erring brothers. "Note that man and have no company with him, that he may be ashamed. Yet count him not as an enemy, but admonish him as a **brother**" (2 Thess. 3. 14, 15). The distinct treatment in either case denotes degrees of discipline —the one excision from the local assembly; the other a deprivation of the social amenities which form part of the fellowship of the saints. I do not think that the exercise of extreme discipline has been the root cause of denominationalism, rather the lack of it; though there are doubtless other causes such as the growth of a party spirit, resulting in attachment to leaders and consequent division. "Also of your own selves shall men arise . . . to draw away disciples after them" (Acts 20. 30), either promulgating error, or magnifying some truth out of all proportion and making it the centre, instead of Christ. Surely those who have formed such sects or who perpetuate them, with their infant sprinkling, clericalism, official ministerialism, cannot be said to be walking according to the scriptural order. Would not Paul's advice to the Lord's servants and people be: "Withdraw yourselves from every brother that walketh disorderly, and not after the tradition that ye have received of us"? Those who seek to carry out these principles will find themselves ostracised as "narrow", but is it to be a matter of surprise, if those who walk in the narrow way, should be dubbed, "narrow", by some? W.H.

Please explain the New Testament teaching of Leviticus 21. 21-22.

Clearly there are physical defects, which, while not hindering a brother breaking bread, would disqualify him from leading the assembly in worship to the Father, e.g., dumbness, excessive stammering, defective organs of speech. I remember a good brother thus afflicted, to whose presence none thought of objecting, but to whose audible exercises, which were frequent, some did take exception. Probably he would have been more in the love of the Spirit, had he but rarely taken audible part in the worship. But the physical defects, enumerated in Lev. 21, as preventing the sons of Aaron from exercising their public priestly functions, would correspond to-day rather to moral defects, which though not bringing the person in question under discipline, would render him unfit to lead the assembly in its priestly worship. How could a brother for instance, who was known to lose his temper in public, or be a quarrelsome person, or had a bad financial record, be indicated as a leader of the saints? How could a bankrupt, who had not paid his creditors, or a man who owed money to the saints or the world, pretend "to offer the bread of God" in the public assembly? The lack of conscience evidenced by attempting to do so, would in itself be but poor proof of the reality of his Christian profession, though he might still be allowed to break the bread, pending possible developments. It might be hoped that his own sense of propriety would keep him silent, but if not, the elder brethren would doubtless feel their responsibility to act. W.H.

Is the discipline exercised on a brother in Matt. 18. 17 equivalent to that exercised in 1 Cor. 5. 11-13?

Let us see what these passages say. In 1 Cor. 5. 11-13 the sinning one is to be "put away from among yourselves," and the saints are not to have fellowship with him in any respect whatsoever. In Matt. 18. 17, when the offender has refused to "hear the church," it is said, "Let him be unto thee as an heathen man and a publican." Our question therefore appears to mean, "Is this man also put away from the assembly as is the former?" and if so, the answer can only be that he is. For how could I be said to treat another "as an heathen man and a publican," if he is still breaking bread with myself and others every Lord's Day? And if the church has not put the man away at v. 17, why should it be said in the following verse, "Whatsoever ye shall bind on earth shall be bound in heaven"?

But it may be asked, why is the expression, "Let him be unto THEE," and not rather "unto YOU" or "unto THE CHURCH"? I suggest that it is because the passage in Matt. 18 is not dealing directly with church procedure at all, but with the attitude of an individual towards one who has sinned against him. The assembly is only introduced incidentally as having to take action in certain circumstances which are mentioned. All the way through from v. 15 an individual is being addressed, and it is not to be wondered at that the same should be the case in v. 17. Yet at the same time, since the matter has now reached a stage where the offender has refused to hear the church, each member of it by that refusal has been practically put into the same position with regard to him as the one first of all concerned, and must act toward him in the same manner.   W.R.

As passages such as Deut. 13. 12; 17. 4 to 7; 19. 17 and 18 teach that it must be the whole assembly that shall exercise discipline, does not the same apply in 1 Cor. 5. 4 and Matt. 18. 15-20? Is it not the cause of much division inside assemblies, that this is not carried out? (1 Cor. 1. 10 to 12). If there are divided opinions as to discipline, is it not more godly to wait on God till all are of the one mind and heart, even though the evidence may seem very plain?

The Lord is with His people at all times, with the two's or three's or the many, as well as with individuals, but the special presence of Matt. 18. 20 is conditioned on their being gathered together to His Name—"eis to onoma"—that is, not promiscuously or for some social end, a meal or conversation, etc., but around His Person for prayer, or worship, or the remembrance of Himself. The same word is used in 1 Cor. 5. 4, though the name is not actually mentioned there as the gathering centre (eis to onoma) but as their authority for gathering (en tō onomati). They were not coming together as an assembly to investigate the case, that had already been done by the Apostle and those responsible, with the help of any immediately concerned, but to carry out the discipline enjoined. There is nothing to lead us to suppose there had been any canvass of the brethren or sisters before this, much less that such was contemplated at their meeting. Nor do I know of any Scripture for a parallel proceeding. Such an idea would imply that all in the assembly are qualified to judge the "pros and cons" of the matter, which is quite contrary to the fact. If all were qualified to be overseers, then there need be none. In the case before us, how could the sad and sordid details be laid bare to all? In the same way in the case of Reception; all who are present hear the name announced for fellowship, and if they know any "just cause or impediment", they should inform the elders, but otherwise they naturally trust in those who have the case in hand. In cases of discipline, there are at times two or three who side with the evil-doer. I know of no Scripture which enjoins that everything must be held up, until these come round to the united judgment of elder brethren. The Apostle puts it in 2 Cor. 2. 6: "Sufficient to such a man is this punishment, which was inflicted of many" (or as R.V. has: "by the many"—margin; Greek "the more"). As Alford suggests, it was very unlikely that the anti-Pauline party were unanimous in the action of 1 Cor. 5. When once disciplinary action has been taken, it is very important that all should respect it. It is indeed grievous when the reverse is the case. It is a curious phenomenon, but there are those who seem automatically to take sides with any who have been dealt with. It is a misplaced charity and a misnamed impartiality, and such only succeed in bolstering up evil-doers, and in undermining the confidence of brethren in themselves.   W.H.

SERVICE

GOSPEL WORK

Is the term "Singing the Gospel" scriptural?

We do not meet with the above phrase in the Scriptures; but we do read of two preachers who sang hymns in the presence of an audience of prisoners; and I should not be surprised if, some day, we discover that more than the jailor and his household got saved on that occasion. I have also myself heard a Gospel preacher, well known in his day, who would stop in his preaching to sing a hymn; and he so did it that no one could doubt he was "singing the Gospel."

On the other hand, I have been in a meeting where it was announced that a brother would sing to us, and although I was seated quite near to him, the only words I could catch were a repetition, at some of the verse ends, of "Christ is dead," the rest of them being, I suppose, swallowed up in the display of musical talent. That sort of thing should not, I submit, be called "singing the Gospel" at all.

Probably the questioner has in mind the tendency, which has been a growing one in Gospel meetings for many years past, of seeking to make up for the lack of the power and presence of God, by introducing various devices, solos, duets, quartets, and all the rest of them, to attract an audience, and hold it. These, as in the old fable of the camel, having got their head in, have pressed on, further and further, until in some instances they monopolise the entire meeting, and the Gospel, like the kindhearted tailor, has been pushed out.

Of such devices, neither the preachers of apostolic days, nor the great gospellers of one or two generations back, ever found any need; and no more will the preacher of to-day, if he preaches from a heart filled with the love of Christ and burdened about the souls of perishing men.

W.R.

An effort is about to be made to create interest amongst young people by the introduction of games and discussions conducted on the lines of a "Brains Trust," followed by an address. Is this new departure commendable?

One would require to be acquainted with all the circumstances before condemning any particular "effort;" but, speaking generally, such things seem to be a confession on the part of those responsible for them, that they have lost faith in the power of the Gospel to draw sinners, young or old, to Christ. God in Deut. 12. 30 foresaw that the Israelites would desire to introduce the ways of the nations into the service of His House, and He warned them against doing so. How needful this warning was, may be seen at various points of their after history. "A new cart" for conveying the heavy Ark, such as the Philistines had used, appeared to David and his captains quite an improvement on the old-fashioned shoulder work of the Levites, (1 Chr. 13. 7; 15. 12-15). And the "fashion" of the altar at Damascus seemed to king Ahaz more likely to attract the "young people" of his day than the plain looking brasen altar in the Temple at home (2 Kin. 16. 10-16). Yet God did not acknowledge either of these innovations, but showed His displeasure. And we have no reason to suppose that He will be more favourable to the "new carts" and "fashionable altars" of our own times.   W.R.

PREACHING AND PROPHESYING
Is preaching the same as prophesying?
I presume the questioner is referring not so much to prophesying in the sense of foretelling, as to prophesying as forth-telling. Certainly foretelling the future was not exactly preaching. Forthtelling was a distinct gift in the primitive Church, enabling those who possessed it to communicate direct revelations from God. It was one of the sign-gifts, and was necessary to the Church in the absence of the complete canon of Scripture. It was a miraculous gift, and was a sign to believers (see 1 Cor. 14. 22). "He that prophesieth speaketh unto men to edification, and exhortation, and comfort" (verse 3). Apostles and prophets were foundation gifts and exist no longer to-day, except in their work in the Holy Scriptures, which they were used to give us. Preaching is a very broad term. Probably the man who prophesied preached, but to-day the term is applied to delivering an address to believers or to proclaiming the Gospel. We have the gifts of evangelist, pastor and teacher with us still, but neither of them is to be confounded with this gift of prophecy.   W.H.

THE LORD'S SERVANTS

In the light of 1 Pet. 2. 5, 9; Rom. 16. 1-6; 1 Thess. 1. 8; Phil. 2. 15, 16, 17; how do you adduce from Num. 18. 24 a class called the Lord's Servants?
This is an important question, but it would have been more impressive had the passages selected as descriptive of service contained the word. Thus verse 9 might at least have been included with 1 Thess. 1. 8, for there you have the word "to serve (**douleuō**) the living and true God" certainly applied to the Thessalonians as a church. They had all turned to God from idols to serve, and were all so far servants of God.

I am not sure that I should use Num. 18. 24 to "adduce a class called the Lord's servants." I think we may quote it, however, to show that in the case of the Levites, who were set apart for a special service (chap. 3. 5-13), and had no inheritance among the other tribes, their needs were to be supplied from the tithes of the children of Israel, which they offered as an heave offering unto the Lord. Of these the Lord said, "I have given to the Levites to inherit." This illustrates the New Testament principle ordained of God, "that they who preach the gospel should live of the gospel" (1 Cor. 9. 14). No doubt every Israelite had a responsibility to serve the Lord, but the Levites were set apart to be His servants in a special sense. The same holds good to-day: every Christian is called to serve (douleuō); but only those who have received special gifts are called to serve (diakoneō) in a public way, as evangelists, pastors or teachers. Such are not made so by special studies, though these, if kept in their place and of the right sort, may be very useful, nor by the appointment of their fellow-men, but by the call of God and the qualification of spiritual gifts. There are several words for "serve" and "servant" in the New Testament, but for our present purpose we need only consider two—"doulos", a servant or bondsman (Rev. 6. 15), and "diakonos",* a servant or minister. The former refers to the relation of all believers to the Lord—they all belong to Him and should be at His beck and call. Diakonos is the man in relation to special service. The idea that somehow a deacon is necessarily one who serves (diakoneō) tables as in Acts 6. 2, is one that dies very slowly, but the passage itself is enough to enlighten us, for Peter adds, "We will give ourselves to prayer and to the ministry (diakonia) of the word." So Peter and the other apostles were deacons, as well as Stephen and Philip, but on a different plane, though these latter were also deacons in the spiritual sense, as they afterwards proved. Men may appoint their treasurers or material deacons, because it is their money these are taking care of or distributing, but only Christ can appoint spiritual deacons, for it is His gifts they are using, It was He who appointed Paul and Apollos, of whom we read, "Who is Paul, who is Apollos, but ministers (diakonoi) by whom ye believed, even as the Lord gave to every man?" (1 Cor. 3. 5). Phebe in Rom. 16. 1 is the deaconess of the church of Cenchrea. She had had definite spiritual work entrusted to her. The Lord Himself "was a Deacon of the circumcision for the truth of God." Surely this one text should suffice to dispel the old idea of one serving tables or transacting mere business. We have the words in close proximity in Phil. 1. 1: "Paul and Timotheus, the servants of Jesus Christ, to all the saints in Christ Jesus which are at Philippi, with the bishops

---

* This is not derived, as is sometimes asserted, from dia and konis—a man who runs through the dust—because the "a" in dia is short, and that in diakonos, long, but from the same root as dioko—to pursue—a man who pursues a certain course.

and **deacons**"—that is, the overseeing and ministering brethren, those who are recognised as qualified to minister the Word. They must be men of a certain character (1 Tim. 3. 8); sound in the faith (v. 9). They should be tested, and if found blameless, be encouraged to do whatever ministry they are qualified for (v. 10). To sum up, though all the Lord's people have a service to render to Him as His **douloi-** bondmen, all are not called to public service in the church as His **diakonoi,** spoken of in a sense as "the Lord's servants."   W.H.

Should the Lord's servant, wholly out in the work of the Lord, carry with him a letter of commendation? I know one or two who do, and each assembly they visit date same, to indicate where they were last.

I hardly think any such rule could be substantiated from Scripture, especially in the case of any well-known servant of the Lord. "Need we, **as some,** letters of commendation to you?" In his case it was, or ought to have been quite superfluous, seeing the saints owed their knowledge of the Gospel to him. In the case of those starting out for the first time as separated unto the gospel—they certainly ought to carry with them a letter of commendation from their assembly of origin. But letters of commendation in New Testament days were not so easily won, as they are to-day. For such a letter implied much more then than that a person had been formerly "in fellowship" (i.e., on the roll of a certain assembly). True letters of commendation should imply much more to-day. What has been the course of the one commended? Has his or her behaviour in the house of God been really commendable? or has it been a source of anxiety to the brethren and of friction in the work? It is perfectly right to ask for a letter of commendation, and it is right, too, to be exercised before God to deserve it, by punctuality, assiduity and general godliness. As for one assembly, signing or dating a brother's letter from another, this would be all right if he asked for it, but to insist on such a thing would seem officious and even vexatious.   W.H.

ONE-MAN MINISTRY

Some believers say that one-man ministry is not condemned by the Scriptures, and quote Acts 20. 7; 1 Tim. 3. 15; 1 Tim. 1. 3; and Titus 1. 5; and the expression, "The angel of the churches," in Rev. 2. and 3.

I do not see how these passages, except, perhaps, the last, can possibly favour the idea of one-man ministry as usually understood. First, then, it is important to understand what is meant by this expression. In Acts 20. 7, we learn that "Paul preached to them," that is he ministered the Word on that occasion. No doubt being an apostle, he was incomparably the most gifted man present, and the most fitted in every way.

L

Certainly the Scriptures teach **one man at a time** ministry. Indeed, in 1 Cor. 14, one of the principles of ministry is that it should be one by one; "Ye may all prophecy one by one." There is to be no "mass production" by everybody speaking at the same time, for "God is not the author of confusion." The man who is for the time being teaching the saints, or preaching the gospel, or leading the worship,* should be allowed to do so without interruption. Nor are all called to minister the Word. Some have not received that gift. If a man can teach the saints, it does not follow he is gifted to preach the gospel, and vice versa. What the Scripture condemns is one man being put up by others (or usurping the place himself, which is, if possible, worse), to occupy a position of pre-eminence, where he alone can speak, or teach, or pray, where, in fact, he acts as if he had a monopoly of all the gifts, and so hinders the exercise of priesthood in his fellow saints, except in so far as he gives them leave. This is a denial of the Lordship of Christ, for "He has given gifts to men—some, apostles; and some, prophets; and some, evangelists; and some, pastors and teachers" (Eph. 4. 11), and also of the presence of the Holy Spirit in the midst of the saints (1 Cor. 12. 4, 7, 8, 11-12). That this has been abused by self-willed, unspiritual men, is undeniable, but we are not advocating the **abuse** of gifts or priesthood, but their use. 1 Tim. 3. 15 simply teaches that Paul had written to Timothy in order that he "might know how to behave himself in the house of God." Would that all knew it more! Anything contrary to God's Word and order is "misbehaviour." But that has nothing directly to do with the subject in hand. 1 Tim. 1. 3 is merely a selection by the apostle of Timothy for special service; of course, where God calls a man to a special service, it is for him to do it, and no one else should presume to interfere; but if he is not called to it, his unfitness will then be manifest, and it will not impress anybody for him to claim the liberty of the Spirit to do it. In Titus 1. 5 the same thing applies. These men were apostolic delegates.

In conclusion, for one man to take the place of pre-eminence among his fellow-believers, and monopolise all the gifts in his own person, is surely condemned in 1 Cor. 12, which teaches that all the members are necessary, that the gifts differ, and that it is the Spirit who guides the use of His own gifts (see vv. 4, 7, 8, 11). It would occupy too much space here to discuss the question as to the angels in Rev. 2. and 3. I would suggest in default of proof to the contrary, that as angels are, we know, "sent forth to minister to them that shall be heirs of salvation," they may do this to companies of saints, as well as to individuals, of whom, then, they may be regarded as representative in a mystical sense.   W.H.

---

* There is a great difference between ministry and priesthood. In this answer, however, I have not emphasised this, as we are dealing with general principles

PETER'S CONVERSION AND CALL.

When was Peter saved? Was it when Andrew brought him to the Lord Jesus, or was it when the Lord called him on the shores of the sea of Galilee to become a fisher of men?

The mission of John the Baptist was, amongst other things, to "make ready a people prepared for the Lord" (Luke 1. 17), and, no doubt, Peter, Andrew and the rest of the apostles were all disciples of John, having been baptized by him with the baptism of repentance for the remission of sins, waiting for the One that was to come. Accordingly, when these prepared ones came in contact with the Lord, they were ready to receive Him as Messiah. In John 1, when Andrew brought Peter to the Lord, He did not call him to repentance or faith, for he did already in a manner believe on Him, but gave Him his new name, anticipating the moment when He would build him as a living stone into His Church. This was only the prelude to the scene on the sea of Galilee. Thus Peter was called by John to repentance and faith in the one coming after him; then by the Lord to a place in His Church, and later to His service. We apply the word "saved" to everyone who has received Christ as personal Saviour, though the word carries with it more than forgiveness, namely, deliverance to and from. Peter could not receive Christ in above sense till the Lord was revealed to Israel, but no doubt all the **true** disciples of John, though they did not form part of the Church till Pentecost, were saved persons; they were of the people of God, His own, in a very real sense. In this sense Peter was a saved person before he was introduced to the Lord by Andrew, for he had been already introduced to Him by John the Baptist and had doubtless believed on Him as the One "who should come after him" (Acts 19. 4), as indeed did the Old Testament saints in a minor degree. The Lord knew him by name and was now calling him out of the Jewish fold, to belong to His flock. W.H.

SISTERS' SERVICE

Are Women's Gospel Meetings scriptural, when able brethren are available? Is not this "usurping authority over the man"? (1 Tim. 2. 11-14).

The questioner does not make clear what is meant by "Women's Gospel Meetings." For women to preach to a mixed company such as is found in an ordinary Gospel meeting is unquestionably wrong, in view of the 1 Tim. 2 passage above mentioned; for the earlier verses of the chapter show that the apostle has Gospel testimony definitely in his mind as he writes it. But if the reference be to meetings consisting of women only, then the point as to usurping authority over the man can scarcely be said to arise, and other circumstances require to be taken into consideration. For example, there are, as is well known, countries in which the womenfolk are quite inaccessible to male missionaries; and if a sister can get a few of these together, and give them the Gospel, it would seem unreasonable to condemn her for so doing. So also even in other lands, it may be possible for one or two sisters to gather together of an afternoon women who have an interval just then from their house work, and who would scarcely ever get to an ordinary Gospel meeting, held at the usual time. Here again, would it not be pressing the matter unduly to hinder these sisters from giving the Gospel to them in such a case? Yet when all allowance has been made for special circumstances, it must be acknowledged that the present trend in the outside world for women to claim equality in all things with men, has at times shown itself amongst the Lord's people; and "Sisters' meetings" of one kind or another have been set going, without any real reason for their exist-ence, other than that some of the sisters desire more prominence than they can get in the ordinary meetings of the assembly. Not only so, but even where such meetings have originated from the best of motives, they seem to have an inherent tendency to develop in an unspiritual direction, and to ultimately prove a source of mischief, rather than good, for all concerned.   W.R.

Is it scriptural for sisters in an assembly to teach in the Sunday School, and take part in prayer meetings if brothers are present?

What did the apostle mean when he said, "I suffer not a woman to teach"?

The apostle in chapter 3. 15 gives his reason for writing to Timothy, as he has done in the previous section of the Epistle, including specially it would seem, chapters 2 and 3: "that thou mayest know how thou oughtest to **behave thyself** in the house of God, which is the church of the living God." Conformity to the Apostle's directions is good behaviour in the church of God; the reverse, bad behaviour. Certainly I believe it is the reverse of "good behaviour" for sisters to take part audibly in an assembly prayer meeting; because the direction in chap. 2. 8 is, "I will that **the men** (i.e., the brethren) pray everywhere" (see R.V.). It is not here an exhortation merely to be prayerful, which would apply to brethren and sisters alike, but as to how the prayer meeting should be conducted, who should lead in prayer, etc.. The word in this verse for "men" is **"andres"** (i.e., the males), which excludes the sisters, and is quite distinct from the other word **"anthrōpoi,"** translated "men" in verses 4 and 5, and which equally includes men and women. The position of leadership is not assigned by the Lord to women; and if the woman prays audibly in the prayer meeting, she is leading the meeting for the time being, and is so far violating the Divine order of things (cf. 1 Cor. 11). This is part of the Divine regulation regarding the position of the sexes in the house of God. **"In Christ Jesus** there is neither male nor female" (Gal. 3. 28), but no intelligent person could read this chap. (2nd of 1 Tim.) and not see that a very distinct difference is made between man and woman **in the house of God.** It is the same with the question of teaching or of authority in ver. 12. The woman is not to teach or rule the man, for two reasons—as true to-day as ever they were—man's priority in creation; woman's priority in the fall (see vv. 13 and 14). These directions do not touch the teaching of children in the home or Sunday School, which seems a most suitable service for sisters. How important it is for sisters to respect the divine order in the home. When the reverse is the case, order is upside down there, and too often the sister is found trying to rule the church through her weak husband, and only disorder and sorrow can result, and a very solemn responsibility be incurred. W.H.

Is there any Scripture for commending sisters to the Lord's service at home or abroad?

We have the well known instance (Rom. xvi. 1) of the commendation of Phœbe—"a servant or deaconess (diakonos) of the church which is in Cenchrea." She was a "deaconess" in the sense that she was recognised as one to whom the care of suitable assembly work could be entrusted, *e.g.,* the women's meeting, visiting the sick, etc.. I do not think there is any indication in the Scriptures that Phœbe was journeying to Rome for anything but the Lord's service. She was a "succourer of many," so that we need not suppose she was commended merely for them for material help, but rather for spiritual help in the service she had in hand —"that ye assist her in whatsoever business she hath need of you." Dorcas was another active sister in her proper sphere. How many women's names are found in the list of Rom. xvi besides Phœbe! Priscilla, Mary, Tryphena, Tryphosa, Persis, the mother of Rufus, Julia, the sister of Nereus. The apostle commends several of them in the work of the Lord. On the analogy of Phœbe, one cannot see any difference in the apostle's commending them for the work of the Lord, if they had been moving to some other place. There is much need of godly sisters in the foreign field, especially in spheres such as Zenana work, not open to men, and such sisters would certainly not go uncommended. W.H.

What is the scriptural authority for Sisters' Prayer Meetings? I cannot find any, nor can I find anything against such meetings. Are they permissible?

I do not think that we have any direct Scripture for such a thing, but where have we Scripture for a Sunday School or even Bible-classes? None in so many words, but both are quite in accord with the spirit of the Scriptures. What objection can there be to sisters coming together privately to engage in prayer? I know of none. Such a thing seems to me to be entirely a matter of their Christian liberty. Naturally if the sisters need the use of a room for this purpose, they would ask leave of the brethren, and certainly arrange their meeting so as not to clash with any other. It would clearly not be desirable that any such meeting should be allowed to dispense sisters from attending the assembly prayer meetings, where their presence and fellowship are so helpful.

W.H.

What is the character of Sisters' Meetings, which are springing up among the assemblies? Is there any scriptural sanction for them?

It is not quite clear to what the questioner refers. We are not aware of any special kinds of sisters' meetings, which are appearing now for the first time, unless it be meetings for sisters home from the foreign field, at which only sisters are present. These seem to be of comparatively modern date, but as long as they do not clash with the ordinary missionary meetings, so as to prevent sisters attending them, it is difficult to see what scriptural principle is involved. Certàinly it seems right that sisters, who have been engaged abroad, say in India Zenana work, should have an opportunity of telling their sisters at home, who have sustained them by prayer and fellowship, what God has done by them. It is a simple matter of Christian liberty and arrangement.

But it is sadly true that there is a general revolt in the world, both the social and the religious, against God's order, and we see unprincipled men in high places going out of their way to preach the revolt of women against the relations of the sexes as laid down in the Scriptures, and urging them to claim perfect affranchisement from every so-called "disability." Unfortunately, the counterpart of all this is evident too in the religious organisations of Christendom: women-pastors, women-preachers, women-leaders in public prayer, women-soloists, etc., etc.. Indeed an important plank in certain "bodies", by which they seem to hope to attract numbers to themselves is the perfect equality of men and women, not only in Christ, but in the churches. The reverse is plainly taught in God's Word: "The head of the woman is the man" (1 Cor. 11. 3). This depends, whether people like it or not, on two great immutable facts: the priority of man in creation and the priority of woman in the fall (1 Tim. 2. 13, 14). This being said, we do not discourage; on the contrary, we wish Godspeed to our sisters, in all forms of service to which the Word of God calls them in the home and in the church, among the young, and among their own sex. Was not Dorcas' labour of love among the widows one approved of God? Nor could we say less of the Eunices, the Phœbes, the Priscillas, the Marys, the

Tryphenas, and Tryphosas, the Euodiases and the Syntyches of to-day. (See Acts 9. 36; Rom. 16. 2, 4, 12; Phil. 4. 2, 3 and Titus 2. 3, 4). W.H.

Ought women to pray at prayer meetings?

Certainly; the exhortations in the Scriptures to pray apply to women equally as to men, and if the former are not to pray, why are they present at all? But I suppose the question means, "*lead* in prayer, in the presence of men?" I believe the Scriptures leave no doubt whatever as to the mind of the Lord on this question. The prayer meeting is a church meeting, and when the church comes together as such, the women are enjoined to keep silence. "Let your women keep silence in the churches, for it is not permitted unto them to speak, but they are commanded to be under obedience, as also saith the law" (a reference I believe to Gen. iii. 16) (1 Cor. xiv. 34). Keeping silence and taking any part which involves individual publicity are clearly incompatible. The passage in chap. xi, as to the woman not "praying with her head uncovered", has been taken to be in contradiction to above. But it cannot be speaking here of public prayer. It simply lays down that "the head of the woman is the man," and that therefore what symbolises him (*i.e.*, her head) should be covered, whenever she engages in a set exercise of prayer, either aloud before her own sex only, or silently in a general prayer meeting. Her head, representing man, should be covered; for man has no mediatorial value before God; whereas man's head, representing Christ, should be uncovered and so seen. If the woman then, whose head is the man, were to lead the assembly in prayer, God's order would be reversed, and the assembly, for the time being, topsy-turvy. This is confirmed in 1 Tim. ii and iii, written towards the close of the apostle's ministry. In chap. iii. 14-15, he indicates the object of his writing: "These things, write I unto you, hoping to come unto you shortly, but if I tarry long, that thou mightest know how thou shouldest behave thyself in the house of God, which is the church of the living God, the pillar and ground of the truth." Everything, therefore, not in accord with the order laid down here is ecclesiastical misbehaviour. Have we, then, any teaching in these two chapters whether it is "good behaviour" for sisters to lead in the public prayer meeting? We have, and in such a definite fashion that the whole idea is simply ruled out. The relations of women to men, as here laid down, are not, as has been evilly suggested, the result of some supposed dislike of women on the part of Paul (how, letting alone the denial of Divine inspiration implied in such a suggestion, could anyone who has read Rom. xvi. nourish such an evil surmise?), but depend on two immutable facts—Adam's priority in creation, and Eve's priority in the fall; and the order laid down here is as much "a commandment of the Lord," as that quoted above from 1 Cor. xiv. 34 (see v. 37). What, then, does the Holy Spirit lay down through His servant for our instruction? "I desire therefore that the men* (*i.e.*, *the males*) pray in every place, lifting up holy hands, without wrath and disputing. In like manner (*i.e.*, I desire) that women adorn themselves in modest apparel," etc. (1 Tim. ii. 8, 9, R.V.). If therefore the men be directed to pray "in every place," what place is left for the woman publicly to do so, when the men are present? Submission to these plain directions no doubt requires in these days of lawlessness increasing grace on the part of sisters; but such will have an abundant reward in that day, and will never lack now a sphere of true service.

W.H.

Should a woman sing solos in public Gospel Meetings?

That a woman should not take any part in the assemblies of the saints, involving prominence or authority,† where brethren are in question, is perfectly clear from such Scriptures as 1 Cor. 14: "Let your women keep silence in the churches, for it is not permitted unto them to speak; but they are commanded to be under obedience, as also saith the law." This prohibition is extended in the following verse even to asking questions; and it applies to leading in prayer at prayer meetings, for the apostle says by the Spirit, "I will therefore that men (lit., "the men," in the sense of the males, **"andres"**, not **"anthrōpoi"**, as in verses 1, 4 and 5, which includes both sexes) pray everywhere" (1 Tim. 2. 8). It is clear that we must understand, "pray", here in the sense of leading in prayer, for women are not forbidden to pray, of course, in the sense of private prayer or joining inaudibly in the public prayers. But how far does this apply to women singing solos in public before men? Nothing is said of either men or women doing such a thing. Supposing we admit, however, for the sake of argument, that this is permitted to men as a mode of proclaiming the Gospel, surely the analogy of the other prohibitions still holds good, on the same ground, as involving prominence. If as is likely, the whole sex-question ("Adam was first formed, then Eve"— 1 Tim. 2. 13) is behind the Holy Spirit's prohibitions as to the public ministry of women ("Adam was not deceived, but the woman being deceived was in the transgression"—ver. 14), the burden of proof rests with those who would thus push women into a place of prominence before men. I judge that such a custom, as is here referred to, does put women quite out of their proper place, and should certainly be avoided. W.H.

The latest theory of those who would push women into the place of public preachers, is that the prohibitions of the Epistles

---

* '*Andres*', husbands or men quite distinct from *anthrōpoi*, the word used in verses 4 and 5, which includes women.

† "Usurp authority" (authenteō), in 1 Tim. 2, is a mistranslation, and the Revised Version gives more correctly, "have dominion." The word in later Greek writers meant "to do a thing oneself," "to act on one's own authority," or initiative. Such a thing is the very opposite of the place of quietness and subjection inculcated by the Holy Spirit in the Scriptures as the place of the true Christian woman.

as to women speaking and teaching in public, only apply to married women, and not to virgins or unmarried sisters. Is it true, as these teachers suggest, that the word "gunē," translated, "women", in 1 Cor. 14. 34, 35 and 1 Tim. 2, ought always to be translated "wife"?

On the face of it, this new theory is very improbable, for doth not nature itself teach that married women ought, if anything, to have more prominence than virgins? No one denies that the word, "gunē", can sometimes be properly translated "wife," but to say that this is always the case is not tenable by anyone who can turn up the occurrences of the word in the New Testament. Let us consider only a few of these from the Gospels. It is clear that the prohibition of Matt. 5. 28 is not limited to married women, yet the word used is "gunē." Clearly the woman (gunē) of chap. 9. 20 was not necessarily a wife. It would be strange to translate chap. 13. 33, "which a wife took." There is nothing to say that Mary of Bethany who anointed our Lord with ointment was a married woman, yet she is called a "gunē." We never hear of her husband. In Luke 1. 27 another word is used to describe Mary as a virgin—but in the next verse she is spoken of as a woman (gunē) too—which shews that "gunē" is not limited to married women. Martha also is spoken of as a "gunē" in Luke 10. 38, but there is no proof that she was married; and so we could go on, with proof after proof. These, taken only from the synoptic Gospels, suffice to shew that "gunē" is the generic term, simply denoting the female sex, so that the directions of 1 Cor. 14. 34 and 1 Tim. 2 apply to all sisters, married or unmarried alike. We note in passing that this new theory, besides being contrary to the usage of the word "gunē," entirely abandons the old arguments which, however groundless, have done duty for years, namely, that the "speaking" forbidden in 1 Cor. 14. 34 was "chattering," or that in 1 Tim. 2, "women" (gunē) may lead in public prayer, provided they are suitably attired. The same double meaning attaches to the word "anēr"— a husband, or a person of the male sex—a "man"—as it should be translated in such passages as 1 Tim. 2. 8: "I will therefore that the men pray everywhere"—the male believers, where it would be out of the question to read—"I would that the husbands pray everywhere." Also in 1 Cor. 14. 35, "Let them ask their husbands at home," might equally well be translated to meet the case of unmarried sisters, "Let them ask their men-folk at home." The only conclusion is that the new theory is an invention of the human mind without any scriptural authority. W.H.

CHILD-BIRTH

Some assert that if a woman dies in child-birth she goes to heaven, basing this on 1 Tim. 2. 15. What does that passage really teach?

The most certain thing about the passage named is that it does **not** teach what is suggested. God has but one way of saving sinners from hell and fitting them for heaven, and that way is through faith in His beloved Son. As to what it does teach, various commentators have given various replies, several of which, though differing, do not necessarily exclude one another. For it is quite probable that more thoughts than one were in the apostle's mind as he penned the words, "She shall be saved through the childbearing, if they continue in faith, and love, and sanctification, with sobriety" (R.V.). To understand them we must take into consideration the entire paragraph, from verse 8 onwards, in which Paul teaches that men have a place of public testimony to fill, from which women are definitely debarred. For this prohibition he assigns two reasons: (1) that the man was first in creation, v. 13, and (2) that the woman was first in transgression, v. 14. That verse 15 is closely connected with verse 14, the "Notwithstanding" with which it begins makes quite evident, and there can therefore be no doubt that when using the expression, "through the childbearing," the apostle has in mind the sentence pronounced by the Lord on the woman in Gen. 3. 16. In that sentence there were two parts: (1) that she was to have sorrow in childbearing, and (2) that she was to be subjected to the man. The latter of these is in keeping with the principle upon which Paul has been just before insisting; while as to the former he has, in this 15th verse, something to add, in which warning and encouragement are combined. For, just as the curse pronounced on the woman was associated with her childbearing, so also, in the words addressed to the Serpent in the preceding verse, was the provision for her salvation in the promised "Seed." Therefore the right path for her, the path in which "she shall be saved" (chiefly in the present sense of that word, so common in the epistles), is the very opposite of that public and prominent one forbidden her in verses 11 and 12. It is the path of home life and subjection; by keeping in which the very curse of Gen. 3 is turned into blessing. Compare those other words of the apostle in chap. 5. 13-15, where the dangers besetting young women who have no home cares are vividly depicted, and the way to be saved therefrom is the same as here. In fact he even uses there the verbal form of this word "childbearing," of which neither noun nor verb is found anywhere else in the New Testament. Observe also, by way of contrast, how the young man Timothy, in chap. 4. 16, is to be "saved" by going on diligently with his public ministry of the Word.   W.R.

ADORNMENT

Do the exhortations in 1 Peter 3. 3, and 1 Timothy 2. 9 refer to sisters only, or is it scriptural for a brother to adorn himself with a beautiful chain and badges, bracelet watch and gold rings?

One has heard it remarked, and that by way of warning, that we too often read the exhortations of the Bible for other people, rather than for ourselves. Thus parents know all the Scriptures about the obedience of children, but there are exhortations to parents and specially to fathers. Likewise with masters and servants, let each study first in the fear of God their own special duties and then both will run more easily. Certainly, 1 Peter 3. 3 does primarily apply to the wives—the exhortation running on, as is clear, from ver. 1: "Likewise ye wives," and I presume, then to women in general, but in verse 7 we read, "Likewise ye husbands", and certain exhortations are then addressed to them which are very important. So in 1 Tim. 2: "the men" (i.e. brethren) are to pray in every place—that is of course—lead in prayer—"holding up holy hands, without wrath and doubting." Then the apostle expresses the will of God to the women, and begins with the manner in which they should attire themselves. We might have said with our natural will and intelligence, that men needed the exhortation as much as women, but clearly the Holy Spirit judges otherwise. Some men may be effeminate and very vain, but there is clearly as a rule a stronger tendency in the female temperament, to adorn herself in the way forbidden, than in the opposite sex.

As for the brother who wears this "beautiful chain and badges, watch, bracelet, etc.," one would really have to see them before judging, but such adornment does not sound very spiritual, or characteristic of his pilgrim character. Perhaps he is not conscious of any unseemly display. We ought all to be exercised before the Lord "to adorn the doctrine of God our Saviour in all things," and that includes dress. The Christian is not called to wear a uniform, nor yet to be peculiar or eccentric in attire (there is nothing necessarily spiritual in abjuring the use of a collar, as one has seen here and there), and much less to follow the passing fashions of the day—but to dress quietly and in a way not noticeable. Let each cleanse his way in this respect according to the Word. I remember reading of the late Mr. J. N. Darby, that, on one occasion, at a time when the fashions of the world decreed that feathers should be worn, he was asked to speak to a sister who was wearing a rather prominent feather in her hat and his reply was, "the moulting time will come." We may hope that if there be brethren, who are excessively adorned in the way complained of, they will one day shed these excrescences and maybe sell them and disburse to some poor worldling, or better still, to some needy saint, and thus lay up treasure in heaven.   W.H.

MISCELLANEOUS SUBJECTS

THE GOSPEL

Is it true to say that there are two Gospels, Paul's and Peter's, each with a different aspect of the Lord's Return in view; the former described in 1 Thess. 4. 17, the latter, in Acts 1. 11 and 3. 20?

Certainly Paul's Apostolate was chiefly to the Gentiles, and Peter's to the Jews, and no doubt the **presentation** of the Gospel would vary accordingly. Compare Paul's address at Antioch in Acts 13 and that on Mars' Hill to an Athenian audience. The former is full of Jewish history and of Old Testament quotations, the latter contains neither the one nor the other. Such references would have had no special weight with Gentiles, but the Gospel in both is centred on the same Person— the Lord Jesus, and on the same work—His death and resurrection. It was the same Gospel in a different setting. Naturally things in the Acts were in a transition state, especially in the earlier chapters. An offer was still being made to the nation of Israel on the ground of resurrection, in which certainly Paul had no part, not being yet an apostle. Had they repented and been converted, no doubt the Lord would have been sent back to them (see chap. 3. 20), but the nation did not repent and so was set on one side, and God's greater purpose "from before the foundation of the world," was gradually unfolded. Paul did become the special minister of this—the mystery of Christ—but he in no way claimed the monopoly of it, which some would attribute to him, as his words in Eph. 3. 5 with reference to that mystery, show: "Which in other ages was not made known to the sons of men. AS IT IS NOW REVEALED UNTO HIS HOLY APOSTLES AND PROPHETS BY THE SPIRIT." It was revealed to them, as well as to Paul, but he became the spokesman. To say that Peter continued to the end to limit his hope to the return of Christ to the earth, is both arbitrary and unscriptural. He certainly does deal with that aspect of the Lords' return in his second epistle, but in his first epistle he speaks of "a living hope . . . to an inheritance reserved in heaven for you." This is not an earthly hope any more than the "revelation of Jesus Christ" in chap. 1. 13, or the appearance of the Chief Shepherd in chap. 5. 4. In both these it will be the revelation of Christ to the Church.   W.H.

Is it correct to say that the Old Testament saints had the Gospel preached to them as we know it? (see Gal. 3. 8). Did Abraham

know when he offered up Isaac, that his son was a type of the Son of God? or did Isaiah know when speaking of the sufferings of Christ, that He was the Son of God? or again, did Job know that his Redeemer was the Son of God?

It is not possible, it seems to me, for anyone to search the hearts and understandings of these Old Testament saints, and define the exact extent of their spiritual apprehension of the Person of whom they spake. Spiritual truths are spiritually apprehended.

Certainly the Gospel preached to Abraham was not the Good News as we know it, but it contained it, for its promise of salvation was alone through Christ. Probably the apprehension of Patriarchs and Prophets was much greater than we might naturally suppose. For instance, would it not be difficult to define the limitations of our Lord's words in John 8. 56: "Your father Abraham rejoiced to see my day: and he saw it, and was glad." This seems to refer to a special occasion, as the verbs are all in the aorist and speak of a point of time in the past, probably to the great deliverance on Mount Moriah. Abraham might have called the name of the place "Jehovah-rahah"—the Lord has provided, had he thought all was over. Evidently he perceived that what had just taken place was the figure of a greater deliverance and so he called it "Jehovah-Jireh"—the Lord **will** provide. Whether Isaiah and the prophets knew that the Messiah about whom they wrote was to be actually the Son of God, it seems profitless to enquire. They knew they were inspired by the Spirit of Christ testifying in them, and that they were speaking for us, concerning "the sufferings of Christ and the glory that should follow" (1 Pet. 1. 11). Their difficulty was not to know of whom they spake, but of what manner of time. As for Job's wonderful words, "I know that my Redeemer liveth," he would be a bold man (which boldness I neither share nor desire to share), who would undertake to limit this prophecy. It seems to me that in these words God gave His tried servant to understand a bit of "Romans" truth—"My Redeemer"; a bit of "Corinthian" truth —"He shall stand in the latter day upon the earth"; a bit of "Thessalonian" truth—"In My flesh I shall see God"; a bit of "Colossian" truth—"My Redeemer is God"; and a bit of "Timothy" truth—"I know." W.H.

THE SABBATH AND THE LORD'S DAY

Is there any Scripture for making the first day of the week or the Lord's Day, a Sabbath, on the ground that the Sabbath has been changed from the seventh to the first day?

None whatever; the Sabbath never was changed from the seventh to the first day of the week by any divine revelation in the Scriptures. The two days are quite distinct.* The former was the Jews' day, and we read in the Acts that the apostles would improve the occasion, by going to the Jewish synagogues on the Sabbath to get an opportunity for testimony (Acts 13. 42; 18. 4), and then on the first day of the week, break bread with the disciples (Acts 20.). Their idea of the Sabbath was a well earned physical rest after six days of work, but true spiritual rest they never earned. The true rest, that of the Lord's Day—the resurrection day—is rest **in Him.** We begin with this rest, and then work throughout the week. The two days ran concurrently in the Acts period, but there is not a line to show that the first day of the week was a physical rest-day. Probably the reason why the early disciples broke bread at night was that they were working all day. A certain legal sect gets a great advantage over denominational Christians owing to this common, mistaken notion. Its adherents point out that God never changed the seventh to the first day, and therefore, as they are legal to the core, they enforce on all literal obedience to what is to them the greatest commandment of all— Sabbath observance. Yet they themselves do not strictly keep it as the law enjoins, but are content with an approximate obedience, as long as you join the ranks of their denomination. It is perfectly true that "God rested on the seventh day from all His works," as recorded in Gen. 2. 2, but though God blessed the seventh day and sanctified it, there is no mention that it was instituted as a rest day for man till Millenniums later, nor have we a single case recorded in the history of the antediluvian patriarchs, nor of Abraham, Isaac or Jacob, of Sabbatical observance. What we read of Sabbatical resting in Gen. 2. 2 was no doubt coincidental with creation, but Genesis was only written by Moses, toward the end of the sojourn in Egypt. The Sabbath was not formally enjoined upon Israel till the giving of the law at Sinai in Exod. 20, though shortly before, when God gave the Manna, He arranged for a double quantity to be collected on the sixth day, "in view of the rest of the holy Sabbath," so soon to be instituted. The collecting of the manna was to go on right through the desert wanderings, so that the question was settled at the start by anticipation, how manna was to be collected for the Sabbath's consumption, preparatory to the institution of the day, in chap. 20. Later, in chap. 31. the true import of the Sabbath is explained (verses 13, 16: "Verily My Sabbaths ye shall keep, for it is a sign between me and you throughout your generations; that ye may know that I am the Lord that doth sanctify you. . . . It is a sign between Me and the **children of Israel for ever"**). The death-penalty was attached to a failure to observe it in every particular, e.g., the man found gathering sticks on the Sabbath. Nor were Israelites allowed to light a fire on the seventh day. But the Sabbath with its stringent laws was never given to the Gentile nations and still less to the church. The question as to

* The Italian Saturday is still Il Sabato.

the advantages of one day's rest in seven is not disputed here. There can be no doubt at all that in practice some such rest is called for. Doubtless governments have a perfect right to decree such cessation from work on the pattern of the Jewish Sabbath, but that is totally different from enforcing a sort of Sunday Sabbath as a religious obligation, which is one of the pillars of Christendom under the title of "Sabbath Observance" (see Colossians 2. 16). What then is the Lord's day?* It is the first day of the week, the resurrection day, on which the early disciples came together to break bread (Acts 20), and on which they were enjoined to lay by them in store as God prospered them, to avoid special collections when the apostle arrived (1 Cor. 16. 2). But because the day is not the Jews' day, it is not for that "**my** day," any more than any other day is "**my** day." This is negative, but is there no positive enforcement? The first day is what no other is said to be: "the Lord's day," and though there is not a line of Scripture, known to the writer, which enjoins a legal or Sabbatical observance of the day on anyone, if it is His day, it is peculiarly fitting to regard it as such, and to avoid anything which would unnecessarily make the day common. The way we spend the Lord's day may well be the straw which shews how the wind blows. The man who deliberately flouts the Lord's day, flouts the Lordship of Christ, and shews the direction in which his whole life is trending.

W.H.

BIBLE TRANSLATIONS

What do you think of the American Revised Version?

I do not know of any volume called the American Revised Version. The Revision of 1881 is the Anglo-American Revision. Our Revisors, numbering as active members 52, began their work in 1871; theirs, numbering only 27, a year later. As our representatives accomplished their work, it was passed on to the American Committee, who agreed, it is believed, to the larger part of the English-proposed changes, and so till the end of the second reading of revision. At the close a list was made out of American suggestions that our Revisors could not accept, though they did, we understand, incorporate in the R.V. many such suggestions: how many we shall never know. In fact the only fair way to regard the R.V. is as a joint work of the two Committees. Some of the points where the American suggestions were not finally acceptable on this side were for a more radical treatment of what are called "innocent archaisms", such as "wot" for "wist", "drag" or "drag away" for "hale", "know" for "knew". Some valuable suggestions might well have been accepted:

---

* We find this expression in Rev. 1. 10: "on the Lord's day" (kuriakē hēmera, cf. the Lord's Supper, 1 Cor. 11. 20. Kuriakos denotes, "belonging to and instituted by the Lord"). This expression is quite distinct from "the day of the Lord." The one is the first day of the week, the other a future period of judgment.

"try" or "make trial" for "tempt", where enticement to do wrong is not clearly indicated; also "demons" for "devils". The Americans would retain "we have peace with God" (Rom. 5. 1) instead of "let us have peace with God". This many scholars, e.g., the late Dr. Handley Moule, of Durham, hold to. Perhaps we may say that on the whole, the Americans were slightly more conservative than our Revisors. However, there was not much difference between the two Companies. They were all, no doubt, great scholars, but "even the wise and prudent" know nothing as such of the things of God, and "great ecclesiastics" are not generally prepared to take their place in the infant class of the babes, to whom God reveals His secrets. Unfortunately, on the crucial changes, e.g., 1 Tim. 3. 16; 2 Tim. 3. 16, the majorities of the two Companies were agreed. The moving spirit of the American Company was Dr. Philip Schaff, L.L.D., of the Union Theological Sem., New York, a very learned man of "broad" and "high" sympathies, corresponding to Drs. Westcott and Hort, the dominant spirits of the English Company, both sacerdotalists and doctrinally unsound, with whom he was closely allied. He was President of the American O.T. and N.T. Companies, and a working member of the latter. There was not much room for great divergence of thought among these three, and they no doubt exercised a determinant influence in their respective Companies. It will be seen that the question to which we have been replying is really based on a misunderstanding. Only two questions, strictly speaking, can be legitimately asked: "What do you think of the R.V.?" and "What do you think of those American suggestions, given at the end of the R.V. volume, which were not accepted by the English Company?"

W.H.

Is the Revised Version of 1881 a more accurate version than the Authorised?

Certainly in some ways it is. A number of corrections long known to be needed were made, but often the changes were unnecessary, slavishly literal and pedantic. The Revisors were only commissioned to make really necessary connections, they had no mandate to make a new translation, or 36,000 changes. Very often they have introduced alterations, which have spoiled the rhythm of the translation, without appreciably improving it. In some places they have gone out of their way to alter translations, such as 2 Tim. 3. 16, contrary to the principle adopted by themselves with analogous phrases in other places, and contrary to what many devout scholars believe to be the true sense. Certain good friends are devotees of the R.V. and read it in public with an almost childlike pleasure; but such a practice hardly tends to general edification. I remember one of these brethren reading out in a public meeting with the greatest gusto 1 Tim. 6. 12: "Fight the good fight of **the** faith, lay hold on the life eternal, whereunto thou wast called and didst confess the good confession, etc." Such literal translation is contrary to the genius of the English language. Why not, "Above all, taking the shield of the faith," or "All men have not the faith"? The differences between A.V. and R.V. may be summarised as follows: the former contains a certain number of archaisms and defective renderings, though in the main it is trustworthy and excellent: the latter offers a certain number of improvements, along with a mass of needless or harmful changes. We can no more reject the A.V. for its few blemishes, than accept the R.V. for its few betterments.   W.H.

Is it safe to use Weymouth's Translation, since it contains such error as is found in the note upon Heb. 10. 27 (page 560)?

It has been pointed out that the notes in this version are not by Dr. R. F. Weymouth, but by E. Hampden-Cook, M.A., who is said to have "Edited and partly revised" the work. In my edition of 1910 the very unsound note on Heb. 10. 27 referred to above is on page 616; and it is by no means the only one of the kind; the notes on this subject always being in the interests of what is known as, "Annihilationism," a very serious and growing heresy to-day. This teaching, however, is not confined to the notes, but occurs in the text. Wherever, apparently, the translator (or do we owe these touches to the "part revision" of Mr. Cook?) comes upon the question of the future of the wicked, the same influence can be noted: e.g., Matt. 25. 46 which is translated, "And these shall go away into the punishment of the ages, but the righteous into the life of the ages," which is the ordinary meaningless and erroneous language affected by the Annihilationist teachers. How this book found its way into my small library, I have no idea; but I neither use it myself, nor would I advise anyone to do so. The Lord's words apply here, "Take heed what ye hear," and I am convinced that all this talk about "æonian" and "the ages" is everywhere a danger-signal for those who desire to hold fast the whole revelation of God and the doctrine of Christ.   W.H.

OLD TESTAMENT SAINT

Is not the claim altogether unreasonable, that we of the present dispensation, though so inferior to faithful Abraham, and not worthy of a quarter of his reward, are a different class of saint?

It is a very serious thing to let go dispensational differences. God is sovereign, and works all things after the counsel of His own will. Supposing we admit the above estimate of Abraham's merits, as is cer-

M

tainly correct in the case of many Christians, even then our questioner's conclusion is based on a fallacy. It involves a confusion between individual rewards for faithfulness, and the place in the kingdom will depend on that, and the calling of God, which is entirely of grace. Grace is free to bestow positions of privilege, quite apart from personal merit. The character of collective blessing depends on the character of the dispensation. Thus the blessings of Israel were in one sense material blessings in earthly places, those of the Church are spiritual blessings in heavenly places. One day Israel will be the head of the nations, and instruments of blessing to the whole world, but they were never in the Church. For the differences between Jew and Gentile were very definite in Old Testament times. The building of the Church was future even in our Lord's time:—"I will build my church." But this does not say that individual saints of the Old Testament: Abraham, Moses, Joshua, David, etc., will not have a far higher individual reward, than many of the Church. An illustration may serve. At the opening of Parliament, the King on his throne, is surrounded by Peers of the Realm, Statesmen, High Officials, and Dignitaries of State, many of whom owe their position to personal merit, for having served well their King and country. But by his side is one seated nearer than any other, accorded that place, not by personal merit exactly, but by the choice of the King, to whom she occupies a relationship nearer than the Prime Minister. On the steps of the throne are the Royal Princes and Princesses, including the little grandchildren, who certainly have done nothing to deserve that honour, but they were born to it. How foolish it would then be to raise the question of their merit! Some present may have made their mark by leadership or statecraft, but that is something over and above their birthright. We must distinguish them. The Kingdom will be a sphere of rewards as well as of blessings. All believers will be in it, that is, in the earthly or heavenly side of it, but all will not enjoy the same reward. Relationships, then, depends upon grace. We do not become members of the Church by merit, but by God's own purpose and grace, and by the baptism in the Holy Spirit. The rewards of faithfulness will be crowns and positions in the kingdom.   W.H.

Were the Old Testament saints born again?

I should think there could be no doubt that all the Old Testament saints were born of God, for how else could they have had communion with Him? The carnal mind (or the minding of the flesh) is enmity against God. How could David then have had the "desire to dwell in the house of the Lord," or "thirst for the living God" unless he had received a new nature? The Old Testament saints were saved on the principle of faith, and no doubt God was revealed to their souls according to the measure of light bestowed. Our Lord speaks of Abraham and Isaac and Jacob sitting down in the Kingdom of Heaven with many from the east and the west (Matt. 8. 11), and in John 3, he lays down to Nicodemus the law of entrance into that Kingdom, namely, the reception of the new life: "Except a man be born again he cannot see the Kingdom of God." Surely this shews conclusively that Old Testament saints will only enter the Kingdom as born of the Spirit. Of course, we make a difference between that—the bestowal of new life, and the indwelling of the Spirit or the baptism in the Spirit; these belong uniquely to New Testament saints. Nor do the Old Testament saints belong to the church, but they were undoubtedly individually regenerated. As for us, it seems safer and more practical to confine ourselves to what the Word reveals. No doubt the Spirit does work on men's souls. It is just here that the mistake arises. It is to assume that the first work of the Spirit is to communicate life, whereas it is rather to create a sense of sin or at least of need. The natural man is dead in trespasses and sins, but this does not mean that he has no conscience or responsibility or capacity to listen. I have heard it said that the 3000 at Pentecost were "born of God" when they cried, "Men and brethren, what shall we do?" and, if I mistake not, that Nicodemus, to whom the Lord uttered the words "Ye must be born again," was already born again, or he would not have come to the Lord. That a theory should entail such conclusions suffices, I think, for its refutation. The reception of the new life is connected with the reception of Christ, or the revelation of God proper to the dispensation. "As many as received Him, to them gave He the power (or right) to become children of God." There the order seems clearly—faith first, then life, because the new words are "even to as many as believed (not "had believed") on His name"—"believing" is only another way of saying "receiving." I think Hebrews 6, for instance, shews us how far men may go in the things of God, and yet never have been born again, and so with other passages. Alas, how many have evinced some interest in the things of God, and even like the stony ground hearers have received the Word with joy, but it has proved later to have been in appearance rather than in reality. How solemn the call to each is, to make our calling and election sure! W.H.

SAINTS

Will you please explain the meaning of the term "Saints"? Does it apply to all believers?

A saint is one who is sanctified and the root meaning of the Hebrew and Greek words, translated "Sanctify," is to set apart for a particular purpose, the nature of which is not specified. It may be good, it may even be bad. Perhaps Psa. 4. 3 is one of the best definitions of scriptural sanctification: "But know that the Lord **hath set apart him that is godly for himself,**"—the word, "godly", being a descriptive title of the people of God—those who belong to God. Compare Psa. 50. 5: "Gather **my saints** together unto Me, those that have made a covenant with me by sacrifice." This includes all the people of God. Holiness of conduct is clearly the end in view, but we must not confuse the way and the destination. We get into great confusion if we forget this distinction, that sanctification does not in itself denote a change of character or conduct, but that in some cases it leads to that.

(1) Thus, "sanctify", is applied to inanimate objects, which cannot experience a change of character—e.g., the gold sanctified by the temple and the gifts by the altar (Matt. 23. 17, 18).

(2) It is applied to unconverted persons, whose character presumably remains unchanged. The unbelieving husband is sanctified by the wife and unconverted children by the parents (1 Cor. 7. 14).

(3) It is applied to the Lord who never needed a change of character. "Say ye of Him whom the Father hath sanctified and sent into the world." "For their sakes I sanctify myself" (John 10. 36; 17. 19).

Progressive sanctification is the continued response of the believer, whom God has set apart, to His purpose for him. Joseph was set apart by Pharaoh to rule Egypt, so he did not go back to the prison but gave himself to the work. Paul was set apart for God's service and he was "not disobedient unto the heavenly vision." If God has sanctified us at the moment of our conversion, it is for us to sanctify ourselves, and this will undoubtedly shew itself in our conduct. It is a very sad thing when believers can talk of sanctification and yet are but little sanctified in their ways. True sanctification consists in conforming our ways to what God has revealed in His Word for us. The Scriptures meditated upon are a great means in the hands of the Spirit for sanctifying the people of God (John 17. 17).   W.H.

DISCIPLESHIP

Is there any difference between a Christian and a disciple? (John 6. 66). Are all Christians disciples? (Luke 14. 27, "cannot"). Can one be a disciple and not a Christian? What of Judas (John 12. 4). Can we speak correctly of "discipleship" as a call distinct from conversion?

In Acts 11. 26 we read "that the **disciples** were called Christians first in Antioch," so here the two terms are not to be separated, especially when one remembers that, as I firmly believe, the new name was God-given. The verse runs as in the Revised Version: "And it came to pass, that even for a whole year they were gathered together with the church, and taught much people; and that the disciples were called Christians first in Antioch," so that the "gathering together," "the teaching," and the naming of the disciples in the new way, were three concomitant facts of spiritual significance. The English word, "dis-ciple," is from the Latin, **"dis-co,"** "I learn by study," and is the equivalent in the New Testament of **"mathētēs,"** "a learner" (from **"man-thanō,"** "I learn"). It is certainly used in two meanings like our word "scholar." A boy goes to school and becomes at once "de facto" a scholar in that school, though he may not yet have learnt anything, but he is regarded according to the intention of his being there. He may not become a "scholar," in the deeper sense of being proficient for years to come; in fact he may never deserve the name. So we read in John 4. 1, "Jesus made and baptized more disciples than John." They became disciples by obeying the Lord's call. They professed themselves His followers and they were **marked** as such by baptism. But of some such we read in John 6. 66, "Many of His disciples went back and walked no more with Him." But did this take the Lord by surprise? In no way was He surprised, for in ver. 64 we read, "But there are some of you that believe not. For Jesus knew from the beginning who they were that believed not and who should betray him." When these special disciples became such the Lord knew they were not real. It is the same to-day. Perhaps one of the best proofs that we ever did believe in the Lord Jesus is to be continuing daily to believe on Him. There is, it is to be feared in these days of easy profession, a possibility of taking ourselves too easily for granted. The exhortation is "that they that have believed in God might be careful to maintain good works" for "faith without works is dead" (Titus 3. 8; James 2. 20). However, there were many who proved themselves true disciples, in the primary sense, but such were called to go on and become disciples in the fuller meaning. To do so meant and ever means a costly thing, as Luke 14. 26-33 testifies. It involves the sacrifice of natural ties, of self, yea, of all. Though the word "disciple" does not occur in the New Testament after Acts 21. 16, the verb **manthanō** occurs often, e.g. Eph. 4. 20; Phil. 4. 11; 1 Tim. 2. 11; 2 Tim. 3. 14 (and for the false thing, see 2 Tim. 3. 7); and the commission of Matt. 28. 19, "Go ye therefore, and teach all nations" (marg. "make disciples of"), carries the thought on throughout the present dispensation, and the truth is prominent in the Epistles. Philippians 3 is a good example of true discipleship: "What things were gain to me (i.e., as a religious Jew) those I counted (lit. I have counted: **hēgēmai**) loss for Christ. Yea doubtless and I am counting (**hēgoumai**) all things but loss . . . but dung, that I may win Christ" (vv. 7, 8).

A man said to a friend of the writer, "I would give the world to have what you've got." "Well," replied my friend, with a smile, "that is about what it cost."   W.H.

DIVORCE

Is it clear from Scripture, as some affirm, that divorced persons can under no circumstances be remarried, till the death of one partner?

This is a question that is often being raised in these days, in which the sacredness of the marriage tie has fallen so low in the eyes of an ungodly world, that divorce is treated as a light thing of no account. We may be sure that God's thoughts on the subject have not changed since He wrote by the prophet Malachi, "The Lord, the God of Israel, saith that He hateth putting away," as He terms divorce or "dealing treacherously," (Mal. 2. 16). In reply to the Pharisees, our Lord explains that, if Moses suffered (a man) to write a bill of divorcement and put his wife away, it was a permission "for the hardness of their heart," but not at all according to the original purpose of God, who made man and wife to be one and remain one, as long as life lasted. He concluded with the clear and determinate words: "What therefore God hath joined together, let not man put asunder" (Mark 10. 4-9).

Are there, then, no circumstances in which God Himself puts asunder what he has joined together? I believe there is one which our Lord points out clearly in Matt. 5. 32, and again in chap. 19. 9, in both of which verses, while emphasising the sacredness of the marriage tie, and the sin of divorce, He does make an exception—"saving for the cause of fornication," and "except it be for fornication." When that cause arises and is clearly proved, divorce should take place, and when this is so, it is not man putting asunder what God hath joined, but God himself. If so, then the parties are henceforth as truly no longer married, as though they had never been united, or as though one was dead. The question of the remarriage of the guilty party is not under discussion. We have nothing to do with it, for one guilty in so gross a manner clearly must cease from the fellowship of the saints, and be put away into the outside place; but as for the offended party, I believe he or she is free before God to remarry, though only in the Lord.   W.H.

What should be our attitude towards a brother who is divorced and remarried, while his first partner is alive? Should he be allowed to minister the Word to the saints? What saith the Scriptures?

It entirely depends on the circumstances of the case. If the person in question was granted a divorce by the Courts against his wife, on account of marital unfaithfulness, then I believe the divorce was according to Scripture, because the above cause is specifically admitted as sufficient by our Lord·Himself (see Matt. 5. 32; 19. 9). In this case the divorced persons are not to be regarded as merely separated, but as no longer married. If this were so in the case before us, then I hold the brother was quite free to remarry, and should certainly be allowed to minister to the saints, if otherwise qualified to do so. But if he were the guilty party, or if he obtained a divorce on any less plea than the scriptural one mentioned above, he violated God's Word in being remarried; he is an adulterer (see Matt. 19. 9), and should not be allowed to break bread, and, of course, not to minister to the saints.

W.H.

FAITH

Did our Lord always use the Hebrew word, " 'emunah," for "faith"? Does it mean not a doctrinal belief but a heart attachment to someone? Did our Lord use the Hebrew word in a Greek form, as the New Testament was written in Greek, not Hebrew?

It seems impossible to say what word the Lord used for "faith," as He is generally supposed to have spoken in Aramaic—a Syriac language allied to Hebrew but not identical with it. The Greek Septuagint translates the Hebrew **'emunah** by **pistis**—faith, and also the Hebrews **'emeth** and **'amanah**—all kindred words. Who can say which of these three words He used? I question whether we can rightly say that **pistis** necessarily implies heart attachment to a Person, though that is the result if we believe the word of a great Benefactor. If we believe God we shall trust and love Him. W.H.

POLITICS

Is it right for a Christian to give a vote to a candidate in a Parliamentary Election?

We certainly have duties to perform to those who occupy positions of rule in our midst, one is to **obey** the laws they make. If I do not, I shall get a bad conscience and I shall pay the penalty. "For this cause **pay** ye tribute also: for they are God's ministers, attending continually on this very thing." So I must pay taxes, and rates, and custom dues when I enter the country (see Romans 13. 5-7). Then I am enjoined to **pray** "for Kings and all that are in authority, that we may lead a quiet and peaceable life in all godliness and honesty" (1 Tim. 2. 2). I am, moreover, to "**honour** the King" and indeed all to whom honour is due, but as far as entering into the political contests of the country, I see no directions in God's Word, and I believe the whole thing is alien to our position as "strangers and pilgrims" in the world. If it be retorted, "What would become of the country, if all believers were of this opinion?" my reply is, it would become neither better nor worse by such a contingency, but the believers would become much better. What wordly associations would they be spared! What unequal yokes with the ungodly! "Let the dead bury their dead, but go thou and preach the gospel," or pray that God may overrule. "The effectual fervent

prayer of a righteous man availeth much," which cannot be said of the
political work of a righteous man; the only effect of which is to shear
him of his locks, and bereave him of his joy and testimony. "Our citizenship is in heaven." "As the Father hath sent me into the world, even so
I send you." All agree that the Lord did not enter into political movements. He was not sent for that,—are we? All the various political
combinations will never succeed in really making the world better,
for there is a factor, they do not recognise, and certainly cannot neutralise
—sin. It is a solemn thought that when at last all political differences
are sunk, and the whole world cemented in one great alliance, it will
be in deadly, open opposition to God and His Christ.   W.H.

ASTRONOMY

As one interested in astronomy I should value some light on
"Joshua's long day", the shadow on Ahaz' dial, and the Star
of Bethlehem. What do you judge the last-named was? How
could the day be prolonged or the shadow be reversed, except
by the arrest of the rotation of the earth? And if so why was
not everybody jerked off it?

These have long been stumbling blocks to many, and every effort
has been made to deny or explain them away. I have heard it stated that
all that happened was that thick clouds shielded the combatants from
the heat of the sun; but how could this be described as "the sun hasted
not to go down about a whole day" (Josh. 10. 13), or as a unique event
in the history of the world? (see ver. 14).

It is no more necessary, I judge, to take literally the **standing still**
of the sun and the moon in the account of the Divine miracle granted to
Joshua, than to admit that the sun literally rises and sets. The Astron-
omer Royal and the "Nautical Almanack" use such conventional
phrases, without going sponsor for their scientific accuracy. The point
of the expression in Joshua 10. 13, is that the putting forth of Divine
power produced the result of the sun, etc., continuing above the horizon,
and not hastening to go down by the space of a whole day. I do not think
the length of the day would be directly affected were the sun to stand
still literally, for of course that depends, as the questioner points out,
on the rotation of the earth on its axis.

That a mighty miracle was performed we know (Josh. 10. 13, 14),
how, we know not, but if the Esquimaux can enjoy each year a day of
6 months, owing to the declension of the polar axis, and the curvature
of the earth's surface, might not a slight temporary increase in the
former produce the necessary prolongation of the day at the latitude of
Gibeon—31.50 N.?

As for the shadow on the dial of Ahaz, one would suggest that the
shadow might be made to travel back ten degrees, without the earth's

rotation being arrested or reversed, by the slight temporary depression or elevation of the panel of the dial. Such depressions and elevations have no doubt taken place over immense areas in the history of the earth, and the solution suggested would be very simple to Divine power. There is, however, this against it, that whatever happened seems to have had a wide-spread effect noticeable to an astronomical people like the Chaldeans living at some distance, for the scientific mission by the ambassadors of the princes of Babylon was to "enquire of the wonder that was done in the land." Whatever may be the way in which God was pleased to perform these two wonders, we are safe, I am sure, in affirming that no one was "jerked off the earth" in consequence. If we accept the great miracle of Gen. i. i, and we do unhesitatingly, is it difficult to believe that the Creator can control the movements of the earth and of the heavenly bodies?

As for the Star of Bethlehem, I think the only thing to be said which conforms to the scriptural account is that it was a special heavenly body, which the Magi had no difficulty in recognising as HIS star or in following, and that it led them to Bethlehem where the young Child lay. There are many things in the heavens "which are not dreamt of in our philosophy," and where so little is really known, especially in the present collapse of the Newtonian system, is not the best and safest reply, "I do not explain, I believe"?   W.H.

OLD TESTAMENT

GENESIS

In Gen. 1. 20 we read, "Let the waters bring forth . . . fowls that may fly"; but in Gen. 2. 19, "Out of the ground the Lord God formed . . . every fowl of the air." How may these two statements, in which there is a seeming contradiction, be reconciled?

In Gen. 2. 19 it is stated definitely that the fowls were formed "out of the ground"; but there is no such statement made with regard to the waters in Gen. 1. 20, of which the second clause should be rendered, as in the R.V., Newberry, Young, etc., "And let fowl fly above the earth in the face of the expanse of the heavens." Even in our A.V. this is suggested by the italics used for the second "that," and is given in the margin as the correct Hebrew rendering.   W.R.

What is the meaning of "Replenish the earth" (Gen. 1. 28)? Is it to restock or refill? Does this prove that human beings were on the earth prior to Genesis 1?

"Replenish" in English has the sense of restocking, but the Hebrew **millē**—here so translated, means simply "to fill," as in verse 22 of sea-creatures, "**fill** the water in the seas"; or in Gen. 6. 13, "the earth was **filled** with violence," where there is no sense of "re-filling," any more than here. Adam is definitely called "the first man" (1 Cor. 15.45), and we are on the only safe ground in holding to that. All the rest is the merest speculation. Scientists differ by millions of years as to the age of the skeletons or fragments of skulls they find, but we cannot go into that question here.   W.H.

Has "the tree of knowledge of good and evil" (Gen. 2. 9) any connection with the command to "be fruitful and replenish the earth"?

I do not think there is any possible connection between the command "to be fruitful and multiply" and the "tree of knowledge." One they were told to do, the other to abstain from. The account in Gen. 1 is the general account of man's creation as a human being—the head of the lower creation; the second chapter gives us the same thing in detail. Man is here viewed as a moral creature in relation with Jehovah-Elohim, and responsible to Him. As such he must be tested. Obedience or disobedience is impossible in the absence of a distinct command or prohibition. Accordingly Jehovah proposes a test of the very simplest description, including three things which made it very easy to pass it— (1) a **permission**: "of every tree of the garden, thou mayest freely eat"; (2) a **prohibition**: "but of the tree of the knowledge of good and evil thou shalt not eat of it"; (3) **a warning**: "for in the day that thou eatest thereof thou shalt surely die." I do not think there was anything peculiar about the tree. It may have been a pomegranate or an apple of some kind, we are not told. God chose it and appointed it to be the test tree. Hence certain results would ensue from partaking of it. Had man obeyed God and abstained from the forbidden fruit, he would not, I believe have needed another test, but would have become, with all his descendants, immune from sin and death. It was "by one man sin entered into the world, and death by sin." But may we not say that man got one thing by the fall—a conscience, that is the knowledge of good, without attaining to it, and of evil, without avoiding it.   W.H.

Is there anything in the Scriptures to show that there is a lengthy period of time between verses 1 and 2 of Gen. 1?

I think there certainly is. The first chapter of Genesis does not describe the creation of the heavens and the earth, that is limited to verse 1. Rather, it describes the re-creation of its surface conditions in preparation for the creation of man. If verse 2 describes the original condition of "heaven and the earth," why is all reference to the heavens omitted, and the earth alone singled out? It may well be to remind ourselves that Genesis was written in Hebrew, which, like other languages has its rules, which cannot be ignored. By Hebrew use, the "and" at the beginning of ver. 2, shows that verse 1 does not stand as a mere summary of what follows, indeed it precludes such a notion. Verse 1 stands as a fact by itself. To this is added another fact: "And the earth was (in the past, but at some unexplained time) void and waste." I have before me a paper which professes to give the "wonderful story" of the creation of the earth (it certainly is very wonderful as the author describes it!), in which he asserts "The earth **was created without form or waste and desolate**" (though this is not what the Bible says) and later, "The perfection of the earth in its waste and void form passes all human conception" (!) I think we must agree that for such a condition to be described as "perfect" is certainly inconceivable for sober Christians. "The sons of God shouted for joy," when God laid the foundations of the earth (Job. 38. 7), that is, I take it, as in verse 1, for no such mention of such a thing occurs later in the chapter; but would they have rejoiced over a scene "without form or waste and desolate" and plunged in thick darkness? It takes a powerful imagination to conceive such a thing; that, it must be confessed by most of us, "passes all human conception." Of course, we must not confuse the "heavens and earth," the Universe or stellar heavens and earth of verse 1, with the atmospheric heavens and the surface land of vv. 8 and 9. It is to these latter that reference is made in Exodus 20. 11: "For in six days, the Lord **made** (not created) heaven and earth, the sea and all that in them is." This leaves a long space (between these two distinct works of God: the creation of the "heavens and the earth" in the beginning, and "the making of things on the earth by His own mighty power, to prepare it as a habitation for man) for the laying down of the geological strata, coal measures, etc. The Word of God certainly does not teach us that such (e.g., the 1,300 feet of the Jurassic deposits) were laid down in six days, and the Bible has more to fear from its friends than from its enemies, if they teach so.   W.H.

Ought we to interpret Gen. 1. 1 as referring to the original creation of the universe quite distinct from the rest of the chapter, or is it the summary of what follows?

I certainly believe it is the former. If it were the latter, should we not expect the creation of both the heavens and the earth to be enlarged upon in the rest of the chapter, whereas the "heavens" in the sense of v. 1 are not mentioned again, nor is it the creation of the earth which is brought before us after Gen. 1. 2, but the refurbishing of its surface conditions to prepare it as a habitation for man. The verb, "to create," occurs only twice in the body of the chapter, at the start of animal life and at the start of human life, vv. 21, 27. Does not the fact that the earth alone is described as "without form and void" (**tohû wābhohû**) indicate that something had happened to it, which had not happened to the universe at large? There is nothing in verse 1 to suggest that the original creation was not perfect. That the earth was created a scene of desolation, is distinctly negatived in Isaiah 45. 18: "He created not the earth a waste" (tohû) (R.V.). These Hebrew descriptive words for "without form and void" occur together in only two other places, i.e., Isaiah 34. 11: "the line of confusion (tohû) and the stones of emptiness"(bohû); and Jer. 4. 23: "I saw the earth and lo, without form and void" (tohû wābhohû), and both describe scenes induced by judgment. We are not called to speculate as to why the earth, created as we believe, so perfectly (Gen. 1. 1) that "the sons of God shouted for joy" (Job. 38. 7), became so imperfect. We cannot imagine them doing this, if the creation they witnessed was a waste of desolation, covered with waters and pitch darkness. Between verses 1 and 3 may occur a period of untold millions of years, sufficient for the laying down of the stratified, fossiliferous and cretaceous, rocks, the coal measures, etc.

But is this division of the chapter a mere arbitrary device, or is it justified by the form of the Hebrew employed? I will cite as a reliable witness Dr. E. B. Pusey, for many years Regius professor of Hebrew at Oxford. He discusses the question in the Preface to his "Lectures on Daniel the Prophet," p.p. xvii.-xxiv. He writes, "Of the forms of speech which could have been chosen, to express past time, **that** has been chosen, which least connects the date, when the earth was one vast waste, with the time when God created it." Both were in past time, but there is nothing to connect "those times together." "Had Moses intended to say that the earth was waste and desolate when God created it, the idiom for this would have been "and the earth without form and void" (without the verb) (page xviii.)—What Moses does write "has no force at all, unless it be used to express what was the condition of the earth in a past time previous to the rest of the narrative, but in no connection in time whatever with what precedes." Dr. Pusey also points out that the "and" by which verse 2 is also united to v. 1, shows that v. 1 does not stand as a mere summary of what follows. There are two distinct facts—the primal creation in v. 1, and a subsequent condition of the earth "without form and void."   W.H.

Had the body of Adam physical life, before the Lord God "breathed into his nostrils the breath of life"? (See Gen. 2. 7).

I should consider such an idea most speculative. How do we know what interval, if any, occurred between the formation of Adam's body and the inbreathing of the breath of life? There is no necessary thought of Adam's body lying without breath, but even so, that would here prove nothing, for the body of a person who has just died has still the blood in it, but there is no life in the blood. James by the Spirit distinctly affirms that "the body without the spirit is dead" (chap. 3. 26), therefore Adam's body could not be alive before receiving the spirit. It is striking, but not surprising, how the Bible confirms true science, which are both products of the same divine Mind; but science is a very different thing from "scientists" self-styled, and their theories. Scientists used to make merry at the idea of a body made of the dust of earth. Now it has been discovered that the fourteen elementary substances said to be found in the dust of the earth, do occur also in the human body in greater or lesser quantities. The word for "breath" in Gen. 2. 7 is n^eshāmā, a word only used of God: 2 Sam. 22. 16 (blast); Job. 4. 9; 32. 8; 33. 4; Isa. 30. 33, etc.; or of man: 1 Kings 15. 29; Job 26. 4; Isa. 2. 22; 57. 16, and in contrast with animals—see Joshua 11. 11, 14, where "everything that breathed was slain", but the cattle were left alive.   W.H.

Would it be correct to say that the two trees mentioned in Genesis 2. 9, viz, the "Tree of Life," and the "Tree of the knowledge of good and evil," are only symbols, and not literal trees? Does the latter tree represent the limit or boundary of the liberty God gave to Adam?

Mere statements of opinion, even when said to be shared by "leading theologians," carry no weight, unless supported by scriptural proof. Personally, I have never heard of any theologian or indeed anyone else who held such views as stated above, although of course, modern unbelief hates the story of the fall of man, and would fain get rid of it at any cost. But if the tree of knowledge is only a symbol, representing "the limit or boundary of the liberty God gave to Adam," (!) (whatever this exactly means), of what is the tree of life a symbol? The two trees are mentioned first in Gen. 2. 9: "And out of the ground made the Lord God to grow every tree, that is pleasant to the sight, etc.: the tree of life also in the midst of the garden, and the tree of the knowledge of good and evil." Here the same Hebrew word for tree is used throughout, and in each case the tree is said to have been made to grow out of the ground. Surely they are literal trees all through. Again, in verses 16 and 17 the tree of life is not mentioned apart from the trees whose fruit might be eaten; the only exception being the tree of the knowledge of good and evil. This would be very strange if it were intended to convey the injunction that they might eat of all the literal trees (including the symbolic tree of life), but that they must not eat of the symbolic tree of knowledge. It is the same in chap. 3. 2, "We may eat," says Eve, "of the trees of the garden, but of the fruit of the tree which is in the midst of the garden, God hath said, Ye shall not eat of it." Here we see that the tree of knowledge was like the tree of life, in the most accessible part of the garden, even the midst. How could two abstract symbols be in the midst of the literal garden? Eve clearly understood the tree of knowledge to be a literal tree, and so it is to the end of the chapter—"Hast thou eaten of the tree?" etc. The tree of life certainly was literal too, bearing fruit capable of maintaining the human body in its daily wear and tear—a kind of elixir of life, so much sought after since. I see that Cruden gives an interesting note in his Concordance under "Tree" in this sense: "Tree of life so-called because it was a natural means of preserving man's life and freeing him from all infirmities, etc., during his abode on earth." This agrees with the fact that after the fall God deprived his creatures of access to the tree of life, lest their existence should be indefinitely prolonged in a sin-haunted body. Perhaps the great ages of the early patriarchs resulted from the fact that Adam and Eve had eaten of this life-preserving fruit. What then was the tree of knowledge? We do not know what kind of fruit it bore, except that it was very attractive, but God chose it to be the test tree for their obedience (for every moral creature, angel or man, has had to be tested). Much objection has been raised by unbelief against so much depending on such a simple thing as eating a bit of fruit! But surely the simpler the test, the easier of fulfilment, and the greater the responsibility of failure. If God had chosen to give them only one tree to eat from, and forbidden all the rest, that would have been, of course, perfectly legitimate, but much more difficult for them. Instead God gave man in His love an infinitely easy test, and solemnly warned him of the dreadful consequences of disobedience, but he fell and was alone responsible. How great the contrast of the Second Man! The commandment He received of His Father was to lay down His life. This was a test infinitely difficult of passing, but He came out triumphant: "He was obedient unto death, even the death of the cross. Wherefore God also hath highly exalted Him, and given Him a Name which is above every name," etc. Had Adam passed his easy test, I do not think he would have been put to another, but would for ever have been in blissful harmony with God's will. I think what we have seen shows that we may safely reject the ideas referred to by our questioner, as unsupported by Scripture, and so contrary to the facts. W.H.

Help will be valued upon Genesis 4. 4, 5, where we read that God had "respect" to Abel and his offering and not to Cain and his, and Romans 2. 11, where it is said that there is "no respect of persons with God."

We can be quite sure that this latter verse is ever and absolutely true. The Greek word, "to have respect of persons," means, "to receive the face of a person," i.e. to look at the outward appearance—at the gold ring and the gay clothing, at the feature and the stature, etc., whereas we know that "God looks, not at the outward appearance, but at the heart." When, therefore, we read that God had respect to Abel and his offering, we must divest ourselves of any idea of favouritism or unfair preference on His part. In fact, the Hebrew word in Genesis 4, "to have respect," has no thought of respect of persons, but of looking to someone, or something. The word is used in Psalm 119. 117—"I will **have respect** unto thy statutes continually"; again in 2 Sam. 22. 42—"They **looked** but there was none to save," and also in Isaiah 17. 7—"In that day shall a man **look** to his Maker." We may be sure that had it been righteously possible, God would have accepted Cain as well as Abel. The key to the verse is in Heb. 11. 4—"By faith Abel offered unto God a more excellent sacrifice than Cain . . . God testifying of his gifts." It was not that Abel was "more excellent" than Cain, though very likely he was, but that his sacrifice was more excellent; so that God simply had respect to Abel because of his sacrifice. The expression, "by faith," shows, I think, conclusively that God had revealed how his creatures were to approach him, "for faith cometh by hearing, and hearing by the word of God." No doubt, Cain's sacrifice was beautiful enough, but it was Cain's way, not God's. It was merely the work of his hands— of the same vegetable kingdom as the fig-leaves of which Adam and Eve had made themselves aprons. Abel offered from the first-fruits of the flock and of the fat thereof, i.e. the slain lamb. In Abel's offering there were two things: there was something which spoke of his repentance, it was as though he admitted that he deserved the death of the victim; and there was something, too, which spoke of the lamb of God, without blemish, slain before the foundation of the world. How far Abel apprehended the truth we cannot say; he obeyed and all was known to God. We are blessed according to His appreciation of the infinite Person and work of Christ, not according to ours, which, however, does determine our enjoyment of our blessings.   W.H.

"By faith Abel offered unto God a more excellent sacrifice than Cain . . . God testifying of his gifts, and by it he being dead yet speaketh." Why were Abel and his offering accepted, and Cain and his offering rejected? Does the expression "more excellent" imply that there was something excellent in that of Cain?

The word translated, "more excellent," is literally "more," or "greater," and is used either of quantity or quality, here clearly of the latter. It does not imply any excellence in Cain's offering, otherwise we should not read, "but unto Cain and to his offering **God had not respect.**" Also later God said to him, "If thou doest well (i.e., come like Abel with the slain victim, implying that Cain **had not done well** in offering his fruit of the earth), but if thou doest not well (i.e., persist in thy refusal of that offering;) sin* lieth at the door; i.e., croucheth like a wild beast ready to spring. There can be no reasonable doubt that God had revealed to His fallen creatures how they must approach to Him—even by the **minhah** or approach offering—a lamb of the flock. Clearly this was to be slain, as the expression—"of the fat thereof" shows. . . . Had there been no such revelation, how could Abel have had "faith" to draw near in this way?

I remember years ago seeing a blind Kabyle reading in Braille type by the wayside in North Africa, what I learned to be this fourth chapter of Genesis. When we asked him why God accepted Abel's offering, he replied, "There was something in it which spoke of the Messiah." This is true; no doubt that sacrifice was a type of the Lamb of God slain at Calvary, and foreshadowed the bruising of the Kinsman's heel. Abel confessed himself worthy of death and appropriated the death of the victim in his stead. Cain's offering was of the same vegetable kingdom as the fig-leaves of the aprons of Adam and Eve, and as the host of flour and water, which the Romanist and Ritualist offer on their "altars," all of which are bloodless offerings and powerless to remit sin.   W.H.

---

* Not "the sin-offering" as is sometimes illogically suggested. This is a secondary meaning of the word which came into use much later, e.g., in Leviticus 16, but could not attach to this its first occurrence. Such an interpretation really makes no sense of the passage. If you come with the offering you will be accepted and if you do not, you will still be accepted. No, if you do not, then "be sure your sin will find you out."

Should the word "sin" in Gen. 4. 7 be "sin-offering" as some translators suggest?

The fact is that the same Hebrew word, "ḥaṭṭāth", may be rendered either "sin" or "sin-offering," according to the context in which it occurs. In the Authorised Version it is given, "sin," about 17 times, and as "sin-offering" about 120 times; while it is also in a few places rendered, "punishment" (for sin). All this is of interest, because it suggests that the sin, its punishment, and the offering which atones for it, are in a sense equivalent in value, since one word serves for all three.

But naturally the above fact makes it difficult in a few passages to decide which rendering into English is the proper one. In Gen. 4. 7 the Newberry Bible gives, "sin offering" in its margin; and this rendering well agrees with the verb "lieth" which follows, for this, as the Newberry margin also points out, is a word used of animals "crouching" or lying down. It is the same Hebrew word that occurs in Gen. 49. 14 of an ass crouching down under its load, and in Isa. 17. 2 of flocks lying down to rest.

Of course, the distinction between the various kinds of offerings was not made known at that early time as it was afterwards in Leviticus. Yet God's act in clothing Adam and Eve with coats of the skin of some animal was doubtless an object lesson to them of the necessity for blood-shedding, as pointing the way to remission of sins. Probably most of the sacrifices offered in times prior to Leviticus took in more aspects of truth than the one, and might be considered from different points of view.

If the verse be taken in this sense, the meaning would be, "If thou art a well-doer shalt thou not be accepted? but if not, a lamb or other animal is readily available, lying as it were at thy very door, to be made use of in offering for thy sin."

On the other hand, in Cain's previous "gift-offering" there was no acknowledgement of sinnership on his part. He had assumed the place of a "well-doer," without having a right to it.

An interesting point which would follow on this view of the passage is that Cain, instead of shedding the blood of the readily available animal, that it might cry for mercy on his behalf, went out to shed his brother's blood, which cried for vengeance on him (v. 10).   W.R.

In Genesis 6. 3, "The Lord said, My Spirit shall not always strive with man." Did this apply only to that dispensation?

The words in question are in close connection with the intermarriage of "the sons of God" and "the daughters of men," described in Genesis 6, by which the barrier between the Seth line and the descendants of Cain was broken down. The sons of God did not make the worldly women godly, but the reverse process took place, as is nearly always the case to-day under similar circumstances. A great increase of evil was the result, and the world was filled with violence and corruption. This was foreseen by God, Who gave utterance to the above solemn declaration, adding, "for that he also is flesh." Man had had at least two thousand years to show what "evolution" could do, if such a principle existed. Surely he would have developed into something supremely excellent. Let verse 11 reply: "The earth also was corrupt before God and the earth was filled with violence." Is not such a development more consistent with the doctrine of the fall of man, than of his constant and consistent "evolution" toward a higher ideal? We need not be surprised if the Modernists wish to expunge the first ten chapters of Genesis. To believe in the evolutionary hypothesis one must not only deny the plain statements of Scripture, but shut one's eyes to the facts of history and human experience. However, God adds in grace, "Yet his days shall be an hundred and twenty years"; that is, I take it, there was to be still a respite of that duration. There is no evidence to show that the testimony of Noah, the "preacher of righteousness" ceased before the flood. But as far as I know, God nowhere pledges Himself to continue pleading with men till the end of their careers. Indeed, such emphasis is laid on immediate decision, that it would be the height of folly to count on even one more chance. We know that when the Man of Sin will be revealed God will send on those, who will have refused the truth, a "strong delusion that they may believe the lie" (2 Thess. 2. 10-12). This moment however has not yet arrived, and it would be both unprofitable and presumptuous to attempt to show that the Spirit has ceased to strive with anyone still alive, for this is to invade the divine prerogative, and pretend to "search the heart."

W.H.

Does Gen. 6. 1-5 refer to the marriage of angels with human beings? If not, please give reasons for rejecting this theory.

I believe it is a purely fanciful speculation, without any real base of probability or Scripture. What is in question is rather the intermarriage of men of the Seth line—the godly seed, with women of the Cain line—the worldly seed. Hitherto these had kept apart, as they always should. It is affirmed that the expression, "sons of God," always refers in Scripture to angels. It certainly does, I judge, in Job. 1. 6; 2. 1 and 38. 7. But these are holy angels; Satan with the brazen audacity, which characterises him and his followers, presents himself among them, but there is no reason to suppose he or other fallen beings could thus be described. Or are we asked to believe that holy angels were tempted by lust toward women? The whole idea is grotesque. Angels are of an entirely different order of creation to human beings. But analogous expressions such as, "sons of the Most High," and "sons of the living God" (Psa. 82. 6; Hosea 1. 10), seem to refer to men, and in the New Testament the exact expression is applied to God-fearing men and women (see Matt. 5. 9, 45; Rom. 8. 14, 19). And I judge it is the same here. Then it is stated, but quite incorrectly, that the result of this "unholy union" was n^ephilîm, which is the Hebrew word for "giants" anglicised, so as to convey to our minds something mysterious and monstrous. But a careful reading of the passage shows that these "giants" were already in the earth at the time, **before** these marriages took place, and then we get the words, "And also after that (giving the facts of verse 2), when the sons of God came in unto the daughters of men," the result was "men of renown," not half-angels—half-men, but true human beings, so that the union seemed to succeed, but God only saw increased depravity in the earth.

The only other place where this word, **"n^ephilîm"**, occurs is Numbers 13. 33: "And there we saw the **giants,** the sons of Anak (which come) of the **giants.**" There is not a hint that these were not real men, like the rest of the Anakins, e.g., Goliath and his four brethren, etc. It is asserted that **"n^ephilîm"** is connected with a verb, "to fall," and that these mysterious beings were "fallen"—"apostates," etc., but Gesenius denies this meaning, and says the true meaning is, "fallers on," or "attackers," i.e., violent men. There must, it is supposed, have been a further "angelic intermarriage" after the flood to account for the appearance of these "giants" in the land of Canaan; for all the first company would have been drowned! We may suppose what we like, but there is no hint of such a thing in Scripture. As a matter of fact the whole speculation seems directly opposed to our Lord's own words, when speaking of the resurrection state:—"In the resurrection they neither marry, nor are given in marriage, but are as the angels of God in heaven" (Matt. 22. 30), ergo.—the thing is impossible. This surely ought to suffice to show that "the angels that kept not their first estate," of Jude 6, have nothing to do, as has been affirmed, with the "sons of God" in Genesis 6. Such speculations have no real scriptural ground, and we should avoid them carefully.   W.H.

What do you consider to be the date of the Flood? How do you account for the fact that apparently no Archæologist has ever made reference to it?

Archæology and Palæontology both concern themselves with ancient things, but whereas the latter is chiefly taken up with geological strata and fossils, the former is more occupied with traces of **human** life and activity, such as ancient ruins, inscriptions, clay tablets, pottery, papyri, etc. Thus the discovery in 1887 of the Tel-el-Amarna clay tablets in Egypt, dating before the Exodus, and proving how early the art of writing was known, and the high state of civilisation existing in the times of the patriarchs, was an Archæological discovery. So also was the discovery of the **papyri** letters in Eliphantine, an island in the Nile opposite Assuan, in 1904 and 1907, dated in the time of Nehemiah and containing the very disputed words in Daniel which the Higher Critics asserted could not possibly have been known at his epoch. As for the assertion of our questioner, he would hardly expect a wooden structure like the ark, to survive five or six millenniums. But the American Archæologist, Mr. C. Leonard Woolley, in his actual researches in and around Ur of the Chaldees, has found within the last few months what he and others believe to be conclusive evidence of the flood from the archæological and palæontological stand-points. They had been excavating a royal graveyard outside the walls, resting on what had been many centuries before, the city dust-heaps. Going down 60 feet, they came across still more wonderful graves, and then lower still, unexpectedly, a layer of clay about 8 feet thick, distributed uniformly on all sides, and completely interrupting the civilisation and containing no pottery, indeed evidently laid down in a very brief period all at once. But underneath again were found traces of a much older and quite distinct civilisation. Mr. Woolley had not the slightest doubt that this clay was deposited by the Noachian flood, which has always been supported by such wide-spread and persistent Sumerian and other traditions. Dr. Stephen Langdon, professor of Assyriology at Oxford supports this view. The reality of the flood, of which believers have no doubt, supported as it is by the most explicit account of the Word of God, as well as by universal tradition, and also on geological grounds, which cannot be gone into here, has like every other record of the Scriptures, been questioned or denied by the enemies of the truth. Now in His own good time God allows these archæologists the honour of discovering, on their own lines, indisputable proofs of the truth of His Word, to the confusion of His adversaries; and so it will be, we may be sure, for every disputed Scriptural record.   W.H.

Which of Noah's sons was the eldest?

In Gen. 9. 24 Ham is spoken of as Noah's younger (or "youngest," R.V.) son, though some commentators would connect the expression there with his grandson Canaan because of the prominence given to the latter in the curse of verse 25. This leaves us as the two elder ones, Shem and Japheth, and the decision between them depends on the rendering which is accepted as the correct one of Gen. 10. 21. The A.V. gives it, "Shem . . . the brother of Japheth the elder," which would imply that Japheth was oldest; but the R.V. with more probability translates it, "Shem . . . the elder brother of Japheth," which would give the honour to Shem.   W.R.

Are we to suppose that the injunction to abstain from blood (Gen. 9. 4) holds good to-day? If not, how quote verse 6 to justify capital punishment? Or does 1 Tim. 4. 1-5 allow us to eat all things even blood, so long as we give thanks?

Sometimes we have to complain that the divisions of the chapters in our Bible cut the sense, but in this case the division between chapters 8 and 9, though it may seem awkward, is really useful to the right understanding of the passage. God's covenant with man, guaranteeing him from a recurrence of the deluge "while the earth remaineth," with an uninterrupted continuance of harvests, seasons and diurnal changes is contained in the two closing verses of ch. 8. This is known as the Noachian Covenant. In chapter 9. 1-7 we have God's **blessing** on Noah, accompanied by (1) a promise, v. 2; (2) a provision, v. 3; (3) a prohibition, v. 4; and (4) a penalty, vv. 5, 6, in which penalty was embodied the entrusting of government into the hands of men. All this, however, was apart from the covenant, which is unconditional, and which is brought up again in vv. 9-12, thus: verse 9—its universality; 9-11—its perpetuity, v. 12—its token, the rainbow.

As for the prohibition and penalty attaching to the blessing, we should not know whether they were perpetually binding on man or the children of God, apart from the rest of the Scriptures. As far as I can see, the penalty attaching to murder has never been abrogated and is binding to-day as a governmental act, on rulers to whom God has entrusted the sword for executing justice on evil doers, especially murderers. As for the prohibition to eat blood, it held, as we know, under the law (see Lev. 17. 10, 11), and in the Acts period (15. 20), but has, I believe, been abrogated for us, not only by such a Scripture as the questioner quotes; but by such a verse as 1 Cor. 10. 25: **"Whatsoever is sold in the shambles,** that eat, asking no questions for conscience sake." The heathen knew nothing of slaughtering after the Jewish method, so as to be sure of draining off the blood of the animal.

According to this verse, therefore, a believer might eat whatsoever was put before him, asking no question for conscience sake. Then it does not say, "But if any say unto you, This has the blood in it, eat not," for that question we may infer was of no importance, but rather, "This is offered in sacrifice unto idols, eat not" (v. 28). It is perfectly clear then that the injunction not to eat blood does not apply to Christians to-day. The prohibition in Acts 15 really has nothing to set against this, as things were then in a transition state, and the Corinthian Epistle had not been written.   W.H.

In Gen. xi. 26 we read, "Terah lived seventy years and begat Abram, Nahor, and Haran," and in v. 32, "and the days of Terah were two hundred and five years and Terah died in Haran."

Now, taking 70 from 205, would make Abram 135 years when Terah died, while we know from Gen. xii. 4 that Abram was 75 years old when he left Haran, and from Acts vii. 4 that he did not leave Haran till Terah died.

It is not necessary to believe from Gen. xi. 26 that Abram, Nahor, and Haran were all born in the same year, but simply that Terah had no children till he was 70, and then had three sons born at intervals. In Gen. v. 32, we have an instance of the same thing, when we read that "Noah was five hundred years old, and Noah begat Shem, Ham, and Japheth," and yet Gen. x. 21 tells us Japheth was older than Shem. It is equally clear that Abram was not the eldest of the three brothers. He and Shem are put first because of their importance as the progenitors of the chosen race and the Messiah. It is generally held that Haran was the eldest, born when Terah was 70, and that Abram came into the world 60 years later. This would account for the fact that he and his nephew Lot, son of Haran, seem to have been much of the same standing. Besides, we are distinctly told that Abraham was 75 when at the death of Terah, he departed out of Haran. He was born, therefore, when his father was 130 years of age.   W.H.

What are we to gather from the scriptural reference to Melchizedek? Was he a man of God of his time—a priest of the Most High, indeed, or was he actually the Son of God?

In dealing with this perennial question one wishes to recognize the views of some esteemed brethren who take a contrary view to that expressed here. They believe that this was a Theophany or appearance of the Second Person of the Godhead in a temporary human form (all such theophanies being necessarily Christophanies), and that Melchizedek was actually the Son of God. But is there nothing in the fact that he is said to have been made "**like** unto the Son of God"? You don't say a man is like himself; he **is** himself, but he may closely resemble someone else. However, many such theophanies occur to us—the man who wrestled with Jacob at Jabbok, the man with sword in hand who appeared to Joshua, the angels who appeared to Gideon and Manoah, etc. One thing characterises them all. At first the appearance seems only human—an ordinary man, but at the end the superhuman, nay the Divine, character of the appearance is manifested. Note this in each of the cases referred to above. This is entirely absent in the case before us. In no sense are we informed that Abraham recognised Melchizedek as Divine, but he did recognise him as a king and as a priest of the Most High God, who ministered to his bodily needs and was greater than himself, therefore able to bless him and worthy to receive tithes from him. Again, Christ might have appeared as a King, but surely not as King of a well-known place as Salem or Jerusalem. Whoever Melchizedek was, his office as priest only shews that God in calling Abraham for a certain object, had not for that left all the world in darkness, but still had notable witnesses, outside His purpose concerning His chosen people to be. Those who stand for the deity of Melchizedek rely much on the expressions used by the Spirit of him in Heb. 7, and make rather "in and out" efforts to shew how each expression applies to Christ. I believe the whole effort is in vain, for these expressions if forced to apply to Christ must be interpreted either of Him in incarnation or of Him before incarnation, and this cannot be done. As a matter of fact, I believe there is one point and only one which the Holy Ghost would emphasise by His **silence** in Gen. 14 concerning the parentage, genealogy, birth and death of Melchizedek, and that is the **conventional** continuity and endless character of His priesthood. The meaning is not that this man was actually without parents nor that he is alive somewhere to-day, but that by the fact that he appears suddenly on the page of Scripture and that no mention is made of his decease, he is thus qualified to be an apt figure of Him Who is Priest for ever after the order of Melchizedek and Whose Priesthood can never pass to another. W.H.

Abraham believed God as to his seed, and it was "counted unto him for righteousness" (Gen. 15. 6), but when promised the land he asked for a sign. Would he not have had it at once had he believed, without having to wait four hundred years for his descendants to inherit it?

I do not think there was necessarily any unbelief in Abraham's asking whereby he should know that he should inherit it. God often dealt thus with his servants of old—with Moses, Gideon, Hezekiah, etc., and granted them signs to strengthen their faith. As a matter of fact, Abraham did not ask for a sign. His question brought out the basis on which God was acting, namely, on the ground of covenant. The heifer, the she-goat, and the other sacrificial victims, all spoke of Christ the One true covenant Victim. Verse 18 makes it clear that the terms of this covenant assured the land, not personally to Abraham, but to his seed, and this was, we need not doubt, the original purpose of God. Stephen understood it so, for he emphasises the fact that "God gave Abraham none inheritance in the land, no, not so much as to set his foot on" (Acts 7. 5), nor does He in any way attribute this to Abraham's unbelief. It would clearly have been premature for a single family to inherit a vast territory, like that indicated in Gen. 15. 18-21; nor had God's time come to expel the owners of the soil, for "the iniquity of the Amorites was not yet full." W.H.

How many years were the children of Israel in bondage in Egypt? Gen. xv. 13 and Acts vii. 6 indicate that the Israelites

would be afflicted 400 years. Exod. xii. 40 states the sojourning of the children of Israel in Egypt was 430 years; Gal. iii. 17 states that from the giving of the promise to Abraham to the giving of the law by Moses was 430 years. How can the above Scriptures be reconciled to one another? What does Gen. xv. 16 mean?

There is no real discrepancy, but we must note what is said in each case, and take into consideration the universal permission of an occasional use of round numbers. The difficulty of Gen. xv. 13 arises from limiting the "four hundred years" to the AFFLICTIONS in Egypt, whereas the expression governs the whole verse, and I feel sure that the earlier expression, "thy seed shall be a stranger in a land that is not theirs," would go further back even than Egypt, to what characterised the lives of Isaac and Jacob and his sons, even before they went down there. That this number—400 years—then is to be taken in this general and round number way, seems clear from Gal. iii. 17, which dates the 430 years exactly from the promise to Abraham (Gen. xv.) to the giving of the law in the third month of the Exodus (see Exod. xix. 1). This tallies with the 430 years of Exod. xii. 41, a verse generally read as though it affirmed that the children of Israel sojourned that period in Egypt, whereas it says that the sojourning (*i.e.*, I take it as including the whole period of their sojournings either in Canaan or Egypt) of the children of Israel (who dwelt in Egypt) was 430 years. That is, they were always characteristically "sojourners." This is shown, I believe, to be the case in Gen. xv. 16, where the Exodus is specified as to occur not 400 years after their arrival, but "IN THE FOURTH GENERATION." This harmonises with the genealogies of Exod. vi, where we learn that Kohath was a son of Levi, and that Amram, the father of Moses and Aaron, was the son of Kohath, *i.e.*, four generations. Notice the ages of Levi (v. 16), of Kohath (v. 18), of Amram (v. 20), which specify this.   W.H.

Why is it said of Abram in Gen. 15. 9-10, "The birds divided he not"? Why were the animals divided, but not the birds?

We see in verse 9 that, preparatory to making a covenant with Abram, the Lord God directed him to take certain sacrificial victims—a heifer of three years old, a she-goat of three years old, a ram of three years old, a turtle dove and a young pigeon. On the slain carcases of these the covenant was to be made. Evidently God had given general directions as to sacrifices and the clean animals to be offered up, as we gather from the knowledge of such things displayed, for example, by Noah, who knew the animals that were clean, that is, fit for sacrifice, and unclean—unfit (see Gen. 7. 2, 3); and the same with the fowls—of the unclean two would suffice, but the clean were to go in "by sevens"—as these latter would be needed for sacrifice (chap. 8. 20). No doubt, too, the order to be followed was divinely revealed. The very word for covenant,

"bᵉrîth," from an unused root, "bārath" means "to cut, to hew"—
that is, the victims were divided—he who made the covenant had to
pass between the victims. In Jer. 34. 19, those who made the covenant
passed between the calves—all typical of Christ, the Mediator of the
New Covenant. According to Heb. 9. 17 the covenant is always made
on the ground of dead things (i.e. sacrifices). I am convinced that the
idea at the back of this whole passage is that of a covenant, not a testament or will in our modern sense, as the next verse seems clearly to
show. If we turn to Exodus 24, there is no thought of a will being made,
but of a covenant being established between Jehovah and Israel. How
then could the second covenant be a testament? The R.V., although
somewhat hesitatingly retaining "covenant" up to verse 15, translates
verse 17: "For a testament is of force where there hath been death"
(margin, "over the dead"). The word, "dead," is plural, and therefore
must, one would judge, refer to the covenant victims, rather than to
the testator of a will—who is a single individual. I suppose that the
reason Abram did not divide the birds is that they formed one offering
in two parts—one of which was placed on each side, representing a
cut victim. To those who have a deeper appreciation of the work of
Christ, the Word divides the victim even between the . . . joints and
marrow (Heb. 4. 12). W.H.

Was the mountain in the land of Moriah, upon which Isaac was offered, the mountain on which our Lord was crucified?

It is important to notice the exact wording of Scripture. Abraham
was told to go "INTO THE LAND OF MORIAH" and offer Isaac there "UPON
ONE OF THE MOUNTAINS WHICH I WILL TELL THEE OF," so that the exact
place is unknown. Probably the principal height was Moriah, and the
scene of Gen. xxii one of the lower spurs of the mountain. Mount
Moriah or Zion is actually at Jerusalem, and in 2 Chron. iii. 1 we learn
that Solomon's temple was there. Now, it is nowhere said in Scripture
that Calvary was a mountain, or even a "green hill," but is simply called
"a place." But then it must be remembered that the whole of Jerusalem
and its suburbs is a mountainous district. We read of "the mountains
round about Jerusalem" (Psa. cxxv. 2), so that though our Lord was
crucified outside Jerusalem, and not actually on Moriah, it MAY have
been the spot where Isaac was offered. All the verbs of John viii. 56
are in the aorist tense, and thus connect Abraham's joy with a special
incident, when "he rejoiced to see the day of Christ." And he called
the name of the place "Jehovah-Jireh" i.e. "in the mount of the Lord
it shall be seen." The word, "mount," is the Hebrew for "mountain"
(har), and includes a mountainous district, properly describing "the
place called Calvary." However, we must not be too dogmatic on the
point raised. W.H.

What is the special significance of Joseph's second dream (Gen. xxxvii. 9-10)?

Both the dreams of Joseph look forward to the day when the One of whom he is so striking a picture, the Lord Jesus, "the man of sorrows," "despised and rejected of men," crucified, but now exalted, will be recognised and owned even by those who once refused him. The first dream, of course, had its literal fulfilment in Egypt, when Joseph's brethren bowed at his feet. It will also have its further fulfilment "when He comes whose right it is," and "they shall look on Him whom they pierced," and shall "mourn because of Him." Then the affecting scenes between Joseph and his brethren will be re-enacted in deeper measure between Christ and the saved remnant of Israel (Zech. xii. 10, 11), which will form the nucleus of the nation, over which He will reign for ever. "The Lord God shall give Him the throne of His father David, and He shall reign over the house of Jacob for ever, and of His kingdom there shall be no end" (Luke i. 32, 33). This is the earthly kingdom—the sheaves speak of a harvest—"the field is the world." The second dream has had no fulfilment yet. Rachel had already passed away. Jacob never bowed to Joseph, but he will to the greater than Joseph. If "the sheaves" point to an earthly sphere, the sun, moon, and stars point to another, the heavenly. This goes further and higher than the first. The earthly kingdom is everlasting, but not unlimited (see Ps. 72. 8). The second will be universal, as well as everlasting. It will include the other, but go beyond it. Of that kingdom, too, Christ will be the Crown, the Centre, and the Sum.   W.H.

Are we to understand from Gen. 44. 5, 18 that Joseph actually used divination?

Though divination was common in Egypt, it is hard to suppose that a pious believer in the true God like Joseph should use such practices. Moreover, as one in close touch with God and an interpreter of dreams, etc., what drawing could he have to descend to such heathenish customs?

The cup may very well have been similar to those used for this purpose, but it is noticeable that Joseph only says to his brethren, "wot ye not that such a man as I can certainly divine?" (v. 15), without affirming that he did. It must be admitted that his word through his steward does seem to go further. The true explanation may be that in order to keep up his character before his brethren, as an orthodox Egyptian, so as the more effectually to carry out his deliberate plan for their conviction and restoration, he might feel justified in conveying this momentary impression that he divined. If he did so, it is not commended nor is it specifically blamed. We are aware in reading the Old Testament that even men of God had not the same standards of truthfulness, that are binding on us to-day. The word here for "divine" (**niḥēsh**) is translated, "I have learned by experience" (Gen. 30. 27), and "did diligently observe" (1 Kings 20. 33), but generally, "to use enchantments" (2 Kings 17. 17; 21. 6). Such divination is strictly forbidden later in the Word of God (see Lev. 19. 26; Deut. 18. 10).

W.H.

EXODUS

In Exodus 4. 10, Moses complained of "slowness of speech" but Stephen in Acts 7. 22, says he was "mighty in words and in deeds." Is there not a contradiction here?

Someone has said that Moses took forty years in Egypt learning all the wisdom of the Egyptians, then forty years in Midian learning that he knew nothing after all, and then forty years in the wilderness in learning what God could do with a man who had learned he knew nothing. There is no contradiction here, or anywhere else in the Scriptures. We read first what Stephen says of Moses, that he was "mighty in words and deeds," that is, during his Egyptian period; then what Moses says of himself. Perhaps there are good speakers to-day who are genuinely diffident, and are quite unaware they are eloquent. It does not matter, if they think so, as long as they are all the more cast upon God and fulfil their ministry. Possibly the reverse is true of some of us. We think we can speak and would do well to be more often silent. In fact, the word is addressed to all "Let every man be swift to hear, slow to speak, slow to wrath."

W.H.

Why do so many preachers speak of "the destroying angel," in Exodus 12?

It seems due to a mistaken idea of what took place on the Passover night, based on a careless reading of the whole passage. Exodus 11. 1 speaks of "one plague more." Exod. 12. 13 refers to "the plague" and ver. 23 to "the destroyer," but there is no such agent mentioned, either in Exodus, Heb. 11, or elsewhere in Scripture, as "the destroying angel," in connection with the deliverance from Egypt. Moses says in chap. 11.4—"Thus saith the Lord, about midnight will I go out into the midst of Egypt"; see, too, ch. 12. 12: "I will pass through the land of Egypt this night, and will smite all the firstborn in the land . . . I will excute judgment"; and v. 23: "For the Lord will pass through to smite the Egyptians, and when He seeth the blood . . . the Lord will pass over the door, and will not suffer the destroyer to come into your houses to smite you." God is Light and God is Love—God is at once "Avenger" and "Redeemer," and neither work does He entrust to an angel, however exalted. It was God vindicating His holy claims against sin, who passed through the land in judgment; it was God who intervened in mercy wherever He saw the blood of His own providing, sprinkled. The two words for "passing through" ('ābar), and "passing over" (pāṣaḥ), are quite distinct. This latter is found again in Isaiah 31. 5: "As birds flying, so will the Lord of hosts defend Jerusalem; defending also He will deliver it and **passing over** (pāṣaḥ) He will preserve it." That is, He will interpose between the enemy, who, it may be suggested, will then be attacking Jerusalem from the air, and His people.   W.H.

How is it proved that what became the first month in Ex. 12 was formerly the seventh month of the year?

This happens to be a very appropriate question, for the very day on which the answer is being penned (October 5th), the Jewish New Year commences. According to the Jewish Calendar, it is the 1st of Tisri in the 5,690th year since the creation of Adam. Thus the Jewish civil year begins to-day (one finds many of their shops closed in consequence), but the month Abib or Nisan is the first of the sacred year. Clearly a change took place at the first Passover, or else why should the Lord say, "This month shall be unto you the beginning (or head) of months, it shall be the first month of the year to you"? It was to be the **chief** month of the year and the **first** month. To say that January was to be the first month to us would mean nothing, but to say it of July would change our reckoning altogether. Thus it is when a man is born-again; all that is past is cut off as nothing worth, and he now begins to live. So the Redeemed Nation was as though "born in a day"; they began to live Godward. Josephus in his "Antiquities" mentions this change of month as a well-known historical fact, but that Tisri remained the first month as before, for civil contracts. The terms for "month" and "moon" are allied in Hebrew as in English. The Jewish month was a lunar one of 30 days and the 14th of Abib was the full moon. There were 12 months in the year, amounting to 360 days about, and every third year there was an additional or intercalary month, Veadar, or "the additional Adar," though this is not referred to in the Bible.

The months were usually designated by their numerical order, e.g. "the second month" (Gen. 7. 11); "the fourth month" (2 Kings 25. 3), and this number was generally added to the name of the month, e.g. "in the month Zif, which is the second month" (1 Kings 6. 1), or "in the third month that is the month Sivan" (Esther 8. 9). This system was also used in naming the days of the week, Monday was "one of the sabbaths," Tuesday "two," Wednesday "three" and so on, translated as we have it, the first, second, and third days of the week. The question has been raised as to whether the months in Genesis 7. 11; 8. 4, 5, 13, 14 date from Abib or Tisri. The latter would certainly seem more likely, as any records kept by Noah would naturally have been dated thus. If that is so, then the flood began on the 17th of Bul (October-November), and the Ark rested on Ararat on the 17th of Abib (March-April), the tops of the mountains were seen on the first of Thammuz (June-July); on the 1st of Tisri (September-October) the waters had disappeared, and on the 27th of Bul the earth dried.

Perhaps a table of the months with their corresponding Feasts and modern months would be helpful to enable readers to enter more intelligently into the Bible references.

SACRED YEAR.	FEASTS.	Corresponding Modern Months.	Months of Civil Year.
1. NISAN or ABIB (green ears). Exod. 13. 4; Deut. 16. 1	14th Passover. 16th First Fruits. Barley Sheaf. Lev. 23. 10. 15th-21st Days of Unleavened Bread	Mar.-Apr.	7th
2. ZIF or IYAR (Splendour). 1 Kings 6. 1.	14th Little Passover. Num. 9. 10, 11.	Apr.-May	8th
3. SIVAN. Esther 8. 9.	Feast of Weeks or First Fruits of Wheat. Lev. 23. 17. Pentecost.	May-June	9th
4. THAMMUZ.	Fast to remember the taking of Jerusalem. 2 Kings 25. 3; Zech. 8. 19.	June-July	10th
5. AB.	Fast. Zech. 8. 19.	July-Aug.	11th
6. ELUL. Neh. 6. 15.	1st Feast of Trumpets, Lev. 23. 24.	Aug.-Sept.	12th
7. TISRI or ETHANIM 1 Kings 8. 2.		Sept.-Oct.	1st
	10th "Day of Atonement"; "the Fast." Acts 27. 9; Zech. 8. 19.		
	15th-21st Feast of Ingathering or Tabernacles, Lev. 23. 34-36.		

SACRED YEAR.	FEASTS.	Corresponding Modern Months.	Months of Civil Year.
8. BUL or MARCHE-SHVAN. (Rain). 1 Kings 6. 38.		Oct.-Nov.	2nd
9. CHISLEU. Neh. 1. 1.		Nov.-Dec.	3rd
10. TEBETH. Esther 2. 16	Fast. Zech. 8. 19.	Dec.-Jan.	4th
11. SHEBAT. Zech. 1. 7.		Jan.-Feb.	5th
12. ADAR. Esther 3. 7; 9. 17.	14-15th Feast of Purim.	Feb.-Mar.	6th

Inter-calary month, every 3 years, Ve-Adar (extra-Adar).

W.H.

Please say why the Fourth Commandment is dealt with as being morally different from the rest. It will be agreed that it is wrong for Christians to steal, murder, etc. Why should it not be morally wrong for Christians not to observe the seventh day of rest?

We regard the Fourth Commandment as being morally different from the others, because apart from God's revealed will for Israel as regards it, no natural conscience could possibly know that it was wrong to work on the seventh day, as is found to be the case by missionaries in heathen lands. The nations round Israel were never put under the Sabbath law, knew nothing about it, and are never held responsible for not keeping it. At least, I know of no place in the Prophets where not keeping the Sabbath is charged home on them. A Gentile who sets himself to keep the Sabbath is doing himself a wrong, as he is now a debtor to do the whole law. He is taking on himself that which in no way appertains to him. He is going beyond what is written, which is wrong, just as coming short is, too. The Sabbath was a sign between Jehovah and the children of Israel for ever, and was never given to the Gentiles at all (Exodus 31. 16, 17). All the other Commandments are repeated in substance in the New Testament, but the Sabbath is only referred to in Colossians 2. 16, to warn believers not to allow themselves to be placed under bondage in that respect—"Let no man judge you," etc. A certain modern heretical sect, of which Sabbath-keeping is a distinguishing feature, is so far right, in maintaining that the Sabbath was never changed from the seventh day to the first. The first day of the week, on which our Lord rose from the dead, is not a Sabbath at all; it is the Lord's Day; though believers, are glad to profit by the usual freedom from secular employment on that day, to occupy themselves with the Lord's service. The breaking of bread was usually in the evening (e.g. Acts 20), because believers were at work all day in those times. Really a fictitious conscience has grown up as regards this question. We ought not to violate our conscience or that of others, by forcing or disregarding it, but to get an enlightened conscience from the Word of God. W.H.

What do the words in Exod. 30. 32, with reference to the Holy Anointing Oil—"Upon man's flesh shall it not be poured"—mean? Were the priests the only exceptions to this rule, or were the Levites also anointed?

I do not think it is correct to speak of the priests as **exceptions** to the rule. The Holy Anointing Oil was specially made for their anointing, and as far as I can find out, we never read of the Levites being anointed with it. This was called "an oil of holy ointment," and it was compounded after the art of the apothecary of the four principal spices: pure myrrh, 500 shekels;* sweet cinnamon, 250; sweet calamus, 250; and cassia, 500, "after the shekel of the sanctuary," compounded "with a hin"† of oil. The ointment represents the perfections of Christ, as revealed in the Gospels, and applied to the believer in the power of the Holy Ghost. All believers possess this anointing (2 Cor. 1. 21; 1 John 2. 20). Here in this chapter we see that the tabernacle itself, the ark of the testimony, the table with all his vessels, the candlestick with his vessels, the altar of incense, the altar of burnt offering with all his vessels, and the laver and his foot (seven objects in all)—all speaking of Christ, were set apart to be most holy unto the Lord; and whatsoever toucheth them must correspond with their holy character and be holy also. Then in v. 30 the anointing of Aaron and his sons is directed, and Moses is told to say to the children of Israel that Jehovah ordained, "This shall be an holy anointing oil unto Me, throughout your generations" (that is, it was only to be used for sacred anointing). "Upon man's flesh it shall not be poured" (that is, it was not to be used for ordinary purposes or ordinary persons). "Neither shall ye make any other like it" (It was not to be imitated.). "Whosoever compoundeth any like it, or putteth any part of it upon a stranger, shall even be cut off from his people" (vv. 31-33). This is a warning against imitating the unction of the Holy Ghost, when out of communion with Him, through unjudged, uncon-

---

* A Shekel weighs just over ½ oz.

† A hin of oil, according to Josephus, equals a little over one-and two-fifths of a gallon.

fessed sin, or of professing to give the Holy Spirit, as "bishops" of the Church of England do, to their candidates for "confirmation," many of whom are not only unregenerate, but have never even been taught the necessity of the new birth, except in the sense of "baptismal regeneration," that terrible and soul-destroying delusion.

The HOLY OIL was also used for the anointing of God's kings, e.g., Psa. 89. 20: "I have found David, My servant; with My holy oil have I anointed him"; though we should not have known from 1 Sam. 16. 1 that the oil that Samuel used was "holy oil." In 1 Kings 19. 16 Elijah is directed by Jehovah to anoint Elisha, the son of Shaphat of Abel-Meholah, to be prophet in his place. God had his successor ready, but we are not told whether this was always done in the case of God's prophets, and if so, whether it was done with holy oil.

In the case of our Lord, we know that He was born the Christ, i.e., the anointed One. "To you is born this day in the City of David a Saviour, which is **Christ** the Lord." Later, He was anointed as God's prophet on Jordan's banks, when the Holy Spirit descended upon Him: "God **anointed** Jesus of Nazareth, with the Holy Ghost, and with power" (Acts 10. 38; see also Isa. 61. 1; Luke 4. 18). In Acts 2. 36, Peter tells the people, "God hath made that same Jesus, Whom ye have crucified, both Lord and **Christ**." Clearly also is the Lord God's anointed King, e.g., Psa. 132. 17: "There will I make the horn of David to bud: I have ordained a lamp for Mine anointed."   W.H.

What Tabernacle is referred to in Exodus 33. 7-11? According to the sequence of the chapters, the Tabernacle was not yet built. Some have inferred from Deut. 10. 1-5 that Moses made the Ark during this interval, between his destruction of the first tables and the bringing down of the second, as a receptacle for the second tables which could not be entrusted to Israel. What do you say to this?

Certainly Deut. 10. 1 to 5 would bear the above interpretation, "and I made an ark of shittim wood . . . and I put them (the tables of the Lord) in the Ark which I had made." Yet we must remember that in Deuteronomy, Moses is admittedly only giving a summary of things, so that events spread over a period, are compressed, as occurring almost synchronously. For dates and details we must consult Exodus and Numbers. In Exod. 25. 10 the directions as to making the Ark are given to Moses, during his first sojourn on the Mount, but were only communicated to the children of Israel in chap. 35. 12, after his second sojourn there. Only in chap. 37. 1 does Bezaleel actually make the Ark of shittim wood, in which the tables were eventually placed. We cannot admit that there were two Arks; for it is evident in Deut. 10. 5 that the tables were to be permanently in the Ark which Moses is said to have made for them—"and there they be as the Lord commanded me." This was actually done in Exod. 40. 20: "And he took and put the testimony into the ark." There is nothing really contradictory to this in the passages quoted. As for the tabernacle mentioned in Exod. 33. 7-11, it could only have been a temporary tent of meeting called "The tabernacle of the congregation" (Exod. 33. 7), to which anyone went, who sought the Lord." After the sin of the golden calf, God would not go up in the midst of the people, so this tent was pitched without the camp. When the actual Tabernacle was constructed and erected, Jehovah once more took His place in the midst of His people (Exod. 25. 8; 29. 45; Num. 2. 2), no doubt, on the ground of sacrifice. The other temporary tent would naturally fall into disuse.   W.H.

LEVITICUS

Heb. 9. 22 states that "almost all things are by the law purged with blood," and Wm. Lincoln has pointed out that the only sin offering which did not involve blood-shedding was that of Lev. 5. 11. The peace-offering was never made without the burnt-offering and then blood was shed. Who paid for the burnt offering? Did one offering avail for two persons?

To reply to the last parts of the question first: I judge from Lev. 1. 2, that each offerer brought his burnt-offering at his own expense, and if so, it was an individual offering. There was, however, the continual burnt offering (see chap. 6. 9-13), and I should think that was provided by the priests from the offerings to them by the people. I do not think the peace-offering was necessarily accompanied by a burnt-offering. They were quite distinct, but it would be true to say that the burnt-offering, representing the whole offering of Himself by Christ to God, was constantly accompanied by a meal-offering (see Num. 28. 11-13; ch. 29; Jud. 13. 16-19), representing the spotless humanity of our Lord Jesus Christ, tested in every possible way. The bloodless offering to which Mr. Lincoln refers was the tenth part of an ephah of fine-flour offered for a sin-offering (Lev. 5. 11). This represents the lowest form of sin-offering. Really there was only one—representing Christ. The different degrees of offering in Lev. 4 and 5 represent the different degrees of appreciation of the offering by different classes of offerers. Some, like the high priest, would offer the bullock—that would entail a very high estimate of Christ; this also availed for the whole congregation. It will take the whole of the redeemed fully to appreciate Christ. The ram would stand for a lower, though still high, appreciation of Christ, and so down to the turtle doves, but in these all the offerer would have the sense of the need and value of the blood of Christ.

The handful of flour would be Christ too, but Christ little understood, little appreciated, "a touching of the hem of His garment," a coming to Him, a trusting Him, but with no sense of His atoning sacrifice. Some, perhaps many, to-day, begin like that, they come to the right Person, but they do not yet apprehend Him in the right way, and which of us can say that we do this as we ought to? One thing we may say in the case of the fine flour, the offering would be almost unseen, but in the case of the bullock it would be the offerer who might be almost unseen; and the higher our thoughts of Christ, the smaller **we** will become. We cannot think much of Christ, and of ourselves at the same time. "He must increase, I must decrease!"   W.H.

Why was it enjoined in Lev. 6. 24-30 that the priest who offered the sin-offering should eat the flesh, but not when the blood thereof was brought into the tabernacle to reconcile withal in the Holy Place, when the flesh was burnt in the fire? (Lev. 4. 12, 21).

The seven or eight varieties of the sin-offering in Lev. 4 and 5 from the bullock to "the tenth of an ephah of fine flour", all point to Christ, according to the varying degrees of the individual offerer's estimate of Him. The "fine flour" would thus represent the one who has but a low appreciation of Him, and so on up to the bullock, which would represent the highest estimate of His Person and work. The smaller offerings would scarcely be seen, the offerer would loom so large; behind the larger, the bullock for instance, the offerer could scarcely be seen, for the offering would loom so large. So, when self fills the mind, Christ seems small; where Christ is much, self disappears. Only in the case of the first two sin-offerings for the priest and the congregation respectively was the blood brought into the Sanctuary to reconcile* withal, and the flesh was burnt (saraph, the burning of judgment) without the camp. This happened for the priest, it would seem, only on the day of atonement, but there a goat was offered for the people. On this day the actual death of Christ at the Cross was represented, where sin was dealt with in His holy Person—root and branch. This is the great foundation on which all rests. Here we see God working for His own glory, and all the claims of His throne fully met. **This is Atonement.** But in the other sin-offerings detailed in Lev. 4 and 5 we see the individual sinner **appropriating** the sin-offering for his personal sin and being forgiven; and in this case the priest **appreciates** increasingly its exceeding value, and the glory which accrues to God, and feeds on the Person and work of Christ. On the day of the setting apart of the priests, the blood of the kid of the sin-offering was not brought into the Sanctuary to reconcile withal, and its flesh ought to have been eaten in

---

* The word for "reconcile" is caphar, usually translated "atone."

the holy place, but in the confusion was wrongly burnt (Lev. 10. 16-18). This is like seeking to repeat the sacrifice of Christ, or like a person truly saved who, instead of feeding on Christ with adoring gratitude and worship in the presence of the Father, is trying to get saved again.

W.H.

What is the significance of the different use of the "lamb" and the "goat" with regard to the offerings etc., in the Old Testament? and in what aspect is the "goat" a type of Christ? How does it compare with the goat used in Matt. 25 as a type of professors and unbelievers?

Goats divide the hoof and chew the cud, and so were equally clean, and eligible for sacrifice as sheep. They formed part of the flock (Lev. 1. 2, 10). The various grades of sacrifices represented typically the varied estimates of Christ and of the needs of different offerers. The bullock-offerer had an exalted view, the lamb or kid-offerer a lower, and the bird-offerer still less. The "handful of meal-" offerer in the grades of the sin-offering represents one who has but little appreciation of His work, but only a sense of need of Him. There may be very many such. Perhaps the fact of the choice being left between a lamb and a kid would be to emphasise the gracious desire of Jehovah, that no one should find himself unable to bring a sacrifice. Christ is for all, everywhere, in every age, for the smallest faith, for the least intelligence, for the youngest believer. We should grow in our appreciation of Him; we need never fear to exhaust His fulness. As for the figure in Matt. 25, the point on which emphasis is laid is simply the facility with which Christ will divide the nations, as a shepherd divides the sheep from the goats, placing the two companies, one on His right and the other on His left; but I do not think this touches the sacrificial value of the goat.

W.H.

In the New Danish translation of the Old Testament, "clean place," in our version of Lev. 6. 11, is rendered, "unclean"; and I see on looking up "a critical translation" that the translators state that it may be just as correct to translate it "unclean" as otherwise, and that this holds good in other places of the same kind in Leviticus. Is this so? What guide is there as to a correct rendering?

Though it may seem a hard saying to the critics, whoever they may be, they must be criticised as freely as they criticise, as they have no monopoly either of learning, or of the critical faculty.

Of course, one cannot say what authority this so-called "critical translation" really has, but as far as our Authorised Version and Revised Version are concerned, it has not their support. The Hebrew adjective, tāhôr, translated "clean" in above passage, occurs more than 90 times in the Old Testament and is not once translated, "unclean," in our Authorised, but always "clean." It is used of persons, places, and animals, in which last case it is often contrasted with "unclean," e.g., Lev. 10. 10; 11. 47; 20. 25; and it is also often used for the pure gold of the tabernacle, e.g., Exod. 25. 11; 37. 17; and then of moral purity, e.g., Psa. 12. 6; 19. 9; Prov. 22. 11. The verbal form, tāhēr, occurs even more frequently, and is always translated "cleanse," "purge," "purify," and never the reverse, any more than tāhôr above. The witness of the Revised Version is the same, at any rate in all the occurrences in the book of Leviticus (which I have looked up).

Gesenius, the well-known Hebrew Lexicographer, though himself unhappily of the higher critical school, gives us the meaning: (a) "clean" ("fair," A.V.) as opposed to filthy (of a garment) (Zec. 3. 5); (b) "un-alloyed"—of gold (Exod. 25. 11); (c) in a Levitical sense, "clean" as opposed to unclean, polluted (Lev. 13. 17); (d) in a moral sense (Job. 14. 4), and Dr. Tregelles in his Hebrew Students' Manual agrees. Indeed, one cannot find a single authority to favour the idea in question. We have thought it worth while to take up this question to show how little value need be attached to the statements of this school of critics, to whom questioning and denying seems "more than their necessary food." It is difficult to suppose, however, that they can make such subversive statements without some authority, but it cannot be very weighty, since it is completely ignored by the scholars I have quoted above.   W.H.

Do the two loaves of Lev. 23. 17 represent Jews and Gentiles? And why were they "baken with leaven," which speaks of what is evil?

The feast of Lev. 23. 15-21, called in Deut. 16. 10, etc., "The Feast of Weeks"; in Acts 2. 1, etc., "The Day of Pentecost": and in Num. 28. 26, "The Day of the First-fruits"; is doubtless, as C. H. M. expresses it, "a type of God's people, gathered by the Holy Ghost, and presented before Him in connection with all the preciousness of Christ." This being so, the presence of leaven in the two loaves is, as he further says, "because they were intended to foreshadow those who, though filled with the Holy Ghost, and adorned with His gifts and graces, had nevertheless evil dwelling in them." But the leaven was not burnt on the altar to God, either in this case or any other (see v. 20). That the number "two" may represent the elements, Jew and Gentile, out of which the Church is formed, seems reasonable enough.   W.R.

DEUTERONOMY

When Moses in Deut. 6. 4 says, "Hear, O Israel, The LORD our God is one LORD," are we to understand that therefore Jesus Christ is the only Person in the Godhead?

No, it would be a very serious and fundamental error to do so, upsetting and dislocating the whole revealed truth concerning the Godhead, as it has pleased God to reveal Himself in His Word.

This is the teaching of a certain fearful system of error, which we need not name, but which has, alas, adherents to-day; but I question whether there is one point of God's revealed truth on which they are sound. It is a false system built on lies.

Moses' words are perfectly true: "The LORD our God is One LORD," but in that Unity there are three distinct Divine Persons or Subsistences —Father, Son and Spirit—co-equal, co-eternal, co-substantial (see e.g. Matt. 3. 16, 17; 28. 19; 2 Cor. 13. 14; Rev. 1. 4-6, etc., etc.). The last expression means that each glorious Person of the Triune God possesses the entire Divine Substance or Essence. God is Spirit and as such is invisible. "No man hath seen God at any time, the only-begotten Son, who is in the bosom of the Father, He hath **declared** Him." "In the beginning was the Word and the Word was with God and the Word was God." . . . "and the Word became flesh and dwelt among us and we beheld His glory, the glory of the Only-begotten of the Father full of grace and truth" (John 1. 1, 14). He was "the express image of God's Person"; "the image of the Invisible God" (John 1. 14, 18; Heb. 1. 3; Col. 1. 15). Only in the Lord Jesus Christ is the Father revealed by the Spirit. Let us not reason about it, but bow and worship. If we do not understand our own tripartite nature, how can we claim to comprehend the Infinite, the "**One** God in **Three** Persons"?

W.H.

Could you throw any light on the apparent contradictions between the 12th and the 44th verses of Deut. 28? We often hear the former quoted in support of the Jews being money-lenders down the course of time. The position in verse 44 is in exactly the opposite order from that of verse 12.

That is so. In verse 12 we read: "Thou shalt lend unto many nations, and thou shalt not borrow," and in verse 44: "He (i.e. the stranger that is within thee) shall lend to thee and thou shalt not lend to him." The positions are reversed, because the conditions are altered. In verse 12, Moses is enumerating the blessings which will accrue to Israel upon obedience, and though the obedience of the nation was very far from perfect, yet for the sake of the godly, and especially of the Messiah,

God did accord them a measure of prosperity, though whether we ever hear of Israel actually lending "to many nations," I very much doubt. But in verse 44 (beginning back from verse 15) Moses is enumerating the disabilities—the cursings on those who disobey, and these have been terribly realised in the great majority of the people. The idea that all Jews are wealthy is a superficial one. Many have accumulated wealth, it is true, in countries like our own and the United States, where they live and carry on business on equal terms with others. In many lands, however, they are hampered and handicapped, with the result that the mass of Jews at the present day are very far from being able to lend, and are reduced to living on a very low scale, on the debtor rather than on the creditor side, if ever the latter. Verse 12 is, moreover, national; verse 44, individual. I think when above considerations are weighed, even the appearance of a contradiction disappears.   W.H.

JOSHUA

Joshua 7. 21. What would the "Babylonish garment and two hundred shekels of silver and the wedge of gold of fifty shekels weight" represent? What is the teaching in this verse?

I think they would stand for what most attracts the eye and fills the heart of the natural man; for what is more desirable to the flesh than fine clothes to deck oneself withal, and gold and silver, which will purchase "everything except peace of mind, and entrance anywhere except to heaven"! "Babylonish garment" is literally "a garment of **Shinar**," the locality where Babylon was built, renowned, it is said, for its beautiful robes. The word for "garment," is from a root meaning, "wide," hence an ample covering, a cloak. It is used of Elijah's mantle and also of the royal robe the King of Nineveh doffed in sign of repentance (Jonah 3. 6). Gesenius says these "cloaks of **Shinar**" were "variegated with figures, or interwoven with various colours, having the figures of men and beasts," reminding one of the great copes worn by ecclesiastics to-day at their religious ceremonials—true "cloaks of **Shinar**" those! Let all see to it, lest fine clothes, ministering to the pride of life, or silver and gold, ministering to its "many foolish and hurtful lusts," occupy our hearts! "But thou, O man of God, flee these things, and follow after righteousness, godliness, faith, love, patience, meekness."   W.H.

Was Caleb (see Josh. 14. 6) an Israelite?

The Lord's injunction in Num. 13. 2 (R.V.) with regard to the sending of the spies was, "Send thou men . . . of every tribe of their fathers shall ye send a man, every one a prince among them." In obedience to this, Moses "sent them according to the commandment of the Lord, all of them men who were heads of the children of Israel" (v. 3). There follows a list of their names and tribes, in which is included, "Of the tribe of Judah, Caleb the son of Jephunneh" (v. 6). Thus in this passage, the first in which Caleb is mentioned, it is affirmed, not only that he was of the tribe of Judah, but that he was a "prince" and "head" of that tribe.

His being called "the Kenezite" (or "Kenizzite") in Num. 32. 12 and Josh. 14. 6, 14 has led some to assert that he was not an Israelite, but one of that Canaanitish race called "Kenizzites" in Gen. 15. 19; while others have associated this patronymic with Kenaz the grandson of Esau (Gen. 16. 11, 15), thus making him out to be an Edomite. But when we find that Caleb's younger brother was called Kenaz (Josh. 15. 17; etc.), and that Caleb's grandson was also called Kenaz (1 Chron. 4. 15), it becomes evident that the name was a popular one in the family to which he belonged, and that the term "Kenezite" in his own case merely connects him with some earlier Kenaz amongst his ancestors.

W.R.

In an Article, "World bordering and its Evils" by J. G. Bellett, in referring to the Altar set up by the two and a half tribes, the writer says it was set up in Gilead, while Joshua 22. 10 states it was erected in the land of Canaan. Again, in verse 11 it says, "over against the land of Canaan," which seems to support Mr. Bellett's article. Please say upon what side of the Jordan, East or West it was erected.

The position of the altar certainly does seem ambiguous from verses 10 and 11 of Joshua 22, as they stand in the Authorised Version. Verse 10 says it was "when they came into the borders of Jordan, that are IN the land of Canaan, . . . they built there an altar by Jordan, a great altar to see to," and then in verse 11 this position is described as "over against the land of Canaan in the borders of Jordan, at the passage of the children of Israel." These descriptions are the determining factors, not what our esteemed brother J. G. Bellett may have written, for what he wrote must be tested by "what is written in the Book." If the altar had been for sacrifice, it would naturally have been erected in the land to the east of Jordan, where the two and a half tribes would conveniently offer sacrifices; if for a witness, its natural place would be on the west, where the other tribes could see it. As we know, Reuben and his companion deprecated any idea of sacrifice, and insisted it was only to be as a witness between them and the main body of Israel that the LORD is God. The Revised Version favours this view for it leaves verse 10 as in the Authorised Version, but makes a notable change in verse 11, the latter part of which ends thus (they) "have built an altar in the forefront of (instead of "over against") the land of Canaan, in the region about Jordan, **on the side that pertaineth to the children of Israel**" (i.e. the West of Jordan). As far as one can judge from the Hebrew usage this seems more correct. The word is scarcely ever translated as in the Authorised Version, "passage," and such a translation is certainly hard of interpretation. I judge the altar was built on the west side of the Jordan, close to the river. It would thus be an indisputable proof that the two and a half tribes had been at one time over there in force. The only argument against this seems to be the fear of Israel lest it meant setting up a new sacrificial altar, for an altar with this end in view must be available for the sacrifices of the two and a half tribes, i.e. on that side of Jordan. This was, however, a mistaken fear and does not counterbalance the arguments on the other side. Had Reuben and the others been in touch with Jehovah, they would not have been content with anything short of the promised land. Material advantage was their snare, but it exposed them specially to the attacks of Moab and Ammon (see "Judges"), and other enemies from the East. Gilead, the possession of Gad, was amongst the first to be led captive by Tiglath-Pileser (2 Kings 15. 29). These tribes are true examples of world-borderers, or of those who for material advantage refuse to go all lengths. They did fight for the other tribes, but did not possess the land for themselves. They are like people who fight for principles and truths they never enjoy. It is sad when believers are content to be so far from God's centre, that they have to erect some great building "to see to," to show that they have some connection with Christ.   W.H.

JUDGES

Please explain Judges 11. 31: "Shall surely be the Lord's, and I will offer it up for a burnt offering."

We know the story of Jephthah's vow. It has been the subject of much heart searching and enquiry. Certainly there is something mysterious about it as it stands. Was Jephthah's daughter really offered up as a burnt offering? This has been taken for granted and the story has been quoted to show the low morality of the times and the general need of humanity for the blessings of further "evolution" in their religious beliefs and practices! That the daughter was ever offered up as a burnt offering, however, can be proved neither by the story nor the morality of the times, **but** only that she bewailed her virginity. That is, she is supposed to have been thinking of this, when she might well have been thinking of losing her life. It would be like a convict about to lose his head, bewailing that they had cut his hair too close. I think the morality of Jephthah and his fellow-Israelites would probably compare very favourably with that of London or any other great modern city, and would certainly be better than that of some of the evolutionary, modernistic teachers, who while accepting a salary to preach what at the most solemn moment of their lives, they declared they unfeignedly believed, are now using their influence to undermine—the foundation truths of Creation, the Fall, Atonement, the true Deity of Christ, etc. All that we learn is that Jephthah is said to have met his daughter, and to have exclaimed: "I have been brought very low." This was because she was his only child and therefore the only one by whom his name could be preserved. No doubt he was deeply moved: "I have opened my mouth unto the Lord and I cannot go back," and the daughter, a true woman of faith, accepts the situation, and only asks that she may be allowed two months that she may go up and down and bewail—her life? No, again, her virginity. She returns at the end of the time, and "her father did with her according to his vow which he had vowed," with what result? that she had died bravely and was buried? No, again we say, but that she never entered the married state. One would think this an unnecessary piece of information, if, in fact, she had been burnt alive, as some would have us believe. I will give one or two further reasons for believing that this is not the true meaning. (1) Human sacrifices were abhorrent to God's mind. As for passing children through the fire in his honour, it was absolutely foreign to His intention. Jehovah's words of this very thing are, "I commanded them not, neither came into My mind that they should do this abomination, to cause Judah to sin" (see Jer. 32. 35, also Ezek. 16. 20, 21; 20. 26, 31). Can we suppose this man of God to do "such a thing"? (2) For Jephthah was, we see, a man of God, by verse 11, and also by the character of his remonstrance to the king of Ammon. His name, too, occurs among the heroes of faith of Heb. 11. (3) It is distinctly said that "the Spirit of God came upon him" before this incident. Can we then suppose he would have been permitted to sacrifice his daughter in the way supposed, entirely out of harmony with the will of God? (4) I think the true solution is found in the margin of our Bibles, "Shall surely be the Lord's, OR I will offer it up for a burnt offering." Had it been his dog or other unclean animal, how could he have offered it up as a burnt offering? No, but he might have sold it and given the price to the Lord. This marginal reading is borne out by the disjunctive use of Waw ("and") in Hebrew, which also has the force of "OR," as in Ex. 21. 16 ("selleth him, OR if he be found in his hand"), Ex. 21. 17 ("father OR mother"), Deut. 24. 7 ("maketh merchandise of him, OR selleth him"); and of "WHETHER ... OR," as in Ex. 21. 31 ("WHETHER he have gored a son, OR have gored a daughter"). In all these passages, "and" would be out of place. It would seem clear that in Jephthah's intention, to be "the Lord's", entailed a life of celibacy. There may have been some such custom current, to judge from this passage, though we know not of any command to confirm it. It is interesting to note the marginal reading of "lament" in the last verse of the chapter—"talk with"—the same verb, "tinnēh" which is translated "rehearse" in Judges 5. 11.

W.H.

Did Jephthah really offer his daughter as a burnt offering to the Lord? (Judges 11. 29-40).

To this one would fain be able to reply, as not a few commentators and others have done, with a definite NO. Their reasons and arguments have been so clearly set forth in a recent article elsewhere, that we cannot here do better than enumerate them in the order given. (1) It is pointed out that human sacrifices were expressly forbidden by the Law (Deut. 18. 9, 10). (2) In verse 31, the marginal reading "or" (of the A.V., not R.V., as stated) is adopted, as showing that two alternatives were in Jephthah's mind: "Whatsoever cometh forth . . . shall surely be the Lord's, or I will offer it up for a burnt offering." And it is remarked that, according to Lev. 27. 4, a person thus vowed might be redeemed for money. (3) The daughter's words, "that I may bewail my virginity" (v. 37), are taken to imply that this was the real outcome of the vow, that she was pledged by her father to perpetual celibacy; and further proof of this is found in the statement of verse 39, "And she knew no man." (4) At verse 40 the reading, "talk with", of the A.V. margin, is given preference to the textual reading, "lament"; and it is suggested that for four days in each year the daughters of Israel went to talk with Jephthah's daughter. We may hope, if only for Jephthah's own sake, that this view is correct; but there are difficulties in connection with each of the points mentioned which may not be ignored. If we enumerate these also, we shall perhaps put the questioner and others in a position to form their own judgment as to what really took place. (1) While there can be no doubt as to the Lord's disapproval of human sacrifices, our passage nowhere states that Jephthah's action met with His approval; and the question is not what the Law forbade, but what a man such as Jephthah, who had lived for some time among the idolatrous Syrians of Tob, might say and might do. (2) The "and" in verse 31 is the common Hebrew particle which is similarly translated some thousands of times elsewhere; and although there are a few passages in which it is employed disjunctively and rendered, "or," the wording of its context in such instances usually indicates this, which is not so here. Moreover, the statement, "shall surely be the Lord's, or I will offer it up for a burnt offering," is not very intelligible, because its being offered as a burnt offering did not mean that it was any less "the Lord's." Neither is it easy to understand why Jephthah should expect an animal, rather than a person, to be first out of the doors of his house to meet him on his return from the war. (3) Why should Jephthah's daughter require two preliminary months to bewail her virginity, if she was going to have years of a lifetime afterwards to bewail it as much as she pleased? As to verse 39, it may be mentioned that the R.V. reads it, "And she had not known man." (4) In verse 40, the R.V. rendering, "celebrate," is probably the most exact of any, especially as the only other occurrence of this Hebrew word in the same form is in Judges 5. 11, where it is translated "rehearse." If the meaning be that the daughters of Israel, while Jephthah's daughter was still alive, went to talk with her, why should they have limited their conversations with her to four days in each year? Some may perhaps attach less importance to these difficulties than others will; but they exist, and must be faced fairly before one can confidently assert that Jephthah did not slay his daughter, but merely compelled her to remain unmarried.   W.R.

1 & 2 SAMUEL

What is meant by the reference to the Ark in 1 Sam. 14. 18? Was it at this time being carried about with Saul's army, as seems to be implied?

I think the key to the difficulty in this verse is found in the reading given in the R.V. margin, which is that of the Septuagint, a Greek version of the Old Testament, made from the Hebrew original before the time of Christ, and sometimes cited by the apostles, instead of the Hebrew. It is, "Saul said unto Ahiah, Bring hither the Ephod: for he (i.e. the priest Ahiah) wore the Ephod at that time before Israel." This reading is in keeping with verse 3, in which it is stated that Ahiah was with Saul at that period, and was wearing an ephod.

It is also in keeping with the fact that it was in connection with the Ephod or robe, upon which were the Breastplate and the Twelve Stones—the Urim and Thummim, rather than in connection with the Ark, that inquiries were made of God through the priest. Compare chapter 23. 9 and chapter 30. 7, in both which we have again the very words, "Bring hither the ephod." But David in them was the speaker instead of Saul, for the priest Abiathar, when fleeing from the latter, had brought the Ephod with him (chap. 23. 6).

Moreover, the expression, "Bring hither the Ark of God," is unnatural, since the Ark was much too heavy for a single priest to carry about with him. It would more probably have been, "Draw near to the Ark," had the Ark been meant. Possibly in writing the words as we now have them, some scribe mistook the word he was copying, as "Ark" and "Ephod" in Hebrew are somewhat similar.

From the time that the Ark was brought to Kirjath-jearim in chap.

7. 1, I do not think it was moved again until David brought it thence to Zion in 2 Sam. 6. They "enquired not at it in the days of Saul," we are told in 1 Chron. 13. 3.   W.R.

How are we to reconcile 1 Sam. 16. 2 with verse 1, where the object of Samuel's mission was "to anoint a King"? Was the former the secret object and the sacrifice the public one?

The two objects were not incompatible, though they may appear to be at first sight. In verse 1 the primary object of the mission is told to Samuel. But the further directions as to the way in which the main object was to be carried out, are only given in reply to Samuel's enquiry, "**How** can I go?" Samuel's words did not convey unwillingness on his part; it was not, "How **can** I go?" but a desire for further instruction—"**How** can I go?" The Lord is a compassionate Master, and would not send His servant into the lion's jaws. The sacrifice was to be the natural public setting, in which the anointing, the secret purpose, was to be carried out.   W.H.

We read in 1 Sam. 17. 50 that David slew the giant, and then it is again stated in the following verse that he slew him, as though he slew him twice. Is it a different word that is used, are there two accounts, or how explain the repetition?

The word is the same—the ordinary Hebrew word—"**mûth**" for "to die," here in the causal mood, "make to die"—"slay." It is the same verb again at close of v. 51, "was dead." I think the explanation is very simple. The second account, as it appears, is simply the explanation in a parenthesis if you will, as to how, seeing David had no sword of his own, he could slay the giant. We may put it in brackets: [Therefore David ran and stood upon the Philistine and took his sword and slew him]. The Scriptures are not written in rounded sentences, which, as one has said, are apt to roll off as fast as they roll on, but in a simple colloquial style, which is never in a hurry, but never lengthy.   W.H.

Did Samuel really come back when Saul consulted the witch of Endor (1 Sam. 28)?

Attempts have been made to prove the contrary, in order to avoid even the appearance of justifying the practice of Spiritism. But this is a weak argument. We must not manipulate the Word of God even on the plea of defending the truth. That is doing evil that good may come. It is a poor heresy that cannot allege some fancied support in Scripture.

I have not the slightest doubt that Samuel did really come back and hold intercourse with Saul by the sovereign permission of God. Really, the reappearance of Samuel does not touch the question of Spiritism or justify men in seeking intercourse with the dead. This is implicitly condemned earlier in the very chapter when Saul, as we are told, cut off those who had dealings with familiar spirits—and yet so hardened was he that "he sware to the witch by the Lord saying, As the Lord liveth there shall no punishment happen to thee for this thing." He obeyed God, as long as it suited him. When Saul had overcome the witch's fears, he told her to call up Samuel. She was in no way perturbed at that, for she knew her familiar spirit would be there to impersonate whomsoever was called up, with greater or less accuracy. Samuel being so widely known, would not be a difficult subject for deception. But when she saw the real Samuel rising out of the earth in a spirit-form, rendered visible to her eyes, she cried out. This was something outside her experience and beyond her ken. (1 Sam. 28. 12).

It is interesting to note her description—"I see gods ('elohim—mighty ones—sometimes according to Gesenius, used in the singular)—ascending out of the earth." Clearly the spirit of the departed prophet had taken on a grandeur and majesty befitting a Paradise-dweller, but for purposes of identification, he was seen as he had been known for many years in the days of his flesh, as an old man, clad in his prophetic mantle, and it was in this latter guise that she described him. There was no trickery about this, as there must always be in spiritism whether in the familiar spirit—or in the medium. She was sure what appeared to her was not her familiar spirit. Saul was sure by the description it was truly Samuel. The spirit of Samuel spake like Samuel, going back to the very judgment, which he had been charged to pass on Saul, for his disobedience in the case of Amalek. What is more, the words of Samuel came true.

God did not let his servant's words fall to the ground now, any more than when he was alive in the flesh. It really is surprising that otherwise well-taught Christians should be found to question all this.

This consultation of the witch by Saul was the consummation of Saul's disobedience. He is reproved for enquiring of the witch and not God. He did ask of God in a formal way, but not in the earnest way in which he sought the witch (see 1 Chron. 10. 13, 14, where distinct words for the two "enquires" mark this). W.H.

Please explain 1 Sam. 28. 15-19 in the light of Eccles. 9. 5. Does this give ground for to-day's teaching of Spiritism?

The story of 1 Sam. 28 in no way justifies the practice of Spiritism in this or in any other age.

As for Ecclesiastes 9. 5, it expresses the general rule, "The dead know not anything"; the above story of the witch of Endor is the exception, by God's special permission, as I shall seek to show. "The dead know not anything," i.e., of what is going on on the earth, but they know what is going on where they are, as the story of the ex-rich man and

Lazarus shows (Luke 16). The former and Abraham knew each other, and the former recognised Lazarus and remembered his own five brethren.

I have not the slightest doubt Samuel was really permitted by God to respond to the call. This was less, I doubt not, of a surprise to Saul the dupe, than to the witch, the deceiver. To her the attendant spirit was familiar, but she seems to have been completely taken aback by the appearance of the strange visitant that Samuel was, for "she cried with a loud voice," and did not know him, though by some peculiar intuition she at once became aware of the identity of Saul. Samuel was a true prophet, and could foretell the morrow's happenings, but we have no justification for supposing that wicked spirits can foretell the future.

That this response to Saul's evil action does not justify modern Spiritism is clear, from the fact that it did not justify his own recourse to this medium, for it is specifically mentioned in 1 Chronicles 10. 13 as one of the two causes of his final downfall: (1) "his transgression" i.e., in sparing Amalek, and also (2) his "asking counsel of one that had a familiar spirit, to enquire of it. And he enquired not of the Lord, therefore He slew him." He did ask of the Lord (shā'al), as indeed of the witch, but he did so in a merely formal way in the former case and he did not enquire (dārash) of Him, as he did of the witch; for in her case he put himself to all pains to get information. Saul knew perfectly well the distinct prohibition of Jehovah to any kind of occult practices—consulting spirits, etc. (see Lev. 19. 31; 20. 6, 27; Deut. 18. 9-12), and had as we know, acted thereon, till he found it convenient to transgress!   W.H.

Is it scriptural to suggest that King Saul is now enjoying the rest of heaven?

Though we should shrink from usurping God's prerogative in such matters, I fear I know no Scripture which would certainly justify such a statement. It is true he was chosen of God to be King over His people, at their demand, as indeed to-day "the powers that be are ordained of God," but without any guarantee as to spiritual condition. He was chosen, but it was to suit the people's choice; he was not a man after God's own heart. He certainly manifested pleasing traits, now and again, especially at the commencement of his reign, when he comes before us as "a choice young man":—in fact one of Adam's best! and he was religious, too, as long as it was convenient, but as soon as any other interest intervened, he broke down lamentably, e.g., in the case of Amalek. He did prophesy on two occasions, but Matthew 7. 21-23 declares plainly that even this is compatible with a dead faith. Like the apostates of Hebrews 6, he tasted of spiritual powers, but he was deprived of these for his sins. He could easily pass over disobedience to

God's commands (e.g., 1 Sam. 14. 32), but when, in the same chapter, the victor Jonathan innocently disobeyed his trivial prohibition, he would have slain him on the spot, had he had his way. The characteristic fruits he bore were envy, jealousy and a murderous spirit to all who opposed him. He had the whole house of Aaron mercilessly and unrighteously butchered in one day, though one of them did escape. He attempted David's innocent life again and again. He deliberately broke God's law in consulting the witch of Endor, and he died by his own hand, without any sign of repentance. It is a sad record. The fact that Samuel's spirit said, "To-morrow thou and thy sons shall be with me," is not out of harmony with the belief that till our Lord's resurrection the Paradise of the departed saints formed one compartment of Hades, the intermediate abode of all the dead.   W.H.

Why in 2 Sam. 24 was it counted a sin in David to number the children of Israel, whereas Moses was commanded by God to do so? (Exod. 30. 12).

Perhaps the very point our questioner notes as to Moses having been **commanded** to take the census of the people goes some way toward solving this difficulty. A thing may be commanded at one time, and not at another. For instance, the Feast of Tabernacles was commanded to be observed on the 15th day of the seventh month, but to keep the feast in the 8th month, as Jeroboam did "out of his own heart," was a flagrant offence (1 Kings 12. 32). So, spurious imitations of God's ordinances to-day become positive acts of disobedience; for instance, baptising infants, or making of the breaking of bread an idolatrous act, the "eucharist" or the mass. Moses was commanded in Exod. 17. 6 to smite the rock, but when he did this in Num. 20. 11, 12, it was counted a sin unto him. In Exodus 30. 12 the Lord gives a direction to be followed when an occasion arose for numbering the people—each one was to give a half shekel as a ransom for his soul unto the Lord. It was, so to speak, a recognition before the Lord that the life numbered was in reality forfeited and needed to be ransomed. There is no mention of this being observed in David's case, though that was a command to the people in general. In Num. 1. 2, 3, Jehovah **commanded** Moses to take the sum of all the congregation of the children of Israel—"From twenty years old and upward, all that are able to go forth to war in Israel." It was clearly a matter of order and importance that the number of the people should be known at the commencement of their desert journeyings, and it is given as 603,550. Then again in chap. 26, Moses and Eleazar were **commanded** to number the people at the close of their wanderings. They actually shewed a decrease of nearly 2,000, surely an eloquent commentary on the effect of their disobedience. Had they taken possession of the land when this was proposed to them they would, no doubt, have shown a large increase over a like period. In the case of David's census, we read that "the anger of the Lord was kindled against Israel and He moved David against them to say, Go, number Israel and Judah" (2 Sam. 24. 1), of which census a man of the world like Joab, and also the captains of the host, saw the futility. Joab's words are remarkable; he expresses the desire that God might add a hundred-fold to the people, that the king might see the increase, i.e. without any need of a census. In 1 Chron. 21. 1 we read, "Satan stood up against Israel," which simply means that Jehovah in inflicting judgment on His people for their transgression, allowed Satan to move in the matter as His agent. Men may make difficulties and cavil at God's ways, but He is Sovereign and He will be justified by all, when His ways and the secrets of men are known. In reality there was no command to David from Jehovah to number the people. It was an arbitrary act of self-will and self-glorying, resulting in the infliction of the plague on the very ones on whom God would inflict judgment. We see, then, in the "Samuel" account God in government carrying out His judgment on David and the people—He is the ultimate cause; but in the "Chronicles," Satan is presented as the instrumental cause—He tempts David to engage in the path of self-will, and the King allows himself to be led astray and is responsible, as he admits himself (2 Sam. 24. 17). David, however, knows the grace of God, as well as His government, and his prayer is: "Let me fall now into the hands of the Lord; for His mercies are great: and let me not fall into the hands of man" (v. 14); and so he is led to build an altar unto the Lord and offer burnt-offerings and peace-offerings, typical of the sacrifice of Christ.   W.H.

What is the meaning of 2 Sam. 3. 33: "Died Abner as a fool dieth?"

Probably the thought is: "Did Abner die like an inexperienced fool, who knew not how to defend himself?" And the intended answer is, "No, he fell victim to a deceitful wicked plot." Compare verse 27, in which the unsuspicious nature of Abner stands in marked contrast to the suspicions Joab had expressed concerning him in verse 25. Notice, too, that he was slain in the last place where it might have been expected he would be, in the gate of Hebron which was a city of refuge (Josh. 20. 7), as well as being the residence of king David at that time.

Yet there is no doubt that Abner did really act as a fool on an earlier occasion, when he made the unwise choice of chap. 2. 8, 9 for Ishbosheth and against David, and did so deliberately though he well knew (see chap. 3. 9, 10) what the mind of God in the matter was.   W.R.

What was the wise woman's line of reasoning in 2 Sam. 14. 4-14?

The woman followed the example of the prophet Nathan in chapter 12. 1-7, by getting the king to decide a hypothetical case which Joab and she had invented. When he did so, she told him (v. 13) that he was setting a bad example to the people of God, by not acting himself in accordance with the decision he had given in the case of others, and bringing home the banished Absalom. In verse 14 she backs this with another argument. God Himself, she points out, has devised means that His banished be not expelled from Him (referring doubtless to the cities of refuge which God had provided so that the manslayer should not have to leave the country). Why then should not David act as God does?

She thus struck two chords that were sure to find an echo in David's heart. He would wish to set God's people a good example, and he surely would like to act as God did. Had he not shortly before sought out the grandson of his bitter enemy, Saul, in order that he might show "the kindness of God" to him (chap. 9. 3)? Of course her reasoning was bad, for she was persuading him to act at the expense of justice; and God's "means" were not for wilful murderers such as Absalom. But "the king's heart was toward Absalom" (v. 1), so he was not difficult to persuade. His son was brought back, and all seemed well. But two factors had been ignored, the claims of God's broken Law, and the unchanged heart of the offender; and the result was a harvest of sorrow to be reaped later.

With regard to the first two clauses of v. 14, she apparently meant to suggest that, like water spilt on the ground, that which was past, i.e. the death of Amnon, could not be recalled. Possibly also, that life is too short to be wasted in a prolonged quarrel.   W.R.

1 & 2 KINGS

According to 1 Kings xv. 33 Baasha began to reign over Israel in the third year of Asa, king of Judah, and reigned twenty-four years, making his death occur in the twenty-seventh year of Asa's reign. In 2 Chron. xvi. 1, however, we read that Baasha came up against Judah in the thirty-sixth year of Asa's reign, i.e., nine years after his death, according to the chronology in 1 Kings. How can this discrepancy be explained?

The natural way of explaining such a difficulty would be to say that there has evidently been a transcriber's error—"thirty-sixth year of Asa" in 2 Chron. xvi. 1, for **thirty-sixth** year. Baasha would then have become king early in the 3rd year of Asa, and reigned 24 years, a part of a year counting a year. Baasha would then have died probably toward the close of Asa's 26th year, and have been succeeded by Elah

P

his son in the same year. Such an error would in no way affect the inspiration of the Bible, but only manifest the carelessness of the transcriber. I once found in a new French Bible the following sentence: "God resists the humble and gives grace to the proud." I at once wrote to the B. & F.B.S., and far from accusing me of attacking the inspiration of the Scriptures, they thanked me and had a new sheet printed and inserted in the First Epistle of Peter in this French edition. It is certain that, apart from the inspiration of God, by which the chronicler wrote, he, as a man, had access to the Books of Kings, etc., and was quite as capable of noticing the discrepancy as the present questioner and answerer. Besides, if it was a transcriber's error, why was it left and why did no variety of reading spring up? Again, the numbers "thirty-six" and "twenty-six" are very distinct in the Hebrew, and are given not in numbers, but in words, "twenty" being " 'esrîm," and "thirty," "sheloshîm," which are not easily confused, so why should we not seek some other explanation? There are good authorities who believe that the thirty-sixth year of Asa in Chronicles really refers to the year of the division of the kingdoms, which would be the 16th year of his reign. This fits in much better with the time necessary for the wars between Asa and Baasha, the building of Ramah; and this mode of reckoning was, in all likelihood, in general use at the time. In any case, if we knew all, all would be plain, and we can fall back with confidence on the words of the Apostle, "All Scripture," (or Every Scripture) is given by inspiration of God."   W.H.

How can we reconcile with human ideas of justice the destruction of the two captains and their fifties? Were they not only doing their duty in carrying out the orders of their king? Why should they be destroyed with lightning for that? (see 2 Kings 1).

The key to this difficulty is found, I believe, in ver. 15, in reference to the third captain, who was spared. "Go down with him," the angel said, **"be not afraid of him."** It seems clear from this that Elijah did well to be afraid of the other two captains and their companies, who would have exceeded their mandate, which was simply to bring the prophet to the king, by killing him themselves:—lynching him in fact. Elijah thus acted in his own defence in the spirit of a prophet of judgment, enforcing the law and its penalties. What was fitting for him was not so for James and John, the servants of the Saviour of men, for they were "of His Spirit."   W.H.

In 2 Kings 5. 18, 19, was Elisha leaving Naaman to choose his own path in not prohibiting him going into the house of Rimmon? What is the spiritual lesson to learn?

We have a beautiful picture here of the true grace of God, and one we would do well to lay to heart. God's grace not only saves, but teaches. Naaman was cleansed, and converted to God: "Henceforth he would offer neither burnt offering nor sacrifice unto other gods, but unto the Lord" (v. 17). This was the fruit of the Spirit acting on the new nature. But he also had an exercised conscience; he remembers that his duties to his king would, in the ordinary way, lead him into an equivocal position. The prophet with true spiritual instinct casts him back on God. It would have been easy to put him under law; it was better "that his heart be established with grace." The prophet does not give him a dispensation to do what his conscience told him was wrong, but leaves the Spirit to do His work. We may be sure Naaman never did go again into the house of Rimmon. Probably the King at once dispensed with him. It was not letting Naaman choose his own path, but trusting God to lead him in His.   W.H.

In 2 Kings 8. 26, and the parallel passage in 2 Chronicles, we read that Athaliah, mother of Ahaziah, was the "daughter of Omri, king of Israel." Was she not rather the daughter of Ahab and Jezebel?

Yes, she is called the daughter of Ahab in v. 18, of this same chapter, and was thus the granddaughter of Omri, who was Ahab's father. The explanation of this and other similar difficulties is that the terms, "son" and "daughter," were often used by the Israelites of relationship to a direct ancestor, however remote he might be. Thus the publican Zacchæus was a "son of Abraham" (Luke 19. 9), and the infirm woman was a "daughter of Abraham" (Luke 13. 16). And in the Old Testament, Jehu, who slew Athaliah's relatives, is oftenest spoken of as "the son of Nimshi," although 2 Kings 9. 2 shows that Nimshi was actually his grandfather. The linking of Athaliah with Omri in the verses referred to in the question may be due to his being the first of that wicked line to become king; and to his being a greater man than his son Ahab ever was. See the reference to his "might" in 1 Kings 16. 27, and to his "statutes" in Micah 6. 16.   W.R.

PSALMS

How are we to explain the use of Alphabetical Psalms in the Holy Scriptures?

I am not sure that it needs more explanation than the use of the alphabet itself, or of ordinary language. Divine inspiration speaks to men in tongues and forms they can understand and appreciate. In the Scriptures we have great variety. Most of the forms in which men communicate their thoughts to one another are to be found in them—historical, didactic, poetical, etc. In this latter, the Holy Spirit would use the forms with which those addressed were familiar, and one of these was the acrostic form based on the letters of the alphabet, with one of which each verse of the alphabetical psalm, i.e., Psalms 25, 34, 37, 111, 112, 145, and notably Psa. 119 (in sections of eight verses), respectively begins. Also Prov. 31. 10-31, and the book of Lamentations, are mainly in the acrostic form. This book, however, presents some curious anomalies. Thus, chap. 1 follows the simple order of the alphabet, whereas in chapters 2, 3, and 4 there is a transposition of the 16th and 17th letters, 'ayin and pe, and it will be noticed that the third chapter is a threefold acrostic beginning with three alephs, then three b's, three g's, etc., which accounts for the number of verses being 66—thrice the number of the letters in the Hebrew alphabet. Dr. J. B. Lightfoot suggests that this transposition of letters may be connected with the duration of the Babylonian exile—70 years—that being the numerical value of the letter 'ayin. In the 5th chapter all acrostic arrangements seem completely ignored. Why this is so is a problem that has taxed the ingenuity of expositors, and it has been pointed out by one of our esteemed contributors that the transposed 'ayin is actually in its place in the 17th verse, and that this completes the 7 seventies of the book, the exact 490 years foretold by Gabriel to Daniel as "determined upon his people." This is certainly very ingenious, but it would be more convincing were the other transposed letter—pe—in its proper place in the 16th verse. I am afraid there is another fact which tends to discount this explanation, and it is that the same letter 'ayin, which is the crucial letter, occurs in four other places in the chapter besides the 17th verse, namely the 5th, 8th, 10th and 18th, which suggests that its appearance at the 17th is a mere coincidence, 'ayin being a common initial letter. If this be so, the problem still remains unsolved. Perhaps the lack of acrostic order in the last chapter may signify the scattered condition of Israel during the present dispensation, and the quite undefined length of it. In the meanwhile let me suggest two other minor problems. Why in Psalm 34, is the letter **waw** or **v** omitted after verse 6? and why does the final verse of the psalm begin with a repetition of the **pe** or **p** of verse 17? And why in Psa. 145, is the **nun** or **n** omitted after verse 13, and the number of the verses cut down to 21 instead of 22, as in other acrostic Psalms?   W.H.

What Asaph is it who wrote the Psalms bearing such a name?

There seems no reasonable room for doubt that the Psalmist is Asaph —son of Berachiah, a Levite of the family of Gershon, one of the leaders of David's choir (see 1 Chron. 6. 39). The only other Asaph is generally known as "the Recorder," but this seems to be based on a mistake, owing to a certain ambiguity in the English version—it seems more correct to understand Joah as the recorder, of whom Asaph (quite possibly the one mentioned above) was the father or progenitor. In any case, if they are distinct persons, the role of psalmist fits in better with the first named. He was then the author of Psa. 50, and of the first eleven Psalms of Book Three. There are passages which must be understood prophetically whether the author lived in the days of David or of Hezekiah (e.g., Psa. 74. 6; 80. 16). There is a didactic, historic character about Asaph's Psalms. He was, like Apollos, "mighty in the Scriptures," and he applied them to the present need.   W.H.

Is there any scriptural authority for the assertion that Hezekiah wrote some of the Psalms?

Though ecclesiastical commentators seem to be attracted by such theories, we do not know of any authority, scriptural or other, for above assertion, It is enough to read an article in some Bible Dictionary, on the authorship of the anonymous Psalms, to be aware how precarious are the theories advanced. Some psalms speaking of desolation and judgment may be made to fit in with Sennacherib's invasion, as also with any other invasion.

I believe it is possible to assign authorship to a few of the anonymous Psalms, following Psalms by well-known authors, on internal evidence. Thus it seems clear that Psa. 43, is by the author of Psa. 42 (the same phrase "Why art thou cast down, oh my soul?" occurring in both); Psa. 91, by the author of Psa. 90; and Psa. 104, by that of Psa. 103, but as a rule it is safer not to attempt to be wise above that which is written. We believe the Holy Spirit spake by David and the other psalmists: that is the chief point. However, to return to our question, I read the following in a well-known Bible Dictionary,* as a whole reliable: "Book II. (i.e., of Psalms) appears by the date of its latest (!) psalm, Psa. 46, to have been compiled in the reign of King Hezekiah." We turn with interest to see on what this statement rests, and we find NIL. The real reason comes out later in the same article as to why Hezekiah's name is brought in. It comes, I believe, from a misreading of the closing words of Psa. 72, "the prayers of David, the son of Jesse, are ended." But there are at least fifteen subsequent psalms, e.g., Nos. 86, 103, 110, 142, which are entitled "Psalms of David," i.e., these must be by some descendant of David, so the theory runs, Hezekiah, Josiah, or Zerubbabel, in fact you may take your choice. Now, this will never do, because in the case of Psa. 142—the place where David wrote it is indicated, and the Lord definitely ascribes to David the authorship of Psa. 110, and as far as we know, though Hezekiah wrote a prayer, neither he,

* Sir Wm. Smith, LL.D. Article on the Psalms.

nor the others wrote psalms, and certainly not in a cave. The explanation is simple: the word, **Kālāh,** translated "ended" in Psa. 72 means also fulfilled or consummated; e.g., Ezra 1. 1; Ezek. 5. 13; Dan. 11. 36; 12. 7. The words then refer to the prophetic subject of the Psalm, the Millennial Reign of David's "Greater Son." In that hope David's prayers reached their zenith. He could not sing of anything higher. That infinitely greater Kingdom—the mystery of God's will—was unknown to Him, when "in the dispensation of the fulness of times (i.e., the eternal state and the everlasting Kingdom of our Lord and Saviour Jesus Christ) all things in heaven and earth shall be headed up in Christ" (Eph. 1. 10). David prayed many subsequent prayers, but **he** could never reach a higher level than in that psalm.   W.H.

What is the true sense of Psalm 2. 7? There is no verse quoted so often as referring to the Incarnation by deniers of the Eternal Sonship of our Lord. Have they sufficient ground for this?

No, for to do so merely begs the question; it is exactly what has to be proved. The Psalm begins prophetically much later than the Incarnation, namely, with the rejection of Christ, for the apostles by the Spirit quote verse 1, as fulfilled in His rejection by "both Herod and Pontius Pilate, with the Gentiles and the people of Israel" (Acts 4. 27). The Psalm is divided into four sections: (1) Verses 1-3—the language of the rebels against Jehovah; (2) Verses 4-6—Jehovah's answer of derision and wrath. So sure is His purpose, that it is as if already executed: "Yet have I set My King upon My Holy hill of Zion," though naturally this purpose did not begin then; (3) Verses 7-9—the King Himself speaks: "I will declare the decree." What decree? Would the Lord refer at such a juncture to His incarnation, which to the eyes of **men** has proved a failure by His rejection? No, it was the Eternal Decree, on which all God's purposes rest, concerning the Eternal generation of the Son. "Thou art My Son, this day have I begotten Thee"; (4) Verses 10-12— words of the Holy Ghost through David to **living** kings and judges of the earth, to be wise and serve the Lord NOW, and rejoice before Him. "Kiss the Son* lest He be angry and ye perish from the way when His wrath is kindled but a little, blessed are all they that put their trust in Him." The word "NOW" shows that this closing section is not prophetic at all, but was, we might say, a lesson drawn by David to his fellow-kings. In the language of to-day, he is turning the occasion to profit to lead them to repentance and reconciliation to the Divine Son. In "NOW" the sense is adversative, in contrast with what has gone before, and

---

* That the word here is "Bar" not "Ben" does not invalidate the argument, for as Gesenius notes, Bar is Son in Psa. 2. 12, in the sense of one begotten, and is applied to Jehovah, the King, and Tregelles adds, "that is Christ." Gesenius goes on to compare the word here, with the more usual word, Ben, in Isa. 9. 6. Indeed, here again we must note that the Son was not born at Bethlehem—but given ("A child was born"), that is, the Lord did not become Son by His human birth. He was born a true human child. The Word became flesh.

with the future reign, when it will be too late to turn. David warns his brother rulers of their **present duty.** Surely such an appeal, addressed in about 1030 B.C., to kings living at that date, to "kiss the Son," (evidently a Divine Person, the equal of Jehovah), does bear witness to the Eternal Sonship of Him who was at once the progenitor of David, and later "made of his seed, according to the flesh." How shallow then are the thoughts of those who deny the relation of the Son to our Lord in the Divine Trinity, on the ground that such a relation is not recognised in the Old Testament Scriptures! How soon, alas, the Scriptures become so far a closed book to those who close their eyes to its teachings!

Now, let us return to the immediate object of our consideration, namely, the words, "Thou art My Son, this day have I begotten Thee," and enquire whether these words do indeed refer to the Incarnation. If so, we should expect to find them addressed to the Lord in the manger, or at any rate that some allusion to them would be found in the herald angels' annoucement, but we search in vain for any reference to such a thing. All they say is, "Unto you is born this day in the City of David, a Saviour, which is Christ the Lord," but there is no hint that in that birth, a Divine Person, hitherto unknown, had become the Son of God. Not even do the words of Gabriel to Mary bear this meaning. In answer to Mary's legitimate question, he makes a double statement: (1) "The Holy Ghost shall come upon thee," that is, "the Holy Ghost will become to thee the Divine Agent of thy conception," or in the words of Matthew 1, "Thou shalt be found with child of the Holy Ghost." But that conception, unlike any other human birth, was to be of One who had already existed in another form, and who, by the fact of human birth, would enter into manhood. Hence we read: (2) "The power of the Highest shall overshadow thee," that is, a Divine Person shall, at the moment of the human conception by the Spirit, become flesh, or in other words, the Eternal Son will take to Himself perfect human nature in the womb of the Virgin. Hence the words of the Angel Gabriel: "Therefore that holy thing that shall be born of thee shall be called the Son of God." To assert that Christ only became "the mighty God" at the Incarnation would be to deny His Deity; to assert that He only then became the Son of God is to deny His person. If the Babe were only Son of God by human birth, then the Incarnation was an exaltation, not a humbling, and must be the predominant truth of the New Testament, though we know that neither our Lord nor His disciples ever grounded their testimony to His Sonship on it. The Lord in the words of Jehovah's decree, "Thou art My Son, this day have I begotten Thee," goes back to the Eternal truth of Him as the Son. This He was "declared to be with power by the resurrection," which, as Alford shows, is not less the subject of Romans 1, because foreshadowed by resurrections on a lower plane. It does not mean that the Lord became Son at the resurrection, any more than at the Holy Mount, or at the Jordan, but that He was then "declared to be the Son of God with power." Recognition of His Divine Sonship is repeated again and again, but the relation was Eternal.

Now, in considering the three-fold quotation of the words in the New Testament, if the Incarnation be ruled out in one case, it must be in all. Acts 13. 33 must refer to resurrection. In verse 23, certainly incarnation is in view, and the word in the best texts is **agō**="to lead, to bring." "God hath **raised** unto Israel a Saviour." In verse 30, a general word is used for "raised" (**egeirō**), the same verb as in verse 22 of David's appointment as king, but in verses 33 and 34 we have another verb altogether (**anistēmi**), which is found eleven times in the Acts, of resurrection, while the substantive **"anastasis"** is translated "resurrection" thirty-nine times, out of its forty-one occurrences. As Alford says, "The meaning, 'raised from the dead,' in verses 33 and 34 is absolutely required by the context, both because the word is repeated with, 'from among the dead,' verse 34, and because the emphasis throughout is on the resurrection."

In Heb. 1. 5 the reference is not only to resurrection, but to that eternal past, when He, the Risen, Glorified One, had received a name, that of Son, more excellent than angels, by inheritance. He was Son, before He was "appointed Heir of all things," and before He created all things.

In Heb. 5. 5 the subject is Christ's call to priesthood. This could not be by the fact of incarnation, seeing He was not of the priestly tribe of Aaron. He must first ascend, where another order reigns—that of Melchizedek, "made like unto the Son of God"—the chief point of which likeness, if not the only point, consisting in the fact that His eternity in the past as Son goes equally with His eternity in the future.

Some have attempted to divide the decree into two: "Thou art My Son," referring to the Eternal Sonship; and "This day have I begotten Thee," to the Incarnation. To our mind, this seems forced and unjustified by the context. It arises from a fear of applying the word,"begetting," to the eternal past, but this was Arius' objection, and can only be justified by applying laws of time to eternal truths. When we can fathom the mystery of the Divine Being without beginning, then we may be able to solve the eternal begetting without beginning. To what "day," then, does the Spirit of God refer in Psa. 2. 7? We have been reminded so often of the varied meanings of "day" in Scripture that we hardly need insist on this—indeed it is sometimes used so broadly that the question of time hardly enters into it. This, we believe, is the case here: "The use of **sēmeron** (the Greek word which here in the LXX, as also in the New Testament, is translated 'to-day' and 'this day') in

the sense of 'eternally' or 'in eternity' is well established (it is found in Philo). Consequently an orthodox reader would understand it: 'Thou art My Son, I have **eternally** begotten Thee' " (cf. Heb. 1. 5)*
This fits in with the New Testament quotations—a testimony in time to a fact beyond time, in the eternal NOW of a past eternity.   W.H.

Does the reference to "the sword" in Psalm 22. 20, find its fulfilment in John 19. 34, where one of the soldiers with a spear pierced His side? and to what does the expression "dogs" refer?

The words referred to in the Psalm are, "Deliver my soul from the sword!" I cannot think that there is any reference here to the soldier's spear! For one thing, the Lord did not pray to be delivered from the spear-thrust, for He was already dead, nor could He be said to be delivered from it, seeing it pierced Him, and was necessary for the fulfilment of the prophecy of Zech. 12. 10, "They shall look upon Me whom they have pierced." No doubt, this was permitted for a secondary reason, as an ocular demonstration to all of the reality of His death in the outpouring of all His blood. The water coming out visibly after the blood would indicate that the fountain of that life-blood was entirely exhausted: "He poured out his soul unto death" (Isa. 53. 12). Then what could the sword be to which reference is made in verse 20, and from which the Lord prayed that His soul might be delivered? It was something terribly real, the pressure of which our Lord felt to His innermost soul. There was only one sword at Calvary, and that was the sword of which Zechariah spake—the sword of Jehovah—"Awake, O sword, against my shepherd, and against the man that is my fellow, saith the Lord of Hosts" (chap. 13. 7). This was the sword of Eden that turned every way (Gen. 3), "the sore and great and strong sword" of Isa. 27. 1, with which "Leviathan, the piercing serpent" will one day be punished—the sword of divine justice meted out against sin, and with which the Holy Victim was smitten, "when He bore our sins in His own body on the tree," and was treated as the sinner deserved.

As to the second part of the question, the expression "dog" refers, I think, to the Gentile element among those who crucified the Lord. It was they who administered the physical sufferings of the cross. "For dogs have compassed me, they pierced my hands and my feet"—clearly refers to the Roman soldiers, the crucifiers; and then follows v. 18: "They part my garments among them." The moral sufferings of our Lord at the hand of Israel are depicted in vv. 6-8. But the sword of Jehovah surpassed them all, and it was being brought through that judgment unto the resurrection ground, which constituted the "deliverance from the sword" prayed for in Psalm 22. 20.   W.H.

* "Creeds or No Creeds." Dr. Charles Harris. Page 368.

What is the application of Psa. 45? Is the Bride mentioned in the Psalm Israel or the Church? How are we to understand the expressions, "unto the king" and "unto thee" in v. 14?

In order to fully understand Psa. 45, it will have to be accepted that its principal application, so far as the Bride is concerned, is not to the Church but to Israel. The expressions, "King's daughters," "the daughter of Tyne," and "the rich among the people," etc., are more easily explained when we think of Israel in her future exaltation above the other nations, and acknowledged as Bride by the Lord, in keeping with His promises of Isa. 54. 5; 62. 5; Hos. 2. 19, 20, etc., than when we think of the Church. Yet there are, no doubt, one or two expressions, such as, "Forget also thine own people" and "raiment of needlework" (as compared with Rev. 19. 8, R.V.), which appear to suit the Church better, although they can perhaps be understood of Israel also.

Of course, some take it for granted that if the Church is the Bride, Israel cannot be; and if Israel is the Bride, the Church cannot be; but this is to lose sight of the fact that the term is figurative, and there is no reason why the figure should not be used of Israel in the Old Testament and of the Church in the New Testament. This is the case with other figures, e.g., Israel is the Vine of the Old Testament (Psa. 80. 8, etc.), while the Church in union with Christ is the Vine in the New Testament; Israel is the House in the Old Testament, while the Church is the House in the New Testament (Num. 12. 7; Heb. 3. 6). Even the term, "Body," which we usually look upon as the exclusive property of the Church, had been used of Israel in Isa. 26. 19 (where the italics should be omitted).

Moreover, it may be that these early pictures, like the early prophecies of the Messiah's coming, in which events separated (as we now know) by many years, are joined together as if one—are so worded by the Holy Ghost as to include applications both to Israel and the Church, some details being more suited to the one application, and some to the other. This would be helpful in studying the Song of Songs, of which Psa. 45 seems to be the germ.

I consider this to be a better way of looking at the matter, than to accept the view suggested in Newberry's Bible, where he distinguishes two women, the "Queen" (Israel), to whom he applies vv. 9-12, and the "King's daughter" (the Church) to whom he applies vv. 13-15. I could agree that the Israel aspect of the picture is prominent in the former verses, and the Church aspect in the latter; but I cannot see two separate Brides in the Psalm definitely distinguished from one another.

With regard to v. 14, I think that the "unto the King" at the beginning of the verse, and the "unto thee" at the end of it, refer to the same person. It is only an example of what is very common in the Psalms, in

Isa. 53, and elsewhere, that is, an abrupt change from speaking about the Lord, to speaking to Him. And this speaking to Him is continued into verse 16, which, as well as verse 17, is addressed to the King, not to the Bride, although in our A.V. it looks as if it were.   W.R.

Please explain Psalm 49. 8.

Verses 6 and 7 circumscribe the power of riches; for all the wealth of the world cannot redeem a brother, nor give to God a ransom for him. The word for "redeem" is not the more usual word gā'al (subst. gō'ēl. Job. 19. 25; Jer. 50. 34), but pādāh—to loose, hence to redeem by paying a price, to let go—preserve (Num. 18. 15; Psa. 25. 22). The word for "ransom" is the atonement word—Kōpher.

Now comes the subject of the question (v. 8): "For the redemption (pidyôn, same root as pādāh) of their soul is precious, and it ceaseth for ever." This certainly seems ambiguous, but the R.V. is an improvement, if more correct: "For the redemption of their soul is costly, and must be let alone for ever." This almost goes back to the English version known as "the Great Bible" brought out in 1539, under the superintendance of Miles Coverdale (subsequent to his own well-known translation), the Psalter of which is still found embedded in the "Book of Common Prayer" of the "Established Church." This version runs: "It cost more to redeem their souls, so that he must let that alone for ever." The meaning then seems plain; Redemption is beyond man's means, so it is wiser to let that alone. But verse 15 comes in as the positive solution. "But God will redeem (pādāh) my soul from the power of the grave, for He will receive me."   W.H.

The R.V. of Psalm 68. 11: "The women that publish the tidings are a great host," has been used in favour of public preaching of the Gospel by women. What is its real meaning?

Psalm 68 is primarily connected with the bringing up of the Ark by David to the "resting place" (Psa. 132. 8, R.V.) which he had, in accordance with his boyhood's vow, prepared for it; though, of course, prophetically it looks forward to events far beyond that. It begins in v. 1 with the words uttered by Moses on the occasions when the Ark was being taken up to move onward through the wilderness (Num. 10. 35); and in its earlier verses it recounts in few words the bright side of Israel's past history, as connected with what the Ark symbolised—the presence and power of God with His people. Their march through the desert; their arrival in the promised inheritance; and their victories over the nations that dwelt there, and those others that surrounded it; are pictured as won by the Presence of God with them. On various occasions these were celebrated in song, especially by their women-folk; and it is to such celebrations that the words quoted in the question refer.

See examples of them, in Exod. 15. 20, 21, after the Red Sea crossing; in Judges 5. 1-31, after Barak's defeat of the host of Sisera; and in 1 Sam. 18. 6, 7, after David's own victory over Goliath. Also compare the rejoicing on this occasion of the bringing up of the Ark as described in 2 Sam. 6. 15-22. It is worthy of note that in many respects our psalm may be compared with the above-mentioned Song of Deborah.

Those who advocate that women should do what in the New Testament they are forbidden to do, must be hard bestead for proof, if they have to come to Psalm 68. 11 for it.   **W.R.**

In what sense, if any, did our Lord confess His people's sins? Is Psalm 69. 5 distinctly applicable to Him? How are we to understand the phrase, "He was made sin for us"? (2 Cor. 5. 21).

These questions open out very important points which are spoken of very loosely to-day and which need careful handling. As for the first, I believe it to be far from scriptural to assert any such thing. Hymn-writers have said so, and the saints have allowed themselves at their bidding, to sing wrong doctrine. I have long shrunk from singing the words of J. G. Deck's, otherwise beautiful hymn,

> "Our sins, our guilt, in love divine
> **Confessed** and borne by Thee."

To confess sins makes them our own, and that the Lord never did. Is it necessary or proper for one paying a debt for a friend, to confess that he incurred it himself? It would be untrue and quite gratuitous and would detract from the favour. The words in question, might be altered to some such phrase as, "All known and borne by Thee." Our Lord Jesus was always the sinless One, and He suffered **vicariously** for our sins; but they were always ours, not His "Who His own self bare our sins in His own body on the tree" (1 Peter 2. 24). There was always a vast distinction between the Saviour and the sinner, He became surety for sin, but never identical with the sinner. As for applying Psalm 69. 5 to our Lord—"O God, Thou knowest my foolishness; and my sins (Heb. guiltiness) are not hid from Thee"—it is, I believe, most improper to do so. We must remember that even the Messianic Psalms represent to a certain degree the experience of the writer, but go beyond this to any godly ones, brought low before God, on account of their sins, especially the faithful remnant of the last days. Bearing this in mind, there is much of the Psalm which can be applied to Christ. But it is exceedingly dangerous, in my judgment, to attempt to apply all to Him. Fancy applying such words as above to "Christ the **Wisdom** of God" and "the **Holy One** of God"!

As for 2 Cor. 5. 21, we can perhaps best see its meaning by negatives, it cannot mean that our Lord became personally that abominable thing called sin. But even had such a thing been possible, it would not have helped us in any way; clearly the Lord was made sin, in such a way as to affect us and cause us to become the righteousness of God in Him. There was only one way to effect this, namely, to take our place, or in other words, be treated as we deserved as an offering for sin. Thus He atoned for sin on the cross, and became our righteousness on resurrection ground. W.H.

Is it right to assert that our Lord died of a broken heart, in accordance with the words of Psalm 69. 20?

It is surely very important "rightly to divide" the Psalms, as the rest of Scripture, distinguishing what may represent the actual experiences of the Psalmist, from what goes much further either to those of the future faithful remnant of Israel, or to our Lord Himself. Such a Psalm as the 38th would apply all through, one would judge, to the faithful remnant, and perhaps in parts to Christ, but it is truly a shocking misapplication to attempt, as has been done sometimes, to interpret such words as are used in vv. 5 and 7 of our Holy, spotless Lord. Even in the most clearly Messianic Psalms, a serious mistake is made in applying, or attempting to apply, everything to Christ, e.g., such verses as Psa. 40. 12, and 69. 5 ("Mine iniquities have taken hold upon me . . . they are more than the hairs of my head," and "Oh God, thou knowest my foolishness and my sins are not hid from thee"). It is blessedly true that He bore our sins, but they were "ours" all the time, not His. "He suffered once for sins," but it was also as "the just for the unjust," for even as the sin-offering He was most holy (see Lev. 6. 29). There was never any confusion between Him, the guiltless, Holy One and those for whom He suffered—the guilty and defiled.

As for the special verse in question, I regard it as quite erroneous to maintain that our Lord "died of a broken heart," even though some medical authorities have asserted it; but doctors differ here as elsewhere. How can it be possible to apply the ordinary diagnosis to One whose side had been pierced, since death, with a spear? Any symptoms might occur, one would think, under such circumstances. Above all let it be remembered we are speaking of One who strictly speaking did not "die of anything", but laid down His life. He did not gradually collapse, as an ordinary dying man; "He dismissed His Spirit" (Matt. 27. 50, lit. translation). He died "too soon" in fact, as all testified. He did not die of shock or heart attack, for as He died, He cried with a loud voice and uttered two memorable, articulate sentences: "It is finished," and "Father into Thy hands I commend my Spirit." But this being said, I see no difficulty whatever in applying to our Lord the words in question, "Reproach hath broken my heart." They are clearly used in a figurative sense; for the verse runs on: "I am full of heaviness and I looked for some to take pity but there was none." Is it not evident that our Lord continued to live after His heart was "broken" in this sense? Heart-breaks, as some know, are not always physical, but moral, and they may not be less poignant for that. But this is quite distinct from the sentimental and mistaken view combated above, that our Lord died in any sense from a broken heart.   W.H.

What is the meaning of the text, "Thou has magnified Thy word above all Thy name" (Psa. 138. 2)?

Perhaps this statement will be more easily understood if we use an illustration. The Churches of Macedonia (i.e. the Philippians, etc.) had a good "name" with the Apostle Paul, as liberal givers from their very beginning (Phil. 4. 15, 16). Yet on an occasion when he sought their help for the supply of the need of poor saints in Judæa, they did far beyond his highest expectation, as he tells us in 2 Cor. 8. 1-5. In effect, he says of them: "They have magnified their liberality above all their name for it."

Now, God's "Name" represents the sum of His manifestations of Himself. As has been said by others, it is the product of His deeds, and is according to His historically manifested glory. In plainer words, it is His reputation for lovingkindness to His people, faithfulness to His promise, etc., as may be seen by its use in such passages as Exod. 9. 16 and Josh. 7. 9. David, who according to its title is the author of Psalm 138, has already known much of the name and fame of the Lord, both from the history of His people, and from His previous dealings with himself. But on the occasion for which he gives praise so fervently in this psalm, he feels that God has shown His faithfulness in keeping His word, even beyond all that past experience would have led him to expect, and so he says, "I will . . . praise Thy name for Thy loving-kindness and Thy truth; for Thou has magnified Thy word above all Thy name."

Possibly the occasion may be that which is referred to in 2 Sam. 7, where at least he is found speaking in a strain very similar. He says there, "Thou hast brought me hitherto; and this was yet a small thing in Thy sight, O Lord God; but Thou hast spoken of Thy servant's house for a great while to come; . . . for Thy word's sake . . . hast Thou done all these great things . . . to make Thee a name; . . . and let Thy name be magnified for ever" (2 Sam. 7. 18-26).   W.R.

PROVERBS

What is the meaning of Proverbs 21. 18, "The wicked shall be a ransom for the righteous, and the transgressor for the upright"?

Compare the following passages, in which a similar thought is more clearly expressed:

"The righteous is delivered out of trouble, and the wicked cometh in his stead" (Prov. 11. 8).

"I gave Egypt for thy ransom, . . . I have loved thee, therefore will I give men for thee and people for thy life" (Isa. 43. 3, 4).

"They hanged Haman on the gallows that he had prepared for Mordecai" (Esther 7. 10).

"Those men which had accused Daniel . . . cast . . . into the den of lions" (Dan. 6. 24).

And note the use of the same word "ransom" in the Isaiah passage, and of "in his stead" in Prov. 11.

The above Scriptures, and others which might be added, suggest two things. First, that God may sometimes deliver His own at the cost of severe suffering, or even destruction, to the unsaved. Second, that the wicked at times suffer the very fate which they themselves had prepared for the righteous. Proverbs 21. 18 contains the first of these thoughts, and probably the second as well.   W.R.

ECCLESIASTES

In Ecclesiastes ix. 4, we find these words:—"For to him that is joined to all the living there is hope, for a living dog is better than a dead lion." Does this teach that there is hope as long as life remains?

The Ecclesiast (chap. viii. 16, 17) beholds all the work of God, and desires to understand what God is doing, but not even a wise man can fathom it (**i.e.**, by his natural intelligence). God must make it plain, as He did His WAYS unto Moses (Psa. ciii. 7). But of one thing he is sure, that the righteous and wise are in God's hand (ch. 9. 1). But judged by all they see before them (**i.e.**, by the sight of the eyes), no man can gauge whether love or hatred is his, because, by the fact of sin being in the world, one event—death—comes to all, righteous and wicked, religious and irreligious. Surely that is an evil thing. I think that verse 4 only emphasises this evil—an inevitable death. For while there is life there is hope, "for a living dog"—an unclean animal in the Oriental and Biblical view—"is better than a *dead* lion"—the king of beasts. When Solomon wrote, many problems now revealed were unsolved. "Jesus Christ had not yet brought life and immortality to light through the Gospel." But none the less, the Ecclesiastes is a true revelation from God of the workings of man's mind, so that man may know himself.   W.H.

SONG OF SONGS

Who are the speakers in the Song of Solomon? Some say they are Christ and the Church; others, God and Israel. Who is the questioner in chap. 5. 9?

The Song of Songs is not, of course, a mere love-song; nor is it a song of espousals, but a marriage song. Certain companies of persons are introduced and take part in the dialogue, e.g., the watchmen, the daughters of Jerusalem; but the Bridegroom and the bride are the principals. Who are they? The Church was an unrevealed mystery in the Old Testament, so may safely be ruled out. Surely there can be no doubt that we have in this Book, a beautiful picture of the affections of Jehovah toward the true Israel, and the response of the bride. "I am married to you, saith Jehovah" (Jer. 3. 14). "Thy maker is thy husband" (Isa. 54. 5). The watchmen of the city seem to represent men of the world with no sympathy for the bride, while the daughters of Jerusalem may stand for nominal Israel. These distinctions being made, the inspired language of the Book fits in well with the affections of a believer to-day toward Christ, when enjoying communion with the "Lover of his soul." The spiritual believer knows how to use the Book in this way to his own soul's blessing and to the glory of Christ.

W.H.

ISAIAH

Is there any good ground for the change, advocated by some, of the word "virgin" in Isa. 7. 14 to "young married woman" or "young woman of marriageable age"?

I believe "virgin" can be shown to be the true rendering, along several lines of proof. It is significant that those who propose this change are mostly of Modernist tendencies. Such men deny the miraculous in general, and would gladly get rid of the Virgin Birth of our Lord, and create a discrepancy between Matt. 1. 23 and our verse. Gesenius, the well-known author of the Hebrew and Chaldee Lexicon, a man with a strong Modernistic bias, says, "The true meaning of 'almāh, ("virgin" in Isa. 7. 14) is a girl of marriageable age, with no special reference to her unspotted virginity, which is expressed," he affirms, "by another word, beˤthûlāh"; but that moral purity is surely taken for granted, unless definite proof is alleged to the contrary. He adds, "'almāh is used of a youthful spouse recently married"; but the only place he quotes to prove this is the verse in question, Isa. 7. 14, where he wants to rule out the other meaning, and thus begs the question. He also quotes Canticles 6. 8 to prove his point, but as virgins ('**almōth**) are distinguished there from wives and concubines, we may ask what they do stand for, if not for unmarried girls of unspotted character? Gesenius admits, moreover, that his word "**beṯhûlāh**" is sometimes clearly used of a woman newly married, e.g., in Joel 1. 8. If that word had been used in Isa. 7. 14 he might still have found a loop-hole, and have quoted Joel to show that even "**beṯhûlāh**" was not conclusive. God, however, has raised up to oppose Gesenius a man of equal scholarship, namely, Dr. S. P. Tregelles, of humble evangelical faith, and also of European reputation as a Hebraist. He translated Gesenius' Lexicon from the German, and has added notes in brackets to neutralise, where necessary, the bias of the Lexicon. The following note by Dr. Tregelles occurs under " '**almāh**": "Gesenius' object in view in seeking to undermine the opinion, which would assign the signification of virgin to this word, is clearly to raise a discrepancy between Isa. 7. 14 and Matt. 1. 23. **Nothing which has been stated** (i.e. by Gesenius earlier in the article) **does, however, really give us any ground for assigning another meaning.** . . . '**Almāh** in the Punic language signifies virgin. . . . The absolute authority of the New Testament is, however, quite sufficient to settle the question to a Christian." We may refer here to the words of Matt. 1. 23: "Now all this was done that it might be fulfilled, which was spoken of the Lord by the prophet, saying, Behold, a virgin shall be with child, and shall bring forth a son, and they shall call his name Emmanuel, which is by interpretation, God with us." The Evangelist uses the ordinary Greek word, "**parthenos**," for "virgin," used too in Luke 1. 27, of the Virgin Mary. The Greek Version, the Septuagint, does sometimes translate the word " '**almāh**" otherwise than by "**parthenos**," but here in Isa. 7. 14, where as Tregelles points out "it must to their minds have occasioned a difficulty," they translate by the same word that we have in the Gospels. We may suppose these learned Jews—the translators of their own Scriptures—knew at least as much of Hebrew and Greek as Modernist scholars. Matthew does not appear to have quoted from the LXX, so is an independent witness. We do not, however, in any case, need even the authority of God-fearing scholars. This is a question in which "a wayfaring man, though a fool, shall not err." Let us look at the other occurrences of the word, " '**almāh**," in the Old Testament. It is used in Gen. 24. 43 of Rebecca—the prospective wife of Isaac. The other word, "**beṯhûlāh**," occurs in verse 16, as we might say "virgin" or "maid" indiscriminately. Miriam, in Exod. 2. 8, is called an " '**almāh**," and she was clearly not a young married woman, but a maiden. This suits, too, in Prov. 30. 19. Canticles 1. 3 seems to demand the sense of virgins, as also chap. 6. 8, as we have seen. Psalm 68. 25 we may take as neutral; we cannot affirm the damsels to be virgins, though they might have been. Then there is

Ω

another consideration. The name to be given to the child—"Emmanuel," "God with us"—goes a long way to justify the translation of "virgin" by our Translators and Revisers, as such a birth demanded extra-ordinary concomitant circumstances. The context, too, favours the same conclusion. Jehovah had offered Ahaz any sign he might choose to ask—"in the depth or in the height" above, that is anything comparable with the drying up of the Red Sea or the Jordan, or on the other hand, with Joshua's long day. When Ahaz refused, the prophet replied, "The Lord Himself shall give you a sign. "Behold a* (literally "the") virgin shall conceive and bear a son, and shall call his name Emmanuel." Clearly God's sign would be something extraordinarily arresting. How else would the Eternal Son of God enter into manhood except in the womb of a Virgin? The birth of a son to a young married woman, far from being an arresting sign, would not be a sign at all, but the most natural of events.   W.H.

What is the difference in Isa. 9. 6. between the expressions the "child born" and the "Son given"?

There is an important difference, I believe, and one which the ex-ponents of what they term "the New Light," as to the Eternal Sonship of our Lord, would do well to consider. Why is the "child" said to be "born," but the "Son" not born, but "given"? We read in chap. 7. 14 that God had been pleased to offer to king Ahaz a sign to confirm his doubting soul, that the line of David would not be superseded by the son of Tabeal, according to the Satanic design of Rezin and Pekah, which would have set aside the purpose of God regarding His future King, who must be of the seed of David according to the flesh. Ahaz had liberty of choice; he might ask for any sign in the depth, that is commensurate with the drying up of the Red Sea, or in the height commensurate with the standing still of the sun in answer to Joshua's prayer. The king who was continually tempting God by his disobedience, refused this offer: He would not tempt the Lord, he said. Very well, then, the Lord will give a sign greater than any other known so far in the history of the world—the Virgin Birth of Him who was God: "Behold a virgin shall conceive, and bear a son, and shall call His name Immanuel" (v. 14). A great effort of unbelief has been made to show that the word, " 'almāh," translated "virgin," should be rather rendered "young married woman." Such an objection hardly shows unusual scholarship, so much as a lack of common sense; for the fact of a young married woman having a son would be no sign at all. In this verse, in the phrase "a virgin shall . . . **bear** a son," the same verb is used as in chap. 9. 6, "a child is **born**." Here the Son is viewed as the Son of

* Heb.—"the Virgin," that is the Virgin of prophecy, predestined one day to be the Virgin of history. When people talk of the Virgin to-day, they refer to the Mother of our Lord, and this expression is undoubtedly better.

Mary in the sense of Matt. 1. 25: "She brought forth her first-born Son." Why then is the "Son" said to be **"given"** in Isa. 9. 6? The reason is that there the One born is viewed as the One who had already been Son from all eternity. He could not become that by human birth. The child was born, but God gave His Eternal Son.   W.H.

What is the meaning of Isaiah 33. 14? Most Gospel preachers use it in warning the unsaved but some Bible students hold differently.

I have heard an attempt to interpret "the devouring fire," and 'everlasting burnings," as God's burning love, on the ground that the words in v. 15, "He that walketh righteously, etc.," are an answer to the question of the hypocrites, but it is not an answer at all and the interpretation is purely fantastic. "He that walketh righteously," etc., describes those who will not dwell "with everlasting burnings," but "on high" as in v. 16. Why should the sinners in Zion be afraid or the hypocrites surprised with fearfulness, if they are intended to understand that all that awaits them is the eternal enjoyment of the love of God? No, they get a glimpse of the terrors of a lost eternity and of what awaits them if they pursue their path. It is to call darkness light and light darkness to make v. 14 mean something good and pleasant. I should think only Bible students of the shallowest "Universalist" type could extract such a meaning from the passage. Certainly let evangelists continue to use it as a warning to the ungodly, for that is its legitimate use.

The word "**'ākal**"—here translated "devouring"—means literally "to eat," and is constantly used of devouring or consuming in judgment (Num. 21. 28; Isa. 24. 6; 29. 6). The word for "burnings" is from **"yāqad"**—and is used in Deut. 32. 22; "and shall **burn** to the lowest hell," see also Isa. 10. 16; and 65. 5; Jer. 15. 14 and 17. 4. It is also used of the burnings of the fire on the altar (Lev. 6. 9, 12, 13).   W.H.

Please explain what is meant by "waiting upon the Lord," as in Isaiah xl. 31.

Several Hebrew words are translated, "wait," in the Old Testament. The root used here for "wait upon" is different from that, say in Psa. lxii. 5, and elsewhere, where the R.V. Margin has "to be silent" (**"dāmam"**—properly "to be dumb"). Here the word is **"qāvāh,"** of which the primary meaning is "to be strong," and then "to await" (the idea being perhaps that waiting God's answer does need a certain strength of purpose or endurance). The two roots are found together in Psa. lxii. 5, "My soul **wait (dāmam**—be dumb) thou only upon God, for my expectation (**qāvāh** root) is from Him." Isa. xl. 31 then means that they that come to the Lord and tell Him their needs, and are will-

ing to wait His time for an answer, "shall renew their strength." Waiting
upon God gets the answer some day, and strengthens the soul to-day.
Therefore "wait (qāvāh) on thy God continually" (Hos. xii. 6).

                                                                    W.H.

In Isaiah 53. 7 we read, "He is brought as a lamb to the
slaughter, and as a sheep before her shearers is dumb"; but in
Acts 8. 32 the order is reversed, and it is said to be "as a sheep
led to the slaughter, and like a lamb dumb," etc. How are we
to account for this reversal?

The quotation in Acts is almost word for word from the Septuagint
or Greek version, the LXX, as it is described in letters. The word for
"sheep" in the Hebrew of Isaiah 53. 7 is not the same as that used in
verse 6: "All we like **sheep** (çôn) have gone astray." The word here is
of frequent occurrence, whereas that in v. 7 (rāhēl) occurs only four
times in the whole Old Testament. It comes from an unused root,
perhaps the same as rāham—to cherish—connected with an Arabic
root—to have lambs. The word in the first part of the verse, translated
"lamb" (sēh), is rendered "sheep" in several passages in the Old Testament. It seems, therefore, that the words employed by the Holy Spirit
operating on the mind of Isaiah in this verse 7, are not so precise as to
necessitate their rendering in the LXX translation as "lamb" and "sheep,"
as they appear in our rendering of Isa. 53. 7, but leave a margin of liberty
to reverse the meaning of the words, and put lamb second, and sheep
first, as in Acts 8. It is a question of the words used in the Old Testament verse, which as I have said, are not closely defined and of the
choice of words by the translators of the Greek version, from which the
Eunuch would be reading.   W.H.

Please explain the expressions: "He was taken from prison
and from judgment," and "He made His grave with the wicked,
and with the rich in His death" (Isa. 53. 8, 9).

The R.V. gives, "By oppression and judgment He was taken away,"
which is certainly more easily understood than A.V., and would seem to
mark the fact that the Messiah would be cut off not by that sudden
violence, which often threatened His life, e.g., stoning or casting down
a precipice (see Luke 4. 29; John 5. 16, 18; 8. 59), but by a judicial
though unjust sentence. Dr. Lowth translates: "By an oppressive
judgment He was taken away," which fits in with the Revised Version.
As for the second phrase in question, the R.V. has: "And they made
His grave with the wicked;" and this would no doubt have been the
normal burial of our Lord with the malefactors (a description then true
of both the robbers, without prejudice to the conversion of one later).
Dr. Lowth again translates: "His grave was appointed with the wicked,

but with the rich was His tomb." We should note that **"the wicked"** is plural, **"the rich,"** singular. This is no doubt the meaning of the prophecy. Very few of the Lord's disciples were rich men, fewer still probably had a tomb in their garden, only one had a tomb in a garden close to the scene of the crucifixion, and this was Joseph of Arimathæa, and in him was fulfilled the prophetic word.   W.H.

In Isaiah 53. 12, who are the "great" and the "strong", and in what way does God "divide" to the Messiah a portion with them?

Is it not probable that we place overmuch emphasis on these three words, and that we seek to get more out of them than perhaps they are meant to convey? "Divide" seems to suggest to our minds a cutting up into so many definite shares, of which Christ gets His, and certain others get theirs. But what if we use the word "assign" as is done in Darby's Translation, or render the clause, "I will allot to Him a portion among the mighty", as Gesenius does in his Lexicon! Either of these is quite correct as a rendering, and at the same time does not tie up our thoughts to an actual division of something into two or more parts. This should make it clear to us that the meaning may be no more than as follows: "I will assign to Him such a spoil as is usually that obtained by the great and the strong; and I will do so in recompense for ("Therefore") His having suffered in littleness and weakness (as pictured in v. 7, etc.), and for ("because") His having poured out His soul unto death (middle of v. 12).

Viewed in this way, the words "great" and "strong", which are both plurals, need not refer to any particular individuals, but to the great and strong in general. Compare how the same two words are coupled together in such passages as Isa. 8. 7; Joel 2. 2; and Zech. 8. 22; the word "many" in the first and last of these being the same Hebrew word as "great" in our verse.

The translators of the Septuagint, when turning the passage into Greek, rendered the second clause. "He shall divide the spoils OF the mighty", and left out the "with" of the first clause also; thus suggesting the meaning to be a complete triumph over all His foes, however "many" or "mighty" they were. Various commentators agree with this view of the passage. But whether we take it thus, and think of the great and mighty ones as His enemies, amongst whom He stands out pre-eminent; the basic idea in the statement is much the same—that the One who stooped so low and who suffered so much, has been given a place and an honour beyond all others.   W.R.

Does Isaiah 60. 19 and 20 teach that there will be night during the Millennium, or does it refer to the Eternal State? (See Rev. 21. 23, 24, 25).

Isaiah 60 seems undoubtedly to refer to the millennial glory of the saved nation of Israel. Verse 12 could not apply to the Eternal state, The passage—vv. 19 and 20, does not say there will be no sun or moon, but they will not be **needed** in "the city of the Lord, the Zion of the Holy One of Israel," that is, in the rebuilt Jerusalem, as we see her described by the prophet Ezekiel. The glory of that city will not be her historical associations, nor her unparalleled situation, but the fact that the Lord will be there (Ezekiel 48. 35). Indeed that will give her her new name, "Jehovah-Shammah." (The Lord is there). Though no doubt the sun will continue to rise and set, and the moon to wax and wane over the millennial earth, the prophet says to Israel: "**Thy** sun shall no more go down," that is, the Lord Jesus, reigning as their Messiah in their midst will not cease to lighten His city. He whose face shone as the sun on the Holy Mount, will never be eclipsed, and they will need no other light. As for Rev. 21. 23, 24, 25, it does definitely say "there will be no night there." I believe the whole chapter from verse 9 to the end is a description of "the New Jerusalem," in connection with the New Earth, which will only supersede "the first earth" at the **close** of the millennium.   W.H.

DANIEL

When did the 2,300 days in Daniel 8. 14 commence and end? What sanctuary was to be cleansed at the end of that period?

No doubt, all questions concerning what it has pleased God to reveal to us, have their importance, and so with these, but they gain a certain fictitious importance, whether the questioner knows it or not, owing to the use or rather misuse made of the above passage by the so-called Seventh-day Adventists, to build up their arbitrary and altogether unscriptural system of interpretation, which nullifies the atoning work of Christ in its present application to the believer, and justification by faith alone. The originator of the system was a certain W. Miller, who foretold the return of the Lord to the earth on a certain day in 1844. His followers in white garments were expecting the event on that day. When it failed to realise, Miller was himself rid of his idea and confessed his error, and the whole system would have collapsed had not one of Miller's adepts, a certain Mrs. Ellen White imagined a way of escape to account for the evident failure of Miller's prophecy. A mistake had been made, she affirmed: **the Lord had come,** not to earth, however, but to the most holy place of the sanctuary in heaven to complete (!) the work of atonement. He had till then (i.e., up to 1844) been "pleading in the first apartment" of the sanctuary on behalf of penitent believers, and thus securing their pardon and acceptance with the Father, yet their sins still remained upon the books of record. So that, according to this theory, the sins of believers, though pardoned, **still remained upon the books of record,** and are supposed to be constantly defiling the heavenly sanctuary. Could anyone imagine a more arbitrary, self-contradictory, or unscriptural system? It rejects the efficacy of His blood to cleanse from all sin. It denies that God has not only forgiven, but has also blotted out His people's sins from the book of His remembrance—"Their sins and their iniquities will I remember no more." The whole theory of "the sanctuary" being in heaven, and that our Lord was up to 1844 in the "first apartment" of it, is pure imagination, In any case, "the veil was rent at the cross from the top to the bottom", so that since then, the sanctuary could be no more divided into two apartments, that is, into Holy Place and Holy of Holies. Moreover, Heb. 8. 1 and 9. 24 tell us that the place of our Lord's priestly work is where He is now and has been since His ascension—"on the right hand of the throne of the Majesty in the heavens"; "in heaven itself now to appear in the presence of God for us." That was true when "Hebrews" was written, and there is not a line to prove that any other entrance into any other part of the heavenly sanctuary was ever contemplated or took place, still less that such an event would occur in 1844. I believe the prophecy of Daniel does not deal directly with the church at all, but with God's earthly people, Israel. The sanctuary that is spoken of in chap. 8. 13-14 is the literal sanctuary of the temple at Jerusalem, and "the 2,300 days" are, in fact, **days,** not years. This passage ought to be read with chap. 9. 27, where we see that the period in question is the last "week" or period of seven years, of the 70 weeks of years (lit. Heb., "seven of sevens"*), during which the covenant will be made between the Man of Sin, the last governmental head of the revived Roman Empire, who is called in Dan. 9. 26 "the Prince that shall come", and the last false King of Israel, the Antichrist. This covenant will be broken in the midst of the week (v. 27), that is after 3½ years: the daily sacrifice will be taken away and the Sanctuary of the Temple will in some way be defiled (see Dan. 11. 31) by what is called "the abomination of desolation", or in more usual language, the image of the beast set up in it, "standing in the holy place" (Matt. 24. 15). It is this vile image which will defile the sanctuary, and it will only be cleansed at the coming of the Lord at the end of the 2,300 days. Seven prophetic years is a period of 2,520 days, so that the time will be 220 days, or a little more than 7 months, short of this. This may be accounted for by God's shortening of the days of persecution by the two Beasts for the elect's sake, according to Matt. 24. 22. There are those who fancy that Seventh-day Adventism is a more or less harmless system taken up with

* This is not the same as the day-year theory that every day can be taken for a year, because the word for "week" is a period of "seven", it may be days, weeks or years.

perhaps strange views on the Coming of the Lord. It is a deadly heretical system which denies the fundamentals of the faith, nullifies the atonement, attributes a sinful nature to our Holy Lord, makes Satan the ultimate bearer of Christians' sins, and insists on his final annihilation and that of all the wicked dead.   W.H.

What scriptural reason is there for stating as a fact that the seventieth week was cut off from the rest and is yet to be fulfilled?

The scriptural reason is understood by reading the passage (Dan. ix. 24-27). The seventy "hebdomads," or periods of seven years are said by Gabriel to be "determined upon Daniel's people (the Jews) and the holy city, to punish the transgressors . . . and to anoint the Most Holy." Then, in verse 25, this whole period of 490 years is resolved into its constituents of 49 years (during which building operations were completed), then a further 434 years to the cutting off of the Messiah, that is 483 years in all, or 7 years short of the total 490. Why is this? Because as Zechariah xi. 10 tells us, when "the staff, even Beauty," is cut off (a description of the same event as the cutting off of Messiah), Jehovah's covenant, which he had made with all the people, is broken, so that one period of seven years, or one "hebdomad," still remains to be fulfilled. This will have its place when the prince of the people who destroyed the city (the Romans in 70 A.D.) will confirm a covenant with many for one week or period of seven years. The fact that He will break His covenant in the middle of the period, *i.e.*, after 3½ years, will not override the fact that this "hebdomad" will complete the 490 years determined on the Jews, to end with "anointing the Most Holy," which will take place when Christ returns in glory to reign.   W.H.

I have read somewhere that the Tribulation, a period of seven years, would be shortened by 220 days, which the writer confirmed by a reference to Daniel 8. 13 and 14. Is this so?

I do not think there is the least justification for saying that the Great Tribulation is to last seven years. That is the length of time for which the Covenant is made between the Prince (or last Great Head of the Roman Empire Revived—otherwise known as the first Beast) and many of Israel, under the Antichrist, or second Beast (Dan. 9. and Rev. 13), but it is only when the Covenant is broken in the midst of the week, and the daily sacrifice taken away, that the Great Tribulation and "the time of Jacob's trouble" will occur (Jer. 30. 7; Matt. 24. 21). It is quite clear from the last passage that the days of the Great Tribulation will be shortened—"For the elect's sake those days shall be shortened" (v. 22). But by how much, is another question. I have myself believed that this may be inferred from Dan. 8. 13, 14. The question in the former verse refers to the vision concerning the daily sacrifice and the transgression of desolation (or that maketh desolate), and the answer is, "Unto two thousand and three hundred days—then shall the sanctuary be cleansed" —that is, 220 days less than the full tribulation of 3½ years, but that does not say that the period of seven years will be shortened, but that in some way the years of the Great Tribulation will be. How this will be effected we can safely leave in the hands of God, who alone is sufficient. W.H.

What warrant have we for insisting on a "gap" or parenthesis in Daniel ch. ix, between verses 26 and 27?

There must be a gap, if not between the two verses, at least between v. 27 and the great events in the early part of v. 26, with the consequent scattering of the Jews. This verse seems to work itself out in a long defined period of war and desolation. Then comes v. 27, showing us some one king making a covenant with the many "for a week." Who is this but the prince of v. 26, whose people destroyed Jerusalem centuries before? And who are "the many" but part of the scattered Jews restored to their land, and recognised as a nation? This restoration is taking place before our eyes, for the first time for 1850 years; but no "prince" has yet appeared to make the seven years' covenant, so v. 27 is still future. Neither party will imagine why the covenant will be specially for "one week," but "the wise will understand." W.H.

Does the fact that the year day was fulfilled in Daniel's 70 weeks justify us in applying it to other periods?

In no way. The thought rests on a misapprehension. The Hebrew word, **"shābûa'"** translated, "weeks," or "week" (chap. ix. 24-27), does not necessarily mean weeks of DAYS, but also of years, etc., that is, any "hebdomad," or period of seven. When Daniel in the next chapter, vv. 2 and 3, wishes it to be understood that he was fasting three literal weeks, he uses the expression in the Hebrew, "weeks of DAYS," probably to avoid confusion with the usage in chap. ix. Here seventy "hebdomads" of YEARS are meant. The so-called, "year day" theory—that is, that when we read of definite periods, e.g., 1290 days, 1335 days, 1260 days, &c., we must read, "years," has been fruitful in fantastical reckonings, and is at the basis of much amateur prophecy-mongering. W.H.

ZECHARIAH AND MALACHI

Can we know from the Scriptures who are the three shepherds of Zech. xi. 8?

It would be too much for anyone to affirm that there is no light in the Scripture on any point mentioned therein. All anyone can say is that he has no light. The incident of the three shepherds forms part of a prophetic Scripture, referring to the closing days of Israel's history. As shepherds they would be responsible rulers of Israel, but their names are not indicated here, but no doubt this prophecy will shine out clearly when it is fulfilled. In the meantime students of prophecy, as has well been said, are not called to try to be prophets.   W.H.

In what sense are we to understand Mal. 4. 6, "Lest I come and smite the earth with a curse," seeing that the ground was cursed by God for man's sake in Gen. 3. 17? Surely that has never been recalled.

No, that is clear, but in the former case it was the ground (i.e., the red earth, " ' dāmāh," same root as "Adam"—the man of clay) which was cursed. That is, the soil was rendered, as a governmental act of God, less productive of the fruits of the earth, and productive, for the first time, of thorns and thistles. This word is often translated, "earth" (e.g., Gen. 1. 25), but is quite distinct from the word so translated in v. 1, which is " 'ereç." It is true that this sometimes is translated, "ground," e.g., Gen. 19. 1, but it also refers to the world, as in above, or as in ch. 1. 10—earth as opposed to sea, and again far more commonly it is translated, "land," as in: "the **land** of Egypt," "the **land** of Canaan," "the promised **land**," and this is the word used in Mal. 4. 6, which may refer to the land of Israel or indeed to the whole earth. If the final testimony of Elias is not listened to, then God will pour out His last judgments on the earth as a whole, including **the** land. The words for "curse" are also quite distinct; that in Gen. 3. 17, is "ah-rar," as also in verse 14 and chapter 4. 11. This has a sense of devastation behind it. The word in Mal. 4. 6 is "herem"—signifying a thing devoted to utter destruction. The word in Deut. 21. 23 is quite distinct from either of these. It is from a root, "qālal" "to be light"—"to esteem lightly," and then to curse, to execrate. The verb here is actually an abstract noun, but becomes concrete in this place—"he that is hanged is **the** curse of God." All these words present to us different aspects of God's hatred of and judgment against sin. Just as salvation has its many sides and manifestations, so has damnation in its ultimate issues. There are many curses, for the rebel, as well as many blessings for His own.

W.H.

NEW TESTAMENT

MATTHEW

Why is Joseph's genealogy given in this Gospel, instead of that of Mary, seeing that Joseph was not the father of the Lord Jesus?

There are, as is well known, not one but two genealogies of Christ in the Gospels. In Matt. 1 His royal descent is traced from Abraham, through David and the kings of Judah, down to Joseph, His legal, though not His actual father. But in Luke 3 His natural descent is traced from Mary's own father, Heli, through a different branch of the Davidic family up to Adam. The phrase, "Being, as was supposed, the son of Joseph," which is parenthetically inserted in Luke 3. 23, really answers the questions asked above. For since He was supposed, or legally reckoned, to be Joseph's son, it was necessary that there should be what might be called an official genealogy, through him to David and Abraham, as well as that through His mother, in order that all objections to His claim to be "Son of David" should be silenced. In Matthew's Gospel Joseph is prominent, and in Luke's, Mary, not merely in the genealogies, but in the entire narrative, which in each case is as it should be, in view of the Jewish character of the former, and the Gentile character of the latter.   W.R.

Is Rahab of Jericho the same person as is mentioned in "Ruth" and Matt. 1. 5? Comparing the dates, this would seem impossible.

We certainly believe in their identity. Only one person of the name is known in the Old Testament (the "Rahab" of Psalm 87. 4, etc., being a poetical designation for Egypt); and Matthew mentions a person of that name, living at the same epoch, as the well-known woman, without further description, as though everyone would know who was meant. This seems to point clearly to Rahab of Jericho. In the book of Ruth only three generations are given—Boaz, Obed and Jesse—between Salmon, the prince of Judah, who married Rahab, and David. The story of Ruth does not come chronologically after "Judges," but as v. 1 of chap. 1. tells us, is embedded in its history—"in the days when the judges ruled." Salmon may have married Rahab many years after the taking of Jericho. The 450 years of the judges begin at the partition of the land and go on to Saul (Acts 13. 20). Possibly Boaz was the son of the old age of Salmon and we know he was himself elderly when he married Ruth. There are still serious difficulties, but no doubt if we knew all, all would be plain. Perhaps the desire to find a second Rahab is due to a feeling as to her antecedents. The other women mentioned along with her in our Lord's genealogy had all some disability. At least Rahab and Ruth were trophies of divine grace; and what are we to say of the wicked **men** in the genealogy, Rehoboam, Ahaz, Joram, Jehoiakim, etc.? Indeed, of the best of the links in the chain we must say, "All these once were sinners defiled in His sight." Not one was worthy to be an ancestor of our Lord. But our Lord, though truly man by virgin birth, was completely detached from any inherited taint of the sin of Adam, by the fact of His miraculous conception by the Holy Spirit. He was "that Holy Thing" from His mother's womb. He knew no sin, neither was sin in Him. Let go that, and Christianity must go at once, as far as **we** are concerned.   W.H.

Where did the wise men (Matthew 2. 1) find the child Jesus—in Bethlehem or Nazareth?

I do not think there can be any reasonable doubt that it was in Bethlehem. Verse 1 tells us the narrative happened "when Jesus was born in Bethlehem." It was thither they were directed by the teaching of the elders (vv. 4-6) and sent by Herod. Nazareth is not mentioned. It was in Bethlehem and its borders that the slaughter of the innocents took place (ver. 16), after the Child and Mary and Joseph had departed into Egypt. From verse 22 we learn that after the death of Herod they would have returned into Judæa, but hearing that Archelaus, his son, was reigning in his stead, Joseph was afraid to go thither and being warned of God in a dream, he turned aside into the parts of Galilee and dwelt in a city, now mentioned for the first time—Nazareth.   W.H.

How are we to understand the words in Matt. 2. 23: "He shall be called a Nazarene"? Some connect them with the Nazarite vow, but how did that depend on living in Nazareth?

The exact words quoted are not to be found **verbatim** in any particular Old Testament Prophet, and the evangelist does not assert so much, but only, as it seems, that the sense of his quotation "was spoken by the prophets." The phrase cannot refer to the Nazariteship of the Lord, because His consecration was not on the line of the Jewish vow of the Nazarite. He was not a Nazarite in the literal sense, and had He been, that would not have depended on His living in Nazareth. Indeed, this interpretation may be ruled out, for the words both in Hebrew and Greek are different—that for Nazarite being "Nazir" or "Nazeiraios," whereas an inhabitant of Nazareth is generally "Nazōraios" or else (e.g., Mark 1. 24 or Luke 4. 34) "Nazarēnos." Some have thought the reference is to Nazareth, as a despised place, which would tally so well with our Lord's name of Nazarene, which certainly conveyed the thought of reproach. However this may be, the more probable interpretation seems to be that which connects the words of Matthew with such a passage as Isa. 11. 1, "There shall come forth a rod out of the stem of Jesse, and a **Netzer** (Branch) shall grow out of his roots." The name "Nazareth" is probably derived from Netzer, from the bushes and shrubs which were a feature of the landscape, a fact that would thus recall the prophetic name. W.H.

Is the Sermon on the Mount the rule for the Christian to-day?

The question is not, be it noted, whether the principles of the Sermon on the Mount are applicable to us to-day; but was it intended to be the rule of Christian living? Of course, it is part of God's Word, and as such, is profitable for doctrine, reproof, correction and instruction in righteousness. So, indeed, is the Law of Sinai, and the rest of the Scriptures, but that does not prevent our drawing dispensational differences, and holding that certain parts do not apply to us primarily or directly. The law is not the Christian's rule of life, for we are told again and again (e.g., Romans 7. 4; Galatians 2. 19) that we have died to the law. It would then be difficult to assert that the Sermon on the Mount, which is the quintessence of the law, is the Christian rule of life. It may be questioned whether many who laud it as a code of morals, and make it literally binding as a rule on the Christian, have a very clear idea of its teaching, or really practise it themselves in any exhaustive way. They seem to have in their mind a dozen or so verses about giving to every man that asketh you, letting a man have your cloak who asks for your coat, going with a man two miles if he forces you to go one, and giving your right cheek to the one who has just smitten you on the left. But this is only a very small part of the Sermon, and if no one has ever perfectly obeyed the ten commandments, it is equally certain that no one has ever perfectly carried out the Sermon which deals with the hidden thoughts of the heart, as well as with acts. Indeed, when Paul was before Ananias and was unjustly smitten, he did not turn the other cheek, nor did our Lord Himself before Caiaphas, as He certainly would have done, had He laid down the Sermon on the Mount as the Christian rule of conduct. In the new style of teaching, unfortunately too common, heard in our midst to-day, from men who have but a feeble grasp of any distinctive truth or place, it is often the fashion to belittle dispensational teaching. No doubt this teaching has been exaggerated, but that is no reason for denying it its true place.

To understand rightly the Sermon on the Mount, we must understand the dispensational character of the Gospel of Matthew, and in a less degree of the other Synoptists. It is addressed primarily to Israel; from the first chapter, Christ is offered them as their King—the heir to the throne of David. John the Baptist was the herald of the coming

Kingdom, and so the Lord, the twelve and the seventy; and the miracles, which are so prominent in chapters 8 and 9; were the signs of the Kingdom; it was as King that the Lord presented Himself to Israel in chapter 21 (see vv. 4, 5). The Sermon on the Mount comes in its place, as the rules binding on the children of the Kingdom, while the Kingdom is being set up. When the Kingdom was rejected, and the powers of the King attributed in chaps. 9 and 12, to Satan, then the Lord revealed the mysteries of the Kingdom, namely, how the Kingdom would be set up in men's hearts, during the absence of the rejected King. When the Church is taken away, the testimony of the Kingdom will once more come to the front, and I take it, that during that period, the Sermon on the Mount, will come into very literal force for God's servants among Israel. It has been alleged, on the other hand, that our Lord in His parting commission told His disciples to teach the converts to observe whatsoever He had commanded them, but that that does not apply to the whole of Matthew is clear, for no one would maintain that our Lord's words in Matt. 10. 5 and 6, about not preaching to the Gentiles or the Samaritans, but only to the lost sheep of the children of Israel, should be taught to converts to-day, as a rule for their witness. I only quote this to show that our Lord intends His "Sermon" to be **interpreted** in the light of subsequent revelation; e.g., "Owe no man anything"; "Whiles it remained was it not thine own?" "He that hath no sword, let him sell his garment and buy one"; "If I have done evil, bear witness of the evil, but if well why smitest thou me?"   W.H.

Help would be valued on Matt. 5. 25 and 1 Cor. 6. 9, 10.

Matt. 5. 25 inculates a wise principle of agreement, rather than of dispute and litigation on the part of the one in the wrong. The French have a proverb: "It is difficult to forgive a man, whom you have injured." An unforgiving spirit often advertises a man, as the aggressor. If the wrong-doer refuses to admit his wrong, he will have to suffer the governmental consequences of his refusal, here and now at the hand of God. But the unrepentant sinner, who refuses to humble himself before God and seek forgiveness through Christ will suffer the eternal consequences. 1 Cor. 6. 9, 10 describes some of the ungodly at Corinth. "Such were some of you," says Paul, naming various phases of sin which habitually characterised them, some one sin, some another. A believer might fall into a grave sin, a Noah into drunkenness, a David into adultery, a Peter into cursing and swearing; but these were terrible accidents in their lives, not habitual customs. A lamb might fall into the mire, but it could not rest there; a swine if dragged out of the mire would return to it again. The characteristically unrighteous shall not inherit the Kingdom of God. They must be born again. Such were some of the Corinthians (but not all grossly so), but they were "washed" (i.e., from the defilement), "sanctified" (i.e., from the habit), and "justified (i.e., from the guilt) in the Name of the Lord Jesus, and by the Spirit of our God." W.H.

With reference to the last clauses of Matt. 5. 32 and Luke 16. 18, what should be the attitude of an assembly when such cases arise?

I have never heard of such a case as that referred to in Matt. 5. 32 being brought up. Such a term would probably be used, not openly in the presence of witnesses, but in a private conversation, or in correspondence, marked "private." I should judge that such an incident might fall under the case supposed in Matt. 18. 15-17, which should then be carried out. As for the second case, in Luke 16. 18, unless the putting away had been for the definite cause notified as a justifying **exception** by our Lord in Matt. 5. 32 and 19. 9, it would clearly have to be referred at once to the elders of the assembly and must result in the offender being put away from all fellowship. W.H.

It has been said there are two orders of apostles, one of the Lord's earthly ministry (Matt. 10.; Mark 3.; Luke 9), and another of His heavenly (Eph. 4. 11). Please define the difference, if any?

Of course, Pentecost made a great difference to all believers. They had "life" before, now they had it "more abundantly" (see John 10. 10). Before, they had been individual believers united in a common love and fealty to the same Master. Now their relationship both to Him and to one another had become profoundly modified. During the Lord's ministry, if we except the special mission in Matthew 10, when they received a special enduement of power (v. 1), and a unique commission (v. 6), the apostles came little into prominence. It was the Lord who led and worked; they followed and learned of Him. Now they became perpetually "endued with power from on high," subject to the leading of the Holy Spirit. They were now united to Christ as members of His Body, and for the first time were indwelt by that Spirit. But that the eleven apostles of the Lord's earthly ministry remained, or ever were, a different apostolic order to Paul, and perhaps two or three others mentioned in the Acts has, I believe, no scriptural authority whatever. We know that the eleven apostles of the original twelve, and Matthias, all passed through Pentecost, and Paul was no doubt Spirit-baptised later at his conversion. Pentecost certainly meant for the twelve a vast accession of apostolic power, so that it is quite permissible to view them as given by the risen Christ. "He gave some apostles," though they existed before potentially as apostles. They all became partakers of Ephesian standing and blessing. Now, as he had advised them, the sphere of their action was greatly widened, for they were sent "to preach the gospel to every creature." It seems to me entirely gratuitous and mistaken to assume that Peter and his ten fellow-apostles were not in the will of God in the appointment of Matthias. No hint of this is given in the passage or subsequently. The Lord had given them "Holy Spirit" (John 20. 22) to carry them over the interval between His resurrection and Pentecost—the true "giving of the Holy Spirit." They appointed him on the authority of the Scriptures, after prayerful exercise before God, appealing to Him to dispose the lot, and Matthias is recognised in Acts 2. 14 as completing the original member of the apostles. Not only so, but Paul himself did not acknowledge any difference. He recognised the twelve as "those who were apostles before him" (Gal. 1. 17), and if he insists on his having received his call and gospel from the Lord Himself, it was only to claim equality with the others, but in no way superiority. Some attach great importance to his word, "My gospel," but this proves nothing, as he tells us in Gal. 1. 6-9, that there was only one true gospel, and in chap. 2. 2, that on his return to Jerusalem he checked the gospel he had been preaching with that of the apostles there, lest he had in any way deviated from the true gospel, which was theirs, before it was his. "In conference," he is able to affirm, "they added nothing to me," though they recognised that his special mission was to the Gentiles. So clear is this in this chapter that these mistaken teachers have imagined a theory to account for it that Paul got under Jewish influence at Jerusalem (by that right hand of fellowship given to him by Peter and James and John), and was absolutely switched off his true character of testimony. Certainly this would be strange, considering that in the same context he tells us that he openly withstood his fellow-apostle for Judaising at Antioch. That such a theory should be necessary to uphold their position, is surely enough to demonstrate its unsoundness.   W.H.

Are the "rests" of Matt. 11. 28, 29 two distinct "rests", or does it mean that the rest is not obtained by soul approach, but by taking the yoke, and learning of the Lord?

I judge that two "rests" are indicated, or perhaps I should say, two distinct stages of rest: the one, rest of conscience for the soul who has never known true rest in Christ; and the other, rest from a restless will, unsatisfied desires and self-seeking service. The word for "rest" is the same in both cases (**anapausis**—or up-rest), which might be illustrated by the action of the Good Samaritan: first he relieved the smitten one, pouring in oil and wine, and then set him on his own beast, brought him to an inn (set him down there) and took care of him. This latter action may denote the "rest" (**katapausis**—down-rest) of Hebrews 3 and 4, where this root is always used, except in verse 9: "There remaineth, therefore, a rest for the people of God." The word here means a "Sabbath rest"

(**Sabbatismos**)—the true spiritual thought of the Sabbath—a resting from our own works. This does not describe a future heavenly rest, but a Christ-rest, to be enjoyed here and now by all the people of God. W.H.

Please explain Matt. 12. 43-45, and Luke 11. 24-26; also why does Mr. Newberry insert the word, "it", in his margin for the word, "he", in Luke 11. 24?

There are certain important words in this section which, if understood, will enable us to grasp the general meaning of the passage.

The "house" refers, I believe, to the house of Israel. "Generation" refers to the class of people then living, a people hostile to the Lord Jesus. The unclean spirit is, I believe, the spirit of idolatry which once found a resting place in Israel, but of which Israel were cured as the result of their Babylonian captivity. That idolatrous spirit will find no resting place save in apostate Israel, to which house it will later return, leading them to worship a mere man—the Man of Sin—the worst form of idolatry. This will bring upon them a far more severe judgment than ever hitherto they have known and so their last end will be worse than the first.

What has been effected by Christ Who came to that house is that he swept and garnished it, turning out from it things that hitherto occupied it. The spirit of idolatry in full force (with seven other spirits) will return to that house with, as I have said, disastrous consequences. The "generation" will persist until the end. They would not have Him Who came in His Father's Name: another shall come in his own name and him they will receive. W.R.

Were "the brethren of the Lord" in such passages as Matt. 12. 46, Matt. 13. 55, etc., His actual brethren? or were they his cousins, as some teach?

Were it not for controversial reasons I do not think any such question would ever have been raised. The word for "cousin" is distinct, and that used for the Lord's "brethren," though sometimes meaning "step-brother," is the ordinary one for brother, and there is no hint in the Gospels of Joseph having been married before. This effort to make the word mean "cousin" is supposed to be necessary in order to defend the miraculous birth and the false idea existing that it is holier not to have children, than to have them; whereas the two thoughts—the Virgin Birth and the perpetual virginity of Mary, are quite distinct and independent. While we believe unswervingly in the former, we hold that the testimony of Scripture is against the latter. The expression, "the brethren (adelphoi) of the Lord," occurs nine times in the Gospels and once in the Acts. In Matt. 12. 46 and its parallels in Mark and Luke (where His mother and brethren come to Him); Matt. 13. 55 and its parallel

R

in Mark (where the brethren are named Jacob, Joseph, Simon and Judas, four common Jewish names), in connection with His mother and sisters. The four others are: John 2. 12—"His mother and His brethren," and chap. 7. 3, 5, 10, where His brethren are said not to have believed in Him. However, it is asserted by the advocates of the perpetual virginity of Mary, that "these brethren" were the sons of Alphæus, the husband of the sister of the mother of our Lord, and therefore his cousins. If this were so, it is remarkable that they should be so consistently found with the mother of Jesus, their aunt, rather than with their own mother, the wife of Alphæus or Clopas, who was still alive. Now, it is nowhere affirmed that any of the Lord's brethren were among the twelve apostles; indeed it is plainly stated in John 7, "Neither did His brethren believe on Him." But among the apostles there were at least two sons of Alphæus, James and his brother Judas, and possibly Matthew, who in Mark's Gospel is said to be "the son of Alphæus," and these certainly could not be among those who did not believe on Him. The two things are inconsistent. Afterwards the brothers did believe, but they never entered the ranks of the twelve apostles. In fact they are in some places distinguished from the apostles, e.g., in Acts 1. 14, where they were present in the prayer meeting, but apart from the eleven. See also 1 Cor. 9. 5, "As well as other apostles and as the brethren of the Lord and Cephas." In reality there are two verses in the New Testament which state implicitly that Mary had other children besides our Lord, namely Matt. 1. 25 ("till she had brought forth her first-born son"); and Luke 2. 7 ("And she brought forth her first-born son"). Now, though the Revisers have omitted, "first-born," in Matt. 1. 25, the word is not a plain and clear error, and therefore by the canon of authority laid down for the Revisionists,* it ought to have been left alone. The Luke passage is not disputed and is very emphatic. Had our Lord been the only Child of Mary, He would certainly have been called her only Son—her **"monogenēs."** As it is, He is called in both these passages her first-born, her **"prōtotokos."**   W.H.

Are the words which are translated "brethren" and "sisters" in Matt. 13. 55, 56, such as would imply that the persons mentioned were, in the strict sense, brothers and sisters of the Lord; i.e., children of Mary? Are they similar to that rendered "cousin" in Luke 1. 36?

The Greek "sungenēs," which is rendered "cousin" in the A.V. of Luke 1. 36, is as wide in its meaning as it is possible for a word conveying the thought of relationship to be. Its proper English equivalent in the verse is undoubtedly, "kinswoman," as given in the R.V.. It is employed

---

* It is backed up by good MS. authority and by the bulk of the Fathers—18 in all (See Burgon "Revision Revised," pages 123-4).

by Luke more frequently than by any other New Testament writer; and a comparison of its other occurrences in his Gospel, at chaps. 1. 58; 2. 44; 14. 12; and 21. 16, in all of which the R.V. has "kinsfolk" or "kinsmen," will show how comprehensive is its use.

On the other hand, the words, "adelphoi," and "adelphai," which are rendered "brethren" and "sisters" in Matt. 13. 55, 56, are the normal Greek words for expressing that particular relationship; and indeed the language contains none other. Like our own English word, "brother," the Greek term may, in certain circumstances, be employed in a widened sense; but when this is the case, the context will make plain what is meant. Here in Matt. 13, the fact that the two words, "brethren" and "sisters" are found together, and in conjunction with "son" and "mother" as well, forbids any such wide or vague reference being given to them; and if it were not for preconceived ideas about the perpetual virginity of Mary, it is most unlikely that any interpretation other than the ordinary and simple one would ever have been thought of. Moreever, any such wide reference would render the remark of the cavillers on this occasion almost pointless; for their reasoning evidently is, "We know this man's father, the carpenter. We know his mother, his brothers, and his sisters. There is nothing remarkable about any of these, so it is not from them that he got this wisdom, and these mighty works. Whence then is it?"

That the James, Simon, and Judas, who are here named, are not to be identified with those bearing similar names amongst Christ's disciples, as is taught by some, is made perfectly clear by the statement of John 7. 5, that at that time "neither did His brethren believe in Him." It is also borne out by Matt. 12. 46-50, where these His natural brethren are placed in direct contrast with the disciples, whom He speaks of as His "brethren," spiritually. And that Mary had other children is at least strongly suggested in the phrase, "She brought forth her **first-born** Son" (Luke 2. 7), as compared with that used a few verses before in the case of Elizabeth, "She brought forth a son" (Luke 1. 57). The statement of Matt. 1. 25, that Joseph "knew her not till she had brought forth" her Son, is another hint, pointing in the same direction.

W.R.

We read in Matt. 13. 41: "The Son of Man shall send forth his angels and they shall gather out of his kingdom all things that offend, and them which do iniquity." Are we not right in understanding the angels here to be the Church glorified, and made equal to the angels, seeing we read in Heb. 2. 5, "For unto the angels (the angels of chap. 1.) hath he not put in subjection the world to come, whereof we speak."?

No, it would be a great mistake to confound angels with the Church, as this questioner suggests. I do not know of any passage which teaches that the Church becomes angels, or indeed that any saints do. In Luke 20. 36, where our Lord uses the expression, "equal unto the angels," it is only as to the question of their immortality ("neither shall they die any more"), that the children of the resurrection (not here only the Church) "are equal to the angels." The next words add a point of blessing, in which these surpass the angels, "and are the children of God," which the angels are not. I think Heb. 2. 5 argues rather against, than for, the thesis of the questioner. "The world to come" (i.e., the millennial age) will not be subjected to angels, which is another point of their inferiority to the Church, for that age will be subject to Christ, with Whom God associates not angels, but the many sons whom He is bringing to glory. If the angels are excluded from this rule, how can they be the same as the Church?   W.H.

In Matt. 16. 18 does the Rock represent Christ? or does it mean Truth? of the Word of God? If it is Christ, can you give Scripture to prove this?

No doubt, our questioner is aware that this is a much disputed passage; though personally we believe the true meaning is not far to seek, in the light of the context and of the general analogy of Scripture. The disciples' answer to the Lord's question, "Whom do men say that I the Son of Man am?" led on to His second question, "But whom say ye that I am?" The Lord desired to hear from their own lips their confession of Him. All were addressed, but one—Simon Peter—replied, "Thou art the Christ, the Son of the living God!" And the Lord pronounced him—"Simon Bar-jona"—blessed (lit. happy), for this had not been learned in the schools of men, but direct from His Father. Not only so, but as Simon Peter had confessed his Lord's Name before His fellow-disciples, now on the principle of Luke 12. 8, the Lord confesses **his** name—"And I say also unto thee, that thou art Peter." In other words He confirms to him the name of Petros or a Stone, which He had conferred on him at his introduction by his brother Andrew (John 1. 41). Moreover, the Lord has something more important to dwell on, namely, the noble, God-given confession by Peter of His true Messiahship and glory as the Eternal Son—something bigger than a "Petros," a stone,—a "Petra," a rock. This distinction is common in classical Greek, and though in Aramaic, the language in which our Lord usually spoke, the difference is not shown, both words being **Cepha,** the fact that the inspired evangelist, in translating, brings out the classical difference, seems to show clearly that the Spirit of God intended the difference to be preserved. Peter is never certainly spoken of as a rock (petra) in any other place of Scripture, but he himself speaks of Christ as the **rock** (petra) of offence, and this is the word used in

1 Cor. 10. 4—"They drank of that spiritual **rock** (petra) that followed them, and that **rock** (petra) was Christ." Peter was "a living stone" along with his fellow disciples, but Christ was the living Rock. Our Lord's words accordingly are not, "Thou art Petros, and upon thee I will build my church," but "Thou art Petros and upon this rock (petra) I will build my church." Perhaps we shall be told this is only Protestant and heretical doctrine. But was then Hilary, bishop of Poitiers in the 4th century, heretical? and yet he writes, "The rock petra is the blessed only **rock faith**—confessed by the mouth of Peter." Was Jerome heretical, who writes, "Christ has founded His church on this rock, and it is from this rock that the Apostle Peter has been named"? Chrysostom whom we cannot admit was a heretic, says, "On this rock I will build my church, that is on the faith of the confession of Peter," and so Ambrose of Milan, Basil of Seleucia, and indeed over forty of the early fathers and ecclesiastical writers (not all, we presume, Protestants or heretical teachers) held that the rock was Christ Himself as revealed in the confession of Peter. So Augustine of Hippo: "On this rock (petra) I will build my church, not on Peter, the stone that thou art, but on the rock that thou hast confessed, I will build thee, who in this reply standest for the church." We may thank God that we have something more stable than vacillating Peter upon which to build for eternity.

W.H.

Matt. 18. 8, 9. Are these verses to be understood as a warning against our "offending" others, as in vv. 6, 7?

The R.V. makes the meaning clear by its rendering, "If thy hand or thy foot CAUSETH THEE TO STUMBLE", etc.. Verse 7 connects with the stumbling of others in v. 6, and then in vv. 8, 9 we are warned against cherishing anything which may be a cause of stumbling to ourselves.

It is interesting that the three members named, are those on which in our physical life we would rely to prevent us from stumbling—our feet to hold us up, our eyes to see anything in the way which might stumble us, and our hands in the last resort to grasp something if the feet should fail us. Yet in the spiritual realm, it is the faculties on which we trust that may prove our undoing. Eve's feet carried her to the tree, her eyes saw that it was good for food, her hands took of it that she might eat. The man who has the best hands and feet and eyes is a man of ability, and such a one was the most likely to have caused the dispute as to who is greatest, which occasioned the Lord's words in this chapter.

W.R.

Matthew 18. 18. Does the binding in heaven chronologically precede the binding on earth?

There seems to be nothing in the verse to indicate the precedence alluded to. By the preaching of the Gospel the terms were announced on which sins could be remitted or bound. The action of the individual hearer determines whether or not his sins are remitted or bound. The binding on earth is simultaneous with the binding in heaven.　W.R.

Can we apply Matthew 18. 20 to Bible Readings and Prayer Meetings?

The second part of the question, it can hardly be contested, is answered by the actual context. The preceding verse, "Again I say unto you, That is two of you shall agree on earth as touching any thing that they shall ask, it shall be done for them of my Father which is in heaven," is separated from the previous subject of discipline by its opening words, "AGAIN I SAY UNTO YOU." This is followed immediately by the words, "For where two or three are gathered together in (or unto) My Name, there am I in the midst." This is a meeting for prayer. But the case of the Bible-Reading is not so clear. The exercise of the ministry of teaching here is from God to man, through His servants: and though the Lord is equally the recourse of His people on such an occasion, it seems hardly correct to apply to such a meeting, the description of being gathered to His Name. When the saints are gathered to the Lord's Name, ministry is incidental.

Much confusion has been caused by confounding priesthood and ministry. The former is the common privilege of all believers; ministry alone appertains to those who have the gift for it, and who believe they have a message from the Lord for the edification of the saints, according to the principles laid down in the fourteenth chapter of the first Epistle to the Corinthians. The expression, "an open platform," is ambiguous. If it means that it is open to anyone who chooses to occupy it, it is quite mistaken; but true, if it means open for those gifted and qualified at the moment, to minister the Word.　W.H.

Is the "eternal life" asked for by the young man (Matt. 19. 16) the same "eternal life" spoken of by John in his 1st Epistle, chap. 1. 2, etc? If so, why did the Lord Jesus answer—"Keep the commandments"?

I would judge "eternal life" to be one; there cannot be two kinds, but no doubt there are many manifestations and degrees of it. Eternal life is not mere endless existence, it is that with the added quality of harmony with God. In Psa. 133. 3 we read, "for there the Lord commanded the blessing, even life for evermore", and in Dan. 12. 2 that "Many of them that sleep in the dust of the earth shall awake, some to everlasting life, and some to shame and everlasting contempt." Clearly, the saved of the Gentiles will not enjoy this life in the same degree as the true Israel, nor these as the Church, but all the elect and redeemed will enjoy it in their measure. "This is life eternal that they might know Thee the only true God and Jesus Christ whom Thou hast sent" (John 17. 3). It is, then, to know and enjoy God in Christ. "This is the true God, and eternal life" (1 John 5. 20). "He that believeth on Me hath everlasting life" (John 6. 47). The young man of Matt. 19. 16 was using words he had heard, but of which he knew nothing yet by experience. Of course, you can have eternal life without being able to give any account of it, but your relation to God is changed, though you may not be able to define what has happened. The very needs and cries of an infant prove it has life, and you would not doubt it because the little one could not explain what life was. The Lord, of course, knew all about the young man, his stage of experience and small capacity, and treated him accordingly in His perfect wisdom. He even pressed home the law to its legitimate conclusion—"Thou shalt love they neighbour as thyself" (though this naturally proved beyond the capacity of the Jews), to bring him face to face with his own deep need. Though we do not hear of this young man again, no doubt, "the word that went out of his (Christ's) mouth did not return void." We, too, should seek to diagnose the condition of men, and apply to them the right treatment, in order to bring them to Christ. 						W.H.

What is the meaning of "the last shall be first and the first last, for many are called but few chosen" (Matt. 20. 16)?

The surface meaning of the first sentence, which occurs also in Chap. 19.30, is that the position will be reversed; the last taking the first place and the first taking the last place, but this is not at all what the parable teaches. What is in view is rather the equality of last with first, and of first with last, and I submit that this is exactly what the words mean; the last shall be as the first, and the first as the last. Those called in the early days of our Lord's ministry, and those called in the last days of the Christian era, will be on an equality. The closing words are undoubtedly difficult, but I believe they mean, that, as far as character of service goes, though the number of those called is great, those chosen for special service, like the apostles, are few in number. Such will undoubtedly receive special awards in the Kingdom, e.g., as above, "sitting on twelve thrones judging the twelve tribes of Israel." As far, however, as the common blessings of the redeemed are concerned— Eternal Life, Membership of Christ's Body, Sonship, etc. there will be equality, though the differences implied by rewards will be eternal. 						W.H.

What do the words, "Whosoever shall fall on this stone shall be broken" (Matt. 21. 44), imply?

The meaning seems to be clearly given in such passages as Isa. 8. 14, 15; 1 Pet. 2. 7, 8; and Rom. 9. 32, 33. Those who reject the Gospel (especially Israel), instead of building on the "Living Stone" of 1 Pet. 2. 4, stumble and fall over the "Stone of Stumbling" of v. 8.

The whole picture in Psa. 118 and Matt. 21 is very interesting. The Stone was meant for the foundation, but the builders did not place it there and afterwards could find no place to fit it. So they "rejected" it and cast it aside. Then as they moved about at their work, it lay in their way, and they stumbled over it and fell. Lastly, God Himself takes up the Stone and places it in the most conspicuous place of all, as "Headstone of the corner," and the rejected One becomes the Judge and Punisher of those who rejected Him.   W.R.

What is the meaning of our Lord's words, "He that shall endure unto the end the same shall be saved" (Matt. 24. 13)? Why was this promise made? To what time does it apply?

In interpreting words of Scripture it is very important, before attempting any general application, to understand the original intention of the speaker, that is, first to interpret the words in their context. What then is the "end" spoken of here, and what did the Lord mean by being "saved"? We notice that the disciples' question was, "What shall be the sign of thy coming and of the end of the age?" This word (**sunteleia**) is much the same as is used in the other occurrences of the chapter for "end" (**telos**), and seems to include the general winding up of things. It occurs before in Matt. 13. 39, 40 and 49 as "the end of the age." The Lord in His reply warns against mistaking for the end of the coming storm, its premonitory rumblings—"wars and rumours of wars." "But the end is not yet," He says (v. 6), for wars, famines, pestilences and earthquakes are only "the beginning of sorrows" (v. 8). Before that "end" there must intervene terrible persecutions against the disciples of the Lord (of whom those addressed were the living representatives), and all will not pass through these unscathed: "many shall be offended," and shall even apostatise from the faith. "And many false prophets shall arise, and shall deceive many. And because inquity shall abound, the love of many shall wax cold. But he that shall endure to the end" (i.e. of this great tribulation)—that is, shall not apostatise—"shall be saved," in the sense, I believe, of being preserved alive. Apostasy will not be the means of safety, but standing firm. This sense of physical preservation we find in other places. "God is the Saviour of all men, specially of them that believe," "Eight souls were saved by water" (i.e. Noah and his family); and in this chapter also at verse 22 we read: "Except those days should be shortened, there should no flesh be saved, but for the elect's sake those days shall be shortened"—reminding us of Paul's words on the ship in Acts 27: "Except these (the sailors) abide in the ship, ye cannot be saved." We may notice in closing that the scene of these happenings will be Judaea; the temple will be rebuilt, and when a special sign spoken of by Daniel the prophet is seen, let all the disciples "flee into the mountains" (v. 16). It will be "the time of Jacob's trouble" (Jer. 30. 7). Let them pray that their flight be not on the Sabbath day. Before the end, the Gospel of the Kingdom will be proclaimed everywhere as a witness. No doubt, the words we are considering may be used by extension to-day. The best proof of reality is continuance in the faith. "Enduring to the end" is the outward and visible effect of the new-birth. It is those who are most truly in Christ who will feel most their need of being kept by the power of God, and consequently their faith will be in exercise. There were false professors in the early churches, who forsook the assembling of themselves with their brethren, and it is to be feared that such exist to-day. Jude speaks of them. They may boast of their correct knowledge of God, but alas their works sometimes seem to give the lie to their profession. The prayer of the true believer will be increasingly and to the end, "Hold Thou me up and I shall be safe!" W.H.

"ONE SHALL BE TAKEN"

What is the meaning of Matt. 24. 40?

When our Lord uttered His great prophetic discourse as recorded in Mark 13, Luke 21, and here in Matt. 24, He was addressing the disciples, not as members of the church, which did not then exist, but as representing the godly remnant of Israel, "the people made ready prepared for the Lord" by John the baptist. The disciples had not ceased to be Jews by receiving Christ; that would have been a strange result of receiving the National Messiah. They were better Jews than ever, in fact, the only true Jews. Now, the first coming of Messiah, in humiliation and the second in glory—"the sufferings of Christ and the glory that should follow"—formed the staple theme of the Old Testament prophets (see Isa. 10. and 11; 24. and 25. 9; 35; Daniel 7. 9-14; Zech. 14. 1-8). In all these places, except Isa. 53, it is the coming in power and great glory of the Son of Man to the earth in connection with the deliverance of Israel that is in view, not His coming to take them away from this scene, but to set up His Kingdom for their blessing under His own beneficent sway. In 1 Thess. 4 quite another character of deliverance is in view—a preliminary stage of the Second Coming—not revealed in the Old Testament, but a mystery displayed in the New, which provides for a deliverance of a large number of saints by resurrection, transformation and translation from this scene, in view of the judgment and tribulation about to occur on the earth. These will be "caught up to meet the Lord in the air" (see 1 Thess. 4. 16, 17). To anyone who will carefully read the synoptic chapters referred to above, with the Old Testament passages quoted there and also 1 Thess. 4, there ought not to be much difficulty in settling to which stage of His Second Coming our Lord was referring in His prophetic discourse. There it is the "Son of Man" (6 times repeated) Who is coming, as in Daniel; it will be a coming in an evil day, as in the days of Noah, see Isa. 10. and 11; in connection with Israel, as in Zech. 14. The answers to the three questions asked seem very clear. The two will be in the field at the coming of the Son of Man in glory; one shall be taken away from this world in judgment, the other left in this scene for Millennial blessing.   W.H.

In Matt. 25, the Lord says to the faithful servants, "Well done!" but in Luke 19, only "Well!" There must be a difference intended. What is it?

The difference is only in the translation, for it is the same word in the Greek in either case—the commendatory adverb, "EU," "Well!" Perhaps, "It is well," would do in both places. This question suggests another which is very interesting, but not so easily answered. What is the difference between the two parables? Nothing but the most superficial reading can fail to note that a wide difference exists. In Matt. 25, there are three servants; in Luke, ten. In Matthew the sums entrusted vary, five talents, two and one; in Luke each servant receives the same, one pound or mina. In Matthew the faithful servants gain proportionately to the talents received, the one who had received five doubles it, and so with the recipient of two. In Luke the sums gained vary from ten to one. In the two Gospels, the unfaithful servant received different treatment; in Matthew he is cast into "outer darkness," in other words, he is a lost soul; in Luke all reward is withheld and his pound taken from him and given to him that had gained ten. There is a fourth and very important difference, which throw light on the interpretation of the parables; in Matthew there are only two classes—the faithful and unfaithful servants; in Luke there is a third and distinct class—the citizens who hated their Lord, and were dealt with in condign judgment at His coming. This indicates, I believe, the true key to the parables. In Matthew, the three servants include profession, in fact all men, as we might say—three divisions of humanity, the Jew, the Gentile, and the Church of God. They have all received some talent from God, for which they must give account to Him. A man does not escape responsibility by refusing it. Each man, godly and ungodly alike, will be held responsible for his talents, his faculties of mind, education, privileges, opportunities; and while no one will be saved by these things, there will be a reward for having by grace used them for God. On the other hand, there will be judgment on those "who have not," corresponding to the rebellious citizens of Luke. In the case of the ten servants, they all start with the same amount—a pound. What exactly this corresponds to is uncertain, perhaps the life which each one has to live and make the most of for God. They will be rewarded in proportion to their faithfulness. The unfaithful one is not consigned to the place of punishment, but he is so far deprived of the opportunity of future service, from which it seems evident that the Lord's servants are qualifying in this world for their service in the next. W.H.

Will those who are judged in Matt. 25. 41-46 appear again at the Great White Throne of Rev. 20. 11?

The Scriptures do not, so far as I am aware, give us any further information about them than what is contained in Matt. 25 itself. In verse 41 the command is, "Depart ye cursed, into everlasting fire prepared for the devil and his angels"; and then in verse 46 it is stated, "These shall go away into everlasting punishment"; both of which expressions can scarcely be understood otherwise than of the Lake of Fire. And if they are sent from this judgment to the Lake of Fire directly, it is difficult to see why they should be brought back from it to stand before the Great White Throne; especially as that appears to be entirely a judgment of the dead, whose bodies have been in the earth or sea, and whose souls have been in hell. According to Rev. 19. 20, the beast and the false prophet will be cast alive into the Lake of Fire at the Lord's appearing; and therefore there would be no difficulty in assuming that these of Matt. 25 may be similarly disposed of. W.R.

In Matt. xxvii. 9-10, the writer ascribed to Jeremiah the well known prophecy of Zechariah xi. 12-13. Please explain why he did so.

Was Matthew as a pious Jew, long in the companionship and service of our Lord, and a man of apostolic gifts, likely, quite apart from the inspiration of the Holy Spirit, to confuse the prophets Jeremiah and Zechariah? Here he was engaged under the direct guidance of the Spirit, in writing a book which was to live down the ages, and which he, as a mere man, was perfectly incapable of producing. Infidels have foolishly boasted sometimes that they could write as good a book as the Bible. They ought to do it then, for it would pay them well. It would be a "best seller" for years. Matthew plainly was familiar with Zechariah, as his quotation in chap. xxi. 4-5 shews, and could not have confused the books, even with his own intelligence alone. The probable explanation is the one cited by Lightfoot, that Jeremiah, as considerably the longest of the prophets, had the first place among them, and so his name came to be used for the volume of the prophetical writings. He quotes the learned David Kimchi as his authority. We often speak of the Psalms of David, without affirming he wrote them all. There is another explanation which may also be the true one. The expression, "spoken by Jeremy the prophet," may refer to some well known word of the prophet, just as Paul in Acts xx refers to words of our Lord: "It is more blessed to give than to receive," which are not recorded in the Gospels. The quotation of Matthew does not agree exactly either with the Hebrew or LXX of Zech. xi. Sometimes the prophets did receive messages as to the same events in almost identical language. Supposing, for instance, some New Testament writer had quoted Micah iv. 1-3, and it had not been recorded that Isaiah had said the same words in chap. ii. 2-4 of his prophecy, and we had read that the well-known words of Micah "were spoken by Isaiah the prophet," how eagerly critics would have seized upon it as a mistake! Of one thing we may be sure, Matthew, an inspired apostle, chosen of God for this wonderful ministry, did not make a mistake.   W.H.

Why does it state in Matt. 27. 28 that they put on our Lord "a scarlet robe" and in John 19. 2 "a purple robe"? Are the references to the same garment, and if so, why are they said to be of different colours?

I do not think it is possible to evade the difficulty by maintaining that the reference is to two different robes, for in both cases we read that those who thus clothed our Lord in mockery were the soldiers present at the trial, and the circumstances are the same. But the word translated, "robe," is not the same in the two passages. That employed by John is quite a general word, rather like our word "garment" or "clothes," whereas the "Matthew" word is particularly used for an official military cloke. Some such old uniform might, as has been remarked, be easily found by the soldiers in the Prætorium or barracks, and would be scarlet, the usual colour worn by high Roman officials. Here the word for "scarlet" (kokkinē) is a very definite word. The word translated "purple," on the contrary, is very indefinite.* We might almost say that the "John" word could be adequately translated "bright colour," while the "Matthew" word gives the exact tint—scarlet. We may add that the word translated, "gorgeous," in reference to the robe (again another word) in which Herod arrayed our Lord (Luke 23. 11), does not specify its colour, but rather its brilliancy; it was probably made of some tissue of metallic lustre. I do not think it the least probable that this was the robe in which the soldiers dressed our Lord; it would be very unlikely that they would have access to that. It seems to have been rather a gift worthy of the acceptance of Pilate, and indeed a feeler for his friendship. Thus are the quarrels of the world patched up in a shallow and unrighteous fashion, but the hatred at the bottom of the heart remains.   W.H.

* See Dr. R. C. Trench's Synonyms of N.T. p. 186.

Matt. 27. 52,53 states that "many bodies of the saints which slept arose, and came out of the graves after his resurrection, and went into the holy city, and appeared unto many." Is it known what happened to these saints? Did they go to heaven with Christ or did they return to their graves?

We are not told in the Scriptures, but the resurrection of these saints in connection with that of our Lord leaves little doubt, I think, on the matter. Our Lord Himself was shewn after His resurrection "not to all the people, but unto witnesses chosen before of God" (Acts 10. 41), to make it easier for the people at large to believe in the resurrection. He was the first-fruits. "Many bodies of the saints arose . . . and went into the holy city, and appeared unto many." They could not deny their own senses that they had seen their dead friends alive, and if so, why should not the testimony of the disciples be that Christ had risen? Under such circumstances, it seems very difficult to believe that the resurrection of these saints was anything but a true and lasting resurrection. I believe this was the first stage in the First Resurrection, of which the resurrection of the sleeping saints, when the Lord comes, will be the second stage, and the remaining saints who have died when He returns in glory the final stage. "This is the first resurrection." Had they returned to their graves, it might be said that He did, too. Surely they were part of that captivity which He led captive when he ascended on high. W.H.

What is the correct baptismal formula to use? Is it that given in Matt. xxviii. 19? In Acts ii. 38 Peter says, "In the name of Jesus Christ." In Acts x. 48 we read, "In the Name of the Lord." In Acts xix. 5, "They were baptized in the Name of the Lord Jesus." Does Matt. xxviii. 19 refer to the millennium?

The commission of Matt. xxviii. 19 was given by the Lord to His disciples before leaving them, as their immediate "marching orders," and there is no hint that it was intended for the millennium, some far-off future dispensation, or that it was superseded by some other commission. Indeed, who had the right to supersede it? It is shallow reasoning to infer that because the formula of Matt. xxviii is not specifically mentioned in the Acts, it was not used. Then the formula of blessing in Num. 6. 23-27 was never used in the history of Israel, since it is not once mentioned! On the contrary, it was doubtless often used, and so with the baptismal formula of Matt. xxviii. There are two prepositions used in connection with baptism in the Acts—"en" and "eis." The first means "in", and with "the Name" it simply explains the authority for baptism. Peter commands them "in the Name of the Lord" to be baptized (Acts x. 48)—order of the Greek. The "eis" occurs twice: *i.e.*, in chap. viii. 16, with reference to the Samaritans, and in chap. xix. 5, of the John Baptist disciples at Ephesus, in both of which cases special importance attached to the confession of the right name—"into the Name of the Lord Jesus." But this was in no sense a formula, and we need have no doubt but that the formula of Matt. xxviii, "into the Name of the Father, and of the Son, and of the Holy Holy Ghost," was used in every case. What more appropriate for a Christian dispensation, or less so for a future Jewish economy? The "epi" of Acts ii. 38 has to give way to "en," it is generally agreed. Peter here too refers back to the authority of the Lord for baptizing. And if we are doing something on another person's authority, should we not carry out that person's direction to the letter?   W.H.

Are we to give up the application of Matt. xxviii. 19-20 to this present dispensation? There are some who maintain that baptizing disciples "in the name of the Father, and of the Son, and of the Holy Ghost" applies to some future dispensation only: to maintain this involves making an exception to "teaching them to observe all things whatsoever I have commanded you," and tends to weaken the confidence of the church in these verses, implying a certain vague absence of unity and of continuity between these important verses, and the "Apostle's doctrine" or teaching, of Acts ii. 42.

I have never heard any sane or sober reasons from Scripture for such an idea, but instead, far-fetched inferences and deductions. The result is a dislocation of the Scripture and a setting on one side of the plain instructions of the Lord. His commission in Matt. xxviii. 19 is very clear, "Go ye therefore and make disciples of all nations." This "therefore" goes back to the fact that the Lord had received (not "would receive" at some distant date) all authority in heaven and earth. How the "discipling" was to be accomplished is indicated in Mark xvi. It was by the preaching of the gospel; only thus, the believers became disciples, exactly as ever since. At no future day will nations as such, become disciples. Where is there a hint that such a commission was not of immediate intent and application? The Lord was fully aware that Israel nationally would refuse the post-resurrection testimony of the apostles, and be set on one side temporarily for the calling out of the Church, and the form of words He indicates in Matt. xxviii, "into the name of the Father and of the Son and of the Holy Ghost" (see v. 19) is peculiarly suited to the present dispensation, as it would not be to a Jewish testimony. Luke gives additional details as to the message—"repentance and remission" were to be preached to "all nations" (Luke xxiv. 47), and in Acts i. 2 these "marching orders" are referred to as "commandments given by Him through the Holy Ghost." They were to wait for the promised Spirit, but not for the millennium, and then, beginning at Jerusalem, launch out into Judaea, Samaria, and the uttermost ends of the earth—exactly what they did and what has gone on ever since. It is indeed a most serious perversion of Scripture to set aside all this, and it must be steadfastly resisted. The apostles, I doubt not, used the words the Lord had indicated, and the fact these are never mentioned proves nothing to the contrary. It would be out of harmony with the genius of Scripture to expect otherwise. Not once do we read of Aaron's blessing (Num. vi. 24-26) or of Moses' words (chap. x. 35), or of the prayer the Lord taught the disciples, being used. Are we then to admit that none of these forms of words was ever put into use? Certainly not, they were doubtless continually in use. The formula of Matt. xxviii was never abrogated, and the idea that something else was substituted is due to a very shallow reading of the Scripture. The expressions, "in the name of Jesus Christ," and "into the name of the Lord Jesus," both of which occur twice in the Acts, have been put forward as a rival formula. If so, who gave it and when? No, the one marks the authority on which we baptize, the latter the Person, faith in whom alone justifies the ordinance being administered, and who says to His servant, not "I will be with you two thousand years hence," but "I am with you all the days, even to the end of the age." I believe the teaching referred to in this question is based on fanciful theories, and is subversive of all sane interpretation of Scripture.   W.H.

MATT. 28. 19 AND COL. 3. 17.

Would not Col. 3. 17: "Whatsoever ye do in word or in deed, do all in the name of the Lord Jesus," settle the question that to baptise in "the name of the Lord Jesus" is the correct formula for this dispensation?

While cordially accepting Col. 3. 17, we cannot agree that it has anything to do with the question of baptizing "in (or "into") the name of the Lord Jesus" rather than "into the name of the Father, the Son, and the Holy Spirit." Certainly we baptize "in the name of the Lord Jesus" and for that reason we do it as He laid down in Matthew 28. But we cannot in any way accept the theory that in the Acts some new "formula" took the place of the one He appointed then. There are three points which should be prominent in carrying out the ordin-ance: (1) **The authority on which it is carried out.** We all agree it is "in the name (en tō onomati) of the Lord Jesus", that is, on His authority. The only record we have of the Lord instituting baptism is in Matthew 28 and Mark 16. If these passages are taken from us, we are shut up to some supposed occasion when the Lord gave other direc-tions, of which we have no shadow of a record. Certainly every baptism in the Acts was carried out "in the name." This phrase (en tō onomati), (quite distinct be it noted from that used in Acts 8. 16 and 19. 5, but which the questioner and his friends seem to confuse with it), occurs only twice, that is in Acts 2. 38 and 10. 48. If one of these phrases replaced the usual formula, which is it? or were there two new formulæ given? (2) **The second point is the confession of faith of the believer.** If the servants of the Lord are responsible to baptize believers, the believers are equally responsible to be baptized. (This we have in Mark 16. 16). For that they must confess their faith in Christ. This is embodied in the phrase referred to above as occurring in Acts 8. 16, of the Samaritans, and 19. 5, of the Ephesian disciples. This is "into the Name (eis tò onoma) of the Lord Jesus," the Person into whose name the candidate desired to be baptized. This was specially important in the two cases referred to, because the Samaritans had been cut off from Israel and the Ephesian disciples had been wrongly baptised "unto John's baptism." That the apostle Paul did use the formula of Matt. 28 may, I think, be fairly deduced from the passage. When he learnt that these disciples had not even heard that the Holy Ghost had been given, he asked at once, "Into what then were ye baptized?" He knew immediately they could not have received the right kind of baptism "into the name of the Father and of the Son and of the Holy Ghost," for that would have informed them that the Spirit was revealed. No other form proposed as a substitute for that of Matt. 28 would have told them anything about it. Into this aspect of baptism very suitably fits the teaching of Rom. 6, by which the believer learns that at his baptism he was identified with Christ in His death, burial and resurrection. (3) The third point is **the object of the act of baptism.** This is not in contrast or opposition to the other two phrases, but in harmony—"Into the name of the Father and of the Son and of the Holy Ghost." The neophyte enters by faith into all that the Triune Name contains and implies. These three points have been for years emphasised by the writer in the act of baptizing—" 'In the name of the Lord Jesus' and on your confession of faith in Him, I baptize you 'into the Name of the Father and of the Son and of the Holy Ghost'." The idea that Paul intended in any way to set aside baptism, in saying that "he thanked God he had only baptized a few of them" is certainly a mistake. He merely meant he was glad he had not performed the manual act, "lest they should say he baptized in his own name." As an historical fact he was in the habit of having all converts baptized on confession of faith (see Acts 16. 15, 33; 18. 8).   .V.H.

Is the Commission of Matt. 28. 18-20 for the present dispensation, or only for one yet future?

In reply to this, let me quote from an answer I gave to the same question many years ago. I have found no cause since then to alter my opinion.

"The Lord Jesus before His death made just one appointment with His disciples, which was, to meet Him on a certain mountain in Galilee after He had risen (Matt. 26. 32; Mark 16. 7). Of this fact we are reminded in Matt. 28. 16, the opening verse of the paragraph in which the Commission is contained. There had been some more or less informal meetings elsewhere previous to it, but this was the **specially prearranged meeting,** which naturally would overshadow them all in importance; yet there are those who would ask us to believe that what He told them when He met them there, was not about their own work at all; but that He gave them minute instructions and comforting assurances with regard to the work of some other unknown individuals, who would live two thousand or more years after their time. They would have us believe that when He said, "Go ye and teach," He meant that somebody else was to go and teach; that when He said, "I am with you," He meant, I will be with some other people who will be on earth two thousand years hence; and that when He added, "Even unto the end of the age," He meant, until the end of some other age. Those who can swallow this kind of thing must have good digestion, for I frankly confess I prefer to believe that the Lord meant just what He said.

The statement, which some of these brethren make, that Matthew does not acknowledge the Church period, is absurd. Is it not in Matthew that we have the formal introduction of the Church in chapter 16, and of Church order in chapter 18? Is it not there that we find the Lord's action, so symbolical of turning from Jew to Gentile, in chap. 13. 1; in which after having been definitely rejected by the Jewish leaders in the two previous chapters, it is said, "The same day went Jesus out of the house, and sat by the seaside"? And immediately after, He speaks the Seven Parables of the Mysteries of the Kingdom, which have so often been shown to picture successive stages of this present Church period. That Matthew's Gospel has a Jewish tinge, no one who is a careful reader can doubt; but this is far off from the conclusion that there is nothing in it except for Jews. The Gospel of Luke has a Gentile tinge, but would these brethren suggest that there is nothing for Jews in Luke, nothing about the Tribulation, nothing about Millennial times? As a matter of fact, the Commission as given in the end of the Gospels of Luke and of Mark, has a more Jewish sound about it than the form of it occurring in Matthew.

As illustrating the fact that the Apostles did carry out Matt. 28. 18-20, there is a word worth noting in Acts 14. 21: "They had preached the gospel to that city, and had taught (Gr., discipled) many." It is the very word, "mathēteuō," used in Matt. 28. 19, and this is the only place in the New Testament, apart from Matthew's Gospel, where it occurs. Were they not here carrying out the commission as given in that verse?" W.R.

s

MARK

With reference to the account of the great storm on the lake narrated in Mark 4. 37, a suggestion has been made that power or authority was given to Satan to cause the storm, with the hope of destroying the Son of God, if it were possible. Is Satan himself possessed of such authority? Have such passages as Matt. 4. 8; Eph. 2. 2 any bearing upon this subject?

In default of a direct statement one must not be dogmatic, but it has long seemed to me a legitimate inference that Satan and his angelic powers did intervene here. The greater the spiritual energy on the Divine side, it has often been remarked, the greater that of Satan in opposition; hence his greater activities during the ministry of our Lord. On this occasion, he (Satan) would become acquainted with our Lord's purpose—"Let us pass over to the other side"—and he would naturally fear lest that voyage should result in an interference with his possession of the demoniacs and the inhabitants of Gadara, among whom he held sway, and he would raise a storm to oppose their deliverance. The word used for "storm" is a very strong one, meaning properly, "whirlwind," and it occurs only elsewhere in the parallel passage in Luke 8. 23 and in 2 Pet. 2. 17. This accords with one of the verses our questioner quotes, namely, Eph. 2. 2, where Satan is called "the prince of the power of the air," from which we are led to infer that he has special power in this sphere, which he exercises freely under God's control. It is better, I suggest, to say that Satan is permitted to exercise his power in these directions, than that he is given special power or authority on each occasion. This Satanic attempt only served to manifest more the glory of Christ and His power, as immensely superior to that of Satan. The ship, already full of water, was, by all the laws of floating bodies, hopelessly lost, and yet complete deliverance was granted, and the water-logged vessel and all in it brought safely to land by the mighty power of the Son of God. I think the words used by our Lord in His exercise of power, to the warring elements, show that He was face to face, not only with these, but with personal rebellious powers using them. For in controlling them we read, "He **rebuked** the wind (a word usually employed of persons), and said unto the sea, **"Peace** (only here so translated, usually "hold your peace"!), **be still"** (literally, "be muzzled"! or "be speechless"!). Matthew 4. 8 is certainly a striking testimony to the reality of Satan's power, and the parallel passage, Luke 4. 6, is even stronger, for there he acknowledges that his power is one conferred upon him, though he uses it as a free agent. That Satan's powers have been in a large measure curtailed owing to his grand defeat at Calvary, cannot be questioned, and yet the world will witness in its closing scenes a remarkable recrudescence of these powers. Perhaps the miraculous powers conferred on the two witnesses (Rev. 11) will lead to an increase in Satanic energy (Rev. 13.). W.H.

In Mark 5. 13 we read that the unclean spirits entered the swine, whereon the latter rushed into the sea and were choked. Would it be right to say that these unclean spirits were then consigned to the Abyss?

It is not so stated anywhere. In the parallel passage at Matt. 8. 29, they said to Christ, "Art Thou come to torment us before the time?" and in Luke 8. 31 (R.V.) they entreated Him "that He would not command them to depart into the Abyss." What became of them after they had been the means of the death of the swine, we are not told, and it is idle to speculate. W.R.

How are we to understand the words of Mark 9. 49?

This verse is a difficult one, and opinions are much divided about it. I cannot say that I have any definitely settled view of it.

If the "every one" refers to the unsaved, then it is clearly linked with the previous verse (v. 48) and the term "fire" is the same thing in both, suggesting that the unquenchable fire will preserve while it burns the wicked.

If the "every one" refers to the real disciples, then it is closely linked with the verse that follows (v. 50), and the term "salted" is much the same in both, and suggests the need for the salt of self-judgment hinted at in verses 43, 45, 47, and perhaps also for the "fire" of chastisement by the Lord, to keep His own from becoming savourless. In this case the meaning would be similar to that of Malachi 3. 2, 3.

But since in v. 49 the word "fire" turns our thoughts to v. 48, and the word "salted" turns them the other way to v. 50, it is possible that both the above views are included in the statement, "every one shall be salted with fire", the saved in this present life in one way, and the unsaved in the lake of fire in another way. In this case the verse would be a warning that it must be either the one thing or the other; either to be amongst those who are subject to self-judgment and God's chastisement now, or to be amongst those who will be preserved eternally under God's judgment in the future.

The latter part of v. 49 is in any case an illustration, quoted, of course, from Lev. 2. 13. And it is helpful to remember that vv. 44, 46, 48 are also a quotation from Isa. 66. 24.

As to the 50th verse itself, it is best understood in the light of the parallel passage in Matt. 5. 13, where God's people, persecuted though they are (vv. 10-12), are called the "salt of the earth," because of their hidden influence, and then the "light of the world," because of their more outward influence. There the salt losing its savour is parallel with the light under a bushel. But as v. 15 says, men do **not** light a candle to put it under a bushel, and similarly in the background is the thought that salt which is real and pure does NOT lose its savour.

The "have peace one with another," with which v. 50 ends, refers back to what had led to this talk with them in vv. 33, 34, namely, their dispute as to who should be greatest.   W.R.

In view of our Lord's omniscience, what is the meaning of Mark xiii. 32: "Of that day and that hour knoweth no man, no, not the angels which are in heaven, neither the Son, but the Father"?

This is confessedly a difficult question at first sight, and one that has been wrested by human reasonings to the self-destruction of professors. But of one thing we may be sure, it does not contradict the definite testimony of God's Word to the omniscience of Christ, who knew all men and what was in man (John ii. 24, 25—a Divine prerogative; Jer. xvii. 10), who knew ALL THINGS (John xvi. 30), and who also knew the Father and was the only One who did (Matt. xi. 27), which entails infinite knowledge. Probably the Lord only meant the hour was not part of His message to communicate, or that it was not known to Him officially, even as it was not to any prophet or angelic messenger. That would account for the absence of any mention of the Holy Spirit, to whom all would be known since He is God, but who had not yet come as a Divine witness on the earth. That the verse has nothing to do with any imagined self-emptying of our Lord of His Divine attributes is clear from Acts i. 7, where even in resurrection the Lord speaks of "the times and seasons which the Father hath put in His own power." There are differences of functions in the Divine Persons of the Holy Trinity. To the Father belong the eternal counsels, as to their origination, "the times and seasons" and "the hour" of their fulfilment; to the Son, the accomplishment of redemption; to the Spirit, the making good of all to the redeemed. But God is one, and as such knows all and fulfils all.   W.H.

"There were also women looking on afar off: among whom was Mary Magdalene, and Mary the mother of James the less and of Joses, and Salome" (Mark 15. 40). Can you give any explanation of "the less"?

This James is only mentioned here as "the less" (Greek, the little), either on account of age or stature, to distinguish him, not from James the son of Zebedee, who was already martyred, when Mark wrote his Gospel, but almost certainly from James, the Lord's brother, who became so prominent in the church at Jerusalem in the Acts period, who was also the author of the Epistle of James. Though his (James the less) mother's name was "Mary," she is not to be confused with "Mary, the mother of the Lord." This James was clearly well known, as Mary is mentioned as his mother to distinguish her. She is generally identified with Mary the wife of Cleopas (or Clopas), who comes in in John xix. 25, as the sister of the mother of our Lord, and in much the same connection as Mary the mother of James in Matt. xxvii. 56 and Mark xv. 40. This Cleopas is believed to be the same as Alphæus, so that "James the less" is none other than the apostle, the son of Alphæus (Acts i. 13).   W.H.

LUKE

Is there any ground for stating that the woman of Luke 7. 36-50 is the same as Mary the sister of Lazarus, whose anointing of the Lord is recorded in Matt. 26. 7; Mark 14. 3; and John 12. 3? Or were there two anointings on different occasions?

The entire circumstances of the anointing in Luke 7 are different from those suggested in the other three passages named. The former evidently occurred in Galilee, at a comparatively early stage of the Lord's ministry, since Luke places it previous to His setting off on the last journey to Jerusalem, recorded by him at chap. 9. 51; while the latter took place at Bethany, in Judæa, only a few days before the crucifixion. The former was done by a sinful woman of the city; the latter by Mary, who long before had sat at Jesus' feet and heard His word (Luke 10. 39). The former was spoken of by Christ as betokening the first love of a newly forgiven soul (v. 47); the latter as showing a measure of appreciation of what lay before Him (Mark 14. 8), such as no other disciple possessed at that time. In the former case it was the owner of the house who felt annoyed, and the source of his annoyance was that the Lord had allowed such a character to touch Him; while in the latter, it was Judas, and to some extent other disciples (Matt. 26. 8), who complained, and the complaint was that what had been done was wasteful. Finally, in the former story Christ, though invited to the man's house, was deliberately or carelessly slighted (v. 44); while in the latter He was the guest of honour, for whom the feast was arranged.

The fact that in each story the name of the owner of the house was Simon is unimportant, as it was quite a common name, of which we find some eight or nine possessors in the New Testament.   W.R.

Is Mary of Bethany the same as Mary Magdalene? (See John 11. 2; Matt. 26. 7; Luke 7. 37, 38; Luke 8. 2).

The idea that Mary Magdalene is to be identified with Mary of Bethany rests on no Scriptural authority whatever, that I can discover, but on two or three assumptions, which, if examined in the light of Scripture, seem lacking in force. The first assumption is that Mary Magdalene is to be identified with the woman who was a sinner, of Luke 7. 37, 38. Now, though the Lord did cast out of Mary Magdalene seven devils (Luke 8. 2), there is no proof whatever that she had lived an openly sinful life. The fact that she comes on the scene in chapter 8, for the first time apparently, and is there described as one of the women who went with our Lord and ministered to Him of their substance, without any reference to the events of the previous chapter, shows sufficiently that she is not the woman spoken of there. The next assumption is that the incident in Luke 7 is the same as that described in Matt. 26. and John 12. It is true that the houses in which both incidents occurred belonged to men called Simon, but the one was a Pharisee, and no disciple of the Lord; the other was known as "the Leper," probably one of the several cleansed by our Lord, and seems to have been a disciple. The two incidents, when examined, show marked differences which should be patent to all. Mary of Bethany knew the Lord long before her act of service; in the case of the other, she had been living an immoral life till then; it was the day of her conversion. The actions of the two, though broadly alike, are quite distinct, and the conversation with the Simon of Luke 7 is replaced in Matt. 26 by the murmurings of the disciples. Our conclusion must be that neither of the Marys is found in Luke 7, and that Mary of Bethany is quite distinct from Mary Magdalene.   W.H.

As regards the lawyer's question in Luke 10. 25, as to what he should do to inherit eternal life, and the Lord's reply: "This do and thou shalt live," it has been suggested that "live" here only means long life on the earth. But surely the Lord's answer must correspond to the lawyer's question. If the law had been perfectly kept, would it have given eternal life?

The promises to Israel seldom went beyond this life, so that, no doubt, "life" in the Old Testament did primarily mean long years of existence on the earth. But though little was said about it, it seems clear that long life under the favour of God, would carry with it a promise of the life to come: "There the Lord commanded the blessing, **even life for evermore**" (Psa. 133. 3). "Many of them that sleep in the dust of the earth shall awake, some to everlasting life," etc. (Dan. 12. 2). This will be the case literally in the last days, when the righteous and blessed of the living nations will enter into eternal life after their judgment by the Son of Man (Matt. 25. 46). Certainly the question of the lawyer looked onward to a future existence, and as our questioner remarks, our Lord's reply cannot point to anything short of that. But when we come to the closing part of the question, it seems more speculative than practical. The true answer is, I believe, in such cases—It did not happen! No one ever did perfectly keep the law. The words of Galatians 3. 21 are explicit enough: "If there had been a law given, which could have given life, verily righteousness should have been by the law," but the context rules this out—"But the Scripture hath concluded all under sin (hamartia—or missing the mark), that the promise by faith of Jesus Christ might be given to them that believe" (v. 22). The true function of the law is given in verse 24: "The law was our schoolmaster unto Christ," but not the Saviour of anybody. The lawyer was not a sincere seeker after eternal life. He was merely trying to puzzle the Lord, but he found he got puzzled himself. The Lord throws him back on his professional knowledge of the law, and when he answers aright, simply says, "This do and thou shalt live." Once in our youth in Switzerland we determined to find a more direct route up to a mountain hotel than the way prepared for travellers. Our way went on easily for a few hundred feet, and then we found ourselves at the bottom of a sheer precipice, which blocked all further progress. Scale this, and we should win our goal! but it was impossible, and we had to turn back discomfited. Had we met another traveller bent on finding a self-way, and determined to try for himself, we might perhaps have ironically encouraged him, "Oh, yes, you will find the way easily enough, it is direct. You only have to climb a sheer precipice some few hundred feet high and you will be there!" So it seems that our Lord dealt with this questioner. But in reality "the law made nothing perfect"; "What the law could not do, in that it was weak through the flesh (like "a lever of steel on a fulcrum of sand"), God, sending His own Son in the likeness of sinful flesh, etc. (did)" (Heb. 7. 19; Rom. 8. 3). "The law of the Spirit of life in Christ Jesus hath made me free from the law of sin and death" (v. 2). It would be as possible for a fallen man to create a world, as to love God with all his heart, or his neighbour as himself. The true answer is—To be an heir you must be born one: "The gift of God is eternal life through Jesus Christ our Lord" (Rom. 6. 23).   W.H.

In view of such a scripture as Luke 12. 14, should a Christian serve on a jury?

Luke 12. 14 is hardly relevant, dealing, as it does, with assuming the place of arbitrator between disputants. The duty of a juryman is to hear the evidence for or against an accused, to listen to the summing up of the judge and then, without prejudice, say whether in his opinion the accused is guilty or not. I do not refer to the slight difference in Scottish law. The judge is not obliged to accept the opinion of the jury, especially if the jury-men are not unanimous, and he may order a fresh trial. I should judge that such service would fall under the directions of 1 Pet. 2. 13: "Submit yourselves to every ordinance of man for the Lord's sake: whether it be to the king, as supreme; or unto governors, as unto them that are sent by him for the punishment of evil-doers, and for the praise of them that do well," and also the teachings of Rom. 13. 1-7. The jury system is part of the law of the land, that juries should be chosen from certain ratepayers. The system is recognised as tending to just trials; the service is neither remunerative nor agreeable, and to refuse to serve is not in accordance, in my judgment, with the Scriptures referred to above, and would rightly cause the refusers to "receive unto themselves judgment" (Rom. 13. 2, Gk.).   W.H.

Do not verses 10-21 of Luke 13, which form the closing paragraph of the section which began at chap. 9. 51, indicate that leaven (see v. 21) has here a meaning other than evil, which in Scripture it generally typifies?

It is generally thought that the "order"* which Luke (see chap. 1. 3) by the Spirit proposes as his aim is moral rather than strictly historical, for it is intended to convey certainty, which a mere historical sequence could hardly do in the same way. The early start for Jerusalem, as narrated in chap. 9. 51, presents a problem of considerable difficulty, if an attempt be made to make consecutive history of Luke's account up to ch. 13. 22, where the exact translation is, "he was journeying through." Really, the section does not end there, for in chap. 17. 11 we read, "as he went to Jerusalem"; and again in chap. 18. 31, the Lord says, "Behold we go up to Jerusalem," and this must have been via Jericho, for chap. 19. 1 finds Him there. It is not till chap. 19. 28 that we find the Lord in sight of His goal. He is there seen "ascending up to Jerusalem," and arriving at Bethany in v. 29, from which He proceeds to Jerusalem in his triumphal entry. But be it noted, the Lord had already got as far as Bethany in chap. 10. 38. All this certainly presents a few problems for "careful readers." However, the point of all this in the writer's mind is perhaps to show that verse 23 and onwards in chap. 13 must not be too rigidly detached from the earlier part of the chapter, and that what has gone before may rather lead up to and explain the question and answer of verses 23-30.

Thus the brutal massacre by Pilate might lead some, as survivors, to argue their superior virtues, a thought the Lord solemnly discountenances. They might be surviving on sufferance like the fruitless fig tree. But the afflicted woman, so long bound by Satan, exhibits what is the true guarantee of blessing, namely faith in God; for in that, she, like Zacchæus (19. 9), is of the true Abrahamic seed. Here is one on whom the grace of God can lavish itself. But the general condition of the Kingdom could only be compared to a mustard seed, intended to produce a modest annual, but contrary to nature developing into a mon-

---

* "In order" (kathexēs") is quite distinct from the word employed in verse 1, which is "anatassomai"—"to set in order."

strous perennial, a tree for nesting demons (vv. 18, 19), while on the doctrinal side permeated with the evil doctrine of Pharisee, Sadducee and Herod (vv. 20, 21). I think this interpretation fits well with the question of v. 20. It would, I suggest, lose its point did the growth of v. 19, or the spread of v. 21, represent the energies of true spiritual development. Why then should any question of the paucity of spiritual results be raised? W.H.

Do the ninety and nine sheep of Luke 15. 4 represent saved people?

The parables of Luke 15 were spoken, according to vv. 1-2, on an occasion when the Pharisees and Scribes had murmured (just as the elder brother in the third parable murmured) at Christ's receiving publicans and sinners. Their interpretation, therefore, lies on the very surface of the chapter. The lost sheep, the lost silver, and the son who wandered, all represent the publicans and sinners who were being received by the Lord on their repentance; while the ninety and nine sheep, the nine pieces of silver, and the elder son, represent the Pharisees and Scribes who, in their own estimation, needed no repentance. These, of course, were not really saved people, as their murmuring itself proves.

Other applications of the parables may be made, legitimately enough, but this is quite evidently the primary one. W.R.

Why did the Lord commend the unjust steward in Luke 16. 8?

The verse itself furnishes of course the reply in the words, "because he had done wisely"; but the capital "L" which the questioner uses for "lord" suggests that he has a mistaken idea as to who is meant by that term. Verse 8, forms a part of the parable, and the "lord" in it is not our Lord, but the same person who is so called in verses 3 and 5, that is, the steward's employer. This man, in spite of the loss he has sustained, cannot help admiring the cleverness of his dishonest servant, in thus providing for his own future. See verse 8 in the R.V., or in Weymouth's rendering which is, "And the master praised the dishonest steward for his shrewdness; for in relation to their own contemporaries the men of this age are shrewder than the sons of light."

It is only with the "I say unto you" of verse 9 that Jesus begins to teach His disciples from the parable and He draws from it at least two distinct lessons. In verse 9 He urges them to imitate the steward by providing themselves with friends who would ultimately welcome them, not into their own houses in this life, but into the "everlasting habitations." This is a further development of His exhortation to them in ch. 12. 33 to provide themselves with "bags which wax not old, a treasure in the heavens that faileth not." Then, in verses 10-12 He warns them against imitating the steward in his unfaithfulness; which is in like manner a development of His teaching in ch. 12. 42 about a steward who was wise and faithful at the same time.   W.R.

Please explain Luke 16. 21.

There is not much to explain, I think. The Spirit of God thus portrays the low estate of the poor sufferer. It reminds us of the Syrophenician woman. What she humbled herself to do morally, poor Lazarus did literally. They were both rich in faith however, and were both sustained and eventually comforted by their Lord. The touch about the dogs licking the sufferer's sores adds colour to the picture. The dogs pitied, if no one else did; it was a slender mitigation, too, for there is healing in a dog's tongue, but the whole description only serves to show up in ugly relief the selfishness of the "poor" rich man.

Chapters 15 and 16 of Luke form one address and in each parable, or story, there is something which corresponds to the Pharisees and something to the sinners, of chap. 15. 2. Clearly here Lazarus represents the latter, the rich man the former.   W.H.

LUKE 21. 24.

What does the phrase, "Times of the Gentiles," mean? Do these "times" begin after the Church is taken away, or when?

Certainly they begin not after, but before, for when the rapture takes place, "the Times of the Gentiles" will nearly have run their course. The expression occurs in Luke 21. 24: "Jerusalem shall be trodden down of the Gentiles until **the times of the Gentiles be fulfilled.**" This phrase must, of course, be distinguished from another in Rom. 11. 25: "blindness in part is happened to Israel, until **the fulness of the Gentiles** be come in,"—which means, I think, till the number of the elect of the Gentiles of this dispensation be complete, or in other words, till the last Gentile be added to the Church. The phrase "times of the Gentiles," means the time of the ascendancy of the four great world powers: Babylon, Medo-Persia, Greece and Rome (see Dan. 2. 31-45; 7. 2-7, 17). The "times", then, began when the Kingdom was transferred from Israel to Babylon. We may leave out of account the captivity of the Northern Kingdom, as Assyria is not counted among the above powers. There were three captivities of the Southern Kingdom of Judah: those of Jehoiakim and his son, and finally eleven years later, that of Zedekiah in 586 B.C. It is from this date, I believe, "the times" started. The remnant that returned later was not independent of the Persian Kings, and in our Lord's time we find a Roman Governor at Jerusalem and the city still "trodden down of the Gentiles," as it has been to this day, and is none the less actually so, though under the British mandate. The question of the disciples to the Lord in Acts 1. 6 was not lacking in intelligence, but the answer depended on the nation's response to the apostles' witness to the Resurrection. Had they repented and turned to the Lord, the Lord Jesus would have come back as "the Stone cut out without hands" of Daniel and wrested the kingdom by power from the Gentile kingdoms, pulverised them, and restored it to Israel (Read Acts 3. 19-26 in R.V.). As it is, this is postponed till He comes in glory whose right it is, and all His saints with Him, for Israel, though for the time being put aside (Rom. 11-15, Gr. "apoballō"), is not utterly repudiated (Rom. 11. 1, Gr. "apōtheō").   W.H.

What did the Lord mean when He said, "He that hath no sword, let him sell his garment and buy one"? (Luke 22. 36), and how reconcile such an injunction with His rebuke of Peter's use of a sword a few hours later? (see Matt. 26. 52).

The Lord is here reviewing His methods when He first sent forth His disciples. "Behold," He then said, "I send you forth as lambs among wolves" (at the mercy of their enemies, it seemed), adding, "Carry neither purse, nor scrip, nor shoes" (see Luke 9. 3, and 10. 3. 4). Now in chap. 22. 35, He asks them, "When I sent you without purse, and scrip, and shoes, lacked ye anything?" The unhesitating reply was, "Nothing." (v. 36). The Lord had provided for these twelve, in-numerable simple meals, during their three and a half years with Him, and He had besides, lodged, clothed and protected them. If now He was about to replace His old methods by new ones, it was not because the old had failed, but because a new condition of things was about to arise, and He would adopt new methods. They were no longer to live by direct miracle; they would need a purse and a scrip; they would need to take reasonable precautions for themselves. "But now he that hath a purse, let him take it and likewise his scrip, and he that hath no sword, let him sell his garment and buy one." Two had already had a sword each (v. 38), without rebuke from their Lord; now the exhorta-tion is, "Buy one"!

Some have tried to evade the literal truth of this, but it is difficult to see how the purse and the scrip could be literal (which no one questions), and the sword not. The apostles understood it so, and though an effort has been made to show that our Lord's reply, "It is enough," was in irony, as much as to say, "It is enough to break My heart to have to do with men so slow of understanding," no one seems able to suggest what He did want them to understand. If the reference to the sword was not to be taken literally, what did the Lord mean? It was not at all His way, moreover, to break off a conversation, if misunderstood (see e.g., Mark 8. 17, when they misunderstood His reference to leaven), but patiently to explain.

How, then, reconcile this teaching with our Lord's words to Peter later in the garden, "Put up again thy sword into his place: . . . all they that take the sword shall perish with the sword" (Matt. 26. 52)? It is, I believe, because these words have been misunderstood, that the others have been misinterpreted.

First, we may note that the Lord did not order Peter to throw away his sword, but to sheathe it, as though He would say that this was not the time to draw it. How then are we to understand the words? They cannot apply to all soldiers, nor even to all Christian soldiers, for many a Christian soldier has died in his bed, e.g., General Havelock. The Lord must refer to some special way of taking the sword, and that would be the way Peter was taking it, namely, to defend His Lord's cause. A notable instance of this is Admiral Gaspard de Coligny, the great Christian Frenchman, of the 16th century, who, as we know, took up the sword on behalf of the French Huguenots, and perished with 70,000 others, by the sword of Papist assassins, on the eve of St. Bartholomew. Certainly there is no justification here for a Christian adopting the profession of arms, nor for taking the offensive under any circumstances. How could a sword or two enable eleven men to take the offensive? But it does suggest a modified measure of self-defence. Should we be right in not bolting our front door at night? Would a Christian husband and father be right in allowing marauders to enter his house and brutally attack his wife and children, and never lift a finger in their defence? I trow not. Such a subject shows the importance of "rightly dividing the word of truth" in the Sermon on the Mount, and in such words of our Lord, as Luke 22. 36, when about to leave His disciples.   W.H.

In Luke 24. 30 when the Lord blessed the bread in the house at Emmaus, did He pray? Is it right to say of the resurrected man that He prays?

The Revised Version is certainly more correct here than the Authorised Version, and throws light on our Lord's action. It is not, "as he sat at meat," but, "When he had sat down (lit.—"in sitting down") with them to meat, he took the bread and blessed (it) and brake and gave to them." This does not represent an act of prayer, but the Lord's customary act of giving thanks, before partaking of food.

The word for, "blessed," here, **"eulogeō,"** seems to be used in the Gospels interchangeably with **"eucharisteō,"** usually translated "to give thanks." This becomes clear by comparing how the two words are used. In Matt. 26. 26, 27 and Mark 14. 22, 23, "He **blessed**" (eulogōe) for the **bread**, and **"gave thanks"** (eucharisteō) for the **cup**. In Luke 22. 19 "He took bread and **gave thanks**" (eucharisteō). In 1 Cor. 10. 16 "we **bless**" (eulogeō) the **cup**, or, as Erasmus and others believe it ought to be, "the cup for which we bless," and this seems to agree with the other occurrences. In 1 Cor. 11. 24

"He **gave thanks**" for the **bread**. Again, with reference to the feeding of the five loaves and two small fishes, Matthew, Mark and Luke say, "He blessed," John, that "He gave thanks." What can be deduced from this, but that the Holy Spirit uses the two words interchangeably? and that the "blessing" is not to be understood as an act of consecration but of thanksgiving? If this be so, then the whole fabric of superstition built by Romanist and Ritualist around the so-called "consecration of the elements" is seen to lack solid foundation. In other words, there never was any **consecration** of the elements intended by Christ, any more than of the five loaves and two small fishes of Matt. 14. 19 (eulogeō) or of the seven loaves and few fishes of Matt. 15. 36 (eucharisteō). As for the other question, it seems impossible to divorce the idea of prayer from the Lord's present intercession and advocacy in resurrection. I believe we are right in viewing our Lord's prayer in John 17, as a specimen of His present ministry for His people. Certainly then, though He is not praying for Himself, He is for us. W.H.

JOHN

Does John 1. 13 supply the reason for the "believing" in the previous verse; or does it describe its result? In other words, does new-birth precede belief, or vice-versa?

Much valuable time has been spent in arguing out this point, and I have no wish to spend more, except that a very important principle is at stake, as I view the question. We are reminded by those who assert that new-birth must precede faith, that sinners are dead in trespasses and sins, and how can one dead do anything? I remember one of these brethren saying to me, that if he had twelve unconverted persons before him, it was exactly as though he had twelve stones. But this is a mistaken analogy. A stone has no hearing, no conscience, no will, no responsibility, nothing to appeal to, whereas to spiritually dead ones the prophet said: "Hear, and your soul shall live"; and the Lord lamented, "Ye will not come to me that ye might have life." The Ephesian believers had been "dead in trespasses and sins" (chap. 2. 1), and while in this state, "God, who is rich in mercy" . . . had quickened them (v. 4). But in chap. 1. 13 we have the history of this from the point of view of their responsibility, and we read, "In whom ye also trusted (lit. hoped) having heard (lit.) . . . the gospel of your salvation." Thus they were born again into the family relationship, to which they were predestinated (chap. 1. 5). The order of the words in the first of John is in perfect harmony with this. "As many as received Him, to them gave He the right to become children of God" (R.V.). The next words explain more fully what "receiving Him" means, and then follow the words, "Which were born, not of blood (i.e., not by natural birth) nor of the will of the flesh (no man can give himself this new-life) nor of the will of man (no man can give it him) but of God." To the simple reader these words present the truth in its true moral order. But to evade this difficulty, some of these teachers change the words "which were born," into the pluperfect tense: "which had been born"—but there is no change of tense in the Greek all through—"receive," "gave," "were born," are all in what is called the aorist, signifying an act accomplished at a definite point of past time. Certainly no priority is allotted to the last named act, rather subsequence. Probably the difference of time is indefinitely small, but it is important to hold it fast. It may remind us of the man with the withered hand to whom the Lord said, "Stretch forth thine hand." Logically this was impossible, practically he did it, and in the act his hand was made whole as the other. But someone may say, if the difference be so small why not leave it indeterminate? Because the whole question of man's responsibility is involved. When Nicodemus came to the Lord as an enquirer, we must suppose he was born again according to these teachers, as " 'a stone' does not enquire anything," and yet it was to this very enquirer that the Lord uttered the memorable words, "Ye must be born again," and when Nicodemus asked, "How can these things be?" the Lord did not say, "You are already born again," but presented Himself, lifted up, as the object of His faith, and then no doubt he was born again, though the fruits took some time to show themselves.   W.H.

It is stated in your booklet, "The Eternal Sonship of Christ," that John 1. 18 was enough to prove the truth in question. But many believe that the words, "the only begotten Son which is in the bosom of the Father, He hath declared Him," point to the Incarnation.

Whether what we affirmed is true or not, it does not depend primarily on the sense of the words cited above, nor is it easy to see how in any case they favour the denial of the Eternal Sonship of Christ. This denial, hailed to-day in certain circles as a new light, is the revival of an ancient heresy, of which Cyril of Jerusalem (4th century) warns the saints: "It is the greatest impiety to say that, after deliberation held in time, God became a Father." I trust we are not of those who despise God's servants in every age but their own, or limit light on His Word to their own small circle. Those who are playing with this heresy seem unaware that they are at the same time denying the Eternal Fatherhood of God. But the verse does prove, I think conclusively, that the Sonship of Christ did antedate the Incarnation for, if "no one has seen the Father, at any time," then it was the Son who declared Him in the theophanies of the Old Testament, to Abraham, Moses, Joshua, Gideon, etc. If this be conceded, we cannot logically stop short of the Eternal Sonship. We come now to the words: "Who is in (lit. to) the bosom." Some say the preposition "eis" (to), usually expressive of "motion to," is "put for en" (in), but then why did not the Spirit use "en," as in John 13. 23? Alford well remarks in loco; **"No word or expression is ever put for another"** (in the Bible). Chrysostom believes the phrase to be of deep significance, denoting "relationship and oneness of being;" and Alford, that it carries on the thought of v. 1, "with God," where the preposition, "pros," which also usually denotes "motion to," is used in John 1 as equivalent to, "in relation to." The expression here "in the bosom," not only denotes position, but interpenetration of essence, or in other words, Divine Unity. All this is lost by the sad and fatal denial we hear of to-day. W.H.

Is there any warrant for the assertion that the word, "in" (Greek "eis"), in John 1. 18 conveys the idea of movement "into" the bosom of the Father? The authority of Liddell and Scott's Lexicon has been advanced in support of this.

Liddell and Scott's Greek Lexicon (with, I suppose, all others) states that the radical signification of the preposition "eis" is "direction towards," or "motion to, on, or into." But this is very far from saying that it can never have any other derivative meaning, or that it should always be translated in English by "into." There is in fact a number of New Testament passages in which "in" is the only suitable rendering for it.

For instance, in Matt. 17. 5 the voice from heaven says, "This is My beloved Son in (Greek "en") whom I am well pleased"; but when Peter quotes this saying at 2 Pet. 1. 17, he replaces the "en", which is the usual Greek word for "in," with "eis." Yet who would think of rendering his words, "My beloved Son into whom I am well pleased"? Again, in Matt. 10. 41 we have the phrase, "receiveth a prophet in (Greek "eis") the name of a prophet," which certainly would sound no better were we to read it, "Into the name of a prophet." Nor would it improve Acts 19. 22; "He himself stayed in (Greek "eis") Asia," to render it, "He himself stayed into Asia."

At the same time, there doubtless is some significance in the use of "eis" rather than "en" in John 1. 18; though it is not to be sought by imagining a time past when first the Son came to be in the bosom of the Father, nor even by suggesting, as some have done, a reference to His return to it after His death and resurrection, an idea which would be entirely disconnected from the rest of the verse. It seems rather to convey a hint that the dwelling in the bosom of the Father expresses, not merely a quiescent state, but the active enjoyment of, and entering into this relationship on the part of the Son; and that it was as a result of His intimate face-to-face fellowship with His Father that He was able fully to "declare Him" to those who had not "seen God at any time." Compare how in John 8. 38 He says, "I speak that which I have seen with My Father."

This use of "eis" in John 1. 18 may well be compared with the use of "pros" for "with God" in verses 1 and 2 of our chapter. According to the same authority, Liddell and Scott, the root idea of "pros" with an accusative (as here) is "motion towards, to, or upon." And while no one would think of rendering it, "the Word was towards God," yet the use of "pros" conveys much more as to the relationship of the Word to God, than would "sun," the usual preposition for "with," or "in company with."

It is good that we should endeavour to glean, as fully as we are able, the force of each word that the Holy Spirit uses in the Scriptures, but we need to be ever on our guard lest we read into words what they do not mean.   W.R.

What does "sin" in John 1. 29, ("the sin of the world") mean? Are "sins" in Acts 10. 43 essentially different? Is it true that the only sin the ungodly will have to answer for is their unbelief? Did Christ bear the sins of all men or only of His people?

I do not think there is a real difference between sins in Acts 10. 43 and "sin" in John 1. 29, though when the words occur in the same context as in 1 John 1. 7, 8 "sin" means the root, "sins," the fruit.

It is exceedingly erroneous to hold that unbelief is the only sin men will be judged for at the Great White Throne, for we read in Rev. 20. 12, "the dead were judged out of those things which were written in the books according to their works." Again, in verse 13, "they were judged every man according to their works," and in the next chapter, verse 8, the lost are seen in their individual character, as sinners of their special categories—not only, that is, as unbelievers, but as "abominable, murderers, whoremongers, sorcerers, idolaters and liars."

This could not be, had they been forgiven all their sins, except unbelief. No, unbelief will be the deciding cause of their judgment, for by it salvation is refused, but all sins committed will be the subject of their judgment and will determine its intensity.

In 1 John 2. 2, the words, "for the sins of," are in italics and 'ould be omitted; and "also for the whole world" suffices. The question of Christ bearing sins is for the people of God. We may call it a family secret. It is not for us to speculate as to the number of persons, whose sins were laid on Christ, that is alone known to God. What is revealed is that "through His name, whosoever believeth in Him shall receive remission of sins" (Acts 10. 43). The Atonement is of infinite value. It permits God righteously to offer forgiveness to all, but not all are saved, only those who repent and believe the gospel. Peter writes to believers: "Who His own self bare **our** sins, in His own body on the tree" (1 Pet. 2. 22), and therefore it is said in Heb. 9. 28: "Christ was once offered to bear the sins of many." Isa. 53. 6 is the language of the penitent believer: He gets into the verse by the first "all"—"All we like sheep have gone astray," he enjoys it by the second "all,"—"the Lord hath laid on Him the iniquity of us all." That is, the atonement of Christ is **potentially** sufficient for all, it is **effectively** sufficient for all who believe.

Then, what is the meaning of John 1. 29? Some think that the sin of the world means **original sin.** But were this taken away, infants would not die. Some affirm that it only means that "sin will be taken away during the millenium," but this is not true, for sin will then only be repressed not removed, and is it likely that John at such a moment would be speaking of the millennium?

No doubt, the question of the removal of sins from men's consciences was a burning one. John's baptism could not effect that, but when he points to Jesus the difficulty is solved—"Behold the Lamb of God which taketh away the sin (not only of repentant Israel, but) of the world." This does not mean that sin is actually taken away from anyone till one believes on God's Lamb, but that He is the One to do it—the only One.

There are similar expressions in this Gospel: "The light that lighteth every man that cometh into the world" (chap. 1. 9). Many are not enlightened, because they turn from the light, but they might be. The Sun of righteousness is shining for them. Again in chap. 6. 33, the Lord speaks of Himself as "the Bread of God . . . which giveth life unto the world." It is for that He came, but many remain dead, for they will not partake. Then in verse 51 the Lord says, "The bread that I will give is My flesh, which I will give for the life of the world," but again they must eat that flesh. In John 12, 32 we have yet another example: "I, if I be lifted up from the earth will draw all men unto me." This does not necessarily mean that in each case He draws effectively, but rather that the Spirit can deal with each on the ground of the work of the cross. Happy those who are drawn by the Father, for His drawing is effective (chap. 6. 44). On the same principle—Christ is the Lamb of God's providing to take away a world's sin. He is the only One to do it, if it is to be done. He is willing to do it. He does it effectively for "every one that seeth the Son, and believeth on Him" (chap. 6. 40). We might point to a man in the street as the village doctor or the village blacksmith, but we should only mean that He was the doctor or shoeing-smith for those who consulted him or brought their horses to be shod. So in the Sacrifice of Calvary there is a latent value to meet the need of every sinner, but it only increases the guilt of those who reject it. It enables God righteously to offer pardon and reconciliation to the whole world, and it was for that in His love that He gave His only-begotten Son, but it does not touch them actually, until they repent and believe. The whole question turns on the difference between what is potential and what is actual, a principle that is quite well understood in every-day life and is of simple application.   W.H.

Is it right to assert dogmatically that our Lord did not become "Son of Man" till His incarnation? Do not John 3. 13 and 6. 62 seem to teach the contrary?

I cannot see how the expression, "Son of Man," could possibly be correctly applied to our Lord, till His Incarnation, except indeed prophetically as in Dan. 7. 13, which refers to a time long subsequent to the Incarnation. The expressions referred to in John—"the Son of Man which is in heaven"; "What and if ye shall see the Son of Man ascend up where He was before?" are not inconsistent with this. The Lord Jesus Christ was a Divine Person, for "The Word was God . . . and became flesh," but that Personality was not less connected with His human, than with His Divine Nature. He was truly the "Son of God," and He spake of Himself as such, viewed as a whole and entire Personality (see John 5. 25; 9, 35, 36; 11. 4); but He far more frequently spake of Himself as the "Son of Man," and He was no less, as such, a whole and entire Personality. We do not confound the Natures, nor do we divide the Person. The "Son of Man" did ascend up where He was before as the Eternal "Son of God" only; but now He is there, as Jesus, the Son of Man. He could not be "Son of Man" till He became man.
                                                                      W.H.

What is the meaning of, "I go to prepare a place for you" (John 14. 2)?

The Lord speaks of this to His disciples as something that was to occupy Him (among other things) during His absence. It is as though He would say, "There are many mansions or dwelling places in my Father's house, but none of them will do for you, I go to prepare a place for you." It will be a very wonderful place. He is also preparing a people for that place, and when place and people are both prepared "He will come again" and receive the prepared people into the prepared place. There they will be **with Him** and **all together** for the first time—all like their Lord, a united family in the Father's house, and brought to the Father's presence. Blessed prospect!   W.H.

When in John 14. 2 our Lord said, "In My Father's house are many mansions," was He referring to what He saw before He came forth from the Father into the world? (John 16. 28).

We should avoid seeking explanations as to how our Lord knew things. He was a Divine Person. He was the Wisdom of God. In Him were "hid all the treasures of wisdom and knowledge." A watchmaker may be excused for knowing how one of his own watches works. The Lord knew there were many mansions in the Father's House, because He had created all things in heaven, as on earth, and by Him they had ever since consisted. He was the Lord from heaven when He came forth from the Father (John 16. 28), and could speak first-hand of heavenly things, and certainly He could say, "We speak that we do know, and testify that we have seen." He had possessed Divine glory with the Father before the world was (John 17. 5). That glory He had laid aside, but not the knowledge of it. His omniscience—the common attribute of Divine Persons—is in no way limited by the differences of function in those Persons for the fulfilment of Divine purposes. Thus when it is a question of knowing "times and seasons" in Acts 1. 7, the Lord does not, in answer to His disciples request, undertake to expound that which "the Father had put in His own power," and which belonged in consequence to Him to expound. "It is not for you to know the times and seasons," etc. It is in this direction that the true explanation is found of the much misunderstood words of our Lord in Mark 13. 32. "But of that day and that hour knoweth no man (Greek—no one), no, not the angels which are in heaven, neither the Son, but the Father." It is "no one," be it noted, not merely, no man. Are we then to understand that the Holy Spirit does not know either, He, of whom we are assured in 1 Cor. 2. 10, 11, that "He searcheth all things, yea the deep things of God," and knows "the things of God"? In spite of religious rationalists, who insist on taking these words in Mark "at their face value" (strange what verbal inspirationists they become when it suits them!), we will insist on taking them with the testimony of the Scriptures as a whole at its face value. "He knew all men"—surely a divine prerogative: He knew the Father—knowledge, which in this absolute unique sense does include all other knowledge. Further, the words of the eleven: "Now are we sure that thou knowest (same word as in Mark 13. 32) all things" (John 16. 30), our Lord does not correct by reminding them of the one thing not known to Him, namely, "that day," but accepts the statement, as a proof that they had at last believed: "Do ye now believe?" If the ground of their faith, namely, their persuasion of His omniscience was mistaken, the faith they had attained would also be null and void. It is noticeable that the verse immediately following Mark 13. 32 is, "Take ye heed, watch and pray: for ye know not when the time is." I believe it is true to say that the statement of Mark 13. 32 had nothing to do with any supposed limitation of our Lord's knowledge, as resulting from His incarnation, because the words we have referred to in Acts 1. 5, are true not merely in His condition as the Incarnate One in humiliation, but in all the freshness and fulness of resurrection life.   W.H.

What do the words mean: "He (the Holy Spirit) shall not speak of Himself" (John 16. 13)? Is not Acts 5 a contradiction of this?

Certainly the story of Ananias and Saphira in Acts 5 was given to Luke for narration by the Holy Spirit, and contains teaching concerning that Spirit; as also do several other chapters of the Acts, e.g. Chap. 2: the coming of the Holy Spirit as a Divine Person. To this subject there are several references in the Epistles, e.g., Romans 5. 5; 8. 2, 9, etc. The explanation is very simple; the words, "He shall not speak of (apo) Himself" do not mean, He shall not speak about Himself, but **from** Himself, that is on His own initiative, independent of the Father. The immediate context of the words shows this to be the sense—"But whatsoever He shall hear that shall He speak." It is exactly the same expression in the Greek as is used by our Lord in chapter 7. 17, 18: "or whether I speak of (apo) Myself"; "He that speaketh of, or from (apo), Himself seeketh His own glory." No man should speak from (apo) himself, but should speak as one sent from God, nor should he speak from (ek) himself, that is, "out of" his own resources. When in John 12. 49 the Lord says, "I have not spoken of myself," it is this latter word (ek) that He uses. The truth seems to be, as presented in the Gospels, that the Father speaks both "from" (apo) and "out of" (ek) Himself; the Spirit "out of" (ek) Himself but not "from" (apo), and the Lord neither "apo" nor yet "ek" Himself. This being said, we may remind ourselves that the true ministry of the Holy Spirit is to be distinguished from the spurious, in that it exalts Christ and does not make the Spirit the centre, or virtually obscure Christ by the teaching. It is not by waiting on the Spirit, but by being taken up with Christ, and appropriating Him by faith, that we shall be Spirit-filled. A man who is full of Christ is full of the Holy Spirit.   W.H.

To what period of time did our Lord's "little while" (Jo. 16. 16) refer?

It would be strange indeed if we could not reach a sure conclusion on this point, seeing our Lord Himself undertakes to explain His words. The occurrence of the words "because I go to My Father," in verse 16, need not be insisted on, though supported by a number of versions, for they are lacking in the principal Uncials. The disciples do use them in their interrogatory, but in doing so they refer back to verse 10 where the Lord certainly uses this expression. I think the Lord means by the first "little while," the three days and three nights of His burial, and by the second, "the forty days." This seems plain from verse 23 and onwards, where He speaks of "that day" (i.e., the day He has been speaking about), when He will see them again and they will enjoy the new privileges of prayer direct to the Father, and in His Name, which are characteristic of the present dispensation, and which do not await His future appearing.   W.H.

Did the words of Christ in His prayer to the Father, "I have finished the work Thou gavest Me to do" (John 17. 4), mean His whole work on earth, where He glorified God's name in everything He accomplished, or were they prophetically spoken in direct reference to Calvary, or to both?

It is generally admitted that there is not only a distinctly prophetic element in our Lord's prayer, especially in its closing half, but that it **anticipates** a condition which had not actually supervened. The very name by which it is usual to describe the prayer, as our Lord's **sacerdotal** prayer, proves this—the cross is scarcely hinted at, the glory is in view. The words are spoken as on resurrection ground. In this sense it would be impossible to limit our Lord's words, "I have finished the work, which Thou gavest me to do," to anything less than the full accomplishment of His whole earthly ministry. For does the Lord not claim to be glorified of the Father on the ground of what He had accomplished for His glory on the earth? How could the infinite work of the cross, the fulfilment of God's eternal purpose, be excluded from this? On the other hand, the prayer crowned the Lord's farewell. He is about to leave, but before doing so commits them to a Keeper. In this sense the cross was still future, and the form of our Lord's words in the Greek include this too: "I have glorified (aorist) . . . I have finished (aorist) the work Thou gavest (perf.—lit., Thou hast given) Me to do." This **perfect** has the sense of what is true up to the present. He had finished **up to that day** His commission. We should be safe then, I think, in affirming that the Lord's words include both what He had actually done and by anticipation, His whole earthly ministry.
W.H.

Please explain what the Lord meant in verse 23 of John 20.

The incident and speech recorded in John 20. 22, 23 took place during the Lord's presence with His disciples (See v. 19). This appearing of Him is the same which is related in Luke 24. 36-49, as well as more briefly in Mark 16. 14-18; and I suggest therefore that the three accounts should be read together, and that when this is done some light will be thrown on the incident mentioned by John, and particularly on the 23rd verse.

In both Mark and Luke, instead of John's words, "Whose soever sins ye remit, they are remitted unto them; and whose soever sins ye retain, they are retained;" we find a commission given to the disciples to preach the Gospel (vv. 15, 16 in Mark and vv. 47-49 in Luke). I think therefore that John 20. 22, 23 has close connection with that commission, and took place immediately after it was given them. If so, the remitting and retaining of sins refers, mainly at least, to the apostles' gospel preaching, and to its effect upon the hearers. By the testimony of the apostles, given in the power of the Spirit, the sins of such as accepted their message would be remitted, while the sins of those who turned down the message would be retained.

Looked at in this way, verse 23 is closely similar to the promise given to Peter in Matt. 16. 19, of which Acts 2 and Acts 10 were part of the fulfilment. It is also similar, though in a less degree, to the one given to the church in Matt. 18. 18, in which case the sin in view is that of a "brother," and the binding or loosing is the effect of the effort of the church to set him right.

With regard to John 20. 22; about which you do not ask, but which is really the more difficult verse of the two; I think that Luke's account helps us somewhat there also. In Luke 24. 45 the giving of the commission is introduced with the words, "Then opened He their understandings that they might understand the Scriptures." This in effect meant the bestowal upon them of a gift of the Spirit, the gift of knowledge; just as John 20. 23 implies the bestowal of the gift of discernment between the two classes of sinning ones. And since Luke concludes the commission with the remark, "Behold I send the promise of My Father upon you; but tarry ye in the city of Jerusalem until ye be endued with power from on high;" he enables us to see that what took place in John 20. 22 was not an earlier Pentecost, though it was doubtless a foretaste of Pentecost, and a preparation for it.   W.R.

What would the order of the grave clothes in John xx. 6-7 suggest?

I would suggest that there is a very important point behind the statement in John xx. 6-7, namely, the complete absence of hurry in the resurrection. Had men come to steal away the body of our Lord, while the guard slept, as the priests lyingly concocted, the sepulchre would have been a scene of wild disorder. The robbers would have torn the clothes off the body and taken it away, leaving everything in confusion on the floor. Who could have thought of folding up the napkin in a place by itself? The resurrection was a Divine work, and God is not the author of confusion.   W.H.

In John 21. 15 does our Lord mean the other disciples or the fishes?

It must be admitted that the bulk of interpreters, though not all by any means, believe the Lord was referring to "these" other disciples, and they point to Peter's boast (Matt. 26. 33), that though all should be offended yet would not he, and also to the threefold repetition of the question which tallied so exactly, they say, with the threefold denial. I think we shall see that this latter plea has no real weight. The other might be allowed, although it must be remembered that Peter did not actually say that he **loved** the Lord, more than his other disciples; but may only have claimed more personal courage. Personally, I feel pretty sure that what the Lord referred to was the fish, and that for the following reasons. The question as to whether Peter was to go back to his fishing or carry out his Lord's command to fish for men was the burning one. Peter's, "I go a fishing," had just put back the clock to his conversion, and set on one side at a stroke the Lord's call and training hitherto. "Come ye after Me, I will make you fishers of men," had become a dead letter. This was the crux, not the denial, which must have been gone into in private, when the Lord appeared to him on the resurrection day, and could have been in public had the Lord wished it long before this.

I think Peter's answers to the Lord's questions were quite unthinkable had he understood Him to refer to the other disciples. Would he not rather have deprecated such a comparison!—"No Lord, I cannot say that, I was wrong in boasting." Surely his answer shows that he understood our Lord was comparing his love to Himself, with his love to something else, not his love with the love of others. Hence his reply, "Yea Lord, thou knowest that I love thee," in other words, I love not the fish, but Thee. Had the degree of his love rather than its object been in question, such an answer would have been quite irrelevant. Peter's grief on the third repetition of the Lord's question depended, as most know, not at all on the threefold repetition, but, on the form of the Lord's words. The word used for love in the first question was a strong one—**"agapaō"**; but Peter answers with a more emotional word—**"phileō,"** and so in the second question and answer. But at the third occasion the Lord uses Peter's word (phileō) seeming thus to question whether he did really love Him so fondly as he professed. Peter was grieved because He used this word the third time and casting himself on the Lord's omniscience, cried "Lord, Thou knowest all things Thou knowest that I love Thee." The Lord's replies seem quite consistent with the above explanation and amounted to, "Very well then, if that be so; don't go fishing, but shepherd and feed My sheep and feed My lambs!" W.H.

THE ACTS

Is the "baptism" mentioned in Acts 2. 38 and 41 John's baptism, or Christian baptism?

While the baptism mentioned here had certain characteristics common to John's baptism, it could not rightly be called John's baptism. It is true, each was a confession of sin, and each was with a view to forgiveness, but the baptism of Acts 2 was administered in compliance with the plain injunction of the Lord in Matt. 28 and Mark 16, and was not a continuation of John's baptism. The revelation of the truth concerning the mystery of the Church and the true significance of Christian baptism had not yet been given. In Acts 2, Israel had not yet been formally set aside: that did not occur till the murder of Stephen recorded in Acts 7: thereafter, the gospel went out to the Samaritans (chap. 8) and to the Gentiles (chap. 10). The setting aside of Israel did not occur at the point indicated by Acts, chapter 28: it had occurred much earlier, as Romans 9-11 teaches. Nor did it occur when Titus ransacked Jerusalem in A.D. 70. That was the execution of a judgment long since pronounced.

During the time, therefore, that God was dealing with the nation as such, baptism was regarded as a confession of the specific sin of the rejection and murder of Christ, and was requisite before there could be forgiveness of that wicked deed. The deed had been public: the confession of it must be public. Similarly, Paul is told to be baptized and "wash away his sins."

Chapters 1 to 7 of the book of the Acts are transitional. That transitional period having now long since expired, Christian baptism is not a confession of sins but a confession of Christ. It is not with a view to forgiveness, but because forgiveness already has been received.

It will help if it is recognised that there are overlaps in God's dispensational ways. The Church was formed in chapter 2 of the Acts: therefore the baptism could not have been John's. But the offer to Israel was open until chapter 7. Therefore, the baptism referred to in chapter 2 could not have been purely "Christian." They who were baptized were baptized as repentant Jews. Admittedly they were members of the Body of Christ, but this truth was not then revealed, nor indeed divulged until after Israel had sealed their doom by sending the messenger (Stephen) back after Christ, saying, "We will not have this man to reign over us."   W.R.

With regard to Acts 2. 38, it has been taught that the people there addressed by Peter could not obtain remission of their sins, until they first of all had been baptized in water. The meaning

of the Greek preposition "eis" (A.V., "for"; R.V., "unto") is relied on as proof of this; and the reason adduced for the withholding of the remission is that, since these Jews had rejected the previous testimony of Jesus Himself and had put Him to death, it was necessary for them publicly to renounce their sin in doing so, by submitting to baptism ere forgiveness could be granted them. Is the view correct?

Before further replying to the question, may I suggest that it is unsafe for anyone, not thoroughly conversant with the many shades of meaning possessed by the Greek prepositions, to build a doctrine **upon his view** of what one of them signifies in a particular instance. In this case for example, if the "eis" of the exhortation, "Repent and be baptized . . . unto the remission of your sins", MUST imply that baptism was to precede remission, what shall be said of Matt. 3. 11, "I indeed baptize you with water unto (Greek, "eis") repentance"? By exactly the same reasoning, the "eis" there MUST imply that baptism was to precede repentance; and if it does, John must have been preaching an even cruder form than Peter of salvation by works.

As to the reason mentioned in the question for this strange order of things, it has to be remembered that there were in Peter's audience many "Jews, devout persons out of every nation under heaven". Were these foreign Jews in actual fact any more guilty of rejecting Christ's testimony, and of His murder, than were their Gentile neighbours in the countries from which they came, as named in vv. 9-11?

In Mark 16. 16 occurs the statement, "He that believeth and is baptized shall be saved"; which, taken by itself would seem to imply that baptism is in the strictest sense necessary to salvation. And since it follows the words, "Preach the Gospel to every creature", it cannot here be explained by referring it to any circumstances peculiar to the Jews. What then is the explanation? Is it not simply this, that baptism is linked with the essential thing—believing, not as being itself also essential to salvation, but as being one of the first and most prominent manifestations of the change which believing brings about? Compare how in Rom. 10. 10, "confession with the mouth", is linked to "believing with the heart," and note that in the other half of the statement in Mark, baptism is entirely omitted. There is no "He that is not baptized shall be damned".

Now, if this simple explanation is the only one open to us when dealing with Mark 16. 16, why should it not suffice also in the case of Acts 2. 38; the **REPENTING** being there the essential thing, as the **BELIEVING** is in Mark, and baptism there also being merely an outward manifestation of its reality? Thus viewed, the exhortation will be in accord with the one used by Peter shortly afterwards in ch. 3. 19, where although he is addressing Jews of Jerusalem, he says nothing whatever about baptism. His words are, "Repent ye therefore and be converted" (R.V., "turn again"), the latter expression taking the place of the reference to baptism, and similarly pointing to the outward change that results from true repentance.   W.R.

Is it scriptural to say with reference to Acts 2. 42, that "the apostles' doctrine formed the fellowship, the breaking of bread expressed it and by prayer it was maintained"? Such a statement has been said to be "fundamentally unsound."

It is difficult to say what fundamental doctrine is assailed by such a statement as above. Perhaps the objector takes the "fellowship" here to be the same as that referred to in 1 Cor. 1. 9: "God is faithful, by whom ye were called unto the fellowship of His Son Jesus Christ our Lord," and would argue that it is God Who creates this fellowship and who maintains it. But then it may be asked, in what sense did the early disciples **"continue** in the fellowship"? Does not such an expression suppose the possibility of not continuing in it? Surely their entrance into it depended not only on their faith, but on the confession of their faith? How could the Apostle have known who had received his words, except from the lips of the believers themselves? Would he have baptized on any other conditions? Had there been in all that multitude on the day of Pentecost one who had truly believed but did not confess to some of the apostles his faith, then, though he would have been united to Christ by the fact of his faith and **ipso facto** a partaker of that divine fellowship, he could not be said to have been brought into the circle of fellowship known at Jerusalem, and how could he have "continued" in what he had not entered into? A man brought to Christ on a desert island is truly "in the fellowship of the Son," but in no local fellowship, for such does not exist. Any pretension of any local company of believers to-day to arrogate to itself the title of "the Church of God" is not favoured here and will surely be blown upon by the Lord, sooner or later, but it is because a man is recognised as having been received by Christ into His fellowship, that his brethren in Christ receive him into the fellowship of the saints. If he does not continue in the apostles' doctrine—that is, if he lets go the truth of Christ's Person and work on which that fellowship is based—his continuance therein is in jeopardy. He may be put away as a wicked person, though he may prove afterwards, as in the case of the incestuous of Corinth, to have been all the time in the sight of God, in "the fellowship of His Son Jesus Christ our Lord."   W.H.

Is the fellowship mentioned in Acts 2. 42 the same as that in 1 Cor. 1. 9; or is it fellowship in the local assembly?

The "Fellowship of His Son," of 1 Cor. 1. 9, is clearly that whereunto God called us in saving us; and includes all that we now have, as well as all that we ever shall have by virtue of our union with Christ, and our being "joint-heirs" with Him. Our place and maintenance in that, as the verse itself says, depends on the fact that "God is faithful."

In Acts 2. 42, on the contrary, the "fellowship" is evidently of a kind, continuance in which depended on the stedfastness of the young converts themselves; and no doubt refers to their casting in their lot whole-heartedly with the apostles and the rest of the saints at Jerusalem in all their activities.   W.R.

Is it right to look upon Ananias and Sapphira as true believers? Did they not belong to those spoken of as "the rest" (Acts v.)?

I judge that Ananias and Sapphira were certainly, outwardly at any rate, in the fellowship of the church. Can we imagine Jews, open rejectors of the Lord, having any interest in selling their property and bringing it to the apostles? What could they hope to gain by it? To such, the apostles would be arch-renegades from their faith as Jews. We to-day would not feel happy in accepting gifts from the world for the Lord's work. Can we imagine Peter accepting the price of their land from Ananias and Sapphira if they were unconverted persons? The words, "Of the rest durst no man JOIN HIMSELF with them," simply mean that the solemn incident deterred outsiders from "joining themselves" to the church by a premature confession of faith, and becoming mere "hangers on," as we say. But these words do not follow directly on the incident, and it would be unnatural to suppose that these two sinning ones were representative of a class, as though "the rest" meant the rest of the Ananias's and Sapphira's, rather than quite an exceptional case. The work of the Spirit was certainly not hindered by His holy judgment, but furthered: "BELIEVERS WERE THE MORE ADDED to the Lord," etc. Personally, I could not go so far as to affirm, "Undoubtedly Ananias and Sapphira were true believers," though I may HOPE they were. The fact of their being dealt with in judgment argues in their favour, as the passage in 1 Cor. xi would bear out: "For this cause many are weak and sickly among you and many sleep, FOR WHEN WE ARE JUDGED, WE ARE CHASTENED OF THE LORD that we should not be condemned WITH THE WORLD" (vv. 30, 32). God usually leaves the world alone now for future judgment. But if anyone falls under the judgment of God, or the extreme discipline of the church, we can only "stand in doubt of him." Paul did not call the incestuous man of 1 Cor. v, "our dear brother," but "that wicked person." The effect of discipline is too often hindered, if not altogether marred, by a determination on the part of some, in the name of that much misused word charity, either altogether to oppose the discipline inflicted, or to act toward the object of it at least in social relations as though nothing had happened. A man under discipline should not be received into our houses in a social way, nor should we "bid him God speed." The one who violates this rule becomes, in God's sight, "partaker of his evil deeds" (2 John x.). This is without prejudice to the endeavours of those competent to restore the fallen one. A mere profession of conversion in the past is not the ultimate proof of reality, but a continuance in the doctrine of Christ, and a holy walk are (2 John i. 9; 1 John iii. 6). But are we called to pronounce on them? "The Lord knoweth them that are His, and let everyone that nameth the name of Christ depart from iniquity" (2 Tim. ii. 19). "By their fruits ye shall know them." It is, I should judge, running clean against the purpose of the Spirit in recording this sad incident, to decree of every professor who makes shipwreck, "Oh, he was once a child of God, and so is now." This is going too far. The conclusion may be mistaken, because the premise may never have been true.   W.H.

Was Gamaliel of Acts 5. 34 a saved man?

He was a teacher well known in the Jewish records of those times, and held in honour by the nation as one of their greatest Rabbis. So far as can be ascertained, he lived and died in their religion, though more tolerant in his views than most of them. This tolerance he displayed in the incident of Acts 5; and it is somewhat remarkable that his pupil, Saul of Tarsus (chap. 22. 3), did not take after him in this respect, but became a bitter persecutor. Yet after all, it was the bigoted pupil who got saved, and not his broadminded teacher.

There may, however, be another consideration which helped to cause Gamaliel to take the stand he did in Acts 5. According to verse 17 (read in connection with chap. 4. 1, 2), these earliest persecutions were got up by the Sadducees, who were "grieved that they ... preached through Jesus the resurrection from the dead." And the High Priest of that day was evidently in sympathy with these Sadducees. Now when Gamaliel is first mentioned in verse 34, it is specially noted that he was not a Sadducee but a Pharisee; and it is therefore not unlikely that he was glad of an excuse to oppose them. Compare how, in chap. 23. 6-9, Paul caused an uproar between the same two parties, by declaring himself a Pharisee, who was being called in question because of his belief in the resurrection. And on that occasion the Pharisees used almost the very words of Gamaliel, when they said, "Let us not fight against God" (v. 9, compared with chap. 5. 39).   W.R.

Was the Ethiopian eunuch of Acts 8, a Jew or a Gentile?

In the story of this man we get the only New Testament reference to a race which is frequently mentioned in the Old Testament. The Hebrew word there used for the Ethiopians is "Cush," and it implies their descent from Cush, the son of Ham (Gen. 10. 6). They, therefore, of course were Gentiles; and Amos 9. 7 appears to suggest that they were looked on as amongst the lowest (or perhaps merely, the farthest off) of the Gentiles; while Jer. 13. 23 shows that they were black, or at least dark-skinned. A point of interest is that in Jer. 38 and 39 we read of Ebedmelech, an Old Testament "Ethiopian eunuch," whose heart had evidently been turned to the Lord, as was that of the New Testament one. It is commonly held that the latter was a proselyte, in the wider sense of that word, to the religion of Israel; but all that we can gather from the Scriptures is that he had heard of and reverenced Israel's God. May we not think of him as part of the answer to Solomon's prayer of 1 Kings 8. 41, 43, "Concerning a stranger, that is not of Thy people Israel, but cometh out of a far country . . . hear Thou."

The story of his conversion is one of three, which are told at length in this part of Acts, and in which we see the gospel reaching a representative of each of the three great families of Noah's descendants, amongst whom the earth was divided in Gen. 10; the eunuch of Ethiopia, a son of Ham; Saul the Jew, a son of Shem; and Cornelius the Roman Centurion, a son doubtless of Japheth. They belong to that section of the Acts, reaching from chap. 8. 1 to chap. 13. 1, which deals with what is pre-eminently the transition phase of the early gospel testimony. Until the stoning of Stephen at the end of chap. 7, the preaching had been to Jews only; but in chap. 8, Stephen's companion in service, Philip, preaches Christ, first to the Samaritans, and then to the Gentile eunuch. Then in chap. 9 the Apostle of the Gentiles is saved and commissioned; in chap. 10 the "door of faith" is formally opened to the Gentiles by Peter; and in chap. 11 certain unnamed brethren preach to the Gentiles of Antioch (verses 19-21), with the result that there is a great ingathering. From chap. 13. 1 onwards, this place, Antioch, becomes the centre from which gospel testimony goes out to the Gentiles in general, instead of Jerusalem; and Paul becomes the prominent worker in the record, instead of Peter. How fitting it is that the conversion and baptism of the Ethiopian, a Gentile and a eunuch (see Deut. 23. 1), should have a place in the history of that great change.   W.R.

What is the significance of the change of preposition in Acts 13. 38, 39? "Through (dia) this man is preached unto you the forgiveness of sins and by (en) Him all that believe are justified from all things from which ye could not be justified by (en) the law of Moses."

The ruler of the synagogue at Antioch had invited Paul and Barnabas to give the people "a word of exhortation," a thing they were quite accustomed to, and ready to hear, as religious man always is, on condition he is not required in an unreasonable manner to follow it out. What they got was something quite different: a "word of salvation," the best word of all, but which man, apart from the grace of God, will never accept. This "word of salvation" is split up in our verses into at least two of its great components—forgiveness and justification. Why then is it "through" or "by means of" (dia) this One, in the case of Forgiveness? and "by" or literally, "in" (en) Him, in the case of Justification? Why, too, in the case of the law does Paul use the latter preposition, saying, "from which ye could not be justified by ('en' lit.: 'in' or 'under') the law of Moses"? It is clear that forgiveness depends directly on the work of Christ upon the cross; it is by means of Him. Forgiveness is often linked with the blood of Christ; and so, too, is justification, as far as its ground goes: "justified by His blood." But it is only on resurrection ground, in association with Christ that our justification is manifested. "He was delivered for (or owing to) our offences, and raised again for (or owing to) our justification." In or under law we could be justified from nothing: "For by the deeds of the law there shall no flesh be justified": but in Christ we stand fully acquitted, and with nothing against us, indeed as free from all charge as Christ Himself, for we form part of Him, being "members of His Body." Forgiveness then is received by means of Christ's work: Justification is enjoyed in association with Christ.   W.H.

What work is referred to in Acts 13. 41, in the words, "I work a work in your days, a work which ye shall in no wise believe, though a man declare it unto you"? Is it a work of grace, or a work of judgment?

Acts 13. 41 is, as the previous verse states, a quotation from the prophets. It is taken from Habakkuk 1. 5, and except for the omission of a word or two, it quotes that verse as it is rendered in the Septuagint, the Greek version of the Old Testament. In Habakkuk the succeeding verses make it clear that the "work" which the Lord is about to do, and which they cannot be brought to believe that He will do, is to raise up the Chaldeans as executors of His judgment on sinful Judah. When, therefore, the words are applied by the apostle to his own times, it is but reasonable to think that he has in mind the still greater judgment shortly to be inflicted on the Jewish people by the hands of the Romans. Yet the fact that he employs them by way of warning his hearers against refusing to believe the gospel, suggests that he is thinking of the "work" God is working in a wider way, as including the offering of the message of life to them first, the turning from them to the Gentiles with it when they would prove "despisers," and the pouring out of His wrath upon them for this, as well as for the nation's rejection of Christ Himself. The three words used of the despisers, "Behold, and wonder, and perish," could be more fully understood thus, than if we applied them to the coming judgment only. Their fate would be that of the lord in 2 Kings 7, who refused to believe the "good tidings," and to whom the prophet said something more difficult still to believe, namely, that he would see it with his eyes, but would not eat thereof. Yet, as the end of the chapter says, "So it fell out unto him." He beheld; he wondered; and he perished. Similarly these Jews of Antioch "beheld" on the following Sabbath day something at which they must have "wondered," when "there came almost the whole city together to hear the Word of God" (verse 44). And that they also "perished," seems sadly clear from their attitude (verse 45); as well as from the apostle's denunciation of them (verse 46), when he said, "Seeing ye put it from you, and judge yourselves unworthy of everlasting life, lo, we turn to the Gentiles."

Looked at in this way, it might be said that the "work" which God was at that time doing, and which culminated in the destruction of Jerusalem, was a work both of grace and of judgment; of judgment upon the despisers, but of grace to such as heard the gospel and believed.　　　　　　　　　　　　　　　　　　　　W.R.

A commentary which I have read says that the words in Acts 13. 48. "As many as were ordained to eternal life believed," should be rendered, "As many as were disposed for eternal life believed." Is this correct?

It would not at all be an improvement to change the word in Acts 13. 48 from "ordained" to "disposed." The R.V. retains "ordained," and so does J. N. Darby's translation, while both Young and Weymouth have "appointed," an even stronger expression. And the same Greek word, in the same form, is the one used in the statement of Rom. 13. 1, "The powers that be are ordained of God."

A commentator who would suggest changing to "disposed," in all probability has a bias against the doctrine of election; and the value of the word "disposed" to him arises from its vagueness. It may on the one hand have a strongly verbal force, as it has in the A.V. rendering of Job 34. 13 and 37. 15, where it is practically equivalent to "ordained," and where the context makes clear that the Disposer or Arranger is God. And if it were certain to be understood in that sense by the reader of Acts 13. 48, its introduction there would make little or no difference to the meaning. But "disposed" frequently has a more adjectival signification, as in the A.V. of Acts 18. 27 and of 1 Cor. 10. 27; where it is equivalent to "desirous" or "wishful," and is the rendering of Greek words quite dissimilar from that in Acts 13. 48. So I fear that the commentator, having been able to introduce it, only because it can bear the former meaning, will be "disposed" to explain it in the latter sense.

The truth of election is plainly taught in many Scriptures and cannot be done away with. But in most of these the converse truth of man's own choice is taught alongside it. Thus in Acts 13, verse 48 follows upon verse 46: "Ye put it from you, and judge yourselves unworthy of everlasting life," and the one statement is just as true as the other.

W.R.

In view of Young's and Weymouth's translations, and Newberry's marginal note, what is the meaning of "ordained" in Acts 14. 23?

We have not Young's translation at hand but see that Weymouth has—"selected elders by show of hands," and then in footnote: (1) "Selection, i.e., caused to be elected"; (2) "by show of hands." Newberry gives in margin, "Appointed by stretching forth the hands." Grimm, the New Testament lexicographer, gives as the meaning: (a) to vote by stretching out the hand; (b) to create or appoint by vote; (c) with the loss of the notion of extending the hands, to elect, appoint, create. It will be noticed that this last-named authority does not recognise the causative sense, which Dr. Weymouth suggests, and we may safely ignore it. Such an idea as a church or chapel electing a pastor or minister over it lacks scriptural sanction. The idea of "stretching out the hands," which occurs in all the authorities quoted, comes from the derivation of the word translated "ordain" (cheirotoneō)—"to stretch out the hand." It seems to us that the two important questions are, who are the subjects of the verb "ordain," and what does the action signify?

It is noticeable that this "ordaining" of elders did not take place on the apostle's first visit, when by the ordinary canons of ecclesiastical order the infant churches needed them most, but only on their return visit. Did the apostles then leave them to themselves? No, but "to God and the word of His grace." The apostles had learned the great lesson that the Lord would care for these new-born believers and sustain them and raise up gifts among them. Now in chap. 14. 21, the apostles return once more to Lystra, Iconium and Antioch, but this visit differs from the first in being pastoral, rather than evangelistic; they are occupied rather with the young churches, than with the unsaved world; their work is to confirm the souls of the disciples (v. 22); no routine episcopal visitation is this, to administer some fancy, human rite, but a real strengthening of them by the Word. And all this was the work of Paul and Barnabas, and it is not impossible, but that the action of the following verse—the "ordaining" of the elders—was equally their work.

Now we can see another reason why they had not done this at the first visit, because the Holy Spirit would not have had time, if we may so speak, to manifest those whom He was about to call to the work. I believe that all that the apostles did was to indicate or recognise those who had come to the front during their absence and shown themselves to be those whom "the Holy Ghost had made overseers," as later in the case of Ephesus (see Acts 20. 28). The subject of "returned," "confirmed," "ordained," "prayed," etc., is the same all through. The word "cheirotoneō" here rendered "ordain," is translated, "choose," in its one other occurrence in the New Testament (2 Cor. 8. 19). The apostles "chose" ("indicated," would do quite well) in Acts 14. 23, where "elect by a show of hands" is excluded by the context. There is something grotesque in the idea of Paul and Barnabas "electing by a show of hands."

In the case of the "seven" of Acts 5, the multitude did choose those who were to administer their contributions to the widows' fund, though the apostles appointed them; but we never read of men choosing elders or pastors or teachers or evangelists of a church, to do their preaching for them at so much per annum (much less "the pastor" or "the evangelist" in the singular), because such are administrators of spiritual gifts, bestowed by their Risen Lord, and He alone chooses His almoners.

W.H.

Is it wrong, in view of Acts 15. 20, 29, for a Christian to eat anything which has blood in it?

This is a matter concerning which there have always been differences of opinion among the Lord's people. The fact is that there is much to be said on both sides of the matter; and possibly the fairest way of dealing with it will be to enumerate the chief reasons usually given against and for eating. These are:—

(AGAINST)

(1) The original prohibition was given, not merely to Israel (as was the case with the "fat," Lev. 3. 16, 17, etc.), but to Noah and his descendants, amongst whom we all, Gentiles and Jews alike, are included (Gen. 9. 4).

(2) It was given on the very occasion when the use of flesh as food was first permitted to mankind (v. 3); and was coupled with another injunction against taking human life (vv. 5, 6), the importance and permanence of which are unquestioned.

(3) Its re-affirmation to Gentile converts in Acts 15 is made in the same communication in which their freedom from circumcision and other strictly Jewish ordinances is upheld.

(4) So late as in the messages to the Seven Churches in the Revelation, certain persons are condemned for transgressing the injunctions of Acts 15, not alone with regard to fornication, but also to the eating of meats offered to idols. See chap. 2. 2c, 24, and compare the final

v

clause of the latter verse with Acts 15. 28, as evidence of a close connection between the passages.

(FOR)

(1) Previous to the blessing of Noah, animals had been used for sacrifice but not for food. After it, they were used for both sacrifice and food. It was fitting therefore that, by way of distinction, the blood which symbolised the life should be reserved for sacrificial use only. In our times animal sacrifices are no longer offered, and an ordinance to mark the distinction is no longer needful.

(2) The reasons for the injunctions given in Acts 15 lie on the surface of that passage, and are: (a) that the things named had intimate connections with the idolatry of those days, which idolatry naturally would be an outstanding temptation to Gentile converts, and (b), that to the scattered Jews, accustomed to "Moses . . . being read in the synagogues every sabbath day," these things were so abhorrent as to constitute a barrier, not only to the spread of the Gospel among them, but even to intercourse between the Jewish converts and their Gentile brethren. Note in this connection the "For" by which verse 21 is linked with what goes before. But where these two reasons are no longer operative, as is, generally speaking, the case to-day, the injunctions are no longer required, except in so far as they forbid what is in its very nature immoral and evil.

(3) The teaching concerning food in the Epistles is uniformly in accord with the view of Acts 15 just now presented, and with that given by our Lord Himself in Matt. 15. 11: "Not that which goeth into the mouth defileth a man," as the following quotations will show. "I know . . . that there is nothing unclean of itself, . . . but if thy brother be grieved with thy meat, . . . for the kingdom of God is not meat and drink" (Rom. 14. 14-17). "Meat commendeth us not to God, . . . but take heed lest this liberty of yours become a stumbling block to them that are weak" (1 Cor. 8. 8, 9). "Whatsoever is sold in the shambles, that eat asking no question for conscience sake" (1 Cor. 10. 25). "If ye be dead with Christ . . . why are ye subject to ordinances (touch not, taste not, handle not), which all are to perish with the using" (Col. 2. 20-22). "Commanding to abstain from meats, which God created to be received with thanksgiving . . . for every creature of God is good, and nothing to be refused" (1 Tim. 4. 3, 4). "Meats and drinks . . . imposed on them until the time of reformation . . . but Christ being come" (Heb. 9. 10, 11).

On the other hand, see how in 1 Cor. 6. 13 the apostle draws a clear distinction between the meats and the fornication of Acts 15, the one being in itself entirely and always wrong, the other not so, but sometimes inexpedient; also how in 1 Cor. 10. 20, 25, he further draws a distinction between eating without question meat which has been purchased, and going along to have fellowship with idolatrous worship.

It seems to me that these scriptures, being subsequent to Acts 15, form the Holy Spirit's comment on the meaning and use of what was there enacted; and that therefore no food whatever need be refused by the child of God to-day, except he finds himself in circumstances where partaking would involve (a) fellowship with evil, or (b) a stumbling-block to others. Yet doubtless to some the reasons against may have the more weight, and to such, one can only say in the words of Rom. 14, "Let every man be fully persuaded in his own mind." W.R.

Please explain Acts 15. 22.

There does not seem perhaps very much to explain here. This verse follows on the Conference at Jerusalem held to consider a difficulty which had arisen at Antioch of Syria through the interference of Judaising brethren from Judæa.

The apostles and elders (not the whole church) came together to consider the matter; and after a number had taken part, the discussion was closed by James (the Lord's brother), who gave as his judgment (krinō = I judge) that the Gentiles should not be troubled in the way some would trouble them, but that only four things should be enjoined on them: one, a moral prohibition true for all time, and three ritual prohibitions, which we learn from the Epistles (e.g., 1 Cor. 10. 25-29) were only temporary. This was agreed upon, and then the whole church was informed and identified with the decision of the apostles and elders. Next they chose from their midst two leading brethren to carry the result to the believing Gentiles in Syria and Cilicea, in the form of letters; the contents of which they declared to contain the expressed will of the Holy Spirit, as well as their own decision. It is perfectly open for a church to seek the fellowship and help of an older assembly in some local difficulty of importance, and that church may give counsel, but cannot impose its decision on fellow-believers, as though it possessed apostolic authority, much less assume dogmatically to have infallibly the mind of the Spirit. How much religious tyranny churches might have been spared had men not assumed jurisdiction where they had none, lorded it over the consciences of their brethren, and made of local differences a cause of world-wide division! W.H.

Do you reject Darby's translation of Acts 16. 34?

I am afraid I must plead ignorance of exactly what Mr. Darby's translation of this verse is, as I do not possess his English, but only his French translation. But as this latter was the original, I understand the two are probably much the same. His French runs thus, "Et croyant Dieu, il se réjouit avec toute sa maison," which means, we know: "And believing God, he rejoiced with all his house." I suppose household baptists prefer this order, as it separates believing as far as possible from "the house," which their theory demands; but I know of no real justification for thus shuffling the words out of their original order, which is, as I pointed out in my "Review," "He rejoiced with all his house, having believed in God." I cannot find a single version which favours Darby's order. The R.V. keeps the exact Greek order—"And rejoiced greatly with all his house, having believed in God." The Ostervald French version of 1881 has, "He rejoiced at having believed in God, with all his house." The Italian 1885 edition reads, "And he rejoiced at having with all his house believed in God," and the Spanish Version the same. Luther's German version has, "And rejoiced greatly with his whole house, at having believed in God." The Douay R.C. Version (fair, apart from the notes) has, "And rejoiced with all his house, believing in God." Alford agrees that the form of the Greek, "having believed", must give the ground of his rejoicing. Thus, he adds, the meaning will be, "And rejoiced that he, with all his house, had been led to believe in God." Of course, if any prefer to accept Mr. Darby's arbitrary alteration of the order of the words, in face of all these other versions, they are at liberty to do so. Personally, I cannot see any reason for so doing. There are two other points which may be noticed in the account. First, that all the verbs in verses 33 and 34 are in the singular,—having **taken** them; he **washed** their stripes; he was **baptized**; having **brought** them; he **set** meat; he **rejoiced**; having **believed**. Are we therefore to understand that he was the sole actor all through or that he is mentioned representatively? I think the latter. Then secondly, in the case of his hearing the Word, we know that the household did so also. So with his baptism—"He was baptized, he and all his straightway"; and so with his rejoicing—"He rejoiced with-all-his-house" (Gk. **panoiki**). To my mind, it seems very clear that in the jailor's case, his rejoicing sprang from his believing, and that if his household shared his joy, it was only because they shared his faith. If all but the jailor had rejected the Word of the Lord, how could they have helped rejecting his joy too? The reverse is contrary to all experience. Nothing more conduces to irritate Christ-rejecters, than the joy of a young convert. The jailor's household rejoiced with him, and the inference is overwhelming, that they shared his reason for so doing—they believed with him.   W.H.

In Acts 18. 21 we read of a feast which Paul was anxious to attend at Jerusalem. And in Acts 20. 16 we are told that he hasted to be at Jerusalem for the Day of Pentecost. Was this to remember the Lord in the breaking of bread, or was it some other feast?

It is difficult to understand how anyone can confound the Jewish yearly feasts, Pentecost and others, which were observed at Jerusalem, with the Christian weekly feast of the Lord's Supper, which was observed wherever there was an assembly of the saints. The very chapter in which it is stated that Paul was hasting to be at Jerusalem at Pentecost, tells us that, while on the way going there, he was present at a breaking of bread meeting in Troas (chap. 20. 6-12). Moreover, it is interesting to note that, in order to be present at this meeting in Troas, he had, despite his hurry, to stay there for seven days (vv. 6, 7). Owing to the fact that the vessel in which he crossed the sea from Philippi took longer than was usual for the voyage (contrast the five days of verse 6 with chap. 16. 11, 12, where little more than two days were required for the same journey in the reverse direction), the apostle seems to have just missed by a day being with them on the preceding Lord's Day.

Pentecost is the New Testament name for the feast called in Deut. 16. 9-11, "The Feast of Weeks," which is fully described there and in Lev. 23. 15-21. The unnamed feast referred to in Acts 18. 21 was probably also a Pentecost, some four years earlier than the one named in chap. 20. 16. In going to these feasts the apostle was doubtless seeking to carry out the principle he lays down when, writing to the Cor inthians at a time almost midway between the two occasions, he says, "Unto the Jews I became as a Jew that I might gain the Jews" (1 Cor. 9. 20). Some tell us that in this respect he went further than he should have done; but it is just possible that it is they themselves who go too far, in condemning him where the Scriptures do not. It must be remembered that the entire period covered by the Acts was a period of transition, and in some respects very gradual transition, during which certain things were expedient, which later would not be so.   W.R.

ACTS 18.24-28.

Was Apollos in the local Assembly? If so, how did he get there, as he knew only the baptism of John? If he was not in the assembly, why did the brethren commend him?

Nothing is said at first of Apollos' connection with the assembly at Ephesus. He seems to have been a servant of the Lord pioneering round, which may have been commoner then than now. When he came to Ephesus, likely enough he knew nothing either of the little company of brethren, or of the disciples baptised according to John's baptism, which in a large city like Ephesus would not make a great stir anyway. However, "he spake and taught diligently the things of the Lord," but in a limited measure, for the Spirit adds, "knowing only the baptism of John." We are not told where he preached, probably wherever he could get in a word—open-air, market places, private houses, etc. Verse 26 tells us of a step in advance. "He began to speak boldly in the synagogue." It was here apparently for the first time, that

Aquila and Priscilla heard him, and they noticed his limitations and "took him unto them" (i.e. probably to their lodgings), "and expounded unto him the way of God more perfectly." I should judge that it was at this point that he came into contact with the brethren of the place, through the two saints just mentioned, and it was they who gave him a letter of commendation to Achaia. The question may suggest itself, why was he not re-baptized, as the twelve disciples in the next chapter were? The answer is, I think, that while these had received the baptism of John, since it had been replaced by that of the Lord (see Matt. 28), the conversion and baptism of Apollos went back further, to a period prior to the Lord's death and resurrection, when the baptism of John was still valid. No doubt the apostles were all at first disciples of John and had received his baptism, and we never read of any of them being re-baptized.   W.H.

Please explain why Paul went to Jerusalem after being warned through the Spirit that He should not go (Acts 21. 4).

Though it can be shown that the inspiration of the apostolic writings is included in the terms of 1 Tim. 3. 16—"All Scripture is given by inspiration of God," there is no passage which guarantees to us the infallibility of all the apostles did or said as recorded in the Acts period, and in the Epistles. Thus Peter "was to be blamed" for his course at Antioch (Gal. 2. 11), and Paul in Acts 24. 21 seems clearly to admit his action before the council (see chap. 23.6) was faulty, as also his retort to the high priest (vv. 3, 5). However, this being said, we may well shrink from passing judgment on the apostles, when the Spirit of God does not do so. I believe there is sufficient proof in the case before us, that though it appears on the surface that Paul was forbidden to go to Jerusalem, the words referred to are rather a warning than a prohibition. The first mention of Paul's desire to go to Jerusalem is found in Acts 19. 21. Later "he hastened . . . if it were possible for him to be at Jerusalem the day of Pentecost" (ch. 20. 16). We must remember in this connection, that however clear the divine revelation was as regards Gentile converts, Jewish converts were in a transition state in the Acts, and so we see myriads of these latter still "zealous of the law" (chap. 21. 20), and even Paul still making vows, shaving his head, and attending "feasts." No doubt, he saw himself later on an altogether higher plane, and in no way under law. All converts, Jew or Gentile, were in the only Church known in the New Testament, but they did not yet know their position. The Church was born at Pentecost, but did not come of age till much later. In verses 22 and 23 of chapter 20, we further read Paul's words: "And now, behold, I go bound in the spirit unto Jerusalem, not knowing the things that shall befall me there: save that the Holy Ghost witnesseth in every city (probably by prophets residing there) saying that bonds and afflictions abide me." The expressions, "bound in the spirit," speaks of compulsion. He feels his spirit drawn by a higher power; the inference is, by the leading of God. This throws light on Acts 21. 4, where they said to Paul "through the Spirit, that he should not go up to Jerusalem." Alford (in loco) has an interesting note, to the effect that this illustrates the truth of 1 Cor. 14. 32: "'The spirits of the prophets are subject to the prophets,' i.e., that the revelation made by the Holy Spirit to each man's spirit was under the influence of that man's will and temperament, moulded by and taking the form of his own capacities and resolves. So here: these Tyrian prophets knew by the Spirit, which testified this in every city, that bonds and imprisonment awaited Paul. This appears to have been announced by them, shaped and intensified by their own intense love and anxiety for him. . . . But he paid no regard to the prohibition, being himself under a leading of the same Spirit, too plain for him to mistake it." It was as though God for His servant's sake would spare him, but for His greater glory's sake would let him go. It was a test for the apostle—that he did not take this as an absolute prohibition seems clear. The Agabus incident bears this out. It was again a warning to Paul to count the cost. When he showed his determination to go forward at any sacrifice "for the name of the Lord Jesus," the significant words were altered by those who had hitherto tried to dissuade him: "The will of the Lord be done." Henceforth his way is open; others joined his escort, and he has a royal welcome in Jerusalem. It is true he seems to have followed faulty advice from James, but though this did lead to his arrest, it did not prevent the Lord's approval of His beloved servant. "The night following the Lord stood by him," and instead of reproaching him with having transgressed His will, said, "Be of good cheer, Paul, for as thou hast testified of Me in Jerusalem, so must thou bear witness also at Rome" (chap. 23. 11). We never read subsequently that the apostle had any misgiving, or that he had been mistaken in any way in going up to Jerusalem, nor need we.   W.H.

Please explain Acts 21. 24.

We must remember that the Acts period was one of transition, and it was only very gradually that believing Israelites were becoming emancipated from their allegiance to the Mosaic ceremonial and learning to enjoy the "liberty wherewith Christ had made them free." I believe a mistake has been made in asserting that this change only became clear through what are known as the prison epistles—Ephesian, Philippian, Colossian. It had been revealed more or less clearly in all the epistles, especially the first to the Corinthians, and "the Galatians." But seeing that the whole Mosaic system had been instituted of God Himself, it was especially difficult for believing Jews to see their new place in Christ. At the same time the truth of the One Body had been revealed (see 1 Cor. 12. 13). Paul had taught the truth to the Galatian churches, as well as to the Corinthians. At Jerusalem they were specially backward. There were "myriads of Jews, who believed, and they were all zealous of the law" (chap. 21. 20). James suggests then that Paul should display a certain zeal for legal observances in the way prescribed, and so allay the fears of the zealots. Paul fell in with the suggestion and carried it out, but God's blessing does not seem to have rested on the expedient, for it was indirectly the means of bringing him into the grasp of his enemies. What the actual ceremonial was, does not seem clear. The shaving of the head is by some referred to the ceremonial at the close of the Nazarite vow (Num. 6. 18), but this is not possible here, for Paul had not been keeping the literal Nazarite vow, as far as we know.   W.H.

How can Paul's claim in Acts 22. 25 to Roman citizenship be reconciled with his statement in Phil. 3. 20 (R.V.) that our citizenship is in heaven?

Is any "reconciling" necessary, seeing that both statements were true? If so we shall have also to "reconcile" with each of them his saying in Acts 21. 39 that he was a citizen of Tarsus, his claim in Phil. 3. 5 to be a Hebrew of pure descent, and some other statements as well.

It was doubtless of God's arrangement that Paul had from birth the privileges which in those days were associated with Roman citizenship, for it facilitated in various ways his missionary journeyings throughout the provinces of the empire. But we may be sure that he never made use of these privileges in any way which would conflict with his heavenly citizenship. We are told of only three occasions on which he did claim them; at Philippi in Acts 16. 37, where the probable motive was to render the position more favourable for the converts he left behind him there, and perhaps for the jailor himself; at Jerusalem in Acts 22. 25, where it not only preserved him from being scourged, but lifted his case out of the hands of his bitterest enemies; and at Cæsarea in Acts 25. 10. 11, where his appeal as a Roman to the Emperor was the means of bringing about that which was in the purpose of God for him, his testimony before the highest tribunal at Rome (see Acts 23. 11). That on each of these occasions he was guided by God, I have no doubt; but in the first case this seems to have been specially evident with regard to the time when the claim was made. Had he and Silas declared themselves Roman citizens on the previous evening, they could have escaped the beating and other indignities; but would have missed those wonderful scenes in the jail and in the jailor's house.   W.R.

ROMANS

Does Rom. 2. 14 refer to converted or to unconverted Gentiles?

To understand Rom. 2 (as well as various other passages in Paul's epistles), one has to remember that the apostle at times isolates one particular side or aspect of a subject, and deals with it only. He is just as sure, while he is writing chap. 2, as while he is writing chap. 4, that justification is through faith only; but he does not deal with that in chap. 2; and it is noteworthy that, while "Romans" contains more occurrences of the words "faith" and "believe" than any other of Paul's writings, not one of these is found in chap. 2.

Here he is engaged in vindicating the truth mentioned in v. 6, that God "will render to everyone according to his deeds," a truth which appears in all parts if the Scriptures. (See Job 34. 11; Psa. 62. 12; Prov. 24. 12; Jer. 32. 19; Matt. 16. 27; Rev. 2. 23; 20. 12; 22. 12, etc.). And while it is quite true that no one can carry out fully and literally what is suggested in vv. 7, 10, or 27, except one who has been "born again" through faith in Christ; it is not with that aspect of the matter he is dealing.

As to v. 14, if the statement in it, "do by nature the things contained in the Law," meant the "patient continuance in" these things referred to in v. 7; here, as there, the implication would be that the persons concerned were already "born again." But in that case the phrase, "by nature," would be difficult to explain; and besides there would be little or no connection with the immediate context of vv. 12, 13, 15. Does not v. 14 rather mean that when any Gentiles at any time do, or feel they ought to do, "the things contained in the Law," although they know not that Law; it is proof that there is "the work of the Law written" on their hearts or consciences? Putting it simply, if a person who has never seen or heard of the Ten Commandments feels in himself that he ought to honour his parents, and that he should refrain from stealing, and makes any endeavour to act accordingly, it shows the stirring within him of conscience, however poorly instructed that conscience may be. And this, the Apostle argues, affords a basis for that judgment of God of which the whole passage has so much to say.

W.R.

What is the difference, if any, between the word translated "propitiation" (Rom. 3. 25), which we are told means "mercy-seat," and that translated "propitiation" in 1 John 2. 2?

It is a cause for thankfulness that this question should be asked, as the amended translation in Romans 3. 25 from "propitiation" to "mercy-seat," though disputed by some good authorities, and accepted, as we judged rightly, by most, has so seized the imagination of some Bible students, not familiar with the original Greek of the New Testament, that confusion has resulted. Only the other day, an excellent brother, in our hearing, corrected "propitiation" in 1 John 2. 2, which is **another word from the same root,** into "mercy-seat," too, and made the verse read: "He is the mercy-seat for our sins," which hardly makes sense and cannot be allowed. I would give two reasons for accepting the proposed alteration in Rom. 3. First, it was the same word exactly (neuter-form of "hilastērios") as is used for the literal mercy-seat in the list of tabernacle furniture given in Heb. 9. 5; and secondly, the "mercy-seat" is not the place where atonement was made, but the place where it was displayed by the blood, sprinkled thereon. Wherever in the Old Testament Scriptures you have the Hebrew root for "atone," "mercy-seat," "atonement," this same Greek root* is employed in the Septuagint translation, the Greek of which resembles closely that of the New Testament; so that wherever we have this root in the New Testament, we might equally well, one would suggest, translate it "atonement," "to make atonement," etc. The root occurs five time in the New Testament besides the three places mentioned above, namely, Luke 18.13: "God be merciful to me," which might be translated, "Accept atonement for me"!; 1 John 4. 10, used as in 2. 2 for a propitiation or atonement; Heb. 8. 12: "I will be merciful (or propitious) to; and Matt. 16. 22—Peter's words to our Lord, in a more general sense: "Pity thyself!" These different occurrences of the root exemplify well its usage—the atonement offered, displayed, accepted, and the disposition of Him who provided, etc., the sacrifice—propitious to all who accept it. Truly it befits us to cry, in view of such costly provision for our deep need, "Thanks be unto God for His unspeakable gift!"   W.H.

What is meant by the promise that Abraham would be "heir of the world"? (Rom. iv. 13).

There is no promise in so many words in Genesis that Abraham would be heir of the world. The promise is that he should inherit the promised land, to its utmost covenanted bounds (see chaps. xii., xv., xvii., xxii.). But the promises of chap. xxii. go beyond the promised land. They await their fulfilment in the SEED which is Christ (see vv. 17, 18), and must be co-extensive with the whole world. The fulfilment then of the promises to Abraham is involved in the Messianic glories of the Seed, who has been appointed Heir of all things, and whose kingdom will stretch from shore to shore and from the river to the ends of the earth.   W.H.

---

* hilaskomai, hilastērion, hilasmos.

What does the last clause of Rom. 5. 10 mean? Is it the present aspect of salvation which is in view! Why is there the change of preposition from "dia" to "en"?

The "For" (Gr. gar), with which this verse begins, links it closely to verse 9. The usual force of that connective word is either to introduce a reason for a statement which has gone before, or else to repeat what has been said with additional emphasis or particulars. The latter is evidently its use here, and verse 10 is simply a repetition and enlargement of verse 9. In verse 9, having as sinners been justified by (Gr. en) His blood, much more we shall as justified persons be saved from the coming wrath through (Gr. dia) Him. In verse 10, having as enemies been reconciled through (Gr. dia) His death, much more we shall as reconciled persons be saved by (Gr. en) His life.

Both verses look onward to the full completing of the work He has begun, and in both, the expression, "shall be saved," does not stop short of this glorious completion. We shall be saved from the wrath to come through Him; and we shall be saved for the life to come in Him, for our life is bound up with His life, as our Lord Himself stated in John 14. 19. In neither verse is it merely the present aspect of salvation that is in view, but its perfect and final accomplishment, in which, of course, the present aspect with all that it includes is implied.

As to the change of preposition in the latter part of verse 10, it is interesting to note that both prepositions in verse 10 are changed over from those in the parallel clauses of verse 9, as has been indicated in the paraphrase of the two verses already given. To a certain extent it might be said that "en" and "dia" are interchangeable in these verses; but while the latter merely expresses instrumentality, the "en," having as its primary meaning "in," suggests much more than that, linking us up, in verse 9 with the blood of Christ, and in verse 10 with the life of Christ, in a way that "dia" could not.   W.R.

Does Romans 6. 3 refer to our baptism into the body when we believe, and verse 4 to our baptism in water? Or is it water baptism in both verses? To what baptism does Galatians 3. 27 refer?

I would certainly judge that both verses refer to the initial act of baptism in water. To me it would be very forced and unnatural to divide the verses as the questioner suggests as possible. The apostle is referring these saints back to the well-remembered day of their baptism in water. The other baptism had certainly occurred, but as far as we can judge, outside their own consciousness, as now. Besides, baptism in the Spirit does not seem to be into the death of Christ, but into His mystical body "for in one Spirit were we all baptized into one body" (1 Cor. 12. 13). Gal. 3. 27 refers to water baptism.   W.H.

Does "baptized" in Rom. 6. 3 refer to water baptism, or to Spirit baptism? And does the "So many of us as" imply that some saints were not baptized into Him?

It refers to our baptism in water, as is shown by the phrase "into His death" which accompanies it, by the teaching which the apostle here bases on it, and by the word "likeness" used of it in verse 5.

"So many of us as" is merely a distributive way of saying, "All we who," which is the rendering given in the R.V. here, and is not meant to convey any hint that some of them had not been baptized.   W.R.

Does Rom. 7. 7 teach that if Paul had not coveted, he would not have known sin?

How many difficulties we should be spared by noticing exactly what the Scripture says! The questioner here should read the passage again carefully, for the question is not accurately framed on the Scripture. The apostle is meeting the idea that, because we need to be delivered from the law, therefore the law itself is sin. On the contrary, it is holy, it is it which shows up sin. The apostle does not say, "I should not have HAD sin, but by the law," but "I should have KNOWN it." A savage lusts, but he does not know it is lust until he hears the law, "Thou shalt not covet." Not only so, but so evil is man that the very prohibition increases the lust, as we read in 1 Cor. xv. 56, "The strength of sin is the law", and as is here stated, "when the commandment came SIN REVIVED and I died." In other words, the very prohibition "wrought in men all manner of concupiscence." Without the law sin was dead (*i.e.*, dormant). The commandment also increases the guilt of sin, giving it the aggravated character of transgression. Our strength is not to put ourselves under law as our rule of life, but "to live by faith in the Son of God," who gives all the needed grace.   W.H.

Does Romans 7. 17-24 describe the experience of an unregenerate person?

The statement of verse 22, "I delight in the Law of God after the inward man," is one which certainly could not be made by an unregenerate person, for in such a one there is no "inward man" that delights in God's Law. We must, therefore, conclude that when at verse 14 the apostle drops the past tense of the previous verses, and begins to use the present, he is no longer describing the experience of one who is unsaved, but of one who has been born again.

At the same time, the experience described, in which one always wishes to do the right thing, and yet always, without exception, does the wrong thing, is just as certainly not normal Christian experience. It could not even be called a stage in Christian experience; because the deliverance from it, which is the subject of thanksgiving at verse 25, and the nature of which is opened up to us in chap. 8. 2-4, is by the power of the Spirit of God indwelling the believer, a power which is present and working in each one of them from the very moment he trusts in Christ. One might rather call it a stage in the apostle's reasoning, during which he holds back all mention of the delivering Spirit, until he has made fully clear how helpless and hopeless is the state of things, apart from His intervention.

Yet in actual fact many a saint has had to experience much of what is described in verses 14-24, in order to learn that he has in the one person an "inward man" and an "outward man," which are ever in opposition to each other; and that the scale is weighed down on the right side, only by the power of the Spirit of God that indwells him (Gal. 5. 16-17, R.V.). W.R.

Is the intercession of Romans 8. 26 the same as that of verses 27 and 34?

The word in the original is virtually the same, but the intercession spoken of in verses 26 and 27 is clearly that of the Holy Spirit in the believer, in the sense of helping him in a special way, and that of verse 34 is the intercession of the Lord Jesus Christ at the right hand of God, "Who also maketh intercession for us." The first is a subjective experience which does not take place without cognizance, the other is objective, and takes place whether we remember it or not. This is the same as that spoken of in Heb. 7. 28, "He is able to save to the uttermost all that come unto God by Him (i.e., all His people), seeing He ever liveth to make intercession for them."

The word translated "intercession" means (1) (literally) to light or chance on a person, and then (2) to meet for consultation or supplication—then to pray or intercede for, or, in some places, against. Thus in Acts 25. 24 Festus uses it: "Ye see this man, about whom all the multitude of the Jews have **dealt with me,**" (or it might read, "against whom have interceded with me all the Jews"). It is used thus too in Romans 11. 2, "Wot ye not what the Scriptures saith of Elias? how he **maketh intercession** to God **against** Israel."

In our verses in Romans 8, and in Heb. 7, the preposition **"on our behalf"** is used in each case. In verse 26, it is when we are brought low before God and know not what we should pray for as we ought or how to express ourselves, that the Spirit comes in in this way. He does not then teach us to pray, e.g., Jude 20—"praying in the Holy Ghost," but "makes intercession for us with groanings that cannot be uttered." These groanings would not be intelligible to our fellow men, but they are to God, "Who knoweth what is the mind of the Spirit, because or (better I think as margin), that He maketh intercession for the saints according to the will of God."

The best prayer is not the intelligent prayer, still less the eloquent prayer, still less perhaps the lengthy prayer, but the earnest prayer which cannot express itself in intelligible words.

Of course, when a brother leads the assembly in public prayer he does not pray in this fashion. Rather, he seeks to "pray in the Holy Ghost" as the representative of the assembly, in such a way that all and each may be able to see, "Amen." It is the moment for presenting not individual petitions or thanks, but more general petitions of an interest to those present. Lengthy prayers in public are apt to be wearisome and are inadvisable; in private they may be like the salt promised to Ezra "without prescribing how much." The intercession of Christ is quite distinct. He is praying not in the believer to aid his petition, but for the believers, "to save them to the uttermost," seeing "He ever liveth to make intercession for them." These words "ever liveth" mark the pre-excellence of the Lord's priesthood over the Aaronic. Theirs was not suffered to continue through death or other causes. At any moment the priestly activities might be cut off—they were intermittent. There is no intermittency about the Priesthood of Christ. He is a merciful and faithful High-Priest, and He "ever lives" to make this good. The Lord is our High-priest in our worship. He offers it, so to speak, to God. He is the Advocate of His people in their failures, He intercedes for them in their necessities.   W.H.

Who is the Intercessor in Rom. 8. 27? Is it the Holy Spirit as in verse 26; or is it our risen Lord as in verse 34 of the same chapter?

I do not think there can be any doubt that the Holy Spirit is the Intercessor referred to in Rom. 8. 27. That verse is closely linked with the one going before; while on the other hand, the intercession of Christ seems to be introduced as a new and additional point in verse 34.

Some of the translations other than our A.V. make the connection and meaning of this 27th verse somewhat clearer. For example, Young's Literal Translation gives: "The Spirit Himself maketh intercession for us with groanings unutterable, but He Who is searching the hearts knoweth what is the mind of the Spirit, because according to God He intercedeth for saints." And Weymouth's puts it, "The Spirit Himself pleads for us in yearnings that can find no words, and the Searcher of hearts knows what the Spirit's meaning is, because His intercessions for God's people are in harmony with God's will."

In either of these it is made plain that the Spirit is the Intercessor.
                                                          W.R.

What "law" is meant in Rom. viii. 4?

There can be no reasonable doubt that the law in verse 4 is the same as in verse 3, that is the law given from Sinai. It was "weak" only because of what it had to act upon, the flesh, like a lever of iron on a fulcrum of sand. The law could not bless, but only curse, because no one could "observe it in all things," and moreover it could not condemn sin, without condemning the sinner. But through the sacrifice of Christ, God can justify the sinner, while condemning sin in the flesh. The law is no more our rule of life, than our means of justification, for we died to it with Christ, or "by the body of Christ" (Gal. ii. 19; Rom. vii. 4); but at the same time "the law is holy, and the commandment holy, and just, and good (Rom. 7. 12). The word here for "righteousness" is not "dikaiosunē," the ordinary word for righteousness, but "dikaiōma," the "righteous requirement" (of the law)—the acknowledgment of God's righteous claims over us, that we belong to Him. The law is not viewed here as a legal system, but in its holy essence. All the ten commandments, except the fourth, are repeated in the New Testament, as containing a principle of righteousness for all time, and included in the law of love.

W.H.

In Rom. 8. 20, who is meant by "Him"? (Newberry Bible has the capital H). And what is meant by "subjected the same in hope"?

The "Him," as Newberry and other translators suggest, refers to God, Who having placed the first man in authority over "the works of His hands" (Psa. 8. 6), willed that these (in Rom. 8. the "creature" or "creation") should share in and be marked by the effects of his sin. But He did so with the view ("in hope") that they should ultimately, and to a much greater extent, share in the effects of the redemption obtained by the second Man, the Lord from heaven.

The entire passage, verses 19-25, which for clearness should be read in the R.V., is illustrated by, and gathers together the truth contained in many such Scriptures as Gen. 3. 17, "Cursed is the ground for thy sake"; Isa. 24. 5, "The earth also is defiled under the inhabitants thereof, etc.; Rev. 11. 18, "That Thou shouldest destroy them which destroy the earth"; and, also, in those which speak of the blessed conditions that will prevail in millennial times. These latter will be ushered in at the time of "the manifestation of the sons of God," and, therefore, the apostle pictures the whole creation as eagerly awaiting that event. W.R.

How are we to understand the word "fitted" in Rom. 9. 22? Some, as Alford and Bagster's Lexicon, would give it a passive sense, while Vine regards it as in the Middle Voice, thus making the "fitting" to have been done by themselves.

The word "fitted" is a passive, perfect participle, so that Bagster and Alford are right. But the passive perfect may sometimes be used for the middle voice, and that is why Vine takes it as such. He is, however, quite wrong in assuming that it **must** be the middle voice here, for there is nothing whatever, either in the word itself, or in the passage, to necessitate this.

Probably it is purposely left open, to include any agency on God's side or their own, or any other, which the "fitting" might include. And in this respect it differs from the other word "afore-prepared" (v. 23), which is definitely attributed to God's agency only.   W.R.

What is the meaning of Rom. xi. 5? In what relationship does this "remnant" stand to unbelieving Israel? Is it in the church? Is this the "remnant" mentioned in chap. ix. 27-29?

This remnant, according to the election of grace of Rom. xi. 5, I think can only be the aggregate of believing Jews at this present time, as the words show. Though still nationally Jews, their relation is broken with the Christ-rejecting nation as a whole. These believing Israelites ought not to be called "Hebrew Christians," but simply Christians, exactly like believing Gentiles, with whom they form the church, in which there is neither Jew nor Gentile. Comparing Rom. ix. 27 with vv. 23-24, it seems clear that this remnant is the same as is described in chap. xi. 5, though no doubt Isa. x. 22-23 will have a broader national application later, in the remnant of Israel, which will survive the "time of Jacob's trouble," like Noah in the flood, and form the nucleus of Israel for millennium blessing.   W.H.

Please give help on Romans 11, especially in the verses connected with "grafting." Are the "branches" Israel only? and what does the olive-tree represent?

Chapter 11 of Romans continues the subject of the closing verse of chapter 10. God is still "stretching forth His hands unto a disobedient and gainsaying people"—His earthly people, Israel. In verses 1 to 7, the apostle shows that God has still "a remnant according to the election of grace" from Israel, which remnant is being called out to form part of the church with believing Gentiles; while the rest—the people as a whole, are blinded—a confirmation of Isa. 6. 10 and Psa. 69. 22, 23. They have not, however, been "cast away" (v. 1), that is, finally forsaken (Gr. apōtheō), but put on one side temporarily (v. 15, where the word used is apobolē). It is generally held that the olive-tree stands for the place of privilege and testimony. Israel are God's chosen witnesses on the earth—they are "the natural branches," but have now been cut off from the place of preferential treatment owing to unbelief and the rejection of their Messiah, whereas the Gentiles (and it is in this character that for the nonce the apostle addresses his Roman readers) —branches of a wild olive-tree, are grafted into the good olive-tree. Naturally, you never graft a wild scion into a cultivated stem, but always the reverse; but God in grace acts above nature. The Gentiles, however, have failed no less deplorably than Israel, and they, too, will be cut off from the place of privilege. Their day will last till the "fulness of the Gentiles," i.e., till the last Gentile convert, be brought into the church; then the day of Israel's restoration to favour and testimony will dawn, and when Christ is manifested in glory, all who survive till that hour, will be saved.   W.H.

Please explain Romans 11. 15-26.

This passage cannot be isolated from the rest of the chapter nor indeed from chapters 9 and 10, which together form a parenthesis in the Epistle, explaining and justifying God's ways with Israel since their rejection of the Lord Jesus, as their Messiah. Such a momentous event could not but profoundly modify God's dealings in government with His earthly people. They were nationally set aside, but not "cast away," as finally (apōtheō, v. 1). Paul shows this in two ways; first, by the fact that "even at this present time, there is a remnant according to the election of grace" (v. 5), which is being called out to form, with the elect of the Gentiles "the Church which is His body." The rest are blinded (v. 7). The second proof that the setting aside is not final, is the direct statement that the people are to be restored in the future as God's witness, on the earth (see vv. 12, 15, 23, 26). Now they are fallen and diminished, and the Gentiles are thereby enriched, in the sense of spiritual opportunity and even temporal blessing. It is no longer, as was true historically at the beginning, "to the Jew first." "Now there is no difference." In all this, Paul for the nonce is not addressing the Romans as Christians, but as representative Gentiles. "I speak to you Gentiles" (v. 13), and that "to provoke to jealousy his fellow-country-men." But if the casting-away (apobolē) of Israel be the reconciling of the world (potentially that is), what shall the receiving of them be but life from the dead? That is, though it is now the fall of Israel, which means the rise of the Gentiles, the rise of the former will not mean as in human logic, the fall of the Gentiles, but according to Divine logic, their increased blessing. Only God could affect this, but "His ways pass finding out."

The Olive Tree symbolises the place of testimony for God on the earth, the root being, I would suggest, "the fathers" as called of God. The Gentile wild olive-branches have been grafted contrary to the natural order, into the good olive tree, whereas the natural branches, the nation of Israel, have been broken off through unbelief. Let the former beware lest they be broken off for the same reason. This will occur to the Gentile nations of Christendom, when the blindness in part of Israel is done away, and that will be when the fulness of the Gentiles (i.e., the last Gentile convert of the church era) be come in.

w

Then the natural branches will be grafted in again. A great movement of the Spirit of God will take place through this, and "the great multitude" of Rev. 7 will be gathered in. Then "all Israel will be saved", at the appearing of Christ in glory; that is, all the faithful ones who will be preserved through the closing persecutions and will stand before the Son of Man.   W.H.

What is meant by the two phrases occurring in Rom. 13. 1, "The higher powers," and "The powers that be"?

That the word "powers" (literally, "authorities") has reference in this passage to earthly rulers, is made perfectly clear by verse 3, where the two terms are employed alternately for the same persons. The expression "higher," as used here, simply implies that these authorities, so far as their position is concerned, are higher than we over whom they rule. In other words, they are set over us. The same Greek word is rendered "supreme" in a parallel passage at 1 Peter 2. 13, 14; but there the point made is that the king is "supreme" or "higher" than the subordinate governors appointed by him, a comparison which does not appear in Rom. 13, where we have rulers in general on the one side, and their subjects on the other.

As for the second phrase, "The powers that be," it, of course, means the authorities at present existent. It is through God's arrangement that they are so, and in that sense they are ordained of Him. But it is of interest to note that while here in verse 2 they are "the ordinance (Greek, "arrangement) of God;" in 1 Peter 2. 13 they are "the ordinance (Greek "creation") of man."

Another point of interest in our passage that cannot well be reproduced in any English version is the word-play in it on the Greek verb "tassō" and its derivatives. It means, "set," or "arrange," and in its simple form is rendered "ordained" in verse 1. Prefixed by "hupo" ("under") it is translated "be subject" in verses 1 and 5; and prefixed by "anti" ("against") it is translated "resisteth" in the beginning of verse 2. Lastly, prefixed by "dia" ("through") and turned into noun form it is rendered "ordinance" in verse 2. The effect is as though in English it could be expressed thus:—(Verse 1) Let every soul SET-HIMSELF-UNDER the higher powers; . . . the powers that be have been SET there by God. (Verse 2) Therefore he that SETS-HIMSELF-AGAINST the power withstands the THROUGH-SETTING of God. . . . (Verse 5) Therefore we must needs SET-OURSELVES-UNDER, etc..   W.R.

In view of the persecutions of Christians in Russia and elsewhere, what is the significance of Rom. 13. 3, "For rulers are not a terror to good works, but to the evil"?

This difficulty was as great when the Epistle to the Romans was written as now, for Nero reigned from 54 to 68 A.D., and the date of the Romans falls within those years. Nero was certainly a persecutor and a terror to the early Christians, and they were in no way called to apostatise from their faith in order to win his favour any more than Christians are in the case of the Soviet atheistical government to-day. The fact is, Romans 13 refers to "the things which are Cæsar's"—the laws of the land. Even a Nero would not be displeased with you for keeping his own laws. But the persecution would come when the question arose of "rendering to God the things that be God's"; then Peter's words give guidance: "We ought to obey God rather than man" (see Acts 5. 29). Though I do not believe that the church will pass through "the Great Tribulation," I can see no guarantee in Scripture that she may not have to pass through great tribulation here in England as she is actually doing in various countries. May we all seek grace to be found, faithful, even unto death, should the occasion arise! Nothing but divine grace will carry us through. W.H.

Is it permissible to apply Rom. 16. 17 to mis-guided servants of Christ, when the following verse shows that those spoken of are His enemies?

Even could this premise be accepted as correct, it might still be legitimate to apply the general principle of the verse to division-makers, of whatever category—"Avoid them!" Certainly we could hardly do less than this to any whose teaching tended to divide the saints, even though no question were raised as to their personal Christianity. In the case before us, the language all through seems to apply to men inside the church, and so professedly Christian. We should scarcely need to be exhorted to "avoid" open enemies of Christ. How could it be necessary to say of such, "they serve not our Lord Jesus Christ"? Clearly these professed to do so. They seem to have been men who had got off the lines of truth and soberness, on to some side issue, which they must press wherever they go, e.g., the church and the great tribulation; the partial rapture of the saints; "evening breaking of bread," etc. This naturally causes unrest and dissension. Are such men to be left a free hand till dissension ripens into division? I trow not. As for the expression, "serving their own belly," perhaps the danger among the Lord's servants is greater than might be supposed. How often large centres, where support may be more liberal, are frequented and smaller assemblies neglected, where the need may be greater. This is a subtle snare and one, as to which each servant of the Lord, knowing the utter frailty of the flesh, should be exercised. W.H.

1 CORINTHIANS

Does the expression "judged of no man" (1 Cor. 2. 15), mean that you need no scriptural reference for where you go in service? Also in verse 6 what does the word "perfect" mean?

The question of service does not appear to be in view here, but rather the judging of spiritual things, explained in verse 12 as "the things that are freely given to us of God." Verse 15 is in contrast with the preceding verse, ending with "neither can he know them, because they are spiritually **discerned**" ("anakrinō," lit. "judged of," "sized up," as we say). This is the word translated in our verse, "judgeth" and "judged." The spiritual man "judgeth of all things (i.e. spiritual things), yet he himself is judged of no man." Alford adds here, "i.e. who is not spiritual," but there may be a sense in which the spiritual, in contrast with the carnal man, cannot be judged of by anyone except the Lord. I think this is borne out by chap. 4. 3-4, where after speaking of his stewardship and its responsibilities, Paul adds, "But with me it is a very small thing that I should be judged (anakrinō) of you or of man's judgment (Greek—"day"), yea I **judge** not mine own self. For I know nothing against myself (i.e. of known unfaithfulness to his stewardship), yet am I not hereby justified, but He that judgeth me is the Lord." In general principles the Word of God must guide; in details we cannot always find direct guidance there, but we use our spiritual intelligence or the counsels of spiritual brethren, "in each perplexing path of life," after having definitely sought guidance from the Lord. We are not to judge the servants of the Lord. I think it is very baneful and soul-withering for any to get into the habit of always watching the Lord's servants, and lightly passing judgment on their path. "What is that to thee? follow thou Me." would perhaps be our Lord's word to such. In verse 6 the word "perfect" is "teleios"="full-grown." These gifted Corinthians were "carnal, even babes in Christ." Paul made up his mind to preach to them nothing but "Jesus Christ and Him crucified"; but great as that subject is, he could not but include in the message (where he found men enough "grown up" spiritually, to receive it), "the wisdom of God," even the unsearchable riches of Christ, that eye nor ear, nor heart of man could picture, but which God had revealed concerning Him by His Spirit in the Word.   W.H.

In view of a man's work being burnt, yet he himself being saved (1 Cor. 3. 15), it would seem that a person can be a Christian and yet bear no fruit in his life to God. If so, what is the meaning of James 2. 17, 20-26; John 15. 5, 6; Matt. 7. 16-20?

I think it can be shown that these passages mostly refer to distinct sides of truth. Thus the "James" passage refers to the **works of faith,** which prove faith to be real. Abraham produced one such, when he offered up Isaac; Rahab when she received the spies. The world would call the one act murder, the other, treason. But God's thoughts are not as man's thoughts. The Spirit of God however does not speak of these acts as "fruit" but as "works." The fruit of John 15 is the result of abiding in Christ—"love, joy, peace," etc. In Matt. 7 it is a question of discerning the true and the false. If a plant produces grapes, it is not a thorn; if figs, it is not a thistle. Men are to be known by their fruits. Merely repeating, "Lord, Lord," proves nothing. Men may go to great lengths in religious activities, but it may all be iniquity (Gk. **"anomia,"** lawlessness), i.e., the result of their own self-will (see Matt. 7. 22, 23). In the Corinthian passage it is a question of servants of God building on the one Foundation. If the material they put in has the character of wood, hay and stubble—mere showy, carnal, unscriptural work— it will be consumed in the testing day; but if it be of gold, silver, precious stones, it will pass unscathed through the fire and earn a reward. The others will lose their reward, but be saved though as by fire. The passage does not say they never produced a single fruit for God, for that is impossible, where the Spirit indwells, as He does every child of God. The point is that their service in the assembly was lacking in true quality and cannot be rewarded, though without prejudice to their salvation by Christ, the one Foundation on which they built.   W.H.

Please explain 1 Cor. 3. 17; 1 Cor. 5. 5; and 1 Tim. 1. 20.

In each of the three verses named we have punishment inflicted on certain persons whose evil conduct or evil teaching merits it. In the first, it is inflicted directly by God, no human intervention being suggested. In the second, it is inflicted by apostolic power, combined with the action of the local assembly. In the third, it is inflicted apparently by apostolic power alone, since there is no reference to local action having been taken.

In 1 Cor. 3 a foundation has been laid, upon which building is being carried on, some of it good work, and some of it worthless. The ultimate result for the builders is that at the Judgment Seat of Christ those who have done good work will receive a reward, while the others will suffer loss. At verse 17, however, instead of either a good builder or a bad one, we find a man who is setting himself to destroy the building (i.e. the assembly at Corinth, which was God's temple, as v. 16 shows). His punishment for doing this is that God will destroy him. Although in our A.V. the word is rendered "defile" in the first clause of verse 17, and "destroy" in the second, the same Greek word is used in both, thus showing how God fits the punishment to the crime. A compound form of the same word occurs in a similarly duplicated manner, but in connection with a wider sphere of action, at Rev. 11. 18, where it is said that God shall "destroy them which destroy the earth."

In seeking therefore to understand 1 Cor. 3. 17, there is no necessity to confine within particular limits, either the condition of the guilty person, or the nature of the evil he does, or the time and method of his punishment. The statement is expressed, purposely no doubt, in as wide a form as possible; and whatever kind the mischief wrought may be, the doer of it, be he saved or unsaved, shall sooner or later reap as he has sown. It was a serious matter in Israel for either "priest" or "stranger" to "defile" God's sanctuary which was among them, and it is a serious matter to-day to injure God's assembly.

As to 1 Cor. 5. 5, the context makes clear that a man who was living in immorality was to be "put away" (v. 13) from the assembly; and that Paul, by associating himself with the doing of it, imparted to it a special character, the man being "delivered to Satan for the destruction of the flesh, that the spirit might be saved." In the Old Testament we see Satan permitted (though not as a punishment for evil committed, but by way of testing and training) to bring upon Job many evils, including bodily sickness. And in the New Testament, at 2 Cor. 12. 7, we get Paul's own bodily ailment, whatever it may have been, called a "messenger of Satan." If then for their good Satan was permitted to thus deal with saints who were doing well, one can easily imagine how dreadful would be the plight of a sinning saint delivered over to him by apostolic authority for the purpose.

The statement in 1 Tim. 1. 20 is, of course, to be understood in a similar sense, except that as already remarked, no local "putting away" is mentioned.   W.R.

What is the meaning of the phrase, "wise above that which is written"? Surely it cannot be that we are to be content merely to read the letter of the Scriptures, without seeking to know its meaning or how it points to Christ!

Certainly these words are not used to discourage diligent digging into the mines of Scripture. The phrase does not actually occur in Scripture, but is possibly derived from 1 Cor. 4. 6, which recognises that though servants of Christ should be "esteemed very highly for their works' sake," they should not be made party-leaders, or set on a pedestal, for that would be "above that which is written." We would say again that we ought to meditate upon the word, to learn its meaning, and how it speaks of Christ. The gift of teaching is to help the saints to this end. But teachers must not legislate where the Spirit of God is silent. Much unsettlement has been wrought by this. "The secret things belong unto the Lord our God, but those things which are revealed belong to us

and to our children, **that we may do all the words of this law.**"
There is alas to-day far too much legislation "above that which is
written," e.g., that the evening is the only legitimate hour for breaking
bread, that only unfermented grape-juice, and only unleavened bread
are permissible. The Holy Spirit has not emphasised the hour: "As
oft as ye do it," leaves the time open. The Lord instituted His Supper
on a Thursday, but we do not therefore infer that the early saints in
observing it on the Lord's Day were wrong. As for the plea that all
"ferment" and all "leaven" must be absent from the table, it is a
mere inference, and, I believe, mistaken at that. Leaving aside "ferment,"
which it has not pleased the Holy Spirit to use typically, we know that
leaven typifies evil in its corrupting and permeating character, though
in the thing itself there is no harm whatever, moral or physical. But
when we come to the New Testament, we must not interpret a type by
a type, that is, we are not called to examine the table to find if leaven
be there; but "let a man examine himself," lest that, of which leaven
is typical—insincerity and falsity—be found in his heart and conduct
(See 1 Cor. 5. 6-8). Everything else is putting the Christian back under
law.   W.H.

**What is meant in 1 Cor. 5. 5: "To deliver such an one unto Satan
for the destruction of the flesh, that the spirit may be saved in the
day of the Lord Jesus"? and in 1 Tim. 1. 20: "Whom I have delivered unto Satan, that they may learn not to blas pheme"?**

The expression shows clearly that at least in the early undivided state
of the church, which existed in the apostolic days, excommunication
involved for the one put away a coming under the power of Satan,
which though it could not touch the spiritual life of the one under
discipline, if that one was a true believer, did give Satan power to
inflict bodily disease or even death. In both cases, spiritual good was to
result. In the first, with reference to the future: "That the spirit may
be saved in the day of the Lord Jesus"; and in the latter, with reference
to the present: "That they may learn not to blaspheme." In both cases
the apostle associates himself with this "delivering up." It seemed to
be done on his apostolic authority. I doubt if it would be seemly or right
for any company of Christians, let alone any individual, to assume
such language now.   W.H.

**Do you think that the list in 1 Cor. 5. 11 of excommunicable
sins is intended to be complete? And do you believe that such
expressions as "avoid him," "from such turn away," "keep no
company," mean the same as excommunication?**

No, I do not think the list is supposed to be exhaustive; it may indeed
be representative of even worse sins. A man, for instance, might be

guilty of murder, and conceivably escape the extreme penalty on some technical point; but clearly he would not be fit for fellowship. Nor would the man guilty of habitual lying. There are terrible sins, too, mentioned in chapter 6. 9, 10 and in Leviticus, which would plainly disqualify for fellowship, but which are not mentioned in this passage. However, we must be careful not to enlarge the list **at the other end,** by adding faults which cannot rightly merit such severe treatment as excommunication.

Some Christian brethren's ⸱ ɪre-all seems to be to "cut off"; it is certainly very effective, though at the same time destructive. Besides, one fall does not necessarily constitute a man a railer or a drunkard. No one would style Noah a drunkard or Peter a profane swearer, though we know they both fell into these sins on one occasion. The expressions referred to are by no means to be confounded with excommunication, and are important as showing, that there is a preliminary procedure to be carried out against an erring brother, at all events, for certain failures, before he is cut off from the assembly, which is only the extreme resort. Such a one, may be "avoided," "cut off from our company," etc., though rightly continuing to break bread. But, of course, if his conduct does not improve, these lighter forms of discipline may lead on to excommunication. It is noteworthy that some brethren will cut off from the Lord's table, while showing fellowship in other things, even sometimes in the gospel or ministry of the Word. This is to reverse God's order. The breaking of bread is the last thing to go. You might not feel free to invite a person to a social meeting, owing to his or her looseness of walk or uncertainty of doctrine, with whom you might still be breaking bread for the time being.   W.H.

Is it possible to carry out 1 Cor. 5. 13, where the guilty person simply absents himself, expecting some action to be taken by the assembly? Further, can such be restored to fellowship without any reference being made in the assembly to his lapse?

It would be strange if an erring one could simply baulk all disciplinary action by absenting himself. I do not see how the presence or absence of such a one could be allowed to make any difference. Though physically absent, he is still morally associated with the assembly, until dealt with. Neither is his presence essential, nor his absence detrimental to the action of the assembly. In the Corinthian case the presence of the saints as a whole was necessary ("When ye are gathered together"). The apostle then associated himself with them ("and my spirit"), and all was to be carried out in the presence and power of the Lord ("In the name of our Lord Jesus Christ . . . with the power of our Lord Jesus Christ," ch. 5. 4). His presence was essential, but nothing is said of the wrongdoer being present. The assembly was no doubt informed of the broad facts, otherwise the saints would not have known what was being done. The details were unsuited, as is the case sometimes to-day, for public explanation, but the assembly would have confidence in the elders. There may have been, as in fact there generally is, a minority of sentimental or unspiritual persons who automatically side with the evil doer, and seek to hinder any action, but however patiently they may be considered, they would not be allowed to nullify the action of the assembly as a whole, guided by the elders who have investigated the matter. Paul speaks in 2 Cor. 2. 6 of "this punishment which was inflicted of many" (lit., "the many"), as though there might have been a negligible number of objectors. As for restoration to assembly fellowship, there can certainly be none without some reference being made in the most general terms, it may be, to the lapse. But restoration to be real must be recognised as such. However, I think all would recognise that such reference should be in a general way, so as in no sense unnecessarily to rake up the past, or mar the joy of the occasion.

W.H.

Does 1 Cor. 6. 4 mean that decisions concerning temporal matters should be left to brethren who are of little account among the saints?

A comparison of the A.V. and R.V. renderings of this verse will show that there are two possible ways of taking the apostle's words here; and a look through what various commentators have to say about them will further show that there is much division of opinion as to which way is preferable. If we take them as in the A.V. (and R.V. margin), the command: "Set them to judge who are least esteemed in the church", is evidently meant ironically, the implication being that since the saints are to judge the world (ver. 2), and even angels (ver. 3), the very least of them should be competent to judge matters which comparatively are so small. But taken as in the R.V. text, "Do ye set them to judge who are of no account in the Church?" Paul asks as though in astonishment, 'Is it possible that those who shall judge the world and angels are bringing affairs of so trifling a character before the judges of the heathen courts—men who have no standing in the Church?'

Various points may be adduced in support of each of these views; and whichever be taken, the general drift of the passage remains the same, and is that such squabbles amongst saints are most unbecoming, and should never occur. But personally I incline to the first named view. The word "exoutheneō" ("least esteemed" in A.V.; "of no account" in R.V.) is found eleven times in the New Testament; and since in practically all the other instances it bears the meaning of, "despise," I think it unlikely that the same apostle who wrote Rom. 14. 1-7 concerning the respect due to "the powers that be" would here speak of them as "the despised in the Church." Moreover, the words which follow in verse 7, "I say this to move you to shame" (R.V.), seem to be more suited to the view that verse 6 is a command given ironically, than to that which makes it either a question, or a statement of fact. W.R.

What does 1 Cor. 7. 14 mean? In what sense are the children "holy"?

They are "holy," only in the same sense that the unbelieving husband is said to be **"sanctified** by the wife." The words, "sanctified" and "holy," are from the same Greek root, which means, "to set apart." It does not necessarily imply any moral change in the thing or person sanctified; e.g., the Lord Jesus Christ was said to be "sanctified by the Father" (John 10. 36), and by Himself (Ch. 17. 19), but He did not need any moral change; He was set apart for a certain object. In Matthew 23. 17 and 19, we read of the Temple and the altar sanctifying the gold and the gift on them respectively, but it is clear that such objects could not be morally changed. In our verse, the husband is not morally changed, he still remains an unbeliever, but he is set apart to the wife by the divine ordinance of marriage, and so they might continue to live together. Were it not so, the children too would have to be separated from, as unclean—"else were your children unclean," a contingency which does not seem to have occurred to the minds of anybody. But they too are sanctified or set apart for their believing parents or parent. The question as to their fitness for baptism has been argued from the passage, but to get baptism out of the passage, it must first be put in, for there is no mention of such a thing. The real question is, of fitness to live under the same roof. W.H.

In what sense are we to understand the words in 1 Cor. 7. 14: "else were your children unclean; but now are they holy"?

The apostle had been giving counsel to the saints in the marriage relation. In verse 8 he advises the unmarried and widows to remain as himself, that is unmarried, but if they must, let them marry and they do not sin in so doing (see ver. 28). But in verse 10, he commands the married, though it was not he who did it, but the Lord, who had already spoken on the matter: "Let not the wife depart from her husband . . . and let not the husband put away his wife." But now he comes to a point, on which the Lord had not legislated, as to the relations of husband and wife, when one of them was still unconverted. If, say, this is the case of the husband, let not the wife leave him, for he is sanctified (hagiazō) by the wife, that is, set apart for her by the divine ordinance of matrimony—and she must not count him unclean; and so, when the wife is the unconverted one, else were your children unclean—they would have to be separated from—but now they too are holy (hagioi), but only in the same social sense as the unconverted parent.   W.H.

What is the meaning of the words in 1 Cor. 7. 15: "A brother or a sister is not under bondage in such cases, but God hath called us to peace"?

A good deal of difficulty has, I think, been read into these words by not taking them in their context and also by connecting them with what is not there—the question of divorce. The first section of the chapter, verses 1-9, is taken up mainly with the advantages or disadvantages of marriage, but in verse 10 the apostle addressed himself to the married, commanding the wife not to depart from her husband. Seeing, however, that this is already covered by our Lord's own teaching (e.g., in Matt. 19. 6), he interjects, "Not I, but the Lord." Then he adds, "But and if she depart, let her remain unmarried or be reconciled to her husband, and let not the husband put away his wife." This shows effectively it seems to me that what we should call "desertion" does not terminate the married relation, by setting either party free to remarry. The wife is not free to marry someone else, nor yet the husband; for he is to be ready to receive his wife back again if she returns: he is still her husband. Indeed, the apostle ends the verse by specifically forbidding such a thing as divorce for desertion. "Let not the husband put away his wife" (i.e. in the case before us). In verse 12 Paul takes up a case of another character, and as he is breaking up new ground, he affirms, "To the rest speak I not the Lord," and supposes the case of a brother having a wife that believeth not, one we may suppose whom he had married before his conversion. Must he separate from such a woman, as in the days of Ezra (chap. 10) and Nehemiah (chap. 13)? No, if the unbelieving partner is content to dwell with the believer, let there be no separation, "for the unbelieving husband is sanctified (hagiazomai) by the wife, and the unbelieving wife is sanctified by the husband." This of course, is not sanctification in the spiritual sense, but in the sense of being set apart for one another by the divine ordinance of marriage, and thus enabled, though separated by a great spiritual gulf, to live together under the same roof. Were this not so, another case would arise which they had clearly not contemplated. What about their children? They, too, would have to be separated from as unclean; but on the same reasoning as above they also are "holy," or "set apart" (hagioi—the same root as the word applied to the unconverted parent). We know how this passage has been exploited in the interests of the baptism of the children, either as infants or as part of "the household," but there is not a word about baptism in the whole chapter. Why bring in what is not there? One writer* says of the children in this verse—

* F. C. Jennings in "Is Marriage Terminated Alone by Death?"

"they are set apart from all Jewish and heathen children, by being openly, formally, evidently, accepted (!) with the parent, who now believes in the Lord Jesus . . . accepted in that external position on the earth answering to 'the commonwealth of Israel' (!), as it is with 'thou and thy house' " (!). The writer, however, forgets to mention, if he has ever noticed it, the identity of meaning of the word used of the unconverted parent, with that used of the children, and that therefore the unconverted parent also would be "set apart from all Jewish and heathen parents by being openly, formally, evidently, accepted," etc., which we know to be contrary to the facts. In both cases it is only a question of being able to live together with the converted partner or parent. All else is imaginary. Now verse 15 introduces another supposition—"But if the unbelieving depart, let him depart," adding, "A brother or a sister is not under bondage in such cases." These words, "not under bondage," have been interpreted as meaning that the deserted partner is henceforth free to re-marry; the marriage tie having been automatically severed by the act of desertion. What else can it mean? we are asked, but that the one left is at liberty from what had hitherto bound her, and then Rom. 7. 2, "bound by the law to her husband" is quoted. In reality a wife is not in **bondage** because "**bound** by the law to her husband." The two words are quite distinct both in English and in the original Greek. Anyone in this land who re-married on the ground of desertion would be convicted of bigamy by English law, and would also be acting in flagrant disobedience of verse 11, where speaking of a wife who has left her husband the apostle says, "let not the husband put away his wife." I think the phrase, "not under bondage," simply means, not in an anxious, morbid state, using every effort to get the other back, on the plea, of, "What will become of him or her spiritually"? The apostle answers this in verse 16 which puts things in their true proportion. Even if you could get the deserter back by hook or by crook, "What knowest thou, O wife, whether thou shalt save thy husband? or how knowest thou, O man, whether thou shalt save thy wife?" Leave that to God; He can use whom He will. But God hath called us to peace, or rather "in peace", to live in that as our element, and not allow these untoward circumstances to mar it.

W.H.

What does the apostle mean by saying that he "became all things to all men that he might by all means gain some"? (1 Cor. 9. 22). Does this give us liberty to join the denominations in their work?

As far as I read the passage it cannot be made to favour the above idea, nor has it anything to do with it. Certainly the apostle was not a Mr. Facing-both-ways, nor did he compromise, or preach different gospels to please people, or "get openings," as it is termed. He only means that as far as possible he adapted himself to his audience. Thus Peter's address on the day of Pentecost and Paul's at Antioch, were nearly all quotations from the Old Testament, because they were addressing Jews, who knew it. There was not one such quotation when Paul was speaking to the Athenians, because they were Gentiles, and the Old Testament was quite unknown to them; but he does quote one of their poets—Aratus—whom they would know and understand. He uses a grain of truth from his writings—"For we are also His offspring"—to press home his message. We all know we must try to get a message suitable to our audience, whether children or adults, whether Jews or Gentiles, whether perfectly ignorant or in a measure instructed, but there is only one gospel. W.H.

What is the "race" in 1 Cor. 9. 24? Has it anything to do with the salvation of the soul, and does Matt. 24. 13 refer to this?

The race in 1 Cor. 9. 24; etc., is surely that course "which is set before us" as believers. Those addressed in Heb. 12, were "holy brethren partakers of the heavenly calling" (chap. 3. 1), and those in our Epistle are addressed as "saints" (chap. 1. 2), as washed, sanctified and justified (chap. 6. 11), as "body of Christ" (chap. 12. 27). They had received the gift of eternal life; now they are so to run as to obtain "the incorruptible crown," the reward of faithfulness. Paul had this in view for himself when he wrote, "Forgetting those things which are behind, and reaching forth unto the things which are before, I press toward the mark for the prize of the high-calling of God in Christ Jesus" (Phil. 3. 13-14).

As for Matt. 24. 13, certainly "endurance to the end" is a mark of reality in every dispensation, but this verse has nothing to do with the Christian race, nor is the salvation referred to that of the soul, but rather the preservation of the body. These will be the last days of Israel's testimony and the Church will no longer be in this scene. The great desideratum will be to be carried in safety **through** the persecution of that period, and stand before the Son of Man when He comes at its end. Those who falter will be cut off; those who "endure to the end" will be preserved. This is the true meaning of that sadly misapplied verse, Luke 21. 31. The prayer is not for Christians, that they may be taken away from the great tribulation, as Enoch was from the flood, but for those addressed, representing the future remnant of Israel, that they may be carried through it, like Noah, in safety, and be alive when the Son of Man returns, and share in the glories of the Kingdom.

To resume, what a sad and sorrowful thing it would be for any to be "castaways" (**adokimos**)! The term applied to the unsuccessful candidates in the games, was of this same root (**apodokimazō**). The opening word of chapter 10 ought to be, "For," and introduces an illustration from the history of Israel of what this coming short entails. It may be taken with 1 Cor. 3: "he himself shall be saved; yet so as by fire."   W.H.

It has been stated that in 1st Cor. 10. 16, 17, 21 there is no reference whatever to the Lord's Supper; and the fact that the cup is mentioned before the bread in verse 16 is relied on as one proof of this. Is this view correct?

It is not easy to understand how anyone, with even a superficial knowledge of New Testament instructions regarding the Supper, could hold that the two expressions in 1 Cor. 10. 16, "The cup of blessing which we bless" and "The bread which we break," have no reference to it. To what else could the Corinthian saints, accustomed as they were to the carrying out of these two things week by week when they came together, imagine the apostle's reference to be? And if it be conceded that there is an allusion to the Supper in this verse, it is quite impossible that the two phrases in verse 21, "the cup of the Lord" and "the table of the Lord," should not have a similar reference; since the one verse clearly points back to the other. But of course, just as the word "cup," is used for what is in the cup, so the word "table" is used for the bread that is on the table. Both words had been employed by the Lord Himself at the institution of the ordinance in Luke 22. 20, 21.

Paul is not here setting a theological puzzle for clever ones amongst them to solve; but is giving to the Corinthians plain and practical teaching and warning as to the effects of associating themselves in any degree with the idolatry which was going on around them. And in the symbolism connected with the Lord's Supper he finds an impressive line of reasoning ready to his hand.

The main theme which binds together the whole passage is easily traced. Some of these Corinthians had actually gone into idol temples, and partook there of the meat which had been offered to the idol. Yet they also came to the meetings of the church, and partook of the bread and the wine. So the apostle seeks to set before them how hateful in the Lord's sight such conduct must be; and all the matters upon which he touches in the passage have that end in view.

In verse 8 he reminds them of what befell Israelites who were guilty of a like sin, when they "joined themselves unto Baalpeor, and ate the sacrifices of the dead" (Psa. 106. 28). Yet, as he remarks in verse 18, these Israelites had been partakers of God's altar, when they ate their portion of their own sacrifices. In the verses which are mentioned in our question, he is showing how similar to this was the sin which the Corinthians were committing. He points out to them, first the close relationship between Christ and His people and amongst the saints themselves that is symbolised in the ordinance of the Supper (vv. 16, 17), and next the "fellowship with devils" into which they were drifting when they partook of meat in an idol temple (v. 20). And then he states his conclusion, strongly and plainly, in the words, "Ye cannot drink the cup of the Lord and the cup of devils; ye cannot be partakers of the Lord's table and of the table of devils" (v. 21).

As to the cup and the blood being mentioned in verse 16 before the bread and the body; Paul is not here setting forth the ORDER of the Supper, as is the case in ch. 11. 23-26, but is merely calling attention to lessons suggested by the ordinance; and there can be no reason why he should not mention the cup and the blood first, if it suits his purpose to do so, as wishing to dwell at more length on the symbolic meaning of the loaf.

The distinction between the verses in ch. 10 which we are considering, and those just now mentioned in ch. 11, is not that two different things are in view, the Supper and something else, but that the same thing is being looked at from a different angle. In ch. 11 we learn how the ordinance can be marred by the conduct of the saints while present at it; but in ch. 10 we are taught that it can also be marred by their conduct at other times. Hence there is double need for the exhortation, "Let a man examine himself, and so let him eat of that bread and drink of that cup."

W.R.

Why does the cup precede the loaf in 1 Cor. 10. 16, whereas in chap. 11 the order is reversed?

I think the reason is that in chapter 10 it is a question of communion, and the ground of that is the blood of Christ; so if we are to enjoy it the blood must be prominently in view. We "show His death"—the bread and the wine separated: for the blood flowing in the veins speaks of life, the blood poured out, of death. We are reminded of that on which all our hopes are based, namely, the blood shed. Whereas in the actual order to be followed, it is remembrance, as given in 1 Cor. 11, and the bread comes first, then the wine—now it is the One who shed that blood, with the grace and love that led Him to pour it out for us, which are specially before us. We do this in remembrance of Him.

W.H.

Do the words, "covered" and "uncovered" in 1 Cor. 11. 4, 5, 6, 7 refer to the hair? and do vv. 13-15 allude to the same thing?

It seems very clear that the "covered or uncovered" condition of 1 Corinthians 11 means a covering, in some form of "head-gear" placed over the hair. The word in ver. 15 for "covering"—"her hair is given her for a covering"—is quite distinct from the word used higher up, and means something "thrown round." The word in verses 4, 5, 6, 7, etc., has a sense of "hiding." The woman should have both long hair as a covering round her, and a covering over the hair to conceal her head. This seems quite plain from ver. 6: "If the woman be not covered, let her **also** be shorn." If the hair were the covering referred to, this verse would read, "If she has no hair, let her cut her hair"! which is not sense. But if it be a shame for a woman to be shorn, and no doubt in God's sight, the "bobbing" and "shingling" of the present day is, let her be covered. That is, let her wear her hair long and also cover it. The reason is very important. "The head of every man is Christ and the head of the woman is the man" (verse 3). Therefore in the case of the man, let that (i.e. his head) which speaks of Christ be uncovered; for it is in His name we pray; but in the case of woman, let that which speaks of man (i.e. her head) be covered, for man has no mediatorial or intercessorial virtue before God. She does not lead in prayer, but follows the prayer of the man, and is accepted in Christ, as he is. The chapter is divided into two sections: (a) verses 1-16 and (b) v. 17 to the end. In the first, Paul praises the Corinthians, and adds directions as to the covering of the head without either praise or blame, for from the words, "I would have you know," he seems to be legislating for the first time. In the second section a public church character seems stamped, by the sevenfold repetition of the phrase, "ye come together," which occurs from v. 17 to the close of chap. 14. There is no mention of this in the first section, which would mark it as of a more private character.

W.H.

What has 1 Corinthians 11. 6 to do with the present day? Are Christian women right in having their hair shingled and bobbed?

We cannot admit for a moment that the teaching of 1 Cor. xi. 3-16 was merely temporary. If so, then vv. 18-34 must be so, too, but they hold good "till He come" (v. 26) and so does the beginning of the chapter. Besides, the teaching is based, among other reasons, on God's order in creation (*e.g.*, vv. 8 and 9). Why should this have more to do with the Corinthians than with us? The woman who prays with uncovered head dishonours her head as if she were shorn (v. 6). That this, representing the "bobbing" and "shingling" of to-day, is a shame, is taken for granted by the apostle, as a thing all Christians would at once admit; and, on the other hand, "if a woman have long hair, it is a glory to her" (v. 15). As for v. 16, I believe it can only refer to the custom under review, of a woman praying, with uncovered head. This is the final argument, which clinches the matter. We apostles recognise no such custom nor yet the churches of God.   W.H.

What is the meaning of 1 Cor. 11. 10: "For this cause ought the woman to have power on her head because of the angels"?

Do you not think that verse 15 gives an important clue to the passage, "Her hair is given her for a covering"? Would a bow on the head suffice?

To reply to the second question first, it is important to note that the word for "covering" (v. 15) is quite distinct from the root translated "covered" in verses 4-7. That is a word, **"katakaluptomai,"** with the sense of hidden or veiled in it, of which the word, **"apokalupsis"** (unveiling), is the opposite, whereas the word in verse 15 is **"peribolaion"** which is, not a veil for the head, but a clothing for the body—something cast around. It is the word translated "vesture" of Heb. 1. 12, which is the only other place where the substantive is used. The verbal form is used in Mark 14. 51, of the young man who "had a linen cloth **cast about** his naked body." Failure to notice this has led some to adopt the mistaken idea that the covering intended throughout is simply the woman's own hair, but in any case verse 6 ought to suffice to negative this idea. Clearly the covering there can be donned or doffed at will, which cannot be done with hair.

As for the earlier question, the verse is admittedly difficult, but I think it is assigning only one more reason for the covering of the woman's head. It is a sign of the authority of her husband in the presence of the angels. The ministry of angels, or their relation to the saints, is not one of which much is revealed in the Scriptures, but enough is said to demonstrate its reality. Thus in 1 Tim. 5. 21 the angels are called on as witnesses to the observance of assembly order and responsibility: "I charge thee before God, and the Lord Jesus Christ, and the elect angels," etc. They are invisible and silent witnesses to the orderly relations, or the reverse, of brethren and sisters in the assembly. The covering on the head is a sign to the angels that the wearer is recognising the position assigned to her by God. As for the idea of "a bow" meeting the case of the covering; it might, provided the bow were big enough to cover or hide the head, but as "bows" are not head-coverings, it hardly seems a practical suggestion, or one to which any importance need be attached. W.H.

What does 1 Cor. 11. 21 mean?

I fear it means what it says. They ought to have come together to eat the Lord's Supper, but what they did had lost this character, and had become their own supper, because they made it a meal, to which they brought their viands. Some had little and were hungry and some brought abundance and were surfeited and even drunken. The apostle explains that they had houses in which to eat and drink. The Lord's Supper was to be conducted on lines altogether different from a meal, for it was not a meal, but a memorial. In the verses which follow, the apostle reminds them of the simple ordinance the Lord had instituted. That

x

it was not intended to be a meal is further seen in the fact that its institution took place **after** a meal.   W.H.

Is the word, "broken," in the sentence, "This is my body which is broken for you," the correct reading in 1 Cor. 11. 24?

The first three Gospels are called "synoptics" because they give a synopsis or general account of our Lord's ministry, much from the same point of view, in contrast with the fourth, which covers less ground. But even the synoptics are not mere verbal repetitions of the same events, for if so, why are there three? Rather, they are supplementary, different points being omitted or emphasised according to the purpose of the Holy Spirit through the special evangelist. In Matthew and Mark the Lord says, "Take eat, this is my body," but Luke adds, "which is given for you"—words which though omitted by some MSS., occur in nearly all the versions (i.e., translations of the Scripture into various tongues). A few versions, e.g., Latin Vulgate, both Egyptian and the Ethiopic have also, "given," in 1 Cor. 11. 24; but more authorities have, "broken," and still more omit altogether, and read simply: "This is my body for you," but the sense does not exclude "given" or "broken". Paul received from the ascended Lord his account of the institution, and we need not be anxious to make all the accounts tally verbally, though the choice seems here to be between "given" or **omission** of the word. I incline to the latter.   W.H.

What does the expression, "Let a man examine himself and so let him eat" (1 Cor. 11. 28) mean?

Twice in the New Testament, believers are told to examine themselves: here and in 2 Cor. 13. 5 ("Examine yourselves, whether ye be in the faith"). In the latter context verse 4 is a parenthesis. The exhortation depends directly on the words in verse 3: "Since ye seek a proof of Christ speaking in me"—"examine yourselves whether ye be in the faith," because if so, then the Lord is speaking through me to you, for you are the fruit of my testimony. The apostle is not raising any question as to their conversion, but rather proving his apostleship from their conversion. In the verse before us it is quite a different question. It is not in any way their conversion which is in view, but their communion. Neither is it a question of their reception into fellowship, as though each man must "receive" himself (they are all regarded in this chapter as in full fellowship), but of their worthily breaking the bread. They are **worthy** to take their place at the Supper since they are children of God; but they may not be able to partake **worthily** because of some defilement, therefore they are to examine themselves, but that not to find some merit in themselves, like vain individuals admiring their persons in the glass. They are to search for some defilement, like persons cleansing themselves after a day's work. There may be some unjudged way, some unconfessed sin, which if brought to the gathering would surely hinder worship and blunt spiritual communion. And "so **let him eat** of that bread and drink of that cup," and not stay away, for "if we confess our sins, He is faithful and just to forgive us our sins, and to cleanse us from all unrighteousness." How great a difference would make itself felt in many gatherings of the saints, if this injunction were heeded by all, and each spent a time over the Word in self-judgment and confession where needful, ere coming to the Lord's table!   W.H.

Are the expressions, "weak," "sickly" and "sleep" in 1 Cor. 11. 30, to be understood morally or physically?

I think without doubt that they are to be understood in the latter way. It was on account of the low spiritual state of these saints and their consequent defective observance of the Lord's Supper, that the Lord's chastening hand was upon them in a bodily sense.

The three words represent degrees of bodily affliction: first a general weakness, without definite illness, then some specific complaint, and then, lastly, physical death. The word from which our "cemetery," "a sleeping place," is derived, is translated here, "sleep," and sometimes means literal "sleep" (e.g., Acts 12. 6—of Peter), but it is the usual word for the death of believers, e.g., "Our friend Lazarus sleepeth" (John 11. 11); "Stephen fell asleep" (Acts 7. 60); "Since the fathers fell asleep" (2 Pet. 3. 4); "Christ . . . the first fruits of them that slept"; "We shall not all sleep, but we shall all be changed" (1 Cor. 15. 20, 51). God loves His children too well to let them go on in Christ-dishonouring ways, so He chastens them in various degrees. A professing Christian who can go on lying and defrauding or in other sin, without chastisement is probably a bastard and not a son (Heb. 12. 8). Evidently in the present broken condition of the Church as a collective testimony, the Holy Spirit, because of being grieved, acts not in the same energy either for blessing or for judgment, as in the bright early undivided days of the Church. But we should not conclude that the Lord never chastens His people now physically; I believe He does. Sickness need not necessarily be, but often is, sent as a chastening discipline—and we should seek to be exercised as to why the Lord permits us to be laid aside, lest we miss our lesson. "For when we are judged, we are chastened of the Lord, that we should not be condemned with the world" (1 Cor. 11. 32).   W.H.

Is the "body" in 1 Cor. 12. 13 ("For in one Spirit were we all baptized into one body") the same as in Eph. 4. 4: "There is one body and one Spirit"?

I cannot see any valid reason for doubting their identity, though the truth of 1 Cor. 12 never reaches the spiritual "breadth, length, depth and height" of the Ephesian Epistle, which comes later. The former passage does develop a restricted reference to the local assembly in verse 27, where the Corinthians are for the first time since verse 3 directly addressed in the second person plural: "Now ye are (the) body of Christ and members in particular." But here it is simply, "body," and not "one body"* as in verse 13, where the apostle joins himself with the Corinthians, saying, "For in one Spirit were we all baptized into one body . . . and were all made to drink one Spirit" (lit.). Water baptism is excluded here, as baptism "in one Spirit" is specified, and since Paul was baptized in water at Damascus, he could not have been baptized into the local assembly at Corinth by that act. Baptism in the Spirit certainly has nothing to do with the local assembly. Indeed 1 Cor. 12. 13 describes what takes place for every believer of the present dispensation at the moment of conversion. Paul predicates it for all the Corinthians, carnal though they were as a company. It is true that the Epistle to the Corinthians was written at Ephesus (Acts 19), and the "Ephesians" at Rome (chap. 28), but that a dispensation separates the one from the other, as the ultra-dispensationalists teach, or that the Church of the Acts is quite distinct from that of "Ephesians" is, I believe, "a delusion and a snare." There is a very close analogy indeed between 1 Cor. 12 and Eph. 4; in both there is mention of the "one body" and "one Spirit," and in both the administration of the gifts is in view. There is no mention of two bodies, let alone of some transference from the old one to the new, in the Ephesians. The mystery had been already revealed when Paul wrote "the Romans" (see chap. 16. 25), as had the truth of the one body (chap. 12. 4, 5). It would be as reasonable to assert that King George has had two families: one of young children before his accession, and another of adults subsequent to it, as to reason as do the ultra-dispensationalists. The Acts gives us the history of the founding of the early local churches; the epistles reveal the origin, character and destiny of the Church which is His Body, of which the others were microcosms, or as a drop of water to a lake.   W.H.

In 1 Cor. 12. 13, are the words, "by one Spirit," of the A.V., nearer the original than "in one Spirit," of the R.V., or vice versa? Some suggest that baptism "by the Spirit" in the Corinthian passage is different from baptism "in the Spirit" in Acts 1. 5.

As far as 1 Cor. 12. 13 is concerned, I certainly think it ought to run as in the R.V.—"In one Spirit were we all baptized into one body . . . and were all made to drink of one Spirit." The Spirit is the medium of

---

* The absence of article before body in verse 27 is vital; it may be included in verse 13 in the preposition, "into (the) one body."

the baptism—"We were all immersed in one Spirit," and then the Spirit filled us. On that first occasion, as probably always now at conversion, this happened by the power of God—"they were made to drink"; on subsequent occasions it is for the believer to drink by faith in Christ and to be filled with the Spirit. As for Acts 1. 5, the R.V. text agrees with the A.V., **"with** one Spirit," but gives "in" in the margin. It is difficult to understand why the Revisers, whose boast it was to translate the same Greek word by the same English, should not have been consistent here, as the preposition is exactly the same as in 1 Cor. 12. 13— "in." It is Christ's prerogative to baptize in the Holy Spirit. The following list of all the relevant passages, I think, will make the above clear:

Matt. 3. 6—"Were baptized of him **in** Jordan" (not "with").

Matt. 3. 11—"I indeed baptize you **in** water unto repentance . . . He shall baptize you **in** the Holy Ghost."

Mark 1. 9—"Jesus . . . was baptized by John **into** the Jordan."

John 1. 31—"Therefore am I come baptizing **in** water."

John 1. 33—He that sent me to baptize **in** water (A.V. and R.V. wrongly, "with") . . . the same is He that baptizeth **in** the Holy Spirit" (Both A.V. and R.V. wrongly, "with").

Acts 1. 5—"John indeed baptized with water (no preposition), but ye shall be baptized **in** the Holy Ghost not many days hence."

Acts 11. 16—"Then remembered I the word of the Lord . . . John indeed baptized with water (no preposition), but ye shall be baptized **in** the Holy Ghost."

1 Cor. 10. 2—"They were all baptized unto Moses **in** the cloud and **in** the sea."

1 Cor. 12. 13—"**In** one Spirit were we all baptized into one body."

It would seem that both Authorised Translators and the Revisers were hampered by ecclesiastical prejudices, and so have relegated the "in's" of the Greek to the margin where possible. They have thus tried by their "with's" to justify their sprinkling of infants with a few drops of water, and their ecclesiastical pictures and stained glass windows, which represent our Lord standing up to His ankles in Jordan, and John aspersing Him with water from a scallop shell. Truly, if Jordan were no deeper than that, it was no great miracle for Israel to cross it.   W.H.

What do the words, "When that which is perfect is come," (1 Cor. 13. 10) mean? Do they refer to heaven?

It is the general view that they do, but should we not then read, "When we have come to perfection"? I think besides that the context is against this interpretation.

The apostle is contrasting charity and the sign-gifts. The former never faileth nor falleth into disuse, but prophecies will be nullified or rendered inoperative ("katargeō"); tongues will cease ("pauō"); knowledge—that is of the intuitive order—will be nullified (again, "katargeō"), "for we know in part, and we prophesy in part, but"— and then follow the words we are considering. These I would certainly interpret of the completed canon of Scripture. When Paul wrote "Corinthians" there were at most three New Testament books extant; the two Epistles to the Thessalonians, and probably the Epistle of James. The sign-gifts were therefore needful, being direct revelations from God to man. Prophecy was needful as a sign to believers; tongues, to unbelievers; and "knowledge," for the believer himself in his private apprehension of divine things. "But when that which is perfect is come"; that is, when we have in hand the completed Bible, God's perfect revelation, we shall no longer need the temporary sign-gifts, and they will be done away. It would hardly be necessary to prove that these gifts will be superfluous in heaven. Were you to meet a friend carrying an oil lamp in some dark suburban street, and solemnly to assert that he would no longer need his lamp when the sun rose, he would think you were a dealer in platitudes; but if you said to him, "You wont want your oil affair when the electricity people have completed their local scheme," that would be comprehensible and worthy of attention. This being said, I have no doubt that in the closing sentences of the chapter, there is an extension reaching forward to the heavenly state.   W.H.

Are there "prophets" to-day in the sense of 1 Cor. 14 or do teachers take their place?

Prophets were one of the foundation gifts, as we read in Ephes. 2. 20, and in a building one does not expect to see foundation stones appearing again and again up to the roof. The ordinary gifts are with us: "Evangelists, pastors and teachers," and will be, I doubt not, to the end. We know that prophecy and tongues were sign gifts, the former to believers, the latter to unbelievers (1 Cor. 14. 22); but they failed, at least the latter did (v. 21). No doubt prophesying was a supernatural gift, in the sense of being a direct revelation (v. 30). No teacher could claim to-day to have this, though one has heard beloved brethren, under a mistaken idea, almost go so far. What they meant was that they had a message from God. That is true, but it is quite distinct from having a prophetic **revelation**. These sign gifts were given till "that which is perfect is come," which I believe means the full revelation of God's mind as contained in the completed Canon (1 Cor. 13. 8-10). Then these partial, temporal expedients would be done away; as in fact they did disappear, though counterfeits crop up even in our day. The fact that prophesing is said in 1 Cor. 14. 3 to "edify, exhort, comfort," does not prove that everything that comforts is necessarily prophesying.

That would be an inverted syllogism, as the term is. Peter tells us "there were false prophets also among the people, even as there shall be false **teachers** among you." The prophets now would probably be false, if there were any, but there is none; false teachers take their place.

W.H.

Does the word rendered "sing" in 1 Cor. 14. 15 imply accompaniment with instrumental music, as Young's Concordance suggests (See also Vine's Dictionary)?

The word "psallō," used here and in a few other N.T. passages, has for its primary meaning, "pluck, or twang with the fingers," as one would a bow-string or a stringed musical instrument. But words have a habit of developing in their signification, till in the course of time the root idea in them has been entirely lost sight of; and this has been the case with "psallō," which as used in the N.T., simply means "sing," or at most "sing praise."

Many other examples might be given, both in Greek and in our own language, of words which have thus changed and in certain instances almost reversed their original signification; but it is unnecessary, because the context in 1 Cor. 14: 15 rules out all thought of a musical instrument. The "singing" is to be "with the spirit" and "with the understanding," neither of which qualities is likely to be found in a harp or an organ. The absurdity of the idea is even more clearly brought out in Eph. 5: 19, where the same word "psallō" is translated "making melody," and this is to be done, not "on a harp," but "IN YOUR HEART." If we make good use of this instrument we shall have little need for any other.

W.R.

How could an unbeliever be said to worship God as in 1 Cor. 14. 24, 25?

The word here for "worship" ("proskuneō"), is the ordinary word so translated. In fact, there is only one other word in the New Testament which counts—"latreuō"—which is, however, usually translated "serve" (but in Acts 7. 42; 24. 14; Phil. 3. 3, "worship," and "worshipper," in Heb. 10. 2). Proskuneō, however, is the word used in the great "worship" passages, such as John 4. 20-24, where the word occurs nine times; and Rev. 4. 10; 5. 14, etc., and is, I repeat, the word employed in our verse. But it is important to remember that there are primary as well as secondary meanings to words in the Greek language. Thus proskuneō is very often the equivalent of "prostrating" one's self, in the Septuagint Version. It means properly to kiss the hand toward another in token of reverence, hence among Orientals to fall on the knees and touch the ground with one's forehead: then to do homage to men of superior rank or worthier character (Acts 10. 25;

Rev. 3. 9, and in our passage in 1 Corinthians). But it is also used of homage to God and to Christ, and this none but a believer can render, for it must be offered "in spirit and in truth." But when the presence of God is manifested in a meeting, and the power of His Spirit reveals Christ, through the worship and ministry of the Word, then an unbeliever present may be convinced, do homage to God, and testify that God is truly in the midst, but he will not thereby become a worshipper in the higher sense.   W.H.

Is it in accordance with 1 Cor. 14. 34 for sisters to carry out the breaking of bread in the absence of brethren?

We believe it would be contrary to scriptural order—in fact, misbehaviour in the house of God (see 1 Tim 2. 8-15; 3. 14, 15). How could sisters do this and observe the commandment of the Lord, "Let your women keep silence in the churches, for it is not permitted unto them to speak, etc."? (1 Cor. 14. 34). It would be breaking one command to keep another; "doing evil that good might come." The whole arrangement would take sisters out of their scriptural place, for, supposing a visiting brother presented himself, a sister would have to interview him, and read out his letter of commendation, or, is he to announce himself? On the other hand, if a local brother arrived late, as a sister was giving thanks for the cup, there would be disorder at once. As for ourselves, we cannot see that such a proceeding is ever contemplated in the New Testament. There the word is, "Let all things be done decently and in order," and where this is impossible, it is better not to attempt anything. The cases must be very rare when such a circumstance would arise. If sisters assembled and no brethren came, we believe the godly course would be for the sisters to wait in silence before the Lord, as long as they felt able, and then quietly retire.   W.H.

Kindly explain what is meant in 1 Cor. 14. 33-35.

In the question above it is not very clear wherein the difficulty lies. Verse 33 is not really in close connection with the two which follow, but rather with what has gone before, as is shown in the R.V., by commencing a new paragraph at v. 34. At the same time the principle set forth in it is so wide as to embrace all matters touched upon in the chapter; for "confusion" in the assembly, from whatever source it may arise, is certainly not of God. The last clause of this verse, "as in all churches of the saints," is one of a number of similar expressions, found in 1 Cor. only, in which the Apostle emphasises that a common body of doctrine and practice should characterise assemblies everywhere. Cf. chaps. 4. 17; 7. 17; 11. 16.

The other two verses, 34, 35, referred to in the question, mean just what they say, i.e., that the women are not to address the assembly;

though much ingenuity has been expended in endeavouring to show that they mean something else. One has painful recollection of such explanations, as that the word here translated, "speak,", merely signifies "to twitter as a sparrow"; a rendering anything but complimentary to the sisters in whose defence it was given. The sufficient reply to any such statement is that the word is the same as is rendered "speak" all the chapter through. It occurs in it no less than twenty-four times, and always with reference to taking part publicly in the assembly. Imagine the effect of introducing the aforementioned rendering in such verses as 3, 19, or 29.

Similarly, the word translated, "keep silence" in v. 34 is the same as that so rendered in v. 28 and in v. 30 (R.V.), in both of which it clearly means, "desist from public speaking." And, to clear up another point, it should be noted that the word rendered, "husbands," in v. 35, while often used in that sense, is really the Greek word for "men" as distinct from women. For example its last occurrence previous to this one is at chap. 13. 11, "When I became a man," where the idea of "husband" would be absurd. Here it simply signifies their menfolk at home, whatever the relationship might be. W.R.

Is it permissible for sisters to ask questions at a Bible Reading arranged by the assembly, at which outside Christians and unsaved may be present? Do 1 Cor. xiv. 34, 35, and 1st Tim. ii. 11, 12, apply to this?

It seems difficult, I was going to say impossible, to hold meetings in the assembly hall, open to all, and yet say they are not assembly meetings. It would be rather like holding a public meeting and calling it private. I judge that 1 Cor. xiv. 34, 35, applies to all such meetings. The women are not to take part in leading the assembly teaching, etc., and as for questions, "If they will learn anything, let them ask their husbands at home" (or "men-folk," for the Greek word will bear that meaning, too). Godly women will have no difficulty in submitting to this "commandment of the Lord" (v. 37). Sometimes questions may be used not to elicit, but to impart information. Sometimes they are difficult to answer, on the spur of the moment, and sometimes they raise vexed topics which may prove an apple of discord in the gathering, and not at all for general edification. It is safest to be guided by the directions of 1 Cor. xiv. 35, in my judgment. W.H.

Please reconcile 1 Cor. 11. 5 with 1 Cor. 14. 34 and 1 Tim. 2. 11, 12.

1 Cor. 14. 34 is a plain commandment of the Lord that women are to "keep silence" in the meetings of the churches, and that "it is not permitted unto them to speak" there. The word used for "keep-silence"

is the same which is employed in verse 28 of a speaker in a tongue when no interpreter is present, and in verse 30 (rendered there in A.V., "hold-his-peace") of a prophet when another prophet has a message to deliver. And the word for "speak" is the same which is used of public ministry throughout the chapter, occurring in it twenty-four times altogether. This being so, any attempt to twist either of these words to have a different meaning in verse 34 betrays ignorance or dishonesty.

1 Tim. 2. 11, 12 sets forth a similar prohibition in a more general way, and clearly includes gospel testimony, since that is the subject of the chapter. The word "teach" here in verse 12 links with "teacher" in verse 7, where Paul claims to be a "teacher," not of the saints, but of Gentile sinners. In Acts this same word "teach" occurs sixteen times, and in all but two has reference to gospel preaching.

If these two clear commands are kept in mind when reading 1 Cor. 11. 3-16, there will not be found in that passage anything which runs counter to them. It may be noticed that in no part of it is reference made to a gathered meeting, either of saints or of sinners; and indeed what follows in verse 18, in which the apostle gives a "first-of-all" message, had no exclusive reference to their stated meetings.

At the same time it cannot be claimed that it is a woman's private praying which is in view, for several reasons, of which three may be mentioned.

1. The praying is coupled with prophesying, which from its very nature could not be an entirely private matter.

2. Verse 16 speaks of a "man" as being contentious against what it enjoined, an unlikely development, if it had to do merely with a woman's individual prayers.

3. The main point of Paul's argument is that the practice to which he refers would challenge man's headship, and this would have no weight in the case of a woman praying alone. It is in fact much the same argument which he makes use of in 1 Cor. 14. 34, 35 and in 1 Tim. 2. 11-14 to enforce the prohibitions against her speaking in a public way.

But between the two extreme cases of "in public" and "in private" which we have mentioned, there is surely ample room left for others in which the apostle's warning and rebuke might be needed.

There seems little reason to doubt that some of the Corinthian women were erring in two ways. They were wrong in taking public part in ministry when the saints came together "in church"; but they were in still grosser error when, in praying or prophesying, they uncovered their heads after the manner of the prophetesses or priestesses who were connected with the various heathen Oracles of those times.

And if Paul thought best, or rather was guided by the Spirit of God, to deal first in chapter 11 with their imitation of heathendom, and later in chapter 14 with their intrusion into leadership in the meetings, why should he not do so? Indeed, the epistle contains another somewhat similar example of his method of dealing separately with different aspects of an evil thing, in the two chapters which speak of meats offered in sacrifice to an idol. In ch. 8. 4 he agrees with their contention that in itself an idol is "nothing in the world," and the meat that has been in its temple is nothing the worse for that. But, says the apostle, if partaking of it causes our weaker brother to stumble, this is a quite sufficient reason why we should have nothing to do with it. Yet when he reverts to the matter in ch. 10. 19-22, he points out that, back of the idol, there are "devils" or demons, who are the real objects of heathen worship, and that having fellowship with these is a more serious affair than these Corinthians who claimed to "have knowledge" (ch. 8. 10) were aware of.

W.R.

Are the words in 1 Cor. 14. 34, 35 from the Talmud, and were they imposed by the Judaisers on the Church in Corinth? Did Paul quote them here in order to refute them in verse 36? Do the words in 1 Tim. 2. 11, 12 concern the home life only and not our church position?

I can find no ground whatever for this suggestion about the Talmud, which seems only a loop-hole invented to escape the plain teaching of the passage. The apostle conveying what he calls lower down "the commandments of the Lord" regarding women's position in the churches, writes, "Let your women keep silence in the churches," etc., and confirms this by an **additional** witness, that of the law—"As **also** saith the law," So that, even if the Talmud was referred to, it would only be as an independent authority for what he had just advanced. There is not, however, the slightest proof that the Talmud was meant. There were two Talmuds or codes of instruction, the Palestinian and the Babylonian, the former of which was not redacted at earliest till after the second century A.D., and the other was later still. Seeing that Paul wrote 1 Corinthians in 58 A.D., he could not have been quoting from codes which did not exist, nor could the Judaisers have been imposing such on the churches. The law Paul refers to is no doubt the law of Moses in the general sense of the Pentateuch, of which the whole trend of the teaching as regards the position of women agrees with the apostle's. Some commentators, such as Alford, Brown and Fausset, and Ellicott, believe that the reference is to Gen. 3. 16—words addressed by Jehovah to Eve: "Thy desire shall be to thine husband, and he shall rule over thee." Verse 36 only means, "Were they their own legislators in the things of God, or did God in His Word legislate for them?" Such a question needed no reply. He is not answering anything but their disobedience.

As for the other query, I believe that the words of 1 Tim. 2. 11, 12, "Let the woman learn in quietness with all subjection," etc., though including, no doubt, home relations, do not exclude the assembly, but rather apply there still more. The blessing in the home, regarding child-bearing in ve.se 15, might perfectly well be the reward of good behaviour in the church. Verse 15 of the next chapter bears this out: "That thou mayest know how thou oughtest to behave thyself (not in the home but) in the house of God which is the church of the living God, the pillar and ground of the truth."   W.H.

In view of 1 Cor. 15. 3, 4 and 1 John 2. 2, can we say that the Gospel is for the unsaved; or can we preach to them that Christ bore their sins on the tree, as in 1 Pet. 2. 24?

The reply to the first part of the question cannot be for a moment in doubt. In Mark 16. 15 the apostles were commanded to "go into all the world and preach the Gospel to every creature." Therefore the Gospel must be for every creature; and in many places to which Paul and others since him have carried its message, there were at their arrival none but unsaved ones to hear it.

As to the second part, a clear and well balanced reply to this was given by the late Editor of "The Believers' Magazine" in the July, 1933, issue of that periodical. It is rather long to quote in its entirety, but a few of his points are given below, and with them the present writer is in hearty agreement. He says: "There is sufficient value in the atonement to meet the need of every sinner of the human race that ever breathed; and not only, so, but God 'will have all men to be saved' and . . . is 'not willing that any should perish,' . . . Christ 'gave Himself a ransom for all' . . . Therefore no one will be able to say, 'I wish to be saved, but God had provided no Saviour for me.' Directly our doctrine of election limits the potential application of the work of Christ, or of our Gospel invitation, our doctrine is wrong.

"He (Paul) when he reminds them (the Corinthians) of the Gospel he had preached to them, shows that he did not shrink from saying that 'Christ died for our sins.' Certainly a preacher would be right in following the apostle's example.

"But when it comes to the question of bearing sins, it would not be apostolic nor Scriptural to say to the unconverted, 'All your sins have been borne by Christ.' That is a family secret revealed in the epistles—'Who His own self bare our sins in His own body on the tree.' "

To the above I would only add—Keep closely to the language and phraseology of the Scriptures in your presentation of the Gospel message, and you will always be on safe ground.   W.R.

Does the second clause of 1 Cor. 15. 22, "Even so in Christ shall all be made alive," include both saved and unsaved?

There is much difference of opinion as to this, some holding that the second "all" of the verse be co-extensive with the first one, while others look upon each "all" as qualified by the phrase accompanying it, "all in Adam" in the one case, "all in Christ" in the other. According to the former view the verse would attribute the resurrection of both saved and unsaved to Christ; according to the latter the reference would be to the resurrection of the saved only, they being linked with Christ by spiritual birth, as all men by natural birth are linked with Adam.

That Christ has to do with "the resurrection of damnation" as well as with "the resurrection of life," whether taught here or not, is a truth clearly set forth in John 5. 25; and therefore nothing vital is at stake, whichever view of our verse be taken. But it is evident that throughout 1 Cor. 15 it is the resurrection of the saints the apostle has in mind; and since nowhere else in the chapter is reference made to that of the unsaved, it is unlikely that verse 22 is an exception. Notice especially the comparisons which are made in verses 42-49, comparisons that can only be true of the present and future conditions of the saints; and see how in that passage, as in verses 21, 22, the first Adam and the last Adam stand contrasted, and the word "quickening" which is found there is from the same Greek verb that in verse 22 is rendered "shall-be-made-alive." This word, usually translated "quicken," does not seem to be applicable to the resurrection of the unsaved. Compare its use in Rom. 8. 11.

Notice, too, that in verse 20, with which 22 stands in close connection, the persons in view are described as "them that slept (R.V., sleep)," an expression never employed of the unsaved dead. It occurs also in verses 6, 18, and 51.   W.R.

Please explain, "And when all things shall be subdued unto Him, then shall the Son also Himself be subject unto Him that put all things under Him, that God may be all in all" (1 Cor. 15. 28).

This is usually taken to mean that at the close of a long period, entitled "the ages of the ages," the Lord will eventually put down all His enemies including death, and then deliver up the Kingdom to God and enter into a new relationship with Him by becoming subject to Him, even the Father, that God too may become something new, namely, "All in All." But is not the Lord even now subject to the Father as His Servant? I do not mean that He is so in the sense of inferiority, but of subordination for divine purposes. It does not say, "Then shall the Son also Himself become (but be) subject to Him," and the exact order of the words is, "Then also ('then,' no less than before) will the Son Himself be subject, that God may be (not 'become') All in All." But when will all this happen? It will not be at the end of some imaginary period—"the ages of the ages"—which is the scriptural equivalent of an eternity of which there is no end, but at the conclusion of the Millennial Reign, as we see in Rev. 20. 10-15. Then the devil will be cast into the lake of fire, and doubtless all his angels too; the wicked dead will be dealt with at the Great White Throne, and death (i.e. physical death) and hades will be cast into the lake of fire, having served their temporary purpose. What enemies will then be left to be dealt with later? There will not be a single one. The phrase, "deliver up", is, I am convinced, mistakenly taken to mean "transfer," or "give up," whereas it only means, "restore." The Kingdom will then be restored to the Father by Christ in greatly enhanced glory, but with no thought of His ceasing to reign, as the Viceroy of God and the Father. Is there not some strong scriptural objection to the idea of Christ ceasing to reign? There is indeed, for if there is one truth more clearly taught in Scripture than another, it is the never-endingness of His Kingdom. "It shall never be destroyed, and the Kingdom shall not be left to other people . . . it shall stand for ever" (Dan. 2. 44). This refers to the earthly side of the Eternal Kingdom (of which the Millennium is the first stage) and agrees with Luke 1. 33: "He shall reign over the house of Jacob for ever, and of His Kingdom there shall be no end." Again, it is written: "He shall reign for ever and ever" (Rev. 11. 15), and His Kingdom is described as "the everlasting Kingdom of our Lord and Saviour Jesus Christ" (2 Pet. 1. 11). The throne will always be "the throne of God and of the Lamb" (Rev. 22. 1), and in verse 5 we read that His servants "shall reign for ever and ever," which certainly will only be, because their Lord will be reigning too.   W.H.

What does "baptized for the dead" (1 Cor. 15. 29) mean?

This is an oft recurring question. Perhaps the answers have not sufficiently taken into account the context of the whole passage. There were false teachers at Corinth, who denied the resurrection of the dead (ch. 15. 12). The apostle argues that if there be no resurrection, then Christ Himself would not be risen (v. 13), which he has earlier shown to be a fact testified by many witnesses, the apostles' preaching would be in vain ("kenos"—empty), and the Corinthians' faith vain ("kenos"), too (v. 14). Further, they, the apostles, would be false witnesses for God (v. 15), and the faith of their hearers vain ("mataios" —foolish), since they would still be "in their sins" (v. 17). Those that have "fallen asleep in Christ" must "have perished" (v. 18, R.V.). Indeed, "if in this life only we have hoped in Christ, we are of all men most pitiable" (v. 19, R.V.). But all these are false suppositions—

Christ is risen and as such He is the first-fruits of the great resurrection of His "sleeping" saints, for he is speaking only of such (v. 20). It is true that even **believers** from their bodily connection with the family of Adam are dying, "in Adam all die" (physically), but as already united with Christ they will "all be made alive" (physically, v. 22). To bring in here the death of Adam's race, as in Rom. 5. 14, is contrary to the Greek, for "die" in our passage is not the Aorist (apethanon) "died," but the present—"die" or "are dying" (apothnēskousin). It is not spiritual death and life which are the prominent thoughts in this chapter, but physical death and resurrection. This leads on to the setting up of the Kingdom and the final defeat of every enemy, the last enemy to be destroyed being physical death, which with Hades will be cast into the lake of fire—the second death, which will never be destroyed. Christ will then be able to hand back the Kingdom, purged from every foe, to God, but in no way (as is often mistakenly inferred) in the sense of ceasing to reign—but He will continue even then to be subordinate to the Father. Note the order of the Greek—"then also ("then," no less than before) shall the Son be subject."* This defeat of every foe will not be at the end of an imaginary period called "the ages of ages," but at the close of the thousand years, at the Great White Throne judgment.† In verses 29 and 30 the apostle reinforces the argument for the resurrection by two more arguments, this time on the moral plane rather than the strictly logical, if you will, but none the less valid.

Is it not a proof of the resurrection of the dead that we are willing to come forward and be baptised to take the place of those who have died? Why does Paul himself "stand in jeopardy every hour," "die daily" in fact, or "fight with beasts at Ephesus . . . if the dead rise not?" Could a mere fancy of the brain enable him thus to throw away his life? It has been asserted that the apostle was referring to some religious ceremony which had risen up in the churches, of persons being baptised for those who had died unbaptised. Certainly there is no scriptural direction for such an ordinance, nor is there any proof that such a ceremonial was ever practised in New Testament times, nor if it did, that the apostle would have argued from it in favour of the resurrection. The fact that such a ceremony, based on this verse, is a prominent and important plank in a wholly Satanic system of misbelief in the United States of America, can only weigh as another argument against such an interpretation.   W.H.

Does Rom. 6 help to explain the meaning of being "baptized for the dead" in 1 Cor. 15. 29? Can we say that a believer who goes

* Not "become subject."
† See Rev. 20. 13, 14.

under the waters of baptism is "baptized for the dead," in the sense that he symbolises, as he does so, that he has died with Christ?

The late Mr. Hoste, when replying to a question about the meaning of 1 Cor. 15. 29 spoke of it as "an oft recurring" one. It is also one to which at lease a score of differing answers have been given by various commentators, many of them absurd, and not a few in conflict with the plain teaching of the Scriptures on the subject of baptism elsewhere.

A mere quoting of the verse as given in the R.V. which here is undoubtedly more exact than the A.V., will make clear that the explanation suggested by the questioner will hardly meet the case. "Else what shall they do which are baptized for the dead? If the dead are not raised at all, why then are they baptized for them?" This final "for them," instead of a repeated "for the dead," has behind it the authority of practically all the most ancient MSS., and it renders it impossible to take the words as having reference to the symbolic meaning of the ordinance. So indeed does the phrase "for the dead" itself, when rightly understood. For it must be remembered that the word "dead" is plural here ("for the dead ones"), and that the same word occurs a dozen more times throughout this 15th chapter, always of persons physically dead. One such occurrence is actually found in the middle of v. 29 itself, in the phrase "if the dead rise not"; and it would seem scarcely reasonable to take the first "dead" in the verse as referring to a spiritual reckoning, but the next as relating to a physical fact.

In view of this, the most satisfactory explanation of the words, "baptized for the dead," seems to be that the apostle had in mind such as were from time to time getting saved, and in their baptism coming forward to take the place, with more or less definiteness, of persons who had died—in many instances, though not particularly so at Corinth itself, having been martyred for their faithfulness. That there should still be some found willing to do this, and take up the testimony where those others had laid it down, could only be the outcome of a real and firm belief on their part in resurrection and future reward.

This section of the chapter will be better understood, if it be noticed that in vv. 20-28 we have a connected line of teaching on the order of resurrection, which stands by itself. If this be treated as in a measure parenthetic, it will bring together vv. 18, 19 and vv. 29, 30; and it will be seen that v. 18 associates itself with v. 29 and v. 19 with v. 30, respectively. In v. 18 the apostle had said that if there be no resurrection, "then they also which are fallen asleep in Christ are perished." In v. 29 he points to some who evidently do not believe that they "are perished," since they themselves are coming forward to fill up the ranks, getting baptized and carrying on the testimony in the stead of these "dead ones." Again, in v. 19 he had said that "if in this life only we have hope in Christ, we are of all men most miserable." In v. 30 he points to his own course as that of one who looked stedfastly beyond "this life only," and setting that aspect of the matter in question form, he asks, "Why stand we in jeopardy every hour?"

It will be seen that this view of the passage not only connects vv. 29, 30 with those earlier ones, but also links together the two verses themselves. The phrase, "If the dead rise not," in the middle of v. 29, governs the "Why" of both verses. The one is, If they rise not, **why then** (Gr. "ti kai") are others found willing to take their place? The other is, If they rise not, **why then** ("ti kai" again) are we ourselves willing to face the dangers we do?   W.R.

Is it correct to say that believers are "baptized for the dead"? It is being taught that as dead sinners we were baptized. This might mean that baptism brings life, but this we know comes only from Christ.

There is a sense in which believers may rightly be said to be "baptized for the dead" (see 1 Cor. 15. 29), but this does not, in any case, mean that baptism is for the spiritually dead. The true sense of the words in 1 Cor. 15 has been much disputed. From it has been deduced that living persons can undergo baptism for defunct individuals, who died unbaptized. The fact that this ceremony is a prominent plank in one of the most un-christian sects of Christendom, does not encourage us to accept it as the true Scriptural explanation. I cannot believe that Paul is referring here, in one of his earliest epistles, to some ceremony in connection with baptism, which is nowhere else referred to in the New Testament, and which could not have grown up so soon. I believe the expression only means that believers were ready to come forward openly to confess in baptism their faith in Christ, and thus fill the ranks depleted by death or even by martyrdom, which would demonstrate at least their firm conviction of a future resurrection. Certainly baptism is not on behalf of literally dead persons, nor is it for infants, nor yet for "dead" households. The three households mentioned in the New Testament as having been baptized, namely, those of Stephanas (1 Cor. 1. 16), Lydia and the Jailer (Acts 16. 15, 33) can be shown to a demonstration to have been all believing households, as was that of Crispus in Acts 18. 8. Certainly regenerate households should be baptized unto the Name of the Father, Son and Spirit, on their individual expression of faith in the Lord Jesus.   W.H.

What is "the last trump" of 1 Cor. 15. 52 ("In a moment in the twinkling of an eye, at the last trump")? Does it refer to the last of the seven trumpets in Rev. 11. 15, or if not, when will it sound?

Y

We may take the last part of the question first. A reference to the Corinthian passage shows that it is connected with what had been "a mystery," that is, something hidden and undreamt of till then. Now the coming of Christ as the Son of Man with His saints is spoken of by Daniel—"I saw in the night visions, and behold one like the Son of Man came with the clouds of heaven" (chap. 7. 13); by Zechariah— "The Lord my God shall come and all the saints with Thee" (chap. 14. 5), and by Malachi—"The Lord whom ye seek shall suddenly come to His temple," and so could not be the coming referred to by Paul as a mystery he was then showing. This mystery is a new thing, unheard of before—a prior stage of the Second Coming, corresponding closely to the coming of the Lord, as described in 1 Thess. 4, for His sleeping and living saints and their rapture to be with Him for ever. This will be before the Great Tribulation, for at the close of it they will come again with Christ:—"all the saints with Thee." The rapture of the saints takes place representatively in the person of John at the beginning of Rev. 4. Perhaps the great shout then will be those very words: "Come up hither!" The coming with the saints will take place fifteen chapters later, at the close of the seven vials, which really comprise the seventh trumpet. It is true that "the mystery of God will be finished then" (Rev. 10. 7), but that is the full revelation of Christ and has nothing to do, I believe, with the mystery of the rapture. "The last trump" of 1 Cor. 15. 52 would be the same as the "trump of God" of 1 Thess. 4. 16. The exact date of the Revelation is not known, how then can any argument be based on what is uncertain, namely that Paul had even read the Revelation, when he wrote 1 Cor. 15. 52? As Mr. George Menzies of New Zealand, in a valuable reply to an analogous question in "The Treasury," once pointed out, a thing may be the last of one series and not the last of another. He suggests that the idea of the "last trump" of 1 Cor. 15. 52 is taken from Numbers 10, and would correspond on another plane to the second trumpet there, i.e., the alarm blown for the final setting out of the camps of Israel. If this be so, then there is no direct connection whatever between the trumpets in 1 Cor. 15. 52 and Rev. 10. 15.   W.H.

2 CORINTHIANS

2 Cor. 3. 18: "Beholding as in a glass." The R.V. renders this, "Reflecting as a mirror." Which of these renderings is to be preferred?

I think that "beholding" is a better rendering than "reflecting." "Beholding" suggests the effect upon ourselves which the following words of the verse speak of. But "reflecting" rather suggests the effect upon others who look at us, and is no reason why we should be "changed into the same image from glory to glory." A mirror is not changed by what it reflects.

The "mirror" does not represent us, but the gospel ministry, of which the whole chapter and the beginning of the next one speaks. The glory of the Lord was reflected by the Law but far more so is it reflected by the Gospel. In the one it was the glory of the condemnation of sin, in the other, the glory of the justification of the sinner. The one was transitory and faded away. The other is permanent and increasing.

Alford, the Speaker's Commentary, Ellicott's Commentary, and many others consider "beholding" to be the better rendering. W.R.

What is the application of 2 Cor. 2. 11: "Lest Satan should get an advantage of us: for we are not ignorant of his devices"?

In verse 4 the apostle has referred to his first epistle and specially to the one who was the subject of the fifth chapter—who had committed so grave an offence, and had necessarily been severely dealt with—being "put away from among themselves," as a "wicked person". Now the one, who had caused so much grief, had shown clear signs of repentance, and Paul, who before had to exhort them with apostolic authority to take drastic action in putting him away, is pleading with them to comfort and forgive him. "Sufficient to such a man is this punishment, which was inflicted of many" (lit. "by the more"—v. 6, R.V. marg.), or "the many," or as Grimm renders it, "by the more part." The danger before was that this one should be allowed to go on unhindered in his evil courses; now an opposite danger threatened: "lest perhaps such a one should be swallowed up with over-much sorrow" (v. 7). It was a device of Satan to hinder discipline in the first place; it was equally his device to hinder restoration now. Wherefore the apostle writes, "Ye ought rather to forgive him, and comfort him" (v. 7). He himself would join them in this, having in fact already done so as an individual (v. 10), his reason being "lest Satan (if allowed his way) should get an advantage of us: for we are not ignorant of his devices." W.H.

What does 2 Cor. 2. 16 mean?

The Lord's perfect testimony as the faithful Witness for God did not, as we know, meet with general acceptance; indeed it was usually rejected, though "they that were of God heard His words." But whether rejected or accepted, that testimony came up as a sweet favour to God. It is the same to-day when the Gospel is proclaimed, either publicly or privately. It is more often rejected than accepted, but even so, it is not lost, any more than if accepted. In both cases, it comes up to God as a sweet savour of Christ, being **reminiscent of His testimony,** whether in increasing the guilt of the rejectors or in leading the acceptors to life eternal. A particular scent may recall something smelt years ago, so the true experience of the faithful believer to-day may recall, if we may use the phrase, the ministry of Christ of years ago. It is the fruit of the same Spirit.   W.H.

What is the meaning of the expression, "the letter killeth but the Spirit giveth life"? (2 Cor. 3. 6).

This is usually quoted by people who wish to avoid the plain literal meaning of any Scripture. They excuse their non-acceptance, under the pretext that "the letter killeth"; but they do not say so much about "the Spirit giving life." Rather, they leave one under the incubus of their virtual denial that the verse means what it says, as though the Spirit would deny His own words and mean something quite different to what appears. I think the context shows that this interpretation is mistaken. The contrast is not between the literal and a more vague spiritual meaning, but between the Law engraved in letters on the tables of stone, and the dispensation of grace; for the following verse goes on to say, "if **the ministration of death, written and engraved in stone was glorious** (where clearly the giving of the law by Moses is referred to, when his face shone after receiving it from God), how much more doth **the ministration of righteousness** (i.e., the gospel of the grace of God) exceed in glory?" for that was transient, this is permanent.   W.H.

What is the meaning of 2 Cor. v. 1 to 4? Is this a reference to the Lord's coming for His own?

The truth of the coming of the Lord surely underlies the passage, but is not the prominent thought, which is the dissolution of the body. The first verse of chap. v continues the thought of chapter iv. "For . . . if our earthly house of this tabernacle (*i.e.*, our natural body) were dissolved (*i.e.*, in death), we have *i.e.*, awaiting us, though, as we know, not at once available, a house (in contrast with tabernacle) not made with hands, ETERNAL in the heavens (*i.e.*, a spiritual and glorified body)." "For in this (body) we groan," but what for? We do not groan for dissolution, but for the change incidental to our receiving a body at the coming of the Lord, SEEING THAT (for that is the sense of the expression "*eige kai*") being then at once clothed with the immortal body, we should not have to pass through the disembodied state spoken of here as "naked." For we who still live in the flesh, earnestly desire, not to be disembodied, but embodied in immortality. But so great was the desire of the apostle to be with Christ, that he was willing not to wait for that perfect state, but "to be absent from the body and to be present with the Lord"—words which cannot apply to resurrection, but to the disembodied state, between death and resurrection.   W.H.

It is suggested from 2 Cor. 5 that believers at death, and prior to their resurrection at the Lord's return, are possessed of another body, not the one laid in the grave and not the glorified body to be given at the resurrection. Do you think this is true?

Such a view is to my judgment quite groundless. Those who hold it seem to read the verse, "**when** the earthly house of this tabernacle be dissolved," whereas it is only, "**if.**" A father at the Exodus might have reassured his son, who was expressing regret at leaving their house in Goshen, by saying, "We have another house in Canaan," meaning when we get there, not at once on leaving Egypt. There is no such thing as a temporary body, for the one spoken of here will be "eternal in the heavens," and were one granted in the intermediate state, that is between death and resurection, what sense could we attach to such a phrase as the "naked" or "unclothed" state, or "absent from the body"? These statements negative the idea put forth here. The only body the raised believer will ever have is that which was sown in "corruption," "dishonour," "weakness,"—"a natural body," and which will be raised in "incorruption," "glory," "power," a spiritual body (1 Cor. 15. 42-44). The Lord's resurrection body, though changed, was the very one in which He suffered, for it bore the scars of Calvary. In this body He ascended to the Father and was glorified. Apart from resurrection, the idea of a disembodied spirit having a body of any kind is a contradiction in terms. The body of the departed saints will only be given on the resurrection day and will be "eternal in the heavens."   W.H.

Help will be valued upon 2 Cor. 5. 1-9.

Let us consider this passage verse by verse. Verse 1. The "for" here links the passage with the last words of chap. 4: "the things which are not seen are eternal," giving us at once one of these "eternal things," namely, the glorified body which awaits the believer. Some have thought that the words, "we have," oblige us to take the expression, "a house not made with hands," as being a reference to some sort of temporary body, which the believer has the moment he falls asleep in death, and while he awaits the true resurrection body; but this, I feel convinced, is quite untenable, as the body here is not at all temporary, being qualified as, "eternal in the heavens." Were there a temporary body, between death and resurrection, there would be no "unclothed" state, whereas this is clearly spoken of in the passage, under such expressions as, "found naked," "absent from the body," etc. It could be said of an heir, that he has an inheritance, though he might not be coming into it at once on the death of his father, but only upon his coming of age.

The apostle is not occupied in verse 1 with the intermediate state, but is contrasting the temporary tabernacle of our present earthly body, with the permanent building of the heavenly body. The verse is in fact a general summary of what follows; it is only at verse 2 that the details begin.

Verse 2. "For in this (i.e., tabernacle) we groan, earnestly desiring to be clothed upon (**ependuō**) with our house which is from heaven."

Verse 3. "If so be (**eige**=seeing that*) that being clothed (**enduō**), we shall not be found naked"—i.e., have to pass through the unclothed or disembodied state. The slight difference in these verbs marks the fact that the first describes the process of being clothed, the second, the state. The "clothing upon" will happen at the coming of the Lord, so that those who are alive then will escape the unnatural state of existing as "naked" spirits apart from the body. This condition of nakedness cannot describe some moral condition of being without Christ, as has been asserted, for only those who belong to Christ are contemplated here.

Verse 4 enlarges and explains the same thought: "For we that are in this tabernacle do groan, not that we would be unclothed (or disembodied, in itself not a desirable condition), but clothed upon"—with the glorified body, as will occur at the return of Christ, when this mortal shall put on immortality (see Rom. 8. 11; 1 Cor. 15. 53).

Verse 5. This is God's ultimate purpose, and the gift of the Spirit is the earnest of it.

Verse 6. Here the apostle goes further and reveals an unexpected resolution. The separation of verses 6 and 8, by the parenthetical 7th verse has perhaps obscured to some the fact that they are one sentence, and reveal an unusual spiritual energy in the apostle, which though he does not claim it as unique, and so uses the plural "we," no doubt surpasses the more general experience described in v. 4, "not that we would be unclothed." This experience is the fruit of his continual confidence and conviction that by remaining "at home in the body," he lengthened out his "absence from the Lord," for here "we walk by faith and not by sight"; we are so confident, that we would prefer to enter the unclothed condition and be absent from the body, so as to be at once present with the Lord.

Verse 9. Wherefore we have the ambition, whichever is to be our lot, whether to be present with the Lord by death, or absent from Him by continuing to live in the body, to be well-pleasing to Him.   W.H.

With reference to 2 Cor. 5. 19:—(1) **What was the time when God was "not imputing their trespasses" to the world? Was it when in an unreconciled condition, or as the result of having**

* The word translated in ver. 3, "if so be" is "a compound of two particles meaning, according to the grammarian Winer, 'if that is': quando-quidem, since, seeing that, when no doubt exists." (Ed. Moulton p. 561), or as another says, it is the if "of a thing believed to be correctly assumed." Others, though agreeing that this may be the true sense, think it can only be fully determined by the context. Certainly it would seem that the context in ver. 3 favours Winer here, for if a thing is clothed it cannot at the same time be unclothed or naked.

received the reconciliation, or was it a special characteristic of the ministry of the Lord? Do the words apply to-day and since the Cross? (2) Does the reconciliation mean a change of God's disposition to man, or merely of man's to God?

These are important questions, for on their right understanding depends a true conception of God's righteous ways with men. The "to wit," at the beginning of verse 19 shows that it describes how God acted in order to be able to commit such a ministry of reconcilation to the saints; verse 20 shows the manner in which they carry it out; and verse 21, the ground on which alone it could be proclaimed:—the vicarious work of Christ. The first series of questions has to do with the time when God was "not imputing their trespasses unto them"— the world—(v. 19). God has ever had from the first but one ground on which He could justify a sinner, namely, the Atonement of Christ. It was future in Old Testament times, present at Calvary, and has been retrospective ever since. Directly man fell, God spoke of the woman's seed, which would bruise the serpent's head, but not without being bruised itself. Of this bruising, Abel's offering and every sacrifice in the Old Testament, spoke. All pointed forward to the same righteous ground of reconcilation, namely, the death of Christ.

Though this was more clearly seen during the Lord's earthly ministry, the very words of the verse forbid our limiting this "not imputing" to that period. They are too general (speaking of "the world"), whereas the Lord's special mission was to the lost sheep of the House of Israel. I believe the words describe God's dealings with man from the fall to the final judgments in the Revelation. Adam and Eve were dealt with governmentally, but had their trespass been actually imputed to them, in the sense of being judicially dealt with, they would have been at once eternally banished from God's presence. As no one is yet consigned to the lake of fire, it is safe to say that God has not yet reckoned with any man about his sins. God is now dealing in grace. Now the long-suffering of God is salvation. Mercy holds back the sword of justice, and sinners have still the opportunity to repent and believe the Gospel. But the reckoning day will come for all who reject the Atonement of Christ, and then their trespasses will be imputed to them.

As for the second part of the question, it is often affirmed that God never did need to be reconciled to the sinner—only the sinner to God. This is entirely erroneous, and fails to take account of God's holy claims. God's irreconcilability does not, as men seem to think, impute to Him unreasoning antipathy to the sinner. God loves the sinner, but hates his sin. Between God and him there is the double barrier: his guilt and his enmity against his Creator. God is "of purer eyes than to behold evil." "The carnal mind is enmity against God." These two barriers exist and always will exist between God and the fallen angels.

But as the holiness of God demanded satisfaction for man's sin, His love provided it. Now God's love can go out on righteous ground to the sinner, who humbles himself before Him and believes in the Lord Jesus Christ. By the Spirit the sinner receives forgiveness, and in that moment his attitude to God is profoundly changed, for he then begins to love Him. All rests, however, on the ground of that other love that has saved him by dying for him. But we must not read the call, "Be ye reconciled to God," as though it meant, "Come and make it up with God." Many speak as though the Cross was merely intended to break down man's misconception of God. It was that, but in a totally different sense from what is usually meant. These theorists make nothing of the holiness of God, whereas the Cross makes everything of it. "Christ died for our sins; ... He was buried, and He rose again the third day." There is no other gospel, and the Spirit of God still says of whoso will bring another, "Let him be accursed!" The Cross reveals that the salvation of one sinner was an infinitely difficult problem, taxing, if we may say so, to their uttermost the resources of the Triune God. Nothing but infinite love and power and wisdom could have designed and carried through such a redemption, or saved one sinner. As a matter of fact, the reading—"atonement"—of our version in Rom. 5. 11 is not so far wrong, though "reconciliation" is more exact, for reconciliation carried with it the sense of the righteous atonement. As the late Dr. Handley Moule writes, "That word (katallagē=reconciliation) habitually points to the winning rather the pardon of an offended king, than the consent of the rebel to yield to his kindness. Thus, 'Be ye reconciled to God' (2 Cor. 5. 20) will mean not so much, 'Bend your pride to His unalterable benevolence, as secure while you can His acceptance,' an acceptance connected with the sufferings of His Son."* This is borne out by a reference to non-theological passages, such as Matt. 5. 24, where the difficulty is not on the side of the would-be worshipper, but on the side of the injured absent brother, who needs to be propitiated. See also 1 Sam. 29. 4: "Wherefore should David reconcile himself unto his master?" that is, make amends to his master, for the offences he was charged with, which the Philistines would presume must be real.

To sum up, the words, "not imputing their trespasses unto the world," describe a principle of God's action through Christ, true for all time. God cannot be reconciled to the sinner, unless he acknowledges his sins and receives forgiveness in God's holy appointed way. Nothing else can break down the enmity of the sinner, but this is a consequence of believing.   W.H.

"God was in Christ reconciling the world", 2 Cor. 5. 19. (a) Can these words refer at all to the life of Christ down here or only

* "Outlines of Christian Doctrine," pages 79 and 80.

to His death? (b) Are we to understand the words "world" and "them" in this verse as embracing the same company?

(a) They definitely refer to Christ's death, as the next clause, "not imputing their trespasses unto them," proves. There was nothing in the life of Christ, taken by itself, to enable God to remove the trespasses of man, or to reconcile them to Himself. Compare the same words in Rom. 5. 10, "Reconciled to God **by the death** of His Son."

(b) As to the "them" of the middle of the verse being synonymous with "world" at the beginning of it, it is not exactly that, for it singles out from amongst the "world" those who accept the provision made. Its relationship to "world" is just the same as the relationship between "whosoever" and "world" in John 3. 16.   W.R.

When Paul wrote to the Corinthians, "Be ye reconciled to God" (2 Cor. 5. 20), are we to understand that they still needed to be reconciled?

Certainly not, for they were already reconciled to God. "God hath reconciled us to Himself by Jesus Christ and hath committed to us the ministry of reconciliation" (chap. 5. 18). He is merely narrating the terms of his message to the world of v. 19. This becomes evident, when we note that "you" which occurs twice in italics in v. 12, need not be expressed. Omitting it, the verse would run, "Now then we are ambassadors for Christ, as though God did beseech by us: we pray in Christ's stead, be ye reconciled to God." The last five words give in "direct speech" the exact words he uses to those he is evangelising.   W.H.

What does the expression, "He who knew no sin was made sin for us" mean? Is "sin" here equivalent to "sin-offering"? (see 2 Cor. 5. 21).

It is sometimes easier to see what a verse cannot mean, than what it does mean. An interpretation to be sound, must agree with the general teaching of Scripture (i.e., be "according to the analogy of the faith", Rom. 12. 6, literal), and certainly not be in direct contradiction with any. Now to maintain that our Lord was made "the abominable thing" itself—sin, would be in contradiction to Scripture. He was never more personally holy than when He was on the cross. The sin-offering was "most holy" (Lev. 6. 25, 29). Does it then mean that Christ was made "a sin-offering"? This would be a very simple explanation, were it the right one, which in my judgment it is not, for though the Hebrew equivalent for sin, "hattath", is often used in its **secondary** meaning of "sin-offering"; the first occurrence being Exod. 29. 14 (not Gen. 4. 7 as is often alleged on mistaken grounds, I believe), the Greek word is not properly so used. In its nearly 180 occurrences, "hamartia" ("missing the mark"), the word here used for sin, there is only one place (Rom. 8. 3), where such a meaning as "offering for sin" is even suggested. In A.V. we have, "for sin," in text and in margin, "by a sacrifice for sin," which however is reversed in the R.V.. Grimm, the well-known Greek N.T. Lexicographer takes no notice of such a possible meaning in the New Testament; Alford and Plumptree (Elliott's Com.) deny that such a meaning seems ever to be attached to the word anywhere, either in New Testament or LXX., and the Revisers do not suggest it, not here in 2 Cor. 5, at any rate. However the fact that, as Alford notes, Augustine, Erasmus and one or two less known authorities, do stand for "sin-offering" in this passage, must have its weight in our consideration. We will not condemn those who adopt it. The true meaning seems to me to be that sin is viewed here in the abstract, and that it was charged to Christ when on the cross. Sin was representatively concentrated in His Holy Person. Grimm quotes Rom. 7. 7: "Is the law sin?" as a parallel, and makes, "made sin," as equivalent to "treated as though He were a sinner." I would suggest, **"the sinner,"** or "the embodiment of sin." Gal. 3. 13 would seem a parallel, where "made a curse" means "bearing the curse."   W.H.

What is the meaning of the statement in 2 Cor. 5. 21, "He hath made Him to be sin for us"? Would it be correct to say that Christ bore our guilt, as well as our punishment?

Rightly to understand the above statement, close attention must be given to the context in which it occurs. When this is done it will be noticed, amongst other things, that the word "sin" appears also in the subsidiary clause, "Who knew no sin;" a fact which takes away all probability from the suggestion made by some, that in the former case it should be translated "sin-offering." For thus, in its two occurrences, which in the Greek are separated only by the little phrase rendered "for us," the word would bear two altogether different meanings. It is true that in the Hebrew of the Old Testament a single term is made to serve for "sin" and "sin-offering," according to the connection in which it occurs; but there is no clear example in the New Testament of the Greek word for "sin" being conformed to this Hebrew usage.

But it will also be noticed that the phrase, "made Him to be sin for us," is set over against another one, "made (or, become) the righteousness of God in Him" This being so, the former should be understood in a way which will be applicable to the latter also; for there seems to be no reason why further import should be sought for in the one statement than in the other. Christ was made sin for us in the same sense in which we are made righteousness in Him. Righteousness that is not our own is attributed to us, and so sin that was not His own was attributed or imputed to Him. Indeed this very word "impute" had already been used in our passage at verse 19, in the saying, "not imputing their trespasses unto them;" and it is of this saying that verse 21 appears to be an enlargement. It is as though it were said, "Not imputing their trespasses unto them, but imputing them to the One who had none of His own; and imputing to us His righteousness instead."

As to the second part of this question, "guilt" or "guiltiness" may be defined as "sins viewed with regard to their legal consequences;" and since it is stated in the Scriptures that Christ "bare our sins," why should it not also be said that He bore our guilt? It is but another way of expressing what we so often sing in the hymn,

"He took the guilty sinner's place,
And suffered in his stead."

W.R.

Is the "Paradise" of 2 Cor. 12. 4 the present abode of the spirits of departed believers; and is it the immediate presence or dwelling-place of God?

The Paradise of 2 Cor. 12. 4 is clearly identical with, or included in what is called "The Third Heaven" in verse 2; and the latter expression is generally understood to signify the Heaven which is God's dwelling-place, in contrast with the first, or atmospheric heaven, and the second, or stellar heaven. The fact that Paul, when caught up into it, "heard unspeakable words which it is not lawful for a man to utter," would suggest that nothing less than this could be meant; and so would the term used in verse 1 to describe his experience on this occasion, for he calls it a "vision" and "revelation" of the Lord.

As to the first part of the question, if this "third heaven," or "Paradise," is God's dwelling-place, it is where Christ is; for while in Heb. 4. 14 (R.V.) we read that He "hath passed through the heavens," we further read in Heb. 9. 24 that He entered "into Heaven itself, now to appear in the presence of God for us." And if it is where our Lord is, then it is where the departed believer is, for according to Phil. 1. 23 he is "with Christ," and according to 2 Cor. 5. 8 he is "present with the Lord."

W.R.

GALATIANS

How is it that the Epistle to the Galatians, dated A.D. 58, is said to have been written from Rome, although according to Acts the apostle does not appear to have reached Rome till A.D. 62?

The words, "Written from Rome," are not found in the inspired epistle itself, but in a little note appended to it, which like all other similar subscriptions to Paul's writings, forms no part of what he wrote, but merely expresses the opinion of the copyist or scribe who long afterwards made a copy of the epistle. It is not found in the earliest manuscripts (See the R.V.); and there is no doubt that it is incorrect, because the words, "So soon removed", of chapter 1. 6, imply that only a comparatively short time had elapsed since the conversion of the Galatians.

But of course it must also be understood that the dates as given at the headings in our Bibles, though on the whole fairly reliable, are also but men's opinions, and therefore liable to error.   W.R.

Please explain the meaning of Galatians 2. 20: "I am crucified with Christ, nevertheless I live, yet not I, but Christ liveth in me: and the life which I now live in the flesh I live by the faith of the Son of God, who loved me and gave himself for me." When does this take place? What are the results?

The special departure of the Galatians is greatly misapprehended, especially among so-called Evangelicals. These are very strong, and rightly so, as to justification by faith in Christ alone and they teach that the Galatians were giving this up, whereas the error of the Galatians is the common error to-day of Evangelicals and others, that is making the law their rule of life. The Galatians were being taught, and unfortunately accepting it, that though the law was not the way of life for the sinner, it was the rule of conduct for the saint. Now the gospel is one and indivisible and if you give up one part you virtually give up all, that is logically you do, though you may not admit it practically. A little grace won't make law grace, but a little law will vitiate grace. The Galatians had begun in the Spirit—that is, they had counted on Christ for everything for salvation, but were now seeking to be made perfect in the flesh, counting on self to keep the law. We do not mean that the law is anything but "holy and the commandment holy and just and good" (Rom. 7. 12), but it can only curse the disobedient and can neither give life nor supply strength to believers to keep it. "Ye are become **dead to the law** by the body of Christ that ye should be married to another." "Now we are **delivered from the law,** being dead to that wherein we were held" (Rom. 7. 4, 6). But if the believer has died to the first husband and has been married to another, how can he live by "the rules" of the first husband? The same truth is taught in Gal. 2, where the law is viewed in its entirety as a religious system. Peter did not mean in the least to give up justification by faith, when he withdrew from the Gentile believers, but he virtually denied Christianity by going back to the law as a religious rule to dominate his Christian conduct. This brings out from Paul the ringing apostolic testimony as to the ground of their common salvation—justification by faith in

Christ alone. By thus accepting Christ, he and Peter had virtually destroyed the whole law-system; if he built this up again he showed he was a transgressor, in ever having laid a finger on it. No, he had died to the law by the law—of course in the crucifixion of Christ, when He was "made a curse for us". For, as he explains in the next verse, not only had Christ been crucified for him, but he had been crucified with Christ; nevertheless he lived, yet not he, but Christ liveth in him. Now so far, I believe, every believer can go; for it is equally true of all who have died with Christ through faith that "Christ liveth in them." How then explain the differences amongst Christians? The next phrase replies: "According to your faith be it unto you." Paul now determinedly and resolutely looked away from law and self and lived by counting on Him by faith. We all are in this position of vantage and strength. We all have Christ as our present life, but how few profit by Him as they might! Instead of living by faith in the Son of God, they have the law always before them. Let us rather, like David have the Lord always before us. This life of faith means a close walk and a careful walk of prayer, meditation on the Word, and obedience thereto. As for the results, they will vary with the individual. You can't get olives from fig-trees, or figs from vines (James 3. 12), but each must produce according to its kind.   W.H.

Why are we told in Gal. 6. 2 to "bear one another's burdens and so fulfil the law of Christ," and then in verse 5 that "every man shall bear his own burden"?

The two words are different and the thoughts they represent different, as the context shows. In the first, it is a question of restoring an erring brother who has been overtaken in a fault. He has been tripped up by some sudden circumstance or temptation. It is not a habitual course of evil-doing; it is, so to speak, an accidental slip. We are called in such a case to "restore such an one in a spirit of meekness," and "to bear his burdens"—to seek to help him in lightening his anguish of spirit. I cannot help thinking that Peter himself at Antioch was in this category; he fell into a fault; he was to be blamed; he was rebuked and he was restored, perhaps through Paul himself. But in verse 5, it is not a question of falling into a fault, but of fulfilling our individual service for the Lord. We each have here a personal responsibility, which no one else can bear for us. We cannot pay for a substitute, if God gives us a work to do for Him. "Every one of us shall give account of himself to God" (Rom. 14. 12). Perhaps we might translate the first burden, "troubles," the other, "duties." This describes what our human line of conduct should be. We can still bring both troubles and duties to Him who careth for us.
                                                                W.H.

EPHESIANS

How are we to understand such passages as Eph. 1. 5 and Acts 13. 48?

There is no contrast or marked antithesis between these two passages. In the Ephesian Epistle the apostle is addressing the saints (those set apart by God) and faithful brethren (or believers, as we should say)—the same men from the Godward and human standpoints, and he blesses God for himself and them for the reception from Him of all spiritual blessings in heavenly places in Christ Jesus. Nor are these bestowed in any arbitrary or fortuitous principle, but in the accomplishment of God's eternal purposes—"According as He hath chosen us in Him before the foundation of the world, that we shall be holy and without blame before Him: In love* having predestinated us unto the adoption of sons . . . to Himself." The difference between election and predestination seems to be that the former guarantees eternal blessing to all its objects, whereas the latter determines the character of the blessing. All will be eternally blessed, but not all—elect angels, elect Israel, elect Gentiles, elect church—with the same blessing. But how did these Ephesians enter this place of blessing? Verse 13 of this same chapter supplies the answer; it was by faith in Christ, "In whom ye also trusted, after that ye heard the word of truth, the gospel of your salvation." This is the human explanation of these men being classed among the chosen ones—the way they treated the gospel. In the Acts 13. 48 passage things are reversed. "As many of them as were ordained to eternal life believed." Here the explanation of these Gentiles being found classed among believers is that they were ordained to eternal life. This is equally true with the other. We cannot reason it out; not because it is contrary to reason, but because it is above reason. When we can understand how to fit in Divine Sovereignty with human responsibility on the low plane of everyday occurrences, we may begin to try to do so on the higher plane of eternal realities. We accept them both side by side in earthly matters; we accept them side by side in spiritual matters. Election does not limit the full and free offer of the gospel to every creature; it will "bring many sons unto glory." Divine Sovereignty guaranteed to Paul the safety of all his fellow-passengers (Acts 27. 24). Human responsibility demanded the presence of the sailors on board—"Except these abide in the ship, ye cannot be saved" (v. 31). Directly our doctrine of election induces carelessness as to the use of ordinary means, we are in peril of self-deception.   W.H.

What is the difference between "the Spirit of Promise", Eph. 1. 13, and the "Promise of the Spirit", Gal. 3. 14?

* Many believe the verses should thus be divided.

The difference is that which exists between **the Subject of the Promise**—the Holy Spirit of God—the One who was promised by the Lord to His disciples in His farewell address—"in whom having believed, ye were sealed with that Holy Spirit of promise" (Eph. i. 13), and **the fulfilment of that promise**—"that we might receive the promise of the Spirit" (Gal. 3. 14). The Holy Spirit was the **Spirit of promise,** the One promised from the moment the Lord uttered the words, "He shall give you another Comforter," up to the day of Pentecost, when He came. But this promise was only realised by those who believed. They actually received the promise of the Spirit. We may compare with these words two other phrases: "the blood of sprinkling," which was provided by God at the death of our Lord Jesus Christ, and the "sprinkling of the blood"—the application of that blood, in all the value of God's estimate, to the one who obeys the gospel and believes in Christ. W.H.

Can a man be born again and not sealed with the Spirit (see Eph. i. 13)?

The idea that the sealing of the Spirit is an experience subsequent to conversion has, I believe, no scriptural authority. It seems to have arisen originally from the "after" in Eph. i. 13, as though there were an interval between "the believing" and "the sealing." However, this is an erroneous translation, and the verse ought to run as in the R.V., "in whom having also believed ye were sealed." This is not an attainment of some, but the heritage of all who believe, as is shown in chap. iv. 30: "Grieve not the Holy Spirit of God, whereby YE WERE SEALED, unto the day of redemption." Then, in writing to the Corinthians, Paul takes for granted that they were all sealed by the Spirit, as he was himself. He does indeed refer to God's work in stablishing them, which was going on, but also to three blessings they and he had all received—the anointing, *sealing*, and earnest of the Spirit (2 Cor. i. 21, 22). These are the only three passages in the New Testament which speak of the sealing of believers. Sealing is the attestation of ownership of something for its security. Thus we seal letters, legal transfers, &c. The stone at the Lord's tomb was sealed as a precaution against marauders; the 144,000 in Rev. vii are sealed, ostensibly for safety in the Apocalyptic judgments and persecutions. A shepherd marks his sheep to know them again. So we have the comfort to know that the Lord seals His sheep, to keep them safe "till the day of redemption". W.H.

Ephesians 2. 8. In this verse, is faith the gift of God?

There does seem a certain ambiguity in the verse as it stands in our translation, as to whether it is "faith" which is the gift of God, or something else. As faith is the last thing mentioned it would seem natural to make the "that" apply to it, but the grammar of verse 8 and the closing words of verse 9 point the other way. In the Greek, "faith" is feminine and "that" is neuter, i.e., "this thing." Then again, if it were faith which is said here to be "the gift of God," why should the final words be added, "not of works, lest any man should boast"? I have never heard of anyone teaching that faith is of works. Certainly "faith," like every other good thing, is ultimately the gift of God, and God does give saving faith, i.e., "to them that have obtained (lit. by lot) like precious faith" (2 Pet. 1. 1), but not in a way to deny the fact that faith is usually regarded in the New Testament as the responsibility of those who hear the gospel. "Believe on the Lord Jesus Christ and thou shalt be saved"; "Ye also have seen me and believe not"; "He that believeth not shall be damned." I believe our verse means we are saved by grace on the principle of faith and that (i.e. this salvation) is not of ourselves, it is the gift of God, not out of works lest any man should boast.   W.H.

Please explain Eph. ii. 8, 9; James ii. 14.

Opponents of salvation by grace have alleged that James wrote to counteract Paul. No godly person of course could listen to such evil surmisings for a moment. There is little or no doubt, moreover, that James wrote his epistle before Paul wrote one of his. In any case, there is no contradiction. Paul in Eph. ii is speaking of works—dead works of the law or flesh—as the *ground* of salvation ("not of works, lest any man should boast," v. 8). James is speaking of works—living works of faith—as the *proof* of salvation, and the emphasis is on the *"say;"* ("Though a man *say* he hath faith and have not works, can *that* faith save him?" chap. ii. 14, R.V.). As the following verses show, it is a mere faith of the lips. Mere profession of faith, however correct and right, is not faith. The "works" are viewed here as the buds or fruit, which prove that a tree is alive. "Faith-works," moreover, are not the same as "love-labour"—"doing good unto all men," etc.. Everyone believes in that. But "faith-works" are "folly to the world." Take the two singled out here—the offering of Isaac, and the reception of the spies by Rahab—"murder" and "treason," even for the religious world. But God willed them, and that made all the difference. "Faith-works" are acts of obedience to God's Word—thus: confession of Christ as Lord, believer's baptism, separation to Christ from the world and its ways, breaking of bread according to the Scriptures, preaching the one and only Gospel and the whole truth of God, a holy walk—all or some of which may be the sign of living faith.   W.H.

Is it scriptural to say, in view of such passages as Ephesians 3. 3-10 and 1 Peter 1. 10-12, that in the Old Testament, God designed the church and it is only we in this age can see it there?

Certainly God did not design the church in the Old Testament; its conception dates much further back. "The mystery of Christ"—namely, the union of Gentiles with Jews in one body to form the church, **"in other ages was not made known unto the sons of men"** (Eph. 3. 5). This word, "age," is not the usual word, but one meaning "generation" (genea), namely, I take it, the generations of men from Adam to Pentecost. Besides, these believers to whom Paul wrote, were "chosen in Christ **before the foundation of the world"** (chapter 1. 4), and "the dispensation of the mystery was **hid in God from the beginning of the world"** (lit. from the ages). Certainly there are incidents in the Old Testament, in which we, with our present light, can see figures of the church. These were given by inspiration of God; "Holy men of God spake as they were moved by the Holy Ghost," but whether they are actual **types,** would be difficult to assert. We ought perhaps to be somewhat more chary than we are of our use of the word "type," unless we have New Testament authority for so employing it. We can, of course, freely speak of the Passover lamb as typical of Christ, the lifting up of the brazen serpent, and the incidents in the history of Israel, which "happened unto them for types." In Eph. 3. 11, the word is, "according to the purpose of the ages," and refers to a past eternity before time was. The "Peter" passage refers not to the church, but to God's salvation, "of which salvation the prophets have enquired and searched diligently." Certainly that salvation was partly revealed in the Old Testament. Compare such a passage as Isa. 45. 22: "Look unto me and be ye saved," see also chaps. 52. 10 and 53, but salvation was only fully known in the death and resurrection of Christ.   W.H.

What is the baptism referred to in Eph. iv. 5.

I think the context shows that baptism in water is meant. The apostle has been exhorting believers to "endeavour to keep the unity of the Spirit in the bond of peace," and then he lays down the sevenfold ground on which this is based. "There is one body" (formed, as 1 Cor. xii. 13, R.V., teaches, by the baptism in one Spirit of all believers). Then there is "one Spirit," indwelling the one body; "one hope" for all believers, arising out of their calling. These three great facts stand for a **unity of privilege.** The next three may be said to form a **unity of responsibility:** "one Lord" to acknowledge; "one faith" (*i.e.*, body of doctrine) to hold; and "one baptism" to practise. And lastly, there is a **unity of relationship;** "One God and Father of all who is above all and through all and in you all," the "all" in each case meaning all believers. If, as we have seen, the existence of the body in v. 4 supposes the baptism in the Spirit, it would be not only redundant, but out of place, to bring it in here. Further, no Christian is responsible to receive the baptism in the Spirit; all have received it. The oneness of the baptism

z

is not in contrast with that of the Spirit, which is of quite another order, but with that of John, in which some twelve of them had been baptised, after it had been superseded by that of the Lord, or in our days with such an invention of men as infant sprinkling.   W.H.

Is the baptism spoken of in Eph. 4. 5 water baptism or that of the Spirit?

Certainly I believe the "one baptism" in Eph. 4. 5 refers to water baptism. The apostle is enumerating the seven-fold ground on which the unity of the Spirit can be maintained. It is no mere agreement to differ based on sentimentality, but an experience grounded on seven realities. "There is one body" (not one of Jews and another of Gentiles, but only one, and in this body is contained the truth of baptism in the Spirit, and therefore it would be quite out of place to refer to it lower down as the sixth item of unity), "and one Spirit" (that is indwelling the members of the one body), "even as ye are called in one hope of your calling" (which all share equally). The Word of God knows nothing of the distinctions in the body, which certain teachers would establish—some being worthy of the "hope," and others unworthy—but insists on the oneness of the hope. Then there is "One Lord" to obey; "one faith" (i.e. canon of belief—to receive and hold); "one baptism" (to submit to), and "One God and Father of all who is above all and through all and in all" ("you" is to be omitted). Only believers are in view, so that I believe the exegesis of reality, profession and universality of those who would make here three circles is quite fanciful, seeing that all are connected with "the unity of the Spirit." It is clear why it is the oneness of water baptism, and not Spirit baptism, on which the apostle insists in this place—there cannot be two Spirit baptisms, but there was a rival water baptism in that of John, and there are rival baptisms to-day, infant, household, etc., which we do well to avoid.   W.H.

"Christ loved the church and gave Himself for it (Gk.: her) that He might sanctify and cleanse it with the washing of water by the word . . . that He might present it to Himself a glorious church" (Eph. 5. 26, 27). When and how does this washing take place, and when and where the presentation?

The more correct translation, which I see the R.V. follows, is, "that He might sanctify it, having cleansed it by the washing of water in the word," making the cleansing antecedent to the sanctification. There are three acts in this passage true in the past:—(1) He loved the church—this looks back to a past eternity; (2) He gave Himself for it—to a past time at Calvary; (3) Having cleansed—to a past time at the conversion of the individual members of it. The word for "washing" here is of the same root as the once for all washing or bathing of John 13. It is the washing of regeneration.

Then there are three acts true in the present for the church and its members:—(1) Their sanctification—that is the daily setting them apart for Himself—in all His wonderful ways of wisdom and love, to which it behoves us to respond by setting ourselves apart to Him; (2) Their nourishing (v. 29)— the word used for "bringing children up" in chap. 6. 4; (3) Their cherishing (v. 29)—a very tender word used by Paul of himself in 1 Thess. 2. 7, when he compares himself to a nurse who cherisheth her own children, e.g., as Jochebed cherished the little Moses, her own boy.

Then there is one act regarded in the future, as indeed it is: the presentation of the church to Himself, which will take place in heaven, when her number is complete, and all have been raised or transformed, and caught up together to be for ever with the Lord. Then will take place, we know, the marriage supper of the Lamb (Rev. 19. 7, 9).   W.H.

PHILIPPIANS

Does the latter part of Phil. 1. 23 refer to the Lord's coming?

Certainly not. The apostle in verses 20-26 of this chapter has in mind just two alternatives: (1) Would the imprisonment, in which at that time he lay, end in his being put to death; or (2) Would he be set free for further service. To introduce a third idea, the Lord's coming, is to utterly confuse the sequence of his thoughts as given us in these verses.

The alternatives he first brings before us at verse 20 in the words (we quote as in R.V.), "Whether by life, or by death." In verses 21, 22 he weighs these against one another, while he says, "To live is Christ, and to die is gain . . . then what I shall choose I wot not." In verses 23, 24, which be it noted form a single sentence, he tells us, "But I am in a strait betwixt the two, having (1) the desire to depart and be with Christ, for it is very far better; yet (2) to abide in the flesh is more needful for your sake." And having thus weighed and considered the matter from all sides, he draws his conclusion in vv. 25, 26 by saying, "Having this confidence, I know that I shall abide, yea and abide with you all, for your progress . . . through my presence with you again."

The root idea in the Greek word which is rendered "to depart" in v. 23 is "to unloose"; and from this it came to signify, "to unmoor" (the ropes fastening a ship to land), and "to unhitch" (the ropes fastening a tent), with a view in each case to setting forward on a journey, whether outward ("depart") or homeward ("return"). The latter thought appears in Luke 12. 36, the only other place where this verb is found in the New Testament, while the former is seen in 2 Tim. 4. 6, which is its only occurrence in noun form ("departure"). Here in Phil. 1. 23, "to depart" is clearly the idea, since the expression, "the desire to return and be with Christ," would be meaningless.

It will be noticed too that the connection between what Paul says here, and what he says in 2 Tim. 4. 6, is very close. Here, towards the end of his first Roman imprisonment, he has the desire to "depart" and be with Christ, but he has to remain on earth a little longer, for the help of the saints. In 2 Tim. towards the end of his second Roman imprisonment, his desire is at last about to be fulfilled, and he says, "The time of my departure is come" (R.V.).   W.R.

Were the persons referred to in Phil. 3. 18 Christians who had been "cast down from their excellency," and had "become like them that go down to the pit," or were they unconverted?

I do not think the idea that the persons to whom the apostle here refers had ever known the grace of God in truth can be justified for a moment. They might rather correspond to the "evil workers" of verse 2, against whom Paul warns the saints. No doubt they had made a profession—like those to whom he refers in another place: "They profess that they know God, but in works they deny Him, being abominable and disobedient, and unto every good work reprobate" (Titus 1. 16). Probably they had been brought up in Christian surroundings, and filled with head-knowledge, had early taken their place among the people of God, but without any true repentance, heart acquaintance with Christ, or experience of the new-birth. It is very solemn that it is just among such a class that the worst moral shipwrecks have appeared in these latter days. As for those referred to in the Philippian passage, their lapses were not doctrinal, but moral. They were probably not averse to the doctrine of the Cross of Christ as an easy way of getting to heaven at the last, but they were totally opposed to the present obligations it entailed, and their final end would be according to their works: "Whose end is destruction"—a word translated "perdition" in ch. 1. 28 and elsewhere. Their God, the only God they know and serve, is their belly, and they even go so far as to glory in their shame, as though their defilements did but magnify the grace of God, which would prevail in spite of all. Their whole outlook is earthly. The conclusion of the chapter is in vivid contrast to all this. "Our citizenship," the apostle writes to the saints, is not of earth but "in heaven." Our end is not perdition, but "we look for the Saviour," and full conformity to Him. We live in antinomian days, when we are prone to take ourselves too easily for granted and to confuse tolerance with charity. May we, writer and readers, be kept by the power of God, so as never to be found in the ranks of these whited sepulchres, full of dead men's bones and of all uncleanness!   W.H.

Are the persons described in Phil. 3. 17-19 as "enemies of the Cross of Christ . . . whose end is destruction," Christians or unbelievers? Some affirm the former.

We have been so anxious to maintain the eternal security of the believer (and we cannot be too clear on the point), that there has been sometimes a tendency to confuse profession of faith with faith—two things far from synonymous. I believe that such passages as Heb. 6 and 10 are intended to remind us to what lengths of appearances a professor may go without having been born again. The final test is, "by their fruits ye shall know them." I believe the presence of Judas among the apostles often lent a peculiar character of warning to our Lord's teachings to the twelve. As regards the passage in question, there seem to be three classes before the apostle; those whom he calls the "perfect," or full-grown, who are like-minded with himself (see ver. 15), then those who may be "otherwise minded" and yet have the root of the matter in them. Such are stunted in growth, and backward in understanding, but are to be borne with: God shall reveal to them what is lacking and Paul would not leave them out in the cold or despise them, but adds, "Whereto we have already attained, let us walk by the same rule, let us mind the same thing" (ver. 16). Then there is a third class, alas numerous, the apostle says, of those who do not follow on, even at a distance in the path of the apostle's example, but who answer rather to the solemn description in Titus 1. "They profess that they know God, but in works they deny Him." "The Lord knoweth them that are His," and the mark by which such should be known is that they "depart from iniquity." But where a person is characterised by shady transactions and a lack of conscience, coupled with a glib profession of Christianity, we may well tremble for him. To say that a man who is an "enemy of the cross of Christ, whose end is perdition" ("apōleia": see John 17. 12; 2 Thess. 2. 3; Heb. 10. 39; Rev. 17. 8, 11, etc.), is a Christian, seems to me a serious abuse of language, and most "antinomian" doctrine. The word translated here "weeping" is not the word used of our Lord at the grave of Lazarus—"shedding tears," but the distinct word used of Him, when He lamented over the blinded, doomed city of Jerusalem (Luke 19. 41).   W.H.

COLOSSIANS

Please explain the last four verses of Col. 2.

The saints of the church at Colosse, though in many ways favoured and praised by the apostle for their faith, love and fruitfulness, as also for the "order and the steadfastness of their faith in Christ" (chap. 1. 3-5; 2. 5), were nevertheless giving him cause for anxiety, as he detected evil influences at work, and a tendency among them "to be moved away from the hope of the gospel" (chap. 1. 23); to be "beguiled with enticing words" (chap. 2. 4); to be despoiled "through philospohy and vain deceit" (v. 8); to allow themselves to be "judged in meat or in drink, or in respect of an holy day, or of the new moon, or of the Sabbath days: which are a shadow of things to come; but the body is of Christ" (vv. 16, 17). In fact they were being drawn back to the principles of worldly religion—the Jewish religion—the shadows instead of the substance, Christ.

"Wherefore," argues the apostle, "if ye died with Christ" (Aorist, "apethanete"), as he had shown them was the fact in verse 11, where they are seen as being cut off with Christ in His cutting off (i.e., at the cross), and raised "with Him through the faith of the operation of God, who raised Him from the dead" (v. 12), "why, as though living in the world," i.e., as though you had come back from resurrection ground on to the old worldly plane, "are ye subject to ordinances," such as "touch not, taste not, handle not, which all are to perish with the using . . . "? (vv. 20-22). The reference is to meats and other articles of diet (described above as "meat or drink"), which are appointed by the Creator for destruction (i.e., in their original form) by their using or consumption by man.

The principle of worldly or Jewish religion is that of rules of abstinence as though the Kingdom of God was meat and drink. Certainly these principles, which we have around us to-day in total abstinence from certain things, according to the "commandments and doctrines of men," especially religious men, have indeed "a show (or reputation) for wisdom in will-worship (or voluntary worship), and humility and neglecting of the body (the ascetic-looking, thin-faced person is often spoken of in certain religious circles as 'the saintly father'), but are not in any honour to the satisfying of the flesh" (v. 23), or according to R.V., "not of any value against the indulgence of the flesh." The objection to these renderings is that the A.V. does not convey any clear meaning, and that the meaning of the R.V., while it is intelligible, is difficult to find in the original text. But Dr. Thayer in Grimm favours the rendering of **"pros"** (sometimes "against") which the Revisers adopted, and quotes this passage as a case in point; so I think we may, though with some hesitation, adopt it too. What then is to be the object before the Christian?—not systems of rules and regulations, pledges and covenants, but Christ and what is fitting to Him. "If ye then be risen with Christ, seek those things which are above where Christ sitteth at the right hand of God" (ch. 3. 1).   W.H.

What does "salt" mean in the exhortation, "Let your speech be always with grace seasoned with salt"? (Col. 4. 6).

"Salt is good": It gives savour (Job 6. 6) and preserves from corruption, which accounts for its being offered with all sacrifices (Lev. 2. 13; Mark 9. 49). It is typical of that which preserves from moral corruption, and the Lord says to His disciples, "Ye are the salt of the earth" (Matt. 5. 13). They were also the "light of the world"—that is in their testimony, but "salt" speaks rather of influence. The speech of the Christian should be always with grace, but there are occasions when he must raise his voice against that which is corrupt and "call a spade a spade", as the saying is. If all is grace, then is it soft and savourless; it needs a bit of law too.   W.H.

THESSALONIANS

What is the significance of the phrase, "Will God bring with Him," in 1 Thess. 4. 14?
The object of the Apostle here is to assure the saints that their saved friends who have died will be raised, and will miss nothing of the glories which lie ahead. As the best means of doing so, he links their resurrection with that of the Lord Jesus Himself, as resting upon it and being secured by it. We believe, don't we, that Jesus died and rose again? Well, just as God has "brought again from the dead our Lord Jesus" (Heb. 13. 20), "even so them also which sleep in (or through) Jesus will God bring (from the dead) with Him." I am aware that other thoughts have been read into the phrase, but this, it seems to me, is the simplest way of taking it, and quite satisfies the context.   W.R.

Does not the fact of "the shout," "the voice of an archangel," and "the trump of God," in 1 Thess. iv. 16, dispose of the idea of a "secret rapture," in contradistinction to what will happen at the coming of Christ in judgment in 2 Thess. i? It is distinctly said in the latter passage, that it is "When He is THUS revealed, He finds His people on the earth, and THEN gives them rest." Do not the words translated "to meet," in the clause, "to meet the Lord in the air," always mean "to meet and to come back with the person met" (Acts xxviii. 15, 16)?
The questioner is a Greek brother, but modern Greek is very different from that of the New Testament, to judge from his letter, for there is nothing in the New Testament phrase, *"eis apantēsin,"* to indicate whether those who meet go forward together, or go back together, or stay where they are. This can only be known from the context. In Acts xxviii. 15, the brethren did quite probably turn back with Paul to Rome, but we are left to deduce it. On the other hand, in Matt. xxv. 1 and 6, the only other passage where this exact expression occurs, the reverse

it would seem takes place. There is nothing to show that it was not the bridegroom who turned back with the wise virgins to the wedding. Surely, too, the verb *"apantaō,"* which occurs seven times in the New Testament, would also have this sense, "to meet and come back," whereas it means simply, "to meet," irrespective of what happens afterwards. See *e.g.*, Matt. xxviii. 9: "Jesus met them," but did not turn back with them. So too in Mark v. 2, the demoniac met the Lord, but did not turn back with Him; and so in Luke xiv. 31 and xvii. 12; while in Mark xiv. 13; John iv. 51; and Acts xvi. 16, the other would seem the sense. I think it is clear that no such meaning attaches to this phrase as our questioner alleges, and certainly no Grammarian or Commentator, that I can find, *e.g.*, Grimm, Alford, Parkhurst, etc., seems aware of it. Later, the Lord's people do return with Him when He comes in judgment, but AFTER AN INTERVAL. What, indeed, would be the use of their being caught away to return at once? They are caught away for a most important reason, namely, to escape the Great Tribulation (see Rev. iii. 10). As for the 2 Thess. i passage, our brother does not accurately quote it, but adds his own thought, "When He is THUS revealed He finds His people on the earth, and THEN gives them rest;" but is not this just the point to be proved? I think a simple consideration will help us. This was addressed to the Thessalonian believers nearly 1,900 years ago. Are we then to understand that they are remaining in a state of "unrest," till the Lord comes to take vengeance? Surely not, but only that then the contrast between their state, and that of their persecutors will be *manifested*; they will be at rest, the others in tribulation. In the Greek text of this passage there is no, "When." The phrase should run, "In the revelation of the Lord Jesus." As for the "SECRET rapture," no importance need be attached to the word "secret," though it would be simple for God to speak to His people loudly, and leave the world unaware of it (see John xii. 28, 29). But from 1 Cor. xv, where the scene in 1 Thess. iv is described from another standpoint, we learn that all takes place "in a moment" of time, so it would be all over before any outsider knew what was happening. The differences between 1 Thess, iv and 2 Thess. 1, are important:—

(1) 1 THESS. 4. 15.

(a) The Lord's coming FOR His saints.

(b) "A mystery" (1 Cor. xv. 51).

(c) To raise the sleeping saints, and change the living, and deliver us from the "hour of temptation" (Rev. iii. 10).

(d) Not to the earth, but appearing in the air (1 Thess. 4. 17).

(e) "In the twinkling of an eye" (1 Cor. 15. 52).

(f) "Without sin unto salvation" (Heb. ix. 28).

(2) 2 THESS. i. 15.

(a) With all His saints (Zech. xiv. 5).

(b) No mystery, but rather the subject of prophecy.

(c) To deliver Israel (Zech. xii. 7, 8).

(d) Actually to the earth; His feet shall stand upon the Mount of Olives (Zech. xiv. 4).

(e) "Every eye shall see Him" (Rev. i. 7).

(f) To judge and reign (Rev. xix. 11, etc.). W.H.

THE PASTORAL EPISTLES

1 TIMOTHY

In 1 Tim. 2. 6 we read, "Who (Christ Jesus) gave Himself a ransom (antilutron) for all." Is it therefore correct to say that all are redeemed?

It is a serious error, if we have regard to the Scriptures, and a perversion of the gospel proclaimed by the apostles, who never preached to the unsaved as we to our grief in by-gone days have sometimes heard, "you are all redeemed, but you don't know it." Otherwise all would form part of the redeemed, and not one soul would be lost. Would it were so, but alas to assert it is contrary to numberless Scriptures. One would not for a moment limit God's loving interest in all men, His willingness to save all, and His provision, by which He can righteously do so, if the condition be fulfilled.

Certainly the ransom price was paid in view of all and is sufficient for all. All might potentially be redeemed, but when the Lord made known to His disciples the **effective** object of His mission, it was "to give His life a ransom for **many**" (Mark 10. 45). Here the redeeming is viewed in its actual effect; in Timothy, in its potential effect. This holds good in the epistles. Only believers are told that they are redeemed, e.g. 1 Peter 1. 18, "For as much as ye know that **ye** were not redeemed with corruptible things . . . but with the precious blood of Christ"; Titus 2. 14, "To redeem **us** from all iniquity." To redeem the Church and the saved of all ages did not require less than an infinite ransom, to redeem all men could not require more. It was only true Israelites who were included in the census and who paid the half shekel redemption price, and it was on that redemption silver that the tabernacle was based. In the case of sinners in general it is only those who are willing to be redeemed (lit. luō = to loose), who are effectively delivered. The question is sometimes asked, To whom is the price paid? The true answer is, we believe—to the justice of God by the mercy of God.

W.H.

What is the meaning of the expression, "husband of one wife," in the list of conditions for overseership in 1 Tim. 3. 2?

The same condition is laid down in verse 12 for the work of a deacon or public minister in the church: "Let the deacons be the husbands of one wife." Various meanings have been attributed to these words. Some maintain (perhaps the majority) that they enforce the married state on a bishop or overseer, etc., but this would be, as Alford* points out, "husband of a wife" not "of one wife." And in 1 Cor. 7. 27-33 the unmarried state is recommended by the apostle for those who can deliberately put marriage on one side for the sake of the Lord's service.† Could he do so, if such excluded from the important work of oversight? Some hold that what is enjoined is abstinence from re-marriage for widowers. It is said that the late Queen Victoria held this view, and would not consent to the appointment of any man, as bishop in the Established Church, of which she was secular head, who had married a second time. But to refer again to 1 Cor. 7, the re-marriage of widowers and widows is clearly recognised here, as in other places, e.g., Heb. 13. 2, "Marriage is honourable in all," which cannot exclude the class in question; and no warning or hint is given, as might be expected, of any disability incurred in the above sense. What then is the meaning of the words? In order to reply, we must not forget that though polygamy is illegal in our country, it is not so, generally speaking, in the Mohammedan and heathen lands, and there the government, even when European, makes allowance for the national custom, and recognises, as legal, polygamous marriages. As to how this question should be handled in practice, missionaries have differed. Some have demanded that a polygamist professing conversion should put away all his wives but one. This is the view generally adopted by brethren, who have lived all their lives at home, though what is to become of the poor wives thus suddenly ejected from their hitherto legal position, does not seem to have troubled these brethren. As a matter of fact, it is not explained why a higher standard should be demanded of these ignorant heathen polygamists, than was required of an Abraham, a Jacob, or a David, etc. I believe the opinion is growing in the foreign field that when a man, having several legally-married wives, is brought to Christ, he should be baptised on his confession of faith and received into the church; but **should be disqualified for the exercise of rule or overseership, and for public ministry or deacon work.** When the Gospel has made its way and the Word of God becomes known, the contraction of polygamous marriages by persons professing conversion could not be tolerated for a moment. **W.H.**

---

* Greek New Testament (in loco).

† Some have inferred from v. 7 that Paul himself was unmarried, but he could hardly have been a member of the Sanhedrin if this was the case.

Were the Revisers justified in changing the word, "God," in 1 Tim. 3. 16 into "He who"?

On the contrary they would have been justified, I believe, on principles of textual criticism, by the claims of the context, and by the instructions laid down for their guidance by the Southern Convocation in letting the word, "God," alone. As for textual criticism, I know it is customary to assert that none but experts can form an opinion on such matters, but in reality it is not so difficult for a person of average intelligence, after reading, say, Ellicott's Commentary (Spence) on this passage on the one hand, and on the other, Dr. Burgon's excursus, in his "Revision Revised" (pp. 424-520), to weigh their findings. Thus though some of the earliest known Uncial MSS., do favour **"Hos"** (He Who), the later ones (quite possibly copied from as early or even earlier MSS. than the others) favour **"Theos"** (God) (see Ellicott* in loco.), who adds: "In the great majority of the fathers who cite the passage we certainly find **Theos** as in the received text." The Versions need not be brought into our discussion, for they are so far mostly neutral, favouring another reading—**"Ho"** (that which), which has been introduced to agree with "mystery," which is neuter in Greek. When we come to the "Copies" of Paul's epistles, known as the Cursives; out of 254 which contain the passage, **all except two,** agree in writing **"Theos"**† (God). It must be remembered that these copies were produced in every part of Christendom from older MSS., which must themselves have exhibited the word **"Theos"** (God) in this passage.

To an ordinary person, then, it does not seem clear that the weight of testimony is so unfavourable to **"Theos"** (God), as some would have us believe.

As to the context, it has been suggested, perhaps on very slender grounds, that the passage is a verse of an early Christian hymn. If so, **"Theos,"** would, one would judge, be a more likely "first word," than a mere relative:—"He Who." The sense moreover demands "God," for the passage is not a mere mention of "someone manifest in the flesh," but a statement that "Someone **was manifested** in the flesh." We could say that our Lord Jesus Christ was "God manifest in the flesh," but not "manifested in the flesh," for He was the manifestation—of whom?—of God. Therefore why not let the verse say so clearly? It seems surprising that persons, who presumably believe in the true Deity of Christ, should be so ready to yield the benefit of the doubt to "He who," rather than to "God".

Then again, the Revisers were not left a free hand. Instructions were

---

* Doctor Ellicott was the Chairman of the Revision Committee, and a strong advocate for Hos (He who).

† A. Souter in his edition of the Revised Version Greek text, cites these two in favour of Hos (He who), but, for some unexplained reason, omits any reference to the 252 copies in favour of "Theos."

laid down for their guidance on a very conservative basis. They were to "introduce as few alterations as possible, in the text of the Authorised Version, consistently with faithfulness"; only to remove "plain and clear errors," and "not to alter the Greek Text except where the evidence is decidedly preponderating." Dr. Scrivener, himself a prominent member of the Revision Committee, and generally considered their greatest textual critic, speaks of the passage, which had been a matter of controversy among scholars for 150 years before the Revised Version came out, as "the crux of the critics." Surely then the Revisers ought to have left well alone, or at most, put their contested emendation in the margin.

Instead of that, they have impoverished the Holy Scriptures of one of its most direct testimonies to the Deity of Christ. I know of no passage in the Revised Version in which testimony to this great truth has been **introduced,** where it was not already in substance in the Authorised Version.   W.H.

What does 1 Tim. 5. 9 mean by forbidding a widow to be "taken into the number" under threescore years old, having been the wife of one man"? and does "the number" refer to the assembly or not?

I think "the number" is that of widows in the assembly on the list of those receiving regular help. The whole context shows that the apostle is not speaking of any widows, but of Christian widows in the assembly. But they may be this, and yet not be eligible to be taken on to the list of those being helped. There are conditions. Has the widow in question children or nephews? then let these show piety at home and requite their mother or aunt. Has she reached the age limit, at which she may be supposed to be no longer able to support herself? The apostle puts that at sixty. Has she only had one husband? Had she had more she **ought to have** been sufficiently provided for by these, and the church not be chargeable. Has she proved herself by her diligent service for the saints to be "a widow indeed"? (See vv. 3, 5, 16). Let widows in the assemblies of the saints see to it that they comply with these conditions, then let the assembly take them into the number of those to be materially supported. Of course, this whole question is somewhat modified in Great Britain under the new conditions of old age pensions. I mean that the pension which has been earned by workers by compulsory insurance, etc., is a factor which cannot be ignored.   W.H.

Please explain 1 Tim. 5. 12: "Having damnation, because they have cast off their first faith."

Without saying that this verse has no difficulties, one thing is certain, namely, that the word ("krima") here translated "damnation," properly means "judgment." "Damnation" is from another word ("katakrima"), as in Rom. 8. 1 where it is rendered "condemnation." The two words occur in juxtaposition in 1 Cor. 11. 29 ("krima," where it ought to be translated "judgment"), and v. 32 ("katakrinō," the verb corresponding to "katakrima," and rightly rendered "condemned"—"condemned with the world"). If the younger widows follow a certain course, they expose themselves to the chastening hand of God in judgment. What is it they may fall into—these younger widows?—into wantonness to the detriment of Christ, and then they re-marry, thus breaking faith with the Lord, to whose service they have presumably devoted themselves. Re-marriage, of course, is not forbidden in Scripture, but it would almost seem from our verse that it ought to be undertaken with greater caution even than the first marriage, not with less, as is sometimes the case. For this cause the younger widows are to be refused, i.e., not put on the "list" of widows to be supported, lest they become idlers, gossipers and busybodies. Let them keep well-employed and they will be preserved from mischief. W.H.

To whom does 1st Tim. 6. 15 refer; to the Father or to the Son?

This verse must be read in conjunction with the following one, in which the description of the same glorious Person is continued. And since He is there said to be "Dwelling in the light which no man can approach unto; whom no man hath seen, nor can see;" it is clear that the reference is to God the Father. Compare John 1. 18, "No man hath seen God at any time; the only-begotten Son which is in the bosom of the Father, He hath declared Him," also Exod. 33. 20, "There shall no man see Me and live."

This being so, verse 15 must refer also to the Father, the statement being that "He (the Father) shall in His own times show the King of kings and Lord of lords." And this form of expression, though it may seem strange, is in keeping with Acts 1. 7, where it is said that "The TIMES and the seasons the Father hath put in His own power."

It is of course a fact that in the Revelation two of the terms found in our verse 15 ("King of kings and Lord of lords") are, in a slightly different form, used of Christ; but this is no reason why they should not be applied to the Father here. W.R.

2 TIMOTHY

What is the meaning of the statement, "The husbandman that laboureth, must be first partaker of the fruits"? (2 Tim. 2. 6).

This can be better understood if taken with the two preceding verses. The three are on parallel lines. In each the Christian is viewed in a certain character, called to a certain course, and that with a certain object in view.

Thus in verse 4 he is viewed as a soldier, ("He that warreth"); in verse 5, as an athlete, ("if a man also strive for masteries"); and in verse 6, as a "husbandman."

Again, in each case a certain course of conduct is enjoined. The **soldier** does not involve himself in the affairs of this life—there are to be no entanglements with the world; the **athlete** must strive lawfully —there are to be no infringements of the regulations—he contends "according to the rules"; and the **husbandman** must work—there are to be no evasions of responsibility.

What is the object in each case? (1) to please him who hath chosen him to be a soldier; (2) to attain the victor's crown; (3) to partake of the fruits. This is the reward of his labour. The three verses seem to present three phases of the future reward:—the devoted warrior will have the "well done" for having pleased his Lord; the athlete who has striven lawfully will get the crown; the husbandman that has worked will be the first to taste the sweets of his toil.   W.H.

In 2 Tim. 2. 21, to what does the "these" refer?—to men or things?

This is a difficult point to decide with absolute certainty. There is nothing in the Greek of "these" to decide, for the word might equally mean "these men" or "these things." On the face of it, it would seem that "things" must be meant. You cannot cleanse a vessel by separating it from other vessels—but by removing its own uncleanness, and this is the view held by many. The word then would refer to the "strivings about words" (v. 14), "profane and vain babblings" of v. 16 (Many sermons would fall under this category), and "iniquity" (v. 19). These have, however, already been covered by the exhortations "shun," "depart from," etc. Personally I am inclined, without wishing to be dogmatic, to hold that it was separation from evil teachers the apostle had in view, which seems more consonant with the form of the Greek of "to purge ourselves out of." It is clearly impossible to purge ourselves from evil things, if we condone evil persons and teachers. There must be compromise and contamination. In teaching this the importance of cleansing the "inside of the platter" is not minimised; the reverse is mere Pharisaism; but if we frequent men who are unsound in the faith, we must either testify against their error or tacitly admit it. In the latter case we grieve the Holy Spirit and prevent His filling us so as to be His "vessels unto honour." I cannot, however, accept the common interpretation of "great house," as "the great house of Christendom." It is "in a great house," that is, any great house in Ephesus, and is introduced as an illustration.   W.H.

Please explain 2 Tim. 2. 26.

The object of the first Epistle was that Timothy might know how to "behave himself (not in the world but) in the house of God" (chap. 3. 15); in the second Epistle, though the order of that house has broken down, the writer's thoughts are with those who at any rate "name the name of Christ," rather than with the outside world. Paul has warned Timothy of heretical leaders, such as Hymenæus and Philetus (chap. 2. 17). He says how such are to be dealt with in Titus 3. 10—they are to be "**rejected** after a first and second admonition." This is the same word as is applied to "foolish and unlearned questions," in v. 23 of our chapter; but the persons mentioned here as "opposing themselves" seem to be rather men led astray by the heretical teachings of the leaders. Such are to be treated with meekness and patiently taught better things, "if peradventure God should grant them repentance to the accurate knowledge of the truth," in which they have become befogged. They may "come to," as from a fit of spiritual drunkenness, who have been drugged and ensnared by Satan, taken so to speak alive by him, but now to be set free to do God's pleasure. The subject of the passage is restoration. A dead man might lie alongside a drugged man and it might be hard to distinguish them at a glance, but they differ **toto cœlo.** The former needs life, the latter, the power rightly to use it. I think the exact meaning of some of the Greek words here certainly favours this conclusion.   W.H.

Is the change in 2. Tim. 3. 16, R.V., justifiable?

Whatever we may think generally of the R.V., and no doubt it embodies a number of improvements, long known as necessary by scholars, and is useful as a reference book for those who know enough to use it aright, on one point most are agreed, namely that it greatly exceeded its mandate, and would have effected more had it attempted less. This mandate, dated May 21st, 1870, drawn up for the guidance of the Revisors, by the Committee of Convocation, laid down that they were "to introduce as few alterations as possible into the Text of the A.V., consistently with faithfulness"; "Plain and clear errors" were to be corrected; only "necessary emendations" were to be made. It would be hard to prove that any large proportion of the 30,000 and more alterations made by the Revisors of the New Testament, were forced upon them by **necessity.** Far from correcting only "plain and clear errors," many think they introduced a number, and among them the serious change referred to above, thus disturbing quite unnecessarily a foundation stone of the faith, and introducing ambiguity and doubt, where there ought never to have been any. The R.V. has relegated the A.V., "All Scripture is given by inspiration of God and is profitable," to the obscurity and second rate authority of the margin, and given the place of honour to its own, at best, ambiguous translation—"every Scripture inspired of God is also profitable." Now, what **does** this mean? Does it mean "being inspired of God"? if so, it is a somewhat feebler edition of the A.V., and the passage need not have been meddled with at all; or it may mean, "if inspired of God," which does question the inspiration of some Scripture, and it is in this sense, that most readers understand the words. If it be maintained that the antithesis is between human writings and the Divine oracles, the reply is that the word translated, "Scripture" (graphē) in its New Testament usage, only refers to the "Scriptures" in their technical sense as equivalent to our word "Bible." The word occurs in fifty other places, e.g., Matt. 21. 42; 22. 29; 26. 54, 56, etc., and always thus. Only twice is a descriptive adjective attached (Rom. 1. 2; 16. 26), so familiar is the term. Thus the R.V. is as though it read, "every part of the Bible, if inspired of God, is also profitable"!

We ask in vain for a parallel to such a translation as that of the R.V. here. There are six or seven cases of similar construction in the New Testament, e.g., 1 Tim. 4. 4 and Heb. 4. 13, which would become on the same principle "every creature of God, which is good is also not to be refused," and "all things which are naked are also open to the eyes of Him, with whom we have to do." The Fathers as a whole favour the sense of the A.V., even the chairman of the Revisors, though in favour of R.V., admits "it is very difficult to decide." Where then was the **necessity** for the change? Why of all the similar constructions was this passage alone altered? Dr. C. H. Waller, late head of Highbury College supplies, what one cannot help feeling to be the only admissible answer: "The A.V. would never have been questioned, had not the inspiration of Scripture come into dispute."*

Some who seem to bow to any R.V. change, as almost inspired, try to make out that the R.V. is even stronger than the A.V. in favour of the "plenary inspiration" of the Scriptures. How anything could be stronger than the A.V. is difficult to see. It cannot be questioned which the Modernists prefer. The Revisors by leaving A.V. in the margin show it is at least an alternative translation. It would then have been more agreeable to their mandate to leave A.V. alone and if they must cast any suspicion upon it, at most do so in the margin.

Though primarily the Old Testament was in view, for Timothy as a boy could hardly have known any other, we may believe that the Spirit of God in this Scripture was including that new body of sacred literature, the New Testament, which was already nearing completion, and which had been preauthenticated by the Lord by His promise of the Spirit. This the apostles already recognised as "Scripture"—Paul in the first

* "The Authoritative Inspiration of Holy Scripture," p. 221.

Epistle to Timothy when he quotes Luke and Deuteronomy in one breath as "Scripture" (chap. 5. 18), and Peter when he classes Paul's writings with "the other Scriptures." (2 Peter 3. 16).

SUPPLEMENTARY NOTE

Query re. Answer as to 2 Tim. 3. 16 (R.V.). An esteemed correspondent has written, as a plea for R.V. here, that Timothy did not need to be assured of the inspiration of the Scriptures, seeing this is implied in the term "Sacred writings" (v. 15). But this is hardly conclusive, for those who deny the "Inspiration" of the Scriptures to-day, would not necessarily refuse to them the title of "Sacred." Besides, "no Scripture is of any private interpretation." Paul by the Spirit was writing for the Church of all time, not for Timothy alone. It is suggested, however, that what Timothy did need, was to be warned against "Apocryphal writings," and that this was in effect what Paul is referring to; but this is special pleading based on pure assumption, for such writings are not once referred to in the Epistle. To describe "Apocrypha" and "pseudo-epistles" as "graphai" (Scriptures) would violate the New Testament technical use of the word, which is the unique equivalent for "the Bible," or Biblical quotations.

It has been alleged, in order to bolster up the R.V., that it is only "a going back" to earlier English translations, but is it worth while having a R.V., if it only "goes back"? In any case, here they did not go back far enough, for as Dean Burgon truly remarks: "The ancients clearly so (i.e., as A.V.) understood St. Paul's words."* e.g. Clement of Alexandria, Chrysostom, Gregory of Nyassa, Origen, Tertullian, Basil, Cyril, Theodoret and other fathers. The real trouble about the R.V.'s "inspired of God" here, is that, in the true spirit of ecclesiastical opportunism, which conceived it, THE WORDS MAY BE TAKEN IN TWO SENSES; THEY MAY BE UNDERSTOOD, AS ITS MORE EVANGELICAL ADVOCATES MAINTAIN, "BEING INSPIRED OF GOD," IN WHICH CASE THE A.V. NEED NOT HAVE BEEN MEDDLED WITH, or as is more usually the fashion, certainly among modernists and other loose teachers, as the equivalent of "if inspired of God," casting a doubt on, if not implicitly denying the inspiration of the Bible as a whole. W. HOSTE.

How do we know that the Bible as we have it contains all the "all scripture" referred to in 2 Tim. 3. 16?

Adequately and exhaustively to answer this question would demand an article far in excess of what is here admissible.

The Old Testament is alluded to in the book of the son of Sirach (the most ancient book which time has spared from between Malachi

*"Revision Revised," p 208.

AA

and the Lord Jesus), and by Josephus, as "the Law, the Psalms and the Prophets," to which the Lord Jesus Himself also referred (Luke 24). The validity of the Old Testament books seems to be determined by a succession of prophets, the latter attesting the works of the former. Since the cessation of prophecy no book could claim a place in the Canon of the Old Testament.

As to the New Testament, while the struggle for admission to the Canon was long in the case of some books, yet in the fourth century our present canon may be said to have been universally acknowledged.

As to the Old Testament Apocryphal writings, it may be observed that they were never received into the Canon by the Jews, nor have they the sanction of the Lord Jesus or His Apostles who never quote them.

As to New Testament Apocryphal books, they were not acknowledged as authentic by the early Christians, nor were they ever quoted by heretics as records of authority. They appear in no recognised catalogues. Internally they bear all the marks of spuriousness. They abound in idle and absurd details and narrate miracles utterly destitute of dignity or purpose.

Much more might be said, but we may be satisfied that at this late date in the providence of God we have in our Bible of sixty-six books the entire written revelation of the mind of God concerning all that is past, present, and future.

Many useful works on this matter are available which deal with the question exhaustively. Litton's Guide to the Study of the Scripture may be mentioned as of special usefulness.   W.R.

Am I right in saying that "Demas" in 2 Tim. 4. 10 is short for Demetrius, and refers to the Christian brother of this name of whom we read in 3 John 12?

"Demas" is said to be most probably a contraction of "Demetrius", or possibly of "Demarchus," but even if the former were the case, I do not know of anything to show that Demas is to be identified with the Demetrius of 3 John. We know of another Demetrius in the New Testament, the silver-smith of Ephesus (Acts 19). The name is not very uncommon. Demas is mentioned in Philemon 24 as a companion of Paul at the time of his imprisonment (see also Col. 4. 14). Later he is mentioned in 1 Tim. 4. 10, as having left the apostle, "having loved this present world". The 3rd Epistle of John is thought to have been written toward the close of John's life, and therefore much later than 2 Timothy. It seems really impossible that, had Demetrius been Demas, under a new name, no hint should be given of it, especially in view of his restoration, which must have taken place, seeing that Demetrius there is no lover of the world, but of God's people.   W.H.

In what sense did Paul use the words: "Do the work of an evangelist" (2 Tim. 4. 5)?

Surely in the sense that he recognised Timothy as the possessor of the gift of evangelist, and exhorted him to use it. In both his Epistles to Timothy the apostle refers to a gift his son in the faith had received. Here in chap. 1. 6 he says, "Wherefore I put thee in remembrance that thou stir up the gift of God, which is in thee **by the putting on of my hands**": and in the first Ep. chap. 4. 14, he writes, "Neglect not the gift that is in thee, which was given thee by prophecy **with the laying on of the hands of the presbytery.**" It was, then, "the gift of God." He was the source—Father, Son and Spirit; but it was given "by the putting on of My hands"—Paul was the channel. It was "by means of" (**dia**) the putting on of his hands, but also "with (**meta**) the laying on the hands" of the presbytery. The word here translated "presbytery" occurs in two other places in the New Testament—Acts 22. 5 ("estate of elders"); and Luke 22. 66 ("elders"). Paul associates with himself the elders in the act of bestowal, as he loved to do on other occasions, e.g., when he associates Sosthenes with himself in the authorship of 1st Corinthians. But as we may be sure no passage of the Epistle came from Sosthenes, so no drop of grace flowed from the elders' hands. People sometimes ask, "Why should we not give spiritual gifts"? Certainly, if you can; no one is prohibited. But no one has the power. The imposition of hands to-day, in the sense of giving gift or the Spirit, is indeed "an **imposition.**" Another point may be noticed, namely, that in 1 Tim. 4. 14 the gift is said to have been given him "by prophecy." This seems to refer back to verse 18 of chap. 1: "According to the **prophecies** which went before on thee, that thou by them mightest war a good warfare." To conclude, Paul recognised God's gift by his hands to Timothy, and I would suggest that this gift was primarily that of evangelist. In Eph. 4. 8 we read that the ascended Lord "gave gifts to men," then in verse 11 that He gave to the church these gifted men, "some apostles, some prophets (the temporary gifts) and some evangelists, and some pastors and teachers (the permanent)." No doubt all should be able to testify of the Gospel: all may care for their fellow-saints; all may pass on instruction, but only those gifted of God are "evangelists, pastors and teachers." Not all possess the gifts: it is "some" in each case; but do all these "some" stir up and use their gift? This naturally sounds the death-knell of the "turn and turn about" system of Gospel preaching practised in some halls. Rather let those who have the gift, like Timothy, do the work of evangelist. It has been asked why there are so few gifts to-day in local churches. I would suggest three reasons: (1) There is so little desire, so little "coveting the best gifts"; (2) There is so little stirring up the gift, which we may have; (3) There is so little opportunity afforded for stirring up the gifts in the local churches. The saints have too often itching ears to hear only the best speakers; budding gift is discouraged. Imported speakers are the order of the day, and the local gifts become atrophied.   W.H.

TITUS

"To be ready to every good work" (Titus 3. 1). Does this mean that I must assist the powers that be with information regarding evil doings and murders, or does "good work" here mean something else?

It is unnecessary to build too much on the proximity of this phrase, "be ready to every good work," and the other, "obey magistrates." It is a general list of exhortations to good conduct in various relations. At any rate there is nothing in the sense or context regarding "giving information about evil doers and murders."

As a law-abiding citizen, the Christian is naturally on the side of constituted authority and order. When Paul's nephew heard that an evil conspiracy was formed, he was no doubt perfectly right in making it known. To become aware of the details of a murder and not to divulge them, constitutes a man before the law an "accessory after the fact," and a sharer in the guilt of the crime.

The second part of the question is based on a very common confusion of thought. It is true, we are in a day of grace and even murderers can be saved by the atonement of Christ, and well authenticated cases are known of such, but the law has nothing to do with this and a convicted murderer should suffer the penalty of his crime in any case. The world is not governed on principles of grace, nor was it ever intended to be. God has placed a sword in the magistrate's hand, and "He beareth not the sword in vain" (see Rom. 13). It would be beside the mark for a criminal to plead that he ought to be let off, because it is a day of grace; he would get, I should judge, a severer sentence. The words, "He that sheddeth man's blood, by man shall his blood be shed," form part of God's covenant with the whole earth through Noah, and hold good to-day as much as ever they did.   W.H.

Titus iii. 5: "Not by works of righteousness which we have done, but according to His mercy He saved us, by the washing of regeneration, and renewing of the Holy Ghost." Eternal life is in Christ, and all believers are in Him. In what sense, then, are we to understand the latter clause: "renewing of the Holy Ghost"?

We must all agree that there can be nothing in this verse out of harmony with the possession of eternal life in Christ, nor should we even appear to neutralise one verse with another. The truth, however, is presented here in a very distinct way, as compared with its presentation in John's Gospel or the Roman Epistle. The apostle, by the Spirit, presents salvation, not so much in connection with the death and resurrection of Christ, as in Romans, or as the result of faith as in John, but as linked to the work of the Holy Spirit in regeneration and renewal. The word for **"washing"** here is **loutron**—the once for all **"washing"** of John xiii—"He that is **washed** (louō) needeth not save to bathe his feet but is clean every whit." At the moment of this "washing" the believer is **"renewed,"** but whereas "regeneration" is completed then and there, this **"renewal"** is the first act of a process which continues to the end. This is shown by considering the three other passages in the New Testament, where the root (anakainoō) occurs: "Be transformed by the **renewal** of your mind" (Rom. xii. 2); "The new man, which is **being renewed** in knowledge after the image of Him that created Him" (Col. iii. 10); "The inward man **is being renewed** day by day" (2 Cor. iv. 16). It is not here the salvation of the sinner from guilt and condemnation, as in Romans, nor yet the possession of eternal life through faith in Christ, that is in view. It is deliverance from the manner of life described in verse 2 by the regenerating power of the Holy Spirit, and by His work of renewal, which even at that moment also begins.   W.H.

HEBREWS

Is it correct to say, as in Darby's Translation of Heb. 2. 9, that Christ was "made some little inferior to angels"? If so, in what way was He made inferior to them?

These questions appear to be fully answered in the context of the passage. In verses 6-8 a quotation is given from the 8th Psalm, in which man is spoken of as "made some little inferior to the angels;" and when, immediately after in verse 9, the same words are used of Christ, it is evident that it was by becoming man that this came to be true of Him. He who, as chapter 1 makes so plain, was immeasurably superior to the angels, by His becoming man took a place below them. And He did so, as verse 9 goes on to say, "on account of the suffering of death," a statement which is further explained by verses 14, 15, "since therefore the children partake of blood and flesh, He also in like manner took part in the same," with a view to their deliverance through His death.

I have used Darby's phrasing of the verses, as did the questioner; but I do not see in what way his "inferior to" is any improvement on the "lower than" of the A.V. and R.V.   W.R.

Would it be correct to say that the words, "crowned with glory and honour," Heb. 2. 9, do not refer to our Lord's present glory bestowed on Him as the reward of His sufferings, but to a glory bestowed on Him before His sufferings, to enable Him to undergo them?

It certainly would not, though the interpretation of the verse is admittedly complicated by the claims of various readings, and by the last phrase, "that He by the grace of God should taste death for every man." But does not this show that "the crowning" came before the death? No, for that has just been made dependent on His death by the preceding words. "Owing to the suffering of death." This fact does, I think, render nugatory the interpretation suggested, though it does not free us from difficulty. All depends on the true meaning of the closing words of the verse. They describe not the fact of His sufferings, but their **value**. The "suffering of death" led to the crowning (this corresponds exactly with the truth of Phil. 2: "Therefore God also hath highly exalted Him"), the "crowning" gives value to the death. "If Christ be not raised ye are yet in your sins." The context seems to show that this is the true interpretation. The quotation from Psalm 8, and verses 7 and 8 of Hebrews 2, mark four epoch-making events, of which two are accomplished and two await their fulfilment:—

(1) "Thou madest Him a little lower than the angels"—marking the period of 33½ years of our Lord's ministry and passion.

(2) "Thou crownest Him with glory and honour." Though the Lord did receive honour and glory from the Father, during His ministry, especially on the Holy Mount, He is never said to have been crowned as a Victor then—the word used for it here. He could not receive the victor's reward without being first the Victor. However, now we contemplate Him thus. The crowning followed on His humiliation, this period has lasted just over 1,900 years. There is nothing after this crowning to correspond to the sufferings of Christ, which could not fail to be there, if the theory we oppose were correct.

(3) "Thou settest Him over the works of Thy hands." This points to the future earthly reign of a thousand years.

(4) "Thou didst put all things in subjection under His feet." This describes final subjection of every foe (see Rev. 20) and the beginning of "the Everlasting Kingdom of our Lord and Saviour, Jesus Christ."

Of these two latter epochs the Spirit of God says, "We see not yet all things put under Him."

The verse we are considering can be read in two columns:—

(1) **His Humiliation—**

    (a) "Who was made a little lower than the angels"—The **fact** of His sufferings.

    (b) "The suffering of death"—Their character.

    (c) "That He, by the grace of God, should taste death **for every man**"—Their value.

(2) **His Exaltation—**"Crowned (estephanōmenon—Perfect Participle with continuing result) with glory and honour."   W.H.

Is Heb. 2. 11 ("He that sanctifieth and they who are sanctified are all of one") a reference to Ex. 25. 19; 37. 9, where the words, "of one," are used of the cherubim?

I do not think the expression "are all of one," is in any way connected with the cherubim being of one piece with the mercy-seat. Rather, "He that sanctifieth and they who are sanctified, are all out of one," in the sense of relationship—all derived from one Father. This is true, with a distinction, of Christ and His people, as He says, "My Father and your Father, and My God and your God." Surely this agrees with the context, "*for which cause* he is not ashamed to call them brethren" (Heb. ii. 11).   W.H.

How are we to understand the "Rest" of Heb. 4. 9? Does verse 10 refer to the sinner who comes to Christ? Or is it the resting of the saint who has reached Heaven? Again, is verse 11 an exhortation to saints to strive after some kind of higher life?

The following meanings have been suggested by Commentators for verse 10:—

(1) An explanation of the word rendered "keeping of sabbath" (v. 9 margin) by a reference to literal Sabbath-keeping. (One writer absurdly applies even that word itself to literal Sabbath-keeping, thus making verse 9 to mean that God's people should still keep a weekly Sabbath). Against this view is a lack of connection with the remainder of the passage, and especially as it leaves the phrase, "that rest" in verse 11 meaningless. Against it, also, is the expression, "He having entered into His rest," which is not at all one which would be used of beginning a weekly Sabbath.

(2) A sinner resting from his own works in order to be saved by grace thus entering into rest, as in Matt. 11. 28. But, in that case, the "resting from his own works" would NOT BE "as God did from His" but rather, the exact opposite. God rested when He had completed all and found all good. The sinner rests in Christ's work when he finds his own NO GOOD.

(3) A saint who has reached rest in heaven. In favour of this is Rev. 14. 13, "they rest from their labours." But against it is the fact that if "rest" in this verse means heaven, it would apparently require to mean heaven throughout the chapter. Most Commentators think it does so, but verse 3 says that we "enter it upon believing" and the phrase, "seem to have come short of it," suggests that we should have it already. But the greatest objection to these three views is the difficulty of explaining why the tenses used should be the Aorist Indicative and Participle, which point to a definite act of someone in the PAST. It is literally, "For the one who entered into his rest, rested from his works."

(4) Christ entering into His rest after finishing His works upon earth, including the Cross. So Alford, Weymouth, etc. In favour of this are the tenses, also the words of Isaiah 11. 10—"His rest shall be glorious." Compare John 9. 4. Against it is the awkward way in which Christ would be introduced in the opening clause without any previous mention of Him since chapter 3. 14. But it would contrast with Joshua's failure of v. 8, and would lead on to the statement of v. 14: "Seeing then that we have a Great High Priest, that is passed into the heavens, Jesus the Son of God, let us hold fast our profession."   W.R.

In Heb. 5. 7, do the "prayers and supplications with strong crying and tears" refer to any particular time in our Lord's life; and in what way was He "heard" and "saved from death"?

I think the reference in Heb. 5. 7 is mainly, or perhaps entirely, to the agony in the Garden of Gethsemane. The phrase, "in the days of His flesh", in the beginning of the verse, is not inserted for the purpose of spreading the "prayers and supplications" over His whole life; but by way of contrast with His present exalted position.

It seems to be taken for granted by nearly everyone who reads this passage, that Jesus is said in it to have prayed to be saved from death; and it is because of this that difficulty is felt as to how He was "heard", and in what sense He was saved from death. Yet it does NOT state that He prayed to be saved from death; but that He "offered up prayers, etc., UNTO HIM THAT WAS ABLE TO SAVE HIM FROM DEATH", which is a very different thing. The One to Whom He prayed was One Who was able to save Him from death, had such been His will; but what Christ actually prayed for is not stated in Heb. 5 at all. From Luke 22. 42 we learn that the prayer was, "Father, if Thou be willing, remove this cup from Me; nevertheless not My will but Thine be done." This prayer was a prayer of what the A.V. margin of Heb. 5. 7 calls "piety", and the R.V., "godly fear." That is to say, it was a prayer of submission to His Father's will, and because of that submission or "piety" it was "heard." An answer which would have taken Him out of the path of His Father's will would not really have been an answer to the prayer, for He did not ask or wish for this. The true answer, or at least a very beginning of it, is suggested in the very next verse in Luke, in which we read that an angel was sent from heaven to strengthen Him. Notice how shortly afterwards the Lord said to Peter, "The cup which My Father hath given Me, shall I not drink it?" (John 18. 11).

W.R.

Does Heb. 5. 8 prove that "Jesus had to learn like anyone else"?

It is a curious phenomenon that Modernists, Unitarians, etc., who deny without scruple the accuracy and authority of the Scriptures, when, as is usually the case, they wish to question its teachings, are suddenly transformed into rigorous verbal-inspirationists, when they can find a verse which it seems possible to turn to their advantage. Thus the Higher Critic, who cheerfully deletes whole chapters of the Bible and denies any real authority to the rest, will cling, like a drowning man to a straw, to some phrase such as "He emptied Himself" (the R.V. rendering of Phil. 2. 7), because he thinks he can use it as a jumping-off ground to drag down our Lord to his own level. But he ignores such words of His as, "I and My Father are One," or even the words in this same chapter of the Philippians, a few verses higher up: "Who being in the form of God" (v. 6). "Oh, Paul says so," the critics reply; "but who is Paul?" The same writer, let them note, who says lower down, "He emptied Himself." The only thing which our Lord asked to be restored to Him was His Divine glory (John 17. 5), and it was that—"the insignia of His Majesty," that He laid aside. But a king is no less personally, when wearing ordinary clothes, than when wearing the Coronation robes, and so we may be sure the Lord was no less a Divine Person, the Eternal Son of God, co-equal with the Father, when He laid aside His Divine glory, than when He was fully clothed in it "before the world was" (see John 17. 5). Do Modernists "confess Jesus Christ as Lord to the glory of God the Father"? It is noticeable rather how they avoid doing so. They speak of Him with less respect than of any earthly monarch. They would not call our King simply, "George," but "Jesus" is their habitual address of Him, Who is the "King of kings." When Thomas cried, "My Lord and my God," our Lord did not demur, but replied, "Because thou hast seen Me, thou hast believed, blessed are they that have not seen and yet have believed" (John 20. 28, 29). The case before us illustrates the same principle. The Modernist quotes Heb. 5. 8 as proof that "Jesus had to learn like anyone else," but really he misses the true sense. It does not say that He learned to obey, but that "He learned obedience," that is, what it was to obey. We start by being disobedient, and gradually through many failures learn to obey. The Lord started as the Eternal Son of God, "being in the form of God," and thus equal with God. As such He had never obeyed, He could only command; but in taking the place of a servant He took orders for the first time, and knew for the first time the sensation of obedience. Let me give an illustration from a lower plane. While Peter the Great remained in his country as the Emperor of all the Russians, he could only give orders, but when he took the place of a shipwright on the wharves of Deptford, he had to take orders, and so it was with our Lord. Though He were a Son (and so equal with the Father), yet learned He obedience by the things He underwent, and became obedient unto death, even the death of the cross—the most wonderful exhibition of obedience the universe has ever seen or could see. By this death He became "perfect," not morally, for He was always that, but officially. Apart from His sufferings He could save no one; now He can save all who trust Him. When men deny the atoning death of Christ, they deny Him as Saviour, and sign their eternal death-warrant.   W.H.

Why should the Hebrew believers be charged with being "dull of hearing," and having become babes? (Heb. 5. 11).

The first verse of the next chapter answers the question. These Hebrews were no doubt believers in the Lord Jesus, as their Messiah and Saviour, but they had failed to **go on to perfection**. They were still occupied with the **beginnings** of the doctrine of Christ. In chap. 3. 1, the apostle had addressed them as "Holy brethren, partakers of the **heavenly** calling," but they clung to their **earthly** calling as Jews; and how little do Christians in general rise above that? No doubt the Church was born at Pentecost, but the Acts was a transition period, during which truth was being gradually brought out; but at its close very few believers understood what had been gradually revealed in the Epistles to the Romans (12. 4) and Corinthians (12. 13), and more clearly in the Ephesian Epistle—their union with Christ in one body. They had become dull of hearing and were babies instead of grown men. We learn from history that after the death of Festus, Ananias initiated a persecution against all believing Jews, forcing them to choose either to renounce Jesus Christ altogether, or lose their national place, privileges, and share in the earthly Levitical order of things. This was a severe test. It is hard enough for believers to-day to quit their denominations, and consent to be gathered to the Name of the Lord alone, which is the path of obedience to which the Lord calls His own.

Many shrink from this, although the whole denominational system is condemned in the Scriptures, but here they were called to give up what Jehovah Himself had ordained, which was doubly difficult. To go back to Judaism, however, meant nothing short of final apostasy, and alas some had yielded. This called forth the Epistle; its object being to show that in Christ all was more than made up to them, and that believers in **Him** were immeasurable gainers all along the line; as thousands have found to-day in the path of separation to Himself, from the world and its religious systems. W.H.

What is the "doctrine of baptisms"? (Heb. 6. 2). Does this refer to the baptism in the Spirit, and ought we to seek this as a second experience?

The Apostle is exhorting the Hebrews to "leave the principles of the doctrine of Christ and to go on unto perfection, **not laying again** the foundation of repentence . . . faith . . . of the doctrine or teaching of **baptisms, and of the laying on of hands,** and of resurrection of the dead, and of eternal judgment." No doubt the teaching of baptisms could not be divorced from baptism in the Holy Spirit and in water, but the word is not quite the usual word for Christian baptism, and probably refers primarily to the purifications in Old Testament times, e.g., the washings of the priests on their being set apart to God's service. It is the word used in Heb. 9. 10 ("divers washings"). Certainly there is nothing here about seeking a second baptism in the Spirit; the exhortation to us is rather to leave these first principles. But we must note that this is not in the sense in which a child leaves its cradle for having out-grown it, but in the sense of a mason who leaves the foundation, as he builds up the wall upon it. Baptism in the Spirit is not an experience to be sought by a Christian, it is the work of Christ on his soul in uniting him, the believing sinner, to Himself, the making him a Christian, in fact. A believer is only baptised in the Spirit once, but he can and should be filled again and again. W.H.

Who are those in Heb. 6, of whom it is said that "it is impossible, if they fall away to renew them again unto repentance"? Are they apostates, or is the apostle proving the security of believers—such can never be "renewed," because they can never need it?

I used to hold the latter view and could expound it rather forcibly, as I thought. I remember once doing so to the late Mr. J. R. Caldwell. He said nothing but quietly looked at me, and asked me a brief question: "Does it satisfy you?" On further consideration I was bound to admit that it did not entirely do so. I was led to seek further light, and to-day my personal conviction is that the passage in Hebrews 6 and also the analogous one in chapter 10, both refer to the solemn possibility of apostasy among professing believers. The difference between the two passages is that in the former we see how far a man may go in religious experiences and spiritual attainments and yet never have been truly born again; and in the other how far a man may go in the things of Satan after having made a profession of faith in Christ. We may notice that the subjects of Heb. 6 are said to have been "enlightened," to have "tasted of the heavenly gift," to have been "made partakers of the Holy Ghost," to have "tasted the good word of God and the powers of the world to come" (experiences to which we may find parallels in those of Balaam, Judas, Simon Magus, the stony-ground hearers, and the wonder-workers of Matt. 7), but are not said to have been cleansed or justified or born of the Spirit. The Hebrews had professed faith in Christ and were now under pressure to "forsake the assembling of themselves together" (see 10. 25), and some had unhappily done so and gone back to Judaism. This is apostasy, from which there is no recovery. Clearly it goes much further than the ordinary falling away theory of a true believer, for those who hold this to be possible are equally strong that such fallen ones may be restored. Neither passage is intended to cast doubt on the security of the true believer, for chapter 6 ends with "strong consolation for such," and they are exhorted in chapter 10. "not to cast away their confidence," but to see to it that the reality of their conversion be proved by the reality of their continuance in the faith.   W.H.

Does Heb. 6. 4 refer to a person who has been under conviction by the Holy Spirit, and has professed to be saved; but who afterwards finds out that he is not saved? Will God never convict such a one again?

There can be no doubt that the person in view has been dealt with by the Spirit of God, and has professed to receive Christ. But, more than that, he is one who, after having done so, has deliberately turned away from Christ, and gone back to the "dead works" (v. 1.) of his former religious life; which is what some of these Hebrews seemed to be almost on the verge of doing. That is why such are described in verse 6 as "crucifying to themselves the Son of God afresh." Peter in Acts 3. 17 could say to them of the original crucifixion, "Brethren, I wot that through IGNORANCE ye did it;" but this could not be said of the "crucifying afresh" of verse 6, which was WILFUL. Compare ch. 10. 26-29.

The case of one who has professed conversion and afterwards found out that he has been mistaken is usually very different from that above described. The very finding out of his mistake is itself often the work of the Spirit, and a proof of His renewed activities.   W.R.

Do the first six verses of Heb. vi teach that one who has the experience there described, and then falls away, is lost? Does v. 6 apply to the Christian to-day?

In order to grasp the point of the Hebrew epistle, especially of its warnings, it is important to see the difference between believing in the Lord Jesus during His earthly ministry, or even during the transitional period of the Acts, and believing in Him subsequently to the full revelation of the heavenly calling of the Church being given in the Ephesian and Colossian epistles. The former involved no break with their Jewish hopes and aspirations. It would have been strange had accepting the Jewish Messiah compromised a man's Judaism. Those who accepted the Lord as Saviour and Messiah were better Jews after than before. So, it was, in a modified sense, in the Acts. It was a time of transition, and though the one and only Church was founded at Pentecost by the Lord Himself, believing Jews did not, and were not expected to, understand what had not yet been revealed. But when from the prison-house in Rome those epistles issued, revealing the mystery of Christ, that the middle wall of partition had been broken down, that the calling was heavenly, and that blessing was no longer connected with the nation and earth, at once a new and energetic exercise of faith was called for. Nature clung to the old forms and the old hopes. These believing Hebrews were terribly tempted to draw back. The central note of the epistle is, "Go on unto perfection." They had known ever since their profession of faith in Christ, "the principles of the doctrine of Christ" (not "the word of the beginning of Christ"). They had believed in Him for forgiveness and many other blessings. Now they were to leave these blessings, not as a child leaves its cradle, because it has no further use for it, but as a builder leaves his foundation by building up away from it. Perfection was to be their object in the widest meaning of that embracing word—even the fulness of Christ. Yes, they had to give up, but it was to get far transcending blessings. The six things mentioned here were indispensable, as far as they went, but they did not go far enough. It is, I believe, impossible to apply "the falling away" to "doctrines and principles," as is suggested by the questioner. It applies to any who had *professed* the name of Christ, but might under pressure turn back and prove apostates. Is apostasy an impossibility to-day? Alas! I fear not. W.H.

Does Heb. 6. 4-6 apply to a person who was exercised about his soul and was as it were, near the Kingdom of God but not born again, or is it simply to assure us of believers' security?

I think it applies to persons who may have passed through many religious experiences, attained to considerable knowledge in spiritual things, and made a profession of faith, but were never born again. Far from the purpose of the Holy Spirit being "simply to assure us of believers' security," I should think its effect ought rather to be a call to all and sundry "to make their calling and election sure" by going on to perfection. These severe passages in Hebrews 6 and 10 are a solemn warning to professors, as to how far we may go in intellectual grasp of truth and in enjoyment of spiritual gifts, and yet never have truly "fled for refuge to lay hold on the hope set before us." It is to those that have done this, that God in His lovingkindness offers "a strong consolation." No gifts of exposition, oratory, or philanthropy, can take the place of personal dealings with Christ. Miraculous powers, prophesying in the name of Christ, and successful work do not suffice to prove reality (See Matt. 7. 22). The Hebrews were under strong pressure to go back to Judaism. Some had done so, and had proved themselves apostates, for they had become adversaries of Christ (see chap. 10. 27-30). A true believer may alas get cold and backslide, but the Father will restore such through chastening. "The Lord shall judge His people" (v. 30), leading them to confession, forgiveness and cleansing (1 John 1. 9).	W.H.

Who is the "he" of Hebrews vii. 8?

The point of Heb. vii is to show the superiority of the Melchisedec order of priesthood to which our Lord Jesus belongs, over the Levitical. Before getting to that, but in view of it, the greatness of Melchisedec is first shown, among other ways, by his receiving tithes of Abraham. Now Melchisedec was the royal priest of Salem, and no doubt a real man; but in Gen. xiv he suddenly appears on the pages of Holy Writ and as suddenly leaves it. We believe he was born and died like other men, but the Spirit guides Moses to pass over such detail, and uses these silences in a symbolical way in order to compare him to the Son of God. "THERE" in Heb. vii. 8 would denote the Biblical incident in Gen. xiv, and the "he" would be Melchisedec, a figure of Christ.	W.H.

Is the covenant referred to in Hebrews viii. 9-12 millennial or Christian?

This is a quotation from Jer. xxxi. 31-34, and no doubt primarily refers to the new covenant with the house of Israel and with the house of Judah in the last days. It is introduced in the "Hebrews" broadly to show those addressed that the covenant of works made with their fathers, when they came out of Egypt, in which the nation as a whole gloried, was, by the witness of a Jewish prophet, to be succeeded by a new and better covenant, "established upon better promises," and which breathes God's grace from beginning to end. This will be enjoyed in full measure by the restored nation of Israel in the millennium, but the apostle quotes it here as an encouragement to believing Hebrews, who found it an intense trial to be separated from all their earthly and national traditions and expectations. It is clear that a great deal of this new covenant cannot apply to believing Hebrews at the present time—

"the remnant according to the election of grace"—for in "the church, which is His body," there is neither Jew nor Gentile. But in chap. x, part of this covenant—the closing words—are so applied—"Their sins and their iniquities will I remember no more." As a matter of interpretation, the new covenant belongs to Israel, as a matter of application, believing Hebrews and others can lay hold of it, at least in part, to-day.

W.H.

Seeing that the context both before and after Hebrews 9. 16-17 refers to Divine covenants, may these verses be accurately translated: "For where a covenant is, there must also of necessity be brought in the death of the covenant victim. For a covenant is stable over the dead; since it is of no strength at all while the covenant victim liveth"? (From Newberry's margin, except the word "since").

It is perfectly true that the word "diathēkē"—translated in the Authorised Version.—"Testament" all through this passage, has the double significance of a testament in the sense of "a will," and a covenant. The word occurs 32 times in the New Testament, 13 times as "testament" and 19 as "covenant." Of these I will only give the "Hebrews" occurrences:—Chap. 7. 22; 8. 6, 8, 9, 10; 9. 4, 15, 16, 17, 20; 10. 16, 29; 12. 24; 13. 20; which all can look up for themselves. In not one of these passages is the idea of "a will" certainly present, and how can the Revisers have brought it in, in Heb. 9. 16 and 17, when at least the previous context, as our questioner notes, clearly demands "covenant" as their Version had it till then correctly? Those who bring in the idea of "a will" here, seem to have been misled by the phrase in the Authorised Version, "While the testator liveth, or as the Revised Version: "he that made it liveth." It is certainly going too far to translate "ho diathemenos" as Newberry does, "the covenant victim." It is really one who "makes the covenant,'" the mediator of the covenant. But the Revisers seem to have lost sight of the wonderful truth that, in the case of the New Covenant, He who is the Mediator— the Lord Jesus Christ—is Himself the Covenant Victim. Newberry's margin represents, I believe, a true interpretation, rather than an accurate translation.

W.H.

What do you think of Heb. 9. 4? Were the pot of Manna and Aaron's rod ever in the Ark or only "laid up before the Lord" (i.e., by the side of it)? If the former was the case, how account for their not being there in the days of Solomon?

Really the difficulty is as great either way. Why had the two articles disappeared, if their "laying up before the Lord beside the Ark" had been intended to be permanent?

Neither in Exod. 16. 33, of the pot of manna, nor in Num. 17. 10, of the rod, is it said that they were put in the ark, as is said of the tables in Deut. 10. 2.

But Hebrews 9. 4 makes it perfectly clear to my mind that **all three** were originally placed in the ark—"**wherein** were the golden pot that had manna and Aaron's rod that budded, and the tables of the covenant". Besides, the statements in 1 Kings 8. 9 and 2 Chron. 5. 10 seem to suggest that before, the tables had not been alone in the ark. It is not necessary for us to be able to explain, in order to believe. "By faith we understand," but perhaps the reason is that as established in the land, with the temple, priestly services fully developed and permanent, Israel no longer needed either the remembrance of the desert provision or the sign of God's choice of the Aaronic family.   W.H.

Does Heb. ix. 12 teach that Christ entered heaven with His blood (literal blood taken in), or is it not rather that by means of His blood (death) He entered in?

Some of our beautiful hymns teach the former, e.g., "He sprinkled with His blood the mercy-seat above." This is poetry, but not doctrinally correct. The high priest did carry the blood into the Holiest. He went in virtue of it, and with it, but the former alone is true of our Lord. "Christ, BY MEANS OF OR IN VIRTUE OF His own blood ('dia' with a genitive case), entered in once into the holy-place" (Heb. 9. 12), whereas in v. 25 we read that "the high priest entereth into the holy place every year with blood of others ('en' with a dative case)." By the blood shed at the altar, a symbolical atonement was made, and at the mercy-seat it was presented. At Calvary the true atonement was accomplished. Out of the pierced side of Christ flowed the blood and the water. It was not gathered up, however, to be carried in anywhere. But Christ went in in virtue of His atoning work, and what corresponds to the blood on the earthly mercy-seat, is Christ Himself on the throne of God, bearing in His Person the scars of Calvary.   W.H.

Heb. 9. 22: "And almost all things are by the law purged with blood; and without shedding of blood is no remission." Why the "almost"? What are the exceptions?

The two numbers of this verse are usually taken as in antithesis, the one embodying an exception, the other none. Should we not then have had a "but" before this latter instead of an "and"? Does not "almost" (skedon) qualify the whole verse rather than the first part only? the argument of the following verse then being that, seeing that both cleansing and forgiveness are "by the law" not entirely effected by the blood, "better sacrifices" are needed for the heavenly things themselves. Alford favours the "almost" character of both parts of the verse and translates: "Almost (it might be said) all things are by the law cleansed by blood and apart from shedding blood is no remission (aphesis)." One exception to the **cleansing** by blood would be "the ashes of the heifer sprinkling the unclean" (see verse 13 here and Numb. 19), and one to the **forgiveness** by blood, the handful of fine flour, without oil or incense, burnt on the altar (Lev. 5. 11-13), which was the sin-offering of the poor man who could not afford an animal victim. This may represent the lowest apprehension of Christ's sacrifice—the hem of the garment touch—though ultimately there can be no forgiveness except on the ground of the atoning blood of Christ. I know what may be said for the processes of grinding through which the flour had to pass, but this hardly meets the fact of the exception noted in the Leviticus passage, where "forgiveness" (same root as in Heb. 9. 22) is pronounced by the priest "without shedding of blood." W.H.

What are "the heavenly things themselves" in Heb. 9. 23 which it was necessary to purify with "better sacrifices than these"?

The whole verse seems to go some way towards answering the question, though it may still need further explanation. "It was therefore necessary that the patterns (hupodeigma) of things in the heavens should be purified with these (i.e. Levitical sacrifices), but the heavenly things themselves with better sacrifices than these." The heavenly things themselves are then clearly the heavenly original pattern (tupos) or model shown to Moses on the Mount (see Heb. 8. 5) —"Who (i.e. the earthly priests) serve unto the example (hupodeigma) and shadow (skia) of heavenly things." God did not merely give Moses the specifications of the tabernacle: measurements, materials, etc., but showed Him the Heavenly original, of which the tabernacle was to be the earthly representation. In the Revelation we have references to this—"the altar," ch. 8. 3; "the golden altar," ch. 9. 13 (clearly this is the altar of incense in heaven); "the temple of God opened in heaven," ch. 11. 19, in which was seen "the ark of his testament"; while in ch. 16. 1, "the temple" is again mentioned. It is certain that only the sacrifice of Christ could for one moment avail for such a work, and that it does so perfectly. It does not seem clear why the plural is used here—"with better sacrifices"—unless it refers to the various aspects of the one sacrifice. It is easy to see why the earthly tabernacle needed cleansing, because it stood in a sin-stricken world, and all connected with it, whether priests, levites or people, were sinful. Sin may be viewed as guilt as in Romans, or as defilement as in Hebrews. Where guilt is out of the question, as in the case of a material tabernacle, defilement is possible. Have we not here the explanation of the need of the cleansing of "the heavenly things themselves"? Sin has found an entrance into the heavenly sphere

BB

by the fall of Satan, and his angels, and although the blood of Christ's atonement was not shed to atone for these ("He took not up angels," Heb. 2. 16), yet the contamination must be met and cleansed.   W.H.

Does the expression, "A body hast Thou prepared me" (Heb. 10. 5) justify remarks heard sometimes that "He had a body to live in or to die in," and that "He dwelt in the body which God had prepared Him"?

Such phrases might pass, as long as they do not mean that our Lord's humanity consisted alone in a human body, and that the spiritual part in man was replaced in His case by His Divine Personality. This would be a denial of incarnation, and would be fundamental error. There is an immense difference between the theophanies of the Old Testament, that is, the divine appearances to Joshua, Gideon, Manoah, etc. (which were in every case Christophanies, see John 1. 18), and the Incarnation of Him, who had always existed as the Eternal Son of God, but had now entered into manhood. "The Word became flesh" means—not only that He took a body, but that He became man, with everything that that **unfallen** humanity implied—human spirit, human soul, human will, human body. Unless this were so, Christ could not have been the seed of the woman, of Abraham, or of David. As it was, a Divine Person, with perfect and complete Divine nature took to Himself perfect and complete human nature. In the case of a theophany it was a temporary appearance assumed for the circumstance, in the case of incarnation it is a condition entered into for ever.   W.H.

Do the expressions in Heb. 10. 22: "our hearts sprinkled from an evil conscience, and our bodies washed with pure water," represent part of our standing in Christ, or do they refer to a preparation that we should make each time we come together?

This is an important enquiry in every way. My own belief is that at conversion every Christian has once for all passed through the spiritual experiences represented by the "sprinkling" and "washing," though we may be very slow to apprehend them, and this we ought to do again and again. I think they are clearly in view of priestly service, and represent the initial and closing acts in the setting apart and consecration of Aaron and his sons, as described in Leviticus 8. There we have the "washing" first, representing "regeneration"; and lastly, the "sprinkling" act, denoting the sanctification or setting apart of the believer to God. This may be, I would submit, the **divine** order of things, whereas in Hebrews it is the reverse order, representing our human. apprehension—first the "sprinkling" of the blood and then the "washing." Perhaps we may say that all that happens in Leviticus 8 between these two acts may also be included in the Hebrews verse for us to appropriate. There the first thing is the "washing" of the person of Aaron and his sons (v. 6). Then Aaron was clothed with his garments of glory and beauty, representing the Lord Jesus glorified (vv. 7-9). Next the anointing takes place, corresponding to the giving of the Spirit (vv. 10-12), and the priests are clothed in their linen garments—that is in Christ—their Righteousness (v. 13). Then follow the sacrifices—the work of Christ—on which all depends (vv. 14-21); the ram of consecration, too, is slain, its blood applied to Aaron and his sons, and with parts of it and the unleavened bread the hands of Aaron and his sons are filled. This is consecration—the hands filled with Christ—then the blood of the ram mingled with it is "sprinkled" upon Aaron and his garments and on his sons and their garments, to sanctify or set them fully apart for God. I think the oil represents the special ministry of the Holy Spirit, applying the blood in view of priestly service. We have all been "washed": The word is that used in John 13 where the Lord says: "He that is **bathed** needeth not, save to wash his feet." We do not require to go through these spiritual experiences again, but in the earlier part of the verse, two exercises are noted which we do need to renew and practise. We are to come with a "true heart and full assurance of faith"—not merely "faith" trembling and hardly daring to draw nigh—but "with full assurance of faith," and as for the "true heart"—however important sincerity and genuineness of purpose are, I do not believe that this is what is referred to here. The word is not "true" (alēthēs) as apposed to the false, but "true" (alēthinos) as opposed to the figurative. It was used by our Lord constantly of Himself: "I am the true bread"; "the true vine"; "the true God." It occurs in Hebrews 8. 2, "the true tabernacle"; 9. 24, "the true holy place." What then is a "true heart" in this sense? I believe it is a heart exercised to distinguish earthly things from heavenly, shadows from substance, figures from realities, types from antitypes. For this we need to ponder the Word, to gird up the loins of our mind to discern things that differ, and to see for ourselves where God has placed us—in Christ, and to know what God has made us—"nigh by the blood," "accepted in the Beloved", and constituted a holy priesthood unto God.   W.H.

Kindly explain Heb. 10. 26: "there remaineth no more sacrifice for sins."

The whole teaching of the chapter is to show that in contrast with the Levitical sacrifices, the sacrifice of Christ was never to be repeated, but was sufficient, and so once for all (see chap. 9. 26; 10. 10, 12, 14). Thus there is "no more offering" for sin (v. 18), and "no more sacrifice" for sins (v. 26) either needed or possible. Are we then to have light views, as believers or professing believers, as to the seriousness of sinning? Indeed no, "judgment" must follow in the shape of chastening for the erring believer, and a "fiery indignation" for the apostate adversary; as some who had given up their faith had proved. The chastening would be in view of the restoration of the backsliding child of God; the "fiery indignation" as "vengeance" on the apostate adversary (see v. 30).

W.H.

Has the wilful sin of Heb. 10. 26 any link with the presumptuous sin of Old Testament times; and is it connected with the "forsaking of the assembling of yourselves together," mentioned in the preceding verse?

Under the Law the presumptuous or wilful sin was deliberate disobedience to, or rejection of, the Law. See it described in Numbers 15. 30, 31; and an illustration of it given immediately afterwards— the case of the man who gathered sticks on the Sabbath day. What he did seemed to be a very little thing; and had he been amongst us to-day, we might have described him as staying away from the "gathering together" that he might "gather sticks" instead. So little did it appear in the eyes of the leaders in Israel, that they made special inquiry of the Lord before they stoned him. But it was wilful sin against a known command, and had to be dealt with as such.

Similarly, under the Gospel the wilful sin must be the deliberate flouting and rejection of the Lord Jesus as offered in the Gospel. The "forsaking of the assembling together" may, like the gathering of the sticks, seem a small matter; but it is the rebellious attitude behind this that constitutes the sin.

To commit wilful sin under Law one required to have "the form of KNOWLEDGE and of TRUTH in the Law," spoken of in Rom. 2. 20. To commit wilful sin under the Gospel one must have received "the KNOWLEDGE of the TRUTH" in the Gospel, spoken of in Heb. 10. 26. The statement that follows in the latter verse, "There remaineth no more sacrifice for sins," suggests that the sin is of such a character as turns down the Sacrifice already offered; and this view is borne out by the description in verse 29 of the persons committing it. They have trodden under foot the Son of God, etc.

The "For" at the beginning of verse 26 associates it closely, though by way of contrast, with what has gone before. The professor who proves himself to be really saved is the one who continues to "draw near with a true heart" (v. 22); to "hold fast his confession" (v. 23); to "consider" his brethren that he may show "love and good works" towards them (v. 24) and to "not forsake the assembling together" (v. 25). On the other hand, he who takes the opposite course regarding all these matters proves himself to be not real (v. 26), but an "adversary" (v. 27). And the forsaking of the assembling is often the first clear outward proof of the direction in which such a one is going. A link with the presumptuous sin of the O.T. is implied in verses 28, 29. W.R.

Is it right to interpret the words in Heb. 12. 2: "Who for (anti) the joy that was set before Him, endured the cross despising the shame," as meaning that instead of accepting the joy that was offered Him on the Holy Mount of going back to heaven then and there without dying, He chose rather to die?

I think such a meaning is quite foreign to the verse. Endurance of suffering is the thought of the passage, not avoidance of it. It is true that "instead of," is more in accordance with the common meaning of the preposition "anti." This is a very important sense in such passages as Matt. 20. 28, or Mark 10. 45: "to give His life a ransom for (anti) many," as showing forth the substitutionary character of the death of Christ; at the same time this is not the only meaning of the preposition: there is also the distinct use—as in Matt. 5. 38; 17. 27, which fits in quite well here in Heb. 12. 2—of that **for which** anything is given or endured.

There can, I believe, be no reasonable doubt that this is the sense here. Indeed, I do not think that the suggested interpretation can, for a moment, be justified, though I am aware that a few names can be quoted as teaching it. But on what ground can it be asserted that some offer was made to our Lord of going back to heaven without dying, from the Holy Mount? This is pure speculation and quite unjustified at that, for not only had the Lord spoken clearly of His sufferings in the previous chapter (Luke 9. 22), but on the Mount the subject of His conversation with His servants Moses and Elias was **"His decease which He should accomplish at Jerusalem."** This is just one of those statements that sensation-mongers love to make on public platforms, but which have no scriptural authority. It is quite true that our Lord's death was a voluntary act, in obedience to His Father's command, and that it was not by a fatalistic decree. The Lord could say to Peter, "Thinkest thou that I cannot now pray to my Father and He shall presently give Me more than twelve legions of angels?" but then He adds at once, "but how then shall the Scripture be fulfilled, that thus it must be?" (Matt. 26. 53, 54). It was not the joy of escaping the cross (how could this be said to be set before Him?), but the joy that would result to Him from enduring the cross for the glory of God and for blessing to man. W.H.

What is the meaning of Heb. 12. 29?

In verses 18-24 of this chapter the writer dwells at length on the contrast between the old dispensation and the new, between Mount

Sinai and Mount Sion, between God speaking on earth in the giving of the Law and God speaking from heaven in the giving of His Son. Everything is terrifying in the picture he draws of the former, everything gracious and encouraging in his presentation of the latter.

Then from verse 24 onwards he warns his readers that this difference, instead of making the rejection of God's present testimony less perilous than the refusal of that former testimony, renders it all the more so; because, just as God's speaking in grace in His Son is so perfect that there can be no further addition to it, or repetition of it, such will also be the character of His speaking in wrath through His Son, when that takes place. It, too, will be "once for all."

This warning, and indeed the entire subject which has occupied the main body of the epistle, he concludes with the exhortation of verses 28, 29, "Wherefore, we receiving a kingdom which cannot be moved, let us have grace whereby we may serve God acceptably, with reverence and godly fear; for our God is a consuming fire."

The final clause of this, which forms verse 29, is a quotation from Deut. 4. 24, where it is used by Moses in warning Israel against apostasy, just as here it is used in similar warning to those to whom the epistle is written. The writer wishes to make clear that, though the dispensation may change, God changes not. He is as much a God of devouring fire (that is to say, a God of searching and righteous judgment) to-day as He was at Sinai; and that he has the comparison with its Old Testament occurrence definitely in mind is made plain by his use of a little word which neither the A.V. translators nor the Revisers thought worth rendering into English but which may be seen in Weymouth, Young, Newberry, etc. The clause literally is, "For **also** our God is a consuming fire."

The lesson here conveyed is one which was never perhaps more needed than in the present day; when everywhere is to be found a one-sided and therefore false conception of God, that ignores His character as the Righteous One whose judgment flames forth against all that is evil. The Old Testament examples of this should ever be kept in mind; the fire of God's presence which devoured Nadad and Abihu in Lev. 10. 2; the fire which consumed 250 men in Num. 16. 35, as well as the murmurers of Num. 11. 1; the fire that, in Isa. 33. 12-14, not only burned up Israel's enemies, but caused the sinners in Zion itself to cry out in their agony, "Who among us shall dwell with the devouring Fire?"

It is nice to see, framed on the walls in the homes of God's people, and in their Halls and Meeting Rooms, that wonderful message, "God is Love"; but one could wish at times that over against it were set up these other words, "Our God is a consuming Fire."   W.R.

What is meant by Heb. xiii. 13: "Let us go forth therefore unto him without the camp, bearing his reproach"? Does the word "camp" mean all the professing Church?

To answer this question we must read the immediate context. Verse 11 reminds us that the sin-offerings, of which the blood was brought into the holy place (i.e., for priest and for congregation, Lev. iv. 3. 13), were not eaten, but consumed by fire "without the camp" (see vv. 12 and 21). This happened, too, on the day of Atonement, to the bullock and goat, the blood of which was taken into the holiest (Lev. xvi. 14, 15). Both were burned "without the camp." When all were implicated and identified with the victim, there could be no communion, expressed by eating. The Lord Jesus, too, as the sin-offering, "that He might sanctify the people with His own blood, suffered without the gate," i.e., of "Jerusalem, the city which the Lord did choose . . . to put His Name there" (1 Kings xiv. 21). The Lord, the very embodiment of that Name, consented "to be led to the slaughter," "without the gate"; and there, too, in figure, He was "consumed." "Thou hast brought me into the dust of death" (Psa. xxii. 15). Could a Christian Hebrew find his place or portion in a city whence his Lord had been cast out? It represented the religious centre of the day. Outside that there was no "religion." We remember that they cast out the healed one of John ix, but Jesus found him (being already there Himself), revealed Himself to him, and made Him a worshipper. I cannot but feel that there is a supplementary reference here, namely, to the episode of Exod. xxxiii. 7: "Moses took the tabernacle (the tent of witness, distinct from the tabernacle, not yet set up), and pitched it without the camp . . . and it came to pass that everyone which sought the Lord went out unto the tabernacle of the congregation, which was without the camp." The camp was where the presence of Jehovah had been made known in the cloudy pillar, but it was defiled by the sin of the golden calf, and the pillar could no longer dwell there. Undoubtedly the camp represents the religious world grouped around "the god of this world." Christ is not in it. Is there place for one Christian where He is not? He is outside it all. "Let us go forth therefore (believing Jew or believing Gentile) unto Him, without the camp bearing His reproach." W.H.

Does the exhortation in Heb. 13, 13 to "go forth unto Him without the camp, bearing His reproach," imply that we are to come out from the sects and systems of men unto Christ Himself, and to stay out?

Yes, it certainly should "imply" this, although primarily the "camp," outside which the Hebrew Christians were to go, was that which Paul in Gal. 1. calls "the Jews' religion." If saints had to go outside a religion that bore such credentials as it did, much more should they go out from the modern systems that have no claim whatever to be of divine institution. As for the "staying out," the trouble with these Hebrew Christians was just that they seemed inclined to go back again; and the same trouble exists with many saints to-day.   W.R.

JAMES

Which James wrote the Epistle of that name?

It is generally agreed by those competent to judge, that the development of doctrine in the Epistle we are considering, precludes the authorship of James, the brother of John, who was slain by Herod, so early in the Acts period. This leaves us two other well-known men of this name, the son of Alphæus, one of the twelve apostles (see Matt. 10. 3; Acts 1. 13, etc.), and James, "the Lord's brother," who is called so by Paul in Gal. 1. 19, and is generally supposed to be the "James" to whom the Lord appeared after His resurrection (1 Cor. 15. 7).

Some would identify these two as the same, but surely Matthew 13. 55 precludes this. If it was true then that His brethren did not believe in Him subsequent to the call of the apostles, one of those brethren could not be included in their number. John 7. 5 shows that this James was not a believer in the Lord's Messiahship, at the moment then indicated. But it is likely that, when the Lord appeared to Him, he was converted and through him the rest of the family, who are mentioned in Acts 1. 14, along with the apostles, and Mary the mother of Jesus. The fact that the Epistle is ascribed simply to "James" seems to point to the brother of the Lord as author, for thus is he known in the Acts (chaps. 12. 17; 15. 13; see also Gal. 2. 9). He became a prominent leader—a "pillar"—in the church at Jerusalem (see Acts 21. 18; Gal. 2. 9). His speech to Paul in the former of these two passages gives us the impression of a man attached to the law, moral and ceremonial, a characteristic which fits in well with the practical righteousness (as distinct from legalism) of the Epistle.   W.H.

Please explain the last two verses of James 5. Is the sinner of verse 20 a brother in Christ; and if so how is his soul saved from death? Is it spiritual or physical death that is meant?

This is a passage that presents difficulty, whatever view of it be taken. If we think of the erring one as an unsaved person, we find it by no means easy to explain the first clause of verse 19, "Brethren, if any of you do err from the truth"; while if we look upon him as a real believer who has fallen into error or backsliding, we are up against that middle clause of verse 20, "to save a soul from death."

To meet the latter difficulty it has been suggested by some that the "death" referred to is death of the body, such as befell erring saints in 1 Cor. 11. 30. But one can scarcely imagine that to turn back a sinning Christian from continuance in his wrongdoing, before it causes God to shorten his earthly existence, would be described by the Holy Spirit as "to save a soul from death." Indeed it could not even be described as saving his body from death, since it would only be saving it from dying prematurely. And the unsatisfactory nature of this explanation becomes the more apparent, when we note that the only other occurrence of the word "soul" in James is in the phrase, "the engrafted Word which is able to save your souls"; and the only other use of the word "death" is in the statement, "Sin when it is finished bringeth forth death."

On the other hand, by taking the erring person to be unsaved, our trouble is with the opening clause of verse 19, "Brethren, if any of you." In this case some cut the knot by pointing out that the epistle is addressed to "The Twelve Tribes which are scattered abroad," whom James might well speak to as "brethren" according to the flesh, whether saved or not. Now there are passages in his letter, such as verses 1 to 6 of this last chapter, in which he does address unsaved ones; but, although he uses the word "brethren" more prominently than any other New Testament writer, it is not in these passages that it appears, but where he is evidently speaking to those who claim to be Christians. He makes it clear, however, that he is doing so on the ground of their profession; and while he calls them brethren," he insists that it is their works which must prove them to be real ones.

If then the person mentioned in verse 19 be unconverted, he must at least have been one who professed formerly to hold the truth. The Revised Version helps us a little by rendering the phrase "any of you" as "any among you," thus making it more indefinite; but in any case it is plain from 1 John 3. 14, 15 that a man may be spoken of as "brother," and yet turn out to be no real brother at all.

This interpretation of our verses I think on the whole to be the more probable one, since it is the only one that adequately explains the clause, "Shall save a soul from death" (i.e. by getting him truly converted to God); and it also makes it easier to understand the next clause, "Shall cover (R.V.) a multitude of sins" (i.e. in the same sense in which they are "covered" in Rom. 4. 7, by God's forgiveness).

It might be suggested that the other view, that physical death is meant, has in its favour the reference earlier in the chapter to sickness, which according to verse 15 might or might not be the result of sins committed. But even when the two closing verses are applied to the case of a professor who has turned back, and who is to be sought after with the object of getting him really saved; it is only a further development of the same line of teaching that James has been giving them. The connection of the parts of chapter 5 might be summarised thus. He begins it by pronouncing judgment on certain oppressors of the saints. Then he turns to urge upon the latter that they take these things patiently, as soon to be ended by the coming of the Lord, and as being used of Him for their training in the meantime. This suggests to him Job as an illustration of similar patience; and the mention of the patriarch in turn suggests sickness as part of the trial under which he was placed. That prayer for one another should be introduced at this point, cannot surprise us when we remember that it was when Job prayed for his friends that his own sickness was healed; nor in view of the old argument between them, as to whether sickness was the outcome of sins committed, can we wonder at the reference to this matter in verse 15. The thought of prayer in connection with restoration brings to mind another Old Testament illustration, that of Elijah who, in keeping with such Scriptures as Lev. 26. 19, 20; Deut. 11. 16, 17; and 1 Kings 8. 35, 36; prayed that rain might be withheld, so that by chastisement God's people might be restored in soul. Then, finally, James notices the worse case (if this view be the correct one), of one who by turning back has proved to be a mere professor, but who if rightly dealt with, may even yet be truly converted.   W.R.

Does James 5. 13-20 apply to a sick body or a sick spirit?

It seems to me that the special point of the sickness in this passage is that of a sick spirit in a sick body: and the latter the result of the former. The word here for "sick" (**astheneō**) is the same root as is applied to the Corinthian believers in 1 Cor. 11. 30, and there translated "weak"—the first stage of physical chastening at the hand of God. Not every physical ailment or sickness is to be explained in this way, far from it; but here it is so, as seems proved by the fact that the sick person summons the elders, not the physicians, to diagnose the case. All this is quite consistent with the prayer of faith, the possibility of sins having been committed and the promised forgiveness. In the case that follows in verse 16, there is no need of spiritual diagnosis, the case is too plain for that. Elders are not necessary; the confession of the fault can be made to any brother on the spot, who is also quite qualified to pray for the desired healing, for the prayer of any "righteous man," not necessarily an elder, "availeth much." Though the spiritual need is predominant in this passage, there is no possibility of questioning that physical sickness is there too—the outward and visible sign of the inward and spiritual complaint. The latter needs spiritual healing, the former, physical.   W.H.

I & 2 PETER

Who are meant by "The Dispersion" in 1 Pet. 1. 1 (R.V.), and how were they dispersed? Some say that they were the result of the persecution which arose after Stephen's death; but were they not rather the same as those who are so called in John 7. 35?

Yes, "The Dispersion" in 1 Pet. 1. 1 means the Jews dispersed in foreign countries, some of whose ancestors had been living in these places ever since the Captivity, while others had been scattered from time to time, during the persecutions to which the nation was subjected afterwards. The noun "diaspora," which is used here, occurs in only two other verses in the New Testament, James 1. 1 and John 7. 35; and in both these it is clear that the dispersed Israelites are meant. The verb form, "diaspeirō," is used, it is true, of a dispersion of the Christians in Acts 8. 1, 4 and 11. 19; but the term "The Dispersion" was a well known one among the Jews long before that.

It should be noticed that Peter does not address the "Dispersion" as a whole, but only "The elect who are sojourners of the Dispersion" in the places named; and he proceeds at once to remind them how their "election" took place, and with what result. In other words, he writes to those Jews in these foreign lands who had been saved through the preaching of the Gospel, mainly by Paul and his fellow-workers (see chap. 1. 12); and one of the aims he has before him in doing so, is to confirm them in the truth which Paul and the others had taught them. In pursuance of this he actually sends his epistle by the hand of one of these labourers who had been used amongst them, Silas or Silvanus (see chap. 5. 12).

Perhaps, however, we should not leave altogether out of consideration the fact that Jews from Pontus, Cappadocia, and Asia were present at Pentecost (Acts 2. 9) to hear Peter's own message. Some of these may well have been among the 3,000 converts of that day, and so may have carried back the Gospel to their friends.   W.R.

Does the expression "unto obedience and sprinkling of the blood" in 1 Pet. 1. 2 refer to a definite act, or to a progressive experience?

It refers to that "obedience of faith" by which we accept God's provision for us in the death of His Son, and are thereby brought into covenant relationship with Him. It may thus suggest a combination of the symbolic acts of Exod. 12. 7 and Exod. 24. 8. In the former the people's obedience is to be shown by striking the blood on their doorposts; while in the latter their promise of obedience in verse 7 is ratified by their being sprinkled with the blood in verse 8.

That it can mean nothing less than this is clear from its connection with the two preceding clauses of the verse, in which our election is said to be:—(1) ACCORDING TO the foreknowledge of THE FATHER; (2) THROUGH sanctification of THE SPIRIT; (3) UNTO obedience and sprinkling of the blood of JESUS CHRIST. Compare with this the somewhat similar statement in 2 Thess. 2. 13 "God hath chosen you to salvation, through sanctification of the Spirit, and belief of the truth."

The word "obedience" has frequently this gospel sense elsewhere, as for example in Rom. 1. 5; 15. 18; 16. 26. In 1 Peter we have, later in the epistle, quite a number of references to obedience and disobedience; and most of these are connected with acceptance or refusal of gospel testimony; while the remainder contain at least some hint of it. Thus in ch. 4. 17 we have it clearly before us in the expression "them that obey not the gospel"; and in ch. 3. 1, almost as clearly in, "if any obey not the word," evidently from the context, the word of the gospel. In ch. 2. 7, 8 "disobedient" is equivalent to "gospel rejecters"; while the same word in ch. 3. 20 suggests the turning down by the antediluvians of God's call to them through Noah, rather than their earlier wickedness to which the Flood was due, since it took place "while the Ark was a preparing," and while "the longsuffering of God" was waiting. In ch. 1. 22, "purified your souls in obeying the truth", refers back to the same time as "being born again" in the succeeding verse; and the term "obedient children" of ch. 1. 14 is literally, "children of obedience," that is, those who by the very fact of their coming into the family of God should be characterised by obedience—the opposites of the "children of disobedience" of Eph. 2. 2, etc.

The word used for obedience in verses 14 and 22 of ch. 1 is exactly the same as that in verse 2; and, putting them together, we learn that the obedience to the gospel which brings us into relationship with God, is manifested afterwards in our seeking to be holy as He is (vv. 14-17), and in love shown to others in the same relationship (vv. 22, 23).

W.R.

Does the word, "tradition," in 1 Pet. 1. 18 refer to "redemption by silver or gold" or to "vain conversation"?

There can be no doubt it refers to the latter, meaning I believe, the whole Jewish system of religion, not merely as delivered by God through Moses (though redemption from that legal system was needed), but as falsified and added to by the traditions of the fathers, which made the commandments of God of none effect (Matt. 15. 3, 6, 9). This was the atmosphere in which Peter had been born and brought up. There is always a tendency to add to the commandments of God by man's tradition (1 Tim. 4. 3), and to legislate and systematise where the Word of God is silent. The word to us to-day is "Stand fast therefore in the liberty, wherewith Christ hath made you free and be not entangled again in the yoke of bondage" (Gal. 5. 1). W.H.

Does the term, "a holy priesthood," in 1 Pet. 2. 5, include all Christians, or only those in assembly fellowship?

The matter of assembly fellowship is not given prominence anywhere in 1st Peter. It is a remarkable fact that, with the exception of his friend, Mark, he is the only one of the New Testament writers who never uses the word "Assembly" or "Church." 1 Peter 5. 13 is not a contradiction of this, as the italics there in the A.V. show.

The "holy priesthood" of 1 Peter 2. 5 clearly refers to the same people as the "spiritual house" of the preceding clause; and the method by which "living stones" are built into this "spiritual house," according to verse 6, is by believing on Christ. In verse 7, they are described as "you which believe," and contrasted with Christ-rejecters. In verse 9, the "holy (sacrificing) priesthood" of verse 5 is shown to be also a "royal (testifying) priesthood;" and in verse 10 the same persons are spoken of simply as "the people of God."

The present tense, "are built-up", in verse 5 is not against the above view. It is used, as the word "groweth" is used in Eph. 2. 21, of the progressive adding of more "living stones" to the great Building of which both these passages speak—a process which is still going on. "The Lord added to them, day by day, those that were being saved" (Acts 2. 47, R.V.). W.R.

What is meant by the word "oversight," 1 Pet. 5. 2? Can any brother, old or young, take the place of an overseer, or should a few qualified brethren be recognised?

The verb simply means "to look upon,"—"look after,"—"care for," and the true overseer is one who does it. (See 1 Pet. 5).

Certainly this does not mean that every brother, old and young alike, should be an overseer. The qualifications, laid down in 1 Tim. 3 and Titus 1, forbid this. These should be studied carefully. 1 Tim. 3 gives the moral characteristics necessary: v. 4, the capacity for rule exemplified by ability in the home; v. 6, the words "not a novice"— (lit. a neophyte—that is, a young convert)—limit the work to mature Christians, and he must have "a good report" of the world (v. 7), e.g., not a bankrupt, or one whose name appears in the papers as causing scandals. Again in Titus 1. 9, he must "hold fast the faithful word." When Paul sent for the Ephesian elders, it is clear that these men were known in the local church, and the apostle exhorts them, "Take heed to . . . all the flock, over the which the Holy Ghost hath made you overseers." Men may appoint "officials" over the people of God; only the Holy Ghost can make true overseers.   W.H.

Some teach that 2 Pet. 1. 5 should read as in the American Revision: "Yea, and for this very cause adding on your part all diligence, in your faith supply virtue, and in your virtue knowledge," because they say the Authorised Version: "Add to your faith virtue," "suggests a kind of mathematical process," which "supply" does not. Do you think we ought to have the R.V. quoted to us so frequently?

The American Revision is almost the same as the English R.V., with a few differences on which the two companies could not agree. The American Version is said to be slightly more conservative than the R.V. proper. We on our part do not reject every change in the R.V. simply because it is R.V.; that would be prejudice, and we know some of the changes are improvements, though far too many were made, as most agree. What we believe vitiates the R.V. is an unjustifiable tampering with such passages as 1 Tim. 3. 16 and 2 Tim. 3. 16, and also doubtful and dangerous suggestions in the margins. Supposing a gardener, brought in to dig and generally tidy up our garden where necessary, tried to make a new garden, which he was not asked to do, removing some beautiful rose-trees and sowing tares here and there, one would wish the good man had left the thing alone, and we cannot help sometimes registering this wish in the case before us. However, the above text, "for this very cause," is certainly more correct than, "besides all this," but I do not see that the objection to "add" need be taken too seriously, especially as the R.V. uses it in the line above for "giving" (!) As a matter of fact, "in your faith supply virtue," though doubtless nearer the original, does not seem itself more clear than "add to your faith virtue." I suppose it means—In the exercise of your faith, do not forget to add some other qualities—first virtue, then knowledge, and so forth. As for those who so constantly refer to the R.V. as though it were "the end of all strife," we need not believe it for that, but we must bear with them all the same, and not try their patience too much by quoting the A.V. to them, as though it were the final authority.   W.H.

Are the men mentioned in 2 Pet. 2. 1 really "delivered from the wrath to come," or are they only professors, who have given up their outward profession?

I believe the latter. Those who, bring in "damnable heresies" seem to come under 2 John 9.—"they abide not in the doctrine of Christ and have not God." It is true that they are said to have been **"bought"** by "the Lord" (despotēs), but this is a very general word; it does not say they were redeemed, a term only applied to the Lord's people. These are "false teachers," who through Christian influence and teaching have for a time "escaped the pollution of the world," but they not only have the flesh in them, as every true Christian has to his sorrow, but they are in the flesh, so they only "endure for a time." They never have been born again, though they have taken their place among the people of God and have passed even as preachers and teachers; but terrible to narrate, the proverb is true of them, "the dog is turned to his own vomit again and the sow that was washed to her wallowing in the mire." There was a turning away from sin, but it was only temporary; the dog nature loved it; there was an outward cleansing of the ways, but the **sow** nature, was all that was there.   W.H.

What promise is referred to in 2 Pet. 3. 4? ("Where is the promise of His coming?")

Verse 2 seems to give the key. The apostle reminds the saints "of the words which were spoken before by the holy prophets, and of the commandment of us the apostles of the Lord and Saviour." The order, prophets first, then apostles, shows, I think, that Old Testament prophets are meant.* The rest of the chapter seems to indicate the subject of the words in question—the day of the Lord, the return of Christ in glory, the judgment of God's enemies, and other events extending to the "new heavens and the new earth wherein dwelleth righteousness." The "coming" then referred to in the question would be, in the broadest sense, the Second Coming of Christ with all His saints. The expression, "the commandment of us the apostles," is more difficult, but may simply mean their exhortations to watchfulness and to a behaviour of "all holy conversation and godliness," suited to such an event. Before going into further details, the apostle warns them that in the last days, when these solemn happenings are about to take place, there shall be scoffers, characterised by two things—a life of self-indulgence and a scornful denial of any Personal return of the Lord. Religious scoffers they would be, with a knowledge of the letter of Scripture and of the promises therein contained. They speak of "the fathers" and are "**willingly** ignorant," so that they are not heathen, but men with the Old Testament at least within their reach, telling them, would they but listen, of God's dealings with men in past ages, e.g., at the flood, His present longsuffering and patience, and of His future purposes in judgment. To-day any Personal return of Christ to the earth is strongly denied by the religious world as a whole, on the ground which is demonstrably false, of what they call "continuity." This is a theory, elevated to the place of a dogma among these wise men

* For the reverse see Eph. 2. 20.

of the earth, that things have always continued in a natural fashion, without any direct intervention of a supernatural power, in the established order of things, That the exact opposite is the truth the very stones cry out, as well as history, sacred and profane. Let us, however, the apostle adds, seeing we look for Divine intervention in a very literal sense, in the future as in the past, be "diligent to be found of Him in peace without spot and blameless."   W.H.

What is the difference, if any, between the "Day of the Lord" and "the Day of God," in 2 Peter 3?

That they differ is, I believe, perfectly certain, but the fact is obscured by our A.V. translation, which translates two different Greek prepositions in verses 10 and 12, "en" and "dia," by the same English equivalent—"in which." This makes the "burning up of the earth" to occur both in the day of the Lord and the day of God. As the same unique event cannot take place in different periods, therefore the two periods are the same. The R.V. of verse 10 reads, however, "But **the day of the Lord** will come as a thief in the night; **in the which** the heavens shall pass away with a great noise"; and of verse 12, "the coming of the day of God, **by reason of which** (A.V. has "in the which") the heavens being on fire shall be dissolved." The expression, "by reason of which," is a little ambiguous, but approaches the literal sense—"owing to which," "in view of which," "for the sake of which"; that is, the burning up of the present heavens and earth is in view of the introduction of "the day of God"—quite a new order of things which necessitates a "new heaven and a new earth." "The day of the Lord" is a period in time prolonged but finite; it will end with the Great White Throne judgment, and just prior to that we read, "the earth and the heavens fled away, and there was found no place for them." This describes in figurative language the literal destruction by fire of the heavens and the earth. This will make room for the introduction of "the New Heavens and the New Earth" which will usher in "the Day of God"—the Eternal State. "The Day of the Lord" will not begin till the falling away or apostasy of the religious world, and the revelation of the Man of Sin, "that wicked one" (2 Thess. 2). It will be a very varied period, for it will contain the Apocalyptic judgments, the Great Tribulation and the day of Jacob's trouble, the revelation of the Lord in glory, the setting up of the throne of His glory, the judgment of the nations, and the whole course of the Millennial reign. It is very important to notice the change in the Revised Version in 2 Thessalonians 2. 2. There is practically no MS. authority for the A.V., "that the day of Christ is at hand," which ought to be, "the day of the Lord is now present." It would seem that so great were the persecutions through which the Thessalonians were passing that they thought that the great tribulation was then present. The A.V. makes the passage a strong argument for the pre-advent tribulation—the falling away and the revival of the Wicked One must precede the great tribulation. The apostle appeals to the fact of the "gathering together" (i.e., the rapture and His advent) of the church to show that what is subsequent to that, the tribulation, could not be present. The reading of the R.V. changes one of the strongest arguments for the post-tribulation Coming, into a strong argument for the pre-tribulation Coming. Whenever the apostasy has taken place and the Wicked One works, then will begin the day of the Lord—the greater part of which will be the Millennium —in which "righteousness will reign." In the day of God, all enemies will be put down, and "righteousness will dwell." W.H.

1 JOHN

Does the "beginning" mentioned in 1 John 1. 1 refer to the New Creation only? and was "eternal life" (v. 2) not manifested until the Lord's resurrection?

Before attempting to reply to these questions, which are in essence one, it will be well to say that this expression, "the beginning," in the New Testament is a very indefinite one, the meaning of which can only be determined by a close consideration of the context.

(1) For instance, in John 1. 1, the phrase goes back to a past Eternity, and is another way of saying, There never was a moment when the Word was not—"In the beginning was the Word." It asserts the Eternal Being of the Son. With this we may connect— because God's purposes are as eternal as Himself—the choice of the church (Eph. 3. 11) and the choice of the individual saint (2 Thess. 2. 13).

From that "beginning" we move forward to the "beginning" of Gen. 1. 1—

(2) "In the beginning God created the heavens and the earth." We have no revelation as to how long ago this act occurred. It is sep-arated, we believe, by an immense period from verse 2, which describes the condition of things existing in the earth when the Spirit of God took it in hand to refurbish it in its surface con-ditions. Not a word is said after verse 1 of the creation of the earth as a whole. It is the merest speculation to pretend to know the history of the world between its creation in verse 1 and its preparation for man in the rest of the chapter. It is a secret which belongs to the Lord our God.

(3) Next must be noticed a certain sinister "beginning"—that of sin. "The devil sinneth from the beginning" (1 John 3. 8). As to when this was, we can only say that it must have been between the beginning of creation in Gen. 1. 1 and the creation of man in verse 26. This could not be the devil's own creation, for Ezek. 28. 15 tells us "he was perfect in his ways, from the day that he was created, till iniquity was found in him." The beginning here spoken of is that of sin. Sin began with him. He bears that terrible responsibility.

(4) Next we note the beginning of man described by our Lord in Mark 10. 6, 7 thus: "In the beginning of the creation (i.e. of man) God made them male and female; for this cause shall a man leave his father and mother and cleave to his wife." He here combines two passages from Genesis—chap. 1. 27; 2. 24, conclusively showing that the two chapters do not represent two creations, but two accounts of one, general and detailed.

(5) Not only was Satan a sinner from the beginning, but he was a "murderer from the beginning." We might suppose these at any rate to be the same "beginnings," but if so we should be mistaken, as the word for "murderer" is literally "a slayer of men," which prevents our extending this to the fall of the angels, of which he seems to have been the determinant cause, but limits it to the fall of man.

(6) Now we come to the verse we are considering—1 John 1. 1. Notice, it is not the Person of Christ that is the subject of the sentence, for then it would be "He who"—whereas we read, "That which was from the beginning." I think the rest of the verse clearly shows that the Incarnation is in view, though it goes on to His ministry—their ears heard His voice, their eyes saw Him, they looked on Him, their hands handled of the Word of Life . . . "For the life was manifested and we have seen it and show unto you that eternal life Which was with the Father, and was manifested unto us." The Lord did not become that "eternal life" in resurrection, nor yet at incarnation. He was it from all Eternity and was manifested as such as the Babe at Bethlehem, and through His life and ministry, for men's eyes to behold, for men's hearts to love. In that Babe was manifested a Divine Person—the Mighty God.

There are three other cases of the word "beginning," which we may refer to in closing.

(7) John 15. 27 and 1 John 2. 7 refer back to the "beginning" of our Lord's ministry.

Does the teaching of 1 John 2. 2 in any way clash with the eternal choice of Eph. 1. 4? Is the whole world chosen?

Much time has been wasted in trying to "reconcile" such Scriptures as the ones quoted above. We need not "reconcile," but believe them both equally. We are not called, however, to apprehend them both equally at first. I think we should be right in saying that until we have had to do with the truth of 1 John ii. 2, "He is the propitiation . . . for the whole world" (see R.V.), we have nothing to do with Eph. i. 4, "Chosen in Him before the foundation of the world." We do not come to Christ on the ground of election, as some mistaken people try to do, waiting for some sign or vision that will give them hope that they are of the elect, on which ground they trust that the Lord may receive them. It has been well said, "Directly your belief in election shapes or colours your gospel, you hold election wrongly." It is the glory of Christ's work and of the Gospel that proclaims it, that it is free to all, as well as sufficient for all. "Go into all the world, and preach the Gospel (not to the elect but) to every creature. He that believeth and is baptized shall be saved; he that believeth not shall be damned." "Whosoever will, let him take the water of life freely," is written outside the door of salvation; "Chosen in Him," inside. It is sufficient for all, efficient for all who believe. We hold both truths fully and entirely.   W.H.

Did Christ die for the sins of believers only (in the light of 1 John 2. 2) or could we say to a sinner that Christ died for his sins on the Cross?

I believe it is very serious error to limit the atonement of Christ to believers. "He is the propitiation for our sins **and not for our sins only, but also for the whole world.**" There is sufficient value in the atonement of Christ to meet the need of every sinner of the human race who ever breathed, and not only so, "God will have all men to be saved and to come to the knowledge of the truth"; "He is not willing that any should perish, but that all should come to repentance." Christ "gave Himself a ransom for all." Potentially then all may be saved, therefore the work of Christ must have made this possible to the justice of God. No one will be able to say, I wished to be saved, but God would not save me, for He had provided no Saviour for me. Directly our doctrine of election limits the potential application of the work of Christ or of our gospel invitation, our doctrine is wrong. But when it comes to the question of bearing sins it would not be apostolic or scriptural to say to the unconverted "all your **sins have been borne by Christ.**" That is the family secret revealed in the epistles—"Who His own self bare our sins in His own body on the tree (1 Pet. 2. 24). Isa. 53. 6 is not out of harmony with this. There, the speakers are Jehovah's witnesses, and of course, believers. They admit their wanderings, they self-will, and they glory in the fact that the Lord hath laid on Him the iniquity of them all. The gospel the apostles preached to the unsaved was a proclamation of Christ dead and risen, and through Him, in answer to faith, forgiveness and justification to all; but as we learn from 1 Cor. 15, where he reminds them of the gospel he had preached to them, he did not shrink from saying, "Christ died for our sins, according to the Scriptures; He was buried and the third day He rose again according to the Scriptures."

Certainly a preacher would be right in following the apostle's example. Many illustrations, however, as to payment of debts, etc., are very defective. They make out that Christ in dying has actually paid the debt of every sinner. If so, of course, every sinner's debt is paid, though the Word of God never says such a thing. Further, every sinner is saved whether he believes or not and can claim salvation as a right due to him, which no regenerate soul would ever do. If such a simile must be used, the truth would rather be, that the whole world was hopelessly in debt, that Christ in dying provided a full atonement, amply sufficient to cover the delinquencies of all; but that it is only those who confess their indebtedness, and trust in the Mediator, who share in the benefits of His work, i.e., in having their debts paid.   W.H.

What do the words, "we shall be like Him; for we shall see Him as He is" (1 John 3. 2) imply? Surely this cannot mean that all the saints will be so like the Lord as not to be told apart, and if it is perfect moral likeness, why strive for such now?

We know that, whatever this verse may mean, there will be **bodily** likeness between the redeemed and the Lord, as Phil. 3. 21 shows.

It seems evident, however, that such likeness does not entail a loss of identity, but something corresponding to what we know as family likeness. We are "predestined to be conformed to the image of His Son, that He might be the first-born among many brethren" (Rom. 8. 29), which can only mean that He may be recognised as the first-born by the likeness to Him of all the members of the family. We have important details of this in 1 Cor. 15, in reference, (1) to the resurrection, and, (2) to the changing of living saints. Speaking of the former, the Spirit says of the believer's body—"It is sown a natural body; it is raised a spiritual body" (v. 44). Then again, "As is the earthy, such are they also that are earthy: and as is the heavenly, such are they also that are heavenly. And as we have borne the image of the earthy (and we do all bear the image of the first Adam, in the sense of the family likeness, but not the absolute likeness), we shall also bear the image of the heavenly," (vv. 48, 49), that is, of the last Adam. But then the question arises how about the living saints when the Lord comes?

They will not sleep, but will all be changed. They will put on bodily immortality, whereas the sleeping saints will put on incorruptibility. I do not judge that this entails any difference in the final result. All will have the same spiritual body, but arrived at by the two processes just described. In 1 John 3 it simply says, "we shall be like Him," which seems to include spirit, soul and body—but just as there are degrees of likeness in a human family, probably the degree there will depend upon the degree attained here. **"Homoios"**, the word translated "like" here, does not imply absolute identity with, but something comparable to; as a reference to the following passages will show; see Matt. 11. 16; Matt. 13. 31, 33, 44, etc.; John 9. 9:—"He is **like** Him"; Rev. 1. 13, **"like** unto the Son of Man." W.H.

What is the difference between loving "in word" and "in tongue" (1 John 3. 18)?
It is a case of parallelism; "word" in the first member of the verse corresponding with "deed" in the second, and "tongue" with "truth." The man who loves in "word" is genuine as far as he goes, he really does mean what he says, but he is unpractical, he forgets that something more than words are needed, he forgets to translate them into deeds. He says, "Be ye warmed and filled" (James 2. 16), and supposes some· one else will send the coal and food. The man who loves in "tongue," does not intend to do anything, or put himself out in the least. He does not mean what he says. "Eat and drink, saith he to thee (perhaps); but his heart is not with thee" (Prov. 23. 7). W.H.

Is 1 John 5. 7 an interpolation? Is the weight of authority against its being genuine?
I am sure we cannot be too jealous lest anyone filch from us a single verse that forms part of the Divine revelation. We, by grace, love the Word of our God, and will not yield up one jot or tittle thereof, unless we are persuaded it is an interpolation of man—some careless or officious scribe—who only put a note in the margin, which was afterwards mistakenly incorporated by some succeeding copyist. Now this is, I believe, without doubt, the case with verse 7 of 1 John 5, which treats of the "three heavenly witnesses." These words occur in none of the great uncial manuscripts, Sinaiticus, Alexandrinus, Vaticanus, etc., and only in two "cursive" manuscripts of the 15th and 16th centuries, against 172 which omit them. Dr. Ellicott speaks of these words as "a gloss;" Dr. Alford says "there is not a shadow of a reason for sup-posing them genuine." J. N. Darby omits them in his critical version, and no copy of the Vulgate has them till the eighth century. Bengel is the only commentator of note, I can find, who upholds them. Besides lacking authority, the words hardly seem relevant. The three witnesses

on earth fit in harmoniously with what has just gone before, but the three witnesses in heaven rather interrupt the argument. What do they say and how does it affect what has been said in verse 6? Never in John's writings, nor in any other of the New Testament, do you get "Father" and "Word" together, but "Father" and "Son." How does the witness of the Holy Ghost in heaven add up to that of the Spirit on earth? There is, moreover, no real correspondence between "these three agree in one," and "these three are one." The R.V. omits this verse, but restores the whole of verse 23 of chap. ii, upon which our A.V. translators had wrongly cast doubt by putting it into italics.   W.H.

What is taught in 1 Cor. 11. 30; James 5. 14; 1 John 5. 16? Is it spiritual death, physical death, or are both referred to in these chapters?

Certainly the reference in 1 Cor. 11. 30 is to physical death, and only that; the Lord was judging the Corinthians for their unworthy participation in the Lord's Supper, "that they should not be condemned with the world." But they are not all dealt with at once, or in the same degree; there is a gradation in the Lord's dealings: "For this cause many are weak (that is, they experience physical weakness without definite disease) and sickly among you (these are laid low with known complaints), and many sleep." "Sleep" is the word **Koimaō** from which our word "cemetery" is derived. It is the word habitually used of the passing away of believers; e.g. Lazarus—"our friend Lazarus **sleepeth**" (John 11. 11.); "them that **sleep** by Jesus" (1 Thess. 4. 14), etc. In James 5. 14 the sickness is clearly physical. (The word is from the same root as that translated above—"weak").

The passage in 1 John 5 is more difficult. Some believe that physical death is meant; thus a man may have been chastened by the Lord, as the Corinthians were, and may have paid no heed and refused to amend his ways. He may reach a point where he is past praying for. He is to be cut off in death, or in other words, He will sleep. Though this be true, I am inclined to think both physical and spiritual may be intended. It is not said that "the **brother**" sins a sin unto death. He may grievously depart, but still there is hope. Such an one is not passed praying for; but on the other hand, there is a far more serious sin, which may be mistaken for backsliding, but is widely different. It is for professors the sin of apostasy. The apostate can never be restored; he becomes an adversary and would never seek restoration. In Hebrews 10. 25, there is a "forsaking the assembling," which may mean temporary departure. In that case the Lord will judge His backsliding people, in view of their restoration; but it may develop into total apostasy, and for that there is only "fiery indignation." Of those who have become apostates the solemn word is spoken, "vengeance is mine, I will repay, saith, the Lord"

(vv. 25, 27, 30). This seems more in accord with John's line of thought (e.g., ch. 2. 9) than a question of physical death.   W.H.

What is "the sin unto death" in 1st John 5. 16; and have we any Biblical examples of it?

The view which appears to be generally held with regard to the "sin unto death" is that it is any sin so flagrant, or so persisted in, that because of it the Lord sees fit to cut off the offender by death of the body. If this view be correct, the fate of some of the sinning Corinthians, as mentioned in 1 Cor. 11. 30 ("For this cause . . . many sleep"), is of course an example of it, and so, perhaps, is the death of Ananias and Sapphira.

I cannot say, however, that this view satisfies me. The tone and trend in 1st John are altogether different from that in 1st Corinthians. The latter is mainly occupied with sins and failures of real saints, but the former with the marks which distinguish the children of God from the children of the devil. Moreover, when Paul speaks of "life" (Gr., zoe) he may, and sometimes does, refer to the earthly life, which terminates with the death of the body; but John, in whose writings we get the word no less than 64 times out of 134 it occurs in the New Testament, never once employs it with merely this signification; unless, as the above view would imply, he does so here in 1 John 5. 16. For if the "death" in this passage be the death of the body, the "life" in verse 16 would necessarily be the present life; and I find it not easy to believe that on this one occasion only, John varies from his usual custom, especially as it would render the statement almost meaningless. If as is predicated in the words which precede and which follow the phrase, "He shall give Him life," the case prayed for is that of one who has sinned "NOT unto death," the promise that he shall be given "life" as a result of the prayer seems unnecessary.

I therefore incline to accept the view, suggested by various commentators, that the kind of sin present to John's mind as "sin unto death" is the rejection of Christ's claims as the Son of God. That he thinks of this sin is plain from his references to it in ch. 2. 22, 23; 2nd John 7-11; etc.; and from the fact that his Gospel appears to have the vindication of these claims for its main object (see John 20. 31). Doubtless by the time John's writings were penned, heresies with regard to the "doctrine of Christ" were beginning to arise; and it is clear that the apostle was deeply moved about them, and considered them to be fundamental error, the propagators of which were putting themselves outside the pale of God's mercy, and could only have a "fearful looking for of judgment and fiery indignation, which shall devour the adversaries."

Looked at thus, the "sin unto death" would not be very different in kind from what the Lord Jesus spoke of as blasphemy against the Holy Spirit and in Mark 3, 29, R.V., described as "an eternal sin." For the context there, in verse 22 and especially in verse 30, shows us that in this case too a rejection of the claims of Christ is involved. It would also be to some extent similar in character and effects to the sin described in Heb. 6. 6 and Heb. 10. 29.

I am well aware this view also has its difficulties, but to me at least they appear much less than those besetting the other. And the point usually relied upon, that the person concerned is called in verse 16 a "brother," has no weight with me. It is noticeable that it is only in connection with the alternative of having sinned "NOT UNTO DEATH" this the term is used of him; and besides this, we have in ch. 3. 14, 15 a clear example of one being classed nominally as a "brother," until his conduct proves that he has no claim to the title, because he has not "eternal life abiding in him." Another difficulty, inherent in the first mentioned view, is that of deciding whether or not the sinner has sinned "unto death," but it would scarcely ever arise in connection with the second.   W.R.

3 JOHN

What is the meaning of "taking nothing of the Gentiles," in 3 John 7? How can this apply to the Lord's servants in receipt of gifts from Gentile assemblies, or from individuals, who are not Jews?

The word here translated "Gentiles" is not the usual one for Gentiles or nations, which is **"ethnos,"** whereas this word is an adjectival form, **"ethnikos,"** which occurs only in the following three other places: Matt. 5. 47 (R.V.)—"do not even the Gentiles the same?" Matt. 6. 7 (R.V.)—"use not vain repetitions, as the Gentiles do"; Matt. 18. 17 (R.V.)—"let him be unto thee as the Gentile" (which has better authority than "an heathen man," A.V.).

This word signifies something more than being a Gentile by birth; it implies moral resemblance—"Gentilish" brings out the thought. This agrees with the dictionary meaning assigned to **"ethnikos"**— "savouring of the nature of pagans, alien to the worship of the true God —heathenish" (see Grimm). Naturally we cannot, nor are we expected to divest ourselves of a certain relation to our native land. The Jew continues nationally a Jew, the German a German, the Briton a Briton, but these differences are not recognised in our Church relations. There, "there is neither Jew nor Greek," though churches composed of Gentiles are once, for a special purpose, called "churches of the Gentiles" (Rom. 16. 4). The expression here was a graceful compliment to

Aquila and Priscilla, who though "Jews by nature," had the gratitude of "all the churches of the Gentiles." But even admitting such an expression, the word is "Gentiles" (**ethnē**) not "Gentilish" (**ethnikos**). Where the word is "Gentilish," we could not apply it to Christian Gentiles, for such do lose the characteristic traits which would mark them as "Gentilish," and seek rather to manifest the mind of Christ. In our passage in 3rd John the expression means:—"taking nothing from the world, or its resources". Probably the contrast is between such and heathen priests whose habit it was to make begging tours, and of course accept from all and sundry for their god—a pattern too generally followed to-day. In the Acts the support of a servant of the Lord going forth to the work is never raised. In the epistles the responsibility of his support is attached to his fellow saints, and especially to those who benefit or have benefitted by his spiritual labours. "He who proclaims the gospel should live of the gospel" (1 Cor. 9. 14). This is a right, which Paul did not always use, to stop the mouths of those who accused him of "profiteering." Again, those who were "taught in the word, were to communicate to the teacher in all good things" (Gal. 6. 6); and "the elders that ruled well" were to be "counted worthy of double honour, especially those that labour in the word and doctrine" (1 Tim. 5. 17), where it would seem that the "honour" included support. Paul in several places—Corinth, Ephesus, Thessalonica—worked with his own hands to supply his needs and those of others. No one accused him of stepping aside from the path of faith in so doing, though some to-day would perhaps have done so. Sometimes we hear it said, "If the Lord has sent so and so, He will support him," but the argument is rather:—"therefore we should support him." Let everyone do what he can, and not leave it to the supposed "well-off," who are so few and far between to-day.   W.H.

JUDE

Please explain Jude 16, especially the last clause.

This verse means exactly what it says, and does not appear to present much difficulty. The persons Jude has in mind, and whom he seven times speaks of as "THESE" (verses 7 (R.V.), 8, 10. 12, 14, 16, 19), and describes from various points of view in his little epistle, are in verse 16 pictured as dissatisfied with God, with His people, and with their own lot ("murmurers and complainers"), but well satisfied with themselves ("speaking great swelling words"). There are, however, some to whom they will cringe and give place and honour, those through whose influence they hope to gain something. In the R.V., the final clause of the verse is, "Shewing respect of persons for the sake of advantage," a rendering which links their sin in this matter with that which is so strongly condemned in James 2. 1–10 and other Scriptures, and which, unfortunately, is still all too prevalent amongst certain of the Lord's people.   W.R.

THE REVELATION

Is it correct or scriptural, in view of Rev. 1. 5 and 3. 14, where the Greek word "martus," is used of Him, to state that the Lord Jesus "died a martyr's death?"

It entirely depends on what is meant by that statement. It is one not found in the Scriptures; and when we use phrases concerning Christ's sufferings and death which are NON-Scriptural, we are on unsafe ground, since they may readily turn out to be ANTI-Scriptural as well. And little need there is for our doing so, since there is such a variety of Biblical phrases concerning it among which we may make choice.

The Greek word "martus" means simply a "witness" or "testimony-bearer," and does not in itself convey the slightest suggestion that the testimony borne results in the death of the one who bears it. Out of about 34 times it occurs in the New Testament, there are just three in which our English A.V. renders it "martyr," Acts 22. 20, Rev. 2. 13, and Rev. 17. 6; and the reason it does so in these is evidently because the witnesses referred to did suffer death for their testimony. The R.V. alters to "witness" in the text of the first two, and in the margin of the third; while all recent versions which aim at accuracy, as Darby's, Young's, Rotherham's, Weymouth's, etc., render "witness" in each place.

On the other hand, the English word "martyr," though transliterated from the Aeolic form of the Greek "martus," is never used to signify "witness" merely, but means "one whose witness has resulted in suffering or death." Indeed in colloquial speech it has become further debased to mean no more than "sufferer," as in the expression, "M—— is a martyr to rheumatism." It is therefore a mistake to think of the Greek word "martus" and the English word "martyr" as though they were synonymous.

Now, if a person who states that Christ died a martyr's death means nothing more than that the men who crucified Him did so because of His testimony, it is so far true. But if the statement is meant to convey that His death was nothing more than that of a martyr, it is fundamentally unsound. And since there is a danger that, even though the one who uses the phrase means it in a sense that is sound, the one who hears it or reads it may take it in a sense which is unsound; would it not be safer to refrain from using it at all, and to employ only the phraseology of the Scriptures in speaking of such a subject?   W.R.

Is Alford's translation of Rev. 1. 19—"write the things which thou sawest, and what things they signify, and the things which are about to happen after these"—reliable? If so, the verse does not furnish the divisions of this Book.

Alford based this on a point in the Greek, which is somewhat technical, and either escaped the notice of our translators and of the revisers, or had no real importance in their eyes. Dr. Ellicott too, to mention only one commentator of many, a Greek scholar of authority, takes no notice in his N.T. Commentary of the possibility of such a change. But even if we accepted Alford's translation, we should still, by his own showing, have to begin the next division of the book, at chap. iv. 1; he refers to the "meta tauta" (after these things), which occurs twice in that verse (translated "hereafter" in chap. i. 19), and thus linking the two verses. But if John is told to write "the things he had seen," that is the vision of chap. i, and "*what they signify*"—this latter is contained in the last verse of chap. i, and in that only; it is difficult to see in what sense chaps. ii and iii can be said to give the signification of chap. i. They rather contain a new and distinct subject—the messages of the Lord to the seven churches—representing, as many believe, not only seven Christian churches then existing, but a panorama of the church from early to last days. These two chapters would then be a hiatus, not referred to at all in verse 19. It seems, therefore, more Scriptural and natural to keep the translation as we have it in A.V. and R.V., and our threefold division as usually understood.   W.H.

What does "leaving thy first love" mean? (Rev. 2. 4.)

The Ephesian Church, representing in the panorama of Rev. 2 and 3 the apostolic era, had many things which Christ could approve: works, labour, patience, intolerance of evil persons, careful testing of pretenders to apostolic gifts, etc., but there was one thing the saints had lost, which the Lord desires above all else, and for the lack of which nothing could compensate, namely, their love to Himself. This they had shown at the first in a pre-eminent degree, but their activities had refrigerated their affections. This would never do. The Lord wants our **hearts**, even more than our **hands**, our **love** than our **zeal**. This is touchingly illustrated in the Old Testament by Jehovah's plaint concerning Israel (Jer. 2.): "I remember thee, the kindness of thy youth, the love of thine espousals, when thou wentest after me in the wilderness, in a land that was not sown" (i.e., with no earthly prospects). As the result of their love the people were characterised by that which marked the High-Priestly mitre—"Holiness unto the Lord," and brought joy to His heart, like the first fruits of His increase (see chap. 24. 2). But alas they left their first love, as these others did later. The call then comes to remember whence they had fallen, to repent and do the first works,

or in other words, do their works with the first love; else He will take
their candlestick of testimony out of its place. The Lord adds one word
of approval, showing how He delights to praise His people when possible. They had lost their first love, but not their first hate. "But this
thou hast that thou hatest the deeds of the Nicolaitanes, which I also
hate." The very idea of hating anything seems abhorrent to certain
minds, as quite contrary to Christian love, but the Lord commends
this fallen church at any rate for that.   W.H.

Is it justifiable to say that the word "Nicolaitanes" of Revela-tion (chap. ii. 6. 15) refers to clerisy or priestcraft?

In the letters to the seven churches there is the mystic foretelling of
our Lord, and this is seen not least in the symbols used, such as "Synagogue of Satan," "Balaam," "Satan's throne," "Antipas," "Jezebel,"
"Nicolaitanes." There is no proof that there ever was a sect of the
Nicolaitanes, far less that Nicolas, the "deacon" of Acts vi, founded
it. It has been held by many teachers of God's Word that to get at the
significance of the word, we must consider the meaning of the name,
also its association with the other symbol used in the letter, viz.,
Balaam; "Nicolaitanes" means "the conquerors of the people." Balaam,
"the devourer of the people." In v. 6 the Lord refers to their "deeds,"
here in v. 15, to their "doctrine." Nicolaitan is simply Balaam's Greek
equivalent. What is said concerning the churches in which the symbol
is found helps us much in understanding the symbol, as well as its association with Balaam. In the Pergamos period clerisy was rampant. In
the Ephesian period it was seeking a strong footing. Ignatius wrote a
letter to Ephesus about twelve years after the sending of John's message,
in which he supports clerisy in very extravagant terms, exhorting the
saints to look on their bishop as they would on the Lord Himself. In
his letter to the Magnesians he says, "As the Lord does nothing without
the Father, so the church should do nothing without their bishop,
whether he be presbyter, deacon, or layman." In the Pergamos period,
at the Council of Nice, there were 318 bishops present. These signed
the church over to Constantine, denied the Headship of her Lord, and
accepted by solemn deed and signature the headship of Constantine,
and with it the royal patronage of Rome. Clerisy to-day, as then, makes
all this and more possible, whether it be found in the Great Whore
herself, or in the State Church, her eldest daughter, or in Nonconform-
ity, her younger children. The man of God will flee all this, as that
which the Lord hates.   W.H.

Should there be any doubt in a believer's mind as to the correctness of the exposition, usual amongst us, of Rev. 2 and 3, as setting forth successive phases of the development

of the professing church from the Apostle's days until the Rapture?

There are not a few prophetical expositions amongst us, concerning which some of us have our doubts; but, so far as the present writer is concerned, the applicability of the seven messages in Rev. 2 and 3 to seven successive stages of development in the history of the church is not one of them. The agreement between the one and the other is too close to be accidental; and this will be particularly felt in the case of the first four messages, which deal with times sufficiently remote from our own to permit of an unprejudiced judgment. The period of decline in first love, while as yet truth was manfully contended for; the period of the great persecutions; the period of making alliances with the world and its rulers; the period when religion became fully fledged idolatry; all these are easily identifiable in the messages and in the history.

In ch. 1. 19 John is instructed to write of three separate matters: (1) "the things which thou hast seen"; (2) "the things which are"; and (3) "the things which shall be hereafter (lit., 'after these things')." Now it is evident that No. 1 refers to what John has already described in this first chapter—the vision of Christ Himself. And the words in ch. 4. 1, "Come up . . . I will show thee the things which must be here-after (lit., 'after these things')," imply that it is at this point we pass from No. 2 to No. 3; that is to say, from the present church period with which chapters 2 and 3 are occupied, to the things which take place afterwards. But if this be so, it is only to be expected that chapters 2 and 3 will in some sense cover the whole Church period; and the idea of it doing so in seven successive stages is the most natural one, and is in keeping with the use made afterwards of three more groups of seven—seals, trumpets, and vials—in connection with a later time.

Yet for all this the contemporary and local aspect of the messages should never be lost sight of, which is that the apostle had before his mind seven assemblies then existing, to which they were to be sent, and each of which, in some degree, must have corresponded to the message written concerning it. Nor should the broadest view of all be left out of consideration, namely, that in the seven messages taken together we are given at least some indication of all the evils that ever afflicted or will afflict the church.

Another interesting feature, which seems to have escaped the notice of most commentators, is that by an inverted parallelism amongst the seven messages, the first and seventh, the second and sixth, and the third and fifth, are respectively linked together, while the middle one to Thyatira stands by itself. Compare the loss of "first love" at Ephesus with the "lukewarm" state of Laodicea, and the "I will remove thy candlestick out of his place" with "I will spue thee out of My mouth."

Compare how neither Smyrna nor Philadelphia is found fault with, how in each case reference is made to "them which say they are Jews, but are of the synagogue of Satan," and how to the one it is said, "I will give thee a crown," and to the other, "Let no man take thy crown." And lastly, compare the "I will come and fight," written to Pergamos, with "I will come as a thief," written to Sardis, and the promise, in the one case, of a "white stone" and a "name," and in the other of "white raiment" and a "name."   W.R.

How would you explain the words, "I will not blot out his name out of the book of life"? (Rev. 3. 5). Do they not seem to raise a question out of harmony with John 10. 27, 28: "My sheep . . . shall never perish"? Was the name of Judas ever in the book of life?

Had the statement run, "I will blot out his name, etc.," the question might legitimately have been raised, but as it stands, the promise is framed in the strongest form of negative—"I will never, never blot out his name, etc." Perhaps the difficulty arises from emphasising the "his," as though the names of others could be erased. But such a thing is never contemplated. The only passage that seems to teach it: Rev. 22. 19, ought by every authority to have "tree of life," not "book of life," i.e., such will be shut out from what they had not attained to, rather than deprived of what they had attained to. The state of Sardis was very low. There were no moral scandals, no doctrinal departures, no divisions, but simply "a name to live and yet dead." Not that all were in that state, but many were. As one has said, "the church registers at Sardis had been badly kept," and the names of dead professors must sooner or later be expunged. But to His own, who gave proof of their reality, the Lord gave the strongest assurance, that He would never blot out their names from His book of life.

Dead professors, such as Judas, though they may have had the credit of having their names inscribed in heaven, and have taken for granted it was so themselves, had never been registered in the book of life. The Lord knew from the beginning that he was "a devil," and would betray Him. It is noteworthy that our Lord could say to the seventy on their return, what he did not say to the twelve, "Rejoice because your names are written in heaven": They had no Judas among them. We may well lay to heart the solemn words: "The Lord knoweth them that are His. And, Let every one that nameth the name of Christ depart from iniquity!"   W.H.

It has been said that, "In Revelation 4 we have a picture of heaven void of Christ," or words to that effect. Is such a theory scriptural?

This is rather an involved question, the answer to which depends on the meaning which is attached to these words. Certainly no one is asked to believe that our Lord was corporeally in heaven during His earthly ministry, as He is now; but to say that therefore heaven was empty of Him is a crude and, as we believe, a quite inadmissible statement, demonstrably mistaken in fact, unless indeed, we are asked to accept the altogether heretical view that our Lord was in some way bereft of His Divine attributes during His earthly ministry, and had therefore ceased to be Himself. To say that our Lord retained His Divine attributes, and yet could not be in heaven, when on earth, is to assert and deny in the same breath His Personal omnipresence. It really denies, however unwittingly, that He was a Divine Person, or at any rate it divides His Personality into two—a Divine, which practically ceased to be when He was on earth, and a human, which was in point of fact the sole factor. Such teaching, would of course be also serious heresy. No, He was always a Divine Person, with two whole and perfect natures, with both of which His Personality was equally associated. Corporeally our Lord was on earth, and not in heaven, but who could limit His Divine nature? Nay, He Himself asserts in no uncertain terms "and (linking the words with what have just gone) no man hath ascended into heaven, but He that came down from heaven, even the Son of Man, **which is in heaven**" (John 3. 13*—lit., "**the One being** in heaven"). With this we may compare the words of John 1. 18: "The only Begotten, which is in the bosom of the Father," where the same striking phrase occurs—"**The One being** in the bosom of the Father." Of this, Chrysostom, who may be supposed to be sufficiently acquainted with Greek to express a judgment writes: "The present participle—(the One) **being,** is used to signify **essential truth** without any particular regard to time." Truly the Person of Christ is inscrutable. We may refer to this matter again, but now we will limit ourselves to the enquiry as to whether, on any showing, it can be rightly said that "heaven as described in Rev. 4. was void of Christ." We believe such an idea to be quite erroneous, and that Scripture specifically conveys to us the thought that Christ is both heard and seen in heaven in Revelation 4, which in no sense represents His ministry on earth. At the beginning of the chapter the Apostle John is called up into heaven, by a voice which says, "Come up hither, and I will shew thee things which must be hereafter." What was this heavenly voice?

The Apostle tells us it was "the first voice which he heard, as it were of a trumpet talking with him." This refers us back to chap. 1, where we learn that this voice was that of the Son of Man—the Lord Jesus

---

* The great preponderance of ancient authorities, and of modern editors stand by the statemen in John 3. 13, as it appears both in the Authorised Version and Revised Version texts.

Christ Himself. There he was seen in the midst of the churches, but now in chapter 4, HE IS IN HEAVEN, for His words are not, "Go up thither!" but "Come up hither!" Moreover, not only is He there speaking, but He is seen on the throne in His Creator glory; for what other Divine Person could be thus visible, only the Second Person of the Godhead, the Lord Jesus—"the Son of Man who is in heaven"? Is it not clear that the idea here combated is mistaken, both in a theological and absolute sense? The Lord was in heaven in His Divine Nature, even while He was on earth; He was in heaven also in a corporeal sense at the time described in Revelation 4.   W.H.

Who are the four living creatures of Rev. 4?

Three points are important in considering this question, which, as a matter of interpretation, we have no desire to treat dogmatically. The first is that the cherubim, whom these four beings seem to represent, are always in Scripture the guardians of God's throne. The next is that this guardianship does not seem to be always vested in the same persons. Sometimes they are angelic beings as in Gen. 3—"who kept the way of the tree of life" (Satan himself was one—"the cherub who covered"— in pre-Old Testament times, see Ezek. 28); whereas here they are different from the angels, and join the redemption song with the twenty-four elders. The third point is that the description of heaven in Rev. 4, is not exhaustive; for instance there the sea of glass is untenanted, and it is only in chapter 14 that we see it filled with those who have gained the victory over the Beast (chap. 15. 2, 3). It is not necessary therefore to try to find some company in our chapter to represent the Old Testament saints. My own belief is that they are not seen in this chapter which, following so closely on chapters 2 and 3, shows us the subject of those chapters in their heavenly condition. If so, the twenty-four are the overcomers of those chapters, the true members of the Church from Pentecost to the Rapture.

Who then are the four living creatures? They are said to be "in the midst of the throne, and round about the throne," that is, they are supporting it and looking out, like the twelve oxen under the great laver in the temple, as its royal guardians. The twenty-four elders would represent the overcomers in their **priestly** character, clothed in white raiment—priestly garments—the reward promised to the overcomers at Sardis (chap. 3. 5), also as a royal priesthood, for they are crowned— the reward to Smyrna (chap. 2. 10), and Philadelphia (3. 11); and they are sitting on twelve thrones surrounding God's throne—reminiscent of the reward promised to the overcomers at Laodicea in chap. 3. 21. These two companies are sometimes seen as individuals, the four "living creatures" (chap. 6. 1, 3, 5, 7, R.V.) and the "elders" (chap. 7. 13). Usually they are spoken of as companies, sometimes apart, sometimes associated. Thus in chap. 4. 10 the twenty-four elders in sympathy with the ascription of glory to God by the four living beings, fall down and worship. In chapter 5 both companies unite in ascribing worthiness to the Lamb—"For Thou wast slain and hast redeemed **us** to God by Thy blood out of every kindred and tongue and people and nation; and hast made **us** unto our God kings and priests, and **we** shall reign on the earth" (vv. 9-10). It is right to say that the **"us"** which here occurs twice does not represent any word in the original, and the **"we"** is disputed, though the Vulgate has it: also the old Armenian, and Primas, a bishop of the 6th century. The same authorities practically, read, **"We** shall reign," though some well-known authorities, e.g., Aleph and A, give the third person plural, **"they** shall reign," or **"they** reign." But the fact that the words, "kings and priests," in v. 10 tally exactly with chap. 1. 6, where they refer to the Church, favours our version. These companies are in heaven, and we would judge them to be men, and therefore they must be redeemed. Is it not more likely, then, that they would be praising for their own redemption, than for that of some unknown persons on earth? It is indeed very unlikely that there would be such a numerous company on the earth to be praised for at this moment, so soon after the rapture; whereas the description exactly suits the Church, a vast number of redeemed down the ages from every nation, people and tongue, who are, as we shall see, represented by these praising companies. In such a case, ancient versions, like the Vulgate, might be weightier authorities than the Cod. Sinaiticus itself of the same century.

We merely mention these facts, that readers may see that the substitution of "them" and "they" of the R.V. for "us" and "we" of our Version is not such a foregone conclusion as is generally thought. At all events, the two companies are seen again in chap. 5. 6, 11—living creatures and elders, and in the same order in v. 14; but in chap. 7. 11, though they are seen together, the elders are mentioned first. In chap. 11. 16 the elders are seen alone, but in chap. 14. 3, and 19. 4, they are again associated with the four living creatures. What can we say then of these two companies—so closely linked—so identical in occupation, sympathy and worship, but that they represent the same persons under two aspects—the four living creatures—the Church Universal of the Redeemed, viewed as kings, Royal guardians of the Throne; and the four and twenty elders, the same great company—as priests— Royal assessors of the Redeemer?   W.H.

What saints are those whose prayers are referred to in Rev. 5. 8?

It does not appear to be necessary to limit "the prayers of saints" in Rev. 5. 8 to any particular body of saints, or to any particular period.

Note how the reference to them is associated with the Lamb taking the Book, a symbolic act which seems to be the prelude to taking possession of His Kingdom. For this the saints have been, in some form or other, praying all down the ages; in fact it is the great and final fulfilment of all prayers that were spiritual, whatever their immediate burden may have been. All such will be answered in perfection then.

Compare the closing verse of Psalm 72 in which, after having described Messiah's reign, David says that his prayers are "ended." He has nothing left to ask for, and feels as he did in 2 Sam. 7. 12-25, when after gracious promises had been made to him concerning this very matter, he asks, "What can David say more unto Thee?" (v. 20), and later adds, "Do as Thou hast said" (v. 25). Compare also Psalm 37. 4, where, in a Psalm written to encourage the righteous by pointing them onward to a time when they "shall inherit the earth," it is said, "He shall give thee the desires of thine heart."

Then, coming to the New Testament, compare the disciples' prayer in Matt. 6. 9-13, of which not only the clause, "Thy kingdom come," but the entire substance of it will be most fully accomplished in times of blessing yet future. And compare even John's own prayer of Rev. 22. 20, which is surely on the heart of multitudes of saints to-day, "Even so, come, Lord Jesus."

But we must remember that the taking of His Kingdom necessitates the taking of vengeance upon those who were His opposers and the persecutors of His people; and thus the immediate accompaniment of the opening of the seals of the Book is outpoured judgment upon them. And these inflictions are followed by others still more severe, at the beginning of which, in chap. 8. 2-4, the "prayers of all the saints" are once more referred to; reminding us that even such prayers as those of chap. 6. 9, 10, and the similar ones in many of the Psalms and elsewhere, will also have their answer in the happenings depicted in the latter part of this book.   W.R.

Are the 144,000, in Rev. 7. 4 the same company as those mentioned in Rev. 14. 1?

I am aware that this is a disputed point, and that a great effort has been made to emphasise the differences between them, but such seem to me of no great account. For instance, it has been pointed out that the 144,000 in chap. 7 are said to be sealed in their foreheads, without the character of the seal being specified, whereas in chap. 14 they are said to have "His Father's name written on their foreheads." But this does not entail a serious difference: the process is sealing; the result has the appearance of something written. Of course, it is admitted that much is added in chap. 14, as to the character of the walk and testimony of these faithful Israelites; whereas in chap. 7 they are spoken of merely as "servants of our God." This is very natural, for in chap. 7 they are set apart for the service; sealed to pass immune through the opposition and persecution of those terrible days; but in chap. 14 they have actually been brought through, and their faithful service is described. Someone will perhaps ask, Are not the 144,000 from the tribes of Israel, clearly said in chap. 14. 5 to be "before the throne"? That would not be a serious objection, even were it valid. The words, "before the throne," however, do not occur in the best MSS. This is a fatal reply to those who insist, in contradiction to all dispensational differences, that these 144,000 represent the faithful Christians, who alone have passed the "rapture."

The church's history on earth ends at the beginning of chap. 4, where John is caught up representatively. The last mention we have of the church on the earth is in chap. 3 (if we except the conclusion of the book in Rev. 22. 16). Here the 144,000 are not seen in heaven, but on Mount Zion. Some difficulty may be felt in believing that a company called out in chap. 7, can have survived till chap. 14, but when once God begins to pour out His judgments, "He will make a short work on the earth" (Rom. 9. 28): Events will travel very fast, and the judgments of the trumpets and vials will be condensed into a few years —probably seven at most.   W.H.

Do you think that the half-hour's silence in heaven (Rev. 8. 1) represents the last half of the seven years' covenant with Israel, in which Antichrist will persecute the faithful remnant? This whole period seems spoken of as an "hour" (see Rev. 3. 10). During this time the remnant will, to judge from certain Psalms, cry seemingly in vain to the Lord, for He will keep silence.

The undoubtedly correct translation of words twice found in 1 John 2. 18 as "It is the last **hour**" not "time," might seem to favour above suggestion, as this last "hour" is specifically associated there with the coming of the Antichrist. But that "the silence" in Rev. 8. 1, interesting though the suggestion may be, can be connected with any silence of God to His persecuted people, does not seem feasible to me, because though the Revelation confessedly cannot always be read consecutively, it is difficult to believe that chap. 8. 1 can thus anticipate the final crisis. For note, the silence then is followed by a long series of judgments:—the trumpets and the vials, whereas the silence of God to the prayers of His saints, predicated by our questioner, will only be broken by the appearing of Christ in glory. Surely all that is meant is that a brief silence, denoting intense and awestruck expectation, falls on all in heaven, as they realise the tremendous issues involved in the events just impending.   W.H.

Is the angel of the 10th of Revelation the Lord Jesus Christ? or is it another angel?

In matters of interpretation we must avoid dogmatism, but I have long believed that the "mighty angel" of Revelation 10 could be none other than "the angel of the covenant," the Lord Himself. My reasons are as follows. First, in His description the symbols are those connected with the throne of God. Could any mere angel's face be said to shine as the sun? Secondly, the response to His message is the seven thunders, uttering unspeakable words. Could this be said of any one but the Creator? Thirdly, the character of the message and the manner of its utterance are Divine. Could any but a Divine Person swear by God? whereas this is quite fitting to the mouth of Him who said, "By myself have I sworn." The key to the Revelation is that it is "The Revelation of Jesus Christ."In chapter 5, the Lion of the tribe of Judah is seen as a Lamb. Here (e.g., v. 3) He has lost this character, and takes possession of the inheritance by power, that is, as a Lion.   W.H.

Do the words spoken by the angel, "There shall be time no longer" (Rev. 10. 6), mark the end of time, and the beginning of Eternity? If so, when do the events from chap. xi. to xxi. occur?

The words as given in the margin of the Revised Version are—"Delay shall be no longer," and refer not to the end of time, but to the execution of the judgment of God.   W.H.

Is the first Beast of Rev. 13 the Antichrist?

I think it is an error to confuse the Antichrist—or the second beast of Rev. 13. 11, with the first beast of the earlier part of the chapter. But then again, we must distinguish between the first beast viewed in verses 1 and 2 as the revived Roman Empire, and that empire personified in a man, from verse 3 onward. The empire here depicted will succeed the first three great world empires—Babylon, Medo-Persia, and Greece of Dan. 7, and will be diverse from them all. When, however, in the last days, that empire is revived it will embody certain characteristics of the other empires, the leopard, bear and lion, as we see in Rev. 13. 2. This is how the first beast is seen by John in verse 1—as an Empire. He sees on this monster seven heads and ten crowned horns; then one of the heads wounded to death (v. 3). The word here is literally, "slain" —the same used in chap. 5. 6, "A Lamb that had been **slain.**" By the power of the dragon, however, this "slain" head is revivified. It is a diabolical travesty of the Resurrection. This head now becomes the eighth (chap. 17. 11) and seems not only indwelt by Satan in a peculiar sense, but to be in some mysterious way the re-incarnation of one of the previous heads of the Roman Empire, for he is described in chap. 11

as having "ascended out of the bottomless pit." We may note that it was a widespread belief in the early Church that Nero was destined to play a future role on the earth. Be that as it may, the point here is that this awful human being—Satan's embodiment—becomes the Man of Sin and the empire beast becomes personified in him. His "resurrection" gives him such tremendous prestige that he becomes the Centre and the Sum of all. In the Satanic Triad he occupies, I believe, the place of "the Father." Then the second beast, the religious head, who was out of the land—becomes the Antichrist, the false Messiah of Israel. He takes the place of Christ. This is the true sense of "Antichrist" —not one against Christ, but one who put himself in the place of Christ. He now acts in full concert with the first beast. Both are empowered by Satan, to the full extent, but as Christ sought not His own glory but the Father's, so will the Antichrist merge his own interests in the glory and advancement of the first beast—the Man of Sin. Satan occupies the place of the Spirit—energising both and uniting them one to the other and to himself. W.H.

Who are they that have part in the "First resurrection" of Rev. 20. 5, 6?

The statement, "on such the second death hath no power," which follows immediately in verse 6, makes it clear that those raised are saved people; while at the same time it implies that those still left in their graves until after the thousand years are unsaved people, i.e. those over whom the second death shall have power. And since the Scriptures do not anywhere suggest that saved people will die during millennial times, it follows that the resurrection described in verse 13 as taking place at their close, is of the wicked dead only.

On the other hand, although the immediate connection of verses 5 and 6 is with the martyrs of verse 4 who have suffered death during the period between the coming of the Lord to the air (when all who have died in faith until then will be raised), and His later appearing upon earth, as recorded in chapter 19 (when such as were put to death for their testimony in the meantime will be raised), yet the term "First", by its very nature, must be inclusive of all saints who have been raised at any time until then. Therefore the statement, "This is the first resurrection," of verse 5 is practically equivalent to, "This completes the first resurrection."

In thinking of words such as "first," "last," etc., as they are used in the Scriptures, we must ever remember that their significance is not restricted to the point of time at which an event occurs. There are other and more important kinds of priority. Might we express the matter in this way: from the point of view of the time of occurrence there are many resurrections; but from the point of view of character and out-

come there are but two, the names of which are given us in John 5. 29.
The first resurrection is the "Resurrection of life," the second resurrection is the "Resurrection of damnation." And yet, of course, time is
not altogether ignored, since the first resurrection is completed a thousand
years before the second takes place.   W.R.

As we are told by some teachers that the book of the Revelation is symbolic in its numbers (Rev. 7. 4), measurements
(21. 16), also in such terms as "seals," "vials," "trumpets,"
"beast," "street of gold," "key," "chain," "dragon," why not
hold that the millennial reign is also symbolical and will last
for a quite different period than a thousand years, especially
when we remember that "one day is as a thousand years and a
thousand years as one day"?

Because a book contains symbols, it does not follow that all its statements of fact are symbolical. In fact such teaching as that referred to
above needs to be accepted with much reserve. The "bread and the
wine" are symbolical but the Lord's Supper conveys definite literal
truth. There is a danger, too, of making symbols out of realities. The
Apocalypse is a "Revelation" not a "Mystification." and is intended to
convey definite truth. It is a much safer canon of interpretation to
interpret it literally, whenever possible, and let those who assert
the symbolic interpretation everywhere assume the burden of
proof. Their method has turned the book into a bag of wild guesses
and fanciful interpretations, leading nowhere. The analogy of "the
week" as applied to the history of man, has been so positively
asserted, that it has assumed in some minds the authority of gospel
truth, whereas in reality it has no scriptural authority whatever. If one
thousand years be stated six times in the book of the Revelation to be
the duration of our Lord's future earthly reign, what is gained by saying
this means some other period? The statement in 2 Peter 3. 8 is simply
that "with the Lord one day is as a thousand years and a thousand
years as one day." That is, that with Him time does not exist, all is an
eternal present. He "inhabits eternity." "All His works are known to
Him from the creation of the world." All this is undoubtedly true,
but this does not mean that when He says to us that a certain period
will last a thousand years, He equally means it may last one day, or a
million years. This would be the death-knell of all sane interpretation.
I think there is no valid reason to doubt that the Lord's earthly reign
will last a thousand years, neither more nor less, and His universal
reign for eternity.   W.H.

Is it true that the book of the Revelation is not a real prophecy
of the future? What is the meaning of Rev. 21. 8?

We shall take the last question first. The verse means what it says, in fearful contrast with the previous verse—"He that overcometh shall inherit all things (i.e., the true believer, see 1 John 5. 4, 5); and I will be his God, and he shall be my son." But then follow the ungodly, detailed under eight categories—"the fearful, the unbelieving and the abominable . . . and all liars"—and they "will have their part" (opposed to the blessed inheritance of the others), in the "lake which burneth with fire and brimstone: which is the second death"—the very place where the beast and the false prophet were cast alive, in chapter 19. 20; the devil, in chap. 20. 10; and "whosoever was not found written in the book of life," in v. 15. There is no room for doubt in these matters.

As for the first query, the questioner has been troubled by extracts from some Modernist Sunday paper, which denies the truth as above stated, though allowing that "long ago there was a belief that this book was a prophecy of what would happen at the end of the world." It is not so very long ago, seeing that multitudes to-day believe it to be so in this year of grace 1934, and really only infidels and their confreres, the modernists, deny it. The first verse of the book makes a claim for itself, which we accept with perfect confidence. "The Revelation of Jesus Christ which **God gave unto him** to show unto His servants things which must shortly come to pass . . . blessed is he that readeth . . . for the time is at hand." Perhaps someone may have a difficulty about such expressions as "shortly" and "at hand"; and these are used by rationalistic writers to discredit prophecies which have not been fulfilled even to-day. Peter explains in what sense such expressions are to be understood—in view of mockers who use this very argument, "Where is the promise of His coming? . . . all things continue." "It was to have come at once, but it has not yet come, therefore it is all a mistake," they reason. But no, "The Lord is not slack concerning His promise, as some men count slackness, but is long-suffering to us-ward, etc.," and then he goes on to remind the saints that, "One day is with the Lord as a thousand years and a thousand years as one day." He would have men all down the centuries expect the judgment—"The end of all things is at hand," and yet in mercy He lingers. But unbelieving "religious man" uses the very long-suffering of God as an argument against His veracity and the genuineness of His warnings. The book ends with a terrible warning to him who takes away from its "Prophecy," which might well give pause to objectors and mockers. "God shall take away his part from the tree of life (see R.V.), and out of the holy city, and from the things which are written in this book" (Rev. 22. 19).   W.H.

Can it be correct to describe Rev. 22. 1-5 as "the Eternal State"?

EE

How could there be "nations" to be "healed" with the leaves of the Tree of Life in that state?

I admit this is a difficulty, and yet, though chap. 22 does follow on chap. 21 so closely, there is a distinct break between them, and primary conditions seem modified. No doubt much that is millennial will prove to be also eternal. Certainly, there is an atmosphere of finality about chap. 22 1-5, which does not belong to the millennial kingdom. How could it be possible to say of the latter, "There shall be no more curse," since sin is yet present, Satan is still to be set at liberty, the last rebellion remains to be suppressed, and the great white throne assize is yet future? Then only the New Heaven and the New Earth will be formed, and the kingdom will take on its eternal character—"they shall reign for ever and ever." It is hard to suppose that the nations will exist as such then. May not the reference to the leaves of the Tree of Life in verse 2 be retrospective, and only indicate that, though mentioned here for the first time, it will already have played a role during the millennium? In verse 14, "the tree of life" is mentioned as the right of those "who have washed their robes" (see R.V., undoubtedly right here). This cannot be united to the millennium.   W.H.

Please give an explanation of Rev. 22. 19.

I think these words need rather believing than explaining, but there is one phrase which calls for comment—"the book of life." This would raise the question, whether a name ever written ın the book of life could be erased. The question, however, does not really arise from this verse, as there is practically no manuscript authority for "book," which ought to be as in the margin—"tree of life." The warning is lest the one who takes away from the words of the prophecy of this book, should be shut out from a future sharing in the tree of life, rather than deprived of something already obtained—a place in the book of life. He will never enter the holy city, nor enjoy the things written in this book. I think the words apply primarily to the book of the Apocalypse, and show the importance the Holy Spirit attaches to this closing revelation. If you add to the book as the Pharisaical religious systems do, or if you detract from it as the Sadducean ethical systems do, you do it at your soul's peril. Surely this is a terrible warning to the many to-day who tamper with the solemn teachings of this book as to future punishment. As the Apocalypse may be viewed as the closing chapter of the whole Bible, these words do apply in principle to the whole volume. There is a terrible risk in tampering with any portion of the Word. Rather we should say, "Let God be true and every man a liar!" One test of reality is the treatment we mete out to the Scriptures.   W.H.

INDEX TO SUBJECTS

SCRIPTURE INDEX TO QUESTIONS